CCNA: Cisco Certified Network Associate Study Guide, Seventh Edition

CCNA (640-802) Exam Objectives

OBJECTIVE	CHAPTER
Describe how a network works.	
Describe the purpose and functions of various network devices.	1
Select the components required to meet a network specification.	1
Use the OSI and TCP/IP models and their associated protocols to explain how data flows in a network.	1, 2
Describe common networked applications including web applications.	1
Describe the purpose and basic operation of the protocols in the OSI and TCP models.	1, 3, 11
Describe the impact of applications (Voice over IP and Video over IP) on a network.	1
Interpret network diagrams.	1, 7
Determine the path between two hosts across a network.	8
Describe the components required for network and Internet communications.	1
Identify and correct common network problems at layers 1, 2, 3, and 7 using a layered model approach.	1, 3
Differentiate between LAN/WAN operation and features.	1, 16
Configure, verify, and troubleshoot a switch with VLANs and interswitch communications.	
Select the appropriate media, cables, ports, and connectors to connect switches to other network devices and hosts.	2, 10
Explain the technology and media access control method for Ethernet networks.	2, 10
Explain network segmentation and basic traffic management concepts.	1, 2, 10
Explain basic switching concepts and the operation of Cisco switches.	10
Perform and verify initial switch configuration tasks including remote access management.	10
Verify network status and switch operation using basic utilities (including Ping, Traceroute, Telnet, SSH, ARP, ipconfig), SHOW and DEBUG commands.	10, 11

Sybex®
An Imprint of
WILEY

OBJECTIVE	CHAPTER
Compare and contrast wireless security features and capabilities of WPA security (including open, WEP, WPA-1/2).	14
Identify common issues with implementing wireless networks (including: interface misconfiguration).	14
Identify security threats to a network and describe general methods to mitigate those threats.	
Describe today's increasing network security threats and explain the need to implement a comprehensive security policy to mitigate the threats.	12
Explain general methods to mitigate common security threats to network devices, hosts, and applications.	12
Describe the functions of common security appliances and applications.	12
Describe security recommended practices including initial steps to secure network devices.	12
Implement, verify, and troubleshoot NAT and ACLs in a medium-size enterprise branch office network.	
Describe the purpose and types of ACLs.	12
Configure and apply ACLs based on network filtering requirements (including CLI/SDM).	12
Configure and apply an ACLs to limit Telnet and SSH access to the router using (including SDM/CLI).	12
Verify and monitor ACLs in a network environment.	12
Troubleshoot ACL issues.	12
Explain the basic operation of NAT.	13
Configure NAT for given network requirements (including CLI/SDM).	13
Troubleshoot NAT issues.	13
Implement and verify WAN links.	
Describe different methods for connecting to a WAN.	16
Configure and verify a basic WAN serial connection.	16
Configure and verify Frame Relay on Cisco routers.	16
Troubleshoot WAN implementation issues.	16
Describe VPN technology (including importance, benefits, role, impact, components).	16
Configure and verify a PPP connection between Cisco routers.	16

Exam objectives are subject to change at any time without prior notice and at Cisco's sole discretion. Please visit Cisco's website (`www.cisco.com`) for the most current listing of exam objectives.

OBJECTIVE	CHAPTER
Configure, verify, and troubleshoot basic router operation and routing on Cisco devices.	
Describe basic routing concepts (including: packet forwarding, router lookup process).	8
Describe the operation of Cisco routers (including: router bootup process, POST, router components).	6
Select the appropriate media, cables, ports, and connectors to connect routers to other network devices and hosts.	2
Configure, verify, and troubleshoot RIPv2.	8
Access and utilize the router to set basic parameters (including CLI/SDM).	6, 8, 9
Connect, configure, and verify operation status of a device interface.	6, 8, 9
Verify device configuration and network connectivity using Ping, Traceroute, Telnet, SSH, or other utilities.	6, 8, 9
Perform and verify routing configuration tasks for a static or default route given specific routing requirements.	8, 9
Manage IOS configuration files (including save, edit, upgrade, restore).	7
Manage Cisco IOS.	7
Compare and contrast methods of routing and routing protocols.	8, 9
Configure, verify, and troubleshoot OSPF.	9
Configure, verify, and troubleshoot EIGRP.	9
Verify network connectivity (including using Ping, Traceroute, and Telnet or SSH).	6, 7, 8, 9
Troubleshoot routing issues.	6, 8, 9
Verify router hardware and software operation using SHOW and DEBUG commands.	6, 8, 9
Implement basic router security.	6, 12
Explain and select the appropriate administrative tasks required for a WLAN.	
Describe standards associated with wireless media (including IEEE Wi-Fi Alliance, ITU/FCC).	14
Identify and describe the purpose of the components in a small wireless network (including SSID, BSS, ESS).	14
Identify the basic parameters to configure on a wireless network to ensure that devices connect to the correct access point.	14

Sybex®
An Imprint of
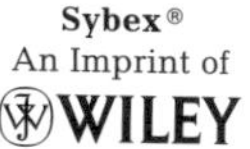
WILEY

OBJECTIVE	CHAPTER
Identify, prescribe, and resolve common switched network media issues, configuration issues, auto-negotiation, and switch hardware failures.	10, 11
Describe enhanced switching technologies (including VTP, RSTP, VLAN, PVSTP, 802.1q).	11
Describe how VLANs create logically separate networks and the need for routing between them.	11
Configure, verify, and troubleshoot VLANs.	11
Configure, verify, and troubleshoot trunking on Cisco switches.	11
Configure, verify, and troubleshoot interVLAN routing.	11
Configure, verify, and troubleshoot VTP.	11
Configure, verify, and troubleshoot RSTP operation.	11
Interpret the output of various show and debug commands to verify the operational status of a Cisco switched network.	7, 11
Implement basic switch security (including port security, trunk access, management vlan other than vlan1, etc.).	10,11
Implement an IP addressing scheme and IP Services to meet network requirements in a medium-size Enterprise branch office network.	
Describe the operation and benefits of using private and public IP addressing.	3, 4
Explain the operation and benefits of using DHCP and DNS.	1
Configure, verify and troubleshoot DHCP and DNS operation on a router (including CLI/SDM).	6
Implement static and dynamic addressing services for hosts in a LAN environment.	4, 5
Calculate and apply an addressing scheme, including VLSM IP addressing design to a network.	5
Determine the appropriate classless addressing scheme using VLSM and summarization to satisfy addressing requirements in a LAN/WAN environment.	5
Describe the technological requirements for running IPv6 in conjunction with IPv4 (including protocols, dual stack, tunneling, etc.).	15
Describe IPv6 addresses.	15
Identify and correct common problems associated with IP addressing and host configurations.	5

Exam objectives are subject to change at any time without prior notice and at Cisco's sole discretion. Please visit Cisco's website (`www.cisco.com`) for the most current listing of exam objectives.

CCNA®

Cisco Certified Network Associate

Study Guide

Seventh Edition

CCNA®

Cisco Certified Network Associate

Study Guide

Seventh Edition

Todd Lammle

Wiley Publishing, Inc.

Acquisitions Editor: Jeff Kellum
Development Editor: Kathi Duggan
Technical Editors: Dan Garfield and John Rouda
Production Editor: Christine O'Connor
Copy Editor: Judy Flynn
Editorial Manager: Pete Gaughan
Production Manager: Tim Tate
Vice President and Executive Group Publisher: Richard Swadley
Vice President and Publisher: Neil Edde
Media Project Manager 1: Laura Moss-Hollister
Media Associate Producer: Shawn Patrick
Media Quality Assurance: Josh Frank
Book Designers: Judy Fung and Bill Gibson
Compositor: Craig Woods, Happenstance Type-O-Rama
Proofreader: Jen Larsen, Word One
Indexer: Robert Swanson
Project Coordinator, Cover: Katherine Crocker
Cover Designer: Ryan Sneed

Published simultaneously in Canada

ISBN: 978-0-470-90107-76

For general information on our other products and services or to obtain technical support, please contact our Customer Care Department within the U.S. at (877) 762-2974, outside the U.S. at (317) 572-3993 or fax (317) 572-4002.

Wiley also publishes its books in a variety of electronic formats. Some content that appears in print may not be available in electronic books.

Library of Congress Cataloging-in-Publication Data

Lammle, Todd.

CCNA : Cisco Certified Network Associate study guide / Todd Lammle. — 7th ed.

p. cm.

ISBN 978-0-470-90107-6 (pbk.)

978-1-118-08804-3 (ebk.)

978-1-118-08805-0 (ebk.)

978-1-118-08806-7 (ebk.)

1. Electronic data processing personnel—Certification. 2. Computer networks—Examinations—Study guides. I. Title. II. Title: Cisco certified network associate study guide.

QA76.3.L348 2011

004.6—dc22

2011004111

10 9 8 7 6 5 4 3 2

Dear Reader,

Thank you for choosing *CCNA: Cisco Certified Associate Study Guide, Seventh Edition.* This book is part of a family of premium-quality Sybex books, all of which are written by outstanding authors who combine practical experience with a gift for teaching.

Sybex was founded in 1976. More than 30 years later, we're still committed to producing consistently exceptional books. With each of our titles, we're working hard to set a new standard for the industry. From the paper we print on, to the authors we work with, our goal is to bring you the best books available.

I hope you see all that reflected in these pages. I'd be very interested to hear your comments and get your feedback on how we're doing. Feel free to let me know what you think about this or any other Sybex book by sending me an email at `nedde@wiley.com`. If you think you've found a technical error in this book, please visit `http://sybex.custhelp.com`. Customer feedback is critical to our efforts at Sybex.

Best regards,

Neil Edde
Vice President and Publisher
Sybex, an Imprint of Wiley

Acknowledgments

My development editor for this book was Kathi Duggan. She was very patient and kind, and easy to work with (as long as I was never late with my submissions!). Thank you, Kathi, for being fun to work with and for being a very hard worker (answering emails literally throughout the night) and making sure everything was done on time and with the very high-quality standard that my Sybex CCNA book has become known for. I'm very happy that you were my new DE for this project, Kathi—we created a great book together!

Next in line to thank was my new technical editor, Dan Garfield. His expertise in the Cisco technical field, and history of networking in general, is second to none. His detailed analysis of my work helped make this my best CCNA book in the last 13 years. Thank you, Dan, for working hard under pressure, with tight deadlines, and for staying the course of delivering high-quality work in a short time frame.

Jeff Kellum is instrumental to my success in the Cisco world and is my acquisitions editor. Jeff, thanks for your guidance and continued patience. I look forward to our continued progress together in the Cisco certification world.

In addition, Christine O'Connor was an excellent production editor, and she worked really hard to get the book done as quickly as possible, without missing the small mistakes that are so easy to overlook. I am always very happy when Christine is on my list of editors for a book project! Judy Flynn, my copy editor, was another return editor for my book who was patient and helpful, and I am happy she worked with me once again. I look forward to having Christine and Judy working with me on my next project.

Last, but in no way least, was Troy McMillian. Troy has become my defacto writer, technical editor, researcher, and he has always comes through on any unreasonable deadline. I always look forward to working with Troy.

Finally a big thanks to Craig Woods at Happenstance-Type-O-Rama and to the CD team.

About the Author

Todd Lammle CCSI, CCNA/CCNA Wireless/CCNP/CCSP/CCVP, MCSE, CEH/CHFI, FCC RF Licensed, is the authority on Cisco certification and internetworking. He is a world-renowned author, speaker, trainer, and consultant. Todd has over 29 years of experience working with LANs, WANs, and large licensed and unlicensed wireless networks and has published over 50 books, including the very popular Sybex *CCNA: Cisco Certified Network Associate Study Guide* and the Sybex *CCNA Wireless Study Guide*. He runs an international training and consulting company based in Colorado and Texas. You can reach Todd through his forum and blog at `www.lammle.com`.

Contents at a Glance

Contents

Introduction

Welcome to the exciting world of Cisco certification! You have picked up this book because you want something better—namely, a better job with more satisfaction. Rest assured that you have made a good decision. Cisco certification can help you get your first networking job or more money and a promotion if you are already in the field.

Cisco certification can also improve your understanding of the internetworking of more than just Cisco products: You will develop a complete understanding of networking and how different network topologies work together to form a network. This is beneficial to every networking job and is the reason Cisco certification is in such high demand, even at companies with few Cisco devices.

Cisco is the king of routing, switching, and security, the Microsoft of the internetworking world. The Cisco certifications reach beyond the popular certifications, such as the CompTIA and Microsoft certifications, to provide you with an indispensable factor in understanding today's network—insight into the Cisco world of internetworking. By deciding that you want to become Cisco certified, you are saying that you want to be the best—the best at routing and the best at switching. This book will lead you in that direction.

For up-to-the-minute updates covering additions or modifications to the CCNA certification exams, as well as additional study tools and review questions, be sure to visit the Todd Lammle forum and website at `www.lammle.com`.

Cisco's Network Certifications

Initially, to secure the coveted Cisco CCIE certification, you took only one test and then you were faced with the (extremely difficult) hands-on lab, an all-or-nothing approach that made it tough to succeed.

In response to a high number of unsuccessful attempts, Cisco created a series of new certifications to help you get the coveted CCIE as well as aid prospective employers in measuring skill levels. With these new certifications, which make for a better approach to preparing for that almighty lab, Cisco opened doors that few were allowed through before.

This book covers everything CCNA routing and switching related. For up-to-date information on the CCENT and CCNA concentrations, as well as CCNP and CCIE certifications, please see `www.lammle.com` and/ or `www.globalnettc.com`.

Cisco Certified Network Associate (CCNA)

The CCNA certification was the first course and exam in the Cisco certification process, and the precursor to all current Cisco certifications. Now you can become a Cisco Certified Network Associate for the meager cost of this book and either one test (640-802) at $250 or two tests (640-816 and 640-822) at $125 each—although the CCNA exams are extremely hard and cover a lot of material, so you have to really know your stuff! Taking a Cisco class or spending months with hands-on experience is not out of the norm.

And once you have your CCNA, you don't have to stop there—you can choose to continue with your studies and achieve a higher certification, called the Cisco Certified Network Professional (CCNP). Someone with a CCNP has all the skills and knowledge they need to attempt the CCIE lab. But just becoming a CCNA can land you that job you've dreamed about.

Why Become a CCNA?

Cisco, not unlike Microsoft and other vendors that provide certification, has created the certification process to give administrators a set of skills and to equip prospective employers with a way to measure those skills or match certain criteria. Becoming a CCNA can be the initial step of a successful journey toward a new, highly rewarding, and sustainable career.

The CCNA program was created to provide a solid introduction not only to the Cisco Internetwork Operating System (IOS) and Cisco hardware, but also to internetworking in general, making it helpful to you in areas that are not exclusively Cisco's. At this point in the certification process, it's not unrealistic that network managers—even those without Cisco equipment—require Cisco certification for their job applicants.

If you make it through the CCNA and are still interested in Cisco and internetworking, you're headed down a path to certain success.

What Skills Do You Need to Become a CCNA?

To meet the CCNA certification skill level, you must be able to understand or do the following:

- Install, configure, and operate LAN, WAN, and wireless access services securely as well as troubleshoot and configure small to medium networks (500 nodes or fewer) for performance.
- Use the protocols IP, IPv6, EIGRP, RIP, RIPv2, and OSPF as well as understand serial connections, Frame Relay, VPN, cable, DSL, PPPoE, LAN switching, VLANs, VTP, STP, Ethernet, security, and access lists.

How Do You Become a CCNA?

The way to become a CCNA is to pass one little test (CCNA Composite exam 640-802). Then—poof!—you're a CCNA. (Don't you wish it were that easy?) True, it can be just one test, but you still have to possess enough knowledge to understand what the test writers are saying.

However, Cisco has a two-step process that you can take in order to become a CCNA that may be easier than taking one longer exam (this book is based on the one-step method, taking the 640-802 exam; however, the information it contains covers all three exams).

The two-test method involves passing the following:

- Exam 640-822: Interconnecting Cisco Networking Devices 1(ICND1)
- Exam 640-816: Introduction to Cisco Networking Devices 2 (ICND2)

I can't stress this enough: it's critical that you have some hands-on experience with Cisco routers. If you can get ahold of some basic routers or Cisco's Packet Tracer software, you're set. But if you can't, I've worked hard to provide hundreds of configuration examples throughout this book to help network administrators (or people who want to become network administrators) learn what they need to know to pass the CCNA exam.

Since the 640-802 exam is so hard, Cisco wants to reward you for taking the two-test approach. Or so it seems. If you take the ICND1 exam, you actually receive a certification called the CCENT (Cisco Certified Entry Networking Technician). This is one step toward your CCNA. To achieve your CCNA, you must still pass your ICND2 exam.

Again, this book was written for the CCNA 640-802 Composite exam—one exam and you get your certification.

For Cisco-authorized hands-on training with CCSI Todd Lammle, please see `www.globalnetc.com`. Each student will get hands-on experience by configuring at least three routers and two switches—no sharing of equipment!

What Does This Book Cover?

This book covers everything you need to know to pass the CCNA 640-802 exam. However, taking the time to study and practice with routers or a router simulator is the real key to success.

You will learn the following information in this book:

- Chapter 1 introduces you to internetworking. You will learn the basics of the Open Systems Interconnection (OSI) model the way Cisco wants you to learn it. There are written labs and plenty of review questions to help you. Do not skip the fundamental written labs in this chapter!
- Chapter 2 will dive into Ethernet networking and standards. Data encapsulation is discussed in detail in this chapter as well. There are written labs and plenty of review questions in this chapter to help you.
- Chapter 3 provides you with the background necessary for success on the exam as well as in the real world by discussing TCP/IP. This in-depth chapter covers the very beginnings of the Internet Protocol stack and then goes all the way to IP addressing

and understanding the difference between a network address and a broadcast address before finally ending with network troubleshooting.

- Chapter 4 introduces you to easy subnetting. You will be able to subnet a network in your head after reading this chapter if you really want to. Plenty of help is found in this chapter if you do not skip the written labs and review questions.
- Chapter 5 will have you learn about Variable Length Subnet Masks (VLSMs) and how to design a network using VLSMs. This chapter will finish with summarization techniques and configurations. As with Chapter 4, plenty of help is found in this chapter if you do not skip the written lab and review questions.
- Chapter 6 introduces you to the Cisco Internetworking Operating System (IOS) and command-line interface (CLI). In this chapter you will learn how to turn on a router and configure the basics of the IOS, including setting passwords, banners, and more. Hands-on labs will help you gain a firm grasp of the concepts taught in the chapter. Before you go through the hands-on labs, be sure to complete the written lab and review questions.
- Chapter 7 provides you with the management skills needed to run a Cisco IOS network. Backing up and restoring the IOS, as well as router configuration, is covered, as are the troubleshooting tools necessary to keep a network up and running. Before performing the hands-on labs in this chapter, complete the written labs and review questions.
- Chapter 8 teaches you about IP routing. This is a fun chapter because we will begin to build our network, add IP addresses, and route data between routers. You will also learn about static, default, and dynamic routing using RIP and RIPv2. Hands-on labs, a written lab, and the review questions will help you understand IP routing to the fullest.
- Chapter 9 dives into the more complex dynamic routing with Enhanced IGRP and OSPF routing. The written lab, hands-on labs, and review questions will help you master these routing protocols.
- Chapter 10 gives you background on layer 2 switching and how switches perform address learning and make forwarding and filtering decisions. Network loops and how to avoid them with the Spanning Tree Protocol (STP) will be discussed as well as the 802.1w RSTP version. Go through the written lab and review questions to make sure you really understand layer 2 switching.
- Chapter 11 covers virtual LANs and how you can use them in your internetwork. This chapter covers the nitty-gritty of VLANs and the different concepts and protocols used with VLANs as well as troubleshooting. Voice VLANs and QoS are also discussed in this all-so-important chapter. The written lab and review questions will reinforce the VLAN material.
- Chapter 12 covers security and access lists, which are created on routers to filter the network. IP standard, extended, and named access lists are covered in detail. Written and hands-on labs, along with review questions, will help you study for the security and access-list portion of the CCNA Composite exam.

- Chapter 13 covers Network Address Translation (NAT). This chapter has been on the Sybex website for a few years as an update to my last CCNA book, but I updated it and added it to this edition. New information, commands, troubleshooting, and hands-on labs will help you nail the NAT CCNA objectives.
- Chapter 14 covers wireless technologies. This is an introductory chapter regarding wireless technologies as Cisco views wireless. However, I also added some advanced wireless topics that cover Cisco's newest gear. At this time, advanced wireless gear is not covered within the Cisco CCNA objectives, but that can change. Make sure you understand basic wireless technologies like access points and clients as well as the difference between 802.11a, b, and g.
- Chapter 15 covers IPv6. This is a fun chapter and has some great information. IPv6 is not the big, bad scary monster that most people think it is. IPv6 is an objective on the latest exam, so study this chapter carefully. Keep an eye out at `www.lammle.com` for late-breaking updates.
- Chapter 16 concentrates on Cisco wide area network (WAN) protocols. This chapter covers HDLC, PPP, and Frame Relay in depth. VPNs and IPSec are also covered in this chapter. You must be proficient in all these protocols to be successful on the CCNA exam. Do not skip the written lab, review questions, or hands-on labs found in this chapter.

How to Use This Book

If you want a solid foundation for the serious effort of preparing for the Cisco Certified Network Associate (CCNA Composite) 640-802 exam, then look no further. I have spent hundreds of hours putting together this book with the sole intention of helping you to pass the CCNA exam and learn how to configure Cisco routers and switches.

This book is loaded with valuable information, and you will get the most out of your studying time if you understand how I put the book together.

To best benefit from this book, I recommend the following study method:

1. Take the assessment test immediately following this introduction. (The answers are at the end of the test.) It's okay if you don't know any of the answers; that's why you bought this book! Carefully read over the explanations for any question you get wrong and note the chapters in which the material is covered. This information should help you plan your study strategy.
2. Study each chapter carefully, making sure you fully understand the information and the test objectives listed at the beginning of each one. Pay extra-close attention to any chapter that includes material covered in questions you missed.
3. Complete the written labs at the end of each chapter. Do *not* skip these written exercises, because they directly relate to the CCNA exam and what you must glean from the chapters in which they appear. Do not just skim these labs! Make sure you understand completely the reason for each answer.

4. Complete all hands-on labs in the chapter, referring to the text of the chapter so that you understand the reason for each step you take. Try to get your hands on some real equipment, but if you don't have Cisco equipment available, try to find Cisco's Packet Tracer for a router simulator that you can use for all the hands-on labs needed for all your Cisco certification needs.
5. Answer all of the review questions related to each chapter. (The answers appear at the end of the chapters.) Note the questions that confuse you and study the topics they cover again. Do not just skim these questions! Make sure you understand completely the reason for each answer. Remember that these will not be the exact questions you find on the exam; they are written to help you understand the chapter material.
6. Try your hand at the practice exams that are included on the companion CD. The questions in these exams appear only on the CD. Check out `www.lammle.com` for more Cisco exam prep questions.
7. Also on the companion CD is the first module from each of the first three CDs from my complete CCNA video series, which covers internetworking, TCP/IP, and subnetting. This is critical information for the CCNA exam. In addition, as an added bonus, I have included an audio section from my CCNA audio program. Do not skip the video and audio section!

Please understand that these are preview editions of the video and audios found at `www.lammlepress.com` and not the full versions, but are still a great value, chock full of information.

8. Test yourself using all the flashcards on the CD. These are brand-new and updated flashcard programs to help you prepare for the CCNA exam. They are a great study tool!

To learn every bit of the material covered in this book, you'll have to apply yourself regularly, and with discipline. Try to set aside the same time period every day to study, and select a comfortable and quiet place to do so. If you work hard, you will be surprised at how quickly you learn this material.

If you follow these steps and really study—*doing hands-on labs every single day*—in addition to using the review questions, the practice exams, the Todd Lammle video/audio sections, and the electronic flashcards, as well as all the written labs, it would be hard to fail the CCNA exam. However, studying for the CCNA exam is like trying to get in shape—and if you do not go to the gym every day, you won't get in shape.

What's on the CD?

The folks at Sybex and I worked hard to provide some really great tools to help you with your certification process. All of the following tools should be loaded on your workstation when you're studying for the test. As a fantastic bonus, I was able to add to the CD included with this book a preview section from both my CCNA video and audio series!

Please understand that these are not the full versions, but they are still a great value for you included free with this book.

The Sybex Test Preparation Software

The test preparation software prepares you to pass the CCNA exam. In the test engine, you will find all the review and assessment questions from the book plus two practice exams with 140 questions that appear exclusively on the CD.

Electronic Flashcards

To prepare for the exam, you can read this book, study the review questions at the end of each chapter, and work through the practice exams included in the book and on the companion CD. But wait, there's more! You can also test yourself with the 200 flashcards included on the CD. If you can get through these difficult questions and understand the answers, you'll know you're ready for the CCNA exam.

The CD includes 200 flashcards specifically written to hit you hard and make sure you are ready for the exam. With the review questions, practice exams, and flashcards on the CD, you'll be more than prepared for the exam.

Bonus Material

The bonus material, found only on the CD, has a wealth of information that covers SDM and CC, recognizing and mitigating security threats, route authentication, layer-3 switching and switching types,and lastly, and probably the most valuable to you as a study tool, is the CCNA Simulation Exam Practice Labs. Do not skip this bonus material when studying for the CCNA exam. Please see my web site and forum at `www.lammle.com` for free up-to-the minute updates and new bonus material.

Todd Lammle Videos

I have created a full CCNA series of videos that can be purchased in either DVD or downloadable format from `www.lammlepress.com`. However, as a bonus included with this book, the first module of this series is included on the CD as a "Preview." Although this isn't the full version, the video is over 1 hour of foundational CCNA information. This is a $149 value! Do not skip this video because it covers the internetworking objectives, TCP/IP, and subnetting, which are very important to the CCNA exam.

Todd Lammle Audio

In addition to the videos included for free on the CD, I have included a "preview" section from my CCNA audio series. The CCNA audio series is a $199 value! This is a great tool to add to your arsenal of study material to help you pass the CCNA exam.

To find more Todd Lammle videos and audios as well as other Cisco study material, please see `www.lammlepress.com`.

Where Do You Take the Exams?

You may take the CCNA Composite exam at any of the Pearson VUE authorized testing centers (`www.vue.com`) or call 877-404-EXAM (3926).

To register for a Cisco Certified Network Associate exam, follow these steps:

1. Determine the number of the exam you want to take. (The CCNA exam number is 640-802.)
2. Register with the nearest Pearson VUE testing center. At this point, you will be asked to pay in advance for the exam. At the time of this writing, the exam is $250 and must be taken within one year of payment. You can schedule exams up to six weeks in advance or as late as the day you want to take it—but if you fail a Cisco exam, you must wait five days before you will be allowed to retake it. If something comes up and you need to cancel or reschedule your exam appointment, contact Pearson VUE at least 24 hours in advance.
3. When you schedule the exam, you'll get instructions regarding all appointment and cancellation procedures, the ID requirements, and information about the testing-center location.

Tips for Taking Your CCNA Exam

The CCNA Composite exam test contains about 55 to 60 questions and must be completed in 75 to 90 minutes or less. This information can change per exam. You must get a score of about 85 percent to pass this exam, but again, each exam can be different.

Many questions on the exam have answer choices that at first glance look identical—especially the syntax questions! Remember to read through the choices carefully because close doesn't cut it. If you get commands in the wrong order or forget one measly character, you'll get the question wrong. So, to practice, do the hands-on exercises at the end of this book's chapters over and over again until they feel natural to you.

Also, never forget that the right answer is the Cisco answer. In many cases, more than one appropriate answer is presented, but the *correct* answer is the one that Cisco recommends. On the exam, it always tells you to pick one, two, or three, never "choose all that apply." The CCNA Composite exam may include the following test formats:

- Multiple-choice single answer
- Multiple-choice multiple answer
- Drag-and-drop
- Fill-in-the-blank
- Router simulations

Cisco proctored exams will not show the steps to follow in completing a router interface configuration; however, they do allow partial command responses. For example, `show config` or `sho config` or `sh conf` would be acceptable. `Router#show ip protocol` or `router#show ip prot` would be acceptable.

Here are some general tips for exam success:

- Arrive early at the exam center so you can relax and review your study materials.

- Read the questions *carefully*. Don't jump to conclusions. Make sure you're clear about *exactly* what each question asks. Read twice, answer once, is what I always tell my students.
- When answering multiple-choice questions that you're not sure about, use the process of elimination to get rid of the obviously incorrect answers first. Doing this greatly improves your odds if you need to make an educated guess.
- You can no longer move forward and backward through the Cisco exams, so double-check your answer before clicking Next since you can't change your mind.

After you complete an exam, you'll get immediate, online notification of your pass or fail status, a printed examination score report that indicates your pass or fail status, and your exam results by section. (The test administrator will give you the printed score report.) Test scores are automatically forwarded to Cisco within five working days after you take the test, so you don't need to send your score to them. If you pass the exam, you'll receive confirmation from Cisco, typically within two to four weeks, sometimes longer.

How to Contact the Author

You can reach Todd Lammle through his forum at `www.lammle.com`.

Assessment Test

1. What protocol does PPP use to identify the Network layer protocol?
   A. NCP
   B. ISDN
   C. HDLC
   D. LCP
2. Each field in an IPv6 address is how many bits long?
   A. 4
   B. 16
   C. 32
   D. 128
3. The RSTP provides which new port role?
   A. Disabled
   B. Enabled
   C. Discarding
   D. Forwarding
4. What does the command `routerA(config)#line cons 0` allow you to perform next?
   A. Set the Telnet password.
   B. Shut down the router.
   C. Set your console password.
   D. Disable console connections.
5. How long is an IPv6 address?
   A. 32 bits
   B. 128 bytes
   C. 64 bits
   D. 128 bits
6. What PPP protocol provides for dynamic addressing, authentication, and multilink?
   A. NCP
   B. HDLC
   C. LCP
   D. X.25

7. What command will display the line, protocol, DLCI, and LMI information of an interface?

   A. `sh pvc`

   B. `show interface`

   C. `show frame-relay pvc`

   D. `sho runn`

8. Which of the following is the valid host range for the subnet on which the IP address 192.168.168.188 255.255.255.192 resides?

   A. 192.168.168.129–190

   B. 192.168.168.129–191

   C. 192.168.168.128–190

   D. 192.168.168.128–192

9. What does the `passive` command provide to the RIP dynamic routing protocol?

   A. Stops an interface from sending or receiving periodic dynamic updates

   B. Stops an interface from sending periodic dynamic updates but not from receiving updates

   C. Stops the router from receiving any dynamic updates

   D. Stops the router from sending any dynamic updates

10. Which protocol does Ping use?

    A. TCP

    B. ARP

    C. ICMP

    D. BootP

11. How many collision domains are created when you segment a network with a 12-port switch?

    A. 1

    B. 2

    C. 5

    D. 12

12. Which of the following commands will allow you to set your Telnet password on a Cisco router?

    A. `line telnet 0 4`

    B. `line aux 0 4`

    C. `line vty 0 4`

    D. `line con 0`

13. Which router command allows you to view the entire contents of all access lists?
    - **A.** `show all access-lists`
    - **B.** `show access-lists`
    - **C.** `show ip interface`
    - **D.** `show interface`

14. What does a VLAN do?
    - **A.** Acts as the fastest port to all servers
    - **B.** Provides multiple collision domains on one switch port
    - **C.** Breaks up broadcast domains in a layer 2 switch internetwork
    - **D.** Provides multiple broadcast domains within a single collision domain

15. If you wanted to delete the configuration stored in NVRAM, what would you type?
    - **A.** `erase startup`
    - **B.** `erase nvram`
    - **C.** `delete nvram`
    - **D.** `erase running`

16. Which protocol is used to send a destination network unknown message back to originating hosts?
    - **A.** TCP
    - **B.** ARP
    - **C.** ICMP
    - **D.** BootP

17. Which class of IP address has the most host addresses available by default?
    - **A.** A
    - **B.** B
    - **C.** C
    - **D.** A and B

18. How often are BPDUs sent from a layer 2 device?
    - **A.** Never
    - **B.** Every 2 seconds
    - **C.** Every 10 minutes
    - **D.** Every 30 seconds

19. Which one of the following is true regarding VLANs?
    - A. Two VLANs are configured by default on all Cisco switches.
    - B. VLANs only work if you have a complete Cisco switched internetwork. No off-brand switches are allowed.
    - C. You should not have more than 10 switches in the same VTP domain.
    - D. VTP is used to send VLAN information to switches in a configured VTP domain.
20. Which WLAN IEEE specification allows up to 54Mbps at 2.4GHz?
    - A. A
    - B. B
    - C. G
    - D. N
21. How many broadcast domains are created when you segment a network with a 12-port switch?
    - A. 1
    - B. 2
    - C. 5
    - D. 12
22. What flavor of Network Address Translation can be used to have one IP address allow many users to connect to the global Internet?
    - A. NAT
    - B. Static
    - C. Dynamic
    - D. PAT
23. What protocols are used to configure trunking on a switch? (Choose two.)
    - A. VLAN Trunking Protocol
    - B. VLAN
    - C. 802.1Q
    - D. ISL
24. What is a stub network?
    - A. A network with more than one exit point
    - B. A network with more than one exit and entry point
    - C. A network with only one entry and no exit point
    - D. A network that has only one entry and exit point

25. Where is a hub specified in the OSI model?
    A. Session layer
    B. Physical layer
    C. Data Link layer
    D. Application layer
26. What are the two main types of access control lists (ACLs)? (Choose two.)
    A. Standard
    B. IEEE
    C. Extended
    D. Specialized
27. To back up an IOS, what command will you use?
    A. `backup IOS disk`
    B. `copy ios tftp`
    C. `copy tftp flash`
    D. `copy flash tftp`
28. What command is used to create a backup configuration?
    A. `copy running backup`
    B. `copy running-config startup-config`
    C. `config mem`
    D. `wr mem`
29. What is the main reason the OSI model was created?
    A. To create a layered model larger than the DoD model
    B. So application developers can change only one layer's protocols at a time
    C. So different networks could communicate
    D. So Cisco could use the model
30. Which protocol does DHCP use at the Transport layer?
    A. IP
    B. TCP
    C. UDP
    D. ARP

31. If your router is facilitating a CSU/DSU, which of the following commands do you need to use to provide the router with a 64000bps serial link?

A. `RouterA(config)#`**`bandwidth 64`**

B. `RouterA(config-if)#`**`bandwidth 64000`**

C. `RouterA(config)#`**`clockrate 64000`**

D. `RouterA(config-if)#`**`clock rate 64`**

E. `RouterA(config-if)#`**`clock rate 64000`**

32. Which command is used to determine if an IP access list is enabled on a particular interface?

A. `show access-lists`

B. `show interface`

C. `show ip interface`

D. `show interface access-lists`

33. Which command is used to upgrade an IOS on a Cisco router?

A. `copy tftp run`

B. `copy tftp start`

C. `config net`

D. `copy tftp flash`

34. The Protocol Data Unit Encapsulation (PDU) is completed in which order?

A. Bits, frames, packets, segments, data

B. Data, bits, segments, frames, packets

C. Data, segments, packets, frames, bits

D. Packets, frames, bits, segments, data

Answers to Assessment Test

1. A. Network Control Protocol is used to help identify the Network layer protocol used in the packet. See Chapter 16 for more information.

2. B. Each field in an IPv6 address is 16 bits long. An IPv6 address is a total of 128 bits. See Chapter 15 for more information.

3. C. The port roles used within RSTP include discarding, learning, and forwarding. The difference between 802.1d and RSTP is the discarding role. See Chapter 10 for more information.

4. C. The command `line console 0` places you at a prompt where you can then set your console user-mode password. See Chapter 6 for more information.

5. D. An IPv6 address is 128 bits long, whereas an IPv4 address is only 32 bits long. See Chapter 15 for more information.

6. C. Link Control Protocol in the PPP stack provides negotiation of dynamic addressing, authentication, and multilink. See Chapter 16 for more information.

7. B. The `show interface` command shows the line, protocol, DLCI, and LMI information of an interface. See Chapter 16 for more information.

8. A. 256 – 192 = 64, so 64 is our block size. Just count in increments of 64 to find our subnet: 64 + 64 = 128. 128 + 64 = 192. The subnet is 128, the broadcast address is 191, and the valid host range is the numbers in between, or 129–190. See Chapter 4 for more information.

9. B. The `passive` command, short for `passive-interface`, stops regular updates from being sent out an interface. However, the interface can still receive updates. See Chapter 8 for more information.

10. C. ICMP is the protocol at the Network layer that is used to send echo requests and replies. See Chapter 3 for more information.

11. D. Layer 2 switching creates individual collision domains per port. See Chapter 1 for more information.

12. C. The command `line vty 0 4` places you in a prompt that will allow you to set or change your Telnet password. See Chapter 6 for more information.

13. B. To see the contents of all access lists, use the `show access-lists` command. See Chapter 12 for more information.

14. C. VLANs break up broadcast domains at layer 2. See Chapter 11 for more information.

15. A. The command `erase startup-config` deletes the configuration stored in NVRAM. See Chapter 6 for more information.

16. C. ICMP is the protocol at the Network layer that is used to send messages back to an originating router. See Chapter 3 for more information.

17. A. Class A addressing provides 24 bits for host addressing. See Chapter 3 for more information.

18. B. Every 2 seconds, BPDUs are sent out from all active bridge ports by default. See Chapter 10 for more information.

19. D. Switches do not propagate VLAN information by default; you must configure the VTP domain for this to occur. VLAN Trunking Protocol (VTP) is used to propagate VLAN information across a trunk link. See Chapter 11 for more information.

20. C. IEEE 802.11bg is in the 2.4GHz range, with a top speed of 54Mbps. See Chapter 14 for more information.

21. A. By default, switches break up collision domains on a per-port basis but are one large broadcast domain. See Chapter 1 for more information.

22. D. Port Address Translation (PAT) allows a one-to-many approach to network address translation. See Chapter 13 for more information.

23. C, D. VTP is not right because it has nothing to do with trunking except that it sends VLAN information across a trunk link. 802.1Q and ISL encapsulations are used to configure trunking on a port. See Chapter 11 for more information.

24. D. Stub networks have only one connection to an internetwork. Default routes should be set on a stub network or network loops may occur; however, there are exceptions to this rule. See Chapter 9 for more information.

25. B. Hubs regenerate electrical signals, which are specified at the Physical layer. See Chapter 1 for more information.

26. A, C. Standard and extended access control lists (ACLs) are used to configure security on a router. See Chapter 12 for more information.

27. D. The command `copy flash tftp` will prompt you to back up an existing file in flash to a TFTP host. See Chapter 7 for more information.

28. B. The command to back up the configuration on a router is `copy running-config startup-config`. See Chapter 7 for more information.

29. C. The primary reason the OSI model was created was so that different networks could interoperate. See Chapter 1 for more information.

30. C. User Datagram Protocol is a connection network service at the Transport layer, and DHCP uses this connectionless service. See Chapter 3 for more information.

31. E. The `clock rate` command is two words, and the speed of the line is in bps. See Chapter 6 for more information.

32. C. The `show ip interface` command will show you if any interfaces have an outbound or inbound access list set. See Chapter 12 for more information.

33. D. The `copy tftp flash` command places a new file in flash memory, which is the default location for the Cisco IOS in Cisco routers. See Chapter 7 for more information.

34. C. The PDU encapsulation method defines how data is encoded as it goes through each layer of the TCP/IP model. Data is segmented at the Transport later, packets created at the Network layer, frames at the Data Link layer, and finally, the Physical layer encodes the 1s and 0s into a digital signal. See Chapter 2 for more information.

Internetworking

THE CCNA EXAM TOPICS COVERED IN THIS CHAPTER INCLUDE THE FOLLOWING:

✓ **Describe how a network works**

- Describe the purpose and functions of various network devices
- Select the components required to meet a network specification
- Use the OSI and TCP/IP models and their associated protocols to explain how data flows in a network
- Describe common networked applications including web applications
- Describe the purpose and basic operation of the protocols in the OSI and TCP models
- Describe the impact of applications (Voice over IP and Video over IP) on a network
- Interpret network diagrams
- Describe the components required for network and Internet communications
- Identify and correct common network problems at layers 1, 2, 3, and 7 using a layered model approach
- Differentiate between LAN/WAN operation and features

✓ **Configure, verify, and troubleshoot a switch with VLANs and interswitch communications**

- Explain network segmentation and basic traffic management concepts

✓ **Implement an IP addressing scheme and IP Services to meet network requirements in a medium-size Enterprise branch office network**

- Explain the operation and benefits of using DHCP and DNS

✓ **Configure, verify, and troubleshoot basic router operation and routing on Cisco devices**

Welcome to the exciting world of internetworking. This first chapter will really help you review your understanding of basic internetworking by focusing on how to connect networks together using Cisco routers and switches. This chapter was written with an assumption that you have already achieved your CompTIA Network+ certification or have the equivalent knowledge, and based on this, I will review internetworking only for the purpose of fully grasping the Cisco CCENT and/or CCNA objectives needed to help you achieve your certifications.

First, you need to know exactly what an internetwork is, right? You create an internetwork when you connect two or more networks via a router and configure a logical network addressing scheme with a protocol such as IP or IPv6.

I'll be reviewing the following in this chapter:

- Internetworking basics
- Network segmentation
- How bridges, switches, and routers are used to physically and logically segment a network
- How routers are employed to create an internetwork

I'm also going to dissect the Open Systems Interconnection (OSI) model and describe each part to you in detail because you really need a good grasp of it for the solid foundation upon which you'll build your Cisco networking knowledge. The OSI model has seven hierarchical layers that were developed to enable different networks to communicate reliably between disparate systems. Since this book is centering upon all things CCNA, it's crucial for you to understand the OSI model as Cisco sees it, so that's how I'll be presenting the seven layers to you.

After you finish reading this chapter, you'll encounter 20 review questions and three written labs. These are given to you to really lock the information from this chapter into your memory. So don't skip them!

To find up-to-the-minute updates for this chapter, please see `www.lammle.com` or `www.sybex.com/go/ccna7e`.

Internetworking Basics

Before we explore internetworking models and the specifications of the OSI reference model, you've got to understand the big picture and learn the answer to the key question: Why is it so important to learn Cisco internetworking?

Networks and networking have grown exponentially over the last 20 years—understandably so. They've had to evolve at light speed just to keep up with huge increases in basic mission-critical user needs such as sharing data and printers as well as more advanced demands such as videoconferencing. Unless everyone who needs to share network resources is located in the same office area (an increasingly uncommon situation), the challenge is to connect the sometimes many relevant networks together so all users can share the networks' wealth.

Starting with a look at Figure 1.1, you get a picture of a basic LAN network that's connected together using a hub. This network is actually one collision domain and one broadcast domain—but no worries if you can't remember what this means right now, because I'm going to talk so much about both collision and broadcast domains throughout this chapter and in Chapter 2 that you'll probably even dream about them!

Okay, about Figure 1.1... How would you say the PC named Bob communicates with the PC named Sally? Well, they're both on the same LAN connected with a multiport repeater (a hub). So does Bob just send out a data message, "Hey Sally, you there?" Or does Bob use Sally's IP address and send a data message like this: "Hey 192.168.0.3, are you there?" Possibly you picked the IP address option, but even if you did, the news is still bad—both answers are wrong! Why? Because Bob is actually going to use Sally's MAC address (known as a hardware address, which is burned right into the network card of Sally's PC) to get ahold of her.

FIGURE 1.1 The basic network

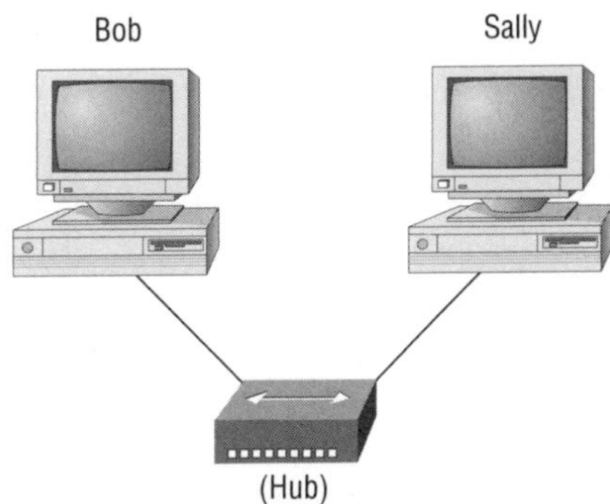
Bob
Sally
(Hub)
The basic network allows devices to share information.
The term computer language refers to binary code (0s or 1s).
The two hosts above communicate using hardware or MAC addresses.

Great, but how does Bob get Sally's MAC address if he knows only Sally's name and doesn't even have her IP address yet? Bob is going to start with name resolution (hostname to IP address resolution), something that's usually accomplished using Domain Name Service (DNS). And of note, if these two are on the same LAN, Bob can just broadcast to Sally asking her for the information (no DNS needed)—welcome to Microsoft Windows!

Here's an output from a network analyzer depicting a simple initiation process from Bob to Sally:

```
Source      Destination    Protocol    Info
    192.168.0.2  192.168.0.255  NBNS  Name query NB SALLY<00>
```

As I already mentioned, since the two hosts are on a local LAN, Windows (Bob) will just broadcast to resolve the name *Sally* (the destination 192.168.0.255 is a broadcast address) and Sally will let Bob know her address is 192.168.0.3 (analyzer output not shown). Let's take a look at the rest of the information:

```
EthernetII,Src:192.168.0.2(00:14:22:be:18:3b),Dst:Broadcast(ff:ff:-ff:ff:ff:ff)
```

What this output shows is that Bob knows his own MAC address and source IP address but not Sally's IP address or MAC address, so Bob sends a broadcast address of all *f*s for the MAC address (a Data Link layer broadcast) and an IP LAN broadcast of 192.168.0.255. Again, don't freak—you're going to learn all about broadcasts in Chapter 3, "Introduction to TCP/IP."

Now Bob has to broadcast on the LAN to get Sally's MAC address so he can finally communicate to her PC and send data:

```
Source      Destination Protocol Info
192.168.0.2 Broadcast  ARP Who has 192.168.0.3? Tell 192.168.0.2
```

Next, check out Sally's response:

```
Source      Destination    Protocol   Info
192.168.0.3 192.168.0.2   ARP  192.168.0.3 is at 00:0b:db:99:d3:5e
192.168.0.3 192.168.0.2 NBNS Name query response NB 192.168.0.3
```

Okay, sweet— Bob now has both Sally's IP address and her MAC address! These are both listed as the source address at this point because this information was sent from Sally back to Bob. So, *finally*, Bob has all the goods he needs to communicate with Sally. And just so you know, I'm going to tell you all about Address Resolution Protocol (ARP) and show you exactly how Sally's IP address was resolved to a MAC address in Chapter 8, "IP Routing."

To complicate things further, it's also likely that at some point you'll have to break up one large network into a bunch of smaller ones because user response will have dwindled to a slow crawl as the network grew and grew. And with all that growth, your LAN's traffic congestion has reached epic proportions. The answer to this is breaking up a really big network into a number of smaller ones—something called *network segmentation*. You do this by using devices like *routers*, *switches*, and *bridges*. Figure 1.2 displays a network that's been segmented with a switch so that each network segment connected to the switch is now a separate collision domain. But make note of the fact that this network is still one broadcast domain.

FIGURE 1.2 A switch can replace the hub, breaking up collision domains.

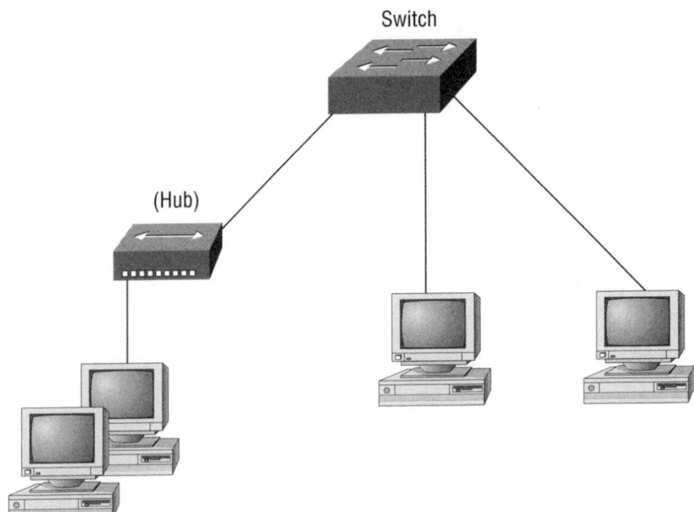

Keep in mind that the hub used in Figure 1.2 just extended the one collision domain from the switch port. Here's a list of some of the things that commonly cause LAN traffic congestion:

- Too many hosts in a broadcast or collision domain
- Broadcast storms
- Too much multicast traffic
- Low bandwidth
- Adding hubs for connectivity to the network

Take another look at Figure 1.2—did you notice that I replaced the main hub from Figure 1.1 with a switch? Whether you did or didn't, the reason I did that is because hubs don't segment a network; they just connect network segments together. So basically, it's an inexpensive way to connect a couple of PCs together, which is great for home use and troubleshooting, but that's about it!

Now, routers are used to connect networks together and route packets of data from one network to another. Cisco became the de facto standard of routers because of its high-quality router products, great selection, and fantastic service. Routers, by default, break up a *broadcast domain*—the set of all devices on a network segment that hear all the broadcasts sent on that segment. Figure 1.3 shows a router in our little network that creates an internetwork and breaks up broadcast domains.

The network in Figure 1.3 is a pretty cool network. Each host is connected to its own collision domain, and the router has created two broadcast domains. And don't forget that the router provides connections to WAN services as well! The router uses something called a serial interface for WAN connections, specifically, a V.35 physical interface on a Cisco router.

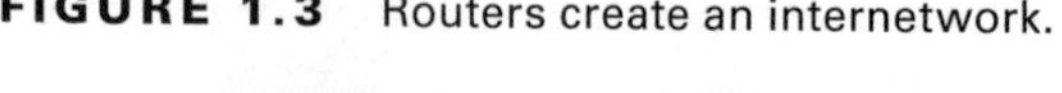

FIGURE 1.3 Routers create an internetwork.

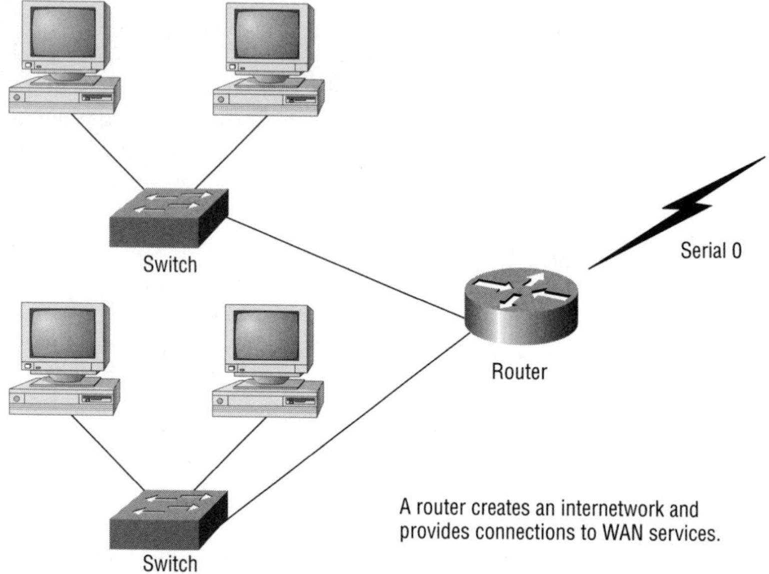
Switch
Serial 0
Router
Switch
A router creates an internetwork and
provides connections to WAN services.

Breaking up a broadcast domain is important because when a host or server sends a network broadcast, every device on the network must read and process that broadcast—unless you've got a router. When the router's interface receives this broadcast, it can respond by basically saying, "Thanks, but no thanks," and discard the broadcast without forwarding it on to other networks. Even though routers are known for breaking up broadcast domains by default, it's important to remember that they break up collision domains as well.

There are two advantages of using routers in your network:

- They don't forward broadcasts by default.
- They can filter the network based on layer 3 (Network layer) information (e.g., IP address).

Four router functions in your network can be listed as follows:

- Packet switching
- Packet filtering
- Internetwork communication
- Path selection

Remember that routers are really switches; they're actually what we call layer 3 switches (we'll talk about layers later in this chapter). Unlike layer 2 switches, which forward or filter frames, routers (or layer 3 switches) use logical addressing and provide what is called packet switching. Routers can also provide packet filtering by using access lists, and when routers connect two or more networks together and use logical addressing (IP or IPv6), this is called an internetwork. Lastly, routers use a routing table (map of the internetwork) to make path selections and to forward packets to remote networks.

Conversely, switches aren't used to create internetworks (they do not break up broadcast domains by default); they're employed to add functionality to a network LAN. The main purpose of a switch is to make a LAN work better—to optimize its performance—providing more bandwidth for the LAN's users. And switches don't forward packets to other networks as routers do. Instead, they only "switch" frames from one port to another within the switched network. Okay, you may be thinking, "Wait a minute, what are frames and packets?" I'll tell you all about them later in this chapter, I promise!

By default, switches break up *collision domains*. This is an Ethernet term used to describe a network scenario wherein one particular device sends a packet on a network segment, forcing every other device on that same segment to pay attention to it. If at the same time a different device tries to transmit, leading to a collision, both devices must retransmit, one at a time. Not very efficient! This situation is typically found in a hub environment where each host segment connects to a hub that represents only one collision domain and only one broadcast domain. By contrast, each and every port on a switch represents its own collision domain.

Switches create separate collision domains but a single broadcast domain. Routers provide a separate broadcast domain for each interface.

The term *bridging* was introduced before routers and hubs were implemented, so it's pretty common to hear people referring to bridges as switches and vice versa. That's because bridges and switches basically do the same thing—break up collision domains on a LAN (in reality, you cannot buy a physical bridge these days, only LAN switches, but they use bridging technologies, so Cisco still refers to them as multiport bridges).

So what this means is that a switch is basically just a multiple-port bridge with more brainpower, right? Well, pretty much, but there are differences. Switches do provide this function, but they do so with greatly enhanced management ability and features. Plus, most of the time, bridges only had 2 or 4 ports. Yes, you could get your hands on a bridge with up to 16 ports, but that's nothing compared to the hundreds available on some switches!

You would use a bridge in a network to reduce collisions within broadcast domains and to increase the number of collision domains in your network. Doing this provides more bandwidth for users. And keep in mind that using hubs in your network can contribute to congestion on your Ethernet network. As always, plan your network design carefully!

Figure 1.4 shows how a network would look with all these internetwork devices in place. Remember that the router will not only break up broadcast domains for every LAN interface, it will break up collision domains as well.

FIGURE 1.4 Internetworking devices

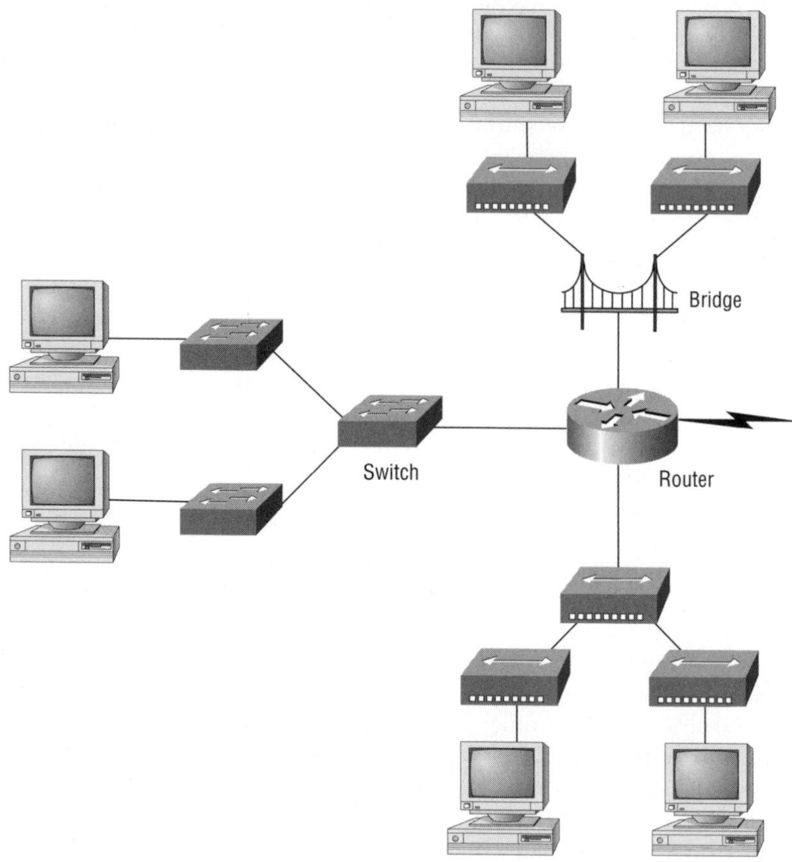

When you looked at Figure 1.4, did you notice that the router is found at center stage and that it connects each physical network together? We have to use this layout because of the older technologies involved—bridges and hubs.

On the top internetwork in Figure 1.4, you'll notice that a bridge was used to connect the hubs to a router. The bridge breaks up collision domains, but all the hosts connected to both hubs are still crammed into the same broadcast domain. Also, the bridge only created two collision domains, so each device connected to a hub is in the same collision domain as every other device connected to that same hub. This is actually pretty lame, but it's still better than having one collision domain for all hosts.

Notice something else: The three hubs at the bottom that are connected also connect to the router, creating one collision domain and one broadcast domain. This makes the bridged network look much better indeed!

Although bridges/switches are used to segment networks, they will not isolate broadcast or multicast packets.

The best network connected to the router is the LAN switch network on the left. Why? Because each port on that switch breaks up collision domains. But it's not all good—all devices are still in the same broadcast domain. Do you remember why this can be a really bad thing? Because all devices must listen to all broadcasts transmitted, that's why. And if your broadcast domains are too large, the users have less bandwidth and are required to process more broadcasts, and network response time will slow to a level that could cause office riots.

Once we have only switches in our network, things change a lot! Figure 1.5 shows the network that is typically found today.

FIGURE 1.5 Switched networks creating an internetwork

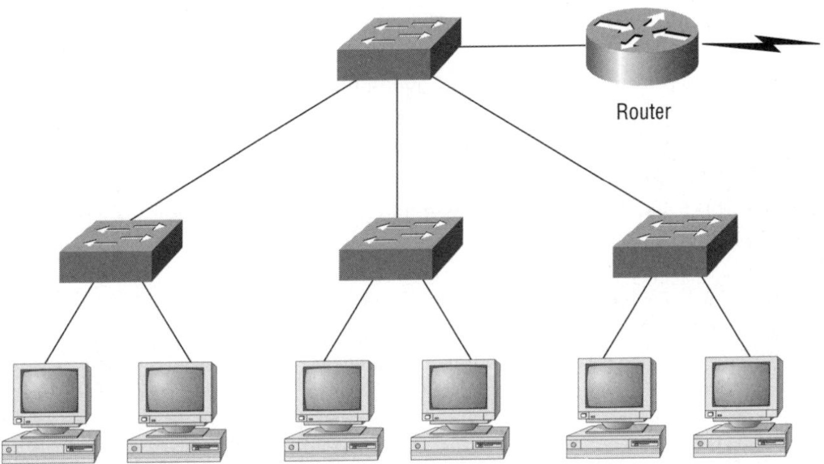

Okay, here I've placed the LAN switches at the center of the network world so the router is connecting only logical networks together. If I implemented this kind of setup, I've created virtual LANs (VLANs), something I'm going to tell you about in Chapter 11. So don't stress. But it is really important to understand that even though you have a switched network, you still need a router (or layer 3 switch) to provide your inter-VLAN communication, or internetworking. Don't forget that!

Obviously, the best network is one that's correctly configured to meet the business requirements of the company it serves. LAN switches with routers, correctly placed in the network, are the best network design. This book will help you understand the basics of routers and switches so you can make good, informed decisions on a case-by-case basis.

Let's go back to Figure 1.4 again. Looking at the figure, how many collision domains and broadcast domains are in this internetwork? Hopefully, you answered nine collision domains and three broadcast domains! The broadcast domains are definitely the easiest to see because only routers break up broadcast domains by default. And since there are three connections, that gives you three broadcast domains. But do you see the nine collision domains? Just in case that's a no, I'll explain. The all-hub network is one collision domain; the bridge network equals three collision domains. Add in the switch network of five collision domains—one for each switch port—and you've got a total of nine.

Now, in Figure 1.5, each port on the switch is a separate collision domain and each VLAN is a separate broadcast domain. But you still need a router for routing between VLANs. How many collision domains do you see here? I'm counting 10—remember that connections between the switches are considered a collision domain!

Real World Scenario

Should I Replace My Existing 10/100Mbps Switches?

You're a network administrator at a large company in San Jose. The boss comes to you and says that he got your requisition to buy all new switches and is not sure about approving the expense; do you really need it?

Well, if you can, absolutely! The newest switches really add a lot of functionality to a network that older 10/100Mbps switches just don't have (yes, five-year-old switches are considered just plain old today). But most of us don't have an unlimited budget to buy all new gigabit switches. 10/100Mbps switches can still create a nice network—that is, of course, if you design and implement the network correctly—but you'll still have to replace these switches eventually.

So do you need 1Gbps or better switch ports for all your users, servers, and other devices? Yes, you *absolutely* need new higher-end switches! With the new Windows networking stack and the IPv6 revolution shortly ahead of us, the server and hosts are no longer the bottlenecks of our internetworks. Our routers and switches are! We need at a minimum gigabit to the desktop and on every router interface—10Gbps would be better, or even higher if you can afford it.

So, go ahead! Put that requisition in to buy all new switches.

So now that you've gotten an introduction to internetworking and the various devices that live in an internetwork, it's time to head into internetworking models.

Internetworking Models

When networks first came into being, computers could typically communicate only with computers from the same manufacturer. For example, companies ran either a complete DECnet solution or an IBM solution—not both together. In the late 1970s, the *Open Systems Interconnection (OSI) reference model* was created by the International Organization for Standardization (ISO) to break this barrier.

The OSI model was meant to help vendors create interoperable network devices and software in the form of protocols so that different vendor networks could work with each other. Like world peace, it'll probably never happen completely, but it's still a great goal.

The OSI model is the primary architectural model for networks. It describes how data and network information are communicated from an application on one computer through the network media to an application on another computer. The OSI reference model breaks this approach into layers.

In the following section, I am going to explain the layered approach and how we can use this approach to help us troubleshoot our internetworks.

The Layered Approach

A *reference model* is a conceptual blueprint of how communications should take place. It addresses all the processes required for effective communication and divides these processes into logical groupings called *layers*. When a communication system is designed in this manner, it's known as *layered architecture*.

Think of it like this: You and some friends want to start a company. One of the first things you'll do is sit down and think through what tasks must be done, who will do them, the order in which they will be done, and how they relate to each other. Ultimately, you might group these tasks into departments. Let's say you decide to have an order-taking department, an inventory department, and a shipping department. Each of your departments has its own unique tasks, keeping its staff members busy and requiring them to focus on only their own duties.

In this scenario, I'm using departments as a metaphor for the layers in a communication system. For things to run smoothly, the staff of each department will have to trust and rely heavily upon the others to do their jobs and competently handle their unique responsibilities. In your planning sessions, you would probably take notes, recording the entire process to facilitate later discussions about standards of operation that will serve as your business blueprint, or reference model.

Once your business is launched, your department heads, each armed with the part of the blueprint relating to their own department, will need to develop practical methods to implement their assigned tasks. These practical methods, or protocols, will need to be compiled into a standard operating procedures manual and followed closely. Each of the various procedures in your manual will have been included for different reasons and have varying degrees of importance and implementation. If you form a partnership or acquire another company, it will be imperative that its business protocols—its business blueprint—match yours (or at least be compatible with it).

Similarly, software developers can use a reference model to understand computer communication processes and see what types of functions need to be accomplished on any one layer. If they are developing a protocol for a certain layer, all they need to concern themselves with is that specific layer's functions, not those of any other layer. Another layer and protocol will handle the other functions. The technical term for this idea is *binding*. The communication processes that are related to each other are bound, or grouped together, at a particular layer.

Advantages of Reference Models

The OSI model is hierarchical, and the same benefits and advantages can apply to any layered model. The primary purpose of all such models, especially the OSI model, is to allow different vendors' networks to interoperate.

Advantages of using the OSI layered model include, but are not limited to, the following:

- It divides the network communication process into smaller and simpler components, thus aiding component development, design, and troubleshooting.
- It allows multiple-vendor development through standardization of network components.
- It encourages industry standardization by defining what functions occur at each layer of the model.
- It allows various types of network hardware and software to communicate.
- It prevents changes in one layer from affecting other layers, so it does not hamper development.

The OSI Reference Model

One of the greatest functions of the OSI specifications is to assist in data transfer between disparate hosts—meaning, for example, that they enable us to transfer data between a Unix host and a PC or a Mac.

The OSI isn't a physical model, though. Rather, it's a set of guidelines that application developers can use to create and implement applications that run on a network. It also provides a framework for creating and implementing networking standards, devices, and internetworking schemes.

The OSI has seven different layers, divided into two groups. The top three layers define how the applications within the end stations will communicate with each other and with users. The bottom four layers define how data is transmitted end to end. Figure 1.6 shows the three upper layers and their functions, and Figure 1.7 shows the four lower layers and their functions.

When you study Figure 1.6, understand that the user interfaces with the computer at the Application layer and also that the upper layers are responsible for applications communicating between hosts. Remember that none of the upper layers knows anything about networking or network addresses. That's the responsibility of the four bottom layers.

In Figure 1.7, you can see that it's the four bottom layers that define how data is transferred through a physical wire or through switches and routers. These bottom layers also determine how to rebuild a data stream from a transmitting host to a destination host's application.

The following network devices operate at all seven layers of the OSI model:

- Network Management Stations (NMSs)
- Web and application servers

- Gateways (not default gateways)
- Network hosts

FIGURE 1.6 The upper layers

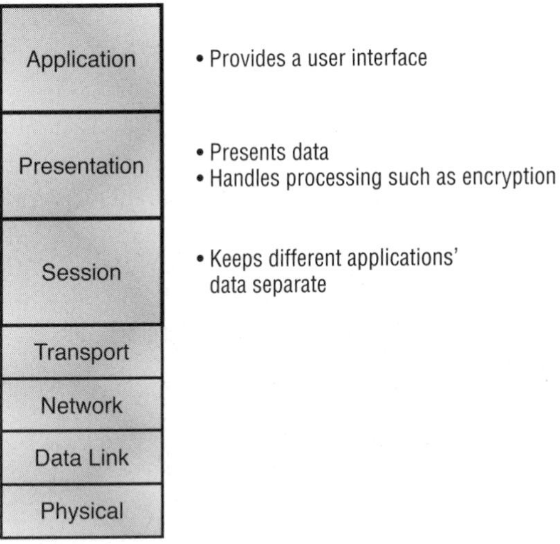

FIGURE 1.7 The lower layers

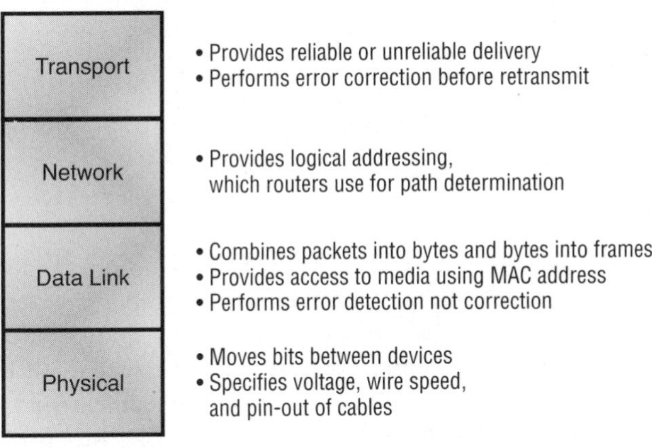

Basically, the ISO is pretty much the Emily Post of the network protocol world. Just as Ms. Post wrote the book setting the standards—or protocols—for human social interaction, the ISO developed the OSI reference model as the precedent and guide for an open network protocol set. Defining the etiquette of communication models, it remains today the most popular means of comparison for protocol suites.

The OSI reference model has the following seven layers:

- Application layer (layer 7)
- Presentation layer (layer 6)
- Session layer (layer 5)
- Transport layer (layer 4)
- Network layer (layer 3)
- Data Link layer (layer 2)
- Physical layer (layer 1)

Figure 1.8 shows a summary of the functions defined at each layer of the OSI model.

FIGURE 1.8 Layer functions

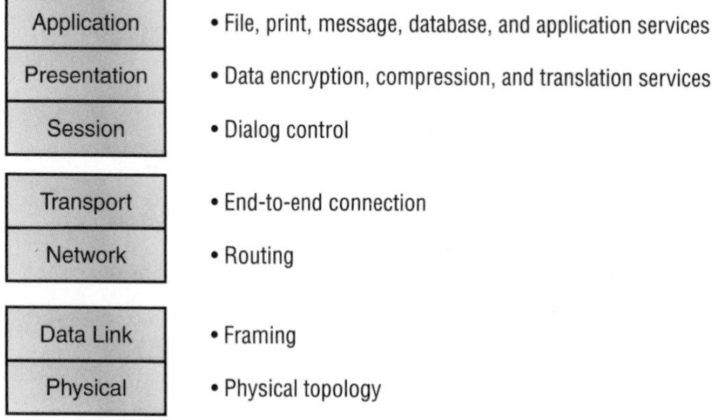

With this in hand, you're now ready to explore each layer's function in detail.

The Application Layer

The *Application layer* of the OSI model marks the spot where users actually communicate to the computer. This layer comes into play only when it's apparent that access to the network is going to be needed soon. Take the case of Internet Explorer (IE). You could uninstall every trace of networking components from a system, such as TCP/IP, NIC card, and so on, and you could still use IE to view a local HTML document—no problem. But things would definitely get messy if you tried to do something like view an HTML document that must be retrieved using HTTP or nab a file with FTP or TFTP. That's because IE will respond to requests such as those by attempting to access the Application layer. And what's happening is that the Application layer is acting as an interface between the actual application program—which isn't at all a part of the layered structure—and the next layer down by providing ways for the application to send information down through the protocol stack. In other words, IE doesn't truly reside within the Application layer—it interfaces with Application layer protocols when it needs to deal with remote resources.

The Application layer is also responsible for identifying and establishing the availability of the intended communication partner and determining whether sufficient resources for the intended communication exist.

These tasks are important because computer applications sometimes require more than only desktop resources. Often, they'll unite communicating components from more than one network application. Prime examples are file transfers and email as well as enabling remote access, network management activities, client/server processes, and information location. Many network applications provide services for communication over enterprise networks, but for present and future internetworking, the need is fast developing to reach beyond the limits of current physical networking.

It's important to remember that the Application layer is acting as an interface between the actual application programs. This means that Microsoft Word, for example, does not reside at the Application layer but instead interfaces with the Application layer protocols. Chapter 3 will present some programs that actually reside at the Application layer—for example, FTP and TFTP.

The Presentation Layer

The *Presentation layer* gets its name from its purpose: It presents data to the Application layer and is responsible for data translation and code formatting.

This layer is essentially a translator and provides coding and conversion functions. A successful data-transfer technique is to adapt the data into a standard format before transmission. Computers are configured to receive this generically formatted data and then convert the data back into its native format for actual reading (for example, EBCDIC to ASCII). By providing translation services, the Presentation layer ensures that data transferred from the Application layer of one system can be read by the Application layer of another one.

The OSI has protocol standards that define how standard data should be formatted. Tasks like data compression, decompression, encryption, and decryption are associated with this layer. Some Presentation layer standards are involved in multimedia operations too.

The Session Layer

The *Session layer* is responsible for setting up, managing, and then tearing down sessions between Presentation layer entities. This layer also provides dialog control between devices, or nodes. It coordinates communication between systems and serves to organize their communication by offering three different modes: *simplex*, *half duplex*, and *full duplex*. To sum up, the Session layer basically keeps different applications' data separate from other applications' data.

The Transport Layer

The *Transport layer* segments and reassembles data into a data stream. Services located in the Transport layer segment and reassemble data from upper-layer applications and unite it into the same data stream. They provide end-to-end data transport services and can establish a logical connection between the sending host and destination host on an internetwork.

Some of you are probably familiar with TCP and UDP already. (But if you're not, no worries—I'll tell you all about them in Chapter 3.) If so, you know that both work at the Transport layer and that TCP is a reliable service and UDP is not. This means that application developers have more options because they have a choice between the two protocols when working with TCP/IP protocols.

The Transport layer is responsible for providing mechanisms for multiplexing upper-layer applications, establishing sessions, and tearing down virtual circuits. It also hides details of any network-dependent information from the higher layers by providing transparent data transfer.

The term *reliable networking* can be used at the Transport layer. It means that acknowledgments, sequencing, and flow control will be used.

The Transport layer can be connectionless or connection oriented. However, Cisco is mostly concerned with you understanding the connection-oriented portion of the Transport layer. The following sections will provide the skinny on the connection-oriented (reliable) protocol of the Transport layer.

Flow Control

Data integrity is ensured at the Transport layer by maintaining *flow control* and by allowing applications to request reliable data transport between systems. Flow control prevents a sending host on one side of the connection from overflowing the buffers in the receiving host—an event that can result in lost data. Reliable data transport employs a connection-oriented communications session between systems, and the protocols involved ensure that the following will be achieved:

- The segments delivered are acknowledged back to the sender upon their reception.
- Any segments not acknowledged are retransmitted.
- Segments are sequenced back into their proper order upon arrival at their destination.
- A manageable data flow is maintained in order to avoid congestion, overloading, and data loss.

The purpose of flow control is to provide a means for the receiver to govern the amount of data sent by the sender.

Connection-Oriented Communication

In reliable transport operation, a device that wants to transmit sets up a connection-oriented communication session with a remote device by creating a session. The transmitting device first establishes a connection-oriented session with its peer system, which is called a *call setup* or a *three-way handshake*. Data is then transferred; when the transfer is finished, a call termination takes place to tear down the virtual circuit.

Figure 1.9 depicts a typical reliable session taking place between sending and receiving systems. Looking at it, you can see that both hosts' application programs begin by notifying their individual operating systems that a connection is about to be initiated. The two operating systems communicate by sending messages over the network confirming that the transfer is approved and that both sides are ready for it to take place. After all of this required synchronization takes place, a connection is fully established and the data transfer begins (this virtual circuit setup is called overhead!).

FIGURE 1.9 Establishing a connection-oriented session

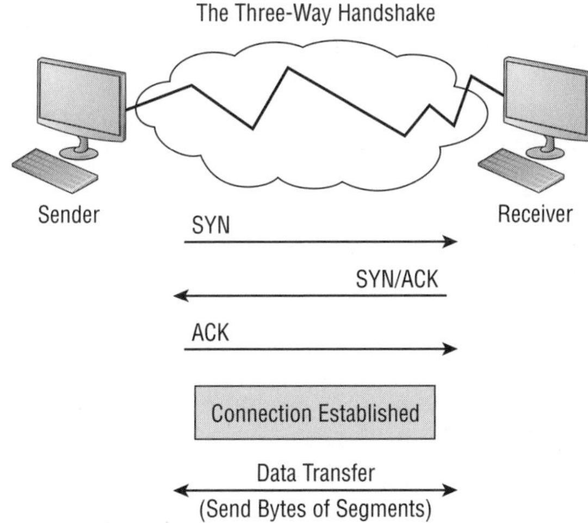

While the information is being transferred between hosts, the two machines periodically check in with each other, communicating through their protocol software to ensure that all is going well and that the data is being received properly.

Here's a summary of the steps in the connection-oriented session—the three-way handshake—pictured in Figure 1.9:

- The first "connection agreement" segment is a request for synchronization.
- The next segments acknowledge the request and establish connection parameters—the rules—between hosts. These segments request that the receiver's sequencing is synchronized here as well so that a bidirectional connection is formed.
- The final segment is also an acknowledgment. It notifies the destination host that the connection agreement has been accepted and that the actual connection has been established. Data transfer can now begin.

Sounds pretty simple, but things don't always flow so smoothly. Sometimes during a transfer, congestion can occur because a high-speed computer is generating data traffic a lot faster than the network can handle transferring. A bunch of computers simultaneously sending datagrams through a single gateway or destination can also botch things up nicely. In the latter case, a gateway or destination can become congested even though no single source caused the problem. In either case, the problem is basically akin to a freeway bottleneck—too much traffic for too small a capacity. It's not usually one car that's the problem; there are simply too many cars on that freeway.

Okay, so what happens when a machine receives a flood of datagrams too quickly for it to process? It stores them in a memory section called a *buffer*. But this buffering action can solve the problem only if the datagrams are part of a small burst. If not, and the datagram deluge continues, a device's memory will eventually be exhausted, its flood capacity will be exceeded, and it will react by discarding any additional datagrams that arrive.

No huge worries here, though. Because of the transport function, network flood control systems really work quite well. Instead of dumping data and allowing data to be lost, the transport can issue a "not ready" indicator to the sender, or source, of the flood (as shown in Figure 1.10). This mechanism works kind of like a stoplight, signaling the sending device to stop transmitting segment traffic to its overwhelmed peer. After the peer receiver processes the segments already in its memory reservoir—its buffer—it sends out a "ready" transport indicator. When the machine waiting to transmit the rest of its datagrams receives this "go" indicator, it resumes its transmission.

FIGURE 1.10 Transmitting segments with flow control

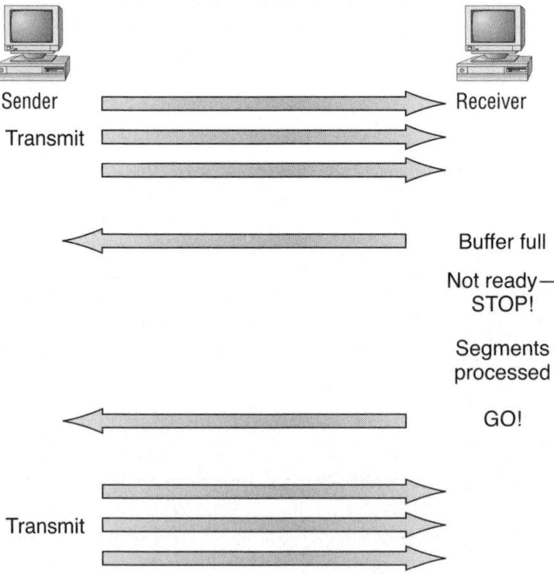

In fundamental, reliable, connection-oriented data transfer, datagrams are delivered to the receiving host in exactly the same sequence they're transmitted—and the transmission fails if this order is breached! If any data segments are lost, duplicated, or damaged along the way, a failure will occur. This problem is solved by having the receiving host acknowledge that it has received each and every data segment.

A service is considered connection oriented if it has the following characteristics:

- A virtual circuit is set up (e.g., a three-way handshake).
- It uses sequencing.
- It uses acknowledgments.
- It uses flow control.

The types of flow control are buffering, windowing, and congestion avoidance.

Windowing

Ideally, data throughput happens quickly and efficiently. And as you can imagine, it would be slow if the transmitting machine had to wait for an acknowledgment after sending each segment. But because there's time available *after* the sender transmits the data segment and *before* it finishes processing acknowledgments from the receiving machine, the sender uses the break as an opportunity to transmit more data. The quantity of data segments (measured in bytes) that the transmitting machine is allowed to send without receiving an acknowledgment for them is called a *window*.

Windows are used to control the amount of outstanding, unacknowledged data segments.

So the size of the window controls how much information is transferred from one end to the other. While some protocols quantify information by observing the number of packets, TCP/IP measures it by counting the number of bytes.

As you can see in Figure 1.11, there are two window sizes—one set to 1 and one set to 3.

When you've configured a window size of 1, the sending machine waits for an acknowledgment for each data segment it transmits before transmitting another. If you've configured a window size of 3, it's allowed to transmit three data segments before an acknowledgment is received.

In this simplified example, both the sending and receiving machines are workstations. In reality, this is not done in simple numbers but in the amount of bytes that can be sent.

If a receiving host fails to receive all the bytes that it should acknowledge, the host can improve the communication session by decreasing the window size.

FIGURE 1.11 Windowing

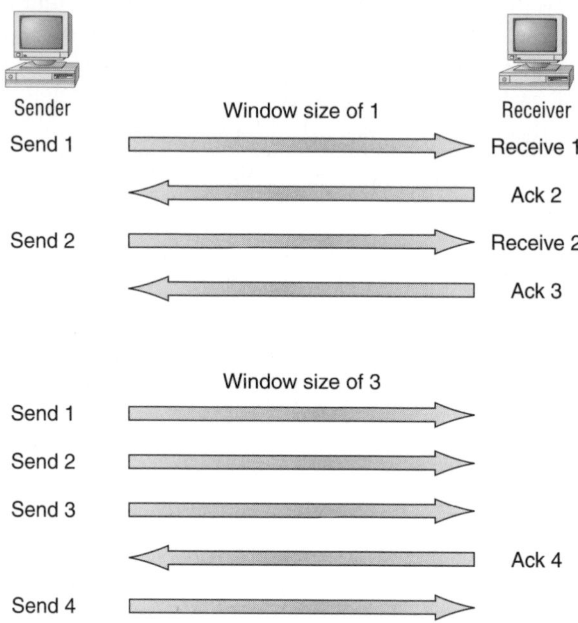

Acknowledgments

Reliable data delivery ensures the integrity of a stream of data sent from one machine to the other through a fully functional data link. It guarantees that the data won't be duplicated or lost. This is achieved through something called *positive acknowledgment with retransmission*—a technique that requires a receiving machine to communicate with the transmitting source by sending an acknowledgment message back to the sender when it receives data. The sender documents each segment measured in bytes; it then sends and waits for this acknowledgment before sending the next segment round of bytes. When it sends a segment, the transmitting machine starts a timer and retransmits if it expires before an acknowledgment is returned from the receiving end.

In Figure 1.12, the sending machine transmits segments 1, 2, and 3. The receiving node acknowledges it has received them by requesting segment 4. When it receives the acknowledgment, the sender then transmits segments 4, 5, and 6. If segment 5 doesn't make it to the destination, the receiving node acknowledges that event with a request for the segment to be resent. The sending machine will then resend the lost segment and wait for an acknowledgment, which it must receive in order to move on to the transmission of segment 7.

The Network Layer

The *Network layer* (also called layer 3) manages device addressing, tracks the location of devices on the network, and determines the best way to move data, which means that the

Network layer must transport traffic between devices that aren't locally attached. Routers (layer 3 devices) are specified at the Network layer and provide the routing services within an internetwork.

FIGURE 1.12 Transport layer reliable delivery

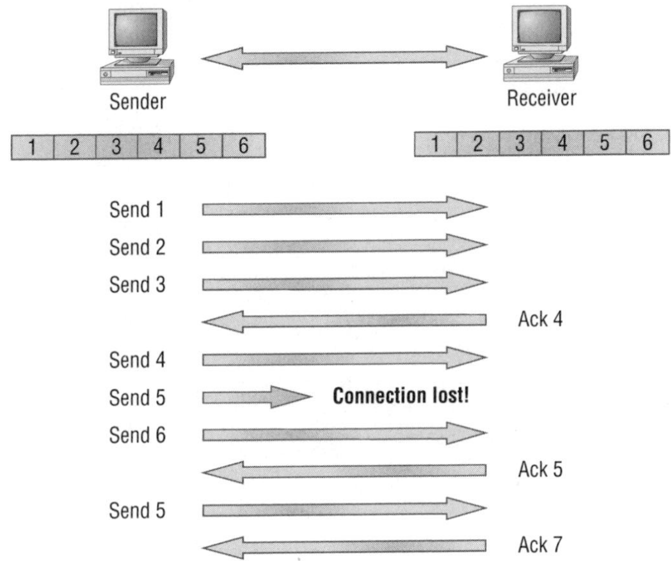

It happens like this: First, when a packet is received on a router interface, the destination IP address is checked. If the packet isn't destined for that particular router, it will look up the destination network address in the routing table. Once the router chooses an exit interface, the packet will be sent to that interface to be framed and sent out on the local network. If the router can't find an entry for the packet's destination network in the routing table, the router drops the packet.

Two types of packets are used at the Network layer: data and route updates.

Data packets Used to transport user data through the internetwork. Protocols used to support data traffic are called *routed protocols*; examples of routed protocols are IP and IPv6. You'll learn about IP addressing in Chapters 3 and 4 and IPv6 in Chapter 15.

Route update packets Used to update neighboring routers about the networks connected to all routers within the internetwork. Protocols that send route update packets are called *routing protocols*; examples of some common ones are RIP, RIPv2, EIGRP, and OSPF. Route update packets are used to help build and maintain routing tables on each router.

Figure 1.13 shows an example of a routing table.

The routing table used in a router includes the following information:

Network addresses Protocol-specific network addresses. A router must maintain a routing table for individual routed protocol because each routed protocol keeps track of a network with a different addressing scheme (IP, IPv6, and IPX, for example). Think of it as a street sign in each of the different languages spoken by the residents that live on a particular street. So, if there were American, Spanish, and French folks on a street named Cat, the sign would read Cat/Gato/Chat.

Interface The exit interface a packet will take when destined for a specific network.

Metric The distance to the remote network. Different routing protocols use different ways of computing this distance. I'm going to cover routing protocols in Chapters 8 and 9, but for now, know that some routing protocols (namely RIP) use something called a *hop count* (the number of routers a packet passes through en route to a remote network), while others use bandwidth, delay of the line, or even tick count (1/18 of a second).

FIGURE 1.13 Routing table used in a router

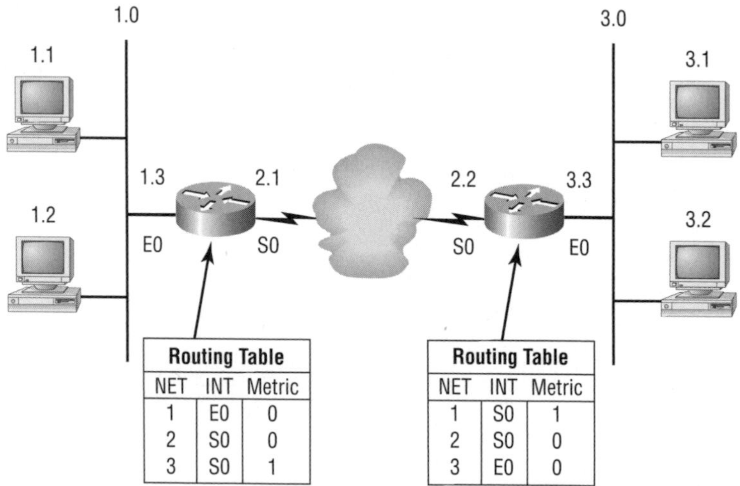

And as I mentioned earlier, routers break up broadcast domains, which means that by default, broadcasts aren't forwarded through a router. Do you remember why this is a good thing? Routers also break up collision domains, but you can also do that using layer 2 (Data Link layer) switches. Because each interface in a router represents a separate network, it must be assigned unique network identification numbers, and each host on the network connected to that router must use the same network number. Figure 1.14 shows how a router works in an internetwork.

Here are some points about routers that you should really commit to memory:

- Routers, by default, will not forward any broadcast or multicast packets.
- Routers use the logical address in a Network layer header to determine the next hop router to forward the packet to.
- Routers can use access lists, created by an administrator, to control security on the types of packets that are allowed to enter or exit an interface.

- Routers can provide layer 2 bridging functions if needed and can simultaneously route through the same interface.
- Layer 3 devices (routers in this case) provide connections between virtual LANs (VLANs).
- Routers can provide quality of service (QoS) for specific types of network traffic.

Switching and VLANs and are covered in Chapter 10, "Layer 2 Switching and Spanning Tree Protocol (STP)," and Chapter 11, "Virtual LANs (VLANs)."

FIGURE 1.14 A router in an internetwork

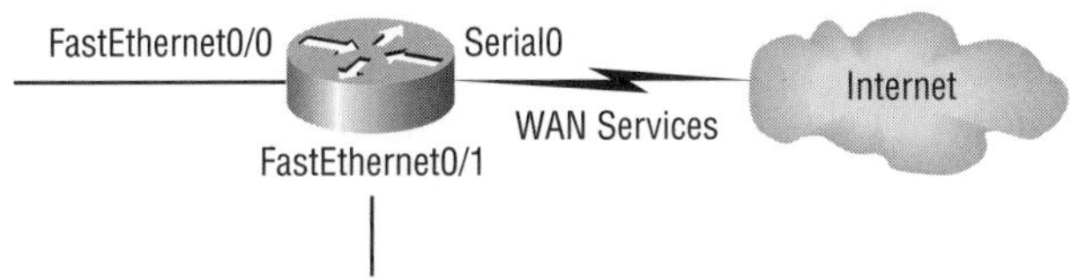
FastEthernet0/0
Serial0
Internet
WAN Services
FastEthernet0/1
Each router interface is a broadcast domain.
Routers break up broadcast domains by
default and provide WAN services.

The Data Link Layer

The *Data Link layer* provides the physical transmission of the data and handles error notification, network topology, and flow control. This means that the Data Link layer will ensure that messages are delivered to the proper device on a LAN using hardware addresses and will translate messages from the Network layer into bits for the Physical layer to transmit.

The Data Link layer formats the message into pieces, each called a *data frame*, and adds a customized header containing the hardware destination and source address. This added information forms a sort of capsule that surrounds the original message in much the same way that engines, navigational devices, and other tools were attached to the lunar modules of the Apollo project. These various pieces of equipment were useful only during certain stages of space flight and were stripped off the module and discarded when their designated stage was complete. Data traveling through networks is similar.

Figure 1.15 shows the Data Link layer with the Ethernet and IEEE specifications. When you check it out, notice that the IEEE 802.2 standard is used in conjunction with and adds functionality to the other IEEE standards.

It's important for you to understand that routers, which work at the Network layer, don't care at all about where a particular host is located. They're only concerned about where networks are located and the best way to reach them—including remote ones. Routers are totally obsessive when it comes to networks. And for once, this is a good thing! It's the Data Link layer that's responsible for the actual unique identification of each device that resides on a local network.

FIGURE 1.15 Data Link layer

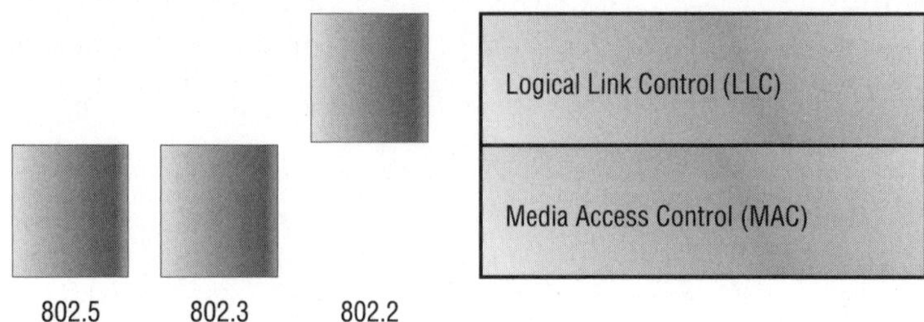

For a host to send packets to individual hosts on a local network as well as transmit packets between routers, the Data Link layer uses hardware addressing. Each time a packet is sent between routers, it's framed with control information at the Data Link layer, but that information is stripped off at the receiving router and only the original packet is left completely intact. This framing of the packet continues for each hop until the packet is finally delivered to the correct receiving host. It's really important to understand that the packet itself is never altered along the route; it's only encapsulated with the type of control information required for it to be properly passed on to the different media types.

The IEEE Ethernet Data Link layer has two sublayers:

Media Access Control (MAC) 802.3 Defines how packets are placed on the media. Contention media access is "first come/first served" access where everyone shares the same bandwidth—hence the name. Physical addressing is defined here as well as logical topologies. What's a logical topology? It's the signal path through a physical topology. Line discipline, error notification (not correction), ordered delivery of frames, and optional flow control can also be used at this sublayer.

Logical Link Control (LLC) 802.2 Responsible for identifying Network layer protocols and then encapsulating them. An LLC header tells the Data Link layer what to do with a packet once a frame is received. It works like this: A host will receive a frame and look in the LLC header to find out where the packet is destined—say, the IP protocol at the Network layer. The LLC can also provide flow control and sequencing of control bits.

The switches and bridges I talked about near the beginning of the chapter both work at the Data Link layer and filter the network using hardware (MAC) addresses. We will look at these in the following section.

Switches and Bridges at the Data Link Layer

Layer 2 switching is considered hardware-based bridging because it uses specialized hardware called an *application-specific integrated circuit (ASIC)*. ASICs can run up to gigabit speeds with very low latency rates.

Latency is the time measured from when a frame enters a port to when it exits a port.

Bridges and switches read each frame as it passes through the network. The layer 2 device then puts the source hardware address in a filter table and keeps track of which port the frame was received on. This information (logged in the bridge's or switch's filter table) is what helps the machine determine the location of the specific sending device. Figure 1.16 shows a switch in an internetwork.

FIGURE 1.16 A switch in an internetwork

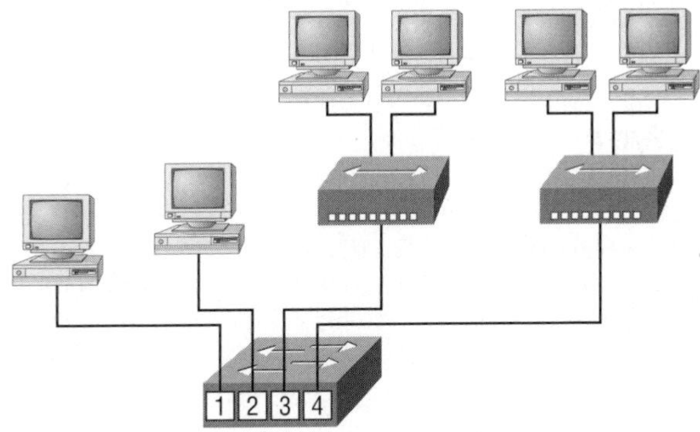

Each segment has its own collision domain.
All segments are in the same broadcast domain.

The real estate business is all about location, location, location, and it's the same way for both layer 2 and layer 3 devices. Though both need to be able to negotiate the network, it's crucial to remember that they're concerned with very different parts of it. Primarily, layer 3 machines (such as routers) need to locate specific networks, whereas layer 2 machines (switches and bridges) need to eventually locate specific devices. So, networks are to routers as individual devices are to switches and bridges. And routing tables that "map" the internetwork are for routers as filter tables that "map" individual devices are for switches and bridges.

After a filter table is built on the layer 2 device, it will forward frames only to the segment where the destination hardware address is located. If the destination device is on the same segment as the frame, the layer 2 device will block the frame from going to any other segments. If the destination is on a different segment, the frame can be transmitted only to that segment. This is called *transparent bridging*.

When a switch interface receives a frame with a destination hardware address that isn't found in the device's filter table, it will forward the frame to all connected segments. If the unknown device that was sent the "mystery frame" replies to this forwarding action, the switch updates its filter table regarding that device's location. But in the event the destination address of the transmitting frame is a broadcast address, the switch will forward all broadcasts to every connected segment by default.

All devices that the broadcast is forwarded to are considered to be in the same broadcast domain. This can be a problem; layer 2 devices propagate layer 2 broadcast storms that choke performance, and the only way to stop a broadcast storm from propagating through an internetwork is with a layer 3 device—a router.

The biggest benefit of using switches instead of hubs in your internetwork is that each switch port is actually its own collision domain. (Conversely, a hub creates one large collision domain.) But even armed with a switch, you still don't break up broadcast domains by default. Neither switches nor bridges will do that. They'll simply forward all broadcasts instead.

Another benefit of LAN switching over hub-centered implementations is that each device on every segment plugged into a switch can transmit simultaneously—at least, they can as long as there is only one host on each port and a hub isn't plugged into a switch port. As you might have guessed, hubs allow only one device per network segment to communicate at a time.

The Physical Layer

Finally arriving at the bottom, we find that the *Physical layer* does two things: It sends bits and receives bits. Bits come only in values of 1 or 0—a Morse code with numerical values. The Physical layer communicates directly with the various types of actual communication media. Different kinds of media represent these bit values in different ways. Some use audio tones, while others employ *state transitions*—changes in voltage from high to low and low to high. Specific protocols are needed for each type of media to describe the proper bit patterns to be used, how data is encoded into media signals, and the various qualities of the physical media's attachment interface.

The Physical layer specifies the electrical, mechanical, procedural, and functional requirements for activating, maintaining, and deactivating a physical link between end systems. This layer is also where you identify the interface between the *data terminal equipment (DTE)* and the *data communication equipment (DCE)*. (Some old phone-company employees still call DCE data circuit-terminating equipment.) The DCE is usually located at the service provider, while the DTE is the attached device. The services available to the DTE are most often accessed via a modem or *channel service unit/data service unit (CSU/DSU)*.

The Physical layer's connectors and different physical topologies are defined by the OSI as standards, allowing disparate systems to communicate. The CCNA objectives are only interested in the IEEE Ethernet standards.

Hubs at the Physical Layer

A *hub* is really a multiple-port repeater. A repeater receives a digital signal and reamplifies or regenerates that signal and then forwards the digital signal out all active ports without looking at any data. An active hub does the same thing. Any digital signal received from a segment on a hub port is regenerated or reamplified and transmitted out all other ports on the hub. This means all devices plugged into a hub are in the same collision domain as well as in the same broadcast domain. Figure 1.17 shows a hub in a network.

Hubs, like repeaters, don't examine any of the traffic as it enters and is then transmitted out to the other parts of the physical media. Every device connected to the hub, or hubs, must listen if a device transmits. A physical star network—where the hub is a central device and cables extend in all directions out from it—is the type of topology a hub creates. Visually, the design really does resemble a star, whereas Ethernet networks run a logical bus topology, meaning that the signal has to run through the network from end to end.

Hubs and repeaters can be used to enlarge the area covered by a single LAN segment, although I do not recommend this. LAN switches are affordable for almost every situation.

FIGURE 1.17 A hub in a network

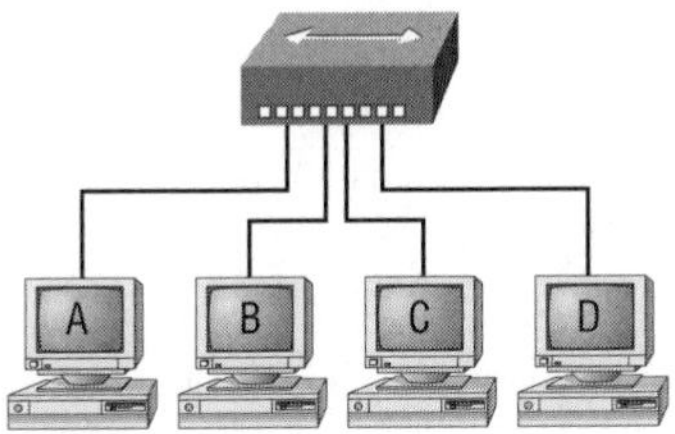

All devices in the same collision domain.
All devices in the same broadcast domain.
Devices share the same bandwidth.

Summary

Whew! I know this seemed like the chapter that wouldn't end, but it did—and you made it through! You're now armed with a ton of fundamental information; you're ready to build upon it and are well on your way to certification.

I started by discussing simple, basic networking and the differences between collision and broadcast domains.

I then discussed the OSI model—the seven-layer model used to help application developers design applications that can run on any type of system or network. Each layer has its special jobs and select responsibilities within the model to ensure that solid, effective communications do, in fact, occur. I provided you with complete details of each layer and discussed how Cisco views the specifications of the OSI model.

In addition, each layer in the OSI model specifies different types of devices, and I described these different devices used at each layer.

Remember that hubs are Physical layer devices and repeat the digital signal to all segments except the one from which it was received. Switches segment the network using hardware addresses and break up collision domains. Routers break up broadcast domains (and collision domains) and use logical addressing to send packets through an internetwork.

Exam Essentials

Identify the possible causes of LAN traffic congestion. Too many hosts in a broadcast domain, broadcast storms, multicasting, and low bandwidth are all possible causes of LAN traffic congestion.

Describe the difference between a collision domain and a broadcast domain. *Collision domain* is an Ethernet term used to describe a network collection of devices in which one particular device sends a packet on a network segment, forcing every other device on that same segment to pay attention to it. On a broadcast domain, a set of all devices on a network segment hear all broadcasts sent on that segment.

Differentiate a MAC address and an IP address and describe how and when each address type is used in a network. A MAC address is a hexadecimal number identifying the physical connection of a host. MAC addresses are said to operate on layer 2 of the OSI model. IP addresses, which can be expressed in binary or decimal format, are logical identifiers that are said to be on layer 3 of the OSI model. Hosts on the same physical segment locate one another with MAC addresses, while IP addresses are used when they reside on different LAN segments or subnets. Even when the hosts are in different subnets, a destination IP address will be converted to a MAC address when the packet reaches the destination network via routing.

Understand the difference between a hub, a bridge, a switch, and a router. Hubs create one collision domain and one broadcast domain. Bridges break up collision domains but create one large broadcast domain. They use hardware addresses to filter the network. Switches are really just multiple-port bridges with more intelligence. They break up collision domains but create one large broadcast domain by default. Switches use hardware addresses to filter the network. Routers break up broadcast domains (and collision domains) and use logical addressing to filter the network.

Identify the functions and advantages of routers. Routers perform packet switching, filtering, and path selection, and they facilitate internetwork communication. One advantage of routers is that they reduce broadcast traffic.

Differentiate connection-oriented and connectionless network services and describe how each is handled during network communications Connection-oriented services use acknowledgments and flow control to create a reliable session. More overhead is used than in a connectionless network service. Connectionless services are used to send data with no acknowledgments or flow control. This is considered unreliable.

Define the OSI layers, understand the function of each, and describe how devices and networking protocols can be mapped to each layer. You must remember the seven layers of the OSI model and what function each layer provides. The Application, Presentation, and Session layers are upper layers and are responsible for communicating from a user interface to an application. The Transport layer provides segmentation, sequencing, and virtual circuits. The Network layer provides logical network addressing and routing through an internetwork. The Data Link layer provides framing and placing of data on the network medium. The Physical layer is responsible for taking 1s and 0s and encoding them into a digital signal for transmission on the network segment.

Written Labs

In this section, you'll complete the following labs to make sure you've got the information and concepts contained within them fully dialed in:

Lab 1.1: OSI Questions

Lab 1.2: Defining the OSI Layers and Devices

Lab 1.3: Identifying Collision and Broadcast Domains

(The answers to the written labs can be found following the answers to the review questions for this chapter.)

Written Lab 1.1: OSI Questions

Answer the following questions about the OSI model:

1. Which layer chooses and determines the availability of communicating partners along with the resources necessary to make the connection, coordinates partnering applications, and forms a consensus on procedures for controlling data integrity and error recovery?
2. Which layer is responsible for converting data packets from the Data Link layer into electrical signals?
3. At which layer is routing implemented, enabling connections and path selection between two end systems?
4. Which layer defines how data is formatted, presented, encoded, and converted for use on the network?
5. Which layer is responsible for creating, managing, and terminating sessions between applications?
6. Which layer ensures the trustworthy transmission of data across a physical link and is primarily concerned with physical addressing, line discipline, network topology, error notification, ordered delivery of frames, and flow control?
7. Which layer is used for reliable communication between end nodes over the network and provides mechanisms for establishing, maintaining, and terminating virtual circuits; transport-fault detection and recovery; and controlling the flow of information?
8. Which layer provides logical addressing that routers will use for path determination?
9. Which layer specifies voltage, wire speed, and pinout cables and moves bits between devices?
10. Which layer combines bits into bytes and bytes into frames, uses MAC addressing, and provides error detection?
11. Which layer is responsible for keeping the data from different applications separate on the network?

12. Which layer is represented by frames?
13. Which layer is represented by segments?
14. Which layer is represented by packets?
15. Which layer is represented by bits?
16. Put the following in order of encapsulation:

    Packets

    Frames

    Bits

    Segments

17. Which layer segments and reassembles data into a data stream?
18. Which layer provides the physical transmission of the data and handles error notification, network topology, and flow control?
19. Which layer manages device addressing, tracks the location of devices on the network, and determines the best way to move data?
20. What is the bit length and expression form of a MAC address?

Written Lab 1.2: Defining the OSI Layers and Devices

Fill in the blanks with the appropriate layer of the OSI or hub, switch, or router device.

Description	Device or OSI Layer
This device sends and receives information about the Network layer.	
This layer creates a virtual circuit before transmitting between two end stations.	
This device uses hardware addresses to filter a network.	
Ethernet is defined at these layers.	
This layer supports flow control, sequencing, and acknowledgments.	
This device can measure the distance to a remote network.	
Logical addressing is used at this layer.	
Hardware addresses are defined at this layer.	

Description	Device or OSI Layer
This device creates one big collision domain and one large broadcast domain.	
This device creates many smaller collision domains, but the network is still one large broadcast domain.	
This device can never run full duplex.	
This device breaks up collision domains and broadcast domains.	

Written Lab 1.3: Identifying Collision and Broadcast Domains

1. In the following exhibit, identify the number of collision domains and broadcast domains in each specified device. Each device is represented by a letter:
   A. Hub
   B. Bridge
   C. Switch
   D. Router

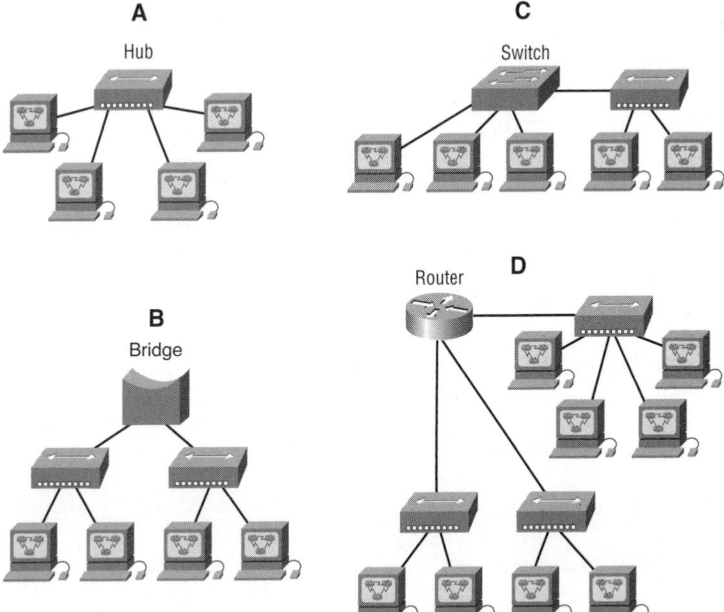

Review Questions

The following questions are designed to test your understanding of this chapter's material. For more information on how to get additional questions, please see this book's introduction.

1. A receiving host has failed to receive all of the segments that it should acknowledge. What can the host do to improve the reliability of this communication session?
   A. Send a different source port number.
   B. Restart the virtual circuit.
   C. Decrease the sequence number.
   D. Decrease the window size.

2. When a station sends a transmission to the MAC address `ff:ff:ff:ff:ff:ff`, what type of transmission is it?
   A. Unicast
   B. Multicast
   C. Anycast
   D. Broadcast

3. Which layer 1 devices can be used to enlarge the area covered by a single LAN segment? (Choose two.)
   A. Switch
   B. NIC
   C. Hub
   D. Repeater
   E. RJ45 transceiver

4. Segmentation of a data stream happens at which layer of the OSI model?
   A. Physical
   B. Data Link
   C. Network
   D. Transport

5. Which of the following describe the main router functions? (Choose four.)
   A. Packet switching
   B. Collision prevention
   C. Packet filtering
   D. Broadcast domain enlargement
   E. Internetwork communication
   F. Broadcast forwarding
   G. Path selection

6. Routers operate at layer ___. LAN switches operate at layer ___. Ethernet hubs operate at layer ___. Word processing operates at layer ___.
   A. 3, 3, 1, 7
   B. 3, 2, 1, none
   C. 3, 2, 1, 7
   D. 2, 3, 1, 7
   E. 3, 3, 2, none

7. When data is encapsulated, which is the correct order?
   A. Data, frame, packet, segment, bit
   B. Segment, data, packet, frame, bit
   C. Data, segment, packet, frame, bit
   D. Data, segment, frame, packet, bit

8. Why does the data communication industry use the layered OSI reference model? (Choose two.)
   A. It divides the network communication process into smaller and simpler components, thus aiding component development, design, and troubleshooting.
   B. It enables equipment from different vendors to use the same electronic components, thus saving research and development funds.
   C. It supports the evolution of multiple competing standards and thus provides business opportunities for equipment manufacturers.
   D. It encourages industry standardization by defining what functions occur at each layer of the model.
   E. It provides a framework by which changes in functionality in one layer require changes in other layers.

9. What are two purposes for segmentation with a bridge?
   A. To add more broadcast domains
   B. To create more collision domains
   C. To add more bandwidth for users
   D. To allow more broadcasts for users

10. Which of the following is *not* a cause of LAN congestion?
    A. Too many hosts in a broadcast domain
    B. Adding switches for connectivity to the network
    C. Broadcast storms
    D. Low bandwidth

11. If a switch has three computers connected to it, with no VLANs present, how many broadcast and collision domains is the switch creating?
    A. Three broadcast and one collision
    B. Three broadcast and three collision
    C. One broadcast and three collision
    D. One broadcast and one collision

12. Acknowledgments, sequencing, and flow control are characteristics of which OSI layer?
    A. Layer 2
    B. Layer 3
    C. Layer 4
    D. Layer 7

13. Which of the following are types of flow control? (Choose all that apply.)
    A. Buffering
    B. Cut-through
    C. Windowing
    D. Congestion avoidance
    E. VLANs

14. If a hub has three computers connected to it, how many broadcast and collision domains is the hub creating?
    A. Three broadcast and one collision
    B. Three broadcast and three collision
    C. One broadcast and three collision
    D. One broadcast and one collision

15. What is the purpose of flow control?
    A. To ensure that data is retransmitted if an acknowledgment is not received
    B. To reassemble segments in the correct order at the destination device
    C. To provide a means for the receiver to govern the amount of data sent by the sender
    D. To regulate the size of each segment

16. Which three statements are true about the operation of a full-duplex Ethernet network?

   A. There are no collisions in full-duplex mode.

   B. A dedicated switch port is required for each full-duplex node.

   C. Ethernet hub ports are preconfigured for full-duplex mode.

   D. In a full-duplex environment, the host network card must check for the availability of the network media before transmitting.

   E. The host network card and the switch port must be capable of operating in full-duplex mode.

17. Which of the following is *not* a benefit of reference models such as the OSI model?

   A. It allows changes on one layer to affect operations on all other layers as well.

   B. It divides the network communication process into smaller and simpler components, thus aiding component development, design, and troubleshooting.

   C. It allows multiple-vendor development through standardization of network components.

   D. It allows various types of network hardware and software to communicate.

18. Which of the following devices do *not* operate at all levels of the OSI model?

   A. Network management stations (NMSs)

   B. Routers

   C. Web and application servers

   D. Network hosts

19. When an HTTP document must be retrieved from a location other than the local machine, what layer of the OSI model must be accessed first?

   A. Presentations

   B. Transport

   C. Application

   D. Network

20. Which layer of the OSI model offers three different modes of communication: *simplex*, *half duplex*, and *full duplex*?

   A. Presentation

   B. Transport

   C. Application

   D. Session

Answers to Review Questions

1. D. A receiving host can control the transmitter by using flow control (TCP uses windowing by default). By decreasing the window size, the receiving host can slow down the transmitting host so the receiving host does not overflow its buffers.

2. D. A transmission to the MAC address `ff:ff:ff:ff:ff:ff` is a broadcast transmission to all stations.

3. C, D. Not that you really want to enlarge a single collision domain, but a hub (multiport repeater) will provide this for you.

4. D. The Transport layer receives large data streams from the upper layers and breaks these up into smaller pieces called segments.

5. A, C, E, G. Routers provide packet switching, packet filtering, internetwork communication, and path selection. Although routers do create or terminate collision domains, this is not the main purpose of a router, so option B is not a correct answer to this question.

6. B. Routers operate at layer 3. LAN switches operate at layer 2. Ethernet hubs operate at layer 1. Word processing applications communicate to the Application layer interface, but do not operate at layer 7, so the answer would be none.

7. C. The encapsulation method is data, segment, packet, frame, bit.

8. A, D. The main advantage of a layered model is that it can allow application developers to change aspects of a program in just one layer of the layer model's specifications. Advantages of using the OSI layered model include, but are not limited to, the following: It divides the network communication process into smaller and simpler components, thus aiding component development, design, and troubleshooting; it allows multiple-vendor development through standardization of network components; it encourages industry standardization by defining what functions occur at each layer of the model; it allows various types of network hardware and software to communicate; and it prevents changes in one layer from affecting other layers, so it does not hamper development.

9. A, D. Unlike full duplex, half-duplex Ethernet operates in a shared collision domain, and it has a lower effective throughput than full duplex.

10. B. Adding switches for connectivity to the network would reduce LAN congestion rather than cause LAN congestion.

11. C. If a switch has three computers connected to it, with no VLANs present, one broadcast and three collision domains are created.

12. C. A reliable Transport layer connection uses acknowledgments to make sure all data is transmitted and received reliably. A reliable connection is defined by a virtual circuit that uses acknowledgments, sequencing, and flow control, which are characteristics of the Transport layer (layer 4).

13. A, C, D. The common types of flow control are buffering, windowing, and congestion avoidance.

14. D. If a hub has three computers connected to it, one broadcast and one collision domain is created.

15. C. Flow control allows the receiving device to control the transmitter so the receiving device's buffer does not overflow.

16. A, B, E. Full duplex means you are using both wire pairs simultaneously to send and receive data. You must have a dedicated switch port for each node, which means you will not have collisions. Both the host network card and the switch port must be capable and set to work in full-duplex mode.

17. A. Reference models prevent, rather than allow, changes on one layer to affect operations on other layers as well, so the model doesn't hamper development.

18. B. Routers operate no higher than layer 3 of the OSI model.

19. C. When an HTTP document must be retrieved from a location other than the local machine, the Application layer must be accessed first.

20. D. The Session layer of the OSI model offers three different modes of communication: *simplex*, *half duplex*, and *full duplex*.

Answers to Written Lab 1.1

1. The Application layer is responsible for finding the network resources broadcast from a server and adding flow control and error control (if the application developer chooses).
2. The Physical layer takes frames from the Data Link layer and encodes the 1s and 0s into a digital signal for transmission on the network medium.
3. The Network layer provides routing through an internetwork and logical addressing.
4. The Presentation layer makes sure that data is in a readable format for the Application layer.
5. The Session layer sets up, maintains, and terminates sessions between applications.
6. PDUs at the Data Link layer are called frames and provide physical addressing, plus other options to place packets on the network medium.
7. The Transport layer uses virtual circuits to create a reliable connection between two hosts.
8. The Network layer provides logical addressing, typically IP addressing and routing.
9. The Physical layer is responsible for the electrical and mechanical connections between devices.
10. The Data Link layer is responsible for the framing of data packets.
11. The Session layer creates sessions between different hosts' applications.
12. The Data Link layer frames packets received from the Network layer.
13. The Transport layer segments user data.
14. The Network layer creates packets out of segments handed down from the Transport layer.
15. The Physical layer is responsible for transporting 1s and 0s (bits) in a digital signal.
16. Segments, packets, frames, bits
17. Transport
18. Data Link
19. Network
20. 48 bits (6 bytes) expressed as a hexadecimal number

Answers to Written Lab 1.2

Description	Device or OSI Layer
This device sends and receives information about the Network layer.	Router
This layer creates a virtual circuit before transmitting between two end stations.	Transport
This device uses hardware addresses to filter a network.	Bridge or switch
Ethernet is defined at these layers.	Data Link and Physical
This layer supports flow control, sequencing, and acknowledgments.	Transport
This device can measure the distance to a remote network.	Router
Logical addressing is used at this layer.	Network
Hardware addresses are defined at this layer.	Data Link (MAC sublayer)
This device creates one big collision domain and one large broadcast domain.	Hub
This device creates many smaller collision domains, but the network is still one large broadcast domain.	Switch or bridge
This device can never run full duplex.	Hub
This device breaks up collision domains and broadcast domains.	Router

Answers to Written Lab 1.3

1. Hub: One collision domain, one broadcast domain
2. Bridge: Two collision domains, one broadcast domain
3. Switch: Four collision domains, one broadcast domain
4. Router: Three collision domains, three broadcast domains

Review of Ethernet Networking and Data Encapsulation

THE CCNA EXAM TOPICS COVERED IN THIS CHAPTER INCLUDE THE FOLLOWING:

✓ **Describe How a Network Works**

✓ **Configure, Verify, and Troubleshoot a Switch with VLANs and Interswitch Communications**

- Use the OSI and TCP/IP models and their associated protocols to explain how data flows in a network
- Select the appropriate media, cables, ports, and connectors to connect switches to other network devices and hosts
- Explain the technology and media access control method for Ethernet networks
- Explain network segmentation and basic traffic management concepts

Before we move on and explore the TCP/IP and DoD models, IP addressing, subnetting, and routing in the upcoming chapters, you've got to understand the big picture of LANs and learn the answers to two key questions: How is Ethernet used in today's networks? and, What are Media Access Control (MAC) addresses and how are they used?

This chapter will answer those questions and more. I'll not only discuss the basics of Ethernet and the way MAC addresses are used on an Ethernet LAN, but I'll cover the protocols used with Ethernet at the Data Link layer as well. You'll also learn about the various Ethernet specifications.

As you learned in Chapter 1, there are a bunch of different types of devices specified at the different layers of the OSI model, and it's very important to understand the many types of cables and connectors used for connecting all those devices to a network. This chapter will review the various cabling used with Cisco devices, describing how to connect to a router or switch and even how to connect a router or switch with a console connection.

Also in this chapter, I'll provide an introduction to encapsulation. Encapsulation is the process of encoding data as it goes down the OSI stack.

The chapter concludes with a discussion of the three-layer hierarchical model that was developed by Cisco to help you design, implement, and troubleshoot internetworks.

After you finish reading this chapter, you'll encounter 20 review questions and four written labs. These are given to you to really lock the information from this chapter into your memory. So don't skip them!

To find up-to-the minute updates for this chapter, please see `www.lammle.com` or `www.sybex.com/go/ccna7e`.

Ethernet Networks in Review

Ethernet is a contention-based media access method that allows all hosts on a network to share the same bandwidth of a link. Ethernet is popular because it's readily scalable, meaning that it's comparatively easy to integrate new technologies, such as upgrading from Fast Ethernet to Gigabit Ethernet, into an existing network infrastructure. It's also relatively simple to implement in the first place, and with it, troubleshooting is reasonably straightforward. Ethernet uses both Data Link and Physical layer specifications, and this chapter will give you both the Data Link layer and Physical layer information you need to effectively implement, troubleshoot, and maintain an Ethernet network.

Collision Domain

As mentioned in Chapter 1, the term *collision domain* is an Ethernet term that refers to a particular network scenario wherein one device sends a packet out on a network segment, thereby forcing every other device on that same physical network segment to pay attention to it. This can be bad because if two devices on one physical segment transmit at the same time, a collision event—a situation where each device's digital signals interfere with another on the wire—occurs and forces the devices to retransmit later. Collisions can have a dramatically negative effect on network performance, so they're definitely something you want to avoid!

The situation I just described is typically found in a hub environment where each host segment connects to a hub that represents only one collision domain and one broadcast domain. This begs the question that we discussed in Chapter 1: What's a broadcast domain?

Broadcast Domain

Here's the written definition: *Broadcast domain* refers to a group of devices on a network segment that hear all the broadcasts sent on that network segment.

Even though a broadcast domain is typically a boundary delimited by physical media like switches and routers, it can also reference a logical division of a network segment where all hosts can reach each other via a Data Link layer (hardware address) broadcast.

That's the basic story, so now let's take a look at a collision detection mechanism used in half-duplex Ethernet.

CSMA/CD

Ethernet networking uses *Carrier Sense Multiple Access with Collision Detection (CSMA/CD)*, a protocol that helps devices share the bandwidth evenly without having two devices transmit at the same time on the network medium. CSMA/CD was created to overcome the problem of those collisions that occur when packets are transmitted simultaneously from different nodes. And trust me—good collision management is crucial, because when a node transmits in a CSMA/CD network, all the other nodes on the network receive and examine that transmission. Only switches and routers can effectively prevent a transmission from propagating throughout the entire network!

So, how does the CSMA/CD protocol work? Let's start by taking a look at Figure 2.1.

When a host wants to transmit over the network, it first checks for the presence of a digital signal on the wire. If all is clear (no other host is transmitting), the host will then proceed with its transmission. But it doesn't stop there. The transmitting host constantly monitors the wire to make sure no other hosts begin transmitting. If the host detects another signal on the wire, it sends out an extended jam signal that causes all nodes on the segment to stop sending data (think busy signal). The nodes respond to that jam signal by waiting a while before attempting to transmit again. Backoff algorithms determine when the colliding stations can retransmit. If collisions keep occurring after 15 tries, the nodes attempting to transmit will then timeout. Pretty clean!

FIGURE 2.1 CSMA/CD

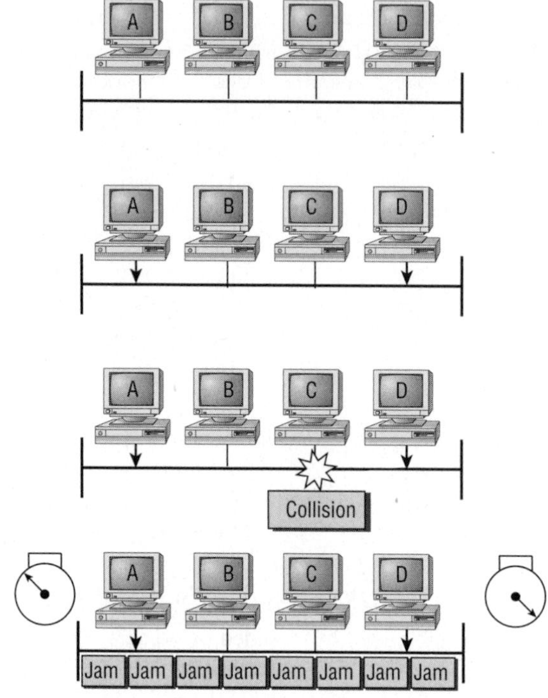

Carrier Sense Multiple Access with Collision Detection (CSMA/CD)

When a collision occurs on an Ethernet LAN, the following happens:

- A jam signal informs all devices that a collision occurred.
- The collision invokes a random backoff algorithm.
- Each device on the Ethernet segment stops transmitting for a short time until their backoff timers expire.
- All hosts have equal priority to transmit after the timers have expired.

The following are the effects of having a CSMA/CD network sustaining heavy collisions:

- Delay
- Low throughput
- Congestion

Backoff on an Ethernet network is the retransmission delay that's enforced when a collision occurs. When a collision occurs, a host will resume transmission after the forced time delay has expired. After this backoff delay period has expired, all stations have equal priority to transmit data.

In the following sections, I am going to cover Ethernet in detail at both the Data Link layer (layer 2) and the Physical layer (layer 1).

Half- and Full-Duplex Ethernet

Half-duplex Ethernet is defined in the original IEEE 802.3 Ethernet specification; Cisco says it uses only one wire pair with a digital signal running in both directions on the wire. Certainly, the IEEE specifications discuss the process of half duplex somewhat differently, but what Cisco is talking about is a general sense of what is happening here with Ethernet.

It also uses the CSMA/CD protocol to help prevent collisions and to permit retransmitting if a collision does occur. If a hub is attached to a switch, it must operate in half-duplex mode because the end stations must be able to detect collisions. Half-duplex Ethernet is only about 30 to 40 percent efficient because a large 100BaseT network will usually only give you 30 to 40Mbps, at most.

But full-duplex Ethernet uses two pairs of wires at the same time instead of one wire pair like half duplex. And full duplex uses a point-to-point connection between the transmitter of the transmitting device and the receiver of the receiving device. This means that with full-duplex data transfer, you get a faster data transfer compared to half duplex. And because the transmitted data is sent on a different set of wires than the received data, no collisions will occur.

The reason you don't need to worry about collisions is because now it's like a freeway with multiple lanes instead of the single-lane road provided by half duplex. Full-duplex Ethernet is supposed to offer 100 percent efficiency in both directions—for example, you can get 20Mbps with a 10Mbps Ethernet running full duplex or 200Mbps for Fast Ethernet. But this rate is something known as an aggregate rate, which translates as "you're supposed to get" 100 percent efficiency. No guarantees, in networking as in life.

Full-duplex Ethernet can be used in the following six situations:

- With a connection from a switch to a host
- With a connection from a switch to a switch
- With a connection from a host to a host using a crossover cable
- With a connection from a switch to a router
- With a connection from a router to a router using a crossover cable
- With a connection from a router to a host using a crossover cable

Full-duplex Ethernet requires a point-to-point connection when only two nodes are present. You can run full-duplex with just about any device except a hub.

Now, if it's capable of all that speed, why wouldn't it deliver? Well, when a full-duplex Ethernet port is powered on, it first connects to the remote end and then negotiates with the other end of the Fast Ethernet link. This is called an *auto-detect mechanism*. This mechanism first decides on the exchange capability, which means it checks to see if it can run at 10, 100, or even 1000Mbps. It then checks to see if it can run full duplex, and if it can't, it will run half duplex.

Remember that half-duplex Ethernet shares a collision domain and provides a lower effective throughput than full-duplex Ethernet, which typically has a private per-port collision domain and a higher effective throughput.

Lastly, remember these important points:

- There are no collisions in full-duplex mode.
- A dedicated switch port is required for each full-duplex node.
- The host network card and the switch port must be capable of operating in full-duplex mode.

Now let's take a look at how Ethernet works at the Data Link layer.

Ethernet at the Data Link Layer

Ethernet at the Data Link layer is responsible for Ethernet addressing, commonly referred to as hardware addressing or MAC addressing. Ethernet is also responsible for framing packets received from the Network layer and preparing them for transmission on the local network through the Ethernet contention-based media access method.

Ethernet Addressing

Here's where we get into how Ethernet addressing works. It uses the *Media Access Control (MAC)* address burned into each and every Ethernet network interface card (NIC). The MAC, or hardware, address is a 48-bit (6-byte) address written in a hexadecimal format.

Figure 2.2 shows the 48-bit MAC addresses and how the bits are divided.

FIGURE 2.2 Ethernet addressing using MAC addresses

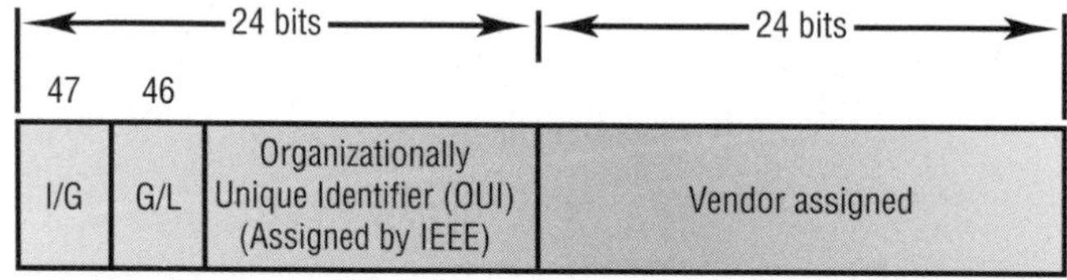

The *organizationally unique identifier (OUI)* is assigned by the IEEE to an organization. It's composed of 24 bits, or 3 bytes. The organization, in turn, assigns a globally administered address (24 bits, or 3 bytes) that is unique (supposedly, again—no guarantees) to each and every adapter it manufactures. Look closely at the figure. The high-order bit is the Individual/Group (I/G) bit. When it has a value of 0, we can assume that the address is the MAC address of a device and may well appear in the source portion of the MAC header. When it is a 1, we can assume that the address represents either a broadcast or multicast address in Ethernet or a broadcast or functional address in Token Ring and FDDI.

The next bit is the global/local bit, or just G/L bit (also known as U/L, where *U* means *universal*). When set to 0, this bit represents a globally administered address (as by the IEEE). When the bit is a 1, it represents a locally governed and administered address. The low-order 24 bits of an Ethernet address represent a locally administered or manufacturer-assigned code. This portion commonly starts with 24 0s for the first card made and continues in order until there are 24 1s for the last (16,777,216th) card made. You'll find that many manufacturers use these same six hex digits as the last six characters of their serial number on the same card.

Binary to Decimal and Hexadecimal Conversion

Before we get into working with the TCP/IP protocol and IP addressing (covered in Chapter 3), it's really important for you to truly understand the differences between binary, decimal, and hexadecimal numbers and how to convert one format into the other.

So we'll start with binary numbering. It's pretty simple, really. The digits used are limited to either a 1 (one) or a 0 (zero), and each digit is called a *bit* (short for *bi*nary digi*t*). Typically, you count either 4 or 8 bits together, with these being referred to as a nibble and a byte, respectively.

What interests us in binary numbering is the value represented in a decimal format—the typical decimal format being the base-10 number scheme that we've all used since kindergarten. The binary numbers are placed in a value spot: starting at the right and moving left, with each spot having double the value of the previous spot.

Table 2.1 shows the decimal values of each bit location in a nibble and a byte. Remember, a nibble is 4 bits and a byte is 8 bits.

TABLE 2.1 Binary values

Nibble Values	Byte Values
8 4 2 1	128 64 32 16 8 4 2 1

What all this means is that if a one digit (1) is placed in a value spot, then the nibble or byte takes on that decimal value and adds it to any other value spots that have a 1. And if a zero (0) is placed in a bit spot, you don't count that value.

Let me clarify things. If we have a 1 placed in each spot of our nibble, we would then add up 8 + 4 + 2 + 1 to give us a maximum value of 15. Another example for our nibble values would be 1010; that means that the 8 bit and the 2 bit are turned on, which equals a decimal value of 10. If we have a nibble binary value of 0110, then our decimal value would be 6, because the 4 and 2 bits are turned on.

But the byte values can add up to a value that's significantly higher than 15. This is how: If we counted every bit as a one (1), then the byte binary value would look like this (remember, 8 bits equal a byte):

11111111

We would then count up every bit spot because each is turned on. It would look like this, which demonstrates the maximum value of a byte:

128 + 64 + 32 + 16 + 8 + 4 + 2 + 1 = 255

There are plenty of other decimal values that a binary number can equal. Let's work through a few examples.

10010110

Which bits are on? The 128, 16, 4, and 2 bits are on, so we'll just add them up: 128 + 16 + 4 + 2 = 150.

01101100

Which bits are on? The 64, 32, 8, and 4 bits are on, so we just need to add them up: 64 + 32 + 8 + 4 = 108.

11101000

Which bits are on? The 128, 64, 32, and 8 bits are on, so just add the values up: 128 + 64 + 32 + 8 = 232.

Table 2.2 is a table you should memorize before braving the IP sections in Chapters 3 and 4.

TABLE 2.2 Binary to decimal memorization chart

Binary Value	Decimal Value
10000000	128
11000000	192
11100000	224
11110000	240
11111000	248
11111100	252
11111110	254
11111111	255

Hexadecimal addressing is completely different than binary or decimal—it's converted by reading nibbles, not bytes. By using a nibble, we can convert these bits to hex pretty simply. First, understand that the hexadecimal addressing scheme uses only the numbers 0 through 9. And since the numbers 10, 11, 12, and so on can't be used (because they are two-digit numbers), the letters *A*, *B*, *C*, *D*, *E*, and *F* are used to represent 10, 11, 12, 13, 14, and 15, respectively.

Hex is short for *hexadecimal*, which is a numbering system that uses the first six letters of the alphabet (*A* through *F*) to extend beyond the available 10 digits in the decimal system.

Table 2.3 shows both the binary value and the decimal value for each hexadecimal digit.

TABLE 2.3 Hex to binary to decimal chart

Hexadecimal Value	Binary Value	Decimal Value
0	0000	0
1	0001	1
2	0010	2
3	0011	3
4	0100	4
5	0101	5
6	0110	6
7	0111	7
8	1000	8
9	1001	9
A	1010	10
B	1011	11
C	1100	12
D	1101	13
E	1110	14
F	1111	15

Did you notice that the first 10 hexadecimal digits (0–9) are the same value as the decimal values? If not, look again. This handy fact makes those values super easy to convert.

So suppose you have something like this: 0x6A. (Sometimes Cisco likes to put *0x* in front of characters so you know that they are a hex value. It doesn't have any other special meaning.) What are the binary and decimal values? All you have to remember is that each hex character is one nibble and two hex characters together make a byte. To figure out the binary value, we need to put the hex characters into two nibbles and then put them together into a byte. 6 = 0110 and A (which is 10 in hex) = 1010, so the complete byte would be 01101010.

To convert from binary to hex, just take the byte and break it into nibbles. Here's what I mean.

Say you have the binary number 01010101. First, break it into nibbles—0101 and 0101—with the value of each nibble being 5 since the 1 and 4 bits are on. This makes the hex answer 0x55. And in decimal format, the binary number is 01010101, which converts to 64 + 16 + 4 + 1 = 85.

Here's another binary number:

11001100

Your answer would be 1100 = 12 and 1100 = 12 (therefore, it's converted to CC in hex). The decimal conversion answer would be 128 + 64 + 8 + 4 = 204.

One more example, then we need to get working on the Physical layer. Suppose you had the following binary number:

10110101

The hex answer would be 0xB5, since 1011 converts to B and 0101 converts to 5 in hex value. The decimal equivalent is 128 + 32 + 16 + 4 + 1 = 181.

See Written Lab 2.1 for more practice with binary/hex/decimal conversion.

Ethernet Frames

The Data Link layer is responsible for combining bits into bytes and bytes into frames. Frames are used at the Data Link layer to encapsulate packets handed down from the Network layer for transmission on a type of media access.

The function of Ethernet stations is to pass data frames between each other using a group of bits known as a MAC frame format. This provides error detection from a *cyclic redundancy check* (*CRC*). But remember—this is error detection, not error correction. The 802.3 frames and Ethernet frame are shown in Figure 2.3.

Encapsulating a frame within a different type of frame is called *tunneling*.

FIGURE 2.3 802.3 and Ethernet frame formats

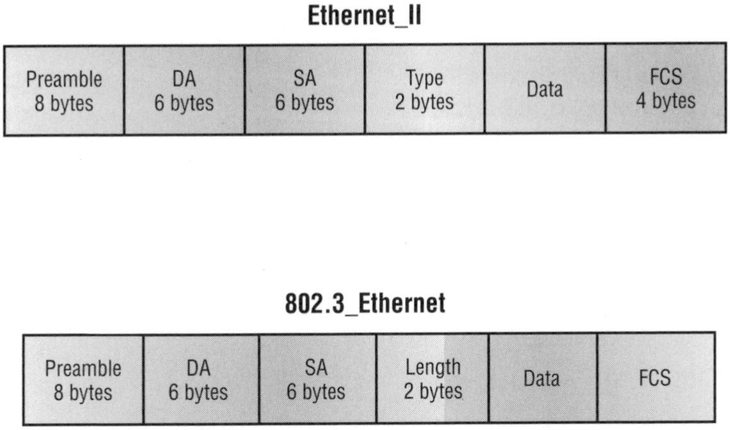

Ethernet_II

Preamble 8 bytes	DA 6 bytes	SA 6 bytes	Type 2 bytes	Data	FCS 4 bytes

802.3_Ethernet

Preamble 8 bytes	DA 6 bytes	SA 6 bytes	Length 2 bytes	Data	FCS

Following are the details of the different fields in the 802.3 and Ethernet frame types:

Preamble An alternating 1,0 pattern provides a 5MHz clock at the start of each packet, which allows the receiving devices to lock the incoming bit stream.

Start Frame Delimiter (SFD)/Synch The preamble is seven octets and the SFD is one octet (synch). The SFD is 10101011, where the last pair of 1s allows the receiver to come into the alternating 1,0 pattern somewhere in the middle and still sync up and detect the beginning of the data.

Destination Address (DA) This transmits a 48-bit value using the least significant bit (LSB) first. The DA is used by receiving stations to determine whether an incoming packet is addressed to a particular node. The destination address can be an individual address or a broadcast or multicast MAC address. Remember that a broadcast is all 1s (or *F*s in hex) and is sent to all devices but a multicast is sent only to a similar subset of nodes on a network.

Source Address (SA) The SA is a 48-bit MAC address used to identify the transmitting device, and it uses the LSB first. Broadcast and multicast address formats are illegal within the SA field.

Length or Type 802.3 uses a Length field, but the Ethernet_II frame uses a Type field to identify the Network layer protocol. 802.3 cannot identify the upper-layer protocol and must be used with a proprietary LAN—IPX, for example.

Data This is a packet sent down to the Data Link layer from the Network layer. The size can vary from 46 to 1,500 bytes.

Frame Check Sequence (FCS) FCS is a field at the end of the frame that's used to store the cyclic redundancy check (CRC) answer. The CRC is a mathematical algorithm that's run when each frame is built. When a receiving host receives the frame and runs the CRC, the answer should be the same. If not, the frame is discarded, assuming errors have occurred.

Let's pause here for a minute and take a look at some frames caught on our trusty network analyzer. You can see that the frame below has only three fields: Destination, Source, and Type (shown as Protocol Type on this analyzer):

```
Destination:    00:60:f5:00:1f:27
Source:         00:60:f5:00:1f:2c
Protocol Type: 08-00 IP
```

This is an Ethernet_II frame. Notice that the Type field is IP, or 08-00 (mostly just referred to as 0x800) in hexadecimal.

The next frame has the same fields, so it must be an Ethernet_II frame too:

```
Destination:    ff:ff:ff:ff:ff:ff Ethernet Broadcast
Source:         02:07:01:22:de:a4
Protocol Type: 08-00 IP
```

Did you notice that this frame was a broadcast? You can tell because the destination hardware address is all 1s in binary, or all *F*s in hexadecimal.

Let's take a look at one more Ethernet_II frame. I'll talk about this next example again when we use IPv6 in Chapter 15, but you can see that the Ethernet frame is the same Ethernet_II frame we use with the IPv4 routed protocol. The Type field has 0x86dd when the frame is carrying IPv6 data, and when we have IPv4 data, the frame uses 0x0800 in the protocol field:

```
Destination: IPv6-Neighbor-Discovery_00:01:00:03 (33:33:00:01:00:03)
Source: Aopen_3e:7f:dd (00:01:80:3e:7f:dd)
Type: IPv6 (0x86dd)
```

This is the beauty of the Ethernet_II frame. Because of the Type field, we can run any Network layer routed protocol and it will carry the data because it can identify the Network layer protocol.

Ethernet at the Physical Layer

Ethernet was first implemented by a group called DIX (Digital, Intel, and Xerox). They created and implemented the first Ethernet LAN specification, which the IEEE used to create the IEEE 802.3 committee. This was a 10Mbps network that ran on coax and then eventually twisted-pair and fiber physical media.

The IEEE extended the 802.3 committee to two new committees known as 802.3u (Fast Ethernet) and 802.3ab (Gigabit Ethernet on category 5) and then finally 802.3ae (10Gbps over fiber and coax).

Figure 2.4 shows the IEEE 802.3 and original Ethernet Physical layer specifications.

When designing your LAN, it's really important to understand the different types of Ethernet media available to you. Sure, it would be great to run Gigabit Ethernet to each desktop and 10Gbps between switches, and you need to figure out how to justify the cost of that network today. But if you mix and match the different types of Ethernet media methods currently available, you can come up with a cost-effective network solution that works great.

FIGURE 2.4 Ethernet Physical layer specifications

Data Link (MAC layer)	Ethernet	802.3						
Physical		10Base2	10Base5	10BaseT	10BaseF	100BaseTX	100BaseFX	100BaseT4

The EIA/TIA (which stands for the Electronic Industries Association and the newer Telecommunications Industry Alliance) is the standards body that creates the Physical layer specifications for Ethernet. The EIA/TIA specifies that Ethernet use a *registered jack (RJ) connector* on *unshielded twisted-pair (UTP)* cabling (RJ45). However, the industry is moving toward calling this just an 8-pin modular connector.

Each Ethernet cable type that is specified by the EIA/TIA has inherent attenuation, which is defined as the loss of signal strength as it travels the length of a cable and is measured in decibels (dB). The cabling used in corporate and home markets is measured in categories. A higher-quality cable will have a higher-rated category and lower attenuation. For example, category 5 is better than category 3 because category 5 cables have more wire twists per foot and therefore less crosstalk. Crosstalk is the unwanted signal interference from adjacent pairs in the cable.

Here are the original IEEE 802.3 standards:

10Base2 10Mbps, baseband technology, up to 185 meters in length. Known as *thinnet* and can support up to 30 workstations on a single segment. Uses a physical and logical bus with BNC connectors and thin coaxial cable. The 10 means 10Mbps, *Base* means baseband technology (which is a digital signaling method for communication on the network), and the 2 means almost 200 meters. 10Base2 Ethernet cards use BNC (British Naval Connector, Bayonet Neill Concelman, or Bayonet Nut Connector), T-connectors, and terminators to connect to a network.

10Base5 10Mbps, baseband technology, up to 500 meters in length using thick coaxial cable. Known as *thicknet*. Uses a physical and logical bus with AUI connectors. Up to 2,500 meters with repeaters and 1,024 users for all segments.

10BaseT 10Mbps using category 3 unshielded twisted pair (UTP) wiring for runs up to 100 meters. Unlike with the 10Base2 and 10Base5 networks, each device must connect into a hub or switch, and you can have only one host per segment or wire. Uses an RJ45 connector (8-pin modular connector) with a physical star topology and a logical bus.

Each of the 802.3 standards defines an AUI, which allows a one-bit-at-a-time transfer to the Physical layer from the Data Link media-access method. This allows the MAC address to remain constant but means the Physical layer can support both existing and new technologies. The thing is, the original AUI interface was a 15-pin connector, which allowed a transceiver (transmitter/receiver) that provided a 15-pin-to-twisted-pair conversion.

There's an issue, though—the AUI interface can't support 100Mbps Ethernet because of the high frequencies involved. So 100BaseT needed a new interface, and the 802.3u specifications created one called the Media Independent Interface (MII), which provides

100Mbps throughput. The MII uses a nibble, which you of course remember is defined as 4 bits. Gigabit Ethernet uses a Gigabit Media Independent Interface (GMII) and transmits 8 bits at a time. 802.3u (Fast Ethernet) is compatible with 802.3 Ethernet because they share the same physical characteristics. Fast Ethernet and Ethernet use the same maximum transmission unit (MTU) and the same MAC mechanisms, and they both preserve the frame format that is used by 10BaseT Ethernet. Basically, Fast Ethernet is just based on an extension to the IEEE 802.3 specification, and because of that, it offers us a speed increase of 10 times that of 10BaseT.

Here are the expanded IEEE Ethernet 802.3 standards, starting with Fast Ethernet:

100Base-TX (IEEE 802.3u) 100Base-TX, most commonly known as Fast Ethernet, uses EIA/TIA category 5, 5E, or 6 UTP two-pair wiring. One user per segment; up to 100 meters long. It uses an RJ45 connector with a physical star topology and a logical bus.

100Base-FX (IEEE 802.3u) Uses fiber cabling 62.5/125-micron multimode fiber. Point-to-point topology; up to 412 meters long. It uses ST and SC connectors, which are media-interface connectors.

1000Base-CX (IEEE 802.3z) Copper twisted-pair called twinax (a balanced coaxial pair) that can run only up to 25 meters and uses a special 9-pin connector known as the High Speed Serial Data Connector (HSSDC).

1000Base-T (IEEE 802.3ab) Category 5, four-pair UTP wiring up to 100 meters long and up to 1Gbps.

1000Base-SX (IEEE 802.3z) The implementation of 1 Gigabit Ethernet running over multimode fiber-optic cable (instead of copper twisted-pair cable) and using short wavelength laser. Multimode fiber (MMF) using 62.5- and 50-micron core; uses an 850 nanometer (nm) laser and can go up to 220 meters with 62.5-micron, 550 meters with 50-micron.

1000Base-LX (IEEE 802.3z) Single-mode fiber that uses a 9-micron core and 1300 nm laser and can go from 3 kilometers up to 10 kilometers.

1000BASE-ZX (Cisco standard) 1000BaseZX (or 1000Base-ZX) is a Cisco specified standard for gigabit Ethernet communication. 1000BaseZX operates on ordinary single-mode fiber-optic link with spans up to 43.5 miles (70 km).

10GBase-T 10GBase-T is a standard proposed by the IEEE 802.3an committee to provide 10Gbps connections over conventional UTP cables (category 5e, 6, or 7 cables). 10GBase-T allows the conventional RJ45 used for Ethernet LANs. It can support signal transmission at the full 100-meter distance specified for LAN wiring.

The following are all part of the IEEE 802.3ae standard.

10GBase-Short Range (SR) An implementation of 10 Gigabit Ethernet that uses short-wavelength lasers at 850 nm over multimode fiber. It has a maximum transmission distance of between 2 and 300 meters, depending on the size and quality of the fiber.

10GBase-Long Range (LR) An implementation of 10 Gigabit Ethernet that uses long-wavelength lasers at 1,310 nm over single-mode fiber. It also has a maximum transmission distance between 2 meters and 10 km, depending on the size and quality of the fiber.

10GBase-Extended Range (ER) An implementation of 10 Gigabit Ethernet running over single-mode fiber. It uses extra-long-wavelength lasers at 1,550 nm. It has the longest transmission distances possible of the 10-Gigabit technologies: anywhere from 2 meters up to 40 km, depending on the size and quality of the fiber used.

10GBase-Short Wavelength (SW) 10GBase-SW, as defined by IEEE 802.3ae, is a mode of 10GBase-S for MMF with an 850 nm laser transceiver with a bandwidth of 10Gbps. It can support up to 300 meters of cable length. This media type is designed to connect to SONET equipment.

10GBase-Long Wavelength (LW) 10GBase-LW is a mode of 10GBase-L supporting a link length of 10 km on standard single-mode fiber (SMF) (G.652). This media type is designed to connect to SONET equipment.

10GBase-Extra Long Wavelength (EW) 10GBase-EW is a mode of 10GBase-E supporting a link length of up to 40 km on SMF based on G.652 using optical-wavelength 1550 nm. This media type is designed to connect to SONET equipment.

If you want to implement a network medium that is not susceptible to electromagnetic interference (EMI), fiber-optic cable provides a more secure, long-distance cable that is not susceptible to EMI at high speeds.

Table 2.4 summarizes the cable types.

TABLE 2.4 Common Ethernet cable types

Ethernet Name	Cable Type	Maximum Speed	Maximum Transmission Distance	Notes
10Base5	Coax	10Mbps	500 meters per segment	Also called thicknet, this cable type uses vampire taps to connect devices to cable.
10Base2	Coax	10Mbps	185 meters per segment	Also called thinnet, a very popular implementation of Ethernet over coax.
10BaseT	UTP	10Mbps	100 meters per segment	One of the most popular network cabling schemes.
100Base-TX	UTP, STP	100Mbps	100 meters per segment	Two pairs of category 5 UTP.

TABLE 2.4 Common Ethernet cable types *(continued)*

Ethernet Name	Cable Type	Maximum Speed	Maximum Transmission Distance	Notes
10Base-FL	Fiber	10Mbps	Varies (ranges from 500 meters to 2,000 meters)	Ethernet over fiber optics to the desktop.
100Base-FX	MMF	100Mbps	2,000 meters	100Mbps Ethernet over fiber optics.
1000Base-T	UTP	1000Mbps	100 meters	Four pairs of category 5e or higher.
1000Base-SX	MMF	1000Mbps	550 meters	Uses SC fiber connectors. Max length depends on fiber size.
1000Base-CX	Balanced, shielded copper	1000Mbps	25 meters	Uses a special connector, the HSSDC.
1000Base-LX	MMF and SMF	1000Mbps	550 meters multimode/ 2,000 meters single mode	Uses longer wavelength laser than 1000Base-SX. Uses SC and LC connectors.
10GBase-T	UTP	10Gbps	100 meters	Connects to the network like a Fast Ethernet link using UTP.
10GBase-SR	MMF	10Gbps	300 meters	850 nm laser. Max length depends on fiber size and quality.
10GBase-LR	SMF	10Gbps	10 kilometers	1,310 nm laser. Max length depends on fiber size and quality.
10GBase-ER	SMF	10Gpbs	40 kilometers	1,550 nm laser. Max length depends on fiber size and quality.
10GBase-SW	MMF	10Gpbs	300 meters	850 nm laser transceiver.
10GBase-LW	SMF	10Gpbs	10 kilometers	Typically used with SONET.
10GBase-EW	SMF	10Gpbs	40 kilometers	1,550 nm optical wavelength.

Armed with the basics covered in this chapter, you're equipped to go to the next level and put Ethernet to work using various Ethernet cabling.

Ethernet Cabling

A discussion about Ethernet cabling is an important one, especially if you are planning on taking the Cisco exams. You need to really understand the following three types of cables:

- Straight-through cable
- Crossover cable
- Rolled cable

We will look at each in the following sections.

Straight-Through Cable

The *straight-through cable* is used to connect the following devices:

- Host to switch or hub
- Router to switch or hub

Four wires are used in straight-through cable to connect Ethernet devices. It is relatively simple to create this type; Figure 2.5 shows the four wires used in a straight-through Ethernet cable.

FIGURE 2.5 Straight-through Ethernet cable

Hub/Switch		Host
1	⟷	1
2	⟷	2
3	⟷	3
6	⟷	6

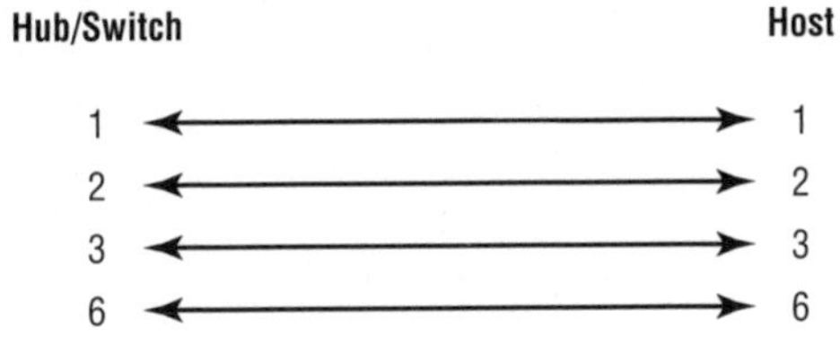

Notice that only pins 1, 2, 3, and 6 are used. Just connect 1 to 1, 2 to 2, 3 to 3, and 6 to 6 and you'll be up and networking in no time. However, remember that this would be an Ethernet-only cable and wouldn't work with voice or other LAN or WAN technology.

Crossover Cable

The *crossover cable* can be used to connect the following devices:

- Switch to switch
- Hub to hub

- Host to host
- Hub to switch
- Router direct to host
- Router to Router via Fast Ethernet ports

The same four wires used in the straight-through cable are used in this cable; we just connect different pins together. Figure 2.6 shows how the four wires are used in a crossover Ethernet cable.

FIGURE 2.6 Crossover Ethernet cable

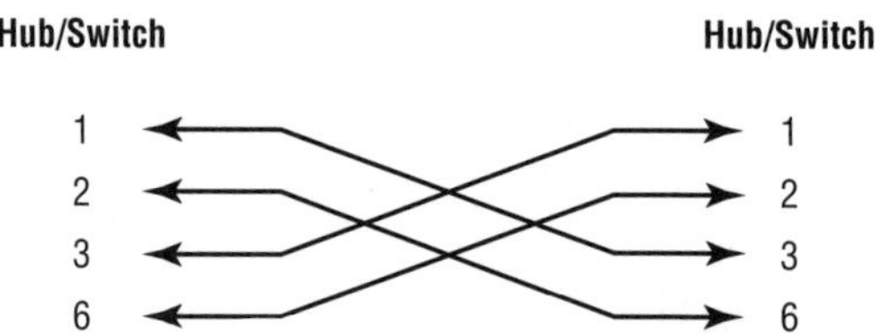

Notice that instead of connecting 1 to 1, 2 to 2, and so on, here we connect pins 1 to 3 and 2 to 6 on each side of the cable.

Rolled Cable

Although *rolled cable* isn't used to connect any Ethernet connections together, you can use a rolled Ethernet cable to connect a host EIA-TIA 232 interface to a router console serial communication (COM) port.

If you have a Cisco router or switch, you would use this cable to connect your PC running HyperTerminal to the Cisco hardware. Eight wires are used in this cable to connect serial devices, although not all eight are used to send information, just as in Ethernet networking. Figure 2.7 shows the eight wires used in a rolled cable.

These are probably the easiest cables to make because you just cut the end off on one side of a straight-through cable, turn it over, and put it back on (with a new connector, of course).

FIGURE 2.7 Rolled Ethernet cable

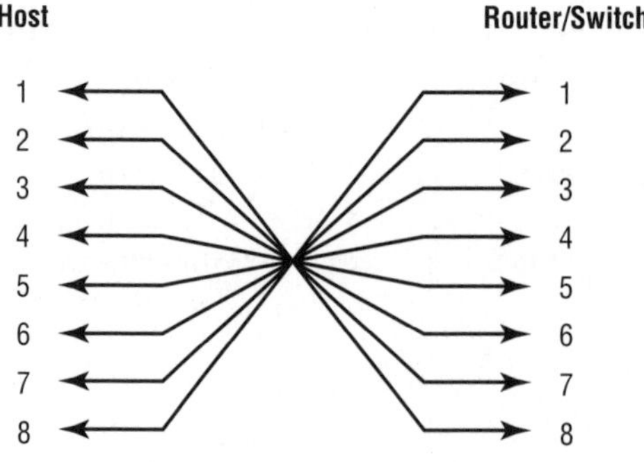

Once you have the correct cable connected from your PC to the Cisco router or switch console port, you can start HyperTerminal to create a console connection and configure the device. Set the configuration as follows:

1. Open HyperTerminal and enter a name for the connection. It is irrelevant what you name it, but I always just use Cisco. Then click OK.

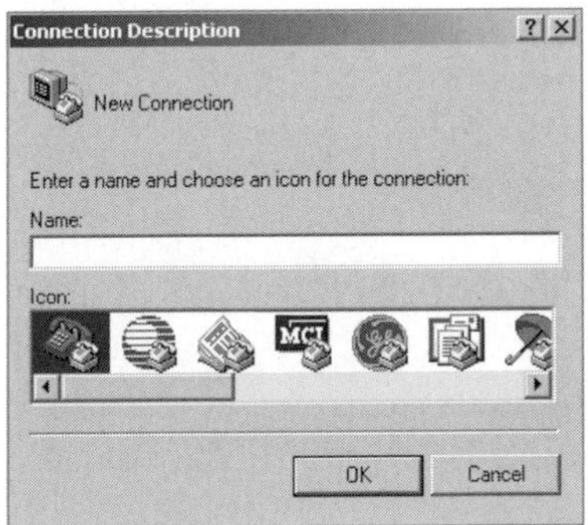

2. Choose the communications port—either COM1 or COM2, whichever is open on your PC.

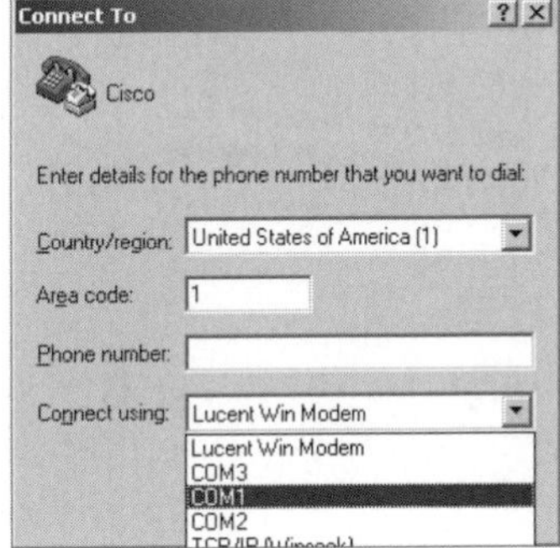

3. Now set the port settings. The default values (2400bps and no flow control hardware) will not work; you must set the port settings as shown in Figure 2.8.

Notice that the bit rate is now set to 9600 and the flow control is set to None. At this point, you can click OK and press the Enter key and you should be connected to your Cisco device console port.

We've taken a look at the various RJ45 unshielded twisted pair (UTP) cables. Keeping this in mind, what cable is used between the switches in Figure 2.9?

In order for host A to ping host B, you need a crossover cable to connect the two switches together. But what types of cables are used in the network shown in Figure 2.10?

FIGURE 2.8 Port settings for a rolled cable connection

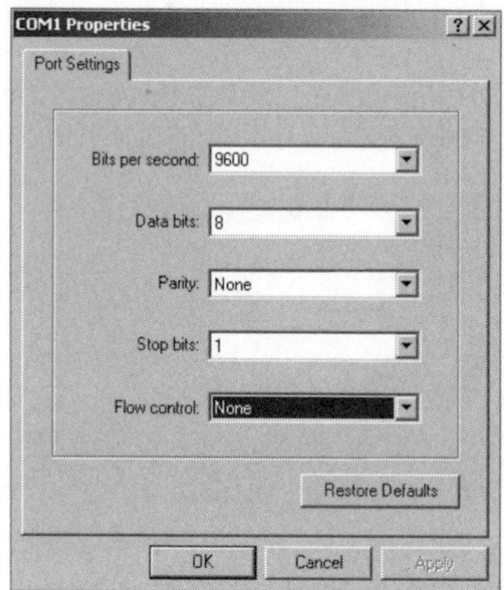

FIGURE 2.9 RJ45 UTP cable question #1

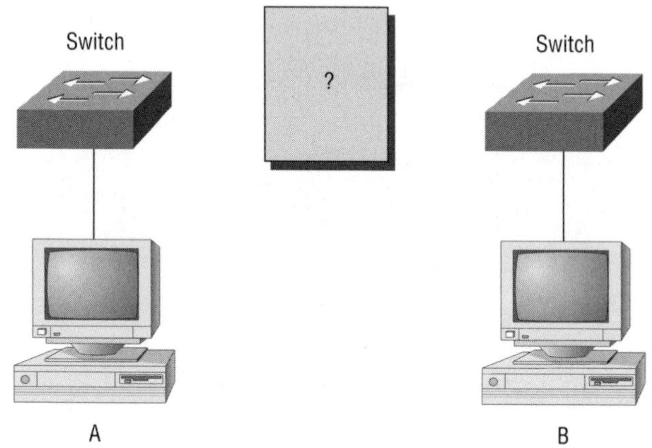

FIGURE 2.10 RJ45 UTP cable question #2

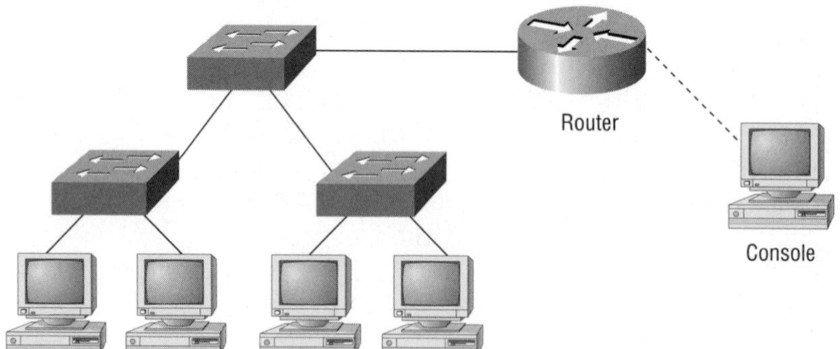

In Figure 2.10, there are a variety of cables in use. For the connection between the switches, we'd obviously use a crossover cable like we saw in Figure 2.6. The trouble is, we have a console connection that uses a rolled cable. Plus, the connection from the router to the switch is a straight-through cable, as is true for the hosts to the switches. Keep in mind that if we had a serial connection (which we don't), it would be a V.35 that we'd use to connect us to a WAN.

Data Encapsulation

When a host transmits data across a network to another device, the data goes through *encapsulation*: It is wrapped with protocol information at each layer of the OSI model. Each layer communicates only with its peer layer on the receiving device.

To communicate and exchange information, each layer uses *Protocol Data Units (PDUs)*. These hold the control information attached to the data at each layer of the model. They are usually attached to the header in front of the data field but can also be at the trailer, or end, of it.

Each PDU attaches to the data by encapsulating it at each layer of the OSI model, and each has a specific name depending on the information provided in each header. This PDU information is read only by the peer layer on the receiving device. After it's read, it's stripped off and the data is then handed to the next layer up.

Figure 2.11 shows the PDUs and how they attach control information to each layer. This figure demonstrates how the upper-layer user data is converted for transmission on the network. The data stream is then handed down to the Transport layer, which sets up a virtual circuit to the receiving device by sending over a synch packet. Next, the data stream is broken up into smaller pieces, and a Transport layer header is created and attached to the header of the data field; now the piece of data is called a *segment* (a *PDU*). Each segment can be sequenced so the data stream can be put back together on the receiving side exactly as it was transmitted.

FIGURE 2.11 Data encapsulation

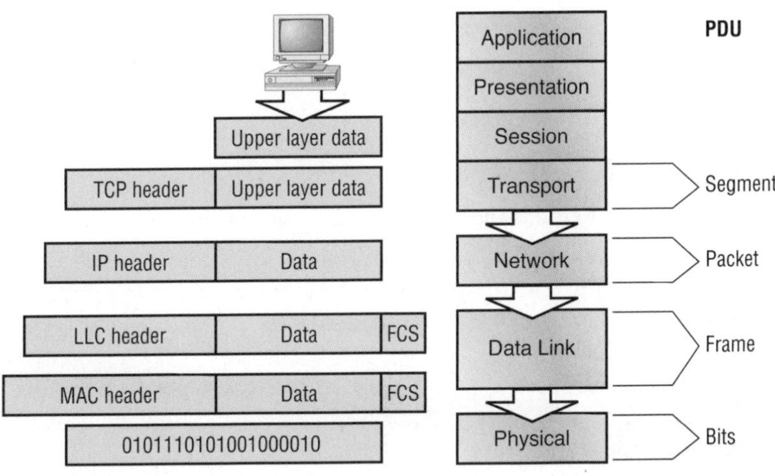

Each segment is then handed to the Network layer for network addressing and routing through the internetwork. Logical addressing (for example, IP) is used to get each segment to the correct network. The Network layer protocol adds a control header to the segment handed down from the Transport layer, and what we have now is called a *packet* or *datagram*. Remember that the Transport and Network layers work together to rebuild a data stream on a receiving host, but it's not part of their work to place their PDUs on a local network segment—which is the only way to get the information to a router or host.

It's the Data Link layer that's responsible for taking packets from the Network layer and placing them on the network medium (cable or wireless). The Data Link layer *encapsulates* each packet in a *frame*, and the frame's header carries the hardware addresses of the source and destination hosts. If the destination device is on a remote network, then the frame is sent to a router to be routed through an internetwork. Once it gets to the destination network, a new frame is used to get the packet to the destination host.

To put this frame on the network, it must first be put into a digital signal. Since a frame is really a logical group of 1s and 0s, the Physical layer is responsible for encoding these digits into a digital signal, which is read by devices on the same local network. The receiving devices will synchronize on the digital signal and extract (decode) the 1s and 0s from the digital signal. At this point, the devices reconstruct the frames, run a CRC, and then check their answer against the answer in the frame's FCS field. If it matches, the packet is pulled from the frame and what's left of the frame is discarded. This process is called *de-encapsulation*. The packet is handed to the Network layer, where the address is checked. If the address matches, the segment is pulled from the packet and what's left of the packet is discarded. The segment is processed at the Transport layer, which rebuilds the data stream and acknowledges to the transmitting station that it received each piece. It then happily hands the data stream to the upper-layer application.

At a transmitting device, the data encapsulation method works like this:

1. User information is converted to data for transmission on the network.
2. Data is converted to segments, and a reliable connection is set up between the transmitting and receiving hosts.
3. Segments are converted to packets or datagrams, and a logical address is placed in the header so each packet can be routed through an internetwork.
4. Packets or datagrams are converted to frames for transmission on the local network. Hardware (Ethernet) addresses are used to uniquely identify hosts on a local network segment.
5. Frames are converted to bits, and a digital encoding and clocking scheme is used.
6. To explain this in more detail using the layer addressing, I'll use Figure 2.12.

Remember that a data stream is handed down from the upper layer to the Transport layer. As technicians, we really don't care who the data stream comes from because that's really a programmer's problem. Our job is to rebuild the data stream reliably and hand it to the upper layers on the receiving device.

Before we go further in our discussion of Figure 2.12, let's discuss port numbers and make sure we understand them. The Transport layer uses port numbers to define both the virtual circuit and the upper-layer processes, as you can see from Figure 2.13.

FIGURE 2.12 PDU and layer addressing

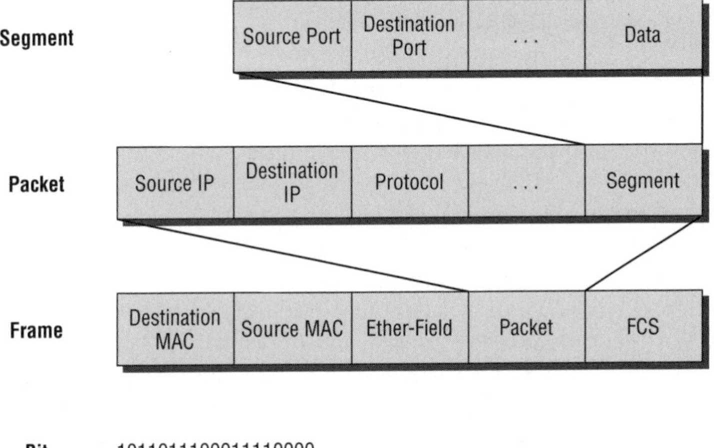

FIGURE 2.13 Port numbers at the Transport layer

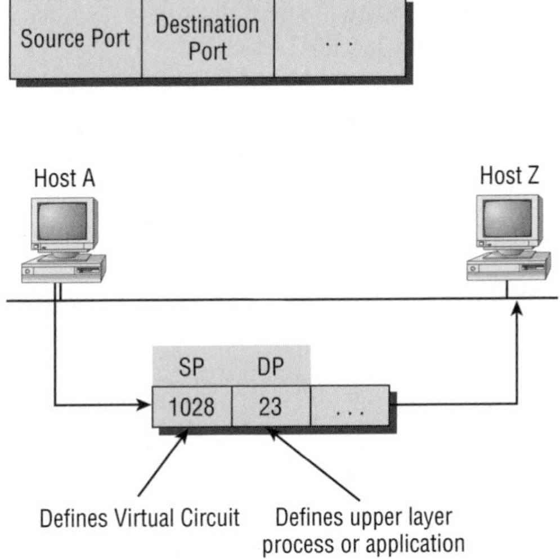

The Transport layer, when using a connection-oriented protocol (i.e., TCP), takes the data stream, makes segments out of it, and establishes a reliable session by creating a virtual circuit. It then sequences (numbers) each segment and uses acknowledgments and flow control. If you're using TCP, the virtual circuit is defined by the source and destination port number as well as source and destination IP address (this is called a socket). Remember, the host just makes this up starting at port number 1024 (0 through 1023 are reserved for well-known port numbers). The destination port number defines the upper-layer process (application) that the data stream is handed to when the data stream is reliably rebuilt on the receiving host.

Now that you understand port numbers and how they are used at the Transport layer, let's go back to Figure 2.12. Once the Transport layer header information is added to the piece of data, it becomes a segment and is handed down to the Network layer along with the destination IP address. (The destination IP address was handed down from the upper layers to the Transport layer with the data stream, and it was discovered through a name resolution method at the upper layers—probably DNS.)

The Network layer adds a header, and adds the logical addressing (IP addresses), to the front of each segment. Once the header is added to the segment, the PDU is called a packet. The packet has a protocol field that describes where the segment came from (either UDP or TCP) so it can hand the segment to the correct protocol at the Transport layer when it reaches the receiving host.

The Network layer is responsible for finding the destination hardware address that dictates where the packet should be sent on the local network. It does this by using the Address Resolution Protocol (ARP)—something I'll talk about more in Chapter 3. IP at the Network layer looks at the destination IP address and compares that address to its own source IP address and subnet mask. If it turns out to be a local network request, the hardware address of the local host is requested via an ARP request. If the packet is destined for a remote host, IP will look for the IP address of the default gateway (router) instead.

The packet, along with the destination hardware address of either the local host or default gateway, is then handed down to the Data Link layer. The Data Link layer will add a header to the front of the packet and the piece of data then becomes a frame. (We call it a frame because both a header and a trailer are added to the packet, which makes it resemble bookends or a frame, if you will.) This is shown in Figure 2.12. The frame uses an Ether-Type field to describe which protocol the packet came from at the Network layer. Now a cyclic redundancy check (CRC) is run on the frame, and the answer to the CRC is placed in the Frame Check Sequence field found in the trailer of the frame.

The frame is now ready to be handed down, one bit at a time, to the Physical layer, which will use bit timing rules to encode the data in a digital signal. Every device on the network segment will synchronize with the clock and extract the 1s and 0s from the digital signal and build a frame. After the frame is rebuilt, a CRC is run to make sure the frame is okay. If everything turns out to be all good, the hosts will check the destination MAC and IP addresses to see if the frame is for them.

If all this is making your eyes cross and your brain freeze, don't freak. I'll be going over exactly how data is encapsulated and routed through an internetwork in Chapter 8.

The Cisco Three-Layer Hierarchical Model

Most of us were exposed to hierarchy early in life. Anyone with older siblings learned what it was like to be at the bottom of the hierarchy. Regardless of where you first discovered hierarchy, today most of us experience it in many aspects of our lives. It is *hierarchy* that helps us understand where things belong, how things fit together, and what functions go where. It brings order and understandability to otherwise complex models. If you want a pay raise, for instance, hierarchy dictates that you ask your boss, not your subordinate. That is the person whose role it is to grant (or deny) your request. So basically, understanding hierarchy helps us discern where we should go to get what we need.

Hierarchy has many of the same benefits in network design that it does in other areas of life. When used properly, it makes networks more predictable. It helps us define which areas should perform certain functions. Likewise, you can use tools such as access lists at certain levels in hierarchical networks and avoid them at others.

Let's face it: Large networks can be extremely complicated, with multiple protocols, detailed configurations, and diverse technologies. Hierarchy helps us summarize a complex collection of details into an understandable model. Then, as specific configurations are needed, the model dictates the appropriate manner in which to apply them.

The Cisco hierarchical model can help you design, implement, and maintain a scalable, reliable, cost-effective hierarchical internetwork. Cisco defines three layers of hierarchy, as shown in Figure 2.14, each with specific functions.

FIGURE 2.14 The Cisco hierarchical model

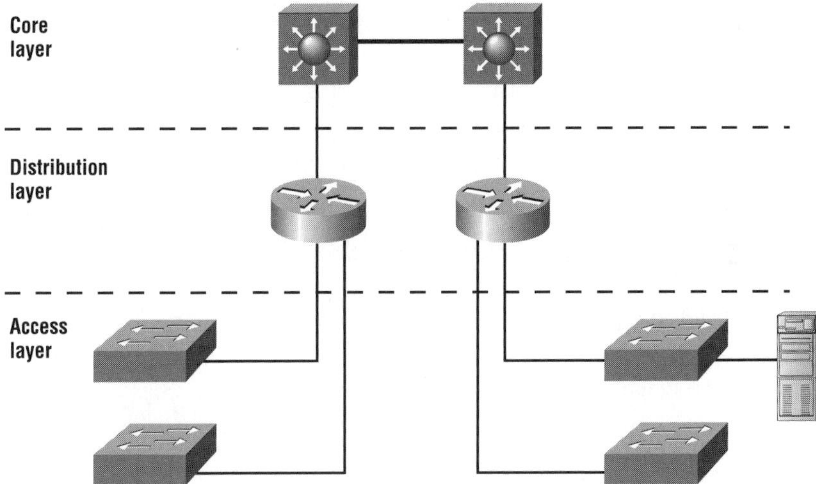

The following are the three layers and their typical functions:

- The core layer: backbone
- The distribution layer: routing
- The access layer: switching

Each layer has specific responsibilities. Remember, however, that the three layers are logical and are not necessarily physical devices. Consider the OSI model, another logical hierarchy. The seven layers describe functions but not necessarily protocols, right? Sometimes a protocol maps to more than one layer of the OSI model, and sometimes multiple protocols communicate within a single layer. In the same way, when we build physical implementations of hierarchical networks, we may have many devices in a single layer, or we might have a single device performing functions at two layers. The definition of the layers is logical, not physical.

Now, let's take a closer look at each of the layers.

The Core Layer

The *core layer* is literally the core of the network. At the top of the hierarchy, the core layer is responsible for transporting large amounts of traffic both reliably and quickly. The only purpose of the network's core layer is to switch traffic as fast as possible. The traffic transported across the core is common to a majority of users. However, remember that user data is processed at the distribution layer, which forwards the requests to the core if needed.

If there is a failure in the core, *every single user* can be affected. Therefore, fault tolerance at this layer is an issue. The core is likely to see large volumes of traffic, so speed and latency are driving concerns here. Given the function of the core, we can now consider some design specifics. Let's start with some things we don't want to do:

- Don't do anything to slow down traffic. This includes using access lists, routing between virtual local area networks (VLANs), and implementing packet filtering.
- Don't support workgroup access here.
- Avoid expanding the core (i.e., adding routers) when the internetwork grows. If performance becomes an issue in the core, give preference to upgrades over expansion.

Now, there are a few things that we want to do as we design the core:

- Design the core for high reliability. Consider data-link technologies that facilitate both speed and redundancy, such as Gigabit Ethernet (with redundant links), or even 10Gigabit Ethernet.
- Design with speed in mind. The core should have very little latency.
- Select routing protocols with lower convergence times. Fast and redundant data-link connectivity is no help if your routing tables are shot!

The Distribution Layer

The *distribution layer* is sometimes referred to as the *workgroup layer* and is the communication point between the access layer and the core. The primary functions of the distribution layer are to provide routing, filtering, and WAN access and to determine how packets can access the core, if needed. The distribution layer must determine the fastest way that network service requests are handled—for example, how a file request is forwarded to a server. After the distribution layer determines the best path, it forwards the request to the core layer if necessary. The core layer then quickly transports the request to the correct service.

The distribution layer is the place to implement policies for the network. Here you can exercise considerable flexibility in defining network operation. There are several actions that generally should be done at the distribution layer:

- Routing
- Implementing tools (such as access lists), packet filtering, and queuing

- Implementing security and network policies, including address translation and firewalls
- Redistributing between routing protocols, including static routing
- Routing between VLANs and other workgroup support functions
- Defining broadcast and multicast domains

Things to avoid at the distribution layer are limited to those functions that exclusively belong to one of the other layers.

The Access Layer

The *access layer* controls user and workgroup access to internetwork resources. The access layer is sometimes referred to as the *desktop layer.* The network resources most users need will be available locally. The distribution layer handles any traffic for remote services. The following are some of the functions to be included at the access layer:

- Continued (from distribution layer) use of access control and policies
- Creation of separate collision domains (segmentation)
- Workgroup connectivity into the distribution layer

Technologies such as Gigabit or Fast Ethernet switching are frequently seen in the access layer.

As already noted, three separate levels does not imply three separate devices. There could be fewer, or there could be more. Remember, this is a *layered* approach.

Summary

In this chapter, you learned the fundamentals of Ethernet networking, how hosts communicate on a network, and how CSMA/CD works in an Ethernet half-duplex network.

I also talked about the differences between half- and full-duplex modes and discussed the collision detection mechanism CSMA/CD.

Also in this chapter was a description of the common Ethernet cable types used in today's networks. And by the way, you'd be wise to study that section really well!

Important enough to not gloss over, this chapter provided an introduction to encapsulation. Encapsulation is the process of encoding data as it goes down the OSI stack.

Last, this chapter covered the Cisco three-layer hierarchical model. I described in detail the three layers and how each is used to help design and implement a Cisco internetwork. We are now going to move on to IP addressing in the next chapter.

Exam Essentials

Describe the operation of Carrier Sense Multiple Access with Collision Detection (CSMA/CD). CSMA/CD is a protocol that helps devices share the bandwidth evenly without having two devices transmit at the same time on the network medium. Although it does not eliminate collisions, it helps to greatly reduce them, which reduces retransmissions, resulting in a more efficient transmission of data for all devices.

Differentiate half-duplex and full-duplex communication and define the requirements to utilize each method. Full-duplex Ethernet uses two pairs of wires instead of one wire pair like half duplex. Full duplex allows for sending and receiving at the same time, using different wires to eliminate collisions, while half duplex can send or receive but not at the same time and still can suffer collisions. To use full duplex, the devices at both ends of the cable must be capable of and configured to perform full duplex.

Describe the sections of a MAC address and the information contained in each section. The MAC, or hardware, address is a 48-bit (6-byte) address written in a hexadecimal format. The first 24 bits or 3 bytes are called the organizationally unique identifier (OUI), which is assigned by the IEEE to the manufacturer of the NIC. The balance of the number uniquely identifies the NIC.

Identify the binary and hexadecimal equivalent of a decimal number. Any number expressed in one format can also be expressed in the other two. The ability to perform this conversion is critical to understanding IP addressing and subnetting. Be sure to go through the written labs covering binary to decimal to hexadecimal conversion.

Identify the fields in the Data Link portion of an Ethernet frame. The fields in the Data Link portion of a frame include the Preamble, Start Frame Delimiter, Destination MAC address, Source MAC address, Length or Type, Data, and Frame Check Sequence.

Identify the IEEE physical standards for Ethernet cabling. These standards describe the capabilities and physical characteristics of various cable types and include but are not limited to 10Base2, 10Base5, and 10Base T.

Differentiate types of Ethernet cabling and identify their proper application. The three types of cables that can be created from an Ethernet cable are straight-through (to connect a PC's or a router's Ethernet interface to a hub or switch), crossover (to connect hub to hub, hub to switch, switch to switch, or PC to PC), and rolled (for a console connection from a PC to a router or switch).

Describe the data encapsulation process and the role it plays in packet creation. Data encapsulation is a process whereby information is added to the frame from each layer of the OSI model. This is also called packet creation. Each layer communicates only with its peer layer on the receiving device.

Understand how to connect a console cable from a PC to a router and start HyperTerminal. Take a rolled cable and connect it from the COM port of the host to the console port of a router. Start HyperTerminal and set the bits per second to 9600 and flow control to None.

Identify the layers in the Cisco three-layer model and describe the ideal function of each layer. The three layers in the Cisco hierarchical model are the core (responsible for transporting large amounts of traffic both reliably and quickly), distribution (provides routing, filtering, and WAN access), and access (workgroup connectivity into the distribution layer).

Written Labs

In this section, you'll complete the following labs to make sure you've got the information and concepts contained within them fully dialed in:

Lab 2.1: Binary/Decimal/Hexadecimal Conversion

Lab 2.2: CSMA/CD Operations

Lab 2.3: Cabling

Lab 2.4: Encapsulation

(The answers to the written labs can be found following the answers to the review questions for this chapter.)

Written Lab 2.1: Binary/Decimal/Hexadecimal Conversion

1. Convert from decimal IP address to binary format.

   Complete the following table to express 192.168.10.15 in binary format.

128	64	32	16	8	4	2	1	Binary

   Complete the following table to express 172.16.20.55 in binary format.

128	64	32	16	8	4	2	1	Binary

Complete the following table to express 10.11.12.99 in binary format.

128	64	32	16	8	4	2	1	**Binary**

2. Convert the following from binary format to decimal IP address.

   Complete the following table to express 11001100.00110011.10101010.01010101 in decimal IP address format.

128	64	32	16	8	4	2	1	**Decimal**

Complete the following table to express 11000110.11010011.00111001.11010001 in decimal IP address format.

128	64	32	16	8	4	2	1	**Decimal**

Complete the following table to express 10000100.11010010.10111000.10100110 in decimal IP address format.

128	64	32	16	8	4	2	1	**Decimal**

3. Convert the following from binary format to hexadecimal.

   Complete the following table to express 11011000.00011011.00111101.01110110 in hexadecimal.

128	64	32	16	8	4	2	1	Hexadecimal

   Complete the following table to express 11001010.11110101.10000011.11101011 in hexadecimal.

128	64	32	16	8	4	2	1	Hexadecimal

   Complete the following table to express 10000100.11010010.01000011.10110011 in hexadecimal.

128	64	32	16	8	4	2	1	Hexadecimal

Written Lab 2.2: CSMA/CD Operations

Carrier Sense Multiple Access with Collision Detection (CSMA/CD) helps to minimize collisions in the network, thereby increasing data transmission efficiency. Place the following steps of its operation in the order in which they occur.

- All hosts have equal priority to transmit after the timers have expired.
- Each device on the Ethernet segment stops transmitting for a short time until the timers expire.
- The collision invokes a random backoff algorithm.
- A jam signal informs all devices that a collision occurred.

Written Lab 2.3: Cabling

For each of the following situations determine whether a straight-through, crossover, or rolled cable would be used.

1. Host to host
2. Host to switch or hub
3. Router direct to host
4. Switch to switch
5. Router to switch or hub
6. Hub to hub
7. Hub to switch
8. Host to a router console serial communication (com) port

Written Lab 2.4: Encapsulation

Place the following steps of the encapsulation process in the proper order.

- Packets or datagrams are converted to frames for transmission on the local network. Hardware (Ethernet) addresses are used to uniquely identify hosts on a local network segment.
- Segments are converted to packets or datagrams, and a logical address is placed in the header so each packet can be routed through an internetwork.
- User information is converted to data for transmission on the network.
- Frames are converted to bits, and a digital encoding and clocking scheme is used.
- Data is converted to segments, and a reliable connection is set up between the transmitting and receiving hosts.

Review Questions

The following questions are designed to test your understanding of this chapter's material. For more information on how to get additional questions, please see this book's introduction.

1. Which fields are contained within an IEEE Ethernet frame? (Choose two.)
   - **A.** Source and destination MAC address
   - **B.** Source and destination network address
   - **C.** Source and destination MAC address and source and destination network address
   - **D.** FCS field
2. Which of the following are unique characteristics of half-duplex Ethernet when compared to full-duplex Ethernet? (Choose two.)
   - **A.** Half-duplex Ethernet operates in a shared collision domain.
   - **B.** Half-duplex Ethernet operates in a private collision domain.
   - **C.** Half-duplex Ethernet has higher effective throughput.
   - **D.** Half-duplex Ethernet has lower effective throughput.
   - **E.** Half-duplex Ethernet operates in a private broadcast domain.
3. You want to implement a network medium that is not susceptible to EMI. Which type of cabling should you use?
   - **A.** Thicknet coax
   - **B.** Thinnet coax
   - **C.** Category 5 UTP cable
   - **D.** Fiber-optic cable
4. Which of the following types of connections can use full duplex? (Choose three.)
   - **A.** Hub to hub
   - **B.** Switch to switch
   - **C.** Host to host
   - **D.** Switch to hub
   - **E.** Switch to host
5. What type of RJ45 UTP cable is used between switches?
   - **A.** Straight-through
   - **B.** Crossover cable
   - **C.** Crossover with a CSU/DSU
   - **D.** Crossover with a router in between the two switches

6. How does a host on an Ethernet LAN know when to transmit after a collision has occurred? (Choose two.)
   - A. In a CSMA/CD collision domain, multiple stations can successfully transmit data simultaneously.
   - B. In a CSMA/CD collision domain, stations must wait until the media is not in use before transmitting.
   - C. You can improve the CSMA/CD network by adding more hubs.
   - D. After a collision, the station that detected the collision has first priority to resend the lost data.
   - E. After a collision, all stations run a random backoff algorithm. When the backoff delay period has expired, all stations have equal priority to transmit data.
   - F. After a collision, all stations involved run an identical backoff algorithm and then synchronize with each other prior to transmitting data.
7. What type of RJ45 UTP cable do you use to connect a PC's COM port to a router or switch console port?
   - A. Straight-through
   - B. Crossover cable
   - C. Crossover with a CSU/DSU
   - D. Rolled
8. You have the following binary number: 10110111. What are the decimal and hexadecimal equivalents?
   - A. 69/0x2102
   - B. 183/B7
   - C. 173/A6
   - D. 83/0xC5
9. Which of the following contention mechanisms is used by Ethernet?
   - A. Token passing
   - B. CSMA/CD
   - C. CSMA/CA
   - D. Host polling
10. In the operation of CSMA/CD, which host(s) have priority after the expiration of the backoff algorithm?
    - A. All hosts have equal priority.
    - B. The two hosts that caused the collision will have equal priority.
    - C. The host that sent the jam signal after the collision.
    - D. The host with the highest MAC address.

11. Which of the following is correct?
    A. Full-duplex Ethernet uses one pair of wires.
    B. Full-duplex Ethernet uses two pairs of wires.
    C. Half-duplex Ethernet uses two pairs of wires.
    D. Full-duplex Ethernet uses three pairs of wires.

12. Which of the following statements is false with respect to full duplex?
    A. There are no collisions in full-duplex mode.
    B. A dedicated switch port is required for each full-duplex node.
    C. There are few collisions in full-duplex mode.
    D. The host network card and the switch port must be capable of operating in full-duplex mode.

13. Which statement is correct with regard to a MAC address?
    A. A MAC, or logical, address is a 48-bit (6-byte) address written in a hexadecimal format.
    B. A MAC, or hardware, address is a 64-bit (6-byte) address written in a hexadecimal format.
    C. A MAC, or hardware, address is a 48-bit (6-byte) address written in a binary format.
    D. A MAC, or hardware, address is a 48-bit (6-byte) address written in a hexadecimal format.

14. Which part of a MAC address is called the organizationally unique identifier (OUI)?
    A. The first 24 bits, or 3 bytes
    B. The first 12 bits, or 3 bytes
    C. The first 24 bits, or 6 bytes
    D. The first 32 bits, or 3 bytes

15. Which layer of the OSI model is responsible for combining bits into bytes and bytes into frames?
    A. Presentation
    B. Data Link
    C. Application
    D. Transport

16. What is the specific term for the unwanted signal interference from adjacent pairs in the cable?
    A. EMI
    B. RFI
    C. Crosstalk
    D. Attenuation

17. Which of the following is part of the IEEE 802.3u standard?
    A. 100Base2
    B. 10Base5
    C. 100Base-TX
    D. 1000Base-T
18. 10GBase-Long Wavelength is known as which IEEE standard?
    A. 802.3F
    B. 802.3z
    C. 802.3ab
    D. 802.3ae
19. 1000Base-T is which IEEE standard?
    A. 802.3F
    B. 802.3z
    C. 802.3ab
    D. 802.3ae
20. When making a HyperTerminal connection, what must the bit rate be set to?
    A. 2400bps
    B. 1200bps
    C. 9600bps
    D. 6400bps

Answers to Review Questions

1. A, D. An Ethernet frame has source and destination MAC addresses, an Ether-Type field to identify the Network layer protocol, the data, and the FCS field that holds the answer to the CRC.
2. A, D. Half-duplex Ethernet works in a shared medium or collision domain. Half duplex provides a lower effective throughput than full duplex.
3. D. Fiber-optic cable provides a more secure, long-distance cable that is not susceptible to EMI interference at high speeds.
4. B, C, E. Hubs cannot run full-duplex Ethernet. Full duplex must be used on a point-to-point connection between two devices capable of running full duplex. Switches and hosts can run full duplex between each other, but a hub can never run full duplex.
5. B. To connect two switches together, you would use a RJ45 UTP crossover cable.
6. B, E. Once transmitting stations on an Ethernet segment hear a collision, they send an extended jam signal to ensure that all stations recognize the collision. After the jamming is complete, each sender waits a predetermined amount of time, plus a random time. After both timers expire, they are free to transmit, but they must make sure the media is clear before transmitting and that they all have equal priority.
7. D. To connect to a router or switch console port, you would use an RJ45 UTP rolled cable.
8. B. You must be able to take a binary number and convert it into both decimal and hexadecimal. To convert to decimal, just add up the 1s using their values. The values that are turned on with the binary number of 10110111 are 128 + 32 + 16 + 4 + 2 + 1 = 183. To get the hexadecimal equivalent, you need to break the eight binary digits into nibbles (4 bits), 1011 and 0111. By adding up these values, you get 11 and 7. In hexadecimal, 11 is B, so the answer is 0xB7.
9. B. Ethernet networking uses Carrier Sense Multiple Access with Collision Detection (CSMA/CD), a protocol that helps devices share the bandwidth evenly without having two devices transmit at the same time on the network medium.
10. A. After the expiration of the backoff algorithm, all hosts have equal priority.
11. B. Full-duplex Ethernet uses two pairs of wires.
12. C. There are no collisions in full-duplex mode.
13. D. A MAC, or hardware, address is a 48-bit (6-byte) address written in a hexadecimal format.
14. A. The first 24 bits, or 3 bytes, of a MAC address is called the organizationally unique identifier (OUI).
15. B. The Data Link layer of the OSI model is responsible for combining bits into bytes and bytes into frames.

16. C. The term for the unwanted signal interference from adjacent pairs in the cable is crosstalk.

17. C. IEEE 802.3.u is Fast Ethernet at 100Mbps and covers 100Base-TX, 100BaseT4, and 100Base-FX.

18. D. IEEE 802.3ae is the standard for 10Gbase-SR, -LR, -ER, -SW, -LW, and -E.

19. C. IEEE 802.3ab is the standard for 1Gbps on twisted-pair.

20. C. When making a HyperTerminal connection, the bit rate must be set to 9600bps.

Answers to Written Lab 2.1

1. Convert from decimal IP address to binary format.

   Complete the following table to express 192.168.10.15 in binary format.

Decimal	128	64	32	16	8	4	2	1	Binary
192	1	1	0	0	0	0	0	0	11000000
168	1	0	1	0	1	0	0	0	10101000
10	0	0	0	0	1	0	1	0	00001010
15	0	0	0	0	1	1	1	1	00001111

   Complete the following table to express 172.16.20.55 in binary format.

Decimal	128	64	32	16	8	4	2	1	Binary
172	1	0	1	0	1	1	0	0	10101100
16	0	0	0	1	0	0	0	0	00010000
20	0	0	0	1	0	1	0	0	00010100
55	0	0	1	1	0	1	1	1	00110111

   Complete the following table to express 10.11.12.99 in binary format.

Decimal	128	64	32	16	8	4	2	1	Binary
10	0	0	0	0	1	0	1	0	00001010
11	0	0	0	0	1	0	1	1	00001011
12	0	0	0	0	1	1	0	0	00001100
99	0	1	1	0	0	0	1	1	01100011

2. Convert the following from binary format to decimal IP address.

Complete the following table to express 11001100.00110011.10101010.01010101 in decimal IP address format.

Binary	128	64	32	16	8	4	2	1	Decimal
11001100	1	1	0	0	1	1	0	0	204
00110011	0	0	1	1	0	0	1	1	51
10101010	1	0	1	0	1	0	1	0	170
01010101	0	1	0	1	0	1	0	1	85

Complete the following table to express 11000110.11010011.00111001.11010001 in decimal IP address format.

Binary	128	64	32	16	8	4	2	1	Decimal
11000110	1	1	0	0	0	1	1	0	198
11010011	1	1	0	1	0	0	1	1	211
00111001	0	0	1	1	1	0	0	1	57
11010001	1	1	0	1	0	0	0	1	209

Complete the following table to express 10000100.11010010.10111000.10100110 in decimal IP address format.

Binary	128	64	32	16	8	4	2	1	Decimal
10000100	1	0	0	0	0	1	0	0	132
11010010	1	1	0	1	0	0	1	0	210
10111000	1	0	1	1	1	0	0	0	184
10100110	1	0	1	0	0	1	1	0	166

3. Convert the following from binary format to hexadecimal.

Complete the following table to express 11011000.00011011.00111101.01110110 in hexadecimal.

Binary	128	64	32	16	8	4	2	1	Hexadecimal
11011000	1	1	0	1	1	0	0	0	D8
00011011	0	0	0	1	1	0	1	1	1B
00111101	0	0	1	1	1	1	0	1	3D
01110110	0	1	1	1	0	1	1	0	76

Complete the following table to express 11001010.11110101.10000011.11101011 in hexadecimal.

Binary	128	64	32	16	8	4	2	1	Hexadecimal
11001010	1	1	0	0	1	0	1	0	CA
11110101	1	1	1	1	0	1	0	1	F5
10000011	1	0	0	0	0	0	1	1	83
11101011	1	1	1	0	1	0	1	1	EB

Complete the following table to express 10000100.11010010.01000011.10110011 in hexadecimal.

Binary	128	64	32	16	8	4	2	1	Hexadecimal
10000100	1	0	0	0	0	1	0	0	84
11010010	1	1	0	1	0	0	1	0	D2
01000011	0	1	0	0	0	0	1	1	43
10110011	1	0	1	1	0	0	1	1	B3

Answers to Written Lab 2.2

When a collision occurs on an Ethernet LAN, the following happens:

1. A jam signal informs all devices that a collision occurred.
2. The collision invokes a random backoff algorithm.
3. Each device on the Ethernet segment stops transmitting for a short time until the timers expire.
4. All hosts have equal priority to transmit after the timers have expired

Answers to Written Lab 2.3

1. Crossover
2. Straight-through
3. Crossover
4. Crossover
5. Straight-through
6. Crossover
7. Crossover
8. Rolled

Answers to Written Lab 2.4

At a transmitting device, the data encapsulation method works like this:

1. User information is converted to data for transmission on the network.
2. Data is converted to segments, and a reliable connection is set up between the transmitting and receiving hosts.
3. Segments are converted to packets or datagrams, and a logical address is placed in the header so each packet can be routed through an internetwork.
4. Packets or datagrams are converted to frames for transmission on the local network. Hardware (Ethernet) addresses are used to uniquely identify hosts on a local network segment.
5. Frames are converted to bits, and a digital encoding and clocking scheme is used.

Introduction to TCP/IP

THE CCNA EXAM TOPICS COVERED IN THIS CHAPTER INCLUDE THE FOLLOWING:

✓ **Describe how a network works**

- Describe the purpose and basic operation of the protocols in the OSI and TCP models.
- Identify and correct common network problems at layers 1, 2, 3, and 7 using a layered model approach.

✓ **Implement an IP addressing scheme and IP Services to meet network requirements in a medium-size Enterprise branch office network.**

- Describe the operation and benefits of using private and public IP addressing.

The *Transmission Control Protocol/Internet Protocol (TCP/IP)* suite was created by the Department of Defense (DoD) to ensure and preserve data integrity as well as maintain communications in the event of catastrophic war. So it follows that if designed and implemented correctly, a TCP/IP network can be a truly dependable and resilient one. In this chapter, I'll cover the protocols of TCP/IP, and throughout this book, you'll learn how to create a marvelous TCP/IP network—using Cisco routers, of course.

We'll begin by taking a look at the DoD's version of TCP/IP and then compare this version and its protocols with the OSI reference model discussed in Chapter 1, "Internetworking."

Once you understand the protocols used at the various levels of the DoD model, I'll cover IP addressing and the different classes of IP addresses used in networks today.

Subnetting will be covered in Chapter 4, "Easy Subnetting."

Last, because IPv4 address types are so important to understanding IP addressing, as well as subnetting and Variable Length Subnet Masks (VLSMs), an understanding of the various flavors of IPv4 addresses is critical. I'll finish the chapter with various types of IPv4 addresses that you just must know.

Internet Protocol version 6 will not be discussed in this chapter; this chapter will focus solely on IPv4. IPv6 will be covered in Chapter 15, "Internet Protocol Version 6 (IPv6)." Also, when I discuss Internet Protocol Version 4, you'll see it written as just IP, not typically IPv4.

For up-to-the-minute updates for this chapter, please see `www.lammle.com` and/or `www.sybex.com/go/ccna7e`.

Introducing TCP/IP

Because TCP/IP is so central to working with the Internet and intranets, it's essential for you to understand it in detail. I'll begin by giving you some background on TCP/IP and how it came about and then move on to describing the important technical goals defined by the original designers. After that, you'll find out how TCP/IP compares to a theoretical model—the Open Systems Interconnection (OSI) model.

A Brief History of TCP/IP

TCP/IP first came on the scene in 1973. Later, in 1978, it was divided into two distinct protocols: TCP and IP. Then, in 1983, TCP/IP replaced the Network Control Protocol (NCP) and was authorized as the official means of data transport for anything connecting to ARPAnet, the Internet's ancestor that was created by ARPA, the DoD's Advanced Research Projects Agency, way back in 1957 in reaction to the Soviet's launching of Sputnik. ARPA was soon redubbed DARPA, and it was divided into ARPAnet and MILNET (also in 1983); both were finally dissolved in 1990.

But contrary to what you might think, most of the development work on TCP/IP happened at UC Berkeley in Northern California, where a group of scientists were simultaneously working on the Berkeley version of UNIX, which soon became known as the BSD, or Berkeley Software Distribution, series of UNIX versions. Of course, because TCP/IP worked so well, it was packaged into subsequent releases of BSD UNIX and offered to other universities and institutions if they bought the distribution tape. So basically, BSD Unix bundled with TCP/IP began as shareware in the world of academia and, as a result, became the basis of the huge success and exponential growth of today's Internet as well as smaller, private and corporate intranets.

As usual, what may have started as a small group of TCP/IP aficionados evolved, and as it did, the U.S. government created a program to test any new published standards and make sure they passed certain criteria. This was to protect TCP/IP's integrity and to ensure that no developer changed anything too dramatically or added any proprietary features. It's this very quality—this open-systems approach to the TCP/IP family of protocols—that pretty much sealed its popularity because it guarantees a solid connection between myriad hardware and software platforms with no strings attached.

TCP/IP and the DoD Model

The DoD model is basically a condensed version of the OSI model—it's composed of four, instead of seven, layers:

- Process/Application layer
- Host-to-Host layer
- Internet layer
- Network Access layer

Figure 3.1 shows a comparison of the DoD model and the OSI reference model. As you can see, the two are similar in concept, but each has a different number of layers with different names.

When the different protocols in the IP stack are discussed, the layers of the OSI and DoD models are interchangeable. In other words, the Internet layer and the Network layer describe the same thing, as do the Host-to-Host layer and the Transport layer.

FIGURE 3.1 The DoD and OSI models

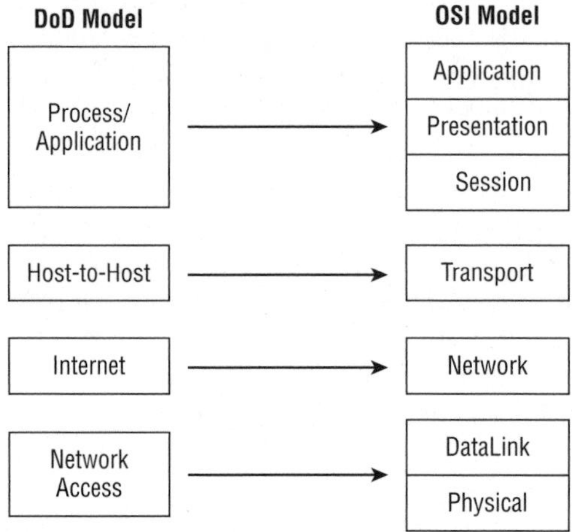

A vast array of protocols combine at the DoD model's *Process/Application layer* to integrate the various activities and duties spanning the focus of the OSI's corresponding top three layers (Application, Presentation, and Session). We'll be looking closely at those protocols in the next part of this chapter. The Process/Application layer defines protocols for node-to-node application communication and also controls user-interface specifications.

The *Host-to-Host layer* parallels the functions of the OSI's Transport layer, defining protocols for setting up the level of transmission service for applications. It tackles issues such as creating reliable end-to-end communication and ensuring the error-free delivery of data. It handles packet sequencing and maintains data integrity.

The *Internet layer* corresponds to the OSI's Network layer, designating the protocols relating to the logical transmission of packets over the entire network. It takes care of the addressing of hosts by giving them an IP (Internet Protocol) address, and it handles the routing of packets among multiple networks.

At the bottom of the DoD model, the *Network Access layer* implements the data exchange between the host and the network. The equivalent of the Data Link and Physical layers of the OSI model, the Network Access layer oversees hardware addressing and defines protocols for the physical transmission of data.

The DoD and OSI models are alike in design and concept and have similar functions in similar layers. Figure 3.2 shows the TCP/IP protocol suite and how its protocols relate to the DoD model layers.

In the following sections, we will look at the different protocols in more detail, starting with the Process/Application layer protocols.

The Process/Application Layer Protocols

In the following sections, I'll describe the different applications and services typically used in IP networks. The following protocols and applications are covered:

- Telnet
- FTP
- TFTP
- NFS
- SMTP
- POP
- IMAP4
- TLS
- SIP (VoIP)
- RTP (VoIP)
- LPD
- X Window
- SNMP
- SSH
- HTTP
- HTTPS
- NTP
- NNTP
- SCP
- LDAP
- IGMP
- LPR
- DNS
- DHCP/BootP

FIGURE 3.2 The TCP/IP protocol suite

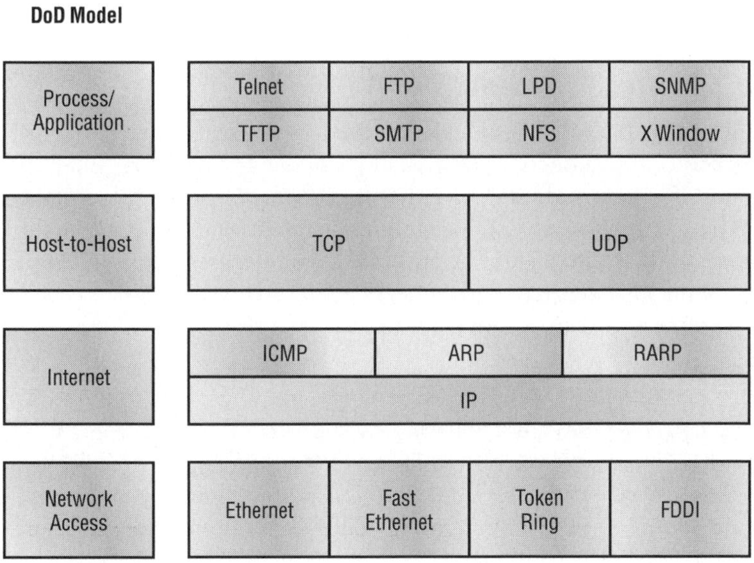

Telnet

Telnet is the chameleon of protocols—its specialty is terminal emulation. It allows a user on a remote client machine, called the Telnet client, to access the resources of another machine, the Telnet server. Telnet achieves this by pulling a fast one on the Telnet server and making the client machine appear as though it were a terminal directly attached to the local network. This projection is actually a software image—a virtual terminal that can interact with the chosen remote host.

These emulated terminals are of the text-mode type and can execute defined procedures such as displaying menus that give users the opportunity to choose options and access the applications on the duped server. Users begin a Telnet session by running the Telnet client software and then logging into the Telnet server.

File Transfer Protocol (FTP)

File Transfer Protocol (FTP) is the protocol that actually lets us transfer files, and it can accomplish this between any two machines using it. But FTP isn't just a protocol; it's also a program. Operating as a protocol, FTP is used by applications. As a program, it's employed by users to perform file tasks by hand. FTP also allows for access to both directories and files and can accomplish certain types of directory operations, such as relocating into different ones.

Accessing a host through FTP is only the first step, though. Users must then be subjected to an authentication login that's probably secured with passwords and usernames implemented by system administrators to restrict access. You can get around this somewhat by adopting the username *anonymous*—though what you'll gain access to will be limited.

Even when employed by users manually as a program, FTP's functions are limited to listing and manipulating directories, typing file contents, and copying files between hosts. It can't execute remote files as programs.

Trivial File Transfer Protocol (TFTP)

Trivial File Transfer Protocol (TFTP) is the stripped-down, stock version of FTP, but it's the protocol of choice if you know exactly what you want and where to find it, plus it's so easy to use and it's fast too! It doesn't give you the abundance of functions that FTP does, though. TFTP has no directory-browsing abilities; it can do nothing but send and receive files. This compact little protocol also skimps in the data department, sending much smaller blocks of data than FTP, and there's no authentication as with FTP, so it's even more insecure. Few sites support it because of the inherent security risks.

Network File System (NFS)

Network File System (NFS) is a jewel of a protocol specializing in file sharing. It allows two different types of file systems to interoperate. It works like this: Suppose the NFS server software is running on a Windows server and the NFS client software is running on a Unix host. NFS allows for a portion of the RAM on the Windows server to transparently store Unix files, which can, in turn, be used by Unix users. Even though the Windows file system and Unix file system are unlike—they have different case sensitivity, filename lengths, security, and so on—both Unix users and Windows users can access that same file with their normal file systems, in their normal way.

Real World Scenario

When Should You Use FTP?

The folks at your San Francisco office need a 50 GB file emailed to them right away. What do you do? Most email servers would reject the email because they have size limits. Even if there's no size limit on the server, it still would take a while to send this big file to SF. FTP to the rescue!

If you need to give someone a large file or you need to get a large file from someone, FTP is a nice choice. Smaller files (less than 5 MB) can just be sent via email if you have the bandwidth of DSL or a cable modem. However, most ISPs don't allow files larger than 5 or 10 MB to be emailed, so FTP is an option you should consider if you are in need of sending and receiving large files (and who isn't these days?). To use FTP, you will need to set up an FTP server on the Internet so that the files can be shared.

Besides, FTP is faster than email, which is another reason to use FTP for sending or receiving large files. In addition, because it uses TCP and is connection-oriented, if the session dies, FTP can sometimes start up where it left off. Try that with your email client!

Simple Mail Transfer Protocol (SMTP)

Simple Mail Transfer Protocol (SMTP), answering our ubiquitous call to email, uses a spooled, or queued, method of mail delivery. Once a message has been sent to a destination, the message is spooled to a device—usually a disk. The server software at the destination posts a vigil, regularly checking the queue for messages. When it detects them, it proceeds to deliver them to their destination. SMTP is used to send mail; POP3 or IMAP is used to receive mail.

Post Office Protocol (POP)

Post Office Protocol (POP) gives us a storage facility for incoming mail, and the latest version is called POP3 (sound familiar?). Basically, how this protocol works is when a client device connects to a POP3 server, messages addressed to that client are released for downloading. It doesn't allow messages to be downloaded selectively, but once they are, the client/server interaction ends and you can delete and tweak your messages locally at will. Lately we're seeing a newer standard, IMAP, being used more and more in place of POP3. Why?

Internet Message Access Protocol, Version 4 (IMAP4)

Because *Internet Message Access Protocol (IMAP)* makes it so you get control over how you download your mail, and with it, you also gain some much-needed security. It lets you peek at the message header or download just a part of a message—you can now just nibble at the bait instead of swallowing it whole and then choking on the hook hidden inside!

With it, you can choose to store messages on the email server hierarchically and link to documents and user groups too. IMAP even gives you search commands to use to hunt for messages based on their subject, header, or content. As you can imagine, it has some serious authentication features—it actually supports the Kerberos authentication scheme that MIT developed. And yes, IMAP4 is the current version.

Transport Layer Security (TLS)

Both *Transport Layer Security (TLS)* and its forerunner, *Secure Sockets Layer (SSL)*, are cryptographic protocols that come in really handy for enabling secure online data-transfer activities like browsing the Web, instant messaging, Internet faxing, and so on. They're so similar it's not within the scope of this book to detail the differences between them.

SIP (VoIP)

Session Initiation Protocol (SIP) is a hugely popular signaling protocol used to construct and deconstruct multimedia communication sessions for many things like voice and video calls, video conferencing, streaming multimedia distribution, instant messaging, presence information, and online games over the Internet.

RTP (VoIP)

Real-time Transport Protocol (RTP) describes a packet-formatting standard for delivering audio and video over the Internet. Although initially designed as a multicast protocol, it's now used for unicast applications too. It's commonly employed for streaming media, video-conferencing, and push-to-talk systems—all things that make it a de facto standard in Voice over IP (VoIP) industries.

Line Printer Daemon (LPD)

The *Line Printer Daemon (LPD)* protocol is designed for printer sharing. The LPD, along with the Line Printer (LPR) program, allows print jobs to be spooled and sent to the network's printers using TCP/IP.

X Window

Designed for client/server operations, *X Window* defines a protocol for writing client/server applications based on a graphical user interface (GUI). The idea is to allow a program, called a client, to run on one computer and have it display things through a window server on another computer.

Simple Network Management Protocol (SNMP)

Simple Network Management Protocol (SNMP) collects and manipulates valuable network information. It gathers data by polling the devices on the network from a management station at fixed or random intervals, requiring them to disclose certain information. When all is well, SNMP receives something called a *baseline*—a report delimiting the operational traits of a healthy network. This protocol can also stand as a watchdog over the network, quickly notifying managers of any sudden turn of events. These network watchdogs are called *agents*, and when aberrations occur, agents send an alert called a *trap* to the management station.

SNMP Versions 1, 2, and 3

SNMP versions 1 and 2 are pretty much obsolete. This doesn't mean you won't see them in a network at some time, but v1 is super old and, well, obsolete. SNMPv2 provided improvements, especially in performance. But one of the best additions was what was called GETBULK, which allowed a host to retrieve a large amount of data at once. However, v2 never really caught on in the networking world. SNMPv3 is now the standard and uses both TCP and UDP, unlike v1, which used only UDP. V3 added even more security and message integrity, authentication, and encryption.

Secure Shell (SSH)

Secure Shell (SSH) protocol sets up a secure Telnet session over a standard TCP/IP connection and is employed for doing things like logging into systems, running programs on remote systems, and moving files from one system to another. And it does all of this while maintaining a nice, strong, encrypted connection. You can think of it as the new-generation protocol that's now used in place of `rsh` and `rlogin`—even Telnet.

Hypertext Transfer Protocol (HTTP)

All those snappy websites comprising a mélange of graphics, text, links, and so on—the *Hypertext Transfer Protocol (HTTP)* is making it all possible. It's used to manage communications between web browsers and web servers and opens the right resource when you click a link, wherever that resource may actually reside.

Hypertext Transfer Protocol Secure (HTTPS)

Hypertext Transfer Protocol Secure (HTTPS) is also known as Secure Hypertext Transfer Protocol. It uses Secure Sockets Layer (SSL). Sometimes you'll see it referred to as SHTTP or S-HTTP (which is an extension of HTTP and doesn't use SSL), but no matter—as indicated, it's a secure version of HTTP that arms you with a whole bunch of security tools for keeping transactions between a web browser and a server secure. It's what your browser needs to fill out forms, sign in, authenticate, and encrypt an HTTP message when you make a reservation or buy something online.

Network Time Protocol (NTP)

Kudos to Professor David Mills of the University of Delaware for coming up with this handy protocol that's used to synchronize the clocks on our computers to one standard time source (typically, an atomic clock). *Network Time Protocol (NTP)* works by synchronizing devices to ensure that all computers on a given network agree on the time. This may sound pretty simple, but it's very important because so many of the transactions done today are time- and date-stamped. Think about your precious databases, for one. It can mess up a server pretty badly if it's out of sync with the machines connected to it, even by mere seconds (think *crash!*). You can't have a transaction entered by a machine at, say, 1:50 a.m. when the server records that transaction as having occurred at 1:45 a.m. So basically, NTP works to prevent "back to the future *sans* DeLorean" from bringing down the network—very important indeed!

Network News Transfer Protocol (NNTP)

Network News Transfer Protocol (NNTP) is how you access the Usenet news servers that hold the legion of specific message boards called *newsgroups*. As you likely know, these groups represent pretty much any special interest humans have under the sun. For instance, if you happen to be a classic car buff or a WWII aircraft enthusiast, odds are good there're lots of newsgroups available to join based upon those interests. NNTP is specified in RFC 977. And because it's complicated to configure a news reader program, lots of websites—even search engines—are the entities we usually depend upon to access these many and varied resources.

Secure Copy Protocol (SCP)

FTP is great. It's a super easy, user-friendly way to transfer files—if you don't need to transfer those files securely. That's because when you use FTP for transferring data, usernames and passwords get sent right along with the file request in the clear for all to see with no encryption whatsoever! Kind of like Hail Mary passes, you basically just throw them out there and hope your information doesn't fall into the wrong hands and get intercepted.

That's where Secure Copy Protocol (SCP) comes to your rescue—its whole purpose is to protect your precious files through SSH. It first establishes and then sustains a secure, encrypted connection between the sending and receiving hosts until file transfer is complete. When armed with SCP, your Hail Mary pass can be caught only by your intended receiver—snap! In today's networks, however, the more robust SFTP is used more commonly than SCP.

Lightweight Directory Access Protocol (LDAP)

If you're the system administrator of any decent-sized network, odds are you've got a type of directory in place that keeps track of all your network resources, such as devices and users. But how do you access those directories? Through the Lightweight Directory Access Protocol (LDAP), that's how. This protocol standardizes how you access directories, and its first and second inceptions are described in RFCs 1487 and 1777, respectively. There were a few glitches in those two earlier versions, so a third version—the one most commonly used today—was created to address those issues, and is described in RFC 3377.

The Requests for Comments (RFCs) form a series of notes, started in 1969, about the Internet (originally the ARPAnet). The notes discuss many aspects of computer communication; they focus on networking protocols, procedures, programs, and concepts but also include meeting notes, opinion, and sometimes humor. You can find the RFCs by visiting `www.iana.org`.

Internet Group Management Protocol (IGMP)

Internet Group Management Protocol (IGMP) is the TCP/IP protocol used for managing IP multicast sessions. It accomplishes this by sending out unique IGMP messages over the network to reveal the multicast-group landscape and to find out which hosts belong to which multicast group. The host machines in an IP network also use IGMP messages to become members of a group and to quit the group, too. IGMP messages come in seriously handy for tracking group memberships as well as active multicast streams.

Line Printer Remote (LPR)

When printing in an unblended, genuine TCP/IP environment, a combination of Line Printer (LPR) and the Line Printer Daemon (LPD) is typically what's used to get the job done. LPD, installed on all printing devices, handles both printers and print jobs. LPR acts on the client, or sending machine, and is used to send the data from a host machine to the network's print resource so you end up with actual printed output.

Domain Name Service (DNS)

Domain Name Service (DNS) resolves hostnames—specifically, Internet names, such as `www.routersim.com`. You don't have to use DNS; you can just type in the IP address of any device you want to communicate with. An IP address identifies hosts on a network and the Internet as well. However, DNS was designed to make our lives easier. Think about this: What would happen if you wanted to move your web page to a different service provider? The IP address would change and no one would know what the new one was. DNS allows you to use a domain name to specify an IP address. You can change the IP address as often as you want and no one will know the difference.

DNS is used to resolve a *fully qualified domain name (FQDN)*—for example, `www.lammle.com` or `todd.lammle.com`. An FQDN is a hierarchy that can logically locate a system based on its domain identifier.

If you want to resolve the name *todd*, you either must type in the FQDN of `todd.lammle.com` or have a device such as a PC or router add the suffix for you. For example, on a Cisco router, you can use the command `ip domain-name lammle.com` to append each request with the `lammle.com` domain. If you don't do that, you'll have to type in the FQDN to get DNS to resolve the name.

An important thing to remember about DNS is that if you can ping a device with an IP address but cannot use its FQDN, then you might have some type of DNS configuration failure.

Dynamic Host Configuration Protocol (DHCP)/Bootstrap Protocol (BootP)

Dynamic Host Configuration Protocol (DHCP) assigns IP addresses to hosts. It allows easier administration and works well in small to even very large network environments. All types of hardware can be used as a DHCP server, including a Cisco router.

DHCP differs from BootP in that BootP assigns an IP address to a host but the host's hardware address must be entered manually in a BootP table. You can think of DHCP as a dynamic BootP. But remember that BootP is also used to send an operating system that a host can boot from. DHCP can't do that.

But there is a lot of information a DHCP server can provide to a host when the host is requesting an IP address from the DHCP server. Here's a list of the information a DHCP server can provide:

- IP address
- Subnet mask
- Domain name
- Default gateway (routers)
- DNS server address
- WINS server address

A DHCP server can give us even more information than this, but the items in the list are the most common.

A client that sends out a DHCP Discover message in order to receive an IP address sends out a broadcast at both layer 2 and layer 3.

- The layer-2 broadcast is all *F*s in hex, which looks like this: FF:FF:FF:FF:FF:FF.
- The layer-3 broadcast is 255.255.255.255, which means all networks and all hosts.

DHCP is connectionless, which means it uses User Datagram Protocol (UDP) at the Transport layer, also known as the Host-to-Host layer, which we'll talk about next.

In case you don't believe me, here's an example of output from my trusty analyzer:

```
Ethernet II, Src: 0.0.0.0 (00:0b:db:99:d3:5e),Dst: Broadcast(ff:ff:ff:ff:ff:ff)
Internet Protocol, Src: 0.0.0.0 (0.0.0.0),Dst: 255.255.255.255(255.255.255.255)
```

The Data Link and Network layers are both sending out "all hands" broadcasts saying, "Help—I don't know my IP address!"

Broadcast addresses will be discussed in more detail at the end of this chapter.

Figure 3.3 shows the process of a client/server relationship using a DHCP connection.

FIGURE 3.3 DHCP client four-step process

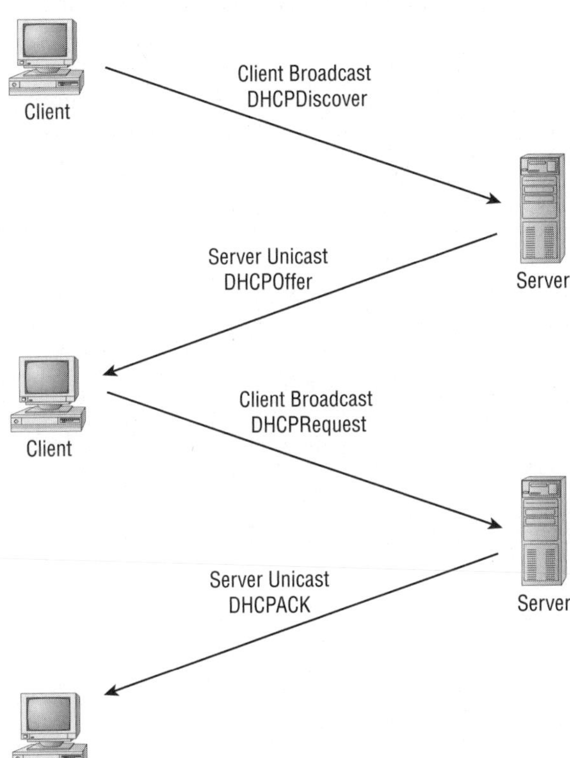

The following is the four-step process a client takes to receive an IP address from a DHCP server:

1. The DHCP client broadcasts a DHCP Discover message looking for a DHCP server (Port 67).
2. The DHCP server that received the DHCP Discover message sends a unicast DHCP Offer message back to the host
3. The client then broadcasts to the server a DHCP Request message asking for the offered IP address and possibly other information.
4. The server finalizes the exchange with a unicast DHCP Acknowledgment message.

DHCP Conflicts

A DHCP address conflict occurs when two hosts use the same IP address. This sounds bad, doesn't it? Well of course it is! We'll never even have to discuss this problem in my IPv6 chapter!

During IP address assignment, a DHCP server checks for conflicts using the ping program to test the availability of the address before it is assigned from the pool. If no host replies, then the DHCP server assumes that the IP address is not already allocated. This helps the server know that it is providing a good address, but what about the host? To provide extra protection against the all-so-terrible IP conflict issue, the host can broadcast for its own address.

A host uses something called a gratuitous ARP to help avoid a possible duplicate address. The DHCP client sends an ARP broadcast out on the local LAN or VLAN using its newly assigned address to solve conflicts before they occur.

So, if an IP address conflict is detected, the address is removed from the DHCP pool (scope), and it is all-so-important to remember that the address will not be assigned to a host until the administrator resolves the conflict by hand.

Please see Chapter 6 to see a DHCP configuration on a Cisco router and also to find out what happens when a DHCP client is on one side of a router and the DHCP server is on the other side (different networks)!

Automatic Private IP Addressing (APIPA)

Okay, so what happens if you have a few hosts connected together with a switch or hub and you don't have a DHCP server? You can add IP information by hand (this is called *static IP addressing*), but Windows provides what is called Automatic Private IP Addressing (APIPA), a feature of later Windows operating systems. With APIPA, clients can automatically self-configure an IP address and subnet mask (basic IP information that hosts use to communicate) when a DHCP server isn't available. The IP address range for APIPA is 169.254.0.1 through 169.254.255.254. The client also configures itself with a default class B subnet mask of 255.255.0.0.

However, when you're in your corporate network working and you have a DHCP server running, and your host shows that it is using this IP address range, this means that either your DHCP client on the host is not working or the server is down or can't be reached because of a network issue. I don't know anyone who's seen a host in this address range and has been happy about it!

Now, let's take a look at the Transport layer, or what the DoD calls the Host-to-Host layer.

The Host-to-Host Layer Protocols

The main purpose of the Host-to-Host layer is to shield the upper-layer applications from the complexities of the network. This layer says to the upper layer, "Just give me your data stream, with any instructions, and I'll begin the process of getting your information ready to send."

The following sections describe the two protocols at this layer:

- Transmission Control Protocol (TCP)
- User Datagram Protocol (UDP)

In addition, we'll look at some of the key host-to-host protocol concepts, as well as the port numbers.

Remember, this is still considered layer 4, and Cisco really likes the way layer 4 can use acknowledgments, sequencing, and flow control.

Transmission Control Protocol (TCP)

Transmission Control Protocol (TCP) takes large blocks of information from an application and breaks them into segments. It numbers and sequences each segment so that the destination's TCP stack can put the segments back into the order the application intended. After these segments are sent, TCP (on the transmitting host) waits for an acknowledgment of the receiving end's TCP virtual circuit session, retransmitting those that aren't acknowledged.

Before a transmitting host starts to send segments down the model, the sender's TCP stack contacts the destination's TCP stack to establish a connection. What is created is known as a *virtual circuit*. This type of communication is called *connection-oriented*. During this initial handshake, the two TCP layers also agree on the amount of information that's going to be sent before the recipient's TCP sends back an acknowledgment. With everything agreed upon in advance, the path is paved for reliable communication to take place.

TCP is a full-duplex, connection-oriented, reliable, and accurate protocol, but establishing all these terms and conditions, in addition to error checking, is no small task. TCP is very complicated and, not surprisingly, costly in terms of network overhead. And since today's networks are much more reliable than those of yore, this added reliability is often unnecessary. Most programmers use TCP because it removes a lot of programming work; however, real-time video and VoIP use UDP because they can't afford the overhead.

TCP Segment Format

Since the upper layers just send a data stream to the protocols in the Transport layers, I'll demonstrate how TCP segments a data stream and prepares it for the Internet layer. When the Internet layer receives the data stream, it routes the segments as packets through an internetwork. The segments are handed to the receiving host's Host-to-Host layer protocol, which rebuilds the data stream to hand to the upper-layer applications or protocols.

Figure 3.4 shows the TCP segment format. The figure shows the different fields within the TCP header.

The TCP header is 20 bytes long, or up to 24 bytes with options. You need to understand what each field in the TCP segment is:

Source port The port number of the application on the host sending the data. (Port numbers will be explained a little later in this section.)

Destination port The port number of the application requested on the destination host.

Sequence number A number used by TCP that puts the data back in the correct order or retransmits missing or damaged data, a process called *sequencing*.

Acknowledgment number The TCP octet that is expected next.

Header length The number of 32-bit words in the TCP header. This indicates where the data begins. The TCP header (even one including options) is an integral number of 32 bits in length.

Reserved Always set to zero.

Code bits/flags Control functions used to set up and terminate a session.

Window The window size the sender is willing to accept, in octets.

Checksum The cyclic redundancy check (CRC), because TCP doesn't trust the lower layers and checks everything. The CRC checks the header and data fields.

Urgent A valid field only if the Urgent pointer in the code bits is set. If so, this value indicates the offset from the current sequence number, in octets, where the segment of non-urgent data begins.

Options May be 0 or a multiple of 32 bits, if any. What this means is that no options have to be present (option size of 0). However, if any options are used that do not cause the option field to total a multiple of 32 bits, padding of 0s must be used to make sure the data begins on a 32-bit boundary.

Data Handed down to the TCP protocol at the Transport layer, which includes the upper-layer headers.

FIGURE 3.4 TCP segment format

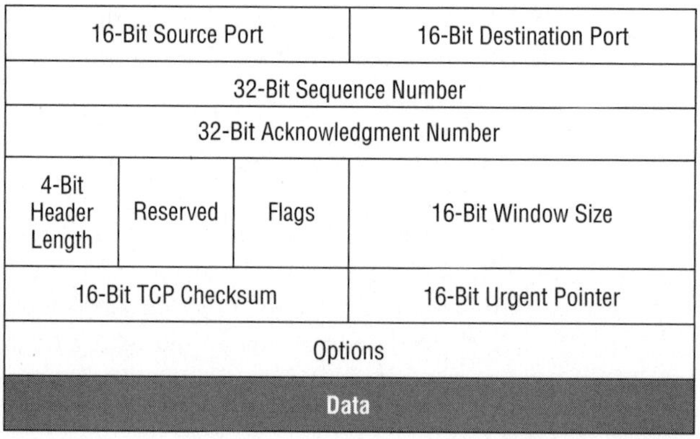

<table>
<tr><td colspan="3">16-Bit Source Port</td><td>16-Bit Destination Port</td></tr>
<tr><td colspan="4">32-Bit Sequence Number</td></tr>
<tr><td colspan="4">32-Bit Acknowledgment Number</td></tr>
<tr><td>4-Bit Header Length</td><td>Reserved</td><td>Flags</td><td>16-Bit Window Size</td></tr>
<tr><td colspan="3">16-Bit TCP Checksum</td><td>16-Bit Urgent Pointer</td></tr>
<tr><td colspan="4">Options</td></tr>
<tr><td colspan="4">Data</td></tr>
</table>

Let's take a look at a TCP segment copied from a network analyzer:

```
TCP - Transport Control Protocol
 Source Port:       5973
 Destination Port: 23
 Sequence Number:  1456389907
 Ack Number:       1242056456
```

```
Offset:           5
Reserved:         %000000
Code:             %011000
     Ack is valid
     Push Request
Window:           61320
Checksum:         0x61a6
Urgent Pointer:   0
No TCP Options
TCP Data Area:
vL.5.+.5.+.5.+.5  76 4c 19 35 11 2b 19 35 11 2b 19 35 11
 2b 19 35 +. 11 2b 19
Frame Check Sequence: 0x0d00000f
```

Did you notice that everything I talked about earlier is in the segment? As you can see from the number of fields in the header, TCP creates a lot of overhead. Application developers may opt for efficiency over reliability to save overhead, so User Datagram Protocol was also defined at the Transport layer as an alternative.

User Datagram Protocol (UDP)

If you were to compare *User Datagram Protocol (UDP)* with TCP, the former is basically the scaled-down economy model that's sometimes referred to as a thin protocol. Like a thin person on a park bench, a thin protocol doesn't take up a lot of room—or in this case, much bandwidth on a network.

UDP doesn't offer all the bells and whistles of TCP either, but it does do a fabulous job of transporting information that doesn't require reliable delivery—and it does so using far fewer network resources. (UDP is covered thoroughly in Request for Comments 768.)

There are some situations in which it would definitely be wise for developers to opt for UDP rather than TCP. One circumstance is when reliability is already handled at the Process/Application layer. Network File System (NFS) handles its own reliability issues, making the use of TCP both impractical and redundant. But ultimately, it's up to the application developer to decide whether to use UDP or TCP, not the user who wants to transfer data faster.

UDP does *not* sequence the segments and does not care in which order the segments arrive at the destination. Rather, UDP sends the segments off and forgets about them. It doesn't follow through, check up on them, or even allow for an acknowledgment of safe arrival—complete abandonment. Because of this, it's referred to as an unreliable protocol. This does not mean that UDP is ineffective, only that it doesn't handle issues of reliability.

Further, UDP doesn't create a virtual circuit, nor does it contact the destination before delivering information to it. Because of this, it's also considered a *connectionless* protocol. Since UDP assumes that the application will use its own reliability method, it doesn't use any. This gives an application developer a choice when running the Internet Protocol stack: TCP for reliability or UDP for faster transfers.

So, it is important to remember how this works because if the segments arrive out of order (very common in IP networks), they'll just be passed up to the next OSI (DoD) layer in whatever order they're received, possibly resulting in some seriously garbled data. On the other hand, TCP sequences the segments so they get put back together in exactly the right order—something UDP just can't do.

UDP Segment Format

Figure 3.5 clearly illustrates UDP's markedly low overhead as compared to TCP's hungry usage. Look at the figure carefully—can you see that UDP doesn't use windowing or provide for acknowledgments in the UDP header?

FIGURE 3.5 UDP segment

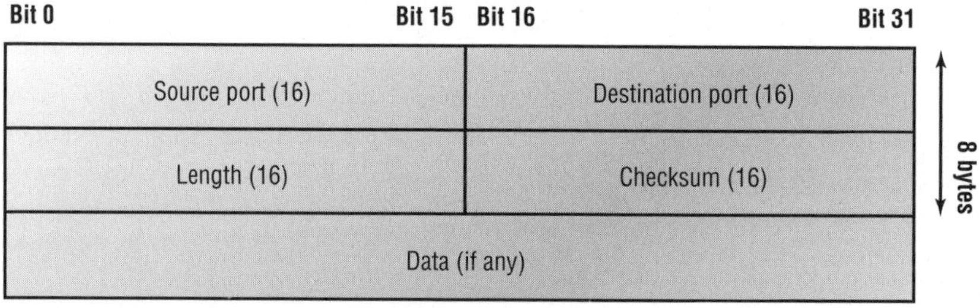

Bit 0 — Bit 15	Bit 16 — Bit 31
Source port (16)	Destination port (16)
Length (16)	Checksum (16)
Data (if any)	

(8 bytes: Source port, Destination port, Length, Checksum)

It's important for you to understand what each field in the UDP segment is:

Source port Port number of the application on the host sending the data

Destination port Port number of the application requested on the destination host

Length Length of UDP header and UDP data

Checksum Checksum of both the UDP header and UDP data fields

Data Upper-layer data

UDP, like TCP, doesn't trust the lower layers and runs its own CRC. Remember that the Frame Check Sequence (FCS) is the field that houses the CRC, which is why you can see the FCS information.

The following shows a UDP segment caught on a network analyzer:

```
UDP - User Datagram Protocol
 Source Port:      1085
 Destination Port: 5136
 Length:           41
 Checksum:         0x7a3c
 UDP Data Area:
 ..Z......00 01 5a 96 00 01 00 00 00 00 00 11 0000 00
...C..2._C._C  2e 03 00 43 02 1e 32 0a 00 0a 00 80 43 00 80
Frame Check Sequence: 0x00000000
```

Notice that low overhead! Try to find the sequence number, ack number, and window size in the UDP segment. You can't because they just aren't there!

Key Concepts of Host-to-Host Protocols

Since you've seen both a connection-oriented (TCP) and connectionless (UDP) protocol in action, it would be good to summarize the two here. Table 3.1 highlights some of the key concepts that you should keep in mind regarding these two protocols. You should memorize this table.

TABLE 3.1 Key features of TCP and UDP

TCP	UDP
Sequenced	Unsequenced
Reliable	Unreliable
Connection-oriented	Connectionless
Virtual circuit	Low overhead
Acknowledgments	No acknowledgment
Windowing flow control	No windowing or flow control of any type

A telephone analogy could really help you understand how TCP works. Most of us know that before you speak to someone on a phone, you must first establish a connection with that other person—wherever they are. This is like a virtual circuit with the TCP protocol. If you were giving someone important information during your conversation, you might say, "You know?" or ask, "Did you get that?" Saying something like this is a lot like a TCP acknowledgment—it's designed to get you verification. From time to time (especially on cell phones), people also ask, "Are you still there?" They end their conversations with a "Goodbye" of some kind, putting closure on the phone call. TCP also performs these types of functions.

Alternately, using UDP is like sending a postcard. To do that, you don't need to contact the other party first. You simply write your message, address the postcard, and mail it. This is analogous to UDP's connectionless orientation. Since the message on the postcard is probably not a matter of life or death, you don't need an acknowledgment of its receipt. Similarly, UDP does not involve acknowledgments.

Let's take a look at another figure, one that includes TCP, UDP, and the applications associated to each protocol: Figure 3.6 (in the next section).

Port Numbers

TCP and UDP must use *port numbers* to communicate with the upper layers because they're what keep track of different conversations crossing the network simultaneously.

Originating-source port numbers are dynamically assigned by the source host and will equal some number starting at 1024. 1023 and below are defined in RFC 3232 (or just see `www.iana.org`), which discusses what are called well-known port numbers.

Virtual circuits that don't use an application with a well-known port number are assigned port numbers randomly from a specific range instead. These port numbers identify the source and destination application or process in the TCP segment.

Figure 3.6 illustrates how both TCP and UDP use port numbers.

FIGURE 3.6 Port numbers for TCP and UDP

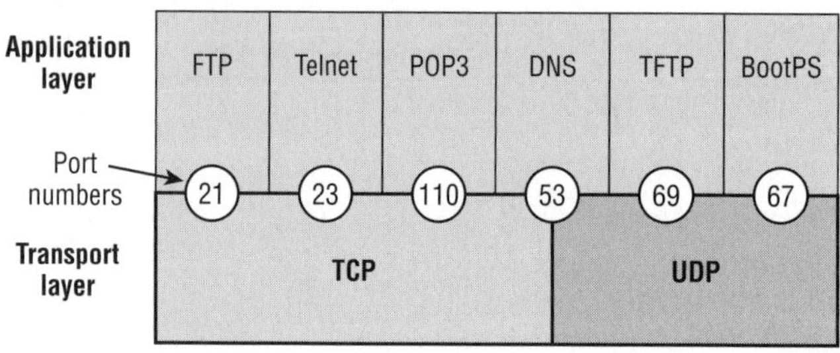

The different port numbers that can be used are explained next:

- Numbers below 1024 are considered well-known port numbers and are defined in RFC 3232.
- Numbers 1024 and above are used by the upper layers to set up sessions with other hosts and by TCP and UDP to use as source and destination addresses in the segment.

In the following sections, we'll take a look at an analyzer output showing a TCP session.

TCP Session: Source Port

The following listing shows a TCP session captured with my analyzer software:

```
TCP - Transport Control Protocol
 Source Port:        5973
 Destination Port: 23
 Sequence Number:  1456389907
 Ack Number:         1242056456
 Offset:             5
 Reserved:           %000000
 Code:               %011000
      Ack is valid
      Push Request
 Window:             61320
 Checksum:           0x61a6
 Urgent Pointer:   0
 No TCP Options
```

```
 TCP Data Area:
 vL.5.+.5.+.5.+.5  76 4c 19 35 11 2b 19 35 11 2b 19 35 11
  2b 19 35 +. 11 2b 19
Frame Check Sequence: 0x0d00000f
```

Notice that the source host makes up the source port, which in this case is 5973. The destination port is 23, which is used to tell the receiving host the purpose of the intended connection (Telnet).

By looking at this session, you can see that the source host makes up the source port by using numbers from 1024 to 65535. But why does the source make up a port number? To differentiate between sessions with different hosts, my friend. How would a server know where information is coming from if it didn't have a different number from a sending host? TCP and the upper layers don't use hardware and logical addresses to understand the sending host's address as the Data Link and Network layer protocols do. Instead, they use port numbers.

TCP Session: Destination Port

You'll sometimes look at an analyzer and see that only the source port is above 1024 and the destination port is a well-known port, as shown in the following trace:

```
TCP - Transport Control Protocol
 Source Port:       1144
 Destination Port: 80 World Wide Web HTTP
 Sequence Number:  9356570
 Ack Number:        0
 Offset:            7
 Reserved:          %000000
 Code:              %000010
      Synch Sequence
 Window:            8192
 Checksum:          0x57E7
 Urgent Pointer:   0
 TCP Options:
  Option Type: 2 Maximum Segment Size
    Length:    4
    MSS:       536
  Option Type: 1 No Operation
  Option Type: 1 No Operation
  Option Type: 4
    Length:    2
    Opt Value:
  No More HTTP Data
Frame Check Sequence: 0x43697363
```

And sure enough, the source port is over 1024, but the destination port is 80, or HTTP service. The server, or receiving host, will change the destination port if it needs to.

In the preceding trace, a "syn" packet is sent to the destination device. The syn sequence is what's telling the remote destination device that it wants to create a session.

TCP Session: Syn Packet Acknowledgment

The next trace shows an acknowledgment to the syn packet:

```
TCP - Transport Control Protocol
 Source Port:       80 World Wide Web HTTP
 Destination Port: 1144
 Sequence Number:  2873580788
 Ack Number:       9356571
 Offset:           6
 Reserved:         %000000
 Code:             %010010
      Ack is valid
      Synch Sequence
 Window:           8576
 Checksum:         0x5F85
 Urgent Pointer:   0
 TCP Options:
  Option Type: 2 Maximum Segment Size
    Length:    4
    MSS:       1460
  No More HTTP Data
Frame Check Sequence: 0x6E203132
```

Notice the *Ack is valid*, which means that the source port was accepted and the device agreed to create a virtual circuit with the originating host.

And here again, you can see that the response from the server shows that the source is 80 and the destination is the 1144 sent from the originating host—all's well.

Table 3.2 gives you a list of the typical applications used in the TCP/IP suite, their well-known port numbers, and the Transport layer protocols used by each application or process. It's important that you study and memorize this table.

TABLE 3.2 Key protocols that use TCP and UDP

TCP	UDP
Telnet 23	SNMP 161
SMTP 25	TFTP 69
HTTP 80	DNS 53

TCP	UDP
FTP 20, 21	BooTPS/DHCP 67
DNS 53	
HTTPS 443	
SSH 22	
POP3 110	
NTP 123	
IMAP4 143	

Notice that DNS uses both TCP and UDP. Whether it opts for one or the other depends on what it's trying to do. Even though it's not the only application that can use both protocols, it's certainly one that you should remember in your studies.

What makes TCP reliable is sequencing, acknowledgments, and flow control (windowing). UDP does not have reliability.

The Internet Layer Protocols

In the DoD model, there are two main reasons for the Internet layer's existence: routing and providing a single network interface to the upper layers.

None of the other upper- or lower-layer protocols have any functions relating to routing—that complex and important task belongs entirely to the Internet layer. The Internet layer's second duty is to provide a single network interface to the upper-layer protocols. Without this layer, application programmers would need to write "hooks" into every one of their applications for each different Network Access protocol. This would not only be a pain in the neck, but it would lead to different versions of each application—one for Ethernet, another one for wireless, and so on. To prevent this, IP provides one single network interface for the upper-layer protocols. That accomplished, it's then the job of IP and the various Network Access protocols to get along and work together.

All network roads don't lead to Rome—they lead to IP. And all the other protocols at this layer, as well as all those at the upper layers, use it. Never forget that. All paths through the DoD model go through IP. The following sections describe the protocols at the Internet layer:

- Internet Protocol (IP)
- Internet Control Message Protocol (ICMP)
- Address Resolution Protocol (ARP)

- Reverse Address Resolution Protocol (RARP)
- Proxy ARP
- Gratuitous ARP

Internet Protocol (IP)

Internet Protocol (IP) essentially is the Internet layer. The other protocols found here merely exist to support it. IP holds the big picture and could be said to "see all," in that it's aware of all the interconnected networks. It can do this because all the machines on the network have a software, or logical, address called an IP address, which I'll cover more thoroughly later in this chapter.

IP looks at each packet's address. Then, using a routing table, it decides where a packet is to be sent next, choosing the best path. The protocols of the Network Access layer at the bottom of the DoD model don't possess IP's enlightened scope of the entire network; they deal only with physical links (local networks).

Identifying devices on networks requires answering these two questions: Which network is it on? And what is its ID on that network? The first answer is the *software address*, or *logical address* (the correct street). The second answer is the hardware address (the correct mailbox). All hosts on a network have a logical ID called an IP address. This is the software, or logical, address and contains valuable encoded information, greatly simplifying the complex task of routing. (IP is discussed in RFC 791.)

IP receives segments from the Host-to-Host layer and fragments them into datagrams (packets) if necessary. IP then reassembles datagrams back into segments on the receiving side. Each datagram is assigned the IP address of the sender and of the recipient. Each router (layer-3 device) that receives a datagram makes routing decisions based on the packet's destination IP address.

Figure 3.7 shows an IP header. This will give you an idea of what the IP protocol has to go through every time user data is sent from the upper layers and is to be sent to a remote network.

The following fields make up the IP header:

Version IP version number.

Header length Header length (HLEN) in 32-bit words.

Priority and Type of Service Type of Service tells how the datagram should be handled. The first 3 bits are the priority bits which is now called the differentiated services bits.

Total length Length of the packet including header and data.

Identification Unique IP-packet value used to differentiate fragmented packets from different datagrams.

Flags Specifies whether fragmentation should occur.

Fragment offset Provides fragmentation and reassembly if the packet is too large to put in a frame. It also allows different maximum transmission units (MTUs) on the Internet.

Time To Live The time to live is set into a packet when it is originally generated. If it doesn't get to where it wants to go before the TTL expires, boom—it's gone. This stops IP packets from continuously circling the network looking for a home.

Protocol Port of upper-layer protocol (TCP is port 6 or UDP is port 17). Also supports Network layer protocols, like ARP and ICMP (this can be called Type field in some analyzers). We'll talk about this field in more detail in a minute.

Header checksum Cyclic redundancy check (CRC) on header only.

Source IP address 32-bit IP address of sending station.

Destination IP address 32-bit IP address of the station this packet is destined for.

Options Used for network testing, debugging, security, and more.

Data After the IP option field will be the upper-layer data.

FIGURE 3.7 IP header

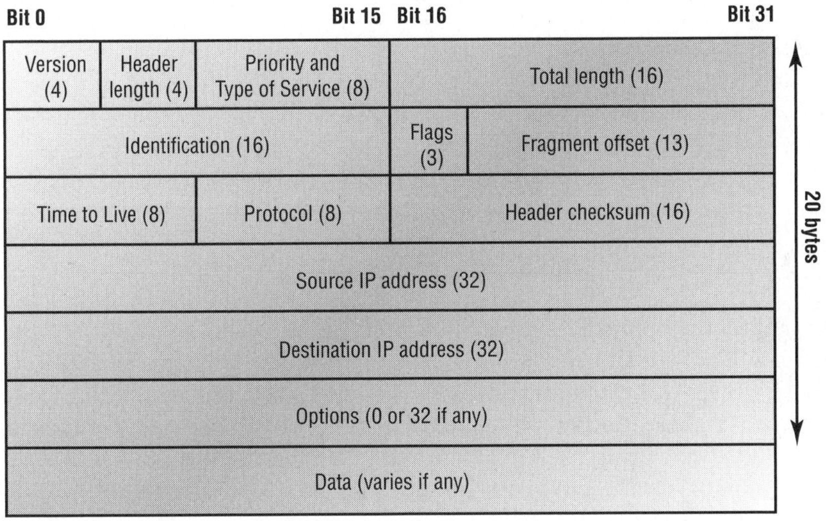

Here's a snapshot of an IP packet caught on a network analyzer (notice that all the header information discussed previously appears here):

```
IP Header - Internet Protocol Datagram
 Version:                4
 Header Length:          5
 Precedence:             0
 Type of Service:        %000
 Unused:                 %00
 Total Length:           187
 Identifier:             22486
```

```
Fragmentation Flags: %010 Do Not Fragment
Fragment Offset:     0
Time To Live:        60
IP Type:             0x06 TCP
Header Checksum:     0xd031
Source IP Address:   10.7.1.30
Dest. IP Address:    10.7.1.10
No Internet Datagram Options
```

The Type field—it's typically a Protocol field, but this analyzer sees it as an IP Type field—is important. If the header didn't carry the protocol information for the next layer, IP wouldn't know what to do with the data carried in the packet. The preceding example tells IP to hand the segment to TCP.

Figure 3.8 demonstrates how the Network layer sees the protocols at the Transport layer when it needs to hand a packet to the upper-layer protocols.

FIGURE 3.8 The Protocol field in an IP header

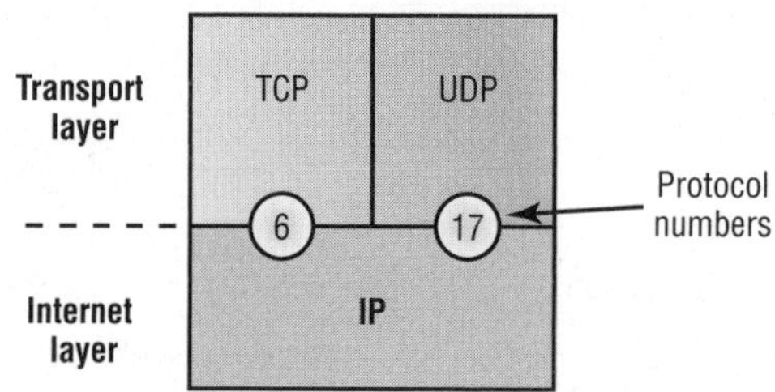

In this example, the Protocol field tells IP to send the data to either TCP port 6 or UDP port 17. But it will only be UDP or TCP if the data is part of a data stream headed for an upper-layer service or application. It could just as easily be destined for Internet Control Message Protocol (ICMP), Address Resolution Protocol (ARP), or some other type of Network layer protocol.

Table 3.3 is a list of some other popular protocols that can be specified in the Protocol field.

TABLE 3.3 Possible protocols found in the Protocol field of an IP header

Protocol	Protocol Number
ICMP	1
IP in IP (tunneling)	4
TCP	6
IGRP	9
UDP	17

Protocol	Protocol Number
EIGRP	88
OSPF	89
IPv6	41
GRE	47
Layer 2 tunnel (L2TP)	115

You can find a complete list of Protocol field numbers at `www.iana.org/assignments/protocol-numbers`.

Internet Control Message Protocol (ICMP)

Internet Control Message Protocol (ICMP) works at the Network layer and is used by IP for many different services. ICMP is a management protocol and messaging service provider for IP. Its messages are carried as IP datagrams. RFC 1256 is an annex to ICMP, which affords hosts extended capability in discovering routes to gateways.

ICMP packets have the following characteristics:

- They can provide hosts with information about network problems.
- They are encapsulated within IP datagrams.

The following are some common events and messages that ICMP relates to:

Destination Unreachable If a router can't send an IP datagram any further, it uses ICMP to send a message back to the sender, advising it of the situation. For example, take a look at Figure 3.9, which shows that interface E0 of the Lab_B router is down.

When Host A sends a packet destined for Host B, the Lab_B router will send an ICMP destination unreachable message back to the sending device (Host A in this example).

Buffer Full/Source Quence If a router's memory buffer for receiving incoming datagrams is full, it will use ICMP to send out this message until the congestion abates.

Hops/Time Exceeded Each IP datagram is allotted a certain number of routers, called hops, to pass through. If it reaches its limit of hops before arriving at its destination, the last router to receive that datagram deletes it. The executioner router then uses ICMP to send an obituary message, informing the sending machine of the demise of its datagram.

Ping Packet Internet Groper (Ping) uses ICMP echo request and reply messages to check the physical and logical connectivity of machines on an internetwork.

Traceroute Using ICMP time-outs, Traceroute is used to discover the path a packet takes as it traverses an internetwork.

FIGURE 3.9 ICMP error message is sent to the sending host from the remote router.

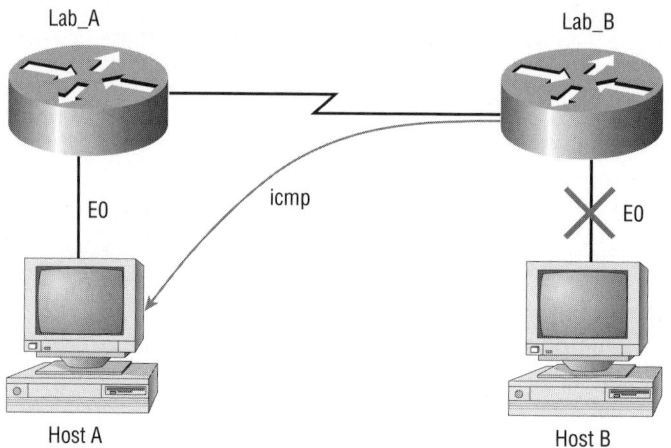
E0 on Lab B is down. Host A is trying to communicate to Host B. What happens?
Lab_A
Lab_B
E0
icmp
E0
Host A
Host B

Both Ping and Traceroute (also just called Trace; Microsoft Windows uses tracert) allow you to verify address configurations in your internetwork.

The following data is from a network analyzer catching an ICMP echo request:

```
Flags:          0x00
 Status:         0x00
 Packet Length: 78
 Timestamp:      14:04:25.967000 12/20/03
Ethernet Header
 Destination: 00:a0:24:6e:0f:a8
 Source:      00:80:c7:a8:f0:3d
 Ether-Type:  08-00 IP
IP Header - Internet Protocol Datagram
 Version:              4
 Header Length:        5
 Precedence:           0
 Type of Service:      %000
 Unused:               %00
 Total Length:         60
 Identifier:           56325
 Fragmentation Flags: %000
 Fragment Offset:      0
```

```
 Time To Live:        32
 IP Type:             0x01 ICMP
 Header Checksum:     0x2df0
 Source IP Address:   100.100.100.2
 Dest. IP Address:    100.100.100.1
 No Internet Datagram Options
ICMP - Internet Control Messages Protocol
 ICMP Type:       8 Echo Request
 Code:            0
 Checksum:        0x395c
 Identifier:      0x0300
 Sequence Number: 4352
 ICMP Data Area:
 abcdefghijklmnop  61 62 63 64 65 66 67 68 69 6a 6b 6c 6d 6e 6f 70
 qrstuvwabcdefghi  71 72 73 74 75 76 77 61 62 63 64 65 66 67 68 69
Frame Check Sequence: 0x00000000
```

Notice anything unusual? Did you catch the fact that even though ICMP works at the Internet (Network) layer, it still uses IP to do the Ping request? The Type field in the IP header is 0x01, which specifies that the data we're carrying is owned by the ICMP protocol. Remember, just as all roads lead to Rome, all segments or data *must* go through IP!

The Ping program uses the alphabet in the data portion of the packet as just a payload, typically around 100 bytes by default, unless, of course, you are pinging from a Windows device, which thinks the alphabet stops at the letter *W* (and doesn't include *X*, *Y*, or *Z*) and then starts at *A* again. Go figure!

If you remember reading about the Data Link layer and the different frame types in Chapter 2, you should be able to look at the preceding trace and tell what type of Ethernet frame this is. The only fields are destination hardware address, source hardware address, and Ether-Type. The only frame that uses an Ether-Type field exclusively is an Ethernet_II frame.

But before we get into the ARP protocol, let's take another look at ICMP in action. Figure 3.10 shows an internetwork (it has a router, so it's an internetwork, right?).

Server1 (10.1.2.2) telnets to 10.1.1.5 from a DOS prompt. What do you think Server1 will receive as a response? Since Server1 will send the Telnet data to the default gateway, which is the router, the router will drop the packet because there isn't a network 10.1.1.0 in the routing table. Because of this, Server1 will receive a destination unreachable back from ICMP.

Address Resolution Protocol (ARP)

Address Resolution Protocol (ARP) finds the hardware address of a host from a known IP address. Here's how it works: When IP has a datagram to send, it must inform a Network Access protocol, such as Ethernet or wireless, of the destination's hardware address on the local network. (It has already been informed by upper-layer protocols of the destination's IP address.) If IP doesn't find the destination host's hardware address in the ARP cache, it uses ARP to find this information.

FIGURE 3.10 ICMP in action

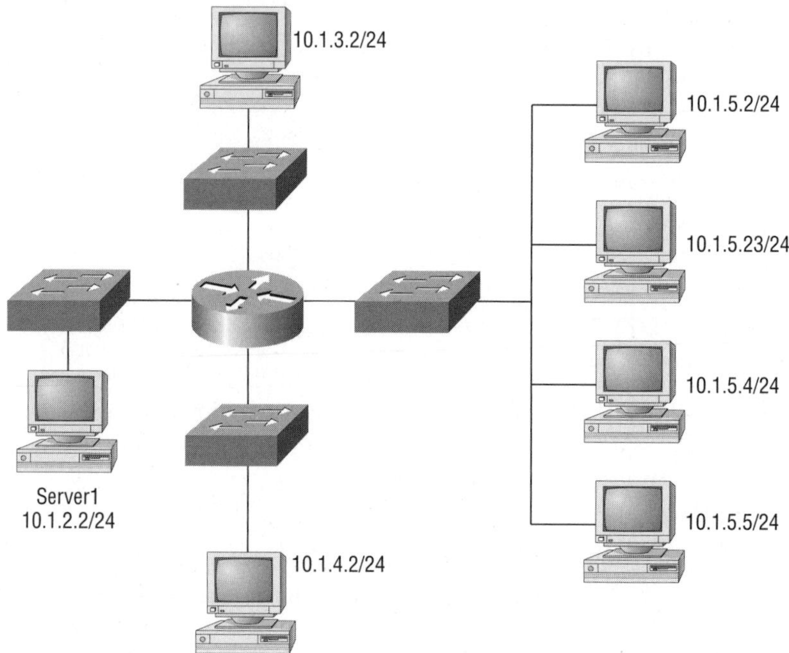

As IP's detective, ARP interrogates the local network by sending out a broadcast asking the machine with the specified IP address to reply with its hardware address. So basically, ARP translates the software (IP) address into a hardware address—for example, the destination machine's Ethernet adapter address—and from it, deduces its whereabouts on the LAN by broadcasting for this address. Figure 3.11 shows how an ARP looks to a local network.

ARP resolves IP addresses to Ethernet (MAC) addresses.

The following trace shows an ARP broadcast—notice that the destination hardware address is unknown and is all *F*s in hex (all 1s in binary)—and is a hardware address broadcast:

```
Flags:          0x00
Status:         0x00
Packet Length: 64
Timestamp:      09:17:29.574000 12/06/03
```

```
Ethernet Header
 Destination:    FF:FF:FF:FF:FF:FF Ethernet Broadcast
 Source:         00:A0:24:48:60:A5
 Protocol Type: 0x0806 IP ARP
ARP - Address Resolution Protocol
 Hardware:                 1 Ethernet (10Mb)
 Protocol:                 0x0800 IP
 Hardware Address Length: 6
 Protocol Address Length: 4
 Operation:                1 ARP Request
 Sender Hardware Address: 00:A0:24:48:60:A5
 Sender Internet Address: 172.16.10.3
 Target Hardware Address: 00:00:00:00:00:00 (ignored)
 Target Internet Address: 172.16.10.10
Extra bytes (Padding):
 ................ 0A 0A 0A 0A 0A 0A 0A 0A 0A 0A 0A 0A 0A
  0A 0A 0A 0A 0A
Frame Check Sequence: 0x00000000
```

FIGURE 3.11 Local ARP broadcast

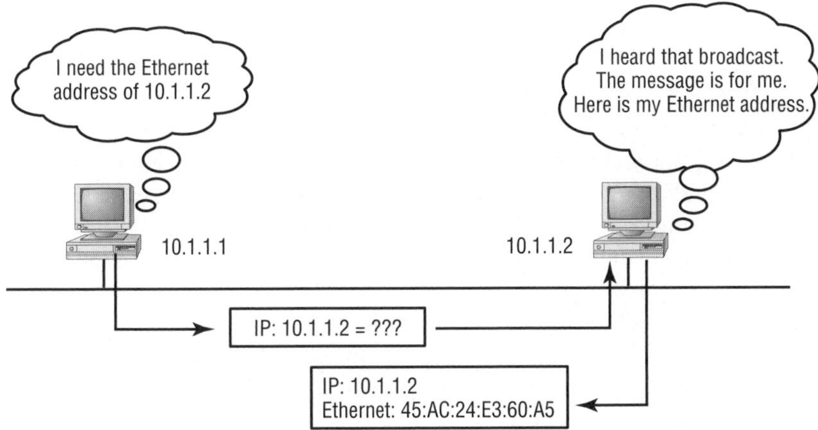

Reverse Address Resolution Protocol (RARP)

When an IP machine happens to be a diskless machine, it has no way of initially knowing its IP address. But it does know its MAC address. *Reverse Address Resolution Protocol (RARP)*, as shown in Figure 3.12, discovers the identity of the IP address for diskless machines by sending out a packet that includes its MAC address and a request for the IP address assigned to that MAC address. A designated machine, called a *RARP server*, responds with the answer and the identity crisis is over. RARP uses the information it does know about the machine's MAC address to learn its IP address and complete the machine's ID portrait.

FIGURE 3.12 RARP broadcast example

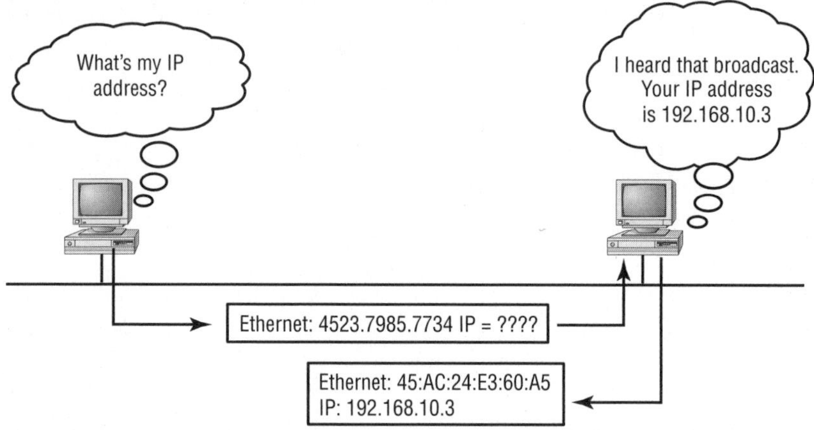

RARP resolves Ethernet (MAC) addresses to IP addresses.

Proxy Address Resolution Protocol (Proxy ARP)

On a network, your hosts can't have more than one default gateway configured. Think about this...What if the default gateway (router) happens to go down? The host won't just start sending to another router automatically—you've got to reconfigure that host. But Proxy ARP can actually help machines on a subnet reach remote subnets without configuring routing or even a default gateway.

One advantage of using Proxy ARP is that it can be added to a single router on a network without disturbing the routing tables of all the other routers that live there too. But there's a serious downside to using Proxy ARP. Using Proxy ARP will definitely increase the amount of traffic on your network segment, and hosts will have a larger ARP table than usual in order to handle all the IP-to-MAC-address mappings. And Proxy ARP is configured on all Cisco routers by default—you should disable it if you don't think you're going to use it.

One last thought on Proxy ARP: Proxy ARP isn't really a separate protocol. It is a service run by routers on behalf of other devices (usually PCs) that are separated from their query to another device by a router, although they think they share the subnet with the remote device.

This lets the router provide its own MAC address in response to ARP queries attempting to resolve a distant IP address to a functional MAC address.

If you can afford it, use Cisco's Hot Standby Router Protocol (HSRP) instead. It means you have to buy two or more of your Cisco device(s), but it is well worth it. Check out the Cisco website for more information on HSRP.

IP Addressing

One of the most important topics in any discussion of TCP/IP is IP addressing. An *IP address* is a numeric identifier assigned to each machine on an IP network. It designates the specific location of a device on the network.

An IP address is a software address, not a hardware address—the latter is hard-coded on a network interface card (NIC) and used for finding hosts on a local network. IP addressing was designed to allow hosts on one network to communicate with a host on a different network regardless of the type of LANs the hosts are participating in.

Before we get into the more complicated aspects of IP addressing, you need to understand some of the basics. First I'm going to explain some of the fundamentals of IP addressing and its terminology. Then you'll learn about the hierarchical IP addressing scheme and private IP addresses.

IP Terminology

Throughout this chapter you'll learn several important terms vital to your understanding of the Internet Protocol. Here are a few to get you started:

Bit A *bit* is one digit, either a 1 or a 0.

Byte A *byte* is 7 or 8 bits, depending on whether parity is used. For the rest of this chapter, always assume a byte is 8 bits.

Octet An octet, made up of 8 bits, is just an ordinary 8-bit binary number. In this chapter, the terms *byte* and *octet* are completely interchangeable.

Network address This is the designation used in routing to send packets to a remote network—for example, 10.0.0.0, 172.16.0.0, and 192.168.10.0.

Broadcast address The address used by applications and hosts to send information to all nodes on a network is called the *broadcast address*. Examples include 255.255.255.255, which is any network, all nodes; 172.16.255.255, which is all subnets and hosts on network 172.16.0.0; and 10.255.255.255, which broadcasts to all subnets and hosts on network 10.0.0.0.

The Hierarchical IP Addressing Scheme

An IP address consists of 32 bits of information. These bits are divided into four sections, referred to as octets or bytes, each containing 1 byte (8 bits). You can depict an IP address using one of three methods:

- Dotted-decimal, as in 172.16.30.56
- Binary, as in 10101100.00010000.00011110.00111000
- Hexadecimal, as in AC.10.1E.38

All these examples truly represent the same IP address. Hexadecimal isn't used as often as dotted-decimal or binary when IP addressing is discussed, but you still might find an IP address stored in hexadecimal in some programs. The Windows Registry is a good example of a program that stores a machine's IP address in hex.

The 32-bit IP address is a structured or hierarchical address, as opposed to a flat or nonhierarchical address. Although either type of addressing scheme could have been used, *hierarchical addressing* was chosen for a good reason. The advantage of this scheme is that it can handle a large number of addresses, namely 4.3 billion (a 32-bit address space with two possible values for each position—either 0 or 1—gives you 2^{32}, or 4,294,967,296). The disadvantage of the flat addressing scheme, and the reason it's not used for IP addressing, relates to routing. If every address were unique, all routers on the Internet would need to store the address of each and every machine on the Internet. This would make efficient routing impossible, even if only a fraction of the possible addresses were used.

The solution to this problem is to use a two- or three-level hierarchical addressing scheme that is structured by network and host or by network, subnet, and host.

This two- or three-level scheme is comparable to a telephone number. The first section, the area code, designates a very large area. The second section, the prefix, narrows the scope to a local calling area. The final segment, the customer number, zooms in on the specific connection. IP addresses use the same type of layered structure. Rather than all 32 bits being treated as a unique identifier, as in flat addressing, a part of the address is designated as the network address and the other part is designated as either the subnet and host or just the node address.

In the following sections, I'm going to discuss IP network addressing and the different classes of address we can use to address our networks.

Network Addressing

The *network address* (which can also be called the network number) uniquely identifies each network. Every machine on the same network shares that network address as part of its IP address. In the IP address 172.16.30.56, for example, 172.16 is the network address.

The *node address* is assigned to, and uniquely identifies, each machine on a network. This part of the address must be unique because it identifies a particular machine—an individual—as opposed to a network, which is a group. This number can also be referred to as a *host address*. In the sample IP address 172.16.30.56, the 30.56 is the node address.

The designers of the Internet decided to create classes of networks based on network size. For the small number of networks possessing a very large number of nodes, they created the rank *Class A network*. At the other extreme is the *Class C network*, which is reserved for the numerous networks with a small number of nodes. The class distinction for networks between very large and very small is predictably called the *Class B network*.

Subdividing an IP address into a network and node address is determined by the class designation of one's network. Figure 3.13 summarizes the three classes of networks—a subject I'll explain in much greater detail throughout this chapter.

FIGURE 3.13 Summary of the three classes of networks

	8 bits	8 bits	8 bits	8 bits
Class A:	Network	Host	Host	Host
Class B:	Network	Network	Host	Host
Class C:	Network	Network	Network	Host
Class D:	Multicast			
Class E:	Research			

To ensure efficient routing, Internet designers defined a mandate for the leading-bits section of the address for each different network class. For example, since a router knows that a Class A network address always starts with a 0, the router might be able to speed a packet on its way after reading only the first bit of its address. This is where the address schemes define the difference between a Class A, a Class B, and a Class C address. In the next sections, I'll discuss the differences between these three classes, followed by a discussion of the Class D and Class E addresses (Classes A, B, and C are the only ranges that are used to address hosts in our networks).

Network Address Range: Class A

The designers of the IP address scheme said that the first bit of the first byte in a Class A network address must always be off, or 0. This means a Class A address must be between 0 and 127 in the first byte, inclusive.

Consider the following network address:

```
0xxxxxxx
```

If we turn the other 7 bits all off and then turn them all on, we'll find the Class A range of network addresses:

```
00000000 = 0
01111111 = 127
```

So, a Class A network is defined in the first octet between 0 and 127, and it can't be less or more. (Yes, I know 0 and 127 are not valid in a Class A network. I'll talk about reserved addresses in a minute.)

Network Address Range: Class B

In a Class B network, the RFCs state that the first bit of the first byte must always be turned on but the second bit must always be turned off. If you turn the other 6 bits all off and then all on, you will find the range for a Class B network:

```
10000000 = 128
10111111 = 191
```

As you can see, a Class B network is defined when the first byte is configured from 128 to 191.

Network Address Range: Class C

For Class C networks, the RFCs define the first 2 bits of the first octet as always turned on, but the third bit can never be on. Following the same process as the previous classes, convert from binary to decimal to find the range. Here's the range for a Class C network:

```
11000000 = 192
11011111 = 223
```

So, if you see an IP address that starts at 192 and goes to 223, you'll know it is a Class C IP address.

Network Address Ranges: Classes D and E

The addresses between 224 to 255 are reserved for Class D and E networks. Class D (224–239) is used for multicast addresses and Class E (240–255) for scientific purposes, but I'm not going into these types of addresses in this book (and you don't need to know them).

Network Addresses: Special Purpose

Some IP addresses are reserved for special purposes, so network administrators can't ever assign these addresses to nodes. Table 3.4 lists the members of this exclusive little club and the reasons why they're included in it.

TABLE 3.4 Reserved IP addresses

Address	Function
Network address of all 0s	Interpreted to mean "this network or segment."
Network address of all 1s	Interpreted to mean "all networks."
Network 127.0.0.1	Reserved for loopback tests. Designates the local node and allows that node to send a test packet to itself without generating network traffic.

Address	Function
Node address of all 0s	Interpreted to mean "network address" or any host on a specified network.
Node address of all 1s	Interpreted to mean "all nodes" on the specified network; for example, 128.2.255.255 means "all nodes" on network 128.2 (Class B address).
Entire IP address set to all 0s	Used by Cisco routers to designate the default route. Could also mean "any network."
Entire IP address set to all 1s (same as 255.255.255.255)	Broadcast to all nodes on the current network; sometimes called an "all 1s broadcast" or limited broadcast.

Class A Addresses

In a Class A network address, the first byte is assigned to the network address and the three remaining bytes are used for the node addresses. The Class A format is as follows:

network.node.node.node

For example, in the IP address 49.22.102.70, the 49 is the network address and 22.102.70 is the node address. Every machine on this particular network would have the distinctive network address of 49.

Class A network addresses are 1 byte long, with the first bit of that byte reserved and the 7 remaining bits available for manipulation (addressing). As a result, the maximum number of Class A networks that can be created is 128. Why? Because each of the 7 bit positions can be either a 0 or a 1, thus 2^7, or 128.

To complicate matters further, the network address of all 0s (0000 0000) is reserved to designate the default route (see Table 3.4 in the previous section). Additionally, the address 127, which is reserved for diagnostics, can't be used either, which means that you can really only use the numbers 1 to 126 to designate Class A network addresses. This means the actual number of usable Class A network addresses is 128 minus 2, or 126.

The IP address 127.0.0.1 is used to test the IP stack on an individual node and cannot be used as a valid host address. However, the loopback address creates a shortcut method for TCP/IP applications and services that run on the same device to communicate with each other.

Each Class A address has 3 bytes (24-bit positions) for the node address of a machine. This means there are 2^{24}—or 16,777,216—unique combinations and, therefore, precisely that many possible unique node addresses for each Class A network. Because node addresses with the two patterns of all 0s and all 1s are reserved, the actual maximum usable number of nodes for a Class A network is 2^{24} minus 2, which equals 16,777,214. Either way, that's a huge number of hosts on a network segment!

Class A Valid Host IDs

Here's an example of how to figure out the valid host IDs in a Class A network address:

- All host bits off is the network address: 10.0.0.0.
- All host bits on is the broadcast address: 10.255.255.255.

The valid hosts are the numbers in between the network address and the broadcast address: 10.0.0.1 through 10.255.255.254. Notice that 0s and 255s can be valid host IDs. All you need to remember when trying to find valid host addresses is that the host bits can't all be turned off or all be on at the same time.

Class B Addresses

In a Class B network address, the first 2 bytes are assigned to the network address and the remaining 2 bytes are used for node addresses. The format is as follows:

network.network.node.node

For example, in the IP address 172.16.30.56, the network address is 172.16 and the node address is 30.56.

With a network address being 2 bytes (8 bits each), there would be 2^{16} unique combinations. But the Internet designers decided that all Class B network addresses should start with the binary digit 1, then 0. This leaves 14 bit positions to manipulate, therefore 16,384 (that is, 2^{14}) unique Class B network addresses.

A Class B address uses 2 bytes for node addresses. This is 2^{16} minus the two reserved patterns (all 0s and all 1s), for a total of 65,534 possible node addresses for each Class B network.

Class B Valid Host IDs

Here's an example of how to find the valid hosts in a Class B network:

- All host bits turned off is the network address: 172.16.0.0.
- All host bits turned on is the broadcast address: 172.16.255.255.

The valid hosts would be the numbers in between the network address and the broadcast address: 172.16.0.1 through 172.16.255.254.

Class C Addresses

The first 3 bytes of a Class C network address are dedicated to the network portion of the address, with only 1 measly byte remaining for the node address. Here's the format:

network.network.network.node

Using the example IP address 192.168.100.102, the network address is 192.168.100 and the node address is 102.

In a Class C network address, the first three bit positions are always the binary 110. The calculation is as follows: 3 bytes, or 24 bits, minus 3 reserved positions leaves 21 positions. Hence, there are 2^{21}, or 2,097,152, possible Class C networks.

Each unique Class C network has 1 byte to use for node addresses. This leads to 2^8, or 256, minus the two reserved patterns of all 0s and all 1s, for a total of 254 node addresses for each Class C network.

Class C Valid Host IDs

Here's an example of how to find a valid host ID in a Class C network:

- All host bits turned off is the network ID: 192.168.100.0.
- All host bits turned on is the broadcast address: 192.168.100.255.

The valid hosts would be the numbers in between the network address and the broadcast address: 192.168.100.1 through 192.168.100.254.

Private IP Addresses

The people who created the IP addressing scheme also created what we call private IP addresses. These addresses can be used on a private network, but they're not routable through the Internet. This is designed for the purpose of creating a measure of well-needed security, but it also conveniently saves valuable IP address space.

If every host on every network had to have real routable IP addresses, we would have run out of IP addresses to hand out years ago. But by using private IP addresses, ISPs, corporations, and home users only need a relatively tiny group of bona fide IP addresses to connect their networks to the Internet. This is economical because they can use private IP addresses on their inside networks and get along just fine.

To accomplish this task, the ISP and the corporation—the end user, no matter who they are—need to use something called *Network Address Translation (NAT)*, which basically takes a private IP address and converts it for use on the Internet. (NAT is covered in Chapter 13, "Network Address Translation.") Many people can use the same real IP address to transmit out onto the Internet. Doing things this way saves megatons of address space—good for us all!

The reserved private addresses are listed in Table 3.5.

TABLE 3.5 Reserved IP address space

Address Class	Reserved Address Space
Class A	10.0.0.0 through 10.255.255.255
Class B	172.16.0.0 through 172.31.255.255
Class C	192.168.0.0 through 192.168.255.255

You must know your private address space to become Cisco certified!

So, What Private IP Address Should I Use?

That's a really great question: Should you use Class A, Class B, or even Class C private addressing when setting up your network? Let's take Acme Corporation in SF as an example. This company is moving into a new building and needs a whole new network (what a treat this is!). It has 14 departments, with about 70 users in each. You could probably squeeze one or two Class C addresses to use, or maybe you could use a Class B, or even a Class A just for fun.

The rule of thumb in the consulting world is, when you're setting up a corporate network—regardless of how small it is—you should use a Class A network address because it gives you the most flexibility and growth options. For example, if you used the 10.0.0.0 network address with a /24 mask, then you'd have 65,536 networks, each with 254 hosts. Lots of room for growth with that network!

But if you're setting up a home network, you'd opt for a Class C address because it is the easiest for people to understand and configure. Using the default Class C mask gives you one network with 254 hosts—plenty for a home network.

With the Acme Corporation, a nice 10.1.*x*.0 with a /24 mask (the *x* is the subnet for each department) makes this easy to design, install, and troubleshoot.

IPv4 Address Types

Most people use the term *broadcast* as a generic term, and most of the time, we understand what they mean. But not always. For example, you might say, "The host broadcasted through a router to a DHCP server," but, well, it's pretty unlikely that this would ever really happen. What you probably mean—using the correct technical jargon—is, "The DHCP client broadcasted for an IP address; a router then forwarded this as a unicast packet to the DHCP server." Oh, and remember that with IPv4, broadcasts are pretty important, but with IPv6, there aren't any broadcasts sent at all—now there's something to get you excited about when you get to Chapter 15!

Okay, I've referred to broadcast addresses throughout Chapters 1 and 2, and even showed you some examples. But I really haven't gone into the different terms and uses associated with them yet, and it's about time I did. So here are the four IPv4 address types that I'd like to define for you:

Layer-2 broadcasts These are sent to all nodes on a LAN.

Broadcasts (layer 3) These are sent to all nodes on the network.

Unicast This is an address for a single interface, and these are used to send packets to a single destination host.

Multicast These are packets sent from a single source and transmitted to many devices on different networks. Referred to as "one-to-many."

Layer-2 Broadcasts

First, understand that layer-2 broadcasts are also known as hardware broadcasts—they only go out on a LAN, and they don't go past the LAN boundary (router).

The typical hardware address is 6 bytes (48 bits) and looks something like 45:AC:24:E3:60:A5. The broadcast would be all 1s in binary, which would be all *F*s in hexadecimal, as in FF.FF.FF.FF.FF.FF.

Layer-3 Broadcasts

Then there are the plain old broadcast addresses at layer 3. Broadcast messages are meant to reach all hosts on a broadcast domain. These are the network broadcasts that have all host bits on.

Here's an example that you're already familiar with: The network address of 172.16.0.0 255.255.0.0 would have a broadcast address of 172.16.255.255—all host bits on. Broadcasts can also be "any network and all hosts," as indicated by 255.255.255.255.

A good example of a broadcast message is an Address Resolution Protocol (ARP) request. When a host has a packet, it knows the logical address (IP) of the destination. To get the packet to the destination, the host needs to forward the packet to a default gateway if the destination resides on a different IP network. If the destination is on the local network, the source will forward the packet directly to the destination. Because the source doesn't have the MAC address to which it needs to forward the frame, it sends out a broadcast, something that every device in the local broadcast domain will listen to. This broadcast says, in essence, "If you are the owner of IP address 192.168.2.3, please forward your MAC address to me," with the source giving the appropriate information.

Unicast Address

A unicast is a single IP address that is assigned to a network interface card and would be the destination IP address in a packet—in other words, directing packets to a specific host. A DHCP client request is a good example of how a unicast works.

Here's an example: Your host on a LAN sends out an FF.FF.FF.FF.FF.FF layer-2 broadcast and destination 255.255.255.255 layer-3 broadcast, looking for a DHCP server on the LAN. The router will see that this is a broadcast meant for the DHCP server because it has a destination port number of 67 (BootP server) and will forward the request to the IP address of the DHCP server on another LAN. So, basically, if your DHCP server IP address is 172.16.10.1, your host just sends out a 255.255.255.255 DHCP client broadcast request, and the router changes that broadcast to the specific destination address of 172.16.10.1. (In order for the router to provide this service, you need to configure the interfaces with the `ip helper-address` command—this is not a default service.)

Multicast Address

Multicast is a different beast entirely. At first glance, it appears to be a hybrid of unicast and broadcast communication, but that isn't quite the case. Multicast does allow point-to-multipoint communication, which is similar to broadcasts, but it happens in a different manner. The crux of *multicast* is that it enables multiple recipients to receive messages without flooding the messages to all hosts on a broadcast domain. However, this is not the default behavior—it's what we *can* do with multicasting if it's configured correctly!

Multicast works by sending messages or data to IP *multicast group* addresses. Routers then forward copies (unlike broadcasts, which are not forwarded) of the packet out to every interface that has hosts *subscribed* to that group address. This is where multicast differs from broadcast messages—with multicast communication, copies of packets, in theory, are sent only to subscribed hosts. When I say in theory, this means that the hosts will receive, for example, a multicast packet destined for 224.0.0.10 (this is an EIGRP packet and only a router running the EIGRP protocol will read these). All hosts on the broadcast LAN (Ethernet is a broadcast multi-access LAN technology) will pick up the frame, read the destination address, and immediately discard the frame, unless they are in the multicast group. This saves PC processing, not LAN bandwidth. Multicasting can cause severe LAN congestion in some instances, if not implemented carefully.

There are several different groups that users or applications can subscribe to. The range of multicast addresses starts with 224.0.0.0 and goes through 239.255.255.255. As you can see, this range of addresses falls within IP Class D address space based on classful IP assignment.

Summary

If you made it this far and understood everything the first time through, you should be proud of yourself. We really covered a lot of ground in this chapter, but understand that the information in this chapter is key to being able to navigate through the rest of this book.

And even if you didn't get a complete understanding the first time around, don't stress. It really wouldn't hurt you to read this chapter more than once. There is still a lot of ground to cover, so make sure you've got it all down, and get ready for more. What we're doing is building a foundation, and you want a strong foundation, right?

After you learned about the DoD model, the layers, and associated protocols, you learned about the oh-so-important IP addressing. I discussed in detail the difference between each class of address and how to find a network address, broadcast address, and valid host range, which is critical information to understand before going on to Chapter 4.

Since you've already come this far, there's no reason to stop now and waste all those brainwaves and new neurons. So don't stop—go through the written lab and review questions at the end of this chapter and make sure you understand each answer's explanation. The best is yet to come!

Exam Essentials

Differentiate the DoD and the OSI network models. The DoD model is a condensed version of the OSI model, composed of four layers instead of seven, but is nonetheless like the OSI model in that it can be used to describe packet creation and devices and protocols can be mapped to its layers.

Identify Process/Application layer protocols. Telnet is a terminal emulation program that allows you to log into a remote host and run programs. File Transfer Protocol (FTP) is a connection-oriented service that allows you to transfer files. Trivial FTP (TFTP) is a connectionless file transfer program. Simple Mail Transfer Protocol (SMTP) is a send-mail program.

Identify Host-to-Host layer protocols. Transmission Control Protocol (TCP) is a connection-oriented protocol that provides reliable network service by using acknowledgments and flow control. User Datagram Protocol (UDP) is a connectionless protocol that provides low overhead and is considered unreliable.

Identify Internet layer protocols. Internet Protocol (IP) is a connectionless protocol that provides network address and routing through an internetwork. Address Resolution Protocol (ARP) finds a hardware address from a known IP address. Reverse ARP (RARP) finds an IP address from a known hardware address. Internet Control Message Protocol (ICMP) provides diagnostics and destination unreachable messages.

Describe the functions of DNS and DHCP in the network. Dynamic Host Configuration Protocol (DHCP) provides network configuration information (including IP addresses) to hosts, eliminating the need to perform the configurations manually. Domain Name Service (DNS) resolves hostnames—both Internet names such as `www.routersim.com` and device names such as Workstation 2 to IP addresses, eliminating the need to know the IP address of a device for connection purposes.

Identify what is contained in the TCP header of a connection-oriented transmission. The fields in the TCP header include the source port, destination port, sequence number, acknowledgment number, header length, a field reserved for future use, code bits, window size, checksum, urgent pointer, options field, and finally the data field.

Identify what is contained in the UDP header of a connectionless transmission. The fields in the UDP header include only the source port, destination port, length, checksum, and data. The smaller number of fields as compared to the TCP header comes at the expense of providing none of the more advanced functions of the TCP frame.

Identify what is contained in the IP header. The fields of an IP header include version, header length, priority or type of service, total length, identification, flags, fragment offset, time to live, protocol, header checksum, source IP address, destination IP address, options, and finally, data.

Compare and contrast UDP and TCP characteristics and features. TCP is connection-oriented, acknowledged, and sequenced and has flow and error control, while UDP is connectionless, unacknowledged, and not sequenced and provides no error or flow control.

Understand the role of port numbers. Port numbers are used to identify the protocol or service that is to be used in the transmission.

Identify the role of ICMP. Internet Control Message Protocol (ICMP) works at the Network layer and is used by IP for many different services. ICMP is a management protocol and messaging service provider for IP.

Define the Class A IP address range. The IP range for a Class A network is 1–126. This provides 8 bits of network addressing and 24 bits of host addressing by default.

Define the Class B IP address range. The IP range for a Class B network is 128–191. Class B addressing provides 16 bits of network addressing and 16 bits of host addressing by default.

Define the Class C IP address range. The IP range for a Class C network is 192 through 223. Class C addressing provides 24 bits of network addressing and 8 bits of host addressing by default.

Identify the private IP ranges. Class A private address range is 10.0.0.0 through 10.255.255.255.

Class B private address range is 172.16.0.0 through 172.31.255.255.

Class C private address range is 192.168.0.0 through 192.168.255.255.

Understand the difference between a broadcast, unicast, and multicast address. A broadcast is all devices in a subnet, a unicast is to one device, and a multicast is to some but not all devices.

Written Labs

In this section, you'll complete the following labs to make sure you've got the information and concepts contained within them fully dialed in:

Lab 3.1: TCP/IP

Lab 3.2: Mapping Applications to the DoD Model

(The answers to the written labs can be found following the answers to the review questions for this chapter.)

Written Lab 3.1: TCP/IP

Answer the following questions about TCP/IP:

1. What is the Class C address range in decimal and in binary?
2. What layer of the DoD model is equivalent to the Transport layer of the OSI model?
3. What is the valid range of a Class A network address?
4. What is the 127.0.0.1 address used for?
5. How do you find the network address from a listed IP address?
6. How do you find the broadcast address from a listed IP address?
7. What is the Class A private IP address space?
8. What is the Class B private IP address space?
9. What is the Class C private IP address space?
10. What are all the available characters that you can use in hexadecimal addressing?

Written Lab 3.2: Mapping Applications to the DoD Model

The four layers of the DoD model are Process/Application, Host-to-Host, Internet, and Network Access. Identify the layer of the DoD model each of these protocols operates.

1. Internet Protocol (IP)
2. Telnet
3. FTP
4. SNMP
5. DNS
6. Address Resolution Protocol (ARP)
7. DHCP/BootP
8. Transmission Control Protocol (TCP)
9. X Window
10. User Datagram Protocol (UDP)
11. NFS
12. Internet Control Message Protocol (ICMP)
13. Reverse Address Resolution Protocol (RARP)
14. Proxy ARP
15. TFTP
16. SMTP
17. LPD

Review Questions

The following questions are designed to test your understanding of this chapter's material. For more information on how to get additional questions, please see this book's Introduction.

1. What must happen if a DHCP IP conflict occurs?
   A. Proxy ARP will fix the issue.
   B. The client uses a gratuitous ARP to fix the issue.
   C. The administrator must fix the conflict by hand at the DHCP server.
   D. The dhcp server will reassign new IP addresses to both computers.
2. Which of the following allows a router to respond to an ARP request that is intended for a remote host?
   A. Gateway DP
   B. Reverse ARP (RARP)
   C. Proxy ARP
   D. Inverse ARP (IARP)
   E. Address Resolution Protocol (ARP)
3. You want to implement a mechanism that automates the IP configuration, including IP address, subnet mask, default gateway, and DNS information. Which protocol will you use to accomplish this?
   A. SMTP
   B. SNMP
   C. DHCP
   D. ARP
4. What protocol is used to find the hardware address of a local device?
   A. RARP
   B. ARP
   C. IP
   D. ICMP
   E. BootP
5. Which of the following are layers in the TCP/IP model? (Choose three.)
   A. Application
   B. Session
   C. Transport
   D. Internet
   E. Data Link
   F. Physical

6. Which class of IP address provides a maximum of only 254 host addresses per network ID?
   - A. Class A
   - B. Class B
   - C. Class C
   - D. Class D
   - E. Class E

7. Which of the following describe the DHCP Discover message? (Choose two.)
   - A. It uses FF:FF:FF:FF:FF:FF as a layer-2 broadcast.
   - B. It uses UDP as the Transport layer protocol.
   - C. It uses TCP as the Transport layer protocol.
   - D. It does not use a layer-2 destination address.

8. Which layer-4 protocol is used for a Telnet connection?
   - A. IP
   - B. TCP
   - C. TCP/IP
   - D. UDP
   - E. ICMP

9. How does a DHCP client ensure that no other computer has its assigned IP address?
   - A. Acknowledge receipt of a TCP segment.
   - B. Ping to its own address to see if a response is detected.
   - C. Broadcast a Proxy ARP
   - D. Broadcast a gratuitous ARP
   - E. Telnet to its own IP address

10. Which of the following services use TCP? (Choose three.)
    - A. DHCP
    - B. SMTP
    - C. SNMP
    - D. FTP
    - E. HTTP
    - F. TFTP

11. Which of the following services use UDP? (Choose three.)
    - A. DHCP
    - B. SMTP
    - C. SNMP
    - D. FTP
    - E. HTTP
    - F. TFTP

12. Which of the following are TCP/IP protocols used at the Application layer of the OSI model? (Choose three.)
    - A. IP
    - B. TCP
    - C. Telnet
    - D. FTP
    - E. TFTP

13. The following illustration shows a data structure header. What protocol is this header from?

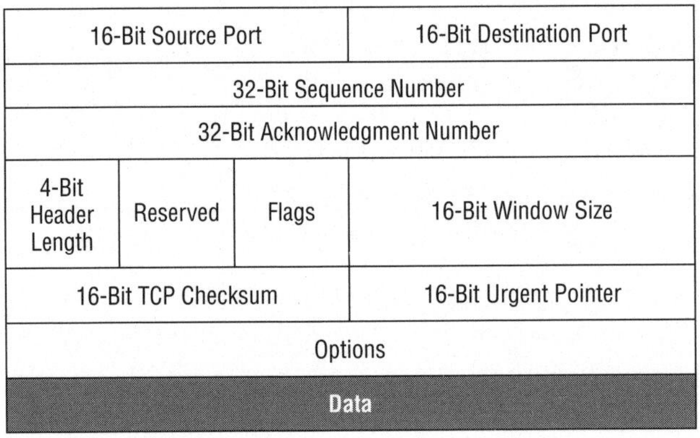

<table>
<tr><td colspan="3">16-Bit Source Port</td><td>16-Bit Destination Port</td></tr>
<tr><td colspan="4">32-Bit Sequence Number</td></tr>
<tr><td colspan="4">32-Bit Acknowledgment Number</td></tr>
<tr><td>4-Bit Header Length</td><td>Reserved</td><td>Flags</td><td>16-Bit Window Size</td></tr>
<tr><td colspan="3">16-Bit TCP Checksum</td><td>16-Bit Urgent Pointer</td></tr>
<tr><td colspan="4">Options</td></tr>
<tr><td colspan="4">Data</td></tr>
</table>

    - A. IP
    - B. ICMP
    - C. TCP
    - D. UDP
    - E. ARP
    - F. RARP

14. If you use either Telnet or FTP, what layer are you using to generate the data?
    - A. Application
    - B. Presentation
    - C. Session
    - D. Transport

15. The DoD model (also called the TCP/IP stack) has four layers. Which layer of the DoD model is equivalent to the Network layer of the OSI model?
    - A. Application
    - B. Host-to-Host
    - C. Internet
    - D. Network Access

16. Which two of the following are private IP addresses?

A. 12.0.0.1

B. 168.172.19.39

C. 172.20.14.36

D. 172.33.194.30

E. 192.168.24.43

17. What layer in the TCP/IP stack is equivalent to the Transport layer of the OSI model?

A. Application

B. Host-to-Host

C. Internet

D. Network Access

18. Which statements are true regarding ICMP packets? (Choose two).

A. ICMP guarantees datagram delivery.

B. ICMP can provide hosts with information about network problems.

C. ICMP is encapsulated within IP datagrams.

D. ICMP is encapsulated within UDP datagrams.

19. What is the address range of a Class B network address in binary?

A. 01*xxxxxx*

B. 0*xxxxxxx*

C. 10*xxxxxx*

D. 110*xxxxx*

20. Which of the following protocols uses both TCP and UDP?

A. FTP

B. SMTP

C. Telnet

D. DNS

Answers to Review Questions

1. C. If a DHCP conflict is detected, either by the server sending a ping and getting a response or by a host using a gratuitous ARP (arp'ing for its own IP address and seeing if a host responds), then the server will hold that address and not use it again until it is fixed by an administrator.

2. C. Proxy ARP can help machines on a subnet reach remote subnets without configuring routing or a default gateway.

3. C. Dynamic Host Configuration Protocol (DHCP) is used to provide IP information to hosts on your network. DHCP can provide a lot of information, but the most common is IP address, subnet mask, default gateway, and DNS information.

4. B. Address Resolution Protocol (ARP) is used to find the hardware address from a known IP address.

5. A, C, D. This seems like a hard question at first because it doesn't make sense. The listed answers are from the OSI model and the question asked about the TCP/IP protocol stack (DoD model). However, let's just look for what is wrong. First, the Session layer is not in the TCP/IP model; neither are the Data Link and Physical layers. This leaves us with the Transport layer (Host-to-Host in the DoD model), Internet layer (Network layer in the OSI), and Application layer (Application/Process in the DoD).

6. C. A Class C network address has only 8 bits for defining hosts: $2^8 - 2 = 254$.

7. A, B. A client that sends out a DHCP Discover message in order to receive an IP address sends out a broadcast at both layer 2 and layer 3. The layer-2 broadcast is all Fs in hex, or FF:FF:FF:FF:FF:FF. The layer-3 broadcast is 255.255.255.255, which means any networks and all hosts. DHCP is connectionless, which means it uses User Datagram Protocol (UDP) at the Transport layer, also called the Host-to-Host layer.

8. B. Although Telnet does use TCP and IP (TCP/IP), the question specifically asks about layer 4, and IP works at layer 3. Telnet uses TCP at layer 4.

9. D. To stop possible address conflicts, a DHCP client will use gratuitous ARP (broadcast an ARP request for its own IP address) to see if another host responds.

10. B, D, E. SMTP, FTP, and HTTP use TCP.

11. A, C, F. DHCP, SNMP, and TFTP use UDP. SMTP, FTP, and HTTP use TCP.

12. C, D, E. Telnet, File Transfer Protocol (FTP), and Trivial FTP (TFTP) are all Application layer protocols. IP is a Network layer protocol. Transmission Control Protocol (TCP) is a Transport layer protocol.

13. C. First, you should know easily that only TCP and UDP work at the Transport layer, so now you have a 50/50 shot. However, since the header has sequencing, acknowledgment, and window numbers, the answer can only be TCP.

14. A. Both FTP and Telnet use TCP at the Transport layer; however, they both are Application layer protocols, so the Application layer is the best answer for this question.

15. C. The four layers of the DoD model are Application/Process, Host-to-Host, Internet, and Network Access. The Internet layer is equivalent to the Network layer of the OSI model.

16. C, E. Class A private address range is 10.0.0.0 through 10.255.255.255. Class B private address range is 172.16.0.0 through 172.31.255.255, and Class C private address range is 192.168.0.0 through 192.168.255.255.

17. B. The four layers of the TCP/IP stack (also called the DoD model) are Application/Process, Host-to-Host, Internet, and Network Access. The Host-to-Host layer is equivalent to the Transport layer of the OSI model.

18. B, C. ICMP is used for diagnostics and destination unreachable messages. ICMP is encapsulated within IP datagrams, and because it is used for diagnostics, it will provide hosts with information about network problems.

19. C. The range of a Class B network address is 128–191. This makes our binary range 10xxxxxx.

20. D. DNS uses TCP for zone exchanges between servers and UDP when a client is trying to resolve a hostname to an IP address.

Answers to Written Lab 3.1

1. 192 through 223, 110*xxxxx*
2. Host-to-Host
3. 1 through 126
4. Loopback or diagnostics
5. Turn all host bits off.
6. Turn all host bits on.
7. 10.0.0.0 through 10.255.255.255
8. 172.16.0.0 through 172.31.255.255
9. 192.168.0.0 through 192.168.255.255
10. 0 through 9 and *A*, *B*, *C*, *D*, *E*, and *F*

Answers to Written Lab 3.2

1. Internet
2. Process/Application
3. Process/Application
4. Process/Application
5. Process/Application
6. Internet
7. Process/Application
8. Host-to-Host
9. Process/Application
10. Host-to-Host
11. Process/Application
12. Internet
13. Internet
14. Internet
15. Process/Application
16. Process/Application
17. Process/Application

Easy Subnetting

THE CCNA EXAM TOPICS COVERED IN THIS CHAPTER INCLUDE THE FOLLOWING:

✓ **Describe how a network works.**

- Interpret network diagrams.

✓ **Implement an IP addressing scheme and IP Services to meet network requirements in a medium-size Enterprise branch office network.**

- Describe the operation and benefits of using private and public IP addressing.
- Implement static and dynamic addressing services for hosts in a LAN environment.

This chapter will pick up right where we left off in the last chapter. We will continue our discussion of IP addressing.

We'll start with subnetting an IP network. You're going to have to really apply yourself because subnetting takes time and practice in order to nail it. So be patient. Do whatever it takes to get this stuff dialed in. This chapter truly is important—possibly the most important chapter in this book for you to understand.

I'll thoroughly cover IP subnetting from the very beginning. I know this might sound weird to you, but I think you'll be much better off if you can try to forget everything you've learned about subnetting before reading this chapter—especially if you've been to a Microsoft class!

So get psyched—you're about to go for quite a ride! This chapter will truly help you understand IP addressing and networking, so don't get discouraged or give up. If you stick with it, I promise that one day you'll look back on this and you'll be really glad you decided to hang on. It's one of those things that after you understand it, you'll wonder why you once thought it was so hard. Ready? Let's go!

For up-to-the-minute updates for this chapter, please see `www.lammle.com` or `www.sybex.com/go/ccna7e`.

Subnetting Basics

In Chapter 3, you learned how to define and find the valid host ranges used in a Class A, Class B, and Class C network address by turning the host bits all off and then all on. This is very good, but here's the catch: You were defining only one network. What happens if you wanted to take one network address and create six networks from it? You would have to do something called *subnetting*, because that's what allows you to take one larger network and break it into a bunch of smaller networks.

There are loads of reasons in favor of subnetting, including the following benefits:

Reduced network traffic We all appreciate less traffic of any kind. Networks are no different. Without trusty routers, packet traffic could grind the entire network down to a near standstill. With routers, most traffic will stay on the local network; only packets destined for other networks will pass through the router. Routers create broadcast domains. The more broadcast domains you create, the smaller the broadcast domains and the less network traffic on each network segment.

Optimized network performance This is a result of reduced network traffic.

Simplified management It's easier to identify and isolate network problems in a group of smaller connected networks than within one gigantic network.

Facilitated spanning of large geographical distances Because WAN links are considerably slower and more expensive than LAN links, a single large network that spans long distances can create problems in every area previously listed. Connecting multiple smaller networks makes the system more efficient.

In the following sections, I am going to move to subnetting a network address. This is the good part—ready?

IP Subnet-Zero

`IP subnet-zero` is not a new command, but in the past, Cisco courseware and Cisco exam objectives, didn't cover it—but it certainly does now! This command allows you to use the first and last subnet in your network design. For example, the Class C mask of 255.255.255.192 provides subnets 64 and 128 (discussed thoroughly later in this chapter), but with the `ip subnet-zero` command, you now get to use subnets 0, 64, 128, and 192. That is two more subnets for every subnet mask we use.

Even though we don't discuss the command line interface (CLI) until Chapter 6, "Cisco's Internetworking Operating System (IOS)," it's important for you to be familiar with this command:

```
P1R1#sh running-config
Building configuration...
Current configuration : 827 bytes
!
hostname Pod1R1
!
ip subnet-zero
!
```

This router output shows that the command `ip subnet-zero` is enabled on the router. Cisco has turned this command on by default starting with Cisco IOS version 12.*x*.

When studying for your Cisco exams, make sure you read very carefully and understand if Cisco is asking you *not* to use `ip subnet-zero`. There are instances where this may happen.

How to Create Subnets

To create subnetworks, you take bits from the host portion of the IP address and reserve them to define the subnet address. This means fewer bits for hosts, so the more subnets, the fewer bits available for defining hosts.

Later in this chapter, you'll learn how to create subnets, starting with Class C addresses. But before you actually implement subnetting, you need to determine your current requirements as well as plan for future conditions.

Before we move on to designing and creating a subnet mask, you need to understand that in this first section, we will be discussing classful routing, which means that all hosts (all nodes) in the network use the exact same subnet mask. When we move on to Variable Length Subnet Masks (VLSMs), I'll discuss classless routing, which means that each network segment *can* use a different subnet mask.

To create a subnet, follow these steps:

1. Determine the number of required network IDs:
   - One for each LAN subnet
   - One for each wide area network connection
2. Determine the number of required host IDs per subnet:
   - One for each TCP/IP host
   - One for each router interface
3. Based on the above requirements, create the following:
   - One subnet mask for your entire network
   - A unique subnet ID for each physical segment
   - A range of host IDs for each subnet

Subnet Masks

For the subnet address scheme to work, every machine on the network must know which part of the host address will be used as the subnet address. This is accomplished by assigning a *subnet mask* to each machine. A subnet mask is a 32-bit value that allows the recipient of IP packets to distinguish the network ID portion of the IP address from the host ID portion of the IP address.

The network administrator creates a 32-bit subnet mask composed of 1s and 0s. The 1s in the subnet mask represent the positions that refer to the network or subnet addresses.

Not all networks need subnets, meaning they use the default subnet mask. This is basically the same as saying that a network doesn't have a subnet address. Table 4.1 shows the default subnet masks for Classes A, B, and C. These default masks cannot change. In other words, you can't make a Class B subnet mask read 255.0.0.0. If you try, the host will read that address as invalid and usually won't even let you type it in. For a Class A network, you can't change the first byte in a subnet mask; it must read 255.0.0.0 at a minimum. Similarly, you cannot assign 255.255.255.255, as this is all 1s—a broadcast address. A Class B address must start with 255.255.0.0, and a Class C has to start with 255.255.255.0.

Understanding the Powers of 2

Powers of 2 are important to understand and memorize for use with IP subnetting. To review powers of 2, remember that when you see a number with another number to its upper right (called an exponent), this means you should multiply the number by itself as many times as the upper number specifies. For example, 2^3 is 2 ´ 2 ´ 2, which equals 8. Here's a list of powers of 2 that you should commit to memory:

$2^1 = 2$

$2^2 = 4$

$2^3 = 8$

$2^4 = 16$

$2^5 = 32$

$2^6 = 64$

$2^7 = 128$

$2^8 = 256$

$2^9 = 512$

$2^{10} = 1,024$

$2^{11} = 2,048$

$2^{12} = 4,096$

$2^{13} = 8,192$

$2^{14} = 16,384$

Before you get stressed out about knowing all these exponents, remember that it's helpful to know them, but it's not absolutely necessary. Here's a little trick since you're working with 2s: Each successive power of 2 is double the previous one.

For example, all you have to do to remember the value of 2^9 is to first know that $2^8 = 256$. Why? Because when you double 2 to the eighth power (256), you get 2^9 (or 512). To determine the value of 2^{10}, simply start at $2^8 = 256$, and then double it twice.

You can go the other way as well. If you needed to know what 2^6 is, for example, you just cut 256 in half two times: once to reach 2^7 and then one more time to reach 2^6.

TABLE 4.1 Default subnet mask

Class	Format	Default Subnet Mask
A	*network.node.node.node*	255.0.0.0
B	*network.network.node.node*	255.255.0.0
C	*network.network.network.node*	255.255.255.0

Classless Inter-Domain Routing (CIDR)

Another term you need to familiarize yourself with is *Classless Inter-Domain Routing (CIDR)*. It's basically the method that ISPs (Internet service providers) use to allocate a number of addresses to a company, a home—a customer. They provide addresses in a certain block size, something I'll be going into in greater detail later in this chapter.

When you receive a block of addresses from an ISP, what you get will look something like this: 192.168.10.32/28. This is telling you what your subnet mask is. The slash notation (/) means how many bits are turned on (1s). Obviously, the maximum could only be /32 because a byte is 8 bits and there are 4 bytes in an IP address: (4 × 8 = 32). But keep in mind that the largest subnet mask available (regardless of the class of address) can only be a /30 because you've got to keep at least 2 bits for host bits.

Take, for example, a Class A default subnet mask, which is 255.0.0.0. This means that the first byte of the subnet mask is all ones (1s), or 11111111. When referring to a slash notation, you need to count all the 1 bits to figure out your mask. The 255.0.0.0 is considered a /8 because it has 8 bits that are 1s—that is, 8 bits that are turned on.

A Class B default mask would be 255.255.0.0, which is a /16 because 16 bits are ones (1s): 11111111.11111111.00000000.00000000.

Table 4.2 has a listing of every available subnet mask and its equivalent CIDR slash notation.

TABLE 4.2 CIDR values

Subnet Mask	CIDR Value
255.0.0.0	/8
255.128.0.0	/9
255.192.0.0	/10
255.224.0.0	/11
255.240.0.0	/12
255.248.0.0	/13
255.252.0.0	/14
255.254.0.0	/15
255.255.0.0	/16
255.255.128.0	/17

Subnet Mask	CIDR Value
255.255.192.0	/18
255.255.224.0	/19
255.255.240.0	/20
255.255.248.0	/21
255.255.252.0	/22
255.255.254.0	/23
255.255.255.0	/24
255.255.255.128	/25
255.255.255.192	/26
255.255.255.224	/27
255.255.255.240	/28
255.255.255.248	/29
255.255.255.252	/30

The /8 through /15 can only be used with Class A network addresses. /16 through /23 can be used by Class A and B network addresses. /24 through /30 can be used by Class A, B, and C network addresses. This is a big reason why most companies use Class A network addresses. Since they can use all subnet masks, they get the maximum flexibility in network design.

No, you cannot configure a Cisco router using this slash format. But wouldn't that be nice? Nevertheless, it's *really* important for you to know subnet masks in the slash notation (CIDR).

Subnetting Class C Addresses

There are many different ways to subnet a network. The right way is the way that works best for you. In a Class C address, only 8 bits are available for defining the hosts. Remember that subnet bits start at the left and go to the right, without skipping bits. This means that the only Class C subnet masks can be the following:

```
Binary     Decimal  CIDR
---------------------------------------------------------
00000000 = 0        /24
10000000 = 128      /25
11000000 = 192      /26
11100000 = 224      /27
11110000 = 240      /28
11111000 = 248      /29
11111100 = 252      /30
```

We can't use a /31 or /32 because we have to have at least 2 host bits for assigning IP addresses to hosts. In the past, I never discussed the /25 in a Class C network. Cisco always had been concerned with having at least 2 subnet bits, but now, because of Cisco recognizing the `ip subnet-zero` command in its curriculum and exam objectives, we can use just 1 subnet bit.

In the following sections, I'm going to teach you an alternate method of subnetting that makes it easier to subnet larger numbers in no time. Trust me, you need to be able to subnet fast!

Subnetting a Class C Address: The Fast Way!

When you've chosen a possible subnet mask for your network and need to determine the number of subnets, valid hosts, and broadcast addresses of a subnet that the mask provides, all you need to do is answer five simple questions:

- How many subnets does the chosen subnet mask produce?
- How many valid hosts per subnet are available?
- What are the valid subnets?
- What's the broadcast address of each subnet?
- What are the valid hosts in each subnet?

At this point, it's important that you both understand and have memorized your powers of 2. Please refer to the sidebar "Understanding the Powers of 2" earlier in this chapter if you need some help. Here's how you get the answers to those five big questions:

- *How many subnets?* 2^x = number of subnets. x is the number of masked bits, or the 1s. For example, in 11000000, the number of 1s gives us 2^2 subnets. In this example, there are 4 subnets.
- *How many hosts per subnet?* $2^y - 2$ = number of hosts per subnet. y is the number of unmasked bits, or the 0s. For example, in 11000000, the number of 0s gives us $2^6 - 2$ hosts. In this example, there are 62 hosts per subnet. You need to subtract 2 for the subnet address and the broadcast address, which are not valid hosts.

- *What are the valid subnets?* 256 – subnet mask = block size, or increment number. An example would be 256 – 192 = 64. The block size of a 192 mask is always 64. Start counting at zero in blocks of 64 until you reach the subnet mask value and these are your subnets. 0, 64, 128, 192. Easy, huh?
- *What's the broadcast address for each subnet?* Now here's the really easy part. Since we counted our subnets in the last section as 0, 64, 128, and 192, the broadcast address is always the number right before the next subnet. For example, the 0 subnet has a broadcast address of 63 because the next subnet is 64. The 64 subnet has a broadcast address of 127 because the next subnet is 128. And so on. And remember, the broadcast address of the last subnet is always 255.
- *What are the valid hosts?* Valid hosts are the numbers between the subnets, omitting the all-0s and all-1s. For example, if 64 is the subnet number and 127 is the broadcast address, then 65–126 is the valid host range—it's *always* the numbers between the subnet address and the broadcast address.

I know this can truly seem confusing. But it really isn't as hard as it seems to be at first—just hang in there! Why not try a few and see for yourself?

Subnetting Practice Examples: Class C Addresses

Here's your opportunity to practice subnetting Class C addresses using the method I just described. Exciting, isn't it! We're going to start with the first Class C subnet mask and work through every subnet that we can using a Class C address. When we're done, I'll show you how easy this is with Class A and B networks too!

Practice Example #1C: 255.255.255.128 (/25)

Since 128 is 10000000 in binary, there is only 1 bit for subnetting and 7 bits for hosts. We're going to subnet the Class C network address 192.168.10.0.

192.168.10.0 = Network address

255.255.255.128 = Subnet mask

Now, let's answer the big five:

- *How many subnets?* Since 128 is 1 bit on (10000000), the answer would be $2^1 = 2$.
- *How many hosts per subnet?* We have 7 host bits off (10000000), so the equation would be $2^7 - 2 = 126$ hosts.
- *What are the valid subnets?* 256 – 128 = 128. Remember, we'll start at zero and count in our block size, so our subnets are 0, 128.
- *What's the broadcast address for each subnet?* The number right before the value of the next subnet is all host bits turned on and equals the broadcast address. For the zero subnet, the next subnet is 128, so the broadcast of the 0 subnet is 127.
- *What are the valid hosts?* These are the numbers between the subnet and broadcast address. The easiest way to find the hosts is to write out the subnet address and the broadcast address. This way, the valid hosts are obvious. The following table shows

the 0 and 128 subnets, the valid host ranges of each, and the broadcast address of both subnets:

Subnet	0	128
First host	1	129
Last host	126	254
Broadcast	127	255

Before moving on to the next example, take a look at Figure 4.1. Okay, looking at a Class C /25, it's pretty clear there are two subnets. But so what—why is this significant? Well actually, it's not, but that's not the right question. What you really want to know is what you would do with this information! You can see in Figure 4.1 that both subnets have been assigned to a router interface, which creates our broadcast domains and assigns our subnets. Use the command show ip route to see the routing table on a router (covered in detail throughout this book).

FIGURE 4.1 Implementing a Class C /25 logical network

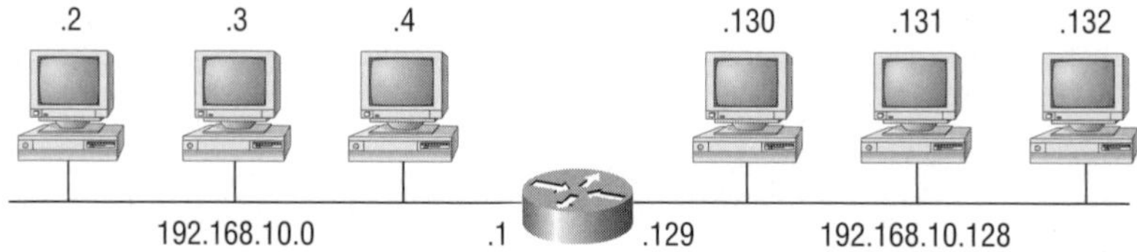


```
Router#show ip route
[output cut]
C 192.168.10.0 is directly connected to Ethernet 0.
C 192.168.10.128 is directly connected to Ethernet 1.
```

I know this isn't exactly everyone's favorite pastime, but it's really important, so just hang in there; we're going to talk about subnetting—period. You need to know that the key to understanding subnetting is to understand the very reason you need to do it. And I'm going to demonstrate this by going through the process of building a physical network—and let's add a router. (We now have an internetwork, as I truly hope you already know!) All right, because we added that router, in order for the hosts on our internetwork to communicate, they must now have a logical network addressing scheme. We could use IPv6, but IPv4 is still the most popular, and it also just happens to be what we're studying at the moment, so that's what we're going with. Okay—now take a look back to Figure 4.1. There are two physical networks, so we're going to implement a logical addressing scheme that allows for two logical networks. As always, it's a really good idea to look ahead and consider likely growth scenarios—both short and long term, but for this example, a /25 will do the trick.

Practice Example #2C: 255.255.255.192 (/26)

In this second example, we're going to subnet the network address 192.168.10.0 using the subnet mask 255.255.255.192.

192.168.10.0 = Network address

255.255.255.192 = Subnet mask

Now, let's answer the big five:

- *How many subnets?* Since 192 is 2 bits on (**11**000000), the answer would be $2^2 = 4$ subnets.
- *How many hosts per subnet?* We have 6 host bits off (11**000000**), so the equation would be $2^6 - 2 = 62$ hosts.
- *What are the valid subnets?* 256 – 192 = 64. Remember, we start at zero and count in our block size, so our subnets are 0, 64, 128, and 192.
- *What's the broadcast address for each subnet?* The number right before the value of the next subnet is all host bits turned on and equals the broadcast address. For the zero subnet, the next subnet is 64, so the broadcast address for the zero subnet is 63.
- *What are the valid hosts?* These are the numbers between the subnet and broadcast address. The easiest way to find the hosts is to write out the subnet address and the broadcast address. This way, the valid hosts are obvious. The following table shows the 0, 64, 128, and 192 subnets, the valid host ranges of each, and the broadcast address of each subnet:

The subnets (do this first)	0	64	128	192
Our first host (perform host addressing last)	1	65	129	193
Our last host	62	126	190	254
The broadcast address (do this second)	63	127	191	255

Okay, again, before getting into the next example, you can see that we can now subnet a /26. And what are you going to do with this fascinating information? Implement it! We'll use Figure 4.2 to practice a /26 network implementation.

The /26 mask provides four subnetworks, and we need a subnet for each router interface. With this mask, in this example, we actually have room to add another router interface.

Practice Example #3C: 255.255.255.224 (/27)

This time, we'll subnet the network address 192.168.10.0 and subnet mask 255.255.255.224.

192.168.10.0 = Network address

255.255.255.224 = Subnet mask

- *How many subnets?* 224 is 11100000, so our equation would be $2^3 = 8$.

- *How many hosts?* $2^5 - 2 = 30$.
- *What are the valid subnets?* 256 – 224 = 32. We just start at zero and count to the subnet mask value in blocks (increments) of 32: 0, 32, 64, 96, 128, 160, 192, and 224.
- *What's the broadcast address for each subnet (always the number right before the next subnet)?*
- *What are the valid hosts (the numbers between the subnet number and the broadcast address)?*

FIGURE 4.2 Implementing a Class C /26 logical network

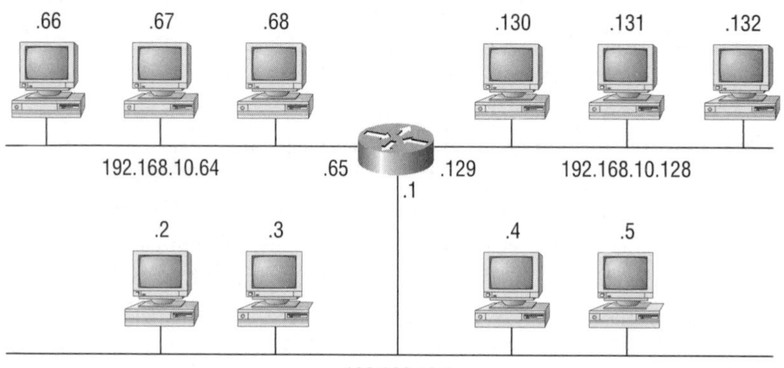
.66
.67
.68
.130
.131
.132
192.168.10.64
.65
.129
192.168.10.128
.1
.2
.3
.4
.5
192.168.10.0
Router#show ip route
[output cut]
C 192.168.10.0 is directly connected to Ethernet 0
C 192.168.10.64 is directly connected to Ethernet 1
C 192.168.10.128 is directly connected to Ethernet 2

To answer the last two questions, first just write out the subnets, then write out the broadcast addresses—the number right before the next subnet. Last, fill in the host addresses. The following table gives you all the subnets for the 255.255.255.224 Class C subnet mask:

The subnet address	0	32	64	96	128	160	192	224
The first valid host	1	33	65	97	129	161	193	225
The last valid host	30	62	94	126	158	190	222	254
The broadcast address	31	63	95	127	159	191	223	255

Practice Example #4C: 255.255.255.240 (/28)

Let's practice on another one:

192.168.10.0 = Network address

255.255.255.240 = Subnet mask

- *Subnets?* 240 is 11110000 in binary. $2^4 = 16$.

- *Hosts?* 4 host bits, or $2^4 - 2 = 14$.
- *Valid subnets?* 256 – 240 = 16. Start at 0: 0 + 16 = 16. 16 + 16 = 32. 32 + 16 = 48. 48 + 16 = 64. 64 + 16 = 80. 80 + 16 = 96. 96 + 16 = 112. 112 + 16 = 128. 128 + 16 = 144. 144 + 16 = 160. 160 + 16 = 176. 176 + 16 = 192. 192 + 16 = 208. 208 + 16 = 224. 224 + 16 = 240.
- *Broadcast address for each subnet?*
- *Valid hosts?*

To answer the last two questions, check out the following table. It gives you the subnets, valid hosts, and broadcast addresses for each subnet. First, find the address of each subnet using the block size (increment). Second, find the broadcast address of each subnet increment (it's always the number right before the next valid subnet), then just fill in the host addresses. The following table shows the available subnets, hosts, and broadcast addresses provided from a Class C 255.255.255.240 mask:

Subnet	0	16	32	48	64	80	96	112	128	144	160	176	192	208	224	240
First host	1	17	33	49	65	81	97	113	129	145	161	177	193	209	225	241
Last host	14	30	46	62	78	94	110	126	142	158	174	190	206	222	238	254
Broadcast	15	31	47	63	79	95	111	127	143	159	175	191	207	223	239	255

Cisco has figured out that most people cannot count in 16s and therefore have a hard time finding valid subnets, hosts, and broadcast addresses with the Class C 255.255.255.240 mask. You'd be wise to study this mask.

Practice Example #5C: 255.255.255.248 (/29)

Let's keep practicing:

192.168.10.0 = Network address

255.255.255.248 = Subnet mask

- *Subnets?* 248 in binary = 11111000. $2^5 = 32$.
- *Hosts?* $2^3 - 2 = 6$.
- *Valid subnets?* 256 – 248 = 0, 8, 16, 24, 32, 40, 48, 56, 64, 72, 80, 88, 96, 104, 112, 120, 128, 136, 144, 152, 160, 168, 176, 184, 192, 200, 208, 216, 224, 232, 240, and 248.
- *Broadcast address for each subnet?*
- *Valid hosts?*

Take a look at the following table. It shows some of the subnets (first four and last four only), valid hosts, and broadcast addresses for the Class C 255.255.255.248 mask:

Subnet	0	8	16	24	…	224	232	240	248
First host	1	9	17	25	…	225	233	241	249

Last host	6	14	22	30	...	230	238	246	254
Broadcast	7	15	23	31	...	231	239	247	255

If you try to configure a router interface with the address 192.168.10.6 255.255.255.248 (for example), and you receive the error

```
Bad mask /29 for address 192.168.10.6
```

This means that `ip subnet-zero` is not enabled. You must be able to subnet to see that the address used in this example is in the zero subnet.

Practice Example #6C: 255.255.255.252 (/30)

Just one more:

192.168.10.0 = Network address

255.255.255.252 = Subnet mask

- *Subnets?* 64.
- *Hosts?* 2.
- *Valid subnets?* 0, 4, 8, 12, etc., all the way to 252.
- *Broadcast address for each subnet (always the number right before the next subnet)?*
- *Valid hosts (the numbers between the subnet number and the broadcast address)?*

The following table shows you the subnet, valid host, and broadcast address of the first four and last four subnets in the 255.255.255.252 Class C subnet:

Subnet	0	4	8	12	...	240	244	248	252
First host	1	5	9	13	...	241	245	249	253
Last host	2	6	10	14	...	242	246	250	254
Broadcast	3	7	11	15	...	243	247	251	255

Subnetting in Your Head: Class C Addresses

It really is possible to subnet in your head. Even if you don't believe me, I'll show you how. And it's not all that hard either—take the following example:

192.168.10.33 = Node address

255.255.255.224 = Subnet mask

First, determine the subnet and broadcast address of the network in which the above IP address resides. You can do this by answering question 3 of the big five questions: 256 – 224 = 32. 0, 32, 64, and so on. The address of 33 falls between the two subnets of

32 and 64 and must be part of the 192.168.10.32 subnet. The next subnet is 64, so the broadcast address of the 32 subnet is 63. (Remember that the broadcast address of a subnet is always the number right before the next subnet.) The valid host range is 33–62 (the numbers between the subnet and broadcast address). This is too easy!

Real World Scenario

Should We Really Use This Mask That Provides Only Two Hosts?

You are the network administrator for Acme Corporation in San Francisco, with dozens of WAN links connecting to your corporate office. Right now your network is a classful network, which means that the same subnet mask is on each host and router interface. You've read about classless routing where you can have different size masks, but don't know what to use on your point-to-point WAN links. Is the 255.255.255.252 (/30) a helpful mask in this situation?

Yes, this is a very helpful mask in wide area networks.

If you use the 255.255.255.0 mask, then each network would have 254 hosts, but you only use 2 addresses with a WAN link! That is a waste of 252 hosts per subnet. If you use the 255.255.255.252 mask, then each subnet has only 2 hosts and you don't waste precious addresses. This is a really important subject, one that we'll address in a lot more detail in the section on VLSM network design in the next chapter.

Okay, let's try another one. We'll subnet another Class C address:

192.168.10.33 = Node address

255.255.255.240 = Subnet mask

What is the subnet and broadcast address of the network of which the above IP address is a member? 256 – 240 = 16. 0, 16, 32, 48, and so on. Bingo—the host address is between the 32 and 48 subnets. The subnet is 192.168.10.32, and the broadcast address is 47 (the next subnet is 48). The valid host range is 33–46 (the numbers between the subnet number and the broadcast address).

Okay, we need to do more, just to make sure you have this down.

You have a node address of 192.168.10.174 with a mask of 255.255.255.240. What is the valid host range?

The mask is 240, so we'd do a 256 – 240 = 16. This is our block size. Just keep adding 16 until we pass the host address of 174, starting at zero, of course: 0, 16, 32, 48, 64, 80, 96, 112, 128, 144, 160, 176, and so on. The host address of 174 is between 160 and 176, so the subnet is 160. The broadcast address is 175; the valid host range is 161–174. That was a tough one.

One more—just for fun. This is the easiest one of all Class C subnetting:

192.168.10.17 = Node address

255.255.255.252 = Subnet mask

What is the subnet and broadcast address of the subnet in which the above IP address resides? 256 – 252 = 0 (always start at zero unless told otherwise), 4, 8, 12, 16, 20, etc. You've got it! The host address is between the 16 and 20 subnets. The subnet is 192.168.10.16, and the broadcast address is 19. The valid host range is 17–18.

Now that you're all over Class C subnetting, let's move on to Class B subnetting. But before we do, let's have a quick review.

What Do We Know?

Okay—here's where you can really apply what you've learned so far and begin committing it all to memory. This is a very cool section that I've been using in my classes for years. It will really help you nail down subnetting!

When you see a subnet mask or slash notation (CIDR), you should know the following:

/25 What do we know about a /25?

- 128 mask
- 1 bit on and 7 bits off (10000000)
- Block size of 128
- 2 subnets, each with 126 hosts

/26 What do we know about a /26?

- 192 mask
- 2 bits on and 6 bits off (11000000)
- Block size of 64
- 4 subnets, each with 62 hosts

/27 What do we know about a /27?

- 224 mask
- 3 bits on and 5 bits off (11100000)
- Block size of 32
- 8 subnets, each with 30 hosts

/28 What do we know about a /28?

- 240 mask
- 4 bits on and 4 bits off
- Block size of 16
- 16 subnets, each with 14 hosts

/29 What do we know about a /29?

- 248 mask
- 5 bits on and 3 bits off
- Block size of 8
- 32 subnets, each with 6 hosts

/30 What do we know about a /30?

- 252 mask
- 6 bits on and 2 bits off
- Block size of 4
- 64 subnets, each with 2 hosts

Regardless of whether you have a Class A, Class B, or Class C address, the /30 mask will provide you with only two hosts, ever. This mask is suited almost exclusively—as well as suggested by Cisco—for use on point-to-point links.

If you can memorize this "What Do We Know?" section, you'll be much better off in your day-to-day job and in your studies. Try saying it out loud, which helps you memorize things—yes, your significant other and/or coworkers will think you've lost it, but they probably already do if you are in the networking field. And if you're not yet in the networking field but are studying all this to break into it, you might as well have people start thinking you're an odd bird now since they will eventually anyway.

It's also helpful to write these on some type of flashcards and have people test your skill. You'd be amazed at how fast you can get subnetting down if you memorize block sizes as well as this "What Do We Know?" section.

Subnetting Class B Addresses

Before we dive into this, let's look at all the possible Class B subnet masks first. Notice that we have a lot more possible subnet masks than we do with a Class C network address:

```
255.255.0.0    (/16)
255.255.128.0  (/17)     255.255.255.0    (/24)
255.255.192.0  (/18)     255.255.255.128  (/25)
255.255.224.0  (/19)     255.255.255.192  (/26)
255.255.240.0  (/20)     255.255.255.224  (/27)
255.255.248.0  (/21)     255.255.255.240  (/28)
255.255.252.0  (/22)     255.255.255.248  (/29)
255.255.254.0  (/23)     255.255.255.252  (/30)
```

We know the Class B network address has 16 bits available for host addressing. This means we can use up to 14 bits for subnetting (because we have to leave at least 2 bits for host addressing). Using a /16 means you are not subnetting with Class B, but it is a mask you can use.

By the way, do you notice anything interesting about that list of subnet values—a pattern, maybe? Ah ha! That's exactly why I had you memorize the binary-to-decimal numbers earlier in the chapter. Since subnet mask bits start on the left and move to the right and bits can't be skipped, the numbers are always the same regardless of the class of address. Memorize this pattern.

The process of subnetting a Class B network is pretty much the same as it is for a Class C, except that you just have more host bits and you start in the third octet.

Use the same subnet numbers for the third octet with Class B that you used for the fourth octet with Class C, but add a zero to the network portion and a 255 to the broadcast section in the fourth octet. The following table shows you an example host range of two subnets used in a Class B 240 (/20) subnet mask:

Subnet Address	16.0	32.0
Broadcast Address	31.255	47.255

Just add the valid hosts between the numbers, and you're set!

The preceding example is true only until you get up to /24. After that, it's numerically exactly like Class C.

Subnetting Practice Examples: Class B Addresses

The following sections will give you an opportunity to practice subnetting Class B addresses. Again, I have to mention that this is the same as subnetting with Class C, except we start in the third octet—with the exact same numbers!

Practice Example #1B: 255.255.128.0 (/17)

172.16.0.0 = Network address

255.255.128.0 = Subnet mask

- *Subnets?* $2^1 = 2$ (same as Class C).
- *Hosts?* $2^{15} - 2 = 32{,}766$ (7 bits in the third octet, and 8 in the fourth).
- *Valid subnets?* 256 – 128 = 128. 0, 128. Remember that subnetting is performed in the third octet, so the subnet numbers are really 0.0 and 128.0, as shown in the next table. These are the exact numbers we used with Class C; we use them in the third octet and add a 0 in the fourth octet for the network address.
- *Broadcast address for each subnet?*
- *Valid hosts?*

The following table shows the two subnets available, the valid host range, and the broadcast address of each:

Subnet	0.0	128.0
First host	0.1	128.1
Last host	127.254	255.254
Broadcast	127.255	255.255

Okay, notice that we just added the fourth octet's lowest and highest values and came up with the answers. And again, it's done exactly the same way as for a Class C subnet. We just use the same numbers in the third octet and added 0 and 255 in the fourth octet—pretty simple, huh? I really can't say this enough: It's just not hard. The numbers never change; we just use them in different octets!

Practice Example #2B: 255.255.192.0 (/18)

172.16.0.0 = Network address

255.255.192.0 = Subnet mask

- *Subnets?* $2^2 = 4$.
- *Hosts?* $2^{14} - 2 = 16,382$ (6 bits in the third octet, and 8 in the fourth).
- *Valid subnets?* 256 – 192 = 64. 0, 64, 128, 192. Remember that the subnetting is performed in the third octet, so the subnet numbers are really 0.0, 64.0, 128.0, and 192.0, as shown in the next table.
- *Broadcast address for each subnet?*
- *Valid hosts?*

The following table shows the four subnets available, the valid host range, and the broadcast address of each:

Subnet	0.0	64.0	128.0	192.0
First host	0.1	64.1	128.1	192.1
Last host	63.254	127.254	191.254	255.254
Broadcast	63.255	127.255	191.255	255.255

Again, it's pretty much the same as it is for a Class C subnet—we just added 0 and 255 in the fourth octet for each subnet in the third octet.

Practice Example #3B: 255.255.240.0 (/20)

172.16.0.0 = Network address

255.255.240.0 = Subnet mask

- *Subnets?* $2^4 = 16$.
- *Hosts?* $2^{12} - 2 = 4094$.
- *Valid subnets?* 256 – 240 = 0, 16, 32, 48, etc., up to 240. Notice that these are the same numbers as a Class C 240 mask—we just put them in the third octet and add a 0 and 255 in the fourth octet.
- *Broadcast address for each subnet?*
- *Valid hosts?*

The following table shows the first four subnets, valid hosts, and broadcast addresses in a Class B 255.255.240.0 mask:

Subnet	0.0	16.0	32.0	48.0
First host	0.1	16.1	32.1	48.1
Last host	15.254	31.254	47.254	63.254
Broadcast	15.255	31.255	47.255	63.255

Practice Example #4B: 255.255.254.0 (/23)

172.16.0.0 = Network address

255.255.254.0 = Subnet mask

- *Subnets?* 2^7 = 128.
- *Hosts?* $2^9 - 2$ = 510.
- *Valid subnets?* 256 – 254 = 0, 2, 4, 6, 8, etc., up to 254.
- *Broadcast address for each subnet?*
- *Valid hosts?*

The following table shows the first five subnets, valid hosts, and broadcast addresses in a Class B 255.255.254.0 mask:

Subnet	0.0	2.0	4.0	6.0	8.0
First host	0.1	2.1	4.1	6.1	8.1
Last host	1.254	3.254	5.254	7.254	9.254
Broadcast	1.255	3.255	5.255	7.255	9.255

Practice Example #5B: 255.255.255.0 (/24)

Contrary to popular belief, 255.255.255.0 used with a Class B network address is not called a Class B network with a Class C subnet mask. It's amazing how many people see this mask used in a Class B network and think it's a Class C subnet mask. This is a Class B subnet mask with 8 bits of subnetting—it's logically different from a Class C mask. Subnetting this address is fairly simple:

172.16.0.0 = Network address

255.255.255.0 = Subnet mask

- *Subnets?* 2^8 = 256.
- *Hosts?* $2^8 - 2$ = 254.
- *Valid subnets?* 256 – 255 = 1. 0, 1, 2, 3, etc., all the way to 255.

- *Broadcast address for each subnet?*
- *Valid hosts?*

The following table shows the first four and last two subnets, the valid hosts, and the broadcast addresses in a Class B 255.255.255.0 mask:

Subnet	0.0	1.0	2.0	3.0	...	254.0	255.0
First host	0.1	1.1	2.1	3.1	...	254.1	255.1
Last host	0.254	1.254	2.254	3.254	...	254.254	255.254
Broadcast	0.255	1.255	2.255	3.255	...	254.255	255.255

Practice Example #6B: 255.255.255.128 (/25)

This is one of the hardest subnet masks you can play with. And worse, it actually is a really good subnet to use in production because it creates over 500 subnets with 126 hosts for each subnet—a nice mixture. So, don't skip over it!

172.16.0.0 = Network address

255.255.255.128 = Subnet mask

- *Subnets?* $2^9 = 512$.
- *Hosts?* $2^7 - 2 = 126$.
- *Valid subnets?* Okay, now for the tricky part. 256 – 255 = 1. 0, 1, 2, 3, etc. for the third octet. But you can't forget the one subnet bit used in the fourth octet. Remember when I showed you how to figure one subnet bit with a Class C mask? You figure this the same way. (Now you know why I showed you the 1-bit subnet mask in the Class C section—to make this part easier.) You actually get two subnets for each third octet value, hence the 512 subnets. For example, if the third octet is showing subnet 3, the two subnets would actually be 3.0 and 3.128.
- *Broadcast address for each subnet?*
- *Valid hosts?*

The following table shows how you can create subnets, valid hosts, and broadcast addresses using the Class B 255.255.255.128 subnet mask (the first eight subnets are shown, and then the last two subnets):

Subnet	0.0	0.128	1.0	1.128	2.0	2.128	3.0	3.128	...	255.0	255.128
First host	0.1	0.129	1.1	1.129	2.1	2.129	3.1	3.129	...	255.1	255.129
Last host	0.126	0.254	1.126	1.254	2.126	2.254	3.126	3.254	...	255.126	255.254
Broadcast	0.127	0.255	1.127	1.255	2.127	2.255	3.127	3.255	...	255.127	255.255

Practice Example #7B: 255.255.255.192 (/26)

Now, this is where Class B subnetting gets easy. Since the third octet has a 255 in the mask section, whatever number is listed in the third octet is a subnet number. However, now that we have a subnet number in the fourth octet, we can subnet this octet just as we did with Class C subnetting. Let's try it out:

172.16.0.0 = Network address

255.255.255.192 = Subnet mask

- *Subnets?* 2^{10} = 1024.
- *Hosts?* $2^6 - 2$ = 62.
- *Valid subnets?* 256 – 192 = 64. The subnets are shown in the following table. Do these numbers look familiar?
- *Broadcast address for each subnet?*
- *Valid hosts?*

The following table shows the first eight subnet ranges, valid hosts, and broadcast addresses:

Subnet	0.0	0.64	0.128	0.192	1.0	1.64	1.128	1.192
First host	0.1	0.65	0.129	0.193	1.1	1.65	1.129	1.193
Last host	0.62	0.126	0.190	0.254	1.62	1.126	1.190	1.254
Broadcast	0.63	0.127	0.191	0.255	1.63	1.127	1.191	1.255

Notice that for each subnet value in the third octet, you get subnets 0, 64, 128, and 192 in the fourth octet.

Practice Example #8B: 255.255.255.224 (/27)

This is done the same way as the preceding subnet mask, except that we just have more subnets and fewer hosts per subnet available.

172.16.0.0 = Network address

255.255.255.224 = Subnet mask

- *Subnets?* 2^{11} = 2048.
- *Hosts?* $2^5 - 2$ = 30.
- *Valid subnets?* 256 – 224 = 32. 0, 32, 64, 96, 128, 160, 192, 224.
- *Broadcast address for each subnet?*
- *Valid hosts?*

The following table shows the first eight subnets:

Subnet	0.0	0.32	0.64	0.96	0.128	0.160	0.192	0.224
First host	0.1	0.33	0.65	0.97	0.129	0.161	0.193	0.225
Last host	0.30	0.62	0.94	0.126	0.158	0.190	0.222	0.254
Broadcast	0.31	0.63	0.95	0.127	0.159	0.191	0.223	0.255

This next table shows the last eight subnets:

Subnet	255.0	255.32	255.64	255.96	255.128	255.160	255.192	255.224
First host	255.1	255.33	255.65	255.97	255.129	255.161	255.193	255.225
Last host	255.30	255.62	255.94	255.126	255.158	255.190	255.222	255.254
Broadcast	255.31	255.63	255.95	255.127	255.159	255.191	255.223	255.255

Subnetting in Your Head: Class B Addresses

Are you nuts? Subnet Class B addresses in our heads? It's actually easier than writing it out—I'm not kidding! Let me show you how:

Question: What is the subnet and broadcast address of the subnet in which 172.16.10.33 /27 resides?

Answer: The interesting octet is the fourth octet. 256 – 224 = 32. 32 + 32 = 64. Bingo: 33 is between 32 and 64. However, remember that the third octet is considered part of the subnet, so the answer would be the 10.32 subnet. The broadcast is 10.63, since 10.64 is the next subnet. That was a pretty easy one.

Question: What subnet and broadcast address is the IP address 172.16.66.10 255.255.192.0 (/18) a member of?

Answer: The interesting octet is the third octet instead of the fourth octet. 256 – 192 = 64. 0, 64, 128. The subnet is 172.16.64.0. The broadcast must be 172.16.127.255 since 128.0 is the next subnet.

Question: What subnet and broadcast address is the IP address 172.16.50.10 255.255.224.0 (/19) a member of?

Answer: 256 – 224 = 0, 32, 64 (remember, we always start counting at zero [0]). The subnet is 172.16.32.0, and the broadcast must be 172.16.63.255 since 64.0 is the next subnet.

Question: What subnet and broadcast address is the IP address 172.16.46.255 255.255.240.0 (/20) a member of?

Answer: 256 – 240 = 16. The third octet is interesting to us. 0, 16, 32, 48. This subnet address must be in the 172.16.32.0 subnet, and the broadcast must be 172.16.47.255 since 48.0 is the next subnet. So, yes, 172.16.46.255 is a valid host.

Question: What subnet and broadcast address is the IP address 172.16.45.14 255.255.255.252 (/30) a member of?

Answer: Where is the interesting octet? 256 – 252 = 0, 4, 8, 12, 16 (in the fourth octet). The subnet is 172.16.45.12, with a broadcast of 172.16.45.15 because the next subnet is 172.16.45.16.

Question: What is the subnet and broadcast address of the host 172.16.88.255/20?

Answer: What is a /20? If you can't answer this, you can't answer this question, can you? A /20 is 255.255.240.0, which gives us a block size of 16 in the third octet, and since no subnet bits are on in the fourth octet, the answer is always 0 and 255 in the fourth octet. 0, 16, 32, 48, 64, 80, 96...bingo. 88 is between 80 and 96, so the subnet is 80.0 and the broadcast address is 95.255.

Question: A router receives a packet on an interface with a destination address of 172.16.46.191/26. What will the router do with this packet?

Answer: Discard it. Do you know why? 172.16.46.191/26 is a 255.255.255.192 mask, which gives us a block size of 64. Our subnets are then 0, 64, 128, 192. 191 is the broadcast address of the 128 subnet, so a router, by default, will discard any broadcast packets.

Subnetting Class A Addresses

Class A subnetting is not performed any differently than Classes B and C, but there are 24 bits to play with instead of the 16 in a Class B address and the 8 in a Class C address.

Let's start by listing all the Class A masks:

```
255.0.0.0     (/8)
255.128.0.0   (/9)      255.255.240.0   (/20)
255.192.0.0   (/10)     255.255.248.0   (/21)
255.224.0.0   (/11)     255.255.252.0   (/22)
255.240.0.0   (/12)     255.255.254.0   (/23)
255.248.0.0   (/13)     255.255.255.0   (/24)
255.252.0.0   (/14)     255.255.255.128   (/25)
255.254.0.0   (/15)     255.255.255.192   (/26)
255.255.0.0   (/16)     255.255.255.224   (/27)
255.255.128.0   (/17)   255.255.255.240   (/28)
255.255.192.0   (/18)   255.255.255.248   (/29)
255.255.224.0   (/19)   255.255.255.252   (/30)
```

That's it. You must leave at least 2 bits for defining hosts. And I hope you can see the pattern by now. Remember, we're going to do this the same way as a Class B or C subnet. It's just that, again, we simply have more host bits and we just use the same subnet numbers we used with Class B and C, but we start using these numbers in the second octet.

Subnetting Practice Examples: Class A Addresses

When you look at an IP address and a subnet mask, you must be able to distinguish the bits used for subnets from the bits used for determining hosts. This is imperative. If you're still struggling with this concept, please reread the section "IP Addressing" in Chapter 3. It shows you how to determine the difference between the subnet and host bits and should help clear things up.

Practice Example #1A: 255.255.0.0 (/16)

Class A addresses use a default mask of 255.0.0.0, which leaves 22 bits for subnetting since you must leave 2 bits for host addressing. The 255.255.0.0 mask with a Class A address is using 8 subnet bits.

- *Subnets?* $2^8 = 256$.
- *Hosts?* $2^{16} - 2 = 65{,}534$.
- *Valid subnets?* What is the interesting octet? 256 – 255 = 1. 0, 1, 2, 3, etc. (all in the second octet). The subnets would be 10.0.0.0, 10.1.0.0, 10.2.0.0, 10.3.0.0, etc., up to 10.255.0.0.
- *Broadcast address for each subnet?*
- *Valid hosts?*

The following table shows the first two and last two subnets, valid host range, and broadcast addresses for the private Class A 10.0.0.0 network:

Subnet	10.0.0.0	10.1.0.0	...	10.254.0.0	10.255.0.0
First host	10.0.0.1	10.1.0.1	...	10.254.0.1	10.255.0.1
Last host	10.0.255.254	10.1.255.254	...	10.254.255.254	10.255.255.254
Broadcast	10.0.255.255	10.1.255.255	...	10.254.255.255	10.255.255.255

Practice Example #2A: 255.255.240.0 (/20)

255.255.240.0 gives us 12 bits of subnetting and leaves us 12 bits for host addressing.

- *Subnets?* $2^{12} = 4096$.
- *Hosts?* $2^{12} - 2 = 4094$.
- *Valid subnets?* What is your interesting octet? 256 – 240 = 16. The subnets in the second octet are a block size of 1 and the subnets in the third octet are 0, 16, 32, etc.
- *Broadcast address for each subnet?*
- *Valid hosts?*

The following table shows some examples of the host ranges—the first three and the last subnets:

Subnet	10.0.0.0	10.0.16.0	10.0.32.0	...	10.255.240.0
First host	10.0.0.1	10.0.16.1	10.0.32.1	...	10.255.240.1
Last host	10.0.15.254	10.0.31.254	10.0.47.254	...	10.255.255.254
Broadcast	10.0.15.255	10.0.31.255	10.0.47.255	...	10.255.255.255

Practice Example #3A: 255.255.255.192 (/26)

Let's do one more example using the second, third, and fourth octets for subnetting.

- *Subnets?* 2^{18} = 262,144.
- *Hosts?* $2^6 - 2$ = 62.
- *Valid subnets?* In the second and third octet, the block size is 1, and in the fourth octet, the block size is 64.
- *Broadcast address for each subnet?*
- *Valid hosts?*

The following table shows the first four subnets and their valid hosts and broadcast addresses in the Class A 255.255.255.192 mask:

Subnet	10.0.0.0	10.0.0.64	10.0.0.128	10.0.0.192
First host	10.0.0.1	10.0.0.65	10.0.0.129	10.0.0.193
Last host	10.0.0.62	10.0.0.126	10.0.0.190	10.0.0.254
Broadcast	10.0.0.63	10.0.0.127	10.0.0.191	10.0.0.255

The following table shows the last four subnets and their valid hosts and broadcast addresses:

Subnet	10.255.255.0	10.255.255.64	10.255.255.128	10.255.255.192
First host	10.255.255.1	10.255.255.65	10.255.255.129	10.255.255.193
Last host	10.255.255.62	10.255.255.126	10.255.255.190	10.255.255.254
Broadcast	10.255.255.63	10.255.255.127	10.255.255.191	10.255.255.255

Subnetting in Your Head: Class A Addresses

This sounds hard, but as with Class C and Class B, the numbers are the same; we just start in the second octet. What makes this easy? You only need to worry about the octet that has the largest block size (typically called the interesting octet; one that is something other than

0 or 255)—for example, 255.255.240.0 (/20) with a Class A network. The second octet has a block size of 1, so any number listed in that octet is a subnet. The third octet is a 240 mask, which means we have a block size of 16 in the third octet. If your host ID is 10.20.80.30, what is your subnet, broadcast address, and valid host range?

The subnet in the second octet is 20 with a block size of 1, but the third octet is in block sizes of 16, so we'll just count them out: 0, 16, 32, 48, 64, 80, 96...voilà! (By the way, you can count by 16s by now, right?) This makes our subnet 10.20.80.0, with a broadcast of 10.20.95.255 because the next subnet is 10.20.96.0. The valid host range is 10.20.80.1 through 10.20.95.254. And yes, no lie! You really can do this in your head if you just get your block sizes nailed!

Okay, let's practice on one more, just for fun!

Host IP: 10.1.3.65/23

First, you can't answer this question if you don't know what a /23 is. It's 255.255.254.0. The interesting octet here is the third one: 256 – 254 = 2. Our subnets in the third octet are 0, 2, 4, 6, etc. The host in this question is in subnet 2.0, and the next subnet is 4.0, so that makes the broadcast address 3.255. And any address between 10.1.2.1 and 10.1.3.254 is considered a valid host.

Summary

Did you read Chapters 3 and 4 and understand everything on the first pass? If so, that is fantastic—congratulations! The thing is, you probably got lost a couple of times—and as I told you, that's what usually happens, so don't stress. Don't feel bad if you have to read each chapter more than once, or even 10 times, before you're truly good to go.

This chapter provided you with an important understanding of IP subnetting. After reading this chapter, you should be able to subnet IP addresses in your head.

This chapter is extremely essential to your Cisco certification process, so if you just skimmed it, please go back and read it and do all the written labs.

Exam Essentials

Identify the advantages of subnetting. Benefits of subnetting a physical network include reduced network traffic, optimized network performance, simplified management, and facilitated spanning of large geographical distances.

Describe the effect of the `ip subnet-zero` command. This command allows you to use the first and last subnet in your network design.

Identify the steps to subnet a classful network. Understand how IP addressing and subnetting work. First, determine your block size by using the 256-subnet mask math. Then count your subnets and determine the broadcast address of each subnet—it is always the number right before the next subnet. Your valid hosts are the numbers between the subnet address and the broadcast address.

Determine possible block sizes. This is an important part of understanding IP addressing and subnetting. The valid block sizes are always 2, 4, 8, 16, 32, 64, 128, etc. You can determine your block size by using the 256-subnet mask math.

Describe the role of a subnet mask in IP addressing. A subnet mask is a 32-bit value that allows the recipient of IP packets to distinguish the network ID portion of the IP address from the host ID portion of the IP address.

Understand and apply the $2^n - 2$ formula. Use this formula to determine the proper subnet mask for a particular size network given the application of that subnet mask to a particular classful network.

Explain the impact of Classless Inter-Domain Routing (CIDR). CIDR allows the creation of networks of a size other than those allowed with the classful subnetting by allowing more than the three classful subnet masks.

Written Labs

In this section, you'll complete the following labs to make sure you've got the information and concepts contained within them fully dialed in:

Lab 4.1: Written Subnet Practice #1

Lab 4.2: Written Subnet Practice #2

Lab 4.3: Written Subnet Practice #3

(The answers to the written labs can be found following the answers to the review questions for this chapter.)

Written Lab 4.1: Written Subnet Practice #1

Write the subnet, broadcast address, and valid host range for question 1 through question 6:

1. 192.168.100.25/30
2. 192.168.100.37/28
3. 192.168.100.66/27
4. 192.168.100.17/29

5. 192.168.100.99/26
6. 192.168.100.99/25
7. You have a Class B network and need 29 subnets. What is your mask?
8. What is the broadcast address of 192.168.192.10/29?
9. How many hosts are available with a Class C /29 mask?
10. What is the subnet for host ID 10.16.3.65/23?

Written Lab 4.2: Written Subnet Practice #2

Given a Class B network and the net bits identified (CIDR), complete the following table to identify the subnet mask and the number of host addresses possible for each mask.

Classful Address	Subnet Mask	Number of Hosts per Subnet ($2^x - 2$)
/16		
/17		
/18		
/19		
/20		
/21		
/22		
/23		
/24		
/25		
/26		
/27		
/28		
/29		
/30		

Written Lab 4.3: Written Subnet Practice #3

Complete the following based on the decimal IP address.

Decimal IP Address	Address Class	Number of Subnet and Host Bits	Number of Subnets (2^x)	Number of Hosts ($2^x - 2$)
10.25.66.154/23				
172.31.254.12/24				
192.168.20.123/28				
63.24.89.21/18				
128.1.1.254/20				
208.100.54.209/30				

Review Questions

The following questions are designed to test your understanding of this chapter's material. For more information on how to get additional questions, please see this book's Introduction.

1. What is the maximum number of IP addresses that can be assigned to hosts on a local subnet that uses the 255.255.255.224 subnet mask?

   A. 14

   B. 15

   C. 16

   D. 30

   E. 31

   F. 62

2. You have a network that needs 29 subnets while maximizing the number of host addresses available on each subnet. How many bits must you borrow from the host field to provide the correct subnet mask?

   A. 2

   B. 3

   C. 4

   D. 5

   E. 6

   F. 7

3. What is the subnetwork address for a host with the IP address 200.10.5.68/28?

   A. 200.10.5.56

   B. 200.10.5.32

   C. 200.10.5.64

   D. 200.10.5.0

4. The network address of 172.16.0.0/19 provides how many subnets and hosts?

   A. 7 subnets, 30 hosts each

   B. 7 subnets, 2,046 hosts each

   C. 7 subnets, 8,190 hosts each

   D. 8 subnets, 30 hosts each

   E. 8 subnets, 2,046 hosts each

   F. 8 subnets, 8,190 hosts each

5. Which two statements describe the IP address 10.16.3.65/23? (Choose two.)
   - A. The subnet address is 10.16.3.0 255.255.254.0.
   - B. The lowest host address in the subnet is 10.16.2.1 255.255.254.0.
   - C. The last valid host address in the subnet is 10.16.2.254 255.255.254.0.
   - D. The broadcast address of the subnet is 10.16.3.255 255.255.254.0.
   - E. The network is not subnetted.
6. If a host on a network has the address 172.16.45.14/30, what is the subnetwork this host belongs to?
   - A. 172.16.45.0
   - B. 172.16.45.4
   - C. 172.16.45.8
   - D. 172.16.45.12
   - E. 172.16.45.16
7. Which mask should you use on point-to-point WAN links in order to reduce the waste of IP addresses?
   - A. /27
   - B. /28
   - C. /29
   - D. /30
   - E. /31
8. What is the subnetwork number of a host with an IP address of 172.16.66.0/21?
   - A. 172.16.36.0
   - B. 172.16.48.0
   - C. 172.16.64.0
   - D. 172.16.0.0
9. You have an interface on a router with the IP address of 192.168.192.10/29. Including the router interface, how many hosts can have IP addresses on the LAN attached to the router interface?
   - A. 6
   - B. 8
   - C. 30
   - D. 62
   - E. 126

10. You need to configure a server that is on the subnet 192.168.19.24/29. The router has the first available host address. Which of the following should you assign to the server?

A. 192.168.19.0 255.255.255.0

B. 192.168.19.33 255.255.255.240

C. 192.168.19.26 255.255.255.248

D. 192.168.19.31 255.255.255.248

E. 192.168.19.34 255.255.255.240

11. You have an interface on a router with the IP address of 192.168.192.10/29. What is the broadcast address the hosts will use on this LAN?

A. 192.168.192.15

B. 192.168.192.31

C. 192.168.192.63

D. 192.168.192.127

E. 192.168.192.255

12. You need to subnet a network that has 5 subnets, each with at least 16 hosts. Which classful subnet mask would you use?

A. 255.255.255.192

B. 255.255.255.224

C. 255.255.255.240

D. 255.255.255.248

13. You configure a router interface with the IP address 192.168.10.62 255.255.255.192 and receive the following error:

```
Bad mask /26 for address 192.168.10.62
```

Why did you receive this error?

A. You typed this mask on a WAN link and that is not allowed.

B. This is not a valid host and subnet mask combination.

C. `ip subnet-zero` is not enabled on the router.

D. The router does not support IP.

14. If an Ethernet port on a router were assigned an IP address of 172.16.112.1/25, what would be the valid subnet address of this interface?

A. 172.16.112.0

B. 172.16.0.0

C. 172.16.96.0

D. 172.16.255.0

E. 172.16.128.0

15. Using the following illustration, what would be the IP address of E0 if you were using the eighth subnet? The network ID is 192.168.10.0/28 and you need to use the last available IP address in the range. The zero subnet should not be considered valid for this question.

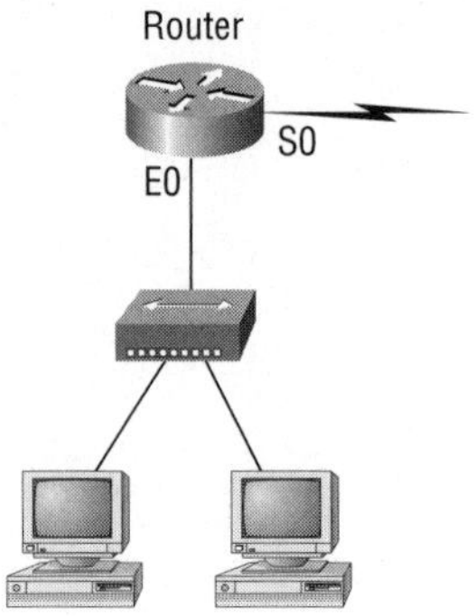

A. 192.168.10.142
B. 192.168.10.66
C. 192.168.100.254
D. 192.168.10.143
E. 192.168.10.126

16. Using the illustration from the previous question, what would be the IP address of S0 if you were using the first subnet? The network ID is 192.168.10.0/28 and you need to use the last available IP address in the range. Again, the zero subnet should not be considered valid for this question.

A. 192.168.10.24
B. 192.168.10.62
C. 192.168.10.30
D. 192.168.10.127

17. Which configuration command must be in effect to allow the use of 8 subnets if the Class C subnet mask is 255.255.255.224?

A. `Router(config)#`**`ip classless`**
B. `Router(config)#`**`ip version 6`**
C. `Router(config)#`**`no ip classful`**
D. `Router(config)#`**`ip unnumbered`**
E. `Router(config)#`**`ip subnet-zero`**
F. `Router(config)#`**`ip all-nets`**

18. You have a network with a subnet of 172.16.17.0/22. Which is the valid host address?

- **A.** 172.16.17.1 255.255.255.252
- **B.** 172.16.0.1 255.255.240.0
- **C.** 172.16.20.1 255.255.254.0
- **D.** 172.16.16.1 255.255.255.240
- **E.** 172.16.18.255 255.255.252.0
- **F.** 172.16.0.1 255.255.255.0

19. Your router has the following IP address on Ethernet0: 172.16.2.1/23. Which of the following can be valid host IDs on the LAN interface attached to the router? (Choose two.)

- **A.** 172.16.0.5
- **B.** 172.16.1.100
- **C.** 172.16.1.198
- **D.** 172.16.2.255
- **E.** 172.16.3.0
- **F.** 172.16.3.255

20. To test the IP stack on your local host, which IP address would you ping?

- **A.** 127.0.0.0
- **B.** 1.0.0.127
- **C.** 127.0.0.1
- **D.** 127.0.0.255
- **E.** 255.255.255.255

Answers to Review Questions

1. D. A /27 (255.255.255.224) is 3 bits on and 5 bits off. This provides 8 subnets, each with 30 hosts. Does it matter if this mask is used with a Class A, B, or C network address? Not at all. The number of host bits would never change.

2. D. A 240 mask is 4 subnet bits and provides 16 subnets, each with 14 hosts. We need more subnets, so let's add subnet bits. One more subnet bit would be a 248 mask. This provides 5 subnet bits (32 subnets) with 3 host bits (6 hosts per subnet). This is the best answer.

3. C. This is a pretty simple question. A /28 is 255.255.255.240, which means that our block size is 16 in the fourth octet. 0, 16, 32, 48, 64, 80, etc. The host is in the 64 subnet.

4. F. A CIDR address of /19 is 255.255.224.0. This is a Class B address, so that is only 3 subnet bits, but it provides 13 host bits, or 8 subnets, each with 8,190 hosts.

5. B, D. The mask 255.255.254.0 (/23) used with a Class A address means that there are 15 subnet bits and 9 host bits. The block size in the third octet is 2 (256 – 254). So this makes the subnets in the interesting octet 0, 2, 4, 6, etc., all the way to 254. The host 10.16.3.65 is in the 2.0 subnet. The next subnet is 4.0, so the broadcast address for the 2.0 subnet is 3.255. The valid host addresses are 2.1 through 3.254.

6. D. A /30, regardless of the class of address, has a 252 in the fourth octet. This means we have a block size of 4 and our subnets are 0, 4, 8, 12, 16, etc. Address 14 is obviously in the 12 subnet.

7. D. A point-to-point link uses only two hosts. A /30, or 255.255.255.252, mask provides two hosts per subnet.

8. C. A /21 is 255.255.248.0, which means we have a block size of 8 in the third octet, so we just count by 8 until we reach 66. The subnet in this question is 64.0. The next subnet is 72.0, so the broadcast address of the 64 subnet is 71.255.

9. A. A /29 (255.255.255.248), regardless of the class of address, has only 3 host bits. Six hosts is the maximum number of hosts on this LAN, including the router interface.

10. C. A /29 is 255.255.255.248, which is a block size of 8 in the fourth octet. The subnets are 0, 8, 16, 24, 32, 40, etc. 192.168.19.24 is the 24 subnet, and since 32 is the next subnet, the broadcast address for the 24 subnet is 31. 192.168.19.26 is the only correct answer.

11. A. A /29 (255.255.255.248) has a block size of 8 in the fourth octet. This means the subnets are 0, 8, 16, 24, etc. 10 is in the 8 subnet. The next subnet is 16, so 15 is the broadcast address.

12. B. You need 5 subnets, each with at least 16 hosts. The mask 255.255.255.240 provides 16 subnets with 14 hosts—this will not work. The mask 255.255.255.224 provides 8 subnets, each with 30 hosts. This is the best answer.

13. C. First, you cannot answer this question if you can't subnet. The 192.168.10.62 with a mask of 255.255.255.192 is a block size of 64 in the fourth octet. The host 192.168.10.62 is in the zero subnet, and the error occurred because `ip subnet-zero` is not enabled on the router.

14. A. A /25 mask is 255.255.255.128. Used with a Class B network, the third and fourth octets are used for subnetting with a total of 9 subnet bits, 8 bits in the third octet and 1 bit in the fourth octet. Since there is only 1 bit in the fourth octet, the bit is either off or on—which is a value of 0 or 128. The host in the question is in the 0 subnet, which has a broadcast address of 127 since 112.128 is the next subnet.

15. A. A /28 is a 255.255.255.240 mask. Let's count to the ninth subnet (we need to find the broadcast address of the eighth subnet, so we need to count to the ninth subnet). Starting at 16 (remember, the question stated that we will not use subnet zero, so we start at 16, not 0), 16, 32, 48, 64, 80, 96, 112, 128, 144. The eighth subnet is 128 and the next subnet is 144, so our broadcast address of the 128 subnet is 143. This makes the host range 129–142. 142 is the last valid host.

16. C. A /28 is a 255.255.255.240 mask. The first subnet is 16 (remember that the question stated not to use subnet zero) and the next subnet is 32, so our broadcast address is 31. This makes our host range 17–30. 30 is the last valid host.

17. E. A Class C subnet mask of 255.255.255.224 is 3 bits on and 5 bits off (11100000) and provides 8 subnets, each with 30 hosts. However, if the command `ip subnet-zero` is not used, then only 6 subnets would be available for use.

18. E. A Class B network ID with a /22 mask is 255.255.252.0, with a block size of 4 in the third octet. The network address in the question is in subnet 172.16.16.0 with a broadcast address of 172.16.19.255. Only option E has the correct subnet mask listed, and 172.16.18.255 is a valid host.

19. D, E. The router's IP address on the E0 interface is 172.16.2.1/23, which is 255.255.254.0. This makes the third octet a block size of 2. The router's interface is in the 2.0 subnet, and the broadcast address is 3.255 because the next subnet is 4.0. The valid host range is 2.1 through 3.254. The router is using the first valid host address in the range.

20. C. To test the local stack on your host, ping the loopback interface of 127.0.0.1.

Answers to Written Lab 4.1

1. 192.168.100.25/30. A /30 is 255.255.255.252. The valid subnet is 192.168.100.24, broadcast is 192.168.100.27, and valid hosts are 192.168.100.25 and 26.
2. 192.168.100.37/28. A /28 is 255.255.255.240. The fourth octet is a block size of 16. Just count by 16s until you pass 37. 0, 16, 32, 48. The host is in the 32 subnet, with a broadcast address of 47. Valid hosts 33–46.
3. A /27 is 255.255.255.224. The fourth octet is a block size of 32. Count by 32s until you pass the host address of 66. 0, 32, 64, 96. The host is in the 64 subnet, and the broadcast address of 95. Valid host range of 65-94.
4. 192.168.100.17/29. A /29 is 255.255.255.248. The fourth octet is a block size of 8. 0, 8, 16, 24. The host is in the 16 subnet, broadcast of 23. Valid hosts 17–22.
5. 192.168.100.99/26. A /26 is 255.255.255.192. The fourth octet has a block size of 64. 0, 64, 128. The host is in the 64 subnet, broadcast of 127. Valid hosts 65–126.
6. 192.168.100.99/25. A /25 is 255.255.255.128. The fourth octet is a block size of 128. 0, 128. The host is in the 0 subnet, broadcast of 127. Valid hosts 1–126.
7. A default Class B is 255.255.0.0. A Class B 255.255.255.0 mask is 256 subnets, each with 254 hosts. We need fewer subnets. If we used 255.255.240.0, this provides 16 subnets. Let's add one more subnet bit. 255.255.248.0. This is 5 bits of subnetting, which provides 32 subnets. This is our best answer, a /21.
8. A /29 is 255.255.255.248. This is a block size of 8 in the fourth octet. 0, 8, 16. The host is in the 8 subnet, broadcast is 15.
9. A /29 is 255.255.255.248, which is 5 subnet bits and 3 host bits. This is only 6 hosts per subnet.
10. A /23 is 255.255.254.0. The third octet is a block size of 2. 0, 2, 4. The subnet is in the 16.2.0 subnet; the broadcast address is 16.3.255.

Answers to Written Lab 4.2

Classful Address	Subnet Mask	Number of Hosts per Subnet ($2^n - 2$)
/16	255.255.0.0	65,534
/17	255.255.128.0	32,766
/18	255.255.192.0	16,382
/19	255.255.224.0	8,190

/20	255.255.240.0	4,094
/21	255.255.248.0	2,046
/22	255.255.252.0	1,022
/23	255.255.254.0	510
/24	255.255.255.0	254
/25	255.255.255.128	126
/26	255.255.255.192	62
/27	255.255.255.224	30
/28	255.255.255.240	14
/29	255.255.255.248	6
/30	255.255.255.252	2

Answers to Written Lab 4.3

Decimal IP Address	Address Class	Number of Subnet and Host Bits	Number of Subnets (2^x)	Number of Hosts ($2^x - 2$)
10.25.66.154/23	A	15/9	32768	510
172.31.254.12/24	B	8/8	256	254
192.168.20.123/28	C	4/4	16	14
63.24.89.21/18	A	10/14	1,024	16,384
128.1.1.254/20	B	4/12	16	4094
208.100.54.209/30	C	6/2	64	2

Variable Length Subnet Masks (VLSMs), Summarization, and Troubleshooting TCP/IP

THE CCNA EXAM TOPICS COVERED IN THIS CHAPTER INCLUDE THE FOLLOWING:

✓ **Implement an IP addressing scheme and IP Services to meet network requirements in a medium-size Enterprise branch office network.**

- Implement static and dynamic addressing services for hosts in a LAN environment.
- Calculate and apply an addressing scheme including VLSM IP addressing design to a network.
- Determine the appropriate classless addressing scheme using VLSM and summarization to satisfy addressing requirements in a LAN/WAN environment.
- Identify and correct common problems associated with IP addressing and host configurations.

After our discussion of IP subnetting in the last two chapters, I'm now going to tell you all about Variable Length Subnet Masks (VLSMs) as well as show you how to design and implement a network using VLSM networks.

Once you have mastered VLSM design and implementation, I'll show you how to summarize classful boundaries. We'll go into this further in Chapter 9, "Enhanced IGRP (EIGRP) and Open Shortest Path First (OSPF)," where I'll demonstrate summarizing using EIGRP and OSPF routing protocols.

I'll wrap up the chapter by going over IP address troubleshooting and take you through the steps Cisco recommends when troubleshooting an IP network.

So get psyched—you're about to go for quite a ride! This chapter will truly help you understand IP addressing and networking, so don't get discouraged or give up. If you stick with it, I promise that one day you'll look back on this and you'll be really glad you decided to hang on. It's one of those things that after you understand it, you'll wonder why you once thought it was so hard. Ready? Let's go!

For up-to-the-minute updates for this chapter, please see `www.lammle.com` or `www.sybex.com/go/ccna7e`.

Variable Length Subnet Masks (VLSMs)

In this chapter I'm going to show you a simple way to take one network and create many networks using subnet masks of different lengths on different types of network designs. This is called VLSM networking, and it does bring up another subject I mentioned in Chapter 4: classful and classless networking.

Neither RIPv1 nor IGRP routing protocols have a field for subnet information, so the subnet information gets dropped. What this means is that if a router running RIP has a subnet mask of a certain value, it assumes that *all* interfaces within the classful address space have the same subnet mask. This is called classful routing, and RIP and IGRP are both considered classful routing protocols. (I'll be talking more about RIP and IGRP in Chapter 8, "IP Routing.") If you mix and match subnet mask lengths in a network running RIP or IGRP, that network just won't work!

Classless routing protocols, however, do support the advertisement of subnet information. Therefore, you can use VLSM with routing protocols such as RIPv2, EIGRP, and OSPF.

(EIGRP and OSPF will be discussed in Chapter 9.) The benefit of this type of network is that you save a bunch of IP address space with it.

As the name suggests, with VLSMs we can have different length subnet masks for different router interfaces. Look at Figure 5.1 to see an example of why classful network designs are inefficient.

FIGURE 5.1 Typical classful network

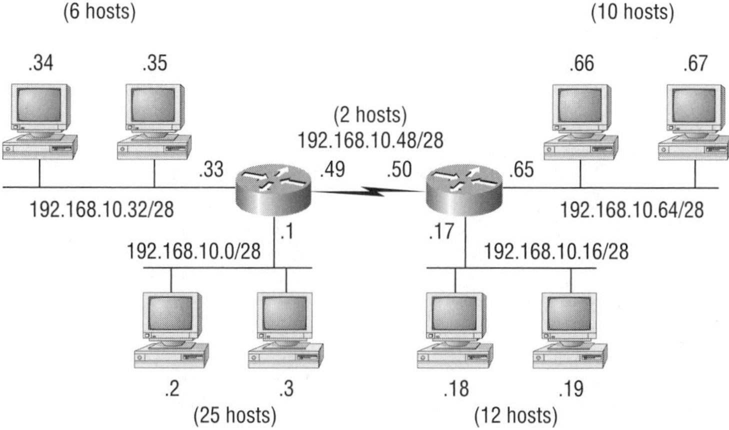

Looking at Figure 5.1, you'll notice that we have two routers, each with two LANs and connected together with a WAN serial link. In a typical classful network design (RIP or IGRP routing protocols), you could subnet a network like this:

192.168.10.0 = Network

255.255.255.240 (/28) = Mask

Our subnets would be (you know this part, right?) 0, 16, 32, 48, 64, 80, etc. This allows us to assign 16 subnets to our internetwork. But how many hosts would be available on each network? Well, as you probably know by now, each subnet provides only 14 hosts. This means that each LAN has 14 valid hosts available—one LAN doesn't even have enough addresses needed for all the hosts! But the point-to-point WAN link also has 14 valid hosts. It's too bad we can't just nick some valid hosts from that WAN link and give them to our LANs!

All hosts and router interfaces have the same subnet mask—again, this is called classful routing. And if we want this network to be more efficient, we definitely need to add different masks to each router interface.

But there's still another problem—the link between the two routers will never use more than two valid hosts! This wastes valuable IP address space, and it's the big reason I'm going to talk to you about VLSM network design.

VLSM Design

Let's take Figure 5.1 and use a classless design...which will become the new network shown in Figure 5.2. In the previous example, we wasted address space—one LAN didn't have enough addresses because every router interface and host used the same subnet mask. Not so good. What would be good is to provide only the needed number of hosts on each router interface. To do this, we use what are referred to as Variable Length Subnet Masks (VLSMs).

FIGURE 5.2 Classless network design

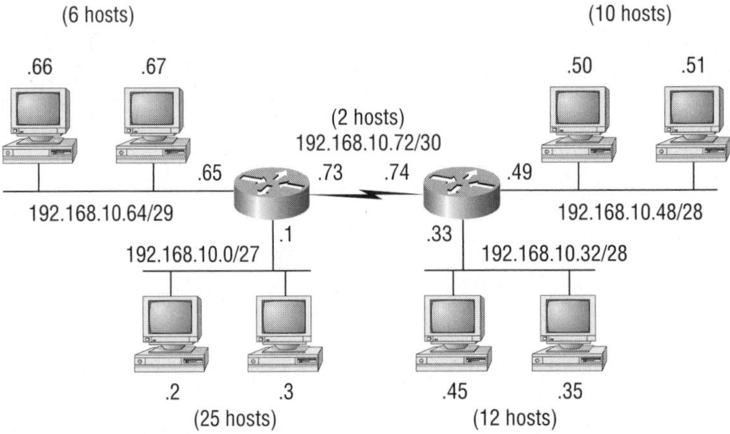

Now remember that we can use different size masks on each router interface. And if we use a /30 on our WAN links and a /27, /28, and /29 on our LANs, we'll get 2 hosts per WAN interface, and 30, 14, and 8 hosts per LAN interface—nice! This makes a huge difference—not only can we get just the right amount of hosts on each LAN, we still have room to add more WANs and LANs using this same network!

Remember, in order to implement a VLSM design on your network, you need to have a routing protocol that sends subnet mask information with the route updates. This would be RIPv2, EIGRP, and OSPF. RIPv1 and IGRP will not work in classless networks and are considered classful routing protocols.

Implementing VLSM Networks

To create VLSMs quickly and efficiently, you need to understand how block sizes and charts work together to create the VLSM masks. Table 5.1 shows you the block sizes used when creating VLSMs with Class C networks. For example, if you need 25 hosts, then you'll need a block size of 32. If you need 11 hosts, you'll use a block size of 16. Need 40 hosts? Then you'll need a block of 64. You cannot just make up block sizes—they've got to be the block sizes shown in Table 5.1. So memorize the block sizes in this table—it's easy. They're the same numbers we used with subnetting!

Real World Scenario

Why Bother with VLSM Design?

You have just been hired by a new company and need to add on to the existing network. There is no problem with starting over with a new IP address scheme. Should you use a VLSM classless network or a classful network?

Let's just say you happen to have plenty of address space because you are using the Class A 10.0.0.0 private network address in your corporate environment and can't even come close to imagining that you'd ever run out of IP addresses. Why would you want to bother with the VLSM design process?

Good question. There's a good answer too!

Because by creating contiguous blocks of addresses to specific areas of your network, you can then easily summarize your network and keep route updates with a routing protocol to a minimum. Why would anyone want to advertise hundreds of networks between buildings when you can just send one summary route between buildings and achieve the same result?

If you're confused about what summary routes are, let me explain. Summarization, also called supernetting, provides route updates in the most efficient way possible by advertising many routes in one advertisement instead of individually. This saves a ton of bandwidth and minimizes router processing. As always, you use blocks of addresses (remember that block sizes are used in all sorts of networks) to configure your summary routes and watch your network's performance hum.

But know that summarization works only if you design your network carefully. If you carelessly hand out IP subnets to any location on the network, you'll notice straight away that you no longer have any summary boundaries. And you won't get very far with creating summary routes without those, so watch your step!

TABLE 5.1 Block sizes

Prefix	Mask	Hosts	Block Size
/25	128	126	128
/26	192	62	64
/27	224	30	32
/28	240	14	16
/29	248	6	8
/30	252	2	4

The next step is to create a VLSM table. Figure 5.3 shows you the table used in creating a VLSM network. The reason we use this table is so we don't accidentally overlap networks.

FIGURE 5.3 The VLSM table

Variable Length Subnet Masks Worksheet

Subnet	Mask	Subnets	Hosts	Block
/26	192	4	62	64
/27	224	8	30	32
/28	240	16	14	16
/29	248	32	6	8
/30	252	64	2	4

Class C Network 192.168.10.0

Network	Hosts	Block	Subnet	Mask
A				
B				
C				
D				
E				
F				
G				
H				
I				
J				
K				
L				

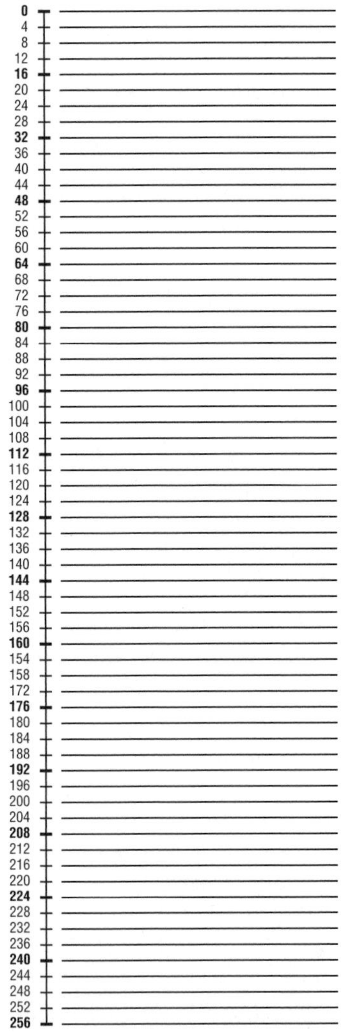

0
4
8
12
16
20
24
28
32
36
40
44
48
52
56
60
64
68
72
76
80
84
88
92
96
100
104
108
112
116
120
124
128
132
136
140
144
148
152
156
160
154
158
172
176
180
184
188
192
196
200
204
208
212
216
220
224
228
232
236
240
244
248
252
256

You'll find the sheet shown in Figure 5.3 very valuable because it lists every block size you can use for a network address. Notice that the block sizes are listed starting from a block size of 4 all the way to a block size of 128. If you have two networks with block sizes of 128, you'll quickly see that you can have only two networks. With a block size of 64, you can have only four networks, and so on, all the way to having 64 networks if you use only block sizes of 4. Remember that this takes into account that you are using the command `ip subnet-zero` in your network design.

Now, just fill in the chart in the lower-left corner, and then add the subnets to the worksheet and you're good to go.

So let's take what we've learned so far about our block sizes and VLSM table and create a VLSM network using a Class C network address 192.168.10.0 for the network in Figure 5.4. Then fill out the VLSM table, as shown in Figure 5.5.

FIGURE 5.4 VLSM network example 1

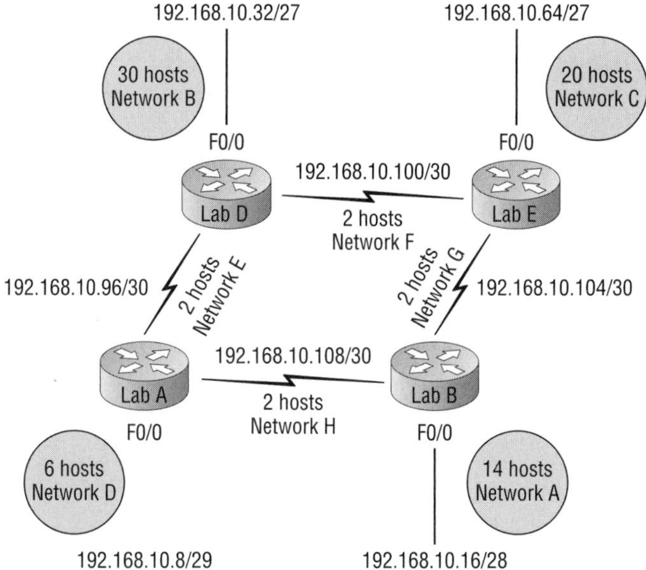

In Figure 5.4, we have four WAN links and four LANs connected together. We need to create a VLSM network that will allow us to save address space. Looks like we have two block sizes of 32, a block size of 16, and a block size of 8, and our WANs each have a block size of 4. Take a look and see how I filled out our VLSM chart in Figure 5.5.

We still have plenty of room for growth with this VLSM network design.

We never could accomplish that with one subnet mask using classful routing. Let's do another one. Figure 5.6 shows a network with 11 networks, two block sizes of 64, one of 32, five of 16, and three of 4.

First, create your VLSM table and use your block size chart to fill in the table with the subnets you need. Figure 5.7 shows a possible solution.

FIGURE 5.5 VLSM table example 1

Variable Length Subnet Masks Worksheet

Subnet	Mask	Subnets	Hosts	Block
/26	192	4	62	64
/27	224	8	30	32
/28	240	16	14	16
/29	248	32	6	8
/30	252	64	2	4

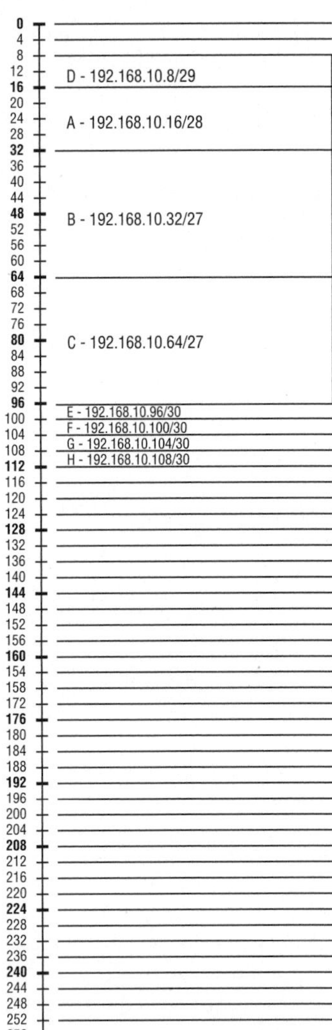

Class C Network 192.16.10.0

Network	Hosts	Block	Subnet	Mask
A	14	16	/28	240
B	30	32	/27	224
C	20	32	/27	224
D	6	8	/29	248
E	2	4	/30	252
F	2	4	/30	252
G	2	4	/30	252
H	2	4	/30	252

Notice that we filled in this entire chart and only have room for one more block size of 4! Only with a VLSM network can you provide this type of address space savings.

Keep in mind that it doesn't matter where you start your block sizes as long as you always count from zero. For example, if you had a block size of 16, you must start at 0 and count from there—0, 16, 32, 48, etc. You can't start a block size of 16 from, say, 40 or anything other than increments of 16.

FIGURE 5.6 VLSM network example 2

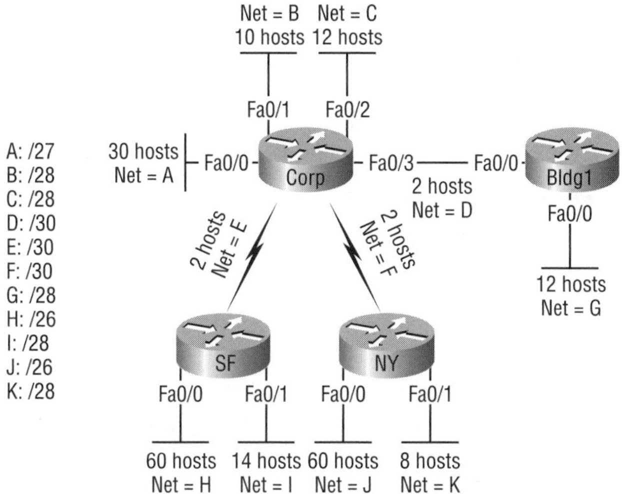

Here's another example. If you had block sizes of 32, you must start at zero like this: 0, 32, 64, 96, etc. Just remember that you don't get to start wherever you want; you must always start counting from zero. In the example in Figure 5.7, I started at 64 and 128, with my two block sizes of 64. I didn't have much choice because my options are 0, 64, 128, and 192. However, I added the block size of 32, 16, 8, and 4 wherever I wanted just as long as they were in the correct increments of that block size.

Okay—you have three locations you need to address, and the IP network you have received is 192.168.55.0 to use as the addressing for the entire network. You'll use `ip subnet-zero` and RIPv2 as the routing protocol. (RIPv2 supports VLSM networks, RIPv1 does not—both of them will be discussed in Chapter 8.) Figure 5.8 shows the network diagram and the IP address of the RouterA S0/0 interface.

From the list of IP addresses on the right of the figure, which IP address will be placed in each router's FastEthernet 0/0 interface and serial 0/1 of RouterB?

To answer this question, first look for clues in Figure 5.8. The first clue is that interface S0/0 on RouterA has IP address 192.168.55.2/30 assigned, which makes for an easy answer. A /30, as you know, is 255.255.255.252, which gives you a block size of 4. Your subnets are 0, 4, 8, etc. Since the known host has an IP address of 2, the only other valid host in the zero subnet is 1, so the third answer down is what you want for the S0/1 interface of RouterB.

The next clues are the listed number of hosts for each of the LANs. RouterA needs 7 hosts, a block size of 16 (/28); RouterB needs 90 hosts, a block size of 128 (/25); and RouterC needs 23 hosts, a block size of 32 (/27).

Figure 5.9 shows the answers to this question.

FIGURE 5.7 VLSM table example 2

Variable Length Subnet Masks Worksheet

Subnet	Mask	Subnets	Hosts	Block
/26	192	4	62	64
/27	224	8	30	32
/28	240	16	14	16
/29	248	32	6	8
/30	252	64	2	4

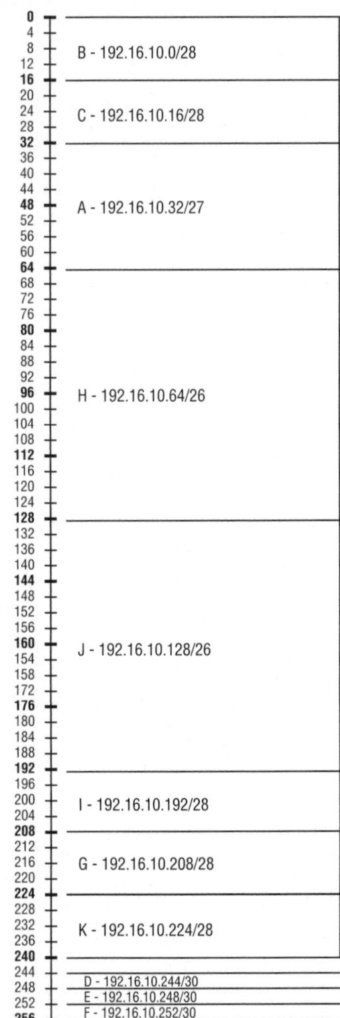

Class C Network 192.168.10.0

Network	Hosts	Block	Subnet	Mask
A	30	32	32	224
B	10	16	0	240
C	12	16	16	240
D	2	4	244	252
E	2	4	248	252
F	2	4	252	252
G	12	16	208	240
H	60	64	64	192
I	14	16	192	240
J	60	64	128	192
K	8	16	224	240

Once you figured out the block size needed for each LAN, this was actually a pretty simple question—all you need to do is look for the right clues and, of course, know your block sizes.

One last example of VLSM design before we move on to summarization. Figure 5.10 shows three routers, all running RIPv2. Which Class C addressing scheme would you use to satisfy the needs of this network yet save as much address space as possible?

FIGURE 5.8 VLSM design example 1

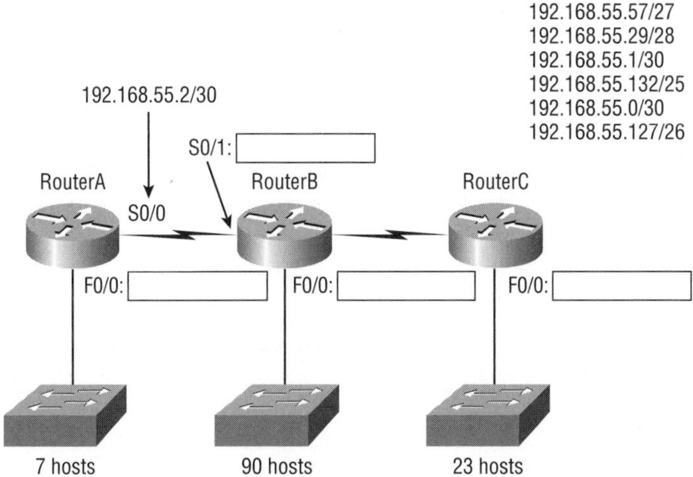

FIGURE 5.9 Solution to VLSM design example 1

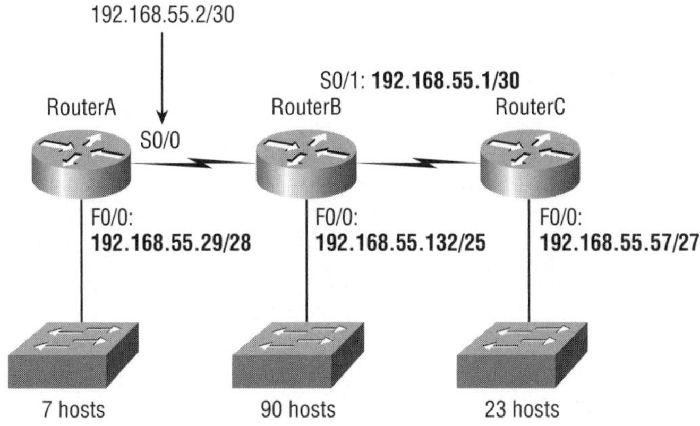

FIGURE 5.10 VLSM design example 2

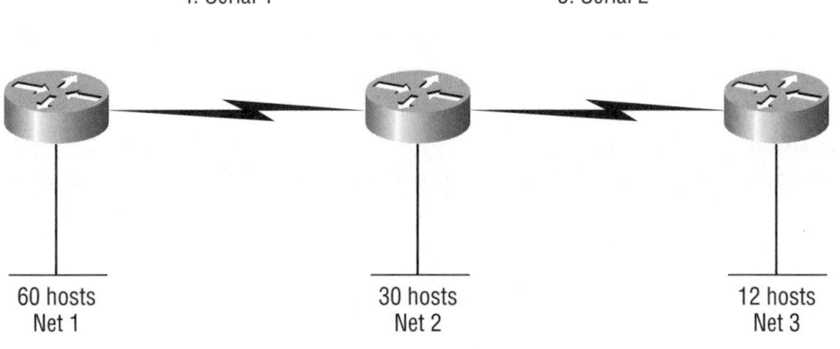

This is a really sweet network, just waiting for you to fill out the chart. There are block sizes of 64, 32, and 16 and two block sizes of 4. This should be a slam dunk for you. Take a look at my answer in Figure 5.11.

FIGURE 5.11 Solution to VLSM design example 2

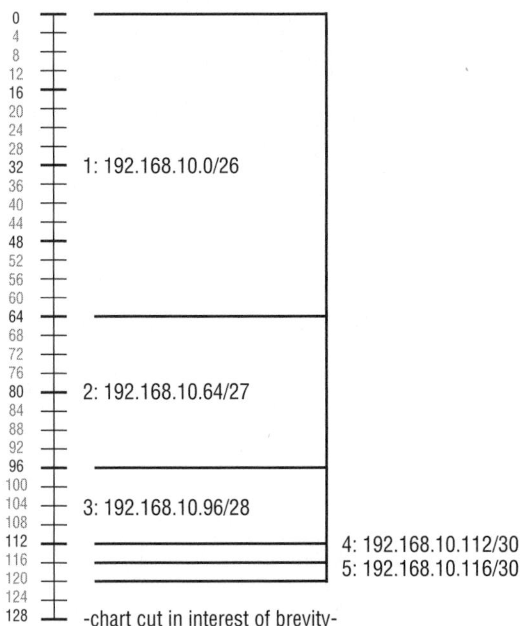

This is what I did: Starting at subnet 0, I used the block size of 64. (I didn't have to—I could have started with a block size of 4, but I usually like to start with the largest block size and move to the smallest.) Okay, then I added the block sizes of 32 and 16 and the two block sizes of 4. There's still a lot of room to add subnets to this network—very cool!

Summarization

Summarization, also called route aggregation, allows routing protocols to advertise many networks as one address. The purpose of this is to reduce the size of routing tables on routers to save memory, which also shortens the amount of time for IP to parse the routing table and find the path to a remote network.

Figure 5.12 shows how a summary address would be used in an internetwork.

FIGURE 5.12 Summary address used in an internetwork

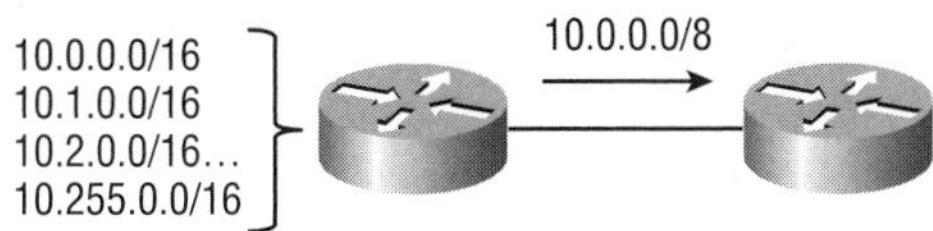

Summarization is actually somewhat simple because all you really need to have down are the block sizes that we just used to learn subnetting and VLSM design. For example, if you wanted to summarize the following networks into one network advertisement, you just have to find the block size first; then you can easily find your answer:

192.168.16.0 through network 192.168.31.0

What's the block size? There are exactly 16 Class C networks, so this neatly fits into a block size of 16.

Okay, now that you know the block size, you can find the network address and mask used to summarize these networks into one advertisement. The network address used to advertise the summary address is always the first network address in the block—in this example, 192.168.16.0. To figure out a summary mask, in this same example, what mask is used to get a block size of 16? Yes, 240 is correct. This 240 would be placed in the third octet—the octet where we are summarizing. So, the mask would be 255.255.240.0.

You'll learn how to apply these summary addresses to a router in Chapter 9.

Here's another example:

Networks 172.16.32.0 through 172.16.50.0

This is not as clean as the previous example because there are two possible answers, and here's why: Since you're starting at network 32, your options for block sizes are 4, 8, 16, 32, 64, etc., and block sizes of 16 and 32 could work as this summary address.

- *Answer #1:* If you used a block size of 16, then the network address is 172.16.32.0 with a mask of 255.255.240.0 (240 provides a block of 16). However, this only summarizes from 32 to 47, which means that networks 48 through 50 would be advertised as single networks. This is probably the best answer, but that depends on your network design. Let's look at the next answer.
- *Answer #2:* If you used a block size of 32, then your summary address would still be 172.16.32.0, but the mask would be 255.255.224.0 (224 provides a block of 32). The possible problem with this answer is that it will summarize networks 32 to 63 and we only have networks 32 to 50. No worries if you're planning on adding networks 51 to 63 later into the same network, but you could have serious problems in your internetwork if somehow networks 51 to 63 were to show up and be advertised from somewhere else in your network! This is the reason answer number one is the safest answer.

Let's take a look at another example, but let's look at it from a host's perspective.

Your summary address is 192.168.144.0/20—what's the range of host addresses that would be forwarded according to this summary? The /20 provides a summary address of 192.168.144.0 and mask of 255.255.240.0.

The third octet has a block size of 16, and starting at summary address 144, the next block of 16 is 160, so our network summary range is 144 to 159 in the third octet (again, you *must* be able to count in 16s!).

A router that has this summary address in the routing table will forward any packet with destination IP addresses of 192.168.144.1 through 192.168.159.254.

Only two more summarization examples, then we'll move on to troubleshooting.

In Figure 5.13, the Ethernet networks connected to router R1 are being summarized to R2 as 192.168.144.0/20. Which range of IP addresses will R2 forward to R1 according to this summary?

FIGURE 5.13 Summarization example 1

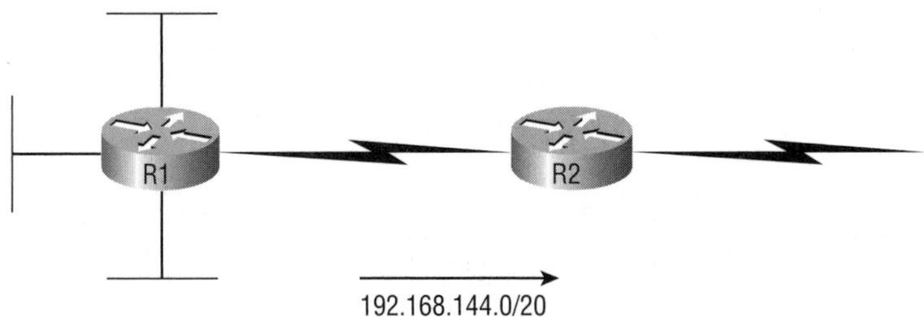
The Ethernet networks connected to router R1 are being summarized to R2 as 192.168.144.0/20.
Which IP addresses will R2 forward to R1 according to this summary?
R1
R2
192.168.144.0/20

No worries—this is really an easier question than it looks. The question actually has the summary address listed: 192.168.144.0/20. You already know that /20 is 255.255.240.0, which means you've got a block size of 16 in the third octet. Starting at 144 (this is also right there in the question), the next block size of 16 is 160, so you can't go above 159 in the third octet. The IP addresses that will be forwarded are 192.168.144.1 through 192.168.159.254.

Okay, last one. In Figure 5.14, there are five networks connected to router R1. What's the best summary address to R2?

FIGURE 5.14 Summarization example 2

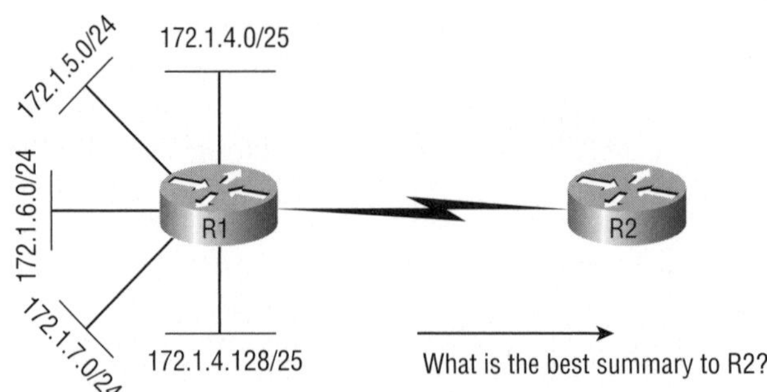
172.1.5.0/24
172.1.4.0/25
172.1.6.0/24
R1
R2
172.1.7.0/24
172.1.4.128/25
What is the best summary to R2?

I'm going to be honest—this is a much harder question than the one in Figure 5.13. You're going to have to look pretty hard to see the answer. The first thing to do with this is to write down all the networks and see if you can find anything in common with all six:

- 172.1.4.128/25
- 172.1.7.0/24
- 172.1.6.0/24
- 172.1.5.0/24
- 172.1.4.0/25

Do you see an octet that looks interesting to you? I do. It's the third octet. 4, 5, 6, 7, and yes, it's a block size of 4. So you can summarize 172.1.4.0 using a mask of 255.255.252.0, which means you will use a block size of 4 in the third octet. The IP addresses forwarded with this summary are 172.1.4.1 through 172.1.7.255.

Now to summarize this summarization section: Basically, if you've nailed down your block sizes, then finding and applying summary addresses and masks is actually fairly easy. But you're going to get bogged down pretty quickly if you don't know what a /20 is or if you can't count by 16s!

Troubleshooting IP Addressing

Troubleshooting IP addressing is obviously an important skill because running into trouble somewhere along the way is pretty much a sure thing, and it's going to happen to you. No—I'm not a pessimist; I'm just keeping it real. Because of this nasty fact, it will be great when you can save the day because you can both figure out (diagnose) the problem and fix it on an IP network whether you're at work or at home!

So this is where I'm going to show you the "Cisco way" of troubleshooting IP addressing. Let's use Figure 5.15 as an example of your basic IP trouble—poor Sally can't log in to the Windows server. Do you deal with this by calling the Microsoft team to tell them their server is a pile of junk and causing all your problems? Probably not such a great idea—let's first double-check our network instead.

Okay let's get started by going over the troubleshooting steps that Cisco follows. They're pretty simple, but important nonetheless. Pretend you're at a customer host and they're complaining that they can't communicate to a server that just happens to be on a remote network. Here are the four troubleshooting steps Cisco recommends:

1. Open a Command window and ping 127.0.0.1. This is the diagnostic, or loopback, address, and if you get a successful ping, your IP stack is considered to be initialized. If it fails, then you have an IP stack failure and need to reinstall TCP/IP on the host.

```
C:\>ping 127.0.0.1
Pinging 127.0.0.1 with 32 bytes of data:
Reply from 127.0.0.1: bytes=32 time<1ms TTL=128
```

```
Reply from 127.0.0.1: bytes=32 time<1ms TTL=128
Reply from 127.0.0.1: bytes=32 time<1ms TTL=128
Reply from 127.0.0.1: bytes=32 time<1ms TTL=128
Ping statistics for 127.0.0.1:
    Packets: Sent = 4, Received = 4, Lost = 0 (0% loss),
Approximate round trip times in milli-seconds:
    Minimum = 0ms, Maximum = 0ms, Average = 0ms
```

FIGURE 5.15 Basic IP troubleshooting

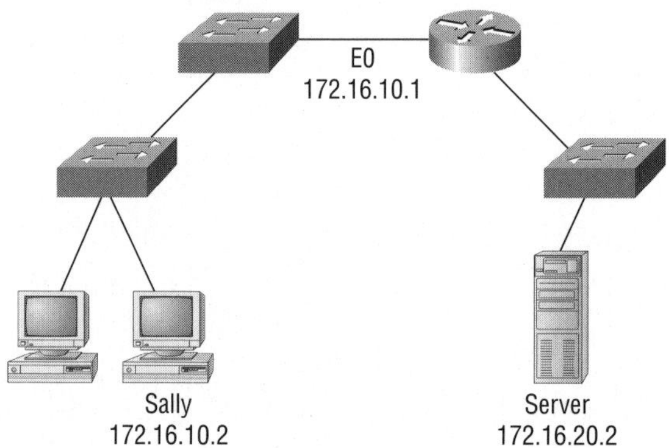

2. From the Command window, ping the IP address of the local host. If that's successful, your network interface card (NIC) is functioning. If it fails, there is a problem with the NIC. Success here doesn't just mean that a cable is plugged into the NIC, only that the IP protocol stack on the host can communicate to the NIC (via the LAN driver).

```
C:\>ping 172.16.10.2
Pinging 172.16.10.2 with 32 bytes of data:
Reply from 172.16.10.2: bytes=32 time<1ms TTL=128
Reply from 172.16.10.2: bytes=32 time<1ms TTL=128
Reply from 172.16.10.2: bytes=32 time<1ms TTL=128
Reply from 172.16.10.2: bytes=32 time<1ms TTL=128
Ping statistics for 172.16.10.2:
    Packets: Sent = 4, Received = 4, Lost = 0 (0% loss),
Approximate round trip times in milli-seconds:
    Minimum = 0ms, Maximum = 0ms, Average = 0ms
```

3. From the DOS window, ping the default gateway (router). If the ping works, it means that the NIC is plugged into the network and can communicate on the local network.

If it fails, you have a local physical network problem that could be anywhere from the NIC to the router.

```
C:\>ping 172.16.10.1
Pinging 172.16.10.1 with 32 bytes of data:
Reply from 172.16.10.1: bytes=32 time<1ms TTL=128
Reply from 172.16.10.1: bytes=32 time<1ms TTL=128
Reply from 172.16.10.1: bytes=32 time<1ms TTL=128
Reply from 172.16.10.1: bytes=32 time<1ms TTL=128
Ping statistics for 172.16.10.1:
    Packets: Sent = 4, Received = 4, Lost = 0 (0% loss),
Approximate round trip times in milli-seconds:
    Minimum = 0ms, Maximum = 0ms, Average = 0ms
```

4. If steps 1 through 3 were successful, try to ping the remote server. If that works, then you know that you have IP communication between the local host and the remote server. You also know that the remote physical network is working.

```
C:\>ping 172.16.20.2
Pinging 172.16.20.2 with 32 bytes of data:
Reply from 172.16.20.2: bytes=32 time<1ms TTL=128
Reply from 172.16.20.2: bytes=32 time<1ms TTL=128
Reply from 172.16.20.2: bytes=32 time<1ms TTL=128
Reply from 172.16.20.2: bytes=32 time<1ms TTL=128
Ping statistics for 172.16.20.2:
    Packets: Sent = 4, Received = 4, Lost = 0 (0% loss),
Approximate round trip times in milli-seconds:
    Minimum = 0ms, Maximum = 0ms, Average = 0ms
```

If the user still can't communicate with the server after steps 1 through 4 are successful, you probably have some type of name resolution problem and need to check your Domain Name System (DNS) settings. But if the ping to the remote server fails, then you know you have some type of remote physical network problem and need to go to the server and work through steps 1 through 3 until you find the snag.

Before we move on to determining IP address problems and how to fix them, I just want to mention some basic commands that you can use to help troubleshoot your network from both a PC and a Cisco router (the commands might do the same thing, but they are implemented differently).

Packet InterNet Groper (`ping`) Uses ICMP echo request and replies to test if a node IP stack is initialized and alive on the network.

`traceroute` Displays the list of routers on a path to a network destination by using TTL time-outs and ICMP error messages. This command will not work from a Command prompt.

`tracert` Same function as `traceroute`, but it's a Microsoft Windows command and will not work on a Cisco router.

`arp -a` Displays IP-to-MAC-address mappings on a Windows PC.

`show ip arp` Same function as `arp -a`, but displays the ARP table on a Cisco router. Like the commands traceroute and tracert, `arp -a` and show ip arp are not interchangeable through DOS and Cisco.

`ipconfig /all` Used only from a Command prompt, shows you the PC network configuration.

Once you've gone through all these steps and used the appropriate DOS commands, if necessary, what do you do if you find a problem? How do you go about fixing an IP address configuration error? Let's move on and discuss how to determine the IP address problems and how to fix them.

Determining IP Address Problems

It's common for a host, router, or other network device to be configured with the wrong IP address, subnet mask, or default gateway. Because this happens way too often, I'm going to teach you how to both determine and fix IP address configuration errors.

Once you've worked through the four basic steps of troubleshooting and determined there's a problem, you obviously then need to find and fix it. It really helps to draw out the network and IP addressing scheme. If it's already done, consider yourself lucky and go buy a lottery ticket because although it should be done, it rarely is. And if it is, it's usually outdated or inaccurate anyway. Typically it is not done, and you'll probably just have to bite the bullet and start from scratch.

I'll show you how to draw out your network using the Cisco Discovery Protocol (CDP) in Chapter 7, "Managing a Cisco Internetwork."

Once you have your network accurately drawn out, including the IP addressing scheme, you need to verify each host's IP address, mask, and default gateway address to determine the problem. (I'm assuming that you don't have a physical layer problem or that if you did, you've already fixed it.)

Let's check out the example illustrated in Figure 5.16. A user in the sales department calls and tells you that she can't get to ServerA in the marketing department. You ask her if she can get to ServerB in the marketing department, but she doesn't know because she doesn't have rights to log on to that server. What do you do?

You ask the client to go through the four troubleshooting steps that you learned about in the preceding section. Steps 1 through 3 work, but step 4 fails. By looking at the figure, can you determine the problem? Look for clues in the network drawing. First, the WAN link between the Lab_A router and the Lab_B router shows the mask as a /27. You should already know that this mask is 255.255.255.224 and then determine that all networks are using this mask. The network address is 192.168.1.0. What are our valid subnets and hosts?

256 – 224 = 32, so this makes our subnets 32, 64, 96, 128, etc. So, by looking at the figure, you can see that subnet 32 is being used by the sales department, the WAN link is using subnet 96, and the marketing department is using subnet 64.

FIGURE 5.16 IP address problem 1

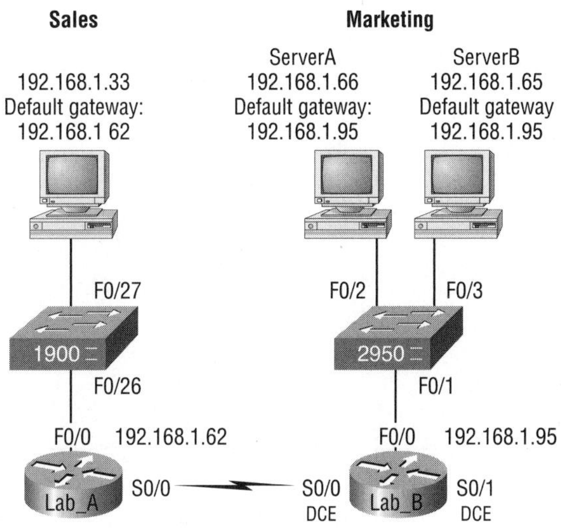

Now you've got to determine what the valid host ranges are for each subnet. From what you learned at the beginning of this chapter, you should now be able to easily determine the subnet address, broadcast addresses, and valid host ranges. The valid hosts for the Sales LAN are 33 through 62—the broadcast address is 63 because the next subnet is 64, right? For the Marketing LAN, the valid hosts are 65 through 94 (broadcast 95), and for the WAN link, 97 through 126 (broadcast 127). By looking at the figure, you can determine that the default gateway on the Lab_B router is incorrect. That address is the broadcast address of the 64 subnet, so there's no way it could be a valid host.

Did you get all that? Maybe we should try another one, just to make sure. Figure 5.17 shows a network problem. A user in the Sales LAN can't get to ServerB. You have the user run through the four basic troubleshooting steps and find that the host can communicate to the local network but not to the remote network. Find and define the IP addressing problem.

If you use the same steps used to solve the last problem, you can see first that the WAN link again provides the subnet mask to use— /29, or 255.255.255.248. Assuming classful addressing, you need to determine what the valid subnets, broadcast addresses, and valid host ranges are to solve this problem.

The 248 mask is a block size of 8 (256 – 248 = 8, as discussed in Chapter 4), so the subnets both start and increment in multiples of 8. By looking at the figure, you see that the Sales LAN is in the 24 subnet, the WAN is in the 40 subnet, and the Marketing LAN is in the 80 subnet. Can you see the problem yet? The valid host range for the Sales LAN is 25–30, and the configuration appears correct. The valid host range for the WAN link is 41–46, and this also appears correct. The valid host range for the 80 subnet is 81–86, with a broadcast address of 87 because the next subnet is 88. ServerB has been configured with the broadcast address of the subnet.

FIGURE 5.17 IP address problem 2

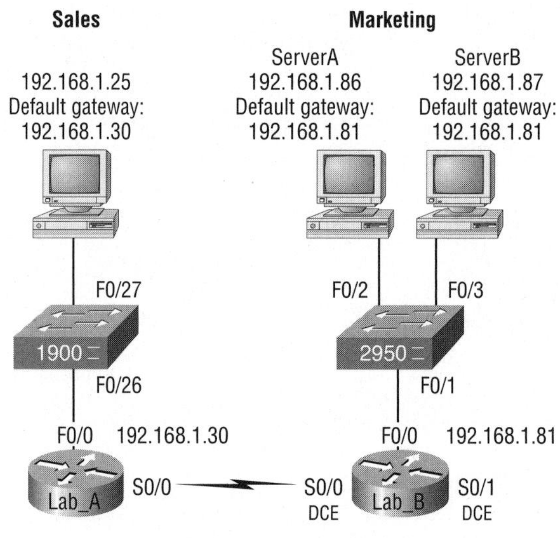

Okay, now that you can figure out misconfigured IP addresses on hosts, what do you do if a host doesn't have an IP address and you need to assign one? What you need to do is look at other hosts on the LAN and figure out the network, mask, and default gateway. Let's take a look at a couple of examples of how to find and apply valid IP addresses to hosts.

You need to assign a server and router IP addresses on a LAN. The subnet assigned on that segment is 192.168.20.24/29, and the router needs to be assigned the first usable address and the server the last valid host ID. What are the IP address, mask, and default gateway assigned to the server?

To answer this, you must know that a /29 is a 255.255.255.248 mask, which provides a block size of 8. The subnet is known as 24, the next subnet in a block of 8 is 32, so the broadcast address of the 24 subnet is 31, which makes the valid host range 25–30.

Server IP address: 192.168.20.30

Server mask: 255.255.255.248

Default gateway: 192.168.20.25 (router's IP address)

As another example, let's take a look at Figure 5.18 and solve this problem.

Look at the router's IP address on Ethernet0. What IP address, subnet mask, and valid host range could be assigned to the host?

FIGURE 5.18 Find the valid host #1.

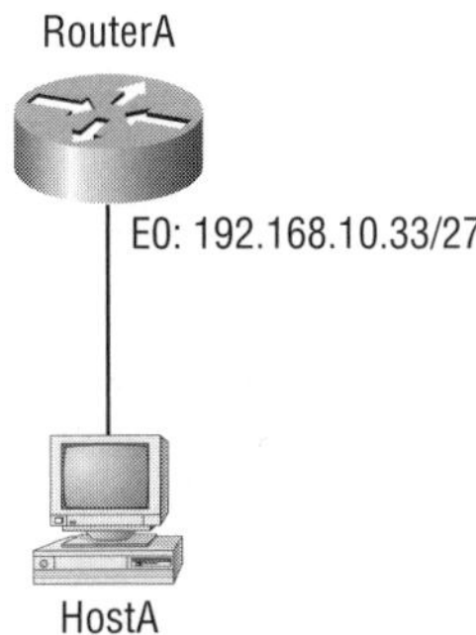

The IP address of the router's Ethernet0 is 192.168.10.33/27. As you already know, a /27 is a 224 mask with a block size of 32. The router's interface is in the 32 subnet. The next subnet is 64, so that makes the broadcast address of the 32 subnet 63 and the valid host range 33–62.

Host IP address: 192.168.10.34–62 (any address in the range except for 33, which is assigned to the router)

Mask: 255.255.255.224

Default gateway: 192.168.10.33

Figure 5.19 shows two routers with Ethernet configurations already assigned. What are the host addresses and subnet masks of hosts A and B?

FIGURE 5.19 Find the valid host #2.

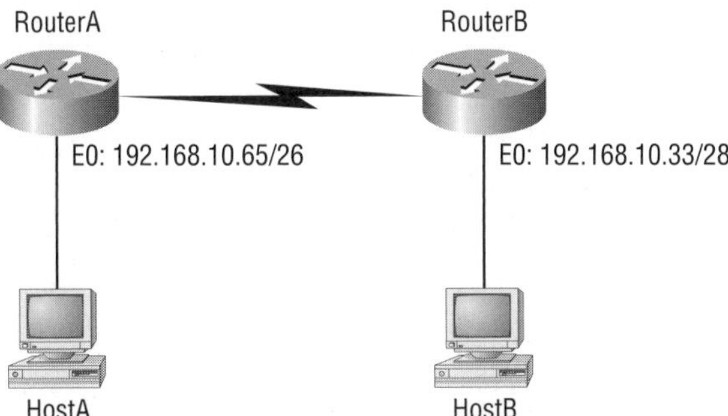

RouterA has an IP address of 192.168.10.65/26 and RouterB has an IP address of 192.168.10.33/28. What are the host configurations? RouterA Ethernet0 is in the 192.168.10.64 subnet and RouterB Ethernet0 is in the 192.168.10.32 network.

Host A IP address: 192.168.10.66–126

Host A mask: 255.255.255.192

Host A default gateway: 192.168.10.65

Host B IP address: 192.168.10.34–46

Host B mask: 255.255.255.240

Host B default gateway: 192.168.10.33

Just a couple more examples and then this chapter is history. Hang in there!

Figure 5.20 shows two routers; you need to configure the S0/0 interface on RouterA. The network assigned to the serial link is 172.16.17.0/22. What IP address can be assigned?

FIGURE 5.20 Find the valid host address #3.

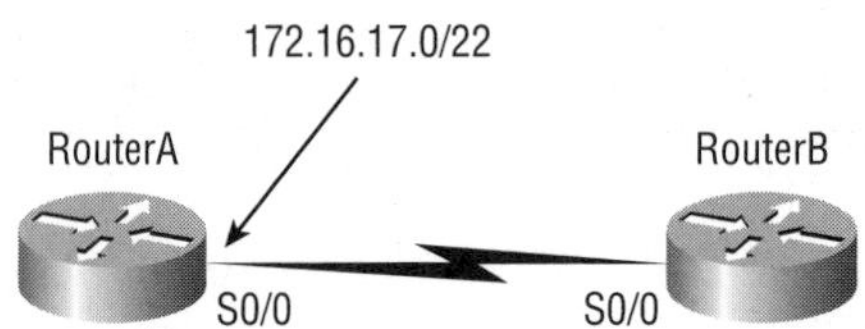

First, you must know that a /22 CIDR is 255.255.252.0, which makes a block size of 4 in the third octet. Since 17 is listed, the available range is 16.1 through 19.254; so, for example, the IP address S0/0 could be 172.16.18.255 since that's within the range.

Okay, last one! You have one Class C network ID and you need to provide one usable subnet per city while allowing enough usable host addresses for each city specified in Figure 5.21. What is your mask?

FIGURE 5.21 Find the valid subnet mask.

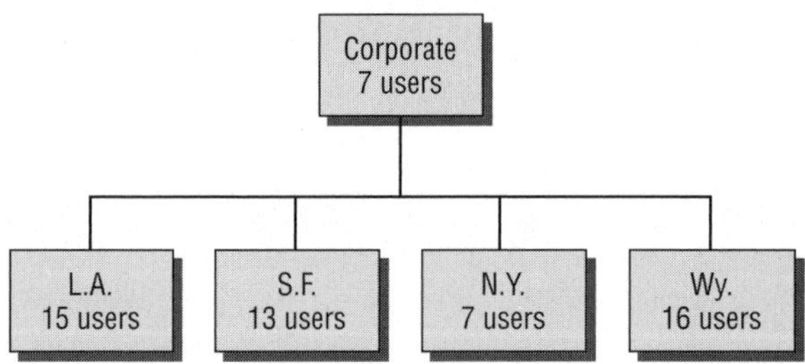

Actually, this is probably the easiest thing you've done all day! I count 5 subnets needed and the Wyoming office needs 16 users (always look for the network that needs the most hosts). What block size is needed for the Wyoming office? 32. (Remember, you cannot use a block size of 16 because you always have to subtract 2!) What mask provides you with a block size of 32? 224. Bingo! This provides 8 subnets, each with 30 hosts.

You're done, the diva has sung, the chicken has crossed the road…whew! Okay, take a good break (but skip the shot and the beer for now), then come back and go through the written lab and review questions.

Summary

Did you read Chapters 3, 4, and 5 and understand everything on the first pass? If so, that is fantastic—congratulations! The thing is, you probably got lost a couple of times—and as I already mentioned, that's what usually happens, so don't stress. Don't feel bad if you have to read each of these chapters more than once, or even 10 times, before you're truly good to go.

This chapter provided you with an important understanding of Variable Length Subnet Masks. You should also know how to design and implement simple VLSM networks and summarization.

You should also understand the Cisco troubleshooting methods. You must remember the four steps that Cisco recommends you take when trying to narrow down exactly where a network/IP addressing problem is and then know how to proceed systematically in order to fix it. In addition, you should be able to find valid IP addresses and subnet masks by looking at a network diagram.

Exam Essentials

Describe the benefits of Variable Length Subnet Masks (VLSMs). VLSMs enable the creation of subnets of specific sizes and allows the division of a classless network into smaller networks that do not need to be equal in size. This makes use of the address space more efficient as many times IP addresses are wasted with classful subnetting.

Understand the relationship between the subnet mask value and the resulting block size and the allowable IP addresses in each resulting subnet. The relationship between the classful network being subdivided and the subnet mask used determines the number of possible hosts or the block size. It also determines where each subnet begins and ends and which IP addresses cannot be assigned to a host within each subnet.

Describe the process of summarization or route aggregation and its relationship to subnetting. Summarization is the combining of subnets derived from a classful network for the purpose of advertising a single route to neighboring routers instead of multiple routes, reducing the size of routing tables and speeding the route process.

Calculate the summary mask that will advertise a single network representing all subnets. The network address used to advertise the summary address is always the first network address in the block of subnets. The mask is the subnet mask value that yields the same block size.

Remember the four diagnostic steps. The four simple steps that Cisco recommends for troubleshooting are ping the loopback address, ping the NIC, ping the default gateway, and ping the remote device.

Identify and mitigate an IP addressing problem. Once you go through the four troubleshooting steps that Cisco recommends, you must be able to determine the IP addressing problem by drawing out the network and finding the valid and invalid hosts addressed in your network.

Understand the troubleshooting tools that you can use from your host and a Cisco router. The `ping 127.0.0.1` command tests your local IP stack, and `tracert` is a Windows DOS command to track the path a packet takes through an internetwork to a destination. Cisco routers use the command `traceroute`, or just `trace` for short. Don't confuse the Windows and Cisco commands. Although they produce the same output, they don't work from the same prompts. The command `ipconfig /all` will display your PC network configuration from a DOS prompt, and `arp -a` (again from a DOS prompt) will display IP-to-MAC-address mapping on a Windows PC.

Written Lab 5

For each of the following sets of networks, determine the summary address and the mask to be used that will summarize the subnets.

1. 192.168.1.0/24 through 192.168.12.0/24
2. 172.144.0.0 through 172.159.0.0
3. 192.168.32.0 through 192.168.63.0
4. 192.168.96.0 through 192.168.111.0
5. 66.66.0.0 through 66.66.15.0
6. 192.168.1.0 through 192.168.120.0
7. 172.16.1.0 through 172.16.7.0
8. 192.168.128.0 through 192.168.190.0
9. 53.60.96.0 through 53.60.127.0
10. 172.16.10.0 through 172.16.63.0

(The answers to Written Lab 5 can be found following the answers to the review questions for this chapter.)

Review Questions

The following questions are designed to test your understanding of this chapter's material. For more information on how to get additional questions, please see this book's Introduction.

1. On a VLSM network, which mask should you use on point-to-point WAN links in order to reduce the waste of IP addresses?
   - **A.** /27
   - **B.** /28
   - **C.** /29
   - **D.** /30
   - **E.** /31
2. To test the IP stack on your local host, which IP address would you ping?
   - **A.** 127.0.0.0
   - **B.** 1.0.0.127
   - **C.** 127.0.0.1
   - **D.** 127.0.0.255
   - **E.** 255.255.255.255
3. What is the only connection type that supports the use of the /30 mask?
   - **A.** Point-to-multipoint
   - **B.** Point-to-point
   - **C.** Multipoint-to-multipoint
   - **D.** Host to switch
4. To use VLSM, what capability must the routing protocols in use possess?
   - **A.** Support for multicast
   - **B.** Multi-protocol support
   - **C.** Transmission of subnet mask information
   - **D.** Support for unequal load balancing
5. What is another term for *route aggregation*?
   - **A.** VLSM
   - **B.** Load balancing
   - **C.** Subnetting
   - **D.** Summarization

6. Which of the following is a result of route aggregation?
   A. Smaller routing tables
   B. More complete routing tables
   C. Increased memory usage
   D. Increased CPU usage
7. The network address used to advertise a summary address is always which of the following?
   A. The last network address in the block
   B. The next to last network in the block
   C. The second network in the block
   D. The first network in the block
8. When a ping to the loopback address fails, what can you assume?
   A. The IP address of the local host is incorrect.
   B. The IP address of the remote host is incorrect.
   C. The NIC is not functional.
   D. The IP stack has failed to initialize.
9. When a ping to the local host IP address fails, what can you assume?
   A. The IP address of the local host is incorrect.
   B. The IP address of the remote host is incorrect.
   C. The NIC is not functional.
   D. The IP stack has failed to initialize.
10. When a ping to the local host IP address succeeds but a ping to the default gateway IP address fails, what can you rule out? (Choose all that apply.)
    A. The IP address of the local host is incorrect.
    B. The IP address of the gateway is incorrect.
    C. The NIC is not functional.
    D. The IP stack has failed to initialize.
11. If a remote host can be pinged, what problems can you rule out?
    A. The IP address of the local host is incorrect.
    B. The IP address of the gateway is incorrect.
    C. The NIC is not functional.
    D. The IP stack has failed to initialize.
    E. All of the above.

12. What network service is the most likely problem if you can ping a computer by IP address but not by name?
    A. DNS
    B. DHCP
    C. ARP
    D. ICMP

13. When you issue the `ping` command, what protocol are you using?
    A. DNS
    B. DHCP
    C. ARP
    D. ICMP

14. Which of the following commands displays the networks traversed on a path to a network destination?
    A. `ping`
    B. `traceroute`
    C. `pingroute`
    D. `pathroute`

15. Which of the following commands uses ICMP echo requests and replies?
    A. `ping`
    B. `traceroute`
    C. `arp`
    D. `tracert`

16. What command is the Windows version of the Cisco command that displays the networks traversed on a path to a network destination?
    A. `ping`
    B. `traceroute`
    C. `arp`
    D. `tracert`

17. Which command displays IP-to-MAC-address mappings on a Windows PC?
    A. `ping`
    B. `traceroute`
    C. `arp -a`
    D. `tracert`

18. What command displays the ARP table on a Cisco router?

A. `show ip arp`

B. `traceroute`

C. `arp -a`

D. `tracert`

19. What switch must be added to the `ipconfig` command on a PC to verify DNS configuration?

A. `/dns`

B. `-dns`

C. `/all`

D. `-all`

20. Which of the following is the best summarization of the following networks: 192.168.128.0 through 192.168.159.0

A. 192.168.0.0/24

B. 192.168.128.0/16

C. 192.168.128.0/19

D. 192.168.128.0/20

Answers to Review Questions

1. D. A point-to-point link uses only two hosts. A /30, or 255.255.255.252, mask provides two hosts per subnet.
2. C. To test the local stack on your host, ping the loopback interface of 127.0.0.1.
3. B. The only connection type that supports the use of the /30 mask is point-to-point.
4. C. To use VLSM, the routing protocols in use possess the capability to transmit subnet mask information.
5. D. Another term for route aggregation is summarization.
6. A. Route aggregation results in smaller routing tables.
7. D. The network address used to advertise a summary address is always the first network in the block.
8. D. When a ping to the loopback address fails, you can assume the IP stack has failed to initialize.
9. C. When a ping to the local host IP address fails, you can assume the NIC is not functional.
10. C, D. If a ping to the local host succeeds, you can rule out IP stack or NIC failure.
11. E. If you can ping a remote host, everything is working locally.
12. A. The most likely problem if you can ping a computer by IP address but not by name is a failure of DNS.
13. D. When you issue the `ping` command, you are using the ICMP protocol.
14. B. The `traceroute` command displays the networks traversed on a path to a network destination.
15. A. The `ping` command uses ICMP echo requests and replies.
16. D. `tracert` is the Windows version of the Cisco command that displays the networks traversed on a path to a network destination.
17. C. The `arp -a` command displays IP-to-MAC-address mappings on a Windows PC.
18. A. The command that displays the ARP table on a Cisco router is `show ip arp`.
19. C. The `/all` switch must be added to the `ipconfig` command on a PC to verify DNS configuration.
20. C. If you start at 192.168.128.0 and go through 192.168.159.0, you can see this is a block of 32 in the third octet. Since the network address is always the first one in the range, the summary address is 192.168.128.0. What mask provides a block of 32 in the third octet?

    The answer is 255.255.224.0, or /19.

Answers to Written Lab 5

1. 192.168.0.0/20.
2. 172.144.0.0 255.240.0.0
3. 192.168.32.0 255.255.224.0
4. 192.168.96.0 255.255.240.0
5. 66.66.0.0 255.255.240.0
6. 192.168.0.0/25
7. 172.16.1.0 255.255.248.0
8. 192.168.128.0 255.255.192.0
9. 53.60.96.0 255.255.224.0
10. 172.16.0.0 255.255.192.0

Cisco's Internetworking Operating System (IOS)

THE CCNA EXAM TOPICS COVERED IN THIS CHAPTER INCLUDE THE FOLLOWING:

✓ **Implement an IP addressing scheme and IP Services to meet network requirements in a medium-size Enterprise branch office network**

- Configure, verify, and troubleshoot DHCP and DNS operation on a router (including CLI/SDM).
- Configure, verify, and troubleshoot basic router operation and routing on Cisco devices.
- Describe the operation of Cisco routers (including: router bootup process, POST, router components).
- Access and utilize the router to set basic parameters (including CLI/SDM).
- Connect, configure, and verify operation status of a device interface.
- Verify device configuration and network connectivity using ping, traceroute, telnet, SSH, or other utilities.
- Verify network connectivity (including: using ping, traceroute, and telnet or SSH).
- Troubleshoot routing issues.
- Verify router hardware and software operation using SHOW and DEBUG commands.

The time has come to introduce you to the Cisco Internetwork Operating System (IOS). The IOS is what runs Cisco routers as well as Cisco's switches, and it's what allows you to configure the devices as well.

So that's what you're going to learn about in this chapter. I'm going to show you how to configure a Cisco IOS router using the Cisco IOS command-line interface (CLI). When you become proficient with this interface, you'll be able to configure hostnames, banners, passwords, and more as well as troubleshoot using the Cisco IOS.

I'm also going to get you up to speed on the vital basics of router configurations and command verifications. Here's a list of the subjects we'll be covering in this chapter:

- Understanding and configuring the Cisco Internetwork Operating System (IOS)
- Connecting to a router
- Bringing up a router
- Logging into a router
- Understanding the router prompts
- Understanding the CLI prompts
- Performing editing and help features
- Gathering basic routing information
- Setting administrative functions
- Setting hostnames
- Setting banners
- Setting passwords
- Setting interface descriptions
- Performing interface configurations

- Viewing, saving, and erasing configurations
- Verifying routing configurations

And just as it was with preceding chapters, the fundamentals that you'll learn in this chapter are foundational building blocks that really need to be in place before you go on to the next chapters in the book.

For up-to-the-minute updates for this chapter, please see `www.lammle.com` or `www.sybex.com/go/ccna7e`.

The IOS User Interface

The *Cisco Internetwork Operating System (IOS)* is the kernel of Cisco routers and most switches. In case you didn't know, a kernel is the basic, indispensable part of an operating system that allocates resources and manages things such as low-level hardware interfaces and security.

In the following sections, I'll show you the Cisco IOS and how to configure a Cisco router using the command-line interface (CLI).

I'm going to save Cisco switch configurations for Chapter 10, "Layer 2 Switching and Spanning Tree Protocol (STP)."

Cisco Router IOS

The Cisco IOS is a proprietary kernel that provides routing, switching, internetworking, and telecommunications features. The first IOS was written by William Yeager in 1986, and it enabled networked applications. It runs on most Cisco routers as well as an ever-increasing number of Cisco Catalyst switches, like the Catalyst 2960 and 3560 series switches.

These are some important things that the Cisco router IOS software is responsible for:

- Carrying network protocols and functions
- Connecting high-speed traffic between devices
- Adding security to control access and stop unauthorized network use
- Providing scalability for ease of network growth and redundancy
- Supplying network reliability for connecting to network resources

You can access the Cisco IOS through the console port of a router, from a modem into the auxiliary (or Aux) port, or even through Telnet. Access to the IOS command line is called an *EXEC session*.

Connecting to a Cisco Router

You can connect to a Cisco router to configure it, verify its configuration, and check statistics. There are different ways to do this, but most often, the first place you would connect to is the console port. The *console port* is usually an RJ-45 (8-pin modular) connection located at the back of the router—by default, there may or may not be a password set. The new ISR routers use *cisco* as the username and *cisco* as the password by default.

See Chapter 2, "Review of Ethernet Networking and Data Encapsulation," for an explanation of how to configure a PC to connect to a router console port.

You can also connect to a Cisco router through an *auxiliary port*—which is really the same thing as a console port, so it follows that you can use it as one. But an auxiliary port also allows you to configure modem commands so that a modem can be connected to the router. This is a cool feature—it lets you dial up a remote router and attach to the auxiliary port if the router is down and you need to configure it *out-of-band* (meaning from outside of the network).

The third way to connect to a Cisco router is in-band, through the program *Telnet*. (*In-band* means configuring the router through the network, the opposite of *out-of-band*.) Telnet is a terminal emulation program that acts as though it's a dumb terminal. You can use Telnet to connect to any active interface on a router, such as an Ethernet or serial port. I'll discuss something called Secure Shell (SSH) later in this chapter, which is a more secure way to connect in-band through the network.

Figure 6.1 shows an illustration of a Cisco 2600 series modular router, which is a cut above routers populating the 2500 series because it has a faster processor and can handle many more interfaces. Both the 2500 and 2600 series routers are end of life (EOL), and you can only buy them used. However, many 2600 series routers are still found in production, so it's important to understand them. Pay close attention to all the different kinds of interfaces and connections.

FIGURE 6.1 A Cisco 2600 router

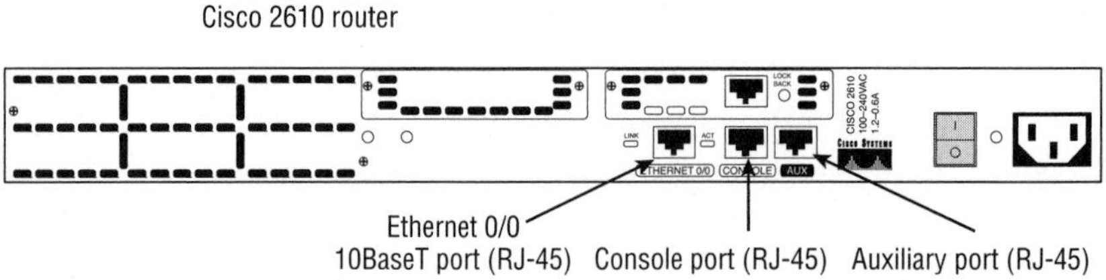

Cisco 2610 router

Ethernet 0/0
10BaseT port (RJ-45)
Console port (RJ-45)
Auxiliary port (RJ-45)

The 2600 series router can have multiple serial interfaces, which can be used for connecting a T1 using a serial V.35 WAN connection. Multiple Ethernet or FastEthernet ports can be used on the router, depending on the model. This router also has one console and one auxiliary connection via RJ-45 connectors.

Another router I want to talk about is the 2800 series (shown in Figure 6.2). This router has replaced the 2600 series router and is referred to as an Integrated Services Router (ISR) but yet again has been updated to the 2900 since my previous edition of this book. The ISR series gets its name because many of the services, like security, are built into it. It's a modular device like the 2600, but it's much faster and a lot more sleek—it's elegantly designed to support a broad new range of interface options.

FIGURE 6.2 A Cisco 2800 router

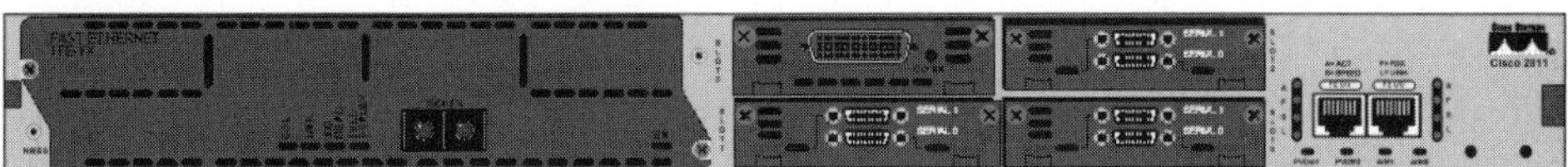

You need to keep in mind that for the most part, you get some serious bang for your buck with the 2800/2900—unless you start adding a lot of interfaces to it. You've got to pony up for each one of those little beauties, and things can really start to add up—fast!

There are a couple of other series of routers that are less expensive than the 2800 series: the 1800/1900 and 800/900 series. You may want to look into these routers if you're looking for a less-expensive alternative to the 2800/2900 but still want to run the same IOS.

Figure 6.3 shows an 1841 router that holds most of the same interfaces as the 2800, but it's smaller and less expensive. The real reason you would opt for a 2800/2900 instead of an 1800/1900 series router comes down to the more advanced interfaces you can run on the 2800/2900—things like the wireless controller and switching modules.

FIGURE 6.3 A Cisco 1841 router

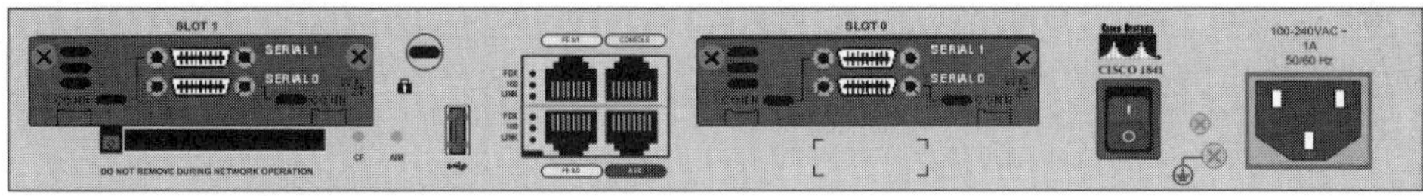

As a heads up, I'm going to be using mostly 2800, 1800, and 800 series routers throughout this book to demonstrate examples of router configurations. But understand that you can use the 2600 and even the older 2500 routers to practice routing principles.

You can find more information about all Cisco routers at `www.cisco.com/en/US/products/hw/routers/index.html`.

Bringing Up a Router

When you first bring up a Cisco router, it will run a power-on self-test (POST). If it passes, it will then look for and load the Cisco IOS from flash memory—if an IOS file is present and expands it into RAM. (Just in case you don't know, flash memory is electronically erasable programmable read-only memory—an EEPROM.) After that, the IOS loads and looks for a valid configuration—the startup-config—that's stored in nonvolatile RAM, or NVRAM.

The following messages appear when you first boot or reload a router (I am using my 2811 router):

```
System Bootstrap, Version 12.4(13r)T, RELEASE SOFTWARE (fc1)
Technical Support: http://www.cisco.com/techsupport
Copyright (c) 2006 by cisco Systems, Inc.
Initializing memory for ECC
c2811 platform with 262144 Kbytes of main memory
Main memory is configured to 64 bit mode with ECC enabled
Upgrade ROMMON initialized
program load complete, entry point: 0x8000f000, size: 0xcb80
program load complete, entry point: 0x8000f000, size: 0xcb80
```

This is the first part of the router boot process output. It's information about the bootstrap program that first runs the POST. It then tells the router how to load, which by default is to find the IOS in flash memory. It also lists the amount of RAM in the router.

The next part shows us that the IOS is being decompressed into RAM:

```
program load complete, entry point: 0x8000f000, size: 0x14b45f8
Self decompressing the image :
   ####################################################################
   ############################################ [OK]
```

The pound signs are telling us that the IOS is being decompressed into RAM. After it is decompressed into RAM, the IOS is loaded and starts running the router, as shown below. Notice that the IOS version is stated as advanced security version 12.4(12):

```
[some output cut]
Cisco IOS Software, 2800 Software (C2800NM-ADVSECURITYK9-M), Version
   12.4(12), RELEASE SOFTWARE (fc1)
Technical Support: http://www.cisco.com/techsupport
Copyright (c) 1986-2006 by Cisco Systems, Inc.
Compiled Fri 17-Nov-06 12:02 by prod_rel_team
Image text-base: 0x40093160, data-base: 0x41AA0000
```

A sweet new feature of the new ISR routers is that the IOS name is no longer cryptic. The filename actually tells you what the IOS can do, as in Advanced Security. Once the

IOS is loaded, the information learned from the POST will be displayed next, as you can see here:

```
[some output cut]
Cisco 2811 (revision 49.46) with 249856K/12288K bytes of memory.
Processor board ID FTX1049A1AB
2 FastEthernet interfaces
4 Serial(sync/async) interfaces
1 Virtual Private Network (VPN) Module
DRAM configuration is 64 bits wide with parity enabled.
239K bytes of non-volatile configuration memory.
62720K bytes of ATA CompactFlash (Read/Write)
```

There are two FastEthernet interfaces, four serial interfaces, plus a VPN module. The amount of RAM, NVRAM, and flash are also displayed. The above router output shows us that there's 256MB of RAM, 239K of NVRAM, and 64MB of flash.

When the IOS is loaded and up and running, a preconfiguration (called startup-config) will be copied from NVRAM into RAM. The copy of this file will be placed in RAM and is called running-config.

My 1841 and 871W routers boot exactly the same as the 2811 router. The 1841 and 871W do show less memory and different interfaces, but other than that, they have the same bootup procedure and the same preconfigured startup-config file.

Bringing Up a Non-ISR Router (a 2600 For Example)

As you're about to see, the boot cycle is about the same for non-ISR routers as for the ISR routers. The following messages appear when you first boot or reload a 2600 router:

```
System Bootstrap, Version 11.3(2)XA4, RELEASE SOFTWARE (fc1)
Copyright (c) 1999 by cisco Systems, Inc.
TAC:Home:SW:IOS:Specials for info
C2600 platform with 65536 Kbytes of main memory
```

The next part shows us that the IOS is being decompressed into RAM:

```
program load complete, entry point:0x80008000, size:0x43b7fc
Self decompressing the image :
#######################################################
#######################################################
#######################################################
#######################################################
```

```
#######################################################
#######################################################
######################################################################## [OK]
```

So far, everything is pretty much the same. Notice below that the IOS version is stated as version 12.3(20):

```
Cisco Internetwork Operating System Software
IOS (tm) C2600 Software (C2600-IK9O3S3-M), Version 12.3(20), RELEASE
   SOFTWARE (fc2)
Technical Support: http://www.cisco.com/techsupport
Copyright (c) 1986-2006 by cisco Systems, Inc.
Compiled Tue 08-Aug-06 20:50 by kesnyder
Image text-base: 0x80008098, data-base: 0x81A0E7A8
```

Just as with the 2800 series, once the IOS is loaded, the information learned from the POST will be displayed:

```
cisco 2610 (MPC860) processor (revision 0x202) with 61440K/4096K bytes
   of memory.
Processor board ID JAD03348593 (1529298102)
M860 processor: part number 0, mask 49
Bridging software.
X.25 software, Version 3.0.0.
1 Ethernet/IEEE 802.3 interface(s)
1 Serial network interface(s)
2 Serial(sync/async) network interface(s)
32K bytes of non-volatile configuration memory.
16384K bytes of processor board System flash (Read/Write)
```

Okay—finally what we see here is one Ethernet interface and three serial interfaces. The amount of RAM and flash is also displayed, and the above router output shows there are 64 MB of RAM and 16 MB of flash.

And as I mentioned, when the IOS is loaded and up and running, a valid configuration called the startup-config will be loaded from NVRAM. But here's where it differs from the default bootup of the ISR routers—if there isn't a configuration in NVRAM, the router will broadcast looking for a valid one on a TFTP host. (This can only happen if the router senses carrier detect, or CD, on any interface.) If the broadcast fails, it will then go into what is called *setup mode*—a step-by-step process to help you configure the router. So you need to remember that if you plug any interface of your router into your network and then boot your router, you may have to wait a couple minutes while the router searches for the configuration.

You can also enter setup mode at any time from the command line by typing the command **setup** from something called privileged mode, which I'll get to in a minute. Setup mode covers only some commands and is generally just unhelpful. Here is an example:

```
Would you like to enter the initial configuration dialog? [yes/no]: y

At any point you may enter a question mark '?' for help.
Use ctrl-c to abort configuration dialog at any prompt.
Default settings are in square brackets '[]'.

Basic management setup configures only enough connectivity
for management of the system, extended setup will ask you
to configure each interface on the system

Would you like to enter basic management setup? [yes/no]: y
Configuring global parameters:

  Enter host name [Router]: Ctrl+C
Configuration aborted, no changes made.
```

You can exit setup mode at any time by pressing Ctrl+C.

I highly recommend going through setup mode once, then never again. You should always use the CLI.

Command-Line Interface (CLI)

I sometimes refer to the CLI as "Cash Line Interface" because if you can create advanced configurations on Cisco routers and switches using the CLI, then you'll get the cash!

Entering the CLI

After the interface status messages appear and you press Enter, the `Router>` prompt will appear. This is called *user exec mode* (user mode), and it's mostly used to view statistics, but it's also a stepping stone to logging in to privileged mode.

You can only view and change the configuration of a Cisco router in *privileged exec mode* (privileged mode), which you can enter with the `enable` command.

Here's how:

```
Router>enable
Router#
```

You now end up with a Router# prompt, which indicates that you're in *privileged mode*, where you can both view and change the router's configuration. You can go back from privileged mode into user mode by using the disable command, as seen here:

```
Router#disable
Router>
```

At this point, you can type **logout** from either mode to exit the console:

```
Router>logout

Router con0 is now available
Press RETURN to get started.
```

In the following sections, I am going to show you how to perform some basic administrative configurations.

Overview of Router Modes

To configure from a CLI, you can make global changes to the router by typing configure terminal (or config t for short), which puts you in global configuration mode and changes what's known as the running-config. A global command (a command run from global config) is set only once and affects the entire router.

You can type config from the privileged-mode prompt and then just press Enter to take the default of terminal, as seen here:

```
Router#config
Configuring from terminal, memory, or network [terminal]? [press enter]
Enter configuration commands, one per line.  End with CNTL/Z.
Router(config)#
```

At this point, you make changes that affect the router as a whole (globally), hence the term *global configuration mode*. To change the running-config—the current configuration running in dynamic RAM (DRAM)—you use the configure terminal command, as I just demonstrated.

Here are some of the other options under the configure command:

```
Router(config)#exit or press cntl-z
Router#config ?
  memory             Configure from NV memory
  network            Configure from a TFTP network host
  overwrite-network  Overwrite NV memory from TFTP network host
  terminal           Configure from the terminal
  <cr>
```

We'll go through these commands in Chapter 7.

CLI Prompts

It's really important that you understand the different prompts you can find when configuring a router. Knowing these well will help you navigate and recognize where you are at any time within configuration mode. In the following sections, I'm going to demonstrate the prompts that are used on a Cisco router and discuss the various terms used. (Always check your prompts before making any changes to a router's configuration!)

I'm not going into every different command prompt offered because doing that would be reaching beyond the scope of this book. Instead, I'm going to describe all the different prompts you'll see throughout this chapter and the rest of the book. These command prompts really are the ones you'll use most in real life anyway; plus, they're the ones you'll need to know for the exam.

Don't freak! It's not important that you understand what each of these command prompts accomplishes yet because I'm going to completely fill you in on all of them really soon. So right now, just relax and focus on becoming familiar with the different prompts available and all will be well!

Interfaces

To make changes to an interface, you use the `interface` command from global configuration mode:

```
Router(config)#interface ?
  Async              Async interface
  BVI                Bridge-Group Virtual Interface
  CDMA-Ix            CDMA Ix interface
  CTunnel            CTunnel interface
  Dialer             Dialer interface
  FastEthernet       FastEthernet IEEE 802.3
  Group-Async        Async Group interface
  Lex                Lex interface
  Loopback           Loopback interface
  MFR                Multilink Frame Relay bundle interface
  Multilink          Multilink-group interface
  Null               Null interface
  Port-channel       Ethernet Channel of interfaces
  Serial             Serial
  Tunnel             Tunnel interface
  Vif                PGM Multicast Host interface
  Virtual-PPP        Virtual PPP interface
  Virtual-Template   Virtual Template interface
```

```
  Virtual-TokenRing  Virtual TokenRing
  range              interface range command
Router(config)#interface fastEthernet 0/0
Router(config-if)#
```

Did you notice that the prompt changed to `Router(config-if)#`? This tells you that you're in *interface configuration mode*. And wouldn't it be nice if the prompt also gave you an indication of what interface you were configuring? Well, at least for now we'll have to live without the prompt information, because it doesn't. One thing is for sure: You really have to pay attention when configuring a router!

Subinterfaces

Subinterfaces allow you to create logical interfaces within the router. The prompt then changes to `Router(config-subif)#`:

```
Router(config-if)#interface f0/0.1
Router(config-subif)#
```

You can read more about subinterfaces in Chapter 11, "Virtual LANs (VLANS)" and Chapter 16, "Wide Area Networks," but don't skip ahead just yet!

Line Commands

To configure user-mode passwords, use the `line` command. The prompt then becomes `Router(config-line)#`:

```
Router#config t
Enter configuration commands, one per line.  End with CNTL/Z.
Router(config)#line ?
  <0-337>  First Line number
  aux      Auxiliary line
  console  Primary terminal line
  tty      Terminal controller
  vty      Virtual terminal
```

The `line console 0` command is known as a major command (also called a *global command*), and any command typed from the `(config-line)` prompt is known as a subcommand.

Routing Protocol Configurations

To configure routing protocols such as RIP and EIGRP, you'll need to get to the prompt `Router(config-router#)`:

```
Router#config t
Enter configuration commands, one per line.  End with CNTL/Z.
```

```
Router(config)#router rip
Router(config-router)#version 2
Router(config-router)#
```

Defining Router Terms

Table 6.1 defines some of the terms we've used so far.

TABLE 6.1 Router terms

Mode	Definition
User EXEC mode	Limited to basic monitoring commands
Privileged EXEC mode	Provides access to all other router commands
Global configuration mode	Commands that affect the entire system
Specific configuration modes	Commands that affect interfaces/processes only
Setup mode	Interactive configuration dialog

Editing and Help Features

You can use the Cisco advanced editing features to help you configure your router. If you type in a question mark (?) at any prompt, you'll be given a list of all the commands available from that prompt:

```
Router#?
Exec commands:
  access-enable     Create a temporary Access-List entry
  access-profile    Apply user-profile to interface
  access-template   Create a temporary Access-List entry
  archive           manage archive files
  auto              Exec level Automation
  bfe               For manual emergency modes setting
  calendar          Manage the hardware calendar
  cd                Change current directory
  clear             Reset functions
  clock             Manage the system clock
  cns               CNS agents
```

```
  configure        Enter configuration mode
  connect          Open a terminal connection
  copy             Copy from one file to another
  crypto           Encryption related commands.
  ct-isdn          Run an ISDN component test command
  debug            Debugging functions (see also 'undebug')
  delete           Delete a file
  dir              List files on a filesystem
  disable          Turn off privileged commands
  disconnect       Disconnect an existing network connection
 --More--
```

Plus, at this point you can press the spacebar to get another page of information, or you can press Enter to go one command at a time. You can also press Q (or any other key, for that matter) to quit and return to the prompt.

Here's a shortcut: To find commands that start with a certain letter, use the letter and the question mark with no space between them:

```
Router#c?
calendar  cd         clear    clock
cns       configure  connect  copy
crypto    ct-isdn

Router#c
```

By typing **c?**, we received a response listing all the commands that start with *c*. Also notice that the Router#c prompt reappears after the list of commands is displayed. This can be helpful when you have long commands and need the next possible command. It would be pretty lame if you had to retype the entire command every time you used a question mark!

To find the next command in a string, type the first command and then a question mark:

```
Router#clock ?
  read-calendar    Read the hardware calendar into the clock
  set              Set the time and date
  update-calendar  Update the hardware calendar from the clock
Router#clock set ?
  hh:mm:ss  Current Time
Router#clock set 11:15:11 ?
  <1-31>  Day of the month
  MONTH   Month of the year
Router#clock set 11:15:11 25 april ?
  <1993-2035>  Year
```

```
Router#clock set 11:15:11 25 april 2011 ?
  <cr>
Router#clock set 11:15:11 25 april 2011
*April 25 11:15:11.000: %SYS-6-CLOCKUPDATE: System clock has been
updated from 18:52:53 UTC Wed Feb 28 2011 to 11:15:11 UTC Sat April 25 2011,
configured from console by cisco on console.
```

By typing the **clock ?** command, you'll get a list of the next possible parameters and what they do. Notice that you should just keep typing a command, a space, and then a question mark until <cr> (carriage return) is your only option.

If you're typing commands and receive

```
Router#clock set 11:15:11
% Incomplete command.
```

you'll know that the command string isn't done yet. Just press the up arrow key to redisplay the last command entered, and then continue with the command by using your question mark.

And if you receive the error

```
Router(config)#access-list 110 permit host 1.1.1.1
                                      ^
% Invalid input detected at '^' marker.
```

you've entered a command incorrectly. See that little caret—the ^? It's a very helpful tool that marks the exact point where you blew it and entered the command incorrectly. Here's another example of when you'll see the caret:

```
Router#sh serial 0/0/0
             ^
% Invalid input detected at '^' marker.
```

This command looks right, but be careful! The problem is that the full command is `show interface serial 0/0/0`.

Now if you receive the error

```
Router#sh ru
% Ambiguous command:  "sh ru"
```

it means there are multiple commands that begin with the string you entered and it's not unique. Use the question mark to find the command you need:

```
Router#sh ru?
rudpv1  running-config
```

As you can see, there are two commands that start with `show ru`.

Table 6.2 lists the enhanced editing commands available on a Cisco router.

TABLE 6.2 Enhanced editing commands

Command	Meaning
Ctrl+A	Moves your cursor to the beginning of the line
Ctrl+E	Moves your cursor to the end of the line
Esc+B	Moves back one word
Ctrl+B	Moves back one character
Ctrl+F	Moves forward one character
Esc+F	Moves forward one word
Ctrl+D	Deletes a single character
Backspace	Deletes a single character
Ctrl+R	Redisplays a line
Ctrl+U	Erases a line
Ctrl+W	Erases a word
Ctrl+Z	Ends configuration mode and returns to EXEC
Tab	Finishes typing a command for you

Another cool editing feature I want to show you is the automatic scrolling of long lines. In the following example, the command typed had reached the right margin and automatically moved 11 spaces to the left (the dollar sign [$] indicates that the line has been scrolled to the left):

```
Router#config t
Enter configuration commands, one per line. End with CNTL/Z.
Router(config)#$110 permit host 171.10.10.10 0.0.0.0 eq 23
```

You can review the router-command history with the commands shown in Table 6.3.

TABLE 6.3 Router-command history

Command	Meaning
Ctrl+P or up arrow	Shows last command entered
Ctrl+N or down arrow	Shows previous commands entered
`show history`	Shows last 20 commands entered by default
`show terminal`	Shows terminal configurations and history buffer size
`terminal history size`	Changes buffer size (max 256)

The following example demonstrates the `show history` command and how to change the history size as well as how to verify it with the `show terminal` command. First, use the `show history` command to see the last 20 commands that were entered on the router, although my router only has 10 commands shown here:

```
Router#show history
 en
 sh history
 show terminal
 sh cdp neig
 sh ver
 sh flash
 sh int fa0
 sh history
 sh int s0/0
 sh int s0/1
```

Now use the `show terminal` command to verify the terminal history size:

```
Router#show terminal
Line 0, Location: "", Type: ""
[output cut]
Modem type is unknown.
Session limit is not set.
Time since activation: 00:21:41
Editing is enabled.
History is enabled, history size is 20.
```

```
DNS resolution in show commands is enabled
Full user help is disabled
Allowed input transports are none.
Allowed output transports are pad telnet rlogin lapb-ta mop v120 ssh.
Preferred transport is telnet.
No output characters are padded
No special data dispatching characters
```

The `terminal history size` command, used from privileged mode, can change the size of the history buffer:

```
Router#terminal history size ?
 <0-256> Size of history buffer
Router#terminal history size 25
```

You verify the change with the `show terminal` command:

```
Router#show terminal
Line 0, Location: "", Type: ""
[output cut]
Editing is enabled.
History is enabled, history size is 25.
Full user help is disabled
Allowed transports are lat pad v120 telnet mop rlogin
  nasi. Preferred is lat.
No output characters are padded
No special data dispatching characters
Group codes:  0
```

When Do You Use the Cisco Editing Features?

A couple of editing features are used quite often and some not so much, if at all. Understand that Cisco didn't make these up; these are just old Unix commands. However, Ctrl+A is really helpful to negate a command.

For example, if you were to put in a long command and then decide you didn't want to use that command in your configuration after all, or if it didn't work, then you could just press your up arrow key to show the last command entered, press Ctrl+A, type **no** and then a space, press Enter—and poof! The command is negated. This doesn't work on every command, but it works on a lot of them.

Gathering Basic Routing Information

The `show version` command will provide basic configuration for the system hardware as well as the software version and the boot images. Here's an example:

```
Router#show version
Cisco IOS Software, 2800 Software (C2800NM-ADVSECURITYK9-M), Version
   12.4(12), RELEASE SOFTWARE (fc1)
Technical Support: http://www.cisco.com/techsupport
Copyright (c) 1986-2006 by Cisco Systems, Inc.
Compiled Fri 17-Nov-06 12:02 by prod_rel_team
```

The preceding section of output describes the Cisco IOS running on the router. The following section describes the read-only memory (ROM) used, which is used to boot the router and holds the POST:

```
ROM: System Bootstrap, Version 12.4(13r)T, RELEASE SOFTWARE (fc1)
```

The next section shows how long the router has been running, how it was restarted (if you see a `system restarted by bus` error, that is a very bad thing), the location from which the Cisco IOS was loaded, and the IOS name. Flash is the default:

```
Router uptime is 2 hours, 30 minutes
System returned to ROM by power-on
System restarted at 09:04:07 UTC Sat Aug 25 2007
System image file is "flash:c2800nm-advsecurityk9-mz.124-12.bin"
```

This next section displays the processor, the amount of DRAM and flash memory, and the interfaces the POST found on the router:

```
[some output cut]
Cisco 2811 (revision 53.50) with 249856K/12288K bytes of memory.
Processor board ID FTX1049A1AB
2 FastEthernet interfaces
4 Serial(sync/async) interfaces
1 Virtual Private Network (VPN) Module
DRAM configuration is 64 bits wide with parity enabled.
239K bytes of non-volatile configuration memory.
62720K bytes of ATA CompactFlash (Read/Write)
Configuration register is 0x2102
```

The configuration register value is listed last—it's something I'll cover in Chapter 7.

In addition, the `show interfaces` and `show ip interface brief` commands are very useful in verifying and troubleshooting a router as well as network issues. These commands are covered later in this chapter. Don't miss it!

Router and Switch Administrative Configurations

Even though the following sections aren't critical to making a router or switch *work* on a network, they're still really important; in them, I'm going to lead you through configuring commands that will help you administer your network.

The administrative functions that you can configure on a router and switch are as follows:

- Hostnames
- Banners
- Passwords
- Interface descriptions

Remember, none of these will make your routers or switches work better or faster, but trust me, your life will be a whole lot better if you just take the time to set these configurations on each of your network devices. That's because doing this makes troubleshooting and maintaining your network sooooo much easier—seriously! In this next section, I'll be demonstrating commands on a Cisco router, but these commands are exactly the same on a Cisco switch.

Hostnames

You can set the identity of the router with the `hostname` command. This is only locally significant, which means that it has no bearing on how the router performs name lookups or how the router works on the internetwork. However, I'll use the hostname in Chapter 16 for authentication purposes when I discuss the WAN protocol PPP.

Here's an example:

```
Router#config t
Enter configuration commands, one per line. End with
  CNTL/Z.
Router(config)#hostname Todd
Todd(config)#hostname Atlanta
Atlanta(config)#hostname Todd
Todd(config)#
```

Even though it's pretty tempting to configure the hostname after your own name, it's definitely a better idea to name the router something pertinent to the location. This is because giving it a hostname that's somehow relevant to where the device actually lives will make finding it a whole lot easier. And it also helps you confirm that you are, indeed, configuring the right device. For this chapter, we'll leave it at *Todd* for now because it's fun.

Banners

A *banner* is more than just a little cool—one very good reason for having a banner is to give any and all who dare attempt to telnet or dial into your internetwork a little security notice. And you can create a banner to give anyone who shows up on the router exactly the information you want them to have.

Make sure you're familiar with these four available banner types: exec process creation banner, incoming terminal line banner, login banner, and message of the day banner (all illustrated in the following code):

```
Todd(config)#banner ?
  LINE            c banner-text c, where 'c' is a delimiting character
  exec            Set EXEC process creation banner
  incoming        Set incoming terminal line banner
  login           Set login banner
  motd            Set Message of the Day banner
  prompt-timeout  Set Message for login authentication timeout
  slip-ppp        Set Message for SLIP/PPP
```

Message of the day (MOTD) is the most extensively used banner. It gives a message to every person dialing into or connecting to the router via Telnet or an auxiliary port, or even through a console port as seen here:

```
Todd(config)#banner motd ?
LINE c banner-text c, where 'c' is a delimiting character
Todd(config)#banner motd #
Enter TEXT message. End with the character '#'.
$ Acme.com network, then you must disconnect immediately.
#
Todd(config)#^Z
Todd#
00:25:12: %SYS-5-CONFIG_I: Configured from console by
  console
Todd#exit

Router con0 is now available

Press RETURN to get started.

If you are not authorized to be in Acme.com network, then you
must disconnect immediately.
Todd#
```

The preceding MOTD banner essentially tells anyone connecting to the router to get lost if they're not on the guest list! The part to understand is the delimiting character—the thing that's used to tell the router when the message is done. You can use any character you want for it, but (I hope this is obvious) you can't use the delimiting character in the message itself. Also, once the message is complete, press Enter, then the delimiting character, and then Enter again. It'll still work if you don't do that, but if you have more than one banner, they'll be combined as one message and put on a single line.

For example, you can set a banner on one line as shown:

```
Todd(config)#banner motd x Unauthorized access prohibited! x
```

This example will work just fine, but if you add another MOTD banner message, they would end up on a single line.

Here are some details of the other banners I mentioned:

Exec banner You can configure a line-activation (exec) banner to be displayed when an EXEC process (such as a line activation or incoming connection to a VTY line) is created. By simply starting a user exec session through a console port, you'll activate the exec banner.

Incoming banner You can configure a banner to be displayed on terminals connected to reverse Telnet lines. This banner is useful for providing instructions to users who use reverse Telnet.

Login banner You can configure a login banner to be displayed on all connected terminals. This banner is displayed after the MOTD banner but before the login prompts. The login banner can't be disabled on a per-line basis, so to globally disable it, you've got to delete it with the `no banner login` command.

Here is an example of a login banner:

```
!
banner login ^C
-----------------------------------------------------------------
Cisco Router and Security Device Manager (SDM) is installed on this device.
This feature requires the one-time use of the username "cisco"
with the password "cisco". The default username and password
have a privilege level of 15.
Please change these publicly known initial credentials using
SDM or the IOS CLI.
Here are the Cisco IOS commands.
username <myuser>  privilege 15 secret 0 <mypassword>
no username cisco
Replace <myuser> and <mypassword> with the username and
password you want to use.
For more information about SDM please follow the instructions
in the QUICK START GUIDE for your router or go to http://www.cisco.com/go/sdm
```

```
---------------------------------------------------------------
^C
!
```

The above login banner could look pretty familiar to anyone who's ever logged into an ISR router—it's the banner that Cisco has in its default configuration for its ISR routers.

The login banner is displayed before the login prompts but after the MOTD banner.

Setting Passwords

Five passwords are used to secure your Cisco routers: console, auxiliary, telnet (VTY), enable password, and enable secret. The enable secret and enable password are used to set the password that's used to secure privileged mode. This will prompt a user for a password when the `enable` command is used. The other three are used to configure a password when user mode is accessed through the console port, through the auxiliary port, or via Telnet.

Let's take a look at each of these now.

Enable Passwords

You set the enable passwords from global configuration mode like this:

```
Todd(config)#enable ?
 last-resort Define enable action if no TACACS servers
             respond
 password    Assign the privileged level password
 secret      Assign the privileged level secret
 use-tacacs  Use TACACS to check enable passwords
```

The following points describe the enable password parameters:

`last-resort` Allows you to still enter the router if you set up authentication through a TACACS server and it's not available. But it isn't used if the TACACS server is working.

`password` Sets the enable password on older, pre-10.3 systems, and isn't ever used if an enable secret is set.

`secret` This is the newer, encrypted password that overrides the enable password if it's set.

`use-tacacs` This tells the router to authenticate through a TACACS server. It's convenient if you have anywhere from a dozen to multitudes of routers because, well, would you like to face the fun task of changing the password on all those routers? If you're sane, no, you wouldn't. So instead, just go through the TACACS server and you only have to change the password once—yeah!

Here's an example of setting the enable passwords:

```
Todd(config)#enable secret todd
Todd(config)#enable password todd
The enable password you have chosen is the same as your
  enable secret. This is not recommended. Re-enter the
  enable password.
```

If you try to set the enable secret and enable passwords the same, the router will give you a nice, polite warning to change the second password. If you don't have older legacy routers, don't even bother to use the enable password.

User-mode passwords are assigned by using the `line` command:

```
Todd(config)#line ?
  <0-337>  First Line number
  aux      Auxiliary line
  console  Primary terminal line
  tty      Terminal controller
  vty      Virtual terminal
```

Here are the lines to be concerned with for the exam objectives:

aux Sets the user-mode password for the auxiliary port. It's usually used for attaching a modem to the router, but it can be used as a console as well.

console Sets a console user-mode password.

vty Sets a Telnet password on the router. If this password isn't set, then Telnet can't be used by default.

To configure the user-mode passwords, you configure the line you want and use either the `login` or `no login` command to tell the router to prompt for authentication. The next sections will provide a line-by-line example of the configuration of each line.

Auxiliary Password

To configure the auxiliary password, go into global configuration mode and type **line aux ?**. You can see here that you only get a choice of 0–0 (that's because there's only one port):

```
Todd#config t
Enter configuration commands, one per line.  End with CNTL/Z.
Todd(config)#line aux ?
  <0-0>  First Line number
Todd(config)#line aux 0
Todd(config-line)#login
% Login disabled on line 1, until 'password' is set
Todd(config-line)#password aux
Todd(config-line)#login
```

It's important to remember to apply the `login` command or the auxiliary port won't prompt for authentication.

Cisco has begun this process of not letting you set the `login` command before a password is set on a line because if you set the `login` command under a line and then don't set a password, the line won't be usable. And it will prompt for a password that doesn't exist. So this is a good thing—a feature, not a hassle!

Definitely remember that although Cisco has this "password feature" on its routers starting in its newer IOS (12.2 and above), it's not in all its IOSs.

Console Password

To set the console password, use the `line console 0` command. But look at what happened when I tried to type **`line console ?`** from the `(config-line)#` prompt—I received an error. You can still type **`line console 0`** and it will accept it, but the help screens just don't work from that prompt. Type **`exit`** to get back one level and you'll find that your help screens now work. This is a "feature." Really.

Here's the example:

```
Todd(config-line)#line console ?
% Unrecognized command
Todd(config-line)#exit
Todd(config)#line console ?
  <0-0>  First Line number
Todd(config-line)#password console
Todd(config-line)#login
```

Since there's only one console port, I can only choose line console 0. You can set all your line passwords to the same password, but for security reasons, I'd recommend that you make them different.

There are a few other important commands to know for the console port.

For one, the `exec-timeout 0 0` command sets the time-out for the console EXEC session to zero, which means to never time out. The default time-out is 10 minutes. (If you're feeling mischievous, try this on people at work: Set it to 0 1. That will make the console time out in 1 second! And to fix it, you have to continually press the down arrow key while changing the time-out time with your free hand!)

`logging synchronous` is a very cool command, and it should be a default command, but it's not. It stops annoying console messages from popping up and disrupting the input you're trying to type. The messages still pop up, but you are returned to your router prompt without your input interrupted. This makes your input messages oh-so-much easier to read.

Here's an example of how to configure both commands:

```
Todd(config-line)#line con 0
Todd(config-line)#exec-timeout ?
```

```
  <0-35791>  Timeout in minutes
Todd(config-line)#exec-timeout 0 ?
  <0-2147483>  Timeout in seconds
  <cr>
Todd(config-line)#exec-timeout 0 0
Todd(config-line)#logging synchronous
```

You can set the console to go from never timing out (0 0) to timing out in 35,791 minutes and 2,147,483 seconds. The default is 10 minutes.

Telnet Password

To set the user-mode password for Telnet access into the router, use the `line vty` command. Routers that aren't running the Enterprise edition of the Cisco IOS default to five VTY lines, 0 through 4. But if you have the Enterprise edition, you'll have significantly more. The best way to find out how many lines you have is to use that question mark:

```
Todd(config-line)#line vty 0 ?
% Unrecognized command
Todd(config-line)#exit
Todd(config)#line vty 0 ?
  <1-1180>  Last Line number
  <cr>
Todd(config)#line vty 0 1180
Todd(config-line)#password telnet
Todd(config-line)#login
```

Remember, you cannot get help from your `(config-line)#` prompt. You must go back to global config mode in order to use the question mark (?).

So what will happen if you try to telnet into a router that doesn't have a VTY password set? You'll receive an error stating that the connection is refused because, well, the password isn't set. So, if you telnet into a router and receive the message

```
Todd#telnet SFRouter
Trying SFRouter (10.0.0.1)…Open

Password required, but none set
[Connection to SFRouter closed by foreign host]
Todd#
```

then the remote router (SFRouter in this example) does not have the VTY (Telnet) password set. But you can get around this and tell the router to allow Telnet connections without a password by using the `no login` command:

```
SFRouter(config-line)#line vty 0 4
SFRouter(config-line)#no login
```

I do not recommend using the `no login` command to allow Telnet connections without a password unless you are in a testing or classroom environment! In a production network, you should always set your VTY password.

After your routers are configured with an IP address, you can use the Telnet program to configure and check your routers instead of having to use a console cable. You can use the Telnet program by typing **telnet** from any command prompt (DOS or Cisco). Anything Telnet is covered more thoroughly in Chapter 7.

Setting Up Secure Shell (SSH)

Instead of Telnet, you can use Secure Shell, which creates a more secure session than the Telnet application that uses an unencrypted data stream. Secure Shell (SSH) uses encryption keys to send data so that your username and password are not sent in the clear.

Here are the steps to setting up SSH:

1. Set your hostname:

   ```
   Router(config)#hostname Todd
   ```

2. Set the domain name (both the hostname and domain name are required for the encryption keys to be generated):

   ```
   Todd(config)#ip domain-name Lammle.com
   ```

3. Set the username to allow SSH client access

   ```
   Todd(config)#username Todd password Lammle
   ```

4. Generate the encryption keys for securing the session:

   ```
   Todd(config)#crypto key generate rsa general-keys modulus ?
     <360-2048>  size of the key modulus [360-2048]
   Todd(config)#crypto key generate rsa general-keys modulus 1024
   The name for the keys will be: Todd.Lammle.com
   % The key modulus size is 1024 bits
   % Generating 1024 bit RSA keys, keys will be non-exportable...[OK]
   *June 24 19:25:30.035: %SSH-5-ENABLED: SSH 1.99 has been enabled
   ```

5. Enable SSH version 2 on the router; although this isn't mandatory it is highly suggested:

```
Todd(config)#ssh version 2
```

6. Connect to the VTY lines of the router:

```
Todd(config)#line vty 0 1180
```

7. Last, configure SSH and then Telnet as access protocols:

```
Todd(config-line)#transport input ssh telnet
```

If you do not use the keyword `telnet` at the end of the command string, then only SSH will work on the router. I am not suggesting you use either way, but just understand that SSH is more secure than Telnet.

Encrypting Your Passwords

Because only the enable secret password is encrypted by default, you'll need to manually configure the user-mode and enable passwords for encryption.

Notice that you can see all the passwords except the enable secret when performing a `show running-config` on a router:

```
Todd#sh running-config
Building configuration...
[output cut]
!
enable secret 5 $1$2R.r$DcRaVo0yBnUJBf7dbG9XE0
enable password todd
!
[output cut]
!
line con 0
 exec-timeout 0 0
 password console
 logging synchronous
 login
line aux 0
 password aux
 login
line vty 0 4

 password telnet
 login
```

```
 transport input telnet ssh
line vty 5 15
password telnet
 login
 transport input telnet ssh
line vty 16 1180
 password telnet
 login
!
end
```

To manually encrypt your passwords, use the `service password-encryption` command. Here's an example of how to do it:

```
Todd#config t
Enter configuration commands, one per line.  End with CNTL/Z.
Todd(config)#service password-encryption
Todd(config)#exit
Todd#sh run
Building configuration...
[output cut]
!
enable secret 5 $1$2R.r$DcRaVo0yBnUJBf7dbG9XE0
enable password 7 131118160F
!
[output cut]
!
line con 0
 exec-timeout 0 0
 password 7 0605002F5F41051C
 logging synchronous
 login
line aux 0
 password 7 03054E13
 login
line vty 0 4
 access-class 23 in
password 7 01070308550E12
 login
 transport input telnet ssh
line vty 5 15
```

```
password 7 01070308550E12
 login
 transport input telnet ssh
line vty 16 1180
 password 7 120D001B1C0E18
 login
!
end

Todd#config t
Todd(config)#no service password-encryption
Todd(config)#^Z
Todd#
```

There you have it! The passwords will now be encrypted. You just encrypt the passwords, perform a `show run`, and then turn off the command. You can see that the enable password and the line passwords are all encrypted.

But before I get into showing you all about setting descriptions on your routers, let's talk about encrypting passwords a bit more. As I said, if you set your passwords and then turn on the `service password-encryption` command, you have to perform a `show running-config` before you turn off the encryption service or your passwords won't be encrypted. You don't have to turn off the encryption service at all; you'd only do that if your router is running low on processes. And if you turn on the service before you set your passwords, then you don't even have to view them to get them encrypted.

Descriptions

Setting descriptions on an interface is helpful to the administrator and, as with the hostname, only locally significant. The `description` command is a helpful one because you can, for instance, use it to keep track of circuit numbers.

Here's an example:

```
Todd#config t
Todd(config)#int s0/0/0
Todd(config-if)#description Wan to SF circuit number 6fdda12345678
Todd(config-if)#int fa0/0
Todd(config-if)#description Sales VLAN
Todd(config-if)#^Z
Todd#
```

You can view the description of an interface with either the `show running-config` command or the `show interface` command:

```
Todd#sh run
[output cut]
```

```
!
interface FastEthernet0/0
 description Sales VLAN
 ip address 10.10.10.1 255.255.255.248
 duplex auto
 speed auto
!
interface Serial0/0/0
 description Wan to SF circuit number 6fdda 12345678
 no ip address
 shutdown
!
[output cut]

Todd#sh int f0/0
FastEthernet0/0 is up, line protocol is down
  Hardware is MV96340 Ethernet, address is 001a.2f55.c9e8 (bia 001a.2f55.c9e8)
  Description: Sales VLAN
 [output cut]

Todd#sh int s0/0/0
Serial0/0/0 is administratively down, line protocol is down
  Hardware is GT96K Serial
  Description: Wan to SF circuit number 6fdda12345678
```

Real World Scenario

description: A Helpful Command

Bob, a senior network administrator at Acme Corporation in San Francisco, has over 50 WAN links to various branches throughout the U.S. and Canada. Whenever an interface goes down, Bob spends a lot of time trying to figure out the circuit number as well as the phone number of the provider of the WAN link.

The interface `description` command would be very helpful to Bob because he can use this command on his LAN links to discern exactly where every router interface is connected. And Bob would benefit tremendously by adding circuit numbers to each and every WAN interface, along with the phone number of the responsible provider.

So by spending the few hours it would take to add this information to each and every router interface, Bob can save a huge amount of precious time when his WAN links go down—and you know they will!

Doing the *do* Command

Beginning with IOS version 12.3, Cisco has finally added a command to the IOS that allows you to view the configuration and statistics from within configuration mode. (In the examples I gave you in the previous section, all show commands were run from privileged mode.)

In fact, with any IOS, you'd get the following error if you tried to view the configuration from global config:

```
Router(config)#sh run
                 ^
% Invalid input detected at '^' marker.
```

Compare that to the output I get from entering that same command on my router that's running the 12.4 IOS and using the "do" syntax:

```
Enter configuration commands, one per line.  End with CNTL/Z.
Todd(config)#do show run
Building configuration...

Current configuration : 3276 bytes
!
[output cut]

Todd(config)#do sh int f0/0
FastEthernet0/0 is up, line protocol is down
  Hardware is MV96340 Ethernet, address is 001a.2f55.c9e8 (bia
    001a.2f55.c9e8)
  Description: Sales VLAN
[output cut]
```

So basically, you can pretty much run any command from any configuration prompt now—cool, huh? Going back to the example of encrypting our passwords, the do command would definitely have gotten the party started sooner—so, my friends, this is a very, very good thing indeed!

Router Interfaces

Interface configuration is one of the most important router configurations because without interfaces, a router is pretty much a completely useless object. Plus, interface configurations must be totally precise to enable communication with other devices. Network layer addresses, media type, bandwidth, and other administrator commands are all used to configure an interface.

Different routers use different methods to choose the interfaces used on them. For instance, the following command shows a Cisco router with 10 serial interfaces, labeled 0 through 9:

```
Router(config)#int serial ?
 <0-9> Serial interface number
```

Now it's time to choose the interface you want to configure. Once you do that, you will be in interface configuration for that specific interface. The following command would be used to choose serial port 5, for example:

```
Router(config)#int serial 5
Router(config)-if)#
```

The old 2522 router I am using in this example has one Ethernet 10BaseT port, and typing **`interface ethernet 0`** can configure that interface, as seen here:

```
Router(config)#int ethernet ?
 <0-0> Ethernet interface number
Router(config)#int ethernet 0
Router(config-if)#
```

As I showed you earlier, the 2500 router is a fixed-configuration router. This means that when you bought that model, you were stuck with that physical configuration—a huge reason why I don't use them much. I certainly never would use them in a production setting anymore, but for studying for your exam they can be used quite effectively at a very low cost.

To configure an interface, we always used the `interface` *`type number`* sequence, but with the 2600 and 2800 series routers (actually, any ISR router for that matter), there's a physical slot in the router, and there's a port number on the module plugged into that slot. So on a modular router, the configuration would be `interface` *`type slot/port`*, as seen here:

```
Router(config)#int fastethernet ?
 <0-1> FastEthernet interface number
Router(config)#int fastethernet 0
% Incomplete command.
Router(config)#int fastethernet 0?
/
Router(config)#int fastethernet 0/?
 <0-1> FastEthernet interface number
```

Make note of the fact that you can't just type **`int fastethernet 0`**. You must type the full command: ***`type slot/port`*** or **`int fastethernet 0/0`** (or **`int fa 0/0`**).

For the ISR series, it's basically the same, only you get even more options. For example, the built-in FastEthernet interfaces work with the same configuration we used with the 2600 series:

```
Todd(config)#int fastEthernet 0/?
  <0-1>  FastEthernet interface number
```

```
Todd(config)#int fastEthernet 0/0
Todd(config-if)#
```

But the rest of the modules are different—they use three numbers instead of two. The first 0 is the router itself, and then you choose the slot, and then the port. Here's an example of a serial interface on my 2811:

```
Todd(config)#interface serial ?
  <0-2>  Serial interface number
Todd(config)#interface serial 0/0/?
  <0-1>  Serial interface number
Todd(config)#interface serial 0/0/0
Todd(config-if)#
```

This can look a little dicey, I know, but I promise it's really not that hard! It helps to remember that you should always view a running-config output first so you know what interfaces you have to deal with. Here's my 2801 output:

```
Todd(config-if)#do show run
Building configuration...
[output cut]
!
interface FastEthernet0/0
 no ip address
 shutdown
 duplex auto
 speed auto
!
interface FastEthernet0/1
 no ip address
 shutdown
 duplex auto
 speed auto
!
interface Serial0/0/0
 no ip address
 shutdown
 no fair-queue
!
interface Serial0/0/1
 no ip address
 shutdown
```

```
!
interface Serial0/1/0
 no ip address
 shutdown
!
interface Serial0/2/0
 no ip address
 shutdown
 clock rate 2000000
!
 [output cut]
```

For the sake of brevity, I didn't include my complete running-config, but I've displayed all you need. You can see the two built-in FastEthernet interfaces, the two serial interfaces in slot 0 (0/0/0 and 0/0/1), the serial interface in slot 1 (0/1/0), and the serial interface in slot 2 (0/2/0). Once you see the interfaces like this, it makes it a lot easier for you to understand how the modules are inserted into the router.

Just understand that if you type **`interface e0`** on a 2500, **`interface fastethernet 0/0`** on a 2600, or **`interface serial 0/1/0`** on a 2800, all you're doing is choosing an interface to configure, and basically, they're all configured the same way after that.

I'm going to continue with our router interface discussion in the next sections, and I'll include how to bring up the interface and set an IP address on it.

Bringing Up an Interface

You can disable an interface with the interface command `shutdown` and enable it with the `no shutdown` command.

If an interface is shut down, it'll display administratively down when you use the `show interfaces` command (`sh int` for short):

```
Todd#sh int f0/1
FastEthernet0/1 is administratively down, line protocol is down
[output cut]
```

Another way to check an interface's status is via the `show running-config` command. All interfaces are shut down by default. You can bring up the interface with the `no shutdown` command (`no shut` for short):

```
Todd#config t
Todd(config)#int f0/1
Todd(config-if)#no shutdown
Todd(config-if)#
*Feb 28 22:45:08.455: %LINK-3-UPDOWN: Interface FastEthernet0/1,
```

```
    changed state to up
Todd(config-if)#do show int f0/1
FastEthernet0/1 is up, line protocol is up
[output cut]
```

Configuring an IP Address on an Interface

Even though you don't have to use IP on your routers, it's most often what people actually do use. To configure IP addresses on an interface, use the `ip address` command from interface configuration mode:

```
Todd(config)#int f0/1
Todd(config-if)#ip address 172.16.10.2 255.255.255.0
```

Don't forget to enable the interface with the `no shutdown` command. Remember to look at the command `show interface` *`int`* to see if the interface is administratively shut down or not. `show running-config` will also give you this information.

The `ip address` *`address mask`* command starts the IP processing on the interface.

If you want to add a second subnet address to an interface, you have to use the `secondary` parameter. If you type another IP address and press Enter, it will replace the existing primary IP address and mask. This is definitely a most excellent feature of the Cisco IOS.

So let's try it. To add a secondary IP address, just use the `secondary` parameter:

```
Todd(config-if)#ip address 172.16.20.2 255.255.255.0 ?
  secondary  Make this IP address a secondary address
  <cr>
Todd(config-if)#ip address 172.16.20.2 255.255.255.0 secondary
Todd(config-if)#^Z
Todd(config-if)#do sh run
Building configuration...
[output cut]

interface FastEthernet0/1
 ip address 172.16.20.2 255.255.255.0 secondary
 ip address 172.16.10.2 255.255.255.0
 duplex auto
 speed auto
!
```

I really wouldn't recommend having multiple IP addresses on an interface because it's ugly and inefficient, but I showed you anyway just in case you someday find yourself dealing with an MIS manager who's in love with really bad network design and makes you administer it! And who knows? Maybe someone will ask you about it someday and you'll get to seem really smart because you know this.

Using the Pipe

No, not that pipe. I mean the output modifier. (Although with some of the router configurations I've seen in my career, sometimes I wonder!) This pipe (|) allows us to wade through all the configurations or other long outputs and get straight to our goods fast. Here's an example:

```
Todd#sh run | ?
  append    Append redirected output to URL (URLs supporting append operation
            only)
  begin     Begin with the line that matches
  exclude   Exclude lines that match
  include   Include lines that match
  redirect  Redirect output to URL
  section   Filter a section of output
  tee       Copy output to URL

Todd#sh run | begin interface
interface FastEthernet0/0
 description Sales VLAN
 ip address 10.10.10.1 255.255.255.248
 duplex auto
 speed auto
!
interface FastEthernet0/1
 ip address 172.16.20.2 255.255.255.0 secondary
 ip address 172.16.10.2 255.255.255.0
 duplex auto
 speed auto
!
interface Serial0/0/0
 description Wan to SF circuit number 6fdda 12345678
 no ip address
!
```

So basically, the pipe symbol (output modifier) is what you need to help you get where you want to go light years faster than mucking around in a router's entire configuration.

I use it a lot when I am looking at a large routing table to find out whether a certain route is in the routing table. Here's an example:

```
Todd#sh ip route | include 192.168.3.32
R       192.168.3.32 [120/2] via 10.10.10.8, 00:00:25, FastEthernet0/0
Todd#
```

First, you need to know that this routing table had over 100 entries, so without my trusty pipe, I'd probably still be looking through that output! It's a powerfully efficient tool that saves you major time and effort by quickly finding a line in a configuration—or as the preceding example shows, a single route in a huge routing table.

Give yourself a little time to play around with the pipe command; get the hang of it, and you'll be seriously high on your newfound ability to quickly parse through router output.

Serial Interface Commands

Wait! Before you just jump in and configure a serial interface, you need some key information—like knowing that the interface will usually be attached to a CSU/DSU type of device that provides clocking for the line to the router, as I've shown in Figure 6.4.

FIGURE 6.4 A typical WAN connection

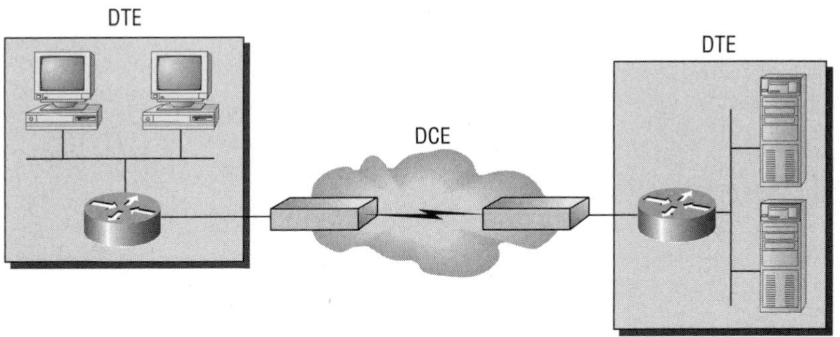

Clocking is typically provided by DCE network to routers.
In nonproduction environments, a DCE network is not always present.

Here you can see that the serial interface is used to connect to a DCE network via a CSU/DSU that provides the clocking to the router interface. But if you have a back-to-back configuration (for example, one that's used in a lab environment like I've shown you in Figure 6.5), one end—the data communication equipment (DCE) end of the cable—must provide clocking!

By default, Cisco router serial interfaces are all data terminal equipment (DTE) devices, which means that you must configure an interface to provide clocking if you need it to act like a DCE device. Again, you would not provide clocking on a production T1 connection, for example, because you would have a CSU/DSU connected to your serial interface, as Figure 6.4 shows.

FIGURE 6.5 Providing clocking on a nonproduction network

Set clock rate if needed.

Todd#config t
Todd(config)#interface serial 0
Todd(config-if)#clock rate 64000

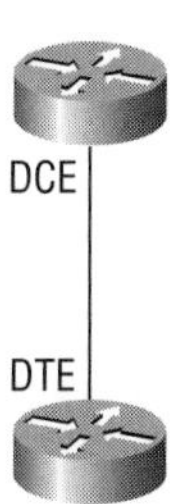

DCE side determined by cable.
Add clocking to DCE side only.

show controllers will show the cable connection type.

You configure a DCE serial interface with the `clock rate` command:

```
Todd#config t
Enter configuration commands, one per line.  End with CNTL/Z.
Todd(config)#int s0/0/0
Todd(config-if)#clock rate ?
        Speed (bits per second)
  1200
  2400
  4800
  9600
  14400
  19200
  28800
  32000
  38400
  48000
  56000
  57600
  64000
  72000
  115200
  125000
  128000
  148000
  192000
  250000
```

```
  256000
  384000
  500000
  512000
  768000
  800000
  1000000
  2000000
  4000000
  5300000
  8000000

  <300-8000000>    Choose clockrate from list above

Todd(config-if)#clock rate 1000000
```

The `clock rate` command is set in bits per second. Besides looking at the cable end to check for a label of DCE or DTE, you can see if a router's serial interface has a DCE cable connected with the `show controllers` *int* command:

```
Todd#sh controllers s0/0/0
Interface Serial0/0/0
Hardware is GT96K
DTE V.35idb at 0x4342FCB0, driver data structure at 0x434373D4
```

Here is an example of an output that shows a DCE connection:

```
Todd#sh controllers s0/2/0
Interface Serial0/2/0
Hardware is GT96K
DCE V.35, clock rate 1000000
```

The next command you need to get acquainted with is the `bandwidth` command. Every Cisco router ships with a default serial link bandwidth of T1 (1.544Mbps). But this has nothing to do with how data is transferred over a link. The bandwidth of a serial link is used by routing protocols such as EIGRP and OSPF to calculate the best cost (path) to a remote network. So if you're using RIP routing, the bandwidth setting of a serial link is irrelevant since RIP uses only hop count to determine that. If you're rereading this part thinking, "Huh—what? Routing protocols? Metrics?"—don't freak! I'm going over all that soon in Chapter 8, "IP Routing."

Here's an example of using the **`bandwidth`** command:

```
Todd#config t
Todd(config)#int s0/0/0
Todd(config-if)#bandwidth ?
```

```
  <1-10000000>  Bandwidth in kilobits
  inherit       Specify that bandwidth is inherited
  receive       Specify receive-side bandwidth
Todd(config-if)#bandwidth 1000
```

Did you notice that, unlike the `clock rate` command, the `bandwidth` command is configured in kilobits per second?

After going through all these configuration examples regarding the clock rate command, understand that the new ISR routers automatically detect DCE connections and set the `clock rate` to 2000000. However, you still need to understand the `clock rate` command for the Cisco objectives, even though the new routers set it for you automatically!

Viewing, Saving, and Erasing Configurations

If you run through setup mode, you'll be asked if you want to use the configuration you just created. If you say yes, then it will copy the configuration running in DRAM (known as the running-config) into NVRAM and name the file `startup-config`. Hopefully, you will always use the CLI and not setup mode.

You can manually save the file from DRAM (usually just called RAM) to NVRAM by using the `copy running-config startup-config` command (you can use the shortcut `copy run start` also):

```
Todd#copy running-config startup-config
Destination filename [startup-config]? [press enter]
Building configuration...
[OK]
Todd#
Building configuration...
```

When you see a question with an answer in `[]`, it means that if you just press Enter, you're choosing the default answer.

Also, when the command asked for the destination filename, the default answer was startup-config. The reason it asks is because you can copy the configuration pretty much anywhere you want. Take a look:

```
Todd#copy running-config ?
  archive:        Copy to archive: file system
```

```
flash:          Copy to flash: file system
ftp:            Copy to ftp: file system
http:           Copy to http: file system
https:          Copy to https: file system
ips-sdf         Update (merge with) IPS signature configuration
null:           Copy to null: file system
nvram:          Copy to nvram: file system
rcp:            Copy to rcp: file system
running-config  Update (merge with) current system configuration
scp:            Copy to scp: file system
startup-config  Copy to startup configuration
syslog:         Copy to syslog: file system
system:         Copy to system: file system
tftp:           Copy to tftp: file system
xmodem:         Copy to xmodem: file system
ymodem:         Copy to ymodem: file system
```

We'll take a closer look at how and where to copy files in Chapter 7.

You can view the files by typing **show running-config** or **show startup-config** from privileged mode. The sh run command, which is a shortcut for show running-config, tells us that we are viewing the current configuration:

```
Todd#show running-config
Building configuration...

Current configuration : 3343 bytes
!
version 12.4
[output cut]
```

The sh start command—one of the shortcuts for the show startup-config command—shows us the configuration that will be used the next time the router is reloaded. It also tells us how much NVRAM is being used to store the startup-config file. Here's an example:

```
Todd#show startup-config
Using 1978 out of 245752 bytes
!
version 12.4
[output cut]
```

Deleting the Configuration and Reloading the Router

You can delete the startup-config file by using the `erase startup-config` command:

```
Todd#erase startup-config
Erasing the nvram filesystem will remove all configuration files!
    Continue? [confirm][enter]
[OK]
Erase of nvram: complete
Todd#
*Feb 28 23:51:21.179: %SYS-7-NV_BLOCK_INIT: Initialized the geometry of nvram
Todd#sh startup-config
startup-config is not present
Todd#reload
Proceed with reload? [confirm]System configuration has been modified.
    Save? [yes/no]: n
```

If you reload or power down and up the router after using the `erase startup-config` command, you'll be offered setup mode because there's no configuration saved in NVRAM. You can press Ctrl+C to exit setup mode at any time (the `reload` command can only be used from privileged mode).

At this point, you shouldn't use setup mode to configure your router. So just say **no** to setup mode, because it's there to help people who don't know how to use the Cash Line Interface (CLI), and this no longer applies to you. Be strong—you can do it!

Verifying Your Configuration

Obviously, `show running-config` would be the best way to verify your configuration and `show startup-config` would be the best way to verify the configuration that'll be used the next time the router is reloaded—right?

Well, once you take a look at the running-config, if all appears well, you can verify your configuration with utilities such as Ping and Telnet. Ping is a program that uses ICMP echo requests and replies. (ICMP is discussed in Chapter 3, "Introduction to TCP/IP.") Ping sends a packet to a remote host, and if that host responds, you know that it's alive. But you don't know if it's alive and also *well*—just because you can ping a Microsoft server does not mean you can log in! Even so, Ping is an awesome starting point for troubleshooting an internetwork.

Did you know that you can ping with different protocols? You can, and you can test this by typing **`ping ?`** at either the router user-mode or privileged-mode prompt:

```
Router#ping ?
  WORD        Ping destination address or hostname
  appletalk   Appletalk echo
  clns        CLNS echo
```

```
decnet    DECnet echo
ip        IP echo
ipv6      IPv6 echo
ipx       Novell/IPX echo
srb       srb echo
tag       Tag encapsulated IP echo
<cr>
```

If you want to find a neighbor's Network layer address, either you need to go to the router or switch itself or you can type **show cdp entry * protocol** to get the Network layer addresses you need for pinging.

You can also use an extended ping to change the default variables, as shown here:

```
Router#ping
Protocol [ip]: [enter]
Target IP address: 1.1.1.1
Repeat count [5]: 100
Datagram size [100]: 1500
Timeout in seconds [2]:
Extended commands [n]: y
Source address or interface: Fastethernet0/0
Type of service [0]:
Set DF bit in IP header? [no]:
Validate reply data? [no]:
Data pattern [0xABCD]:
Loose, Strict, Record, Timestamp, Verbose[none]: verbose
Loose, Strict, Record, Timestamp, Verbose[V]:
Sweep range of sizes [n]:
Type escape sequence to abort.
Sending 100, 1500-byte ICMP Echos to 1.1.1.1, timeout is 2 seconds:
Packet sent with a source address of 10.10.10.1
```

Notice that extended ping allows you to set the repeat count higher than the default of 5 and the datagram size larger, which raises the MTU and allows a better testing of throughput, and one last important piece I'll pull out of the output, the source interface. You can choose which interface the ping is sourced from. This is helpful in some diagnostic situations.

Cisco Discovery Protocol (CDP) is covered in Chapter 7.

Traceroute uses ICMP with IP time to live (TTL) time-outs to track the path a packet takes through an internetwork, in contrast to Ping, which just finds the host and responds. And Traceroute can also be used with multiple protocols.

```
Router#traceroute ?
  WORD       Trace route to destination address or hostname
  appletalk  AppleTalk Trace
  clns       ISO CLNS Trace
  ip         IP Trace
  ipv6       IPv6 Trace
  ipx        IPX Trace
  <cr>
```

Telnet, FTP, and HTTP are really the best tools because they use IP at the Network layer and TCP at the Transport layer to create a session with a remote host. If you can telnet, ftp, or http into a device, your IP connectivity just has to be good.

```
Router#telnet ?
 WORD IP address or hostname of a remote system
 <cr>
```

From the router prompt, you just type a hostname or IP address and it will assume you want to telnet—you don't need to type the actual command, `telnet`.

In the following sections, I am going to show you how to verify the interface statistics.

Verifying with the *show interface* Command

Another way to verify your configuration is by typing `show interface` commands, the first of which is `show interface ?`. That will reveal all the available interfaces to verify and configure.

The `show interfaces` command displays the configurable parameters and statistics of all interfaces on a router.

This command is very useful for verifying and troubleshooting router and network issues.

The following output is from my freshly erased and rebooted 2811 router:

```
Router#sh int ?
  Async              Async interface
  BVI                Bridge-Group Virtual Interface
  CDMA-Ix            CDMA Ix interface
  CTunnel            CTunnel interface
  Dialer             Dialer interface
  FastEthernet       FastEthernet IEEE 802.3
```

```
Loopback            Loopback interface
MFR                 Multilink Frame Relay bundle interface
Multilink           Multilink-group interface
Null                Null interface
Port-channel        Ethernet Channel of interfaces
Serial              Serial
Tunnel              Tunnel interface
Vif                 PGM Multicast Host interface
Virtual-PPP         Virtual PPP interface
Virtual-Template    Virtual Template interface
Virtual-TokenRing   Virtual TokenRing
accounting          Show interface accounting
counters            Show interface counters
crb                 Show interface routing/bridging info
dampening           Show interface dampening info
description         Show interface description
etherchannel        Show interface etherchannel information
irb                 Show interface routing/bridging info
mac-accounting      Show interface MAC accounting info
mpls-exp            Show interface MPLS experimental accounting info
precedence          Show interface precedence accounting info
pruning             Show interface trunk VTP pruning information
rate-limit          Show interface rate-limit info
stats               Show interface packets & octets, in & out, by switching
                    path
status              Show interface line status
summary             Show interface summary
switching           Show interface switching
switchport          Show interface switchport information
trunk               Show interface trunk information
|                   Output modifiers
<cr>
```

The only "real" physical interfaces are FastEthernet, Serial, and Async; the rest are all logical interfaces or commands you can use to verify with.

The next command is show interface fastethernet 0/0. It reveals to us the hardware address, logical address, and encapsulation method as well as statistics on collisions, as seen here:

```
Router#sh int f0/0
FastEthernet0/0 is up, line protocol is up
  Hardware is MV96340 Ethernet, address is 001a.2f55.c9e8 (bia 001a.2f55.c9e8)
```

```
  Internet address is 192.168.1.33/27
MTU 1500 bytes, BW 100000 Kbit, DLY 100 usec,
     reliability 255/255, txload 1/255, rxload 1/255
  Encapsulation ARPA, loopback not set
  Keepalive set (10 sec)
  Auto-duplex, Auto Speed, 100BaseTX/FX
  ARP type: ARPA, ARP Timeout 04:00:00
  Last input never, output 00:02:07, output hang never
  Last clearing of "show interface" counters never
  Input queue: 0/75/0/0 (size/max/drops/flushes); Total output drops: 0
  Queueing strategy: fifo
  Output queue: 0/40 (size/max)
  5 minute input rate 0 bits/sec, 0 packets/sec
  5 minute output rate 0 bits/sec, 0 packets/sec
     0 packets input, 0 bytes
     Received 0 broadcasts, 0 runts, 0 giants, 0 throttles
     0 input errors, 0 CRC, 0 frame, 0 overrun, 0 ignored
     0 watchdog
     0 input packets with dribble condition detected
     16 packets output, 960 bytes, 0 underruns
     0 output errors, 0 collisions, 0 interface resets
     0 babbles, 0 late collision, 0 deferred
     0 lost carrier, 0 no carrier
     0 output buffer failures, 0 output buffers swapped out
Router#
```

As you probably guessed, we're going to discuss the important statistics from this output, but first, for fun (this is all fun, right?), I've got to ask you, what subnet is the FastEthernet 0/0 a member of and what's the broadcast address and valid host range?

And, my friend, you really have to be able to nail these things NASCAR fast! Just in case you didn't, the address is 192.168.1.33/27. And I've gotta be honest—if you don't know what a /27 is at this point, you'll need a miracle to pass the exam. (A /27 is 255.255.255.224.) The fourth octet is a block size of 32. The subnets are 0, 32, 64, etc.; the FastEthernet interface is in the 32 subnet; the broadcast address is 63; and the valid hosts are 33–62.

If you struggled with any of this, please save yourself from certain doom and get yourself back into Chapter 4, "Easy Subnetting," now! Read and reread it until you've got it dialed in!

The preceding interface is working and looks to be in good shape. The `show interfaces` command will show you if you are receiving errors on the interface, and it will show you the maximum transmission unit (MTU), which is the maximum packet size allowed that can transmit on that interface; bandwidth (BW) for use with routing protocols; reliability (255/255 means perfect!); and load (1/255 means no load).

Continuing to use the previous output, what is the bandwidth of the interface? Well, other than the easy giveaway of the interface being called a "FastEthernet" interface, we can see that the bandwidth is 100000 Kbit, which is 100,000,000 (Kbit means to add three zeros), which is 100Mbits per second, or FastEthernet. Gigabit would be 1000000Kbits per second.

The most important statistic of the `show interface` command is the output of the line and Data Link protocol status. If the output reveals that FastEthernet 0/0 is up and the line protocol is up, then the interface is up and running:

```
Router#sh int fa0/0
FastEthernet0/0 is up, line protocol is up
```

The first parameter refers to the Physical layer, and it's up when it receives carrier detect. The second parameter refers to the Data Link layer, and it looks for keepalives from the connecting end. (Keepalives are used between devices to make sure connectivity has not dropped.)

Here's an example of where the problem usually is found—on serial interfaces:

```
Router#sh int s0/0/0
Serial0/0 is up, line protocol is down
```

If you see that the line is up but the protocol is down, as shown here, you're experiencing a clocking (keepalive) or framing problem—possibly an encapsulation mismatch. Check the keepalives on both ends to make sure that they match; that the clock rate is set, if needed; and that the encapsulation type is the same on both ends. The preceding output would be considered a Data Link layer problem.

If you discover that both the line interface and the protocol are down, it's a cable or interface problem. The following output would be considered a Physical layer problem:

```
Router#sh int s0/0/0
Serial0/0 is down, line protocol is down
```

If one end is administratively shut down (as shown next), the remote end would present as down and down:

```
Router#sh int s0/0/0
Serial0/0 is administratively down, line protocol is down
```

To enable the interface, use the command `no shutdown` from interface configuration mode.

The next `show interface serial 0/0/0` command demonstrates the serial line and the maximum transmission unit (MTU)—1,500 bytes by default. It also shows the default bandwidth (BW) on all Cisco serial links: 1.544 Kbps. This is used to determine the bandwidth of the line for routing protocols such as EIGRP and OSPF. Another important configuration to notice is the keepalive, which is 10 seconds by default. Each router sends a keepalive message to its neighbor every 10 seconds, and if both routers aren't configured for the same keepalive time, it won't work.

```
Router#sh int s0/0/0
Serial0/0 is up, line protocol is up
 Hardware is HD64570
 MTU 1500 bytes, BW 1544 Kbit, DLY 20000 usec,
   reliability 255/255, txload 1/255, rxload 1/255
 Encapsulation HDLC, loopback not set, keepalive set
  (10 sec)
 Last input never, output never, output hang never
 Last clearing of "show interface" counters never
 Queueing strategy: fifo
 Output queue 0/40, 0 drops; input queue 0/75, 0 drops
 5 minute input rate 0 bits/sec, 0 packets/sec
 5 minute output rate 0 bits/sec, 0 packets/sec
   0 packets input, 0 bytes, 0 no buffer
   Received 0 broadcasts, 0 runts, 0 giants, 0 throttles
   0 input errors, 0 CRC, 0 frame, 0 overrun, 0 ignored,
   0 abort
   0 packets output, 0 bytes, 0 underruns
   0 output errors, 0 collisions, 16 interface resets
   0 output buffer failures, 0 output buffers swapped out
   0 carrier transitions
   DCD=down DSR=down DTR=down RTS=down CTS=down
```

You can clear the counters on the interface by typing the command **clear counters**:

```
Router#clear counters ?
  Async                Async interface
  BVI                  Bridge-Group Virtual Interface
  CTunnel              CTunnel interface
  Dialer               Dialer interface
  FastEthernet         FastEthernet IEEE 802.3
  Group-Async          Async Group interface
  Line                 Terminal line
  Loopback             Loopback interface
  MFR                  Multilink Frame Relay bundle interface
  Multilink            Multilink-group interface
  Null                 Null interface
  Serial               Serial
  Tunnel               Tunnel interface
```

```
  Vif                 PGM Multicast Host interface
  Virtual-Template    Virtual Template interface
  Virtual-TokenRing   Virtual TokenRing
  <cr>

Router#clear counters s0/0/0
Clear "show interface" counters on this interface
  [confirm][enter]
Router#
00:17:35: %CLEAR-5-COUNTERS: Clear counter on interface
  Serial0/0/0 by console
Router#
```

Verifying with the *show ip interface* Command

The `show ip interface` command will provide you with information regarding the layer 3 configurations of a router's interfaces:

```
Router#sh ip interface
FastEthernet0/0 is up, line protocol is up
  Internet address is 1.1.1.1/24
  Broadcast address is 255.255.255.255
  Address determined by setup command
  MTU is 1500 bytes
  Helper address is not set
  Directed broadcast forwarding is disabled
  Outgoing access list is not set
  Inbound  access list is not set
  Proxy ARP is enabled
  Security level is default
  Split horizon is enabled
[output cut]
```

The status of the interface, the IP address and mask, information on whether an access list is set on the interface, and basic IP information are included in this output.

Using the *show ip interface brief* Command

The `show ip interface brief` command is probably one of the most helpful commands that you can ever use on a Cisco router. This command provides a quick overview of the router's interfaces, including the logical address and status:

```
Router#sh ip int brief
Interface           IP-Address      OK? Method Status   Protocol
```

```
FastEthernet0/0    unassigned    YES unset  up                    up
FastEthernet0/1    unassigned    YES unset  up                    up
Serial0/0/0        unassigned    YES unset  up                    down
Serial0/0/1        unassigned    YES unset  administratively down down
Serial0/1/0        unassigned    YES unset  administratively down down
Serial0/2/0        unassigned    YES unset  administratively down down
```

Remember, administratively down means that you need to type `no shutdown` under the interface. Notice that Serial0/0/0 is up/down, which means that the physical layer is good and carrier detect is sensed but no keepalives are being received from the remote end. In a nonproduction network, like the one I am working with, the clock rate isn't set.

Verifying with the *show protocols* Command

The `show protocols` command is a really helpful command you'd use in order to quickly see the status of layers 1 and 2 of each interface as well as the IP addresses used.

Here's a look at one of my production routers:

```
Router#sh protocols
Global values:
  Internet Protocol routing is enabled
Ethernet0/0 is administratively down, line protocol is down
Serial0/0 is up, line protocol is up
  Internet address is 100.30.31.5/24
Serial0/1 is administratively down, line protocol is down
Serial0/2 is up, line protocol is up
  Internet address is 100.50.31.2/24
Loopback0 is up, line protocol is up
  Internet address is 100.20.31.1/24
```

Using the *show controllers* Command

The `show controllers` command displays information about the physical interface itself. It'll also give you the type of serial cable plugged into a serial port. Usually, this will only be a DTE cable that plugs into a type of data service unit (DSU).

```
Router#sh controllers serial 0/0
HD unit 0, idb = 0x1229E4, driver structure at 0x127E70
buffer size 1524 HD unit 0, V.35 DTE cable

Router#sh controllers serial 0/1
HD unit 1, idb = 0x12C174, driver structure at 0x131600
buffer size 1524 HD unit 1, V.35 DCE cable
```

Notice that serial 0/0 has a DTE cable, whereas the serial 0/1 connection has a DCE cable. Serial 0/1 would have to provide clocking with the `clock rate` command. Serial 0/0 would get its clocking from the DSU.

Let's look at this command again. In Figure 6.6, see the DTE/DCE cable between the two routers? Know that you will not see this in production networks!

FIGURE 6.6 The `show controllers` command

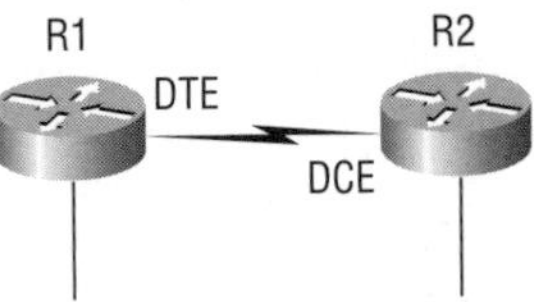

Router R1 has a DTE connection—typically the default for all Cisco routers. Routers R1 and R2 can't communicate. Check out the output of the `show controllers s0/0` command here:

```
R1#sh controllers serial 0/0
HD unit 0, idb = 0x1229E4, driver structure at 0x127E70
buffer size 1524 HD unit 0, V.35 DCE cable
```

The `show controllers s0/0` command shows that the interface is a V.35 DCE cable. This means that R1 needs to provide clocking of the line to router R2. Basically, the interface has the wrong label on the cable on the R1 router's serial interface. But if you add clocking on the R1 router's serial interface, the network should come right up.

Let's check out another issue, shown in Figure 6.7, that you can solve by using the `show controllers` command. Again, routers R1 and R2 can't communicate.

FIGURE 6.7 The `show controllers` command used with the `show ip interface` command

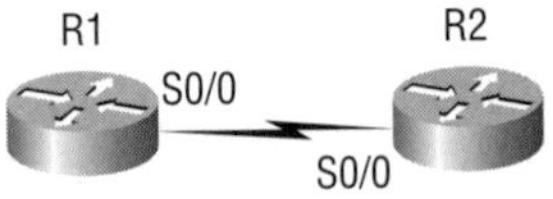

Here's the output of R1's `show controllers s0/0` command and `show ip interface s0/0`:

```
R1#sh controllers s0/0
HD unit 0, idb = 0x1229E4, driver structure at 0x127E70
buffer size 1524 HD unit 0,
DTE V.35 clocks stopped
cpb = 0xE2, eda = 0x4140, cda = 0x4000

R1#sh ip interface s0/0
```

```
Serial0/0 is up, line protocol is down
  Internet address is 192.168.10.2/24
  Broadcast address is 255.255.255.255
```

If you use the `show controllers` command and the `show ip interface` command, you'll see that router R1 isn't receiving clocking of the line. This network is a nonproduction network, so no CSU/DSU is connected to provide clocking of the line. This means the DCE end of the cable will be providing the clock rate—in this case, the R2 router. The `show ip interface` indicates that the interface is up but the protocol is down, which means that no keepalives are being received from the far end. In this example, the likely culprit is the result of bad cable, or no clocking.

Summary

This was a fun chapter! I showed you a lot about the Cisco IOS and I really hope you gained a lot of insight into the Cisco router world. This chapter started off by explaining the Cisco Internetwork Operating System (IOS) and how you can use the IOS to run and configure Cisco routers. You learned how to bring a router up and what setup mode does. Oh, and by the way, since you can now basically configure Cisco routers, you should never use setup mode, right?

After I discussed how to connect to a router with a console and LAN connection, I covered the Cisco help features and how to use the CLI to find commands and command parameters. In addition, I discussed some basic `show` commands to help you verify your configurations.

Administrative functions on a router help you administer your network and verify that you are configuring the correct device. Setting router passwords is one of the most important configurations you can perform on your routers. I showed you the five passwords to set. In addition, I used the hostname, interface description, and banners to help you administer your router.

Well, that concludes your introduction to the Cisco IOS. And, as usual, it's super-important for you to have the basics that we went over in this chapter before you move on to the following chapters.

Exam Essentials

Describe the responsibilities of the IOS. The Cisco router IOS software is responsible for network protocols and providing supporting functions, connecting high-speed traffic between devices, adding security to control access and prevent unauthorized network use, providing scalability for ease of network growth and redundancy, and supplying network reliability for connecting to network resources.

List the options available to connect to a Cisco device for management purposes. The three options available are the console port and auxiliary port and through Telnet. A Telnet connection is not possible until an IP address has been configured and a Telnet username and password have been configured.

Understand the boot sequence of a router. When you first bring up a Cisco router, it will run a power-on self-test (POST), and if that passes, it will look for and load the Cisco IOS from flash memory, if a file is present. The IOS then proceeds to load and looks for a valid configuration in NVRAM called the startup-config. If no file is present in NVRAM, the router will go into setup mode.

Describe the use of setup mode. Setup mode is automatically started if a router boots and no startup-config is in NVRAM. You can also bring up setup mode by typing **`setup`** from privileged mode. Setup provides a minimum amount of configuration in an easy format for someone who does not understand how to configure a Cisco router from the command line.

Differentiate user, privileged, and global configuration modes, both visually and from a command capabilities perspective. User mode, indicated by the `routername>` prompt, provides a command-line interface with very few available commands by default. User mode does not allow the configuration to be viewed or changed. Privileged mode, indicated by the `routername#` prompt, allows a user to both view and change the configuration of a router. You can enter privileged mode by typing the command **`enable`** and entering the enable password or enable secret password, if set. Global configuration mode, indicated by the `routername(config)#` prompt, allows configuration changes to be made that apply to the entire router (as opposed to a configuration change that might affect only one interface, for example).

Recognize additional prompts available in other modes and describe their use. Additional modes are reached via the global configuration prompt, `routername(config)#`, and their prompts include interface, `router(config-if)#`, for making interface settings; subinterface, `router(config-subif)#`, used when a physical interface must be logically subdivided; line configuration mode, `router(config-line)#`, used to set passwords and make other settings to various connection methods; and routing protocol modes for various routing protocols, `router(config-router)#`, used to enable and configure routing protocols.

Access and utilize editing and help features. Make use of typing a question mark at the end of commands for help in using the commands. Additionally, understand how to filter command help with the same question mark and letters. Use the command history to retrieve commands previously utilized without retyping. Understand the meaning of the caret when an incorrect command is rejected. Finally, identify useful hot key combinations.

Identify the information provided by the `show version` command. The `show version` command will provide basic configuration for the system hardware as well as the software version, the names and sources of configuration files, the configuration register setting, and the boot images.

Set the hostname of a router. The command sequence to set the hostname of a router is as follows:

```
enable
config t
hostname Todd
```

Differentiate the enable password and enable secret password. Both of these passwords are used to gain access into privileged mode. However, the enable secret password is newer and is always encrypted by default. Also, if you set the enable password and then set the enable secret, only the enable secret will be used.

Describe the configuration and use of banners. Banners provide information to users accessing the device and can be displayed at various login prompts. They are configured with the `banner` command and a keyword describing the specific type of banner.

Set the enable secret on a router. To set the enable secret, you use the global config command `enable secret`. Do not use `enable secret password` *`password`* or you will set your password to *`password password`*. Here is an example:

```
enable
config t
enable secret todd
```

Set the console password on a router. To set the console password, use the following sequence:

```
enable
config t
line console 0
password todd
login
```

Set the Telnet password on a router. To set the Telnet password, the sequence is as follows:

```
enable
config t
line vty 0 4
password todd
login
```

Describe the advantages of using Secure Shell and list its requirements. Secure Shell (SSH) uses encrypted keys to send data so that usernames and passwords are not sent in the clear. It requires that a hostname and domain name be configured and that encryption keys be generated.

Describe the process of preparing an interface for use. To use an interface, you must configure it with an IP address and subnet mask in the same subnet of the hosts that will be connecting to the switch that is connected to that interface. It also must be enabled with the `no shutdown` command. A serial interface that is connected back-to-back with another router serial interface must also be configured with a clock rate on the DCE end of the serial cable.

Understand how to troubleshoot a serial link problem. If you type **`show interface serial 0`** and see `down, line protocol is down`, this will be considered a Physical layer problem. If you see it as `up, line protocol is down`, then you have a Data Link layer problem.

Understand how to verify your router with the `show interfaces` command. If you type **`show interfaces`**, you can view the statistics for the interfaces on the router, verify whether the interfaces are shut down, and see the IP address of each interface.

Describe how to view, edit, delete, and save a configuration. The `show running-config` command is used to view the current configuration being used by the router. The `show startup-config` command displays the last configuration that was saved and is the one that will be used at next startup. The `copy running-config startup-config` command is used to save changes made to the running configuration in NVRAM. The `erase startup-config` command deletes the saved configuration and will result in the invocation of the setup menu when the router is rebooted because there will be no configuration present.

Written Lab 6

Write out the command or commands for the following questions:

1. What command is used to set a serial interface to provide clocking to another router at 64 Kb?
2. If you telnet into a router and get the response `connection refused, password not set`, what commands would you execute on the destination router to stop receiving this message and not be prompted for a password?
3. If you type **`show inter ethernet 0`** and notice the port is administratively down, what commands would you execute to enable the interface?
4. If you wanted to delete the configuration stored in NVRAM, what command(s) would you type?
5. If you wanted to set the user-mode password to *todd* for the console port, what command(s) would you type?
6. If you wanted to set the enable secret password to *cisco*, what command(s) would you type?
7. If you wanted to determine if serial interface 0/2 should provide clocking, what command would you use?
8. What command would you use to see the terminal history size?
9. You want to reinitialize the router and totally replace the running-config with the current startup-config. What command will you use?
10. How would you set the name of a router to *Chicago*?

(The answers to Written Lab 6 can be found following the answers to the review questions for this chapter.)

Hands-on Labs

In this section, you will perform commands on a Cisco router that will help you understand what you learned in this chapter.

You'll need at least one Cisco router—two would be better, three would be outstanding. The hands-on labs in this section are included for use with real Cisco routers. All of these labs work with the Cisco Packet Tracer router simulator. Lastly, for the CCNA it doesn't matter what series type router you use with these labs (i.e., 2500, 2600, 800, 1800, or 2800).

It is assumed that the router you're going to use has no current configuration present. If necessary, erase any existing configuration with Hands-on Lab 6.1; otherwise, proceed to Hands-on lab 6.2:

Lab 6.1: Erasing an Existing Configuration

Lab 6.2: Exploring User, Privileged, and Configuration Modes

Lab 6.3: Using the Help and Editing Features

Lab 6.4: Saving a Router Configuration

Lab 6.5: Setting Passwords

Lab 6.6: Setting the Hostname, Descriptions, IP Address, and Clock Rate

Hands-on Lab 6.1: Erasing an Existing Configuration

The following lab may require the knowledge of a username and password to enter privileged mode. If the router has a configuration with an unknown username and password for privileged mode, this procedure will not be possible. It is possible to erase a configuration without a privileged mode password, but the exact steps depend on the router model and will not be covered until Chapter 7.

1. Start the router up and when prompted, press Enter.
2. At the `Routername>` prompt, type **`enable`**.
3. If prompted, enter the username and press Enter. Then enter the correct password and press Enter.
4. At the privileged mode prompt, type **`erase startup-config`**.
5. At the privileged mode prompt, type **`reload`**, and when prompted to save the configuration, type **`n`** for no.

Hands-on Lab 6.2: Exploring User, Privileged, and Configuration Modes

1. Turn the router on. If you just erased the configuration as in Hands-on Lab 6.1, when prompted to continue with the configuration dialog, enter **`n`** for no and press Enter. When prompted, press Enter to connect to your router. This will put you into user mode.

2. At the `Router>` prompt, type a question mark (**?**).
3. Notice the `-more-` at the bottom of the screen.
4. Press the Enter key to view the commands line by line. Press the spacebar to view the commands a full screen at a time. You can type **q** at any time to quit.
5. Type **enable** or **en** and press Enter. This will put you into privileged mode where you can change and view the router configuration.
6. At the `Router#` prompt, type a question mark (**?**). Notice how many options are available to you in privileged mode.
7. Type **q** to quit.
8. Type **config** and press Enter.
9. When prompted for a method, press Enter to configure your router using your terminal (which is the default).
10. At the `Router(config)#` prompt, type a question mark (**?**), then **q** to quit, or press the spacebar to view the commands.
11. Type **interface e0** or **int e0** (or even **int fa0/0**) and press Enter. This will allow you to configure interface Ethernet 0.
12. At the `Router(config-if)#` prompt, type a question mark (**?**).
13. Type **int s0 (int s0/0)** or **interface s0** (same as the `interface serial 0` command) and press Enter. This will allow you to configure interface serial 0. Notice that you can go from interface to interface easily.
14. Type **encapsulation ?**.
15. Type **exit**. Notice how this brings you back one level.
16. Press Ctrl+Z. Notice how this brings you out of configuration mode and places you back into privileged mode.
17. Type **disable**. This will put you into user mode.
18. Type **exit**, which will log you out of the router.

Hands-on Lab 6.3: Using the Help and Editing Features

1. Log into the router and go to privileged mode by typing **en** or **enable**.
2. Type a question mark (**?**).
3. Type **cl?** and then press Enter. Notice that you can see all the commands that start with *cl*.
4. Type **clock ?** and press Enter.

Notice the difference between steps 3 and 4. Step 3 has you type letters with no space and a question mark, which will give you all the commands that start with *cl*. Step 4 has you type a command, space, and question mark. By doing this, you will see the next available parameter.

5. Set the router's clock by typing **clock ?** and, following the help screens, setting the router's time and date. The following steps walk you through setting the date and time:
6. Type **clock ?**.
7. Type **clock set ?**.
8. Type **clock set 10:30:30 ?**.
9. Type **clock set 10:30:30 14 May ?**.
10. Type **clock set 10:30:30 14 March 2011**.
11. Press Enter.
12. Type **show clock** to see the time and date.
13. From privileged mode, type **show access-list 10**. Don't press Enter.
14. Press Ctrl+A. This takes you to the beginning of the line.
15. Press Ctrl+E. This should take you back to the end of the line.
16. The Ctrl-A takes you back to the beginning of the line, and then the Ctrl+F moves you forward one character.
17. Press Ctrl+B, which will move you back one character.
18. Press Enter, then press Ctrl+P. This will repeat the last command.
19. Press the up arrow key on your keyboard. This will also repeat the last command.
20. Type **sh history**. This shows you the last 10 commands entered.
21. Type **terminal history size ?**. This changes the history entry size. The ? is the number of allowed lines.
22. Type **show terminal** to gather terminal statistics and history size.
23. Type **terminal no editing**. This turns off advanced editing. Repeat steps 14 through 18 to see that the shortcut editing keys have no effect until you type **terminal editing**.
24. Type **terminal editing** and press Enter to re-enable advanced editing.
25. Type **sh run**, then press your Tab key. This will finish typing the command for you.
26. Type **sh start**, then press your Tab key. This will finish typing the command for you.

Hands-on Lab 6.4: Saving a Router Configuration

1. Log into the router and go into privileged mode by typing **en** or **enable**, then press Enter.
2. To see the configuration stored in NVRAM, type **sh start** and press Tab and Enter, or type **show startup-config** and press Enter. However, if no configuration has been saved, you will get an error message.
3. To save a configuration to NVRAM, which is known as startup-config, you can do one of the following:
   - Type **copy run start** and press Enter.
   - Type **copy running**, press Tab, type **start**, press Tab, and press Enter.
   - Type **copy running-config startup-config** and press Enter.

4. Type **sh start**, press Tab, then press Enter.
5. Type **sh run**, press Tab, then press Enter.
6. Type **erase start**, press Tab, then press Enter.
7. Type **sh start**, press Tab, then press Enter. The router will either tell you that NVRAM is not present, or some other type of message, depending on the IOS and hardware.
8. Type **reload**, then press Enter. Acknowledge the reload by pressing Enter. Wait for the router to reload.
9. Say no to entering setup mode, or just press Ctrl+C.

Hands-on Lab 6.5: Setting Passwords

1. Log into the router and go into privileged mode by typing **en** or **enable**.
2. Type **config t** and press Enter.
3. Type **enable ?**.
4. Set your enable secret password by typing **enable secret *password*** (the third word should be your own personalized password) and pressing Enter. Do not add the parameter `password` after the parameter `secret` (this would make your password the word *password*). An example would be `enable secret todd`.
5. Now let's see what happens when you log all the way out of the router and then log in. Log out by pressing Ctrl+Z, and then type **exit** and press Enter. Go to privileged mode. Before you are allowed to enter privileged mode, you will be asked for a password. If you successfully enter the secret password, you can proceed.
6. Remove the secret password. Go to privileged mode, type **config t**, and press Enter. Type **no enable secret** and press Enter. Log out and then log back in again; now you should not be asked for a password.
7. One more password used to enter privileged mode is called the enable password. It is an older, less secure password and is not used if an enable secret password is set. Here is an example of how to set it:

```
config t
enable password todd1
```

8. Notice that the enable secret and enable passwords are different. They cannot be the same.
9. Type **config t** to be at the right level to set your console and auxiliary passwords, then type **line ?**.
10. Notice that the parameters for the line commands are `auxiliary`, `vty`, and `console`. You will set all three.
11. To set the Telnet or VTY password, type **line vty 0 4** and then press Enter. The `0 4` is the range of the five available virtual lines used to connect with Telnet. If you have an enterprise IOS, the number of lines may vary. Use the question mark to determine the last line number available on your router.

12. The next command is used to set the authentication on or off. Type **login** and press Enter to prompt for a user-mode password when telnetting into the router. You will not be able to telnet into a router if the password is not set.

You can use the no login command to disable the user-mode password prompt when using Telnet.

13. One more command you need to set for your VTY password is password. Type **password *password*** to set the password. (*password* is your password.)
14. Here is an example of how to set the VTY password:

```
config t
line vty 0 4
login
password todd
```

15. Set your auxiliary password by first typing **line auxiliary 0** or **line aux 0**.
16. Type **login**.
17. Type **password password**.
18. Set your console password by first typing **line console 0** or **line con 0**.
19. Type **login**.
20. Type **password *password***. Here is an example of the last two command sequences:

```
config t
line con 0
login
password todd1
line aux 0
login
password todd
```

21. You can add the Exec-timeout 0 0 command to the console 0 line. This will stop the console from timing out and logging you out. The command sequence will now look like this:

```
config t
line con 0
login
password todd2
exec-timeout 0 0
```

22. Set the console prompt to not overwrite the command you're typing with console messages by using the command `logging synchronous`.

```
config t
line con 0
logging synchronous
```

Hands-on Lab 6.6: Setting the Hostname, Descriptions, IP Address, and Clock Rate

1. Log into the router and go into privileged mode by typing **en** or **enable**. If required, enter a username and password.
2. Set your hostname on your router by using the hostname command. Notice that it is one word. Here is an example of setting your hostname:

```
Router#config t
Router(config)#hostname RouterA
RouterA(config)#
```

   Notice that the hostname of the router changed in the prompt as soon as you pressed Enter.
3. Set a banner that the network administrators will see by using the `banner` command, as shown in the following steps.
4. Type **config t**, then **banner ?**.
5. Notice that you can set at least four different banners. For this lab we are only interested in the login and message of the day (MOTD) banners.
6. Set your MOTD banner, which will be displayed when a console, auxiliary, or Telnet connection is made to the router, by typing this:

```
config t
banner motd #
This is an motd banner
#
```

7. The preceding example used a # sign as a delimiting character. This tells the router when the message is done. You cannot use the delimiting character in the message itself.
8. You can remove the MOTD banner by typing the following command:

```
config t
no banner motd
```

9. Set the login banner by typing this:

```
config t
banner login #
This is a login banner
#
```

10. The login banner will display immediately after the MOTD but before the user-mode password prompt. Remember that you set your user-mode passwords by setting the console, auxiliary, and VTY line passwords.
11. You can remove the login banner by typing this:

```
config t
no banner login
```

12. You can add an IP address to an interface with the `ip address` command. You need to get into interface configuration mode first; here is an example of how you do that:

```
config t
int e0 (you can use int Ethernet 0 too)
ip address 1.1.1.1 255.255.0.0
no shutdown
```

Notice that the IP address (`1.1.1.1`) and subnet mask (`255.255.0.0`) are configured on one line. The `no shutdown` (or `no shut` for short) command is used to enable the interface. All interfaces are shut down by default.

13. You can add identification to an interface by using the `description` command. This is useful for adding information about the connection. Here is an example:

```
config t
int s0
ip address 2.2.2.1 255.255.0.0
no shut
description Wan link to Miami
```

14. You can add the bandwidth of a serial link as well as the clock rate when simulating a DCE WAN link. Here is an example:

```
config t
int s0
bandwidth 64
clock rate 64000
```

Review Questions

The following questions are designed to test your understanding of this chapter's material. For more information on how to get additional questions, please see this book's Introduction.

1. You type **show running-config** and get this output:

```
[output cut]
line console 0
      Exec-timeout 1 44
      Password 7 098C0BQR
      Login
[output cut]
```

   What do the two numbers following the `exec-timeout` command mean?

   A. If no command has been typed in 44 seconds, the console connection will be closed.

   B. If no router activity has been detected in 1 hour and 44 minutes, the console will be locked out.

   C. If no commands have been typed in 1 minute and 44 seconds, the console connection will be closed.

   D. If you're connected to the router by a Telnet connection, input must be detected within 1 minute and 44 seconds or the connection will be closed.

2. Which of the following connection methods available to connect to a router is considered *out-of-band*?

   A. Serial port

   B. VTY port

   C. HTTP port

   D. Aux port

3. Which two of the following commands are required when configuring SSH on your router?

   A. `enable secret` *password*

   B. `exec-timeout 0 0`

   C. `ip domain-name` *name*

   D. `username` *name* `password` *password*

   E. `ip ssh version 2`

4. Which command will show you whether a DTE or a DCE cable is plugged into serial 0?

   A. `sh int s0`

   B. `sh int serial 0`

   C. `show controllers s 0`

   D. `show serial 0 controllers`

5. Which of the following is a correct combination of file type and default location in a Cisco router?

   A. IOS/NVRAM

   B. Startup configuration/flash memory

   C. IOS/flash memory

   D. Running configuration/NVRAM

6. You set the console password, but when you display the configuration, the password doesn't show up; it looks like this:

```
[output cut]
Line console 0
      Exec-timeout 1 44
      Password 7 098C0BQR
      Login
[output cut]
```

   What command would configure the password to be stored this way?

   A. `encrypt password`

   B. `service password-encryption`

   C. `service-password-encryption`

   D. `exec-timeout 1 44`

7. Which of the following commands will configure all the default VTY ports on a router?

   A. `Router#`**`line vty 0 4`**

   B. `Router(config)#`**`line vty 0 4`**

   C. `Router(config-if)#`**`line console 0`**

   D. `Router(config)#`**`line vty all`**

8. Which of the following commands sets the secret password to Cisco?

   A. `enable secret password Cisco`

   B. `enable secret cisco`

   C. `enable secret Cisco`

   D. `enable password Cisco`

9. If you wanted administrators to see a message when logging into the router, which command would you use?

   A. `message banner motd`

   B. `banner message motd`

   C. `banner motd`

   D. `message motd`

10. Which of the following prompts indicate that the router is currently in privileged mode?

    A. `router(config)#`

    B. `router>`

    C. `router#`

    D. `router(config-if)`

    ```
    router(config)# -- global configuration mode
    router> -- user mode
    router# -- privileged mode
    router(config-if)# -- interface configuration mode
    ```

11. What command do you type to save the configuration stored in RAM to NVRAM?

    A. `Router(config)#`**`copy current to starting`**

    B. `Router#`**`copy starting to running`**

    C. `Router(config)#`**`copy running-config startup-config`**

    D. `Router#`**`copy run start`**

12. You try to telnet into SFRouter from router Corp and receive this message:

    ```
    Corp#telnet SFRouter
    Trying SFRouter (10.0.0.1)...Open

    Password required, but none set
    [Connection to SFRouter closed by foreign host]
    Corp#
    ```

Which of the following sequences will address this problem correctly?

A. `Corp(config)#line console 0`

`Corp (config-line)#password` *`password`*

`Corp (config-line)#login`

B. `SFRemote(config)#line console 0`

`Corp (config-line)#enable secret` *`password`*

`Corp (config-line)#login`

C. `Corp(config)#line vty 0 4`

`Corp (config-line)#password` *`password`*

`Corp (config-line)#login`

D. `SFRemote(config)#line vty 0 4`

`Corp (config-line)#password` *`password`*

`Corp (config-line)#login`

13. Which command will delete the contents of NVRAM on a router?

A. `delete NVRAM`

B. `delete startup-config`

C. `erase NVRAM`

D. `erase start`

14. What is the problem with an interface if you type **`show interface serial 0`** and receive the following message?

`Serial0 is administratively down, line protocol is down`

A. The keepalives are different times.

B. The administrator has the interface shut down.

C. The administrator is pinging from the interface.

D. No cable is attached.

15. Which of the following commands displays the configurable parameters and statistics of all interfaces on a router?

A. `show running-config`

B. `show startup-config`

C. `show interfaces`

D. `show versions`

16. If you delete the contents of NVRAM and reboot the router, what mode will you be in?

A. Privileged mode

B. Global mode

C. Setup mode

D. NVRAM loaded mode

17. You type the following command into the router and receive the following output:

```
Router#show serial 0/0
                ^
% Invalid input detected at '^' marker.
```

Why was this error message displayed?

A. You need to be in privileged mode.

B. You cannot have a space between serial and 0/0.

C. The router does not have a serial0/0 interface.

D. Part of the command is missing.

18. You type **`Router#sh ru`** and receive a `% ambiguous command` error. Why did you receive this message?

A. The command requires additional options or parameters.

B. There is more than one `show` command that starts with the letters *ru*.

C. There is no `show` command that starts with *ru*.

D. The command is being executed from the wrong router mode.

19. Which of the following commands will display the current IP addressing and the layer 1 and 2 status of an interface? (Choose two.)

A. `show version`

B. `show interfaces`

C. `show controllers`

D. `show ip interface`

E. `show running-config`

20. At which layer of the OSI model would you assume the problem is if you type **`show interface serial 1`** and receive the following message?

`Serial1 is down, line protocol is down`

A. Physical layer

B. Data Link layer

C. Network layer

D. None; it is a router problem.

Answers to Review Questions

1. C. The `exec-timeout` command is set in minutes and seconds.

2. D. The auxiliary port can be configured with modem commands so that a modem can be connected to the router. It lets you dial up a remote router and attach to the auxiliary port if the router is down and you need to configure it out-of-band (meaning out of the network).

3. C, D. To configure SSH on your router, you need to set the `username` command, the `ip domain-name`, `login local`, and the `transport input ssh` under the VTY lines, and the `crypto key` command. However, SSH version 2 is not required, but suggested.

4. C. The `show controllers serial 0` command will show you whether either a DTE or DCE cable is connected to the interface. If it is a DCE connection, you need to add clocking with the `clock rate` command.

5. C. The default locations of the files are IOS in flash memory, startup configuration in NVRAM, and running configuration in RAM.

6. B. The command `service password-encryption`, from global configuration mode, will encrypt the passwords.

7. B. From global configuration mode, use the `line vty 0 4` command to set all five default VTY lines.

8. C. The enable secret password is case sensitive, so the second option is wrong. To set the enable secret password, use the `enable secret` *`password`* command from global configuration mode.

9. C. The typical banner is a message of the day (MOTD) and is set by using the global configuration mode command `banner motd`.

10. C. The prompts offered as options indicate the following modes:

    ```
    router(config)# -- global configuration mode
    router> -- user mode
    router# -- privileged mode
    router(config-if)# -- interface configuration mode
    ```

11. D. To copy the running-config to NVRAM so that it will be used if the router is restarted, use the `copy running-config startup-config` command in privileged mode (`copy run start` for short).

12. D. To allow a VTY (Telnet) session into your router, you must set the VTY password. Option C is wrong because it is setting the password on the wrong router. Notice that the answers you have to set the password before you set the login command. Remember, Cisco may have you set the password before the login command.

13. D. The erase startup-config command erases the contents of NVRAM and will put you in setup mode if the router is restarted.

14. B. If an interface is shut down, the `show interface` command will show the interface as administratively down. (It is possible that no cable is attached, but you can't tell that from this message.)

15. C. With the `show interfaces` command, you can view the configurable parameters, get statistics for the interfaces on the router, verify if the interfaces are shut down, and see the IP address of each interface.

16. C. If you delete the startup-config and reload the router, the router will automatically enter setup mode. You can also type **`setup`** from privileged mode at any time.

17. D. You can view the interface statistics from user mode, but the command is `show interface serial 0/0`.

18. B. The `% ambiguous command` error means that there is more than one possible `show` command that starts with ru. Use a question mark to find the correct command.

19. B, D. The commands `show interfaces` and `show ip interface` will show you the layer 1 and 2 status and the IP addresses of your router's interfaces.

20. A. If you see that a serial interface and the protocol are both down, then you have a Physical layer problem. If you see `serial1 is up, line protocol is down`, then you are not receiving (Data Link) keepalives from the remote end.

Answers to Written Lab 6

1. `router(config)#clock rate 64000`
2. `router#config t`
   `router(config)# line vty 0 4`
   `router(config-line)# no login`
3. `router#config t`
   `router(config)# int e0`
   `router(config-if)#  no shut`
4. `router#erase startup-config`
5. `router#config t`
   `router(config)# line console 0`
   `router(config)# login`
   `router(config)# password todd`
6. `router#config t`
   `router(config)# enable secret cisco`
7. `router#show controllers serial 0/1`
8. `router#show terminal`
9. `router#reload`
10. `router#config t`
    `router(config)#hostname Chicago`

Managing a Cisco Internetwork

THE CCNA EXAM TOPICS COVERED IN THIS CHAPTER INCLUDE THE FOLLOWING:

✓ **Configure, verify, and troubleshoot basic router operation and routing on Cisco devices.**

- Manage IOS configuration files (including: save, edit, upgrade, restore).
- Manage Cisco IOS.
- Verify network connectivity (including: using ping, traceroute, and telnet or SSH).

Here in Chapter 7, I'm going to show you how to manage Cisco routers on an internetwork. The Internetwork Operating System (IOS) and configuration files reside in different locations in a Cisco device, so it's really important to understand both where these files are located and how they work.

You'll be learning about the main components of a router, the router boot sequence, and the configuration register, including how to use the configuration register for password recovery. After that, you'll find out how to manage routers by using the copy command with a TFTP host when using the Cisco IOS File System (IFS).

We'll wrap up the chapter with an exploration of the Cisco Discovery Protocol (CDP), and you'll learn how to resolve hostnames and some important Cisco IOS troubleshooting techniques.

For up-to-the-minute updates for this chapter, please see `www.lammle.com` and/or `www.sybex.com/go/ccna7e`.

The Internal Components of a Cisco Router

To configure and troubleshoot a Cisco internetwork, you need to know the major components of Cisco routers and understand what each one does. Table 7.1 describes the major Cisco router components.

TABLE 7.1 Cisco router components

Component	Description
Bootstrap	Stored in the microcode of the ROM, the bootstrap is used to bring a router up during initialization. It will boot the router and then load the IOS.

Component	Description
POST (power-on self-test)	Stored in the microcode of the ROM, the POST is used to check the basic functionality of the router hardware and determines which interfaces are present.
ROM monitor	Stored in the microcode of the ROM, the ROM monitor is used for manufacturing, testing, and troubleshooting.
Mini-IOS	Called the RXBOOT or bootloader by Cisco, the mini-IOS is a small IOS in ROM that can be used to bring up an interface and load a Cisco IOS into flash memory. The mini-IOS can also perform a few other maintenance operations.
RAM (random access memory)	Used to hold packet buffers, ARP cache, routing tables, and also the software and data structures that allow the router to function. Running-config is stored in RAM, and most routers expand the IOS from flash into RAM upon boot.
ROM (read-only memory)	Used to start and maintain the router. Holds the POST and the bootstrap program as well as the mini-IOS.
Flash memory	Stores the Cisco IOS by default. Flash memory is not erased when the router is reloaded. It is EEPROM (electronically erasable programmable read-only memory) created by Intel.
NVRAM (nonvolatile RAM)	Used to hold the router and switch configuration. NVRAM is not erased when the router or switch is reloaded. Does not store an IOS. The configuration register is stored in NVRAM.
Configuration register	Used to control how the router boots up. This value can be found as the last line of the `show version` command output and by default is set to 0x2102, which tells the router to load the IOS from flash memory as well as to load the configuration from NVRAM.

The Router Boot Sequence

When a router boots up, it performs a series of steps, called the *boot sequence*, to test the hardware and load the necessary software. The boot sequence consists of the following steps:

1. The router performs a POST. The POST tests the hardware to verify that all components of the device are operational and present. For example, the POST checks for the different interfaces on the router. The POST is stored in and run from *ROM (read-only memory)*.
2. The bootstrap then looks for and loads the Cisco IOS software. The bootstrap is a program in ROM that is used to execute programs. The bootstrap program is responsible for finding where each IOS program is located and then loading the file. By default, the IOS software is loaded from flash memory in all Cisco routers.

The default order of an IOS loading from a router is flash, TFTP server, then ROM.

3. The IOS software looks for a valid configuration file stored in NVRAM. This file is called startup-config and is only there if an administrator copies the running-config file into NVRAM. (As you already know, the new ISR routers have a small startup-config file preloaded.)
4. If a startup-config file is in NVRAM, the router will copy this file and place it in RAM and call the file running-config. The router will use this file to run the router. The router should now be operational. If a startup-config file is not in NVRAM, the router will broadcast out any interface that detects carrier detect (CD) for a TFTP host looking for a configuration, and when that fails (typically it will fail—most people won't even realize the router has attempted this process), it will start the setup mode configuration process.

Managing Configuration Register

All Cisco routers have a 16-bit software register that's written into NVRAM. By default, the *configuration register* is set to load the Cisco IOS from *flash memory* and to look for and load the startup-config file from NVRAM. In the following sections, I am going to discuss the configuration register settings and how to use these settings to provide password recovery on your routers.

Understanding the Configuration Register Bits

The 16 bits (2 bytes) of the configuration register are read from 15 to 0, from left to right. The default configuration setting on Cisco routers is 0x2102. This means that bits 13, 8, and 1 are on, as shown in Table 7.2. Notice that each set of 4 bits (called a nibble) is read in binary with a value of 8, 4, 2, 1.

TABLE 7.2 The configuration register bit numbers

Configuration Register			2					1				0			2	
Bit number	15	14	13	12	11	10	9	8	7	6	5	4	3	2	1	0
Binary	0	0	1	0	0	0	0	1	0	0	0	0	0	0	1	0

Add the prefix *0x* to the configuration register address. The *0x* means that the digits that follow are in hexadecimal.

Table 7.3 lists the software configuration bit meanings. Notice that bit 6 can be used to ignore the NVRAM contents. This bit is used for password recovery—something I'll go over with you soon in the section "Recovering Passwords" later in this chapter.

Remember that in hex, the scheme is 0–9 and A–F (A = 10, B = 11, C = 12, D = 13, E = 14, and F = 15). This means that a 210F setting for the configuration register is actually 210(15), or 1111 in binary.

TABLE 7.3 Software configuration meanings

Bit	Hex	Description
0–3	0x0000–0x000F	Boot field (see Table 7.4).
6	0x0040	Ignore NVRAM contents.
7	0x0080	OEM bit enabled.
8	0x101	Break disabled.
10	0x0400	IP broadcast with all zeros.
5, 11–12	0x0800–0x1000	Console line speed.
13	0x2000	Boot default ROM software if network boot fails.
14	0x4000	IP broadcasts do not have net numbers.
15	0x8000	Enable diagnostic messages and ignore NVRAM contents.

The boot field, which consists of bits 0–3 in the configuration register, controls the router boot sequence. Table 7.4 describes the boot field bits.

TABLE 7.4 The boot field (configuration register bits 00–03)

Boot Field	Meaning	Use
00	ROM monitor mode	To boot to ROM monitor mode, set the configuration register to 2100. You must manually boot the router with the b command. The router will show the rommon> prompt.
01	Boot image from ROM	To boot the mini-IOS image stored in ROM, set the configuration register to 2101. The router will show the Router(boot)> prompt.
02–F	Specifies a default boot filename	Any value from 2102 through 210F tells the router to use the boot commands specified in NVRAM.

Checking the Current Configuration Register Value

You can see the current value of the configuration register by using the `show version` command (`sh version` or `show ver` for short), as demonstrated here:

```
Router>sh version
Cisco IOS Software, 2800 Software (C2800NM-ADVSECURITYK9-M), Version
    12.4(12), RELEASE SOFTWARE (fc1)
[output cut]
Configuration register is 0x2102
```

The last information given from this command is the value of the configuration register. In this example, the value is 0x2102—the default setting. The configuration register setting of 0x2102 tells the router to look in NVRAM for the boot sequence.

Notice that the `show version` command also provides the IOS version, and in the preceding example, it shows the IOS version as 12.4(12).

The `show version` command will display system hardware configuration information, software version, and the names of the boot images on a router.

Changing the Configuration Register

You can change the configuration register value to modify how the router boots and runs. These are the main reasons you would want to change the configuration register:

- To force the system into the ROM monitor mode
- To select a boot source
- To enable or disable the `Break` function
- To control broadcast addresses
- To set the console terminal baud rate
- To load operating software from ROM
- To enable booting from a Trivial File Transfer Protocol (TFTP) server

Before you change the configuration register, make sure you know the current configuration register value. Use the `show version` command to get this information.

You can change the configuration register by using the `config-register` command. Here's an example. The following commands tell the router to boot a small IOS from ROM and then show the current configuration register value:

```
Router(config)#config-register 0x2101
Router(config)#^Z
Router#sh ver
[output cut]
Configuration register is 0x2102 (will be 0x2101 at next
  reload)
```

Notice that the `show version` command displays the current configuration register value and also what that value will be when the router reboots. Any change to the configuration register won't take effect until the router is reloaded. The 0x2101 will load the IOS from ROM the next time the router is rebooted. You may see it listed as 0x101—that's basically the same thing, and it can be written either way.

Here is our router after setting the configuration register to 0x2101 and reloading:

```
Router(boot)#sh ver
Cisco IOS Software, 2800 Software (C2800NM-ADVSECURITYK9-M), Version
    12.4(12), RELEASE SOFTWARE (fc1)
[output cut]

ROM: System Bootstrap, Version 12.4(13r)T, RELEASE SOFTWARE (fc1)
```

```
Router uptime is 3 minutes
System returned to ROM by power-on
System image file is "flash:c2800nm-advsecurityk9-mz.124-12.bin"
[output cut]

Configuration register is 0x2101
```

At this point, if you typed **show flash**, you'd still see the IOS in flash memory ready to go. But we told our router to load from ROM, which is why the hostname shows up with (boot).

```
Router(boot)#sh flash
-#- --length-- -----date/time------ path
1     21710744 Jan 2 2007 22:41:14 +00:00 c2800nm-advsecurityk9-mz.124-12.bin
2         1823 Dec 5 2006 14:46:26 +00:00 sdmconfig-2811.cfg
3      4734464 Dec 5 2006 14:47:12 +00:00 sdm.tar
4       833024 Dec 5 2006 14:47:38 +00:00 es.tar
5      1052160 Dec 5 2006 14:48:10 +00:00 common.tar
6         1038 Dec 5 2006 14:48:32 +00:00 home.shtml
7       102400 Dec 5 2006 14:48:54 +00:00 home.tar
8       491213 Dec 5 2006 14:49:22 +00:00 128MB.sdf
9      1684577 Dec 5 2006 14:50:04 +00:00 securedesktop-ios-3.1.1.27-k9.pkg
10      398305 Dec 5 2006 14:50:34 +00:00 sslclient-win-1.1.0.154.pkg

32989184 bytes available (31027200 bytes used)
```

So even though we have our full IOS in flash, we changed the default loading of the router's software by changing the configuration register. If you want to set the configuration register back to the default, just type this:

```
Router(boot)#config t
Router(boot)(config)#config-register 0x2102
Router(boot)(config)#^Z
Router(boot)#reload
```

In the next section, I'll show you how to load the router into ROM monitor mode so you can perform password recovery.

Recovering Passwords

If you're locked out of a router because you forgot the password, you can change the configuration register to help you get back on your feet. As I said earlier, bit 6 in the configuration register is used to tell the router whether to use the contents of NVRAM to load a router configuration.

The default configuration register value is 0x2102, meaning that bit 6 is off. With the default setting, the router will look for and load a router configuration stored in

NVRAM (startup-config). To recover a password, you need to turn on bit 6. Doing this will tell the router to ignore the NVRAM contents. The configuration register value to turn on bit 6 is 0x2142.

Here are the main steps to password recovery:

1. Boot the router and interrupt the boot sequence by performing a break, which will take the router into ROM monitor mode.
2. Change the configuration register to turn on bit 6 (with the value 0x2142).
3. Reload the router.
4. Enter privileged mode.
5. Copy the startup-config file to running-config.
6. Change the password.
7. Reset the configuration register to the default value.
8. Save the router configuration.
9. Reload the router (optional).

I'm going to cover these steps in more detail in the following sections. I'll also show you the commands to restore access to ISR, 2600, and even 2500 series routers. (You can still use 2500s for labs and you never know when you might need this information!)

As I said, you can enter ROM monitor mode by pressing Ctrl+Break during router bootup. But if the IOS is corrupt or missing, if there's no network connectivity available to find a TFTP host, or if the mini-IOS from ROM doesn't load (meaning the default router fallback failed), the router will enter ROM monitor mode by default.

Interrupting the Router Boot Sequence

Your first step is to boot the router and perform a break. This is usually done by pressing the Ctrl+Break key combination when using HyperTerminal (personally, I use SecureCRT or Putty) while the router first reboots.

After you've performed a break, you should see something like this for a 2600 series router (it is pretty much the same output for the ISR series):

```
System Bootstrap, Version 11.3(2)XA4, RELEASE SOFTWARE (fc1)
Copyright (c) 1999 by cisco Systems, Inc.
TAC:Home:SW:IOS:Specials for info
PC = 0xfff0a530, Vector = 0x500, SP = 0x680127b0
C2600 platform with 32768 Kbytes of main memory
PC = 0xfff0a530, Vector = 0x500, SP = 0x80004374
monitor: command "boot" aborted due to user interrupt
rommon 1 >
```

Notice the line `monitor: command "boot" aborted due to user interrupt`. At this point, you will be at the `rommon 1>` prompt, which is called the ROM monitor mode.

Changing the Configuration Register

As I explained earlier, you can change the configuration register from within the IOS by using the `config-register` command. To turn on bit 6, use the configuration register value 0x2142.

Remember that if you change the configuration register to 0x2142, the startup-config will be bypassed and the router will load into setup mode.

Cisco ISR/2600 Series Commands

To change the bit value on a Cisco ISR/2600 series router, you just enter the command at the `rommon 1>` prompt:

```
rommon 1 >confreg 0x2142
You must reset or power cycle for new config to take effect
rommon 2 >reset
```

Cisco 2500 Series Commands

To change the configuration register on a 2500 series router, type **o** after creating a break sequence on the router. This brings up a menu of configuration register option settings. To change the configuration register, enter the command **o/r**, followed by the new register value. Here's an example of turning on bit 6 on a 2501 router:

```
System Bootstrap, Version 11.0(10c), SOFTWARE
Copyright (c) 1986-1996 by cisco Systems
2500 processor with 14336 Kbytes of main memory
Abort at 0x1098FEC (PC)
>o
Configuration register = 0x2102 at last boot
Bit#    Configuration register option settings:
15      Diagnostic mode disabled
14      IP broadcasts do not have network numbers
13      Boot default ROM software if network boot fails
12-11   Console speed is 9600 baud
10      IP broadcasts with ones
08      Break disabled
07      OEM disabled
06      Ignore configuration disabled
03-00   Boot file is cisco2-2500 (or 'boot system' command)
>o/r 0x2142
```

Notice that the last entry in the router output is 03-00. This tells the router what the IOS boot file is. By default, the router will use the first file found in the flash memory, so if you want to boot a different filename, you can use the `boot system flash:ios_name` command. (I'll show you the `boot system` command in a minute.)

Reloading the Router and Entering Privileged Mode

At this point, you need to reset the router like this:

- From the ISR/2600 series router, type **`I`** (for initialize) or **`reset`**.
- From the 2500 series router, type **`I`**.

The router will reload and ask if you want to use setup mode (because no startup-config is used). Answer no to entering setup mode, press Enter to go into user mode, and then type **`enable`** to go into privileged mode.

Viewing and Changing the Configuration

Now you're past the point where you would need to enter the user-mode and privileged-mode passwords in a router. Copy the startup-config file to the running-config file:

```
copy startup-config running-config
```

Or use the shortcut:

```
copy start run
```

The configuration is now running in *random access memory (RAM)*, and you're in privileged mode, meaning that you can now view and change the configuration. But you can't view the enable secret setting for the password since it is encrypted. To change the password, do this:

```
config t
enable secret todd
```

Resetting the Configuration Register and Reloading the Router

After you're finished changing passwords, set the configuration register back to the default value with the `config-register` command:

```
config t
config-register 0x2102
```

Finally, save the new configuration with a `copy running-config startup-config` and `reload` the router.

If you save your configuration and reload the router and it comes up in setup mode, the configuration register setting is probably incorrect.

Boot System Commands

Did you know that you can configure your router to boot another IOS if the flash is corrupted? Well, you can. In fact, you just might want all your routers to boot from a TFTP host each time anyway because that way, you'll never have to upgrade each router individually. This may be a smooth way to go because it allows you to just change one file on a TFTP host to perform an upgrade.

There are some `boot` commands you can play with that will help you manage the way your router boots the Cisco IOS—but remember, we're talking about the router's IOS here, *not* the router's configuration!

```
Router>en
Router#config t
Enter configuration commands, one per line.  End with CNTL/Z.
Router(config)#boot ?
  bootstrap  Bootstrap image file
  config     Configuration file
  host       Router-specific config file
  network    Network-wide config file
  system     System image file
```

The `boot` command truly gives you a wealth of options, but first, I'll show you the typical settings that Cisco recommends. So let's get started—the `boot system` command will allow you to tell the router which file to boot from flash memory. Remember that the router, by default, boots the first file found in flash. You can change that with the following commands:

```
Router(config)#boot system ?
  WORD   TFTP filename or URL
  flash  Boot from flash memory
  ftp    Boot from a server via ftp
  mop    Boot from a Decnet MOP server
  rcp    Boot from a server via rcp
  rom    Boot from rom
  tftp   Boot from a tftp server
Router(config)#boot system flash c2800nm-advsecurityk9-mz.124-12.bin
```

The preceding command configures the router to boot the IOS listed in it. This is a helpful command for when you load a new IOS into flash and want to test it, or even when you want to totally change which IOS is loading by default.

The next command is considered a fall-back routine, but as I said, you can make it a permanent way to have your routers boot from a TFTP host. Personally, I wouldn't necessarily recommend doing this (single point of failure); I'm just showing you that it's possible:

```
Router(config)#boot system tftp ?
  WORD  System image filename
```

```
Router(config)#boot system tftp c2800nm-advsecurityk9-mz.124-12.bin ?
  Hostname or A.B.C.D  Address from which to download the file
  <cr>
Router(config)#boot system tftp c2800nm-advsecurityk9-mz.124-12.bin 1.1.1.2
Router(config)#
```

As your last recommended fall-back option—the one to go to if the IOS in flash doesn't load and the TFTP host does not produce the IOS—load the mini-IOS from ROM like this:

```
Router(config)#boot system rom
Router(config)#do show run | include boot system
boot system flash c2800nm-advsecurityk9-mz.124-12.bin
boot system tftp c2800nm-advsecurityk9-mz.124-12.bin 1.1.1.2
boot system rom
Router(config)#
```

To sum this up, we now have Cisco's suggested IOS backup routine configured on our router: flash, TFTP host, ROM.

Backing Up and Restoring the Cisco IOS

Before you upgrade or restore a Cisco IOS, you really should copy the existing file to a *TFTP host* as a backup just in case the new image crashes and burns.

And you can use any TFTP host to accomplish this. By default, the flash memory in a router is used to store the Cisco IOS. In the following sections, I'll describe how to check the amount of flash memory, how to copy the Cisco IOS from flash memory to a TFTP host, and how to copy the IOS from a TFTP host to flash memory.

You'll learn how to use the Cisco IFS to manage your IOS files after first learning how to manage them with a TFTP host.

But before you back up an IOS image to a network server on your intranet, you've got to do these three things:

- Make sure you can access the network server.
- Ensure that the network server has adequate space for the code image.
- Verify the file naming and path requirement.

And if you have a laptop or workstation's Ethernet port directly connected to a router's Ethernet interface, as shown in Figure 7.1, you need to verify the following before attempting to copy the image to or from the router:

- TFTP server software must be running on the administrator's workstation.
- The Ethernet connection between the router and the workstation must be made with a crossover cable.
- The workstation must be on the same subnet as the router's Ethernet interface.
- The `copy flash tftp` command must be supplied the IP address of the workstation if you are copying from the router flash.
- And if you're copying "into" flash, you need to verify that there's enough room in flash memory to accommodate the file to be copied.

FIGURE 7.1 Copying an IOS from a workstation to a router

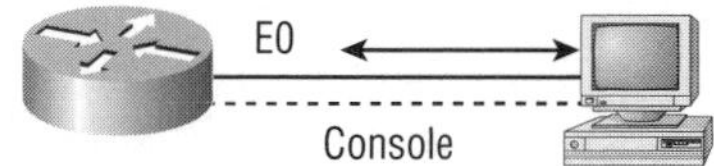

Verifying Flash Memory

Before you attempt to upgrade the Cisco IOS on your router with a new IOS file, it's a good idea to verify that your flash memory has enough room to hold the new image. You verify the amount of flash memory and the file or files being stored in flash memory by using the `show flash` command (`sh flash` for short):

```
Router#sh flash
-#- --length-- -----date/time------ path
1     21710744 Jan 2 2007 22:41:14 +00:00 c2800nm-advsecurityk9-mz.124-12.bin
[output cut]
32989184 bytes available (31027200 bytes used)
```

The router above has 64MB of RAM, and roughly half of the memory is in use.

The `show flash` command will display the amount of memory consumed by the current IOS image as well as tell you if there's enough room available to hold both current and new images. You should know that if there's not enough room for both the old and new image you want to load, the old image will be erased!

The amount of flash is actually easier to tally using the `show version` command on routers:

```
Router#show version
[output cut]
```

```
Cisco 2811 (revision 49.46) with 249856K/12288K bytes of memory.
Processor board ID FTX1049A1AB
2 FastEthernet interfaces
4 Serial(sync/async) interfaces
1 Virtual Private Network (VPN) Module
DRAM configuration is 64 bits wide with parity enabled.
239K bytes of non-volatile configuration memory.
62720K bytes of ATA CompactFlash (Read/Write)
```

You can see that the amount of flash shows up on the last line. By averaging up, we get the amount of flash to 64MB.

Notice that the filename in this example is `c2800nm-advsecurityk9-mz.124-12.bin`. The main difference in the output of the `show flash` and `show version` commands is that the `show flash` command displays all files in flash and the `show version` command shows the actual name of the file that the router is using to run the router.

Backing Up the Cisco IOS

To back up the Cisco IOS to a TFTP server, you use the `copy flash tftp` command. It's a straightforward command that requires only the source filename and the IP address of the TFTP server.

The key to success in this backup routine is to make sure you've got good, solid connectivity to the TFTP server. Check this by pinging the TFTP device from the router console prompt like this:

```
Router#ping 1.1.1.2
Type escape sequence to abort.
Sending 5, 100-byte ICMP Echos to 1.1.1.2, timeout
  is 2 seconds:
!!!!!
Success rate is 100 percent (5/5), round-trip min/avg/max
  = 4/4/8 ms
```

The *Packet Internet Groper (Ping)* utility is used to test network connectivity, and I use it in some of the examples in this chapter. I'll be talking about it in more detail in the section "Checking Network Connectivity and Troubleshooting" later in the chapter.

After you ping the TFTP server to make sure that IP is working, you can use the `copy flash tftp` command to copy the IOS to the TFTP server as shown next:

```
Router#copy flash tftp
Source filename []?c2800nm-advsecurityk9-mz.124-12.bin
Address or name of remote host []?1.1.1.2
```

```
Destination filename [c2800nm-advsecurityk9-mz.124-12.bin]?[enter]
!!!!!!!!!!!!!!!!!!!!!!!!!!!!!!!!!!!!!!!!!!!!!!!!!!!!!!!!!!!!!!!!!!!!!!!!!!!!!!!!
!!!!!!
21710744 bytes copied in 60.724 secs (357532 bytes/sec)
Router#
```

Just copy the IOS filename from either the `show flash` or `show version` command and then paste it when prompted for the source filename.

In the preceding example, the contents of flash memory were copied successfully to the TFTP server. The address of the remote host is the IP address of the TFTP host, and the source filename is the file in flash memory.

The `copy flash tftp` command won't prompt you for the location of any file or ask you where to put the file. TFTP is just a "grab it and place it" program in this situation. This means that the TFTP server must have a default directory specified or it won't work!

Restoring or Upgrading the Cisco Router IOS

What happens if you need to restore the Cisco IOS to flash memory to replace an original file that has been damaged or if you want to upgrade the IOS? You can download the file from a TFTP server to flash memory by using the `copy tftp flash` command. This command requires the IP address of the TFTP host and the name of the file you want to download.

But before you begin, make sure the file you want to place in flash memory is in the default TFTP directory on your host. When you issue the command, TFTP won't ask you where the file is, so if the file you want to use isn't in the default directory of the TFTP host, this just won't work.

```
Router#copy tftp flash
Address or name of remote host []?1.1.1.2
Source filename []?c2800nm-advsecurityk9-mz.124-12.bin
Destination filename [c2800nm-advsecurityk9-mz.124-12.bin]?[enter]
%Warning: There is a file already existing with this name
Do you want to over write? [confirm][enter]
Accessing tftp://1.1.1.2/c2800nm-advsecurityk9-mz.124-12.bin...
Loading c2800nm-advsecurityk9-mz.124-12.bin from 1.1.1.2 (via
   FastEthernet0/0): !!!!!!!!!!!!!!!!!!!!!!!!!!!!!!!!!!!!!!!!!!!!!!!!!!!!!!!!!!!!!
!!!!!!!!!!!!!!
[OK - 21710744 bytes]

21710744 bytes copied in 82.880 secs (261954 bytes/sec)
Router#
```

In the preceding example, I copied the same file into flash memory, so it asked me if I wanted to overwrite it. Remember that we are "playing" with files in flash memory. If I had just corrupted my file by overwriting it, I won't know until I reboot the router. Be careful with this command! If the file is corrupted, you'll need to do an IOS restore from ROM monitor mode.

If you are loading a new file and you don't have enough room in flash memory to store both the new and existing copies, the router will ask to erase the contents of flash memory before writing the new file into flash memory.

A Cisco router can become a TFTP server host for a router system image that's run in flash memory. The global configuration command is `tftp-server flash:ios_name`.

Using the Cisco IOS File System (Cisco IFS)

Cisco has created a file system called Cisco IFS that allows you to work with files and directories just as you would from a Windows DOS prompt. The commands you use are `dir`, `copy`, `more`, `delete`, `erase` or `format`, `cd` and `pwd`, and `mkdir` and `rmdir`.

Working with IFS gives you the ability to view all files—even those on remote servers. And you definitely want to find out if an image on one of your remote servers is valid before you copy it, right? You also need to know how big it is—size matters here! It's also a really good idea to take a look at the remote server's configuration and make sure it's all good before loading that file on your router.

It's very cool that IFS makes the file system user interface universal—it's not platform specific anymore. You now get to use the same syntax for all your commands on all of your routers, no matter the platform!

Sound too good to be true? Well, it kind of is because you'll find out that support for all commands on each file system and platform just isn't there. But it's really no big deal since various file systems differ in the actions they perform; the commands that aren't relevant to a particular file system are the very ones that aren't supported. Be assured that any file system or platform will fully support all the commands you need to manage it.

Another cool IFS feature is that it cuts down on all those obligatory prompts for a lot of the commands. If you want to enter a command, all you have to do is type all the necessary info straight into the command line—no more jumping through hoops of prompts! So, if you want to copy a file to an FTP server, all you'd do is first indicate where the desired source file is on your router, pinpoint where the destination file is to be on the FTP server, determine the username and password you're going to use when you want to connect to that server, and type it all in on one line—sleek! And for those of you resistant to change, you can still have the router prompt you for all the information it needs and enjoy entering a more elegantly minimized version of the command than you did before.

But even in spite of all this, your router might still prompt you—even if you did everything right in your command line. It comes down to how you've got the `file prompt` command configured and which command you're trying to use. But no worries—if that happens, the default value will be entered right there in the command, and all you have to do is hit Enter to verify the correct values.

IFS also lets you explore various directories and inventory files in any directory you want. Plus, you can make subdirectories in flash memory or on a card, but you only get to do that if you're working on one of the more recent platforms.

And get this—the new file system interface uses URLs to determine the whereabouts of a file. So just as they pinpoint places on the Web, URLs now indicate where files are on your Cisco router, or even on a remote file server! You just type URLs right into your commands to identify where the file or directory is. It's really that easy—to copy a file from one place to another, you simply enter the `copy source-url destination-url` command—sweet! IFS URLs are a tad different than what you're used to though, and there's an array of formats to use that vary depending on where, exactly, the file is that you're after.

We're going to use Cisco IFS commands pretty much the same way that we used the `copy` command in the IOS section earlier:

- For backing up the IOS
- For upgrading the IOS
- For viewing text files

Okay—with all that down, let's take a look at the common IFS commands available to us for managing the IOS. I'll get into configuration files soon, but for now I'm going to get you started with going over the basics used to manage the new Cisco IOS.

`dir` Same as with Windows, this command lets you view files in a directory. Type **`dir`**, hit Enter, and by default you get the contents of the `flash:/` directory output.

`copy` This is one popular command, often used to upgrade, restore, or back up an IOS. But as I said, when you use it, it's really important to focus on the details—what you're copying, where it's coming from, and where it's going to land.

`more` Same as with Unix, this will take a text file and let you look at it on a card. You can use it to check out your configuration file or your backup configuration file. I'll go over it more when we get into actual configuration.

`show file` This command will give you the skinny on a specified file or file system, but it's kind of obscure because people don't use it a lot.

`delete` Three guesses—yep, it deletes stuff. But with some types of routers, not as well as you'd think. That's because even though it whacks the file, it doesn't always free up the space it was using. To actually get the space back, you have to use something called the `squeeze` command too.

`erase/format` Use these with care—make sure that when you're copying files, you say no to the dialog that asks you if you want to erase the file system! The type of memory you're using determines if you can nix the flash drive or not.

`cd/pwd` Same as with Unix and DOS, `cd` is the command you use to change directories. Use the `pwd` command to print (show) the working directory.

mkdir/rmdir Use these commands on certain routers and switches to create and delete directories—the mkdir command for creation and the rmdir command for deletion. Use the cd and pwd commands to change into these directories.

Using the Cisco IFS to Upgrade an IOS

Let's take a look at some of these Cisco IFS commands on my ISR router (1841 series) with a hostname of R1.

We'll start with the pwd command to verify our default directory and then use the dir command to verify the contents of the default directory (flash:/):

```
R1#pwd
flash:
R1#dir
Directory of flash:/
    1  -rw-    13937472  Dec 20 2006 19:58:18 +00:00  c1841-ipbase-
   mz.124-1c.bin
    2  -rw-        1821  Dec 20 2006 20:11:24 +00:00  sdmconfig-18xx.cfg
    3  -rw-     4734464  Dec 20 2006 20:12:00 +00:00  sdm.tar
    4  -rw-      833024  Dec 20 2006 20:12:24 +00:00  es.tar
    5  -rw-     1052160  Dec 20 2006 20:12:50 +00:00  common.tar
    6  -rw-        1038  Dec 20 2006 20:13:10 +00:00  home.shtml
    7  -rw-      102400  Dec 20 2006 20:13:30 +00:00  home.tar
    8  -rw-      491213  Dec 20 2006 20:13:56 +00:00  128MB.sdf
    9  -rw-     1684577  Dec 20 2006 20:14:34 +00:00  securedesktop-
   ios-3.1.1.27-k9.pkg
   10  -rw-      398305  Dec 20 2006 20:15:04 +00:00  sslclient-win-
   1.1.0.154.pkg

32071680 bytes total (8818688 bytes free)
```

What we can see here is that we have the basic IP IOS (c1841-ipbase-mz.124-1c.bin). Looks like we need to upgrade our 1841. You've just got to love how Cisco puts the IOS type in the filename now! First, let's check the size of the file that's in flash with the show file command (show flash would also work):

```
R1#show file info flash:c1841-ipbase-mz.124-1c.bin
flash:c1841-ipbase-mz.124-1c.bin:
  type is image (elf) []
  file size is 13937472 bytes, run size is 14103140 bytes
  Runnable image, entry point 0x8000F000, run from ram
```

With a file that size, the existing IOS will have to be erased before we can add our new IOS file (c1841-advipservicesk9-mz.124-12.bin), which is over 21MB. We'll use the delete command, but remember, we can play with any file in flash memory and nothing serious will happen until we reboot—that is, if we made a mistake. So obviously, and as I pointed out earlier, we need to be majorly careful here!

```
R1#delete flash:c1841-ipbase-mz.124-1c.bin
Delete filename [c1841-ipbase-mz.124-1c.bin]?[enter]
Delete flash:c1841-ipbase-mz.124-1c.bin? [confirm][enter]
R1#sh flash
-#- --length-- -----date/time------ path
1         1821 Dec 20 2006 20:11:24 +00:00 sdmconfig-18xx.cfg
2      4734464 Dec 20 2006 20:12:00 +00:00 sdm.tar
3       833024 Dec 20 2006 20:12:24 +00:00 es.tar
4      1052160 Dec 20 2006 20:12:50 +00:00 common.tar
5         1038 Dec 20 2006 20:13:10 +00:00 home.shtml
6       102400 Dec 20 2006 20:13:30 +00:00 home.tar
7       491213 Dec 20 2006 20:13:56 +00:00 128MB.sdf
8      1684577 Dec 20 2006 20:14:34 +00:00 securedesktop-ios-3.1.1.27-k9.pkg
9       398305 Dec 20 2006 20:15:04 +00:00 sslclient-win-1.1.0.154.pkg
22757376 bytes available (9314304 bytes used)
R1#sh file info flash:c1841-ipbase-mz.124-1c.bin
%Error opening flash:c1841-ipbase-mz.124-1c.bin (File not found)
R1#
```

So with the preceding commands, I deleted the existing file and then verified the deletion by using both the `show flash` and `show file` commands. Let's add the new file with the copy command, but again, I'm going to make sure I'm careful because this doesn't make it safer than the first method I showed you earlier:

```
R1#copy tftp://1.1.1.2//c1841-advipservicesk9-mz.124-12.bin/ flash:/
    c1841-advipservicesk9-mz.124-12.bin
Source filename [/c1841-advipservicesk9-mz.124-12.bin/]?[enter]
Destination filename [c1841-advipservicesk9-mz.124-12.bin]?[enter]
Loading /c1841-advipservicesk9-mz.124-12.bin/ from 1.1.1.2 (via
    FastEthernet0/0): !!!!!!!!!!!!!!!!!!!!!!!!!!!!!!!!!!!!!!!!
[output cut]
!!!!!!!!!!!!!!!!!!!!!!!!!!!!!!!!!!!!!!!!!!!!!!!!!!!!!!!
[OK - 22103052 bytes]
22103052 bytes copied in 72.008 secs (306953 bytes/sec)
R1#sh flash
-#- --length-- -----date/time------ path
1         1821 Dec 20 2006 20:11:24 +00:00 sdmconfig-18xx.cfg
2      4734464 Dec 20 2006 20:12:00 +00:00 sdm.tar
3       833024 Dec 20 2006 20:12:24 +00:00 es.tar
4      1052160 Dec 20 2006 20:12:50 +00:00 common.tar
```

```
5          1038 Dec 20 2006 20:13:10 +00:00 home.shtml
6        102400 Dec 20 2006 20:13:30 +00:00 home.tar
7        491213 Dec 20 2006 20:13:56 +00:00 128MB.sdf
8       1684577 Dec 20 2006 20:14:34 +00:00 securedesktop-ios-3.1.1.27-k9.pkg
9        398305 Dec 20 2006 20:15:04 +00:00 sslclient-win-1.1.0.154.pkg
10     22103052 Mar 10 2007 19:40:50 +00:00 c1841-advipservicesk9-mz.124-12.bin
651264 bytes available (31420416 bytes used)
R1#
```

We can check the file information as well with the `show file` command:

```
R1#sh file information flash:c1841-advipservicesk9-mz.124-12.bin
flash:c1841-advipservicesk9-mz.124-12.bin:
  type is image (elf) []
  file size is 22103052 bytes, run size is 22268736 bytes
  Runnable image, entry point 0x8000F000, run from ram
```

Remember that the IOS is expanded into RAM when the router boots, so the new IOS will not run until you reload the router.

I really recommend that you play with the Cisco IFS commands on a router just to get a good feel for them because, as I've said, they can definitely give you some grief at first!

I mention "safer methods" a lot in this chapter. Clearly, I've caused myself some serious pain not being careful enough when working in flash memory! I cannot tell you enough—pay attention when messing around with flash memory!

One of the brilliant features of the ISR routers is that they use the physical flash cards that are accessible from the front or back of any router. You can pull these flash cards out, put them in an appropriate slot in your PC, and the card will show up as a drive. You can then add, change, and delete files. Just put the flash card back in your router and power up—instant upgrade. Nice!

Backing Up and Restoring the Cisco Configuration

Any changes that you make to the router configuration are stored in the running-config file. And if you don't enter a `copy run start` command after you make a change to running-config, that change will go poof if the router reboots or gets powered down. So you probably want to make another backup of the configuration information just in case the router or switch completely dies on you. Even if your machine is healthy and happy, it's good to have for reference and documentation reasons.

In the following sections, I'll describe how to copy the configuration of a router to a TFTP server and how to restore that configuration.

Backing Up the Cisco Router Configuration

To copy the router's configuration from a router to a TFTP server, you can use either the `copy running-config tftp` or the `copy startup-config tftp` command. Either one will back up the router configuration that's currently running in DRAM or that's stored in NVRAM.

Verifying the Current Configuration

To verify the configuration in DRAM, use the `show running-config` command (`sh run` for short) like this:

```
Router#show running-config
Building configuration...

Current configuration : 776 bytes
!
version 12.4
```

The current configuration information indicates that the router is running version 12.4 of the IOS.

Verifying the Stored Configuration

Next, you should check the configuration stored in NVRAM. To see this, use the `show startup-config` command (`sh start` for short) like this:

```
Router#show startup-config
Using 776 out of 245752 bytes
!
version 12.4
```

The first line shows you how much room your backup configuration is using. Here, we can see that NVRAM is 245KB (again, memory is easier to see with the `show version` command when you're using an ISR router) and that only 776 bytes of it are used.

If you're not sure that the files are the same and the running-config file is what you want to use, then use the `copy running-config startup-config command`. This will help you ensure that both files are in fact the same. I'll go through this with you in the next section.

Copying the Current Configuration to NVRAM

By copying running-config to NVRAM as a backup, as shown in the following output, you're assured that your running-config will always be reloaded if the router gets rebooted. In the new IOS version 12.0, you're prompted for the filename you want to use:

```
Router#copy running-config startup-config
Destination filename [startup-config]?[enter]
Building configuration...
[OK]
Router#
```

The reason the filename prompt appears is that there are now so many options you can use when using the copy command:

```
Router#copy running-config ?
  archive:         Copy to archive: file system
  flash:           Copy to flash: file system
  ftp:             Copy to ftp: file system
  http:            Copy to http: file system
  https:           Copy to https: file system
  ips-sdf          Update (merge with) IPS signature configuration
  null:            Copy to null: file system
  nvram:           Copy to nvram: file system
  rcp:             Copy to rcp: file system
  running-config   Update (merge with) current system configuration
  scp:             Copy to scp: file system
  startup-config   Copy to startup configuration
  syslog:          Copy to syslog: file system
  system:          Copy to system: file system
  tftp:            Copy to tftp: file system
  xmodem:          Copy to xmodem: file system
  ymodem:          Copy to ymodem: file system
```

We'll go over the copy command again in a minute.

Copying the Configuration to a TFTP Server

Once the file is copied to NVRAM, you can make a second backup to a TFTP server by using the `copy running-config tftp` command (`copy run tftp` for short), like this:

```
Router#copy running-config tftp
Address or name of remote host []?1.1.1.2
Destination filename [router-confg]?todd-confg
```

```
!!
776 bytes copied in 0.800 secs (970 bytes/sec)
Router#
```

In the preceding example, I named the file `todd-confg` because I had not set a hostname for the router. If you have a hostname already configured, the command will automatically use the hostname plus the extension `-confg` as the name of the file.

Restoring the Cisco Router Configuration

If you've changed your router's running-config file and want to restore the configuration to the version in the startup-config file, the easiest way to do this is to use the `copy startup-config running-config` command (`copy start run` for short). You can also use the older Cisco command `config mem` to restore a configuration. Of course, this will work only if you copied running-config into NVRAM before making any changes!

If you did copy the router's configuration to a TFTP server as a second backup, you can restore the configuration using the `copy tftp running-config` command (`copy tftp run` for short) or the `copy tftp startup-config` command (`copy tftp start` for short), as shown here (the old command that provides this function is `config net`):

```
Router#copy tftp running-config
Address or name of remote host []?1.1.1.2
Source filename []?todd-confg
Destination filename[running-config]?[enter]
Accessing tftp://1.1.1.2/todd-confg...
Loading todd-confg from 1.1.1.2 (via FastEthernet0/0): !
[OK - 776 bytes]
776 bytes copied in 9.212 secs (84 bytes/sec)
Router#
*Mar  7 17:53:34.071: %SYS-5-CONFIG_I: Configured from
    tftp://1.1.1.2/todd-confg by console
Router#
```

The configuration file is an ASCII text file, meaning that before you copy the configuration stored on a TFTP server back to a router, you can make changes to the file with any text editor. Last, notice that the command was changed to a URL of `tftp://1.1.1.2/todd-config`. This is the Cisco IOS File System (IFS)—as discussed earlier—and we'll use that to back up and restore our configuration in a minute.

It is important to remember that when you copy or merge a configuration from a TFTP server to a freshly erased and rebooted router's RAM, the interfaces are shut down by default and you must manually go and enable each interface with the no shutdown command.

Erasing the Configuration

To delete the startup-config file on a Cisco router, use the command `erase startup-config`, like this:

```
Router#erase startup-config
Erasing the nvram filesystem will remove all configuration files!
    Continue? [confirm][enter]
[OK]
Erase of nvram: complete
*Mar  7 17:56:20.407: %SYS-7-NV_BLOCK_INIT: Initialized the geometry of nvram
Router#reload
System configuration has been modified. Save? [yes/no]:n
Proceed with reload? [confirm][enter]
 *Mar  7 17:56:31.059: %SYS-5-RELOAD: Reload requested by console.
    Reload Reason: Reload Command.
```

This command deletes the contents of NVRAM on the router. If you type **reload** at privileged mode and say no to saving changes, the router will reload and come up into setup mode.

Using the Cisco IOS File System to Manage Your Router's Configuration (Cisco IFS)

Using the old, faithful copy command is still useful and I recommend it. However, you still need to know about the Cisco IFS. The first thing we'll do is use the `show file` command to see the contents of NVRAM and RAM:

```
R3#show file information nvram:startup-config
nvram:startup-config:
  type is config
R3#cd nvram:
R3#pwd
nvram:/
R3#dir
Directory of nvram:/

  190  -rw-         830                 <no date>  startup-config
  191  ----           5                 <no date>  private-config
  192  -rw-         830                 <no date>  underlying-config
    1  -rw-           0                 <no date>  ifIndex-table
196600 bytes total (194689 bytes free)
```

There really are no other commands that will actually show us the contents of NVRAM. However, I am not sure how helpful it is to see them either. Let's look at the contents of RAM:

```
R3#cd system:
R3#pwd
system:/
R3#dir ?
  /all              List all files
  /recursive        List files recursively
  all-filesystems   List files on all filesystems
  archive:          Directory or file name
  cns:              Directory or file name
  flash:            Directory or file name
  null:             Directory or file name
  nvram:            Directory or file name
  system:           Directory or file name
  xmodem:           Directory or file name
  ymodem:           Directory or file name
  <cr>
R3#dir
Directory of system:/

    3  dr-x           0                    <no date>  lib
   33  dr-x           0                    <no date>  memory
    1  -rw-         750                    <no date>  running-config
    2  dr-x           0                    <no date>  vfiles
```

Again, not too exciting. Let's use the `copy` command with the Cisco IFS to copy a file from a TFTP host to RAM. First, let's try the old command `config net` that was used for the last 10 years or so to accomplish this same feat:

```
R3#config net
Host or network configuration file [host]?[enter]
This command has been replaced by the command:
         'copy <url> system:/running-config'
Address or name of remote host [255.255.255.255]?
```

Although the output tells us that the old command has been replaced with the new URL command, the old command will still will work. Let's try it with the Cisco IFS:

```
R3#copy tftp://1.1.1.2/todd-confg system://running-config
Destination filename [running-config]?[enter]
Accessing tftp://1.1.1.2/todd-confg...Loading todd-confg from 1.1.1.2
    (via FastEthernet0/0): !
```

```
[OK - 776 bytes]
[OK]
776 bytes copied in 13.816 secs (56 bytes/sec)
R3#
*Mar 10 22:12:59.819: %SYS-5-CONFIG_I:
Configured from tftp://1.1.1.2/todd-confg by console
```

I guess we can say that this was easier than using the `copy tftp run` command—Cisco says it is, so who am I to argue? Maybe it just takes some getting used to.

Using Cisco Discovery Protocol (CDP)

Cisco Discovery Protocol (CDP) is a proprietary protocol designed by Cisco to help administrators collect information about both locally attached and remote devices. By using CDP, you can gather hardware and protocol information about neighbor devices, which is useful info for troubleshooting and documenting the network.

In the following sections, I am going to discuss the CDP timer and CDP commands used to verify your network.

Getting CDP Timers and Holdtime Information

The `show cdp` command (`sh cdp` for short) gives you information about two CDP global parameters that can be configured on Cisco devices:

- *CDP timer* is how often CDP packets are transmitted out all active interfaces.
- *CDP holdtime* is the amount of time that the device will hold packets received from neighbor devices.

Both Cisco routers and Cisco switches use the same parameters.

The output on the Corp router looks like this:

```
Corp#sh cdp
Global CDP information:
        Sending CDP packets every 60 seconds
        Sending a holdtime value of 180 seconds
        Sending CDPv2 advertisements is  enabled
```

Use the global commands `cdp holdtime` and `cdp timer` to configure the CDP holdtime and timer on a router:

```
Corp(config)#cdp ?
  advertise-v2      CDP sends version-2 advertisements
  holdtime          Specify the holdtime (in sec) to be sent in packets
  log               Log messages generated by CDP
```

```
  run               Enable CDP
  source-interface  Insert the interface's IP in all CDP packets
  timer             Specify rate (in sec) at which CDP packets are sent  run
Corp(config)#cdp holdtime ?
  <10-255>  Length  of time  (in sec) that receiver must keep this packet
Corp(config)#cdp timer ?
  <5-254>  Rate at which CDP packets are sent (in  sec)
```

You can turn off CDP completely with the `no cdp run` command from the global configuration mode of a router. To turn CDP off or on for an interface, use the `no cdp enable` and `cdp enable` commands. Be patient—I'll work through these with you in a second.

Gathering Neighbor Information

The `show cdp neighbor` command (`sh cdp nei` for short) delivers information about directly connected devices. It's important to remember that CDP packets aren't passed through a Cisco switch and that you only see what's directly attached. So this means that if your router is connected to a switch, you won't see any of the devices hooked up to that switch.

The following output shows the `show cdp neighbor` command used on my Corp 2811 router:

```
Corp#sh cdp neighbors
Capability Codes: R - Router, T - Trans Bridge, B - Source Route Bridge
                  S - Switch, H - Host, I - IGMP, r - Repeater
Device ID    Local Intrfce   Holdtme    Capability  Platform  Port ID
ap          Fas 0/1          165         T I        AIR-AP124 Fas 0
R2          Ser 0/1/0        140        R S I       2801      Ser 0/2/0
R3          Ser 0/0/1        157        R S I       1841      Ser 0/0/1
R1          Ser 0/2/0        154        R S I       1841      Ser 0/0/1
R1          Ser 0/0/0        154        R S I       1841      Ser 0/0/0
Corp#
```

Okay, we are directly connected with a console cable to the Corp router, and the router is directly connected to four devices. We have two connections to the R1 router. The device ID shows the configured hostname of the connected device, the local interface is our interface, and the port ID is the remote devices' directly connected interface. All you get to view are directly connected devices.

Table 7.5 summarizes the information displayed by the `show cdp neighbor` command for each device.

TABLE 7.5 Output of the show cdp neighbor command

Field	Description
Device ID	The hostname of the device directly connected.
Local Interface	The port or interface on which you are receiving the CDP packet.
Holdtime	The remaining amount of time the router will hold the information before discarding it if no more CDP packets are received.
Capability	The capability of the neighbor, such as the router, switch, or repeater. The capability codes are listed at the top of the command output.
Platform	The type of Cisco device directly connected. In the previous output, a 1240AP, 2801 router, and two 1841 routers are directly connected to the Corp router.
Port ID	The neighbor device's port or interface on which the CDP packets are multicast.

It is imperative that you can look at the output of a show cdp neighbors command and decipher the neighbor's device (capability, i.e., router or switch), model number (platform), your port connecting to that device (local interface), and the port of the neighbor connecting to you (port ID).

Another command that'll deliver the goods on neighbor information is the show cdp neighbors detail command (show cdp nei de for short). This command can be run on both routers and switches, and it displays detailed information about each device connected to the device you're running the command on. Check out this router output for an example:

```
Corp#sh cdp neighbors detail
-------------------------
Device ID: ap
Entry address(es): 10.1.1.2
Platform: cisco AIR-AP1242AG-A-K9    , Capabilities: Trans-Bridge IGMP
Interface: FastEthernet0/1,  Port ID (outgoing port): FastEthernet0
Holdtime : 122 sec

Version :
Cisco IOS Software, C1240 Software (C1240-K9W7-M), Version 12.3(8)JEA,
    RELEASE SOFTWARE (fc2)
```

```
Technical Support: http://www.cisco.com/techsupport
Copyright (c) 1986-2006 by Cisco Systems, Inc.
Compiled Wed 23-Aug-06 16:45 by kellythw

advertisement version: 2
Duplex: full
Power drawn: 15.000 Watts
-------------------------
Device ID: R2
Entry address(es):
  IP address: 10.4.4.2
Platform: Cisco 2801,  Capabilities: Router Switch IGMP
Interface: Serial0/1/0,  Port ID (outgoing port): Serial0/2/0
Holdtime : 135 sec

Version :
Cisco IOS Software, 2801 Software (C2801-ADVENTERPRISEK9-M),
    Experimental Version 12.4(20050525:193634) [jezhao-ani 145]
Copyright (c) 1986-2005 by Cisco Systems, Inc.
Compiled Fri 27-May-05 23:53 by jezhao

advertisement version: 2
VTP Management Domain: ''
-------------------------
Device ID: R3
Entry address(es):
  IP address: 10.5.5.1
Platform: Cisco 1841,  Capabilities: Router Switch IGMP
Interface: Serial0/0/1,  Port ID (outgoing port): Serial0/0/1
Holdtime : 152 sec

Version :
Cisco IOS Software, 1841 Software (C1841-IPBASE-M), Version 12.4(1c),
    RELEASE SOFTWARE (fc1)
Technical Support: http://www.cisco.com/techsupport
Copyright (c) 1986-2005 by Cisco Systems, Inc.
Compiled Tue 25-Oct-05 17:10 by evmiller

advertisement version: 2
VTP Management Domain: ''
```

```
-------------------------
[output cut]
Corp#
```

What are we being shown here? First, we're given the hostname and IP address of all directly connected devices. In addition to the same information displayed by the `show cdp neighbor` command (see Table 7.5), the `show cdp neighbor detail` command gives us the IOS version of the neighbor device.

Remember that you can see the IP address of only directly connected devices.

The `show cdp entry *` command displays the same information as the `show cdp neighbors detail` command. Here's an example of the router output using the `show cdp entry *` command:

```
Corp#sh cdp entry *
-------------------------
Device ID: ap
Entry address(es):
Platform: cisco AIR-AP1242AG-A-K9    ,  Capabilities: Trans-Bridge IGMP
Interface: FastEthernet0/1,  Port ID (outgoing port): FastEthernet0
Holdtime : 160 sec

Version :
Cisco IOS Software, C1240 Software (C1240-K9W7-M), Version 12.3(8)JEA,
    RELEASE SOFTWARE (fc2)
Technical Support: http://www.cisco.com/techsupport
Copyright (c) 1986-2006 by Cisco Systems, Inc.
Compiled Wed 23-Aug-06 16:45 by kellythw

advertisement version: 2
Duplex: full
Power drawn: 15.000 Watts
-------------------------
Device ID: R2
Entry address(es):
  IP address: 10.4.4.2
Platform: Cisco 2801,  Capabilities: Router Switch IGMP
 --More--
[output cut]
```

There isn't any difference between the `show cdp neighbors detail` and `show cdp entry *` commands. However, the `sh cdp entry *` command has two options that the `show cdp neighbors detail` command does not:

```
Corp#sh cdp entry * ?
  protocol  Protocol information
  version   Version information
  |         Output modifiers
  <cr>
Corp#show cdp entry * protocols
Protocol information for ap :
  IP address: 10.1.1.2
Protocol information for R2 :
  IP address: 10.4.4.2
Protocol information for R3 :
  IP address: 10.5.5.1
Protocol information for R1 :
  IP address: 10.3.3.2
Protocol information for R1 :
  IP address: 10.2.2.2
```

The preceding output of the `show cdp entry * protocols` command can show you just the IP addresses of each directly connected neighbor. The `show cdp entry * version` will show you only the IOS version of your directly connected neighbors:

```
Corp#show cdp entry * version
Version information for ap :
  Cisco IOS Software, C1240 Software (C1240-K9W7-M), Version
   12.3(8)JEA, RELEASE SOFTWARE (fc2)
Technical Support: http://www.cisco.com/techsupport
Copyright (c) 1986-2006 by Cisco Systems, Inc.
Compiled Wed 23-Aug-06 16:45 by kellythw

Version information for R2 :
  Cisco IOS Software, 2801 Software (C2801-ADVENTERPRISEK9-M),
   Experimental Version 12.4(20050525:193634) [jezhao-ani 145]
Copyright (c) 1986-2005 by Cisco Systems, Inc.
Compiled Fri 27-May-05 23:53 by jezhao

Version information for R3 :
  Cisco IOS Software, 1841 Software (C1841-IPBASE-M), Version 12.4(1c),
   RELEASE SOFTWARE (fc1)
Technical Support: http://www.cisco.com/techsupport
Copyright (c) 1986-2005 by Cisco Systems, Inc.
```

```
Compiled Tue 25-Oct-05 17:10 by evmiller

 --More--
[output cut]
```

Although the `show cdp neighbors detail` and `show cdp entry` commands are very similar, the `show cdp entry` command allows you to display only one line of output for each directly connected neighbor, whereas the `show cdp neighbor detail` command does not. Next, let's look at the `show cdp traffic` command.

Gathering Interface Traffic Information

The `show cdp traffic` command displays information about interface traffic, including the number of CDP packets sent and received and the errors with CDP.

The following output shows the `show cdp traffic` command used on the Corp router:

```
Corp#sh cdp traffic
CDP counters :
        Total packets output: 911, Input: 524
        Hdr syntax: 0, Chksum error: 0, Encaps failed: 2
        No memory: 0, Invalid packet: 0, Fragmented: 0
        CDP version 1 advertisements output: 0, Input: 0
        CDP version 2 advertisements output: 911, Input: 524
```

This is not really the most important information you can gather from a router, but it does show how many CDP packets are sent and received on a device.

Gathering Port and Interface Information

The `show cdp interface` command gives you the CDP status on router interfaces or switch ports.

As I said earlier, you can turn off CDP completely on a router by using the `no cdp run` command. But remember that you can also turn off CDP on a per-interface basis with the `no cdp enable` command. You enable a port with the `cdp enable` command. All ports and interfaces default to `cdp enable`.

On a router, the `show cdp interface` command displays information about each interface using CDP, including the encapsulation on the line, the timer, and the holdtime for each interface. Here's an example of this command's output on the ISR router:

```
Corp#sh cdp interface
FastEthernet0/0 is administratively down, line protocol is down
  Encapsulation ARPA
  Sending CDP packets every 60 seconds
  Holdtime is 180 seconds
FastEthernet0/1 is up, line protocol is up
```

```
  Encapsulation ARPA
  Sending CDP packets every 60 seconds
  Holdtime is 180 seconds
Serial0/0/0 is up, line protocol is up
  Encapsulation HDLC
  Sending CDP packets every 60 seconds
  Holdtime is 180 seconds
Serial0/0/1 is up, line protocol is up
  Encapsulation HDLC
  Sending CDP packets every 60 seconds
  Holdtime is 180 seconds
Serial0/1/0 is up, line protocol is up
  Encapsulation HDLC
  Sending CDP packets every 60 seconds
  Holdtime is 180 seconds
Serial0/2/0 is up, line protocol is up
  Encapsulation HDLC
  Sending CDP packets every 60 seconds
  Holdtime is 180 seconds
```

The preceding output is nice because it always tells you the interface's status. To turn off CDP on one interface on a router, use the `no cdp enable` command from interface configuration mode:

```
Corp#config t
Corp(config)#int s0/0/0
Corp(config-if)#no cdp enable
Corp(config-if)#do show cdp interface
FastEthernet0/0 is administratively down, line protocol is down
  Encapsulation ARPA
  Sending CDP packets every 60 seconds
  Holdtime is 180 seconds
FastEthernet0/1 is up, line protocol is up
  Encapsulation ARPA
  Sending CDP packets every 60 seconds
  Holdtime is 180 seconds
Serial0/0/1 is up, line protocol is up
  Encapsulation HDLC
  Sending CDP packets every 60 seconds
  Holdtime is 180 seconds
Serial0/1/0 is up, line protocol is up
  Encapsulation HDLC
  Sending CDP packets every 60 seconds
```

```
  Holdtime is 180 seconds
Serial0/2/0 is up, line protocol is up
  Encapsulation HDLC
  Sending CDP packets every 60 seconds
  Holdtime is 180 seconds
Corp(config-if)#
```

Notice that serial 0/0/0 isn't listed in the router output. To get that output, you'd have to perform a `cdp enable` on serial 0/0/0. It would then show up in the output:

```
Corp(config-if)#cdp enable
Corp(config-if)#^Z
Corp#
```

Real World Scenario

CDP Can Save Lives!

Karen has just been hired as a senior network consultant at a large hospital in Dallas, Texas. She is expected to be able to take care of any problem that comes up. No stress here—she only has to worry about people possibly not getting the right health care if the network goes down. Talk about a potential life-or-death situation!

Karen starts her job happily. Soon, of course, the network has some problems. She asks one of the junior administrators for a network map so she can troubleshoot the network. This person tells her that the old senior administrator (who just got fired) had them with him and now no one can find them—ouch!

Doctors are calling every couple of minutes because they can't get the necessary information they need to take care of their patients. What should she do?

CDP to the rescue! Thank God this hospital has all Cisco routers and switches and that CDP is enabled by default on all Cisco devices. Also, luckily, the disgruntled administrator who just got fired didn't turn off CDP on any devices before he left.

All Karen has to do now is to use the show `cdp neighbor detail` command to find all the information she needs about each device to help draw out the hospital network and save lives!

The only snag for you nailing this in your own network is if you don't know the passwords of all those devices. Your only hope then is to somehow find out the access passwords or to perform password recovery on them.

So, use CDP— you never know when you may end up saving someone's life.

This is a true story.

Documenting a Network Topology Using CDP

As the title of this section implies, I'm now going to show you how to document a sample network by using CDP. You'll learn to determine the appropriate router types, interface types, and IP addresses of various interfaces using only CDP commands and the `show running-config` command. And you can only console into the Lab_A router to document the network. You'll have to assign any remote routers the next IP address in each range. Figure 7.2 is what you'll use to complete the documentation.

FIGURE 7.2 Documenting a network topology using CDP

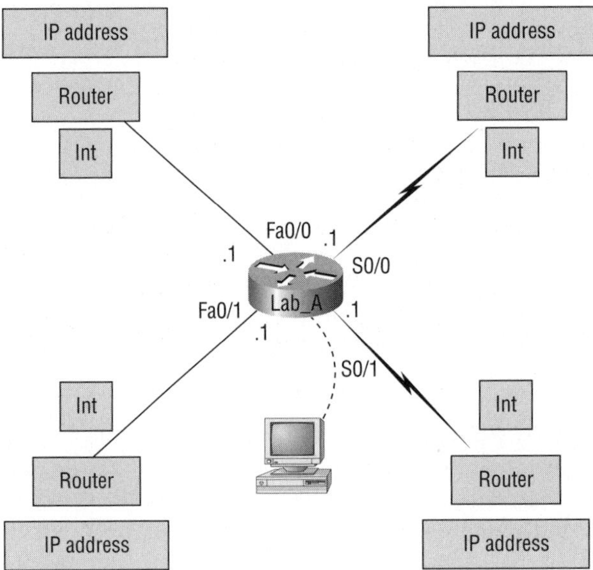

In this output, you can see that you have a router with four interfaces: two FastEthernet and two serial. First, determine the IP addresses of each interface by using the `show running-config` command:

```
Lab_A#sh running-config
Building configuration...

Current configuration : 960 bytes
!
version 12.2
service timestamps debug uptime
service timestamps log uptime
no service password-encryption
!
```

```
hostname Lab_A
!
ip subnet-zero
!
!
interface FastEthernet0/0
 ip address 192.168.21.1 255.255.255.0
 duplex auto
!
interface FastEthernet0/1
 ip address 192.168.18.1 255.255.255.0
 duplex auto
!
interface Serial0/0
ip address 192.168.23.1 255.255.255.0
!
interface Serial0/1
ip address 192.168.28.1 255.255.255.0
!
ip classless
!
line con 0
line aux 0
line vty 0 4
!
end
```

With this step completed, you can now write down the IP addresses of the Lab_A router's four interfaces. Next, you need to determine the type of device on the other end of each of these interfaces. It's easy to do this—just use the `show cdp neighbors` command:

```
Lab_A#sh cdp neighbors
Capability Codes: R - Router, T - Trans Bridge, B - Source Route Bridge
S - Switch, H - Host, I - IGMP, r - Repeater
Device ID   Local Intrfce     Holdtme     Capability Platform   Port ID
Lab_B        Fas 0/0            178          R          2501     E0
Lab_C        Fas 0/1            137          R          2621     Fa0/0
Lab_D        Ser 0/0            178          R          2514     S1
Lab_E        Ser 0/1            137          R          2620     S0/1
Lab_A#
```

You've got a good deal of information now! By using both the `show running-config` and `show cdp neighbors` commands, you know about all the IP addresses of the Lab_A router plus the types of routers connected to each of the Lab_A router's links and all the interfaces of the remote routers.

And by using all the information gathered from `show running-config` and `show cdp neighbors`, we can now create the topology in Figure 7.3.

FIGURE 7.3 Network topology documented

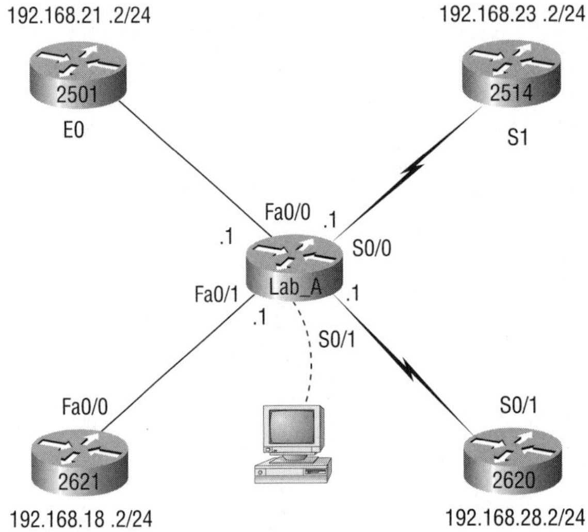

If we needed to, we could've also used the `show cdp neighbors detail` command to view the neighbor's IP addresses. But since we know the IP addresses of each link on the Lab_A router, we already know what the next available IP address is going to be.

Link Layer Discovery Protocol (LLDP)

Before I move away from CDP, I need to discuss a nonproprietary discovery protocol that provides pretty much the same information as CDP but works in multivendor networks.

The IEEE created a new standardized discovery protocol called 802.1AB for Station and Media Access Control Connectivity Discovery. We'll just call it Link Layer Discovery Protocol (LLDP).

LLDP defines basic discovery capabilities, but it was also enhanced to specifically address the voice application, and this version is called LLDP-MED (Media Endpoint Discovery). LLDP and LLDP-MED are not compatible.

More information can be found here:

```
www.cisco.com/en/US/docs/ios/cether/configuration/guide/ce_lldp-med.html
```

And here:

```
www.cisco.com/en/US/technologies/tk652/tk701/technologies_white_
paper0900aecd804cd46d.html
```

Using Telnet

Telnet, part of the TCP/IP protocol suite, is a virtual terminal protocol that allows you to make connections to remote devices, gather information, and run programs.

After your routers and switches are configured, you can use the Telnet program to reconfigure and/or check up on them without using a console cable. You run the Telnet program by typing **telnet** from any command prompt (DOS or Cisco). You need to have VTY passwords set on the routers for this to work.

Remember, you can't use CDP to gather information about routers and switches that aren't directly connected to your device. But you can use the Telnet application to connect to your neighbor devices and then run CDP on those remote devices to get information on them.

You can issue the `telnet` command from any router prompt like this:

```
Corp#telnet 10.2.2.2
Trying 10.2.2.2 ... Open

Password required, but none set

[Connection to 10.2.2.2 closed by foreign host]
Corp#
```

As you can see, I didn't set my passwords—how embarrassing! Remember that the VTY ports on a router are configured as `login`, meaning that we have to either set the VTY passwords or use the `no login` command. (You can review setting passwords in Chapter 6, "Cisco's Internetworking Operating System (IOS)," if you need to.)

If you find you can't telnet into a device, it could be that the password on the remote device hasn't been set. It's also possible that an access control list is filtering the Telnet session.

On a Cisco router, you don't need to use the `telnet` command; you can just type in an IP address from a command prompt and the router will assume that you want to telnet to the device. Here's how that looks using just the IP address:

```
Corp#10.2.2.2
Trying 10.2.2.2 ... Open

Password required, but none set

[Connection to 10.2.2.2 closed by foreign host]
Corp#
```

At this point, it would be a great idea to set those VTY passwords on the router I want to telnet into. Here's what I did on the remote router named R1:

```
R1#config t
Enter configuration commands, one per line.  End with CNTL/Z.
R1(config)#line vty 0 ?
  <1-807>  Last Line number
  <cr>
R1(config)#line vty 0 807
R1(config-line)#password telnet
R1(config-line)#login
R1(config-line)#^Z
```

Now let's try this again. Here I'm connecting to the router from the Corp console:

```
Corp#10.2.2.2
Trying 10.2.2.2 ... Open

User Access Verification

Password:
R1>
```

Remember that the VTY password is the user-mode password, not the enable-mode password. Watch what happens when I try to go into privileged mode after telnetting into router R1:

```
R1>en
% No password set
R1>
```

It is basically saying, "No way!" This is a really good security feature because you don't want anyone telnetting into your device and being able to just type the `enable` command to get into privileged mode. You've got to set your enable-mode password or enable secret password to use Telnet to configure remote devices!

When you telnet into a remote device, you will not see console messages by default. For example, you will not see debugging output. To allow console messages to be sent to your Telnet session, use the `terminal monitor` command.

In the following examples, I am going to show you how to telnet into multiple devices simultaneously and then show you how to use hostnames instead of IP addresses.

Telnetting into Multiple Devices Simultaneously

If you telnet to a router or switch, you can end the connection by typing **exit** at any time. But what if you want to keep your connection to a remote device but still come back to your original router console? To do that, you can press the Ctrl+Shift+6 key combination, release it, and then press X.

Here's an example of connecting to multiple devices from my Corp router console:

```
Corp#10.2.2.2
Trying 10.2.2.2 ... Open

User Access Verification

Password:
R1>Ctrl+Shift+6
Corp#
```

In this example, I telnetted to the R1 router and then typed the password to enter user mode. I next pressed Ctrl+Shift+6, then X (but you can't see any of that because it doesn't show on the screen output). Notice that my command prompt is now back at the Corp router.

Let's run through some verification commands.

Checking Telnet Connections

To see the connections made from your router to a remote device, use the `show sessions` command:

```
Corp#sh sessions
Conn Host                Address             Byte  Idle Conn Name
   1 10.2.2.2            10.2.2.2               0     0 10.2.2.2
*  2 10.1.1.2            10.1.1.2               0     0 10.1.1.2
Corp#
```

See that asterisk (*) next to connection 2? It means that session 2 was your last session. You can return to your last session by pressing Enter twice. You can also return to any session by typing the number of the connection and pressing Enter.

Checking Telnet Users

You can list all active consoles and VTY ports in use on your router with the `show users` command:

```
Corp#sh users
    Line       User       Host(s)              Idle       Location
*  0 con 0                10.1.1.2             00:00:01
                          10.2.2.2             00:01:06
```

In the command's output, con represents the local console. In this example, the console session is connected to two remote IP addresses, or in other words, two devices. In the next example, I typed `sh users` on the ap device that the Corp router had telnetted into and is connected to via line 1:

```
Corp#sh sessions
Conn Host                Address             Byte  Idle Conn Name
   1 10.1.1.2            10.1.1.2               0     0 10.1.1.2
*  2 10.2.2.2            10.2.2.2               0     0 10.2.2.2
Corp#1
[Resuming connection 1 to 10.1.1.2 ... ]
ap>sh users
    Line       User       Host(s)              Idle       Location
*  1 vty 0                idle                 00:00:00 10.1.1.1
ap>
```

This output shows that the console is active and that VTY router line 1 is being used. The asterisk represents the current terminal session from which the `show user` command was entered.

Closing Telnet Sessions

You can end Telnet sessions a few different ways—typing `exit` or `disconnect` is probably the easiest and quickest.

To end a session from a remote device, use the `exit` command:

```
ap>exit
[Connection to 10.1.1.2 closed by foreign host]
Corp#
```

To end a session from a local device, use the `disconnect` command:

```
Corp#sh session
Conn Host                Address             Byte  Idle Conn Name
   *2 10.2.2.2            10.2.2.2              0     0 10.2.2.2
Corp#disconnect ?
  <2-2>  The number of an active network connection
  qdm    Disconnect QDM web-based clients
  ssh    Disconnect an active SSH connection
Corp#disconnect 2
Closing connection to 10.2.2.2 [confirm][enter]
Corp#
```

In this example, I used session number 2 because that was the connection to the R1 router that I wanted to end. As I showed, you can use the `show sessions` command to see the connection number.

Resolving Hostnames

If you want to use a hostname rather than an IP address to connect to a remote device, the device that you are using to make the connection must be able to translate the hostname to an IP address.

There are two ways to resolve hostnames to IP addresses: building a host table on each router or building a Domain Name System (DNS) server, which is similar to a dynamic host table (assuming dynamic DNS).

Building a Host Table

A host table provides name resolution only on the router that it was built upon. The command to build a host table on a router is as follows:

```
ip host host_name [tcp_port_number] ip_address
```

The default is TCP port number 23, but you can create a session using Telnet with a different TCP port number if you want. You can also assign up to eight IP addresses to a hostname.

Here's an example of configuring a host table on the Corp router with two entries to resolve the names for the R1 router and the ap device:

```
Corp#config t
Corp(config)#ip host R1 ?
  <0-65535>   Default telnet port number
  A.B.C.D     Host IP address
  additional  Append addresses
  mx          Configure a MX record
  ns          Configure an NS record
  srv         Configure a SRV record
Corp(config)#ip host R1 10.2.2.2 ?
  A.B.C.D  Host IP address
  <cr>
Corp(config)#ip host R1 10.2.2.2
Corp(config)#ip host ap 10.1.1.2
```

Notice in the preceding router configuration that I can just keep adding IP addresses to reference a host, one after another, up to eight IP addresses. And to see the newly built host table, just use the `show hosts` command:

```
Corp(config)#do show hosts
Default domain is not set
Name/address lookup uses domain service
Name servers are 255.255.255.255

Codes: UN - unknown, EX - expired, OK - OK, ?? - revalidate
       temp - temporary, perm - permanent
       NA - Not Applicable None - Not defined
Host                      Port  Flags      Age Type   Address(es)
ap                        None  (perm, OK)  0   IP    10.1.1.2
R1                        None  (perm, OK)  0   IP    10.2.2.2
Corp(config)#^Z
Corp#
```

You can see the two hostnames plus their associated IP addresses in the preceding router output. The `perm` in the `Flags` column means that the entry is manually configured. If it said `temp`, it would be an entry that was resolved by DNS.

The `show hosts` command provides information on temporary DNS entries and permanent name-to-address mappings created using the `ip host` command.

To verify that the host table resolves names, try typing the hostnames at a router prompt. Remember that if you don't specify the command, the router assumes you want to telnet.

In the following example, I'll use the hostnames to telnet into the remote devices and press Ctrl+Shift+6 and then X to return to the main console of the Corp router:

```
Corp#r1
Trying R1 (10.2.2.2)... Open

User Access Verification

Password:
R1>Ctrl+Shift+6
Corp#ap
Trying ap (10.1.1.2)... Open
```

```
User Access Verification

Password:
ap>Ctrl+Shift+6
Corp#
```

I successfully used entries in the host table to create a session to two devices by using the names to telnet into both devices. Names in the host table are not case sensitive.

Notice that the entries in the following `show sessions` output now display the hostnames and IP addresses instead of just the IP addresses:

```
Corp#sh sessions
Conn Host                Address             Byte  Idle Conn Name
   1 r1                  10.2.2.2               0     1 r1
*  2 ap                  10.1.1.2               0     0 ap
Corp#
```

If you want to remove a hostname from the table, just use the `no ip host` command like this:

```
Corp(config)#no ip host R1
```

The problem with the host table method is that you would need to create a host table on each router to be able to resolve names. And if you have a whole bunch of routers and want to resolve names, using DNS is a much better choice!

Using DNS to Resolve Names

If you have a lot of devices and don't want to create a host table in each device, you can use a DNS server to resolve hostnames.

Any time a Cisco device receives a command it doesn't understand, it will try to resolve it through DNS by default. Watch what happens when I type the special command `todd` at a Cisco router prompt:

```
Corp#todd
Translating "todd"...domain server (255.255.255.255)
Translating "todd"...domain server (255.255.255.255)
Translating "todd"...domain server (255.255.255.255)
% Unknown command or computer name, or unable to find
  computer address
Corp#
```

It doesn't know my name or what command I am trying to type, so it tries to resolve this through DNS. This is really annoying for two reasons: first, because it doesn't know my name <grin>, and second, because I need to hang out and wait for the name lookup to time out. You can get around this and prevent a time-consuming DNS lookup by using the `no ip domain-lookup` command on your router from global configuration mode.

If you have a DNS server on your network, you need to add a few commands to make DNS name resolution work:

- The first command is `ip domain-lookup`, which is turned on by default. It needs to be entered only if you previously turned it off (with the `no ip domain-lookup` command). The command can be used without the hyphen as well (`ip domain lookup`).
- The second command is `ip name-server`. This sets the IP address of the DNS server. You can enter the IP addresses of up to six servers.
- The last command is `ip domain-name`. Although this command is optional, it really should be set. It appends the domain name to the hostname you type in. Since DNS uses a fully qualified domain name (FQDN) system, you must have a second level DNS name, in the form `domain.com`.

Here's an example of using these three commands:

```
Corp#config t
Corp(config)#ip domain-lookup
Corp(config)#ip name-server ?
  A.B.C.D  Domain server IP address (maximum of 6)
Corp(config)#ip name-server 192.168.0.70
Corp(config)#ip domain-name lammle.com
Corp(config)#^Z
Corp#
```

After the DNS configurations are set, you can test the DNS server by using a hostname to ping or telnet a device like this:

```
Corp#ping R1
Translating "R1"...domain server (192.168.0.70) [OK]
Type escape sequence to abort.
Sending 5, 100-byte ICMP Echos to 10.2.2.2, timeout is
  2 seconds:
!!!!!
Success rate is 100 percent (5/5), round-trip min/avg/max
  = 28/31/32 ms
```

Notice that the router uses the DNS server to resolve the name.

After a name is resolved using DNS, use the `show hosts` command to see that the device cached this information in the host table:

```
Corp#sh hosts
Default domain is lammle.com
Name/address lookup uses domain service
Name servers are 192.168.0.70
```

```
Host                      Flags       Age Type   Address(es)
R1                        (temp, OK)  0   IP     10.2.2.2
ap                        (perm, OK)  0   IP     10.1.1.2
Corp#
```

The entry that was resolved is shown as `temp`, but the ap device is still `perm`, meaning that it's a static entry. Notice that the hostname is a full domain name. If I hadn't used the `ip domain-name lammle.com` command, I would have needed to type in `ping r1.lammle.com`, which is a pain.

Real World Scenario

Should You Use a Host Table or a DNS Server?

Karen has finally finished drawing out her network by using CDP and the doctors are much happier. However, Karen is having a difficult time administering the network because she has to look at the network drawing to find an IP address every time she needs to telnet to a remote router.

Karen was thinking about putting host tables on each router, but with literally hundreds of routers, this is a daunting task.

Most networks have a DNS server now anyway, so adding a hundred or so hostnames into it would be an easy way to go—certainly easier then adding these hostnames to each and every router! She can just add the three commands on each router and blammo—she's resolving names.

Using a DNS server makes it easy to update any old entries too—remember, even one little change and off she goes to each and every router to manually update its table if she's using static host tables.

Keep in mind that this has nothing to do with name resolution on the network and nothing to do with what a host on the network is trying to accomplish. This is only used when you're trying to resolve names from the router console.

Checking Network Connectivity and Troubleshooting

You can use the `ping` and `traceroute` commands to test connectivity to remote devices, and both of them can be used with many protocols, not just IP. But don't forget that the `show ip route` command is a good troubleshooting command for verifying your routing table and the `show interfaces` command will show you the status of each interface.

I'm not going to get into the show interfaces commands here because we've already been over that in Chapter 6. But I am going to go over both the debug command and the show processes command you need to troubleshoot a router.

Using the *ping* Command

So far, you've seen many examples of pinging devices to test IP connectivity and name resolution using the DNS server. To see all the different protocols that you can use with the *Ping* program, type ping ?:

```
Corp#ping ?
  WORD  Ping destination address or hostname
  clns  CLNS echo
  ip    IP echo
  srb   srb echo
  tag   Tag encapsulated IP echo
  <cr>
```

The ping output displays the minimum, average, and maximum times it takes for a ping packet to find a specified system and return. Here's an example:

```
Corp#ping R1
Translating "R1"...domain server (192.168.0.70)[OK]
Type escape sequence to abort.
Sending 5, 100-byte ICMP Echos to 10.2.2.2, timeout
  is 2 seconds:
!!!!!
Success rate is 100 percent (5/5), round-trip min/avg/max
  = 1/2/4 ms
Corp#
```

You can see that the DNS server was used to resolve the name, and the device was pinged in a minimum of 1 ms (milliseconds), an average of 2 ms, and up to 4 ms.

The ping command can be used in user and privileged mode but not configuration mode.

Using the *traceroute* Command

Traceroute (the traceroute command, or trace for short) shows the path a packet takes to get to a remote device. It uses time to live (TTL) time-outs and ICMP error messages to outline the path a packet takes through an internetwork to arrive at a remote host.

Trace (the trace command), which can be used from either user mode or privileged mode, allows you to figure out which router in the path to an unreachable network host should be examined more closely for the cause of the network's failure.

To see the protocols that you can use with the traceroute command, type **traceroute ?**:

```
Corp#traceroute ?
  WORD       Trace route to destination address or hostname
  appletalk  AppleTalk Trace
  clns       ISO CLNS Trace
  ip         IP Trace
  ipv6       IPv6 Trace
  ipx        IPX Trace
  <cr>
```

The traceroute command shows the hop or hops that a packet traverses on its way to a remote device. Here's an example:

```
Corp#traceroute r1

Type escape sequence to abort.
Tracing the route to R1 (10.2.2.2)

  1 R1 (10.2.2.2) 4 msec *  0 msec
Corp#
```

You can see that the packet went to only one hop to find the destination.

Do not get confused! You can't use the tracert command—it's a Windows command. For a router, use the traceroute command!

Here's an example of using tracert from a Windows DOS prompt (notice the command tracert!):

```
C:\>tracert www.whitehouse.gov

Tracing route to a1289.g.akamai.net [69.8.201.107]
over a maximum of 30 hops:

  1     *        *        *     Request timed out.
  2    53 ms    61 ms    53 ms  hlrn-dsl-gw15-207.hlrn.qwest.net
      [207.225.112.207]
  3    53 ms    55 ms    54 ms  hlrn-agw1.inet.qwest.net [71.217.188.113]
  4    54 ms    53 ms    54 ms  hlr-core-01.inet.qwest.net [205.171.253.97]
```

```
  5    54 ms    53 ms    54 ms  apa-cntr-01.inet.qwest.net [205.171.253.26]
  6    54 ms    53 ms    53 ms  63.150.160.34
  7    54 ms    54 ms    53 ms  www.whitehouse.gov [69.8.201.107]

Trace complete.
```

Okay, let's move on now and talk about how to troubleshoot your network using the `debug` command.

Debugging

Debug is a troubleshooting command that's available from the privileged exec mode of Cisco IOS. It's used to display information about various router operations and the related traffic generated or received by the router, plus any error messages.

It's a useful and informative tool, but you really need to understand some important facts about its use. Debug is regarded as a very high-overhead task because it can consume a huge amount of resources and the router is forced to process-switch the packets being debugged. So you don't just use debug as a monitoring tool—it's meant to be used for a short period of time and only as a troubleshooting tool. By using it, you can really find out some truly significant facts about both working and faulty software and/or hardware components.

Because debugging output takes priority over other network traffic, and because the **`debug all`** command generates more output than any other `debug` command, it can severely diminish the router's performance—even render it unusable. So in virtually all cases, it's best to use more-specific `debug` commands.

As you can see from the following output, you can't enable debugging from user mode, only privileged mode:

```
Corp>debug ?
% Unrecognized command
Corp>en
Corp#debug ?
  aaa                     AAA Authentication, Authorization and Accounting
  access-expression       Boolean access expression
  adjacency               adjacency
  all                     Enable all debugging
[output cut]
```

If you've got the freedom to pretty much take out a router and you really want to have some fun with debugging, use the `debug all` command:

```
Corp#debug all

This may severely impact network performance. Continue? (yes/[no]):yes
```

```
All possible debugging has been turned on

2d20h: SNMP: HC Timer 824AE5CC fired
2d20h: SNMP: HC Timer 824AE5CC rearmed, delay = 20000
2d20h: Serial0/0: HDLC myseq 4, mineseen 0, yourseen 0, line down
2d20h:
2d20h: Rudpv1 Sent: Pkts 0,  Data Bytes 0,  Data Pkts 0
2d20h: Rudpv1 Rcvd: Pkts 0,  Data Bytes 0,  Data Pkts 0
2d20h: Rudpv1 Discarded: 0,  Retransmitted 0
2d20h:
2d20h: RIP-TIMER: periodic timer expired
2d20h: Serial0/0: HDLC myseq 5, mineseen 0, yourseen 0, line down
2d20h: Serial0/0: attempting to restart
2d20h: PowerQUICC(0/0): DCD is up.
2d20h: is_up: 0 state: 4 sub state: 1 line: 0
2d20h:
2d20h: Rudpv1 Sent: Pkts 0,  Data Bytes 0,  Data Pkts 0
2d20h: Rudpv1 Rcvd: Pkts 0,  Data Bytes 0,  Data Pkts 0
2d20h: Rudpv1 Discarded: 0,  Retransmitted 0
2d20h: un all
All possible debugging has been turned off
Corp#
```

To disable debugging on a router, just use the command `no` in front of the debug command:

```
Corp#no debug all
```

But I typically just use the `undebug all` command since it is so easy when using the shortcut:

```
Corp#un all
```

Remember that instead of using the `debug all` command, it's almost always better to use specific commands—and only for short periods of time. Here's an example of deploying `debug ip rip` that will show you RIP updates being sent and received on a router:

```
Corp#debug ip rip
RIP protocol debugging is on
Corp#
1w4d: RIP: sending v2 update to 224.0.0.9 via Serial0/0 (192.168.12.1)
1w4d: RIP: build update entries
1w4d:   10.10.10.0/24 via 0.0.0.0, metric 2, tag 0
1w4d:   171.16.125.0/24 via 0.0.0.0, metric 3, tag 0
```

```
1w4d:    172.16.12.0/24 via 0.0.0.0, metric 1, tag 0
1w4d:    172.16.125.0/24 via 0.0.0.0, metric 3, tag 0
1w4d: RIP: sending v2 update to 224.0.0.9 via Serial0/2 (172.16.12.1)
1w4d: RIP: build update entries
1w4d:    192.168.12.0/24 via 0.0.0.0, metric 1, tag 0
1w4d:    192.168.22.0/24 via 0.0.0.0, metric 2, tag 0
1w4d: RIP: received v2 update from 192.168.12.2 on Serial0/0
1w4d:     192.168.22.0/24 via 0.0.0.0 in 1 hops
Corp#un all
```

I'm sure you can see that the debug command is one powerful command. And because of this, I'm also sure you realize that before you use any of the debugging commands, you should make sure you check the utilization of your router. This is important because in most cases, you don't want to negatively impact the device's ability to process the packets through on your internetwork. You can determine a specific router's utilization information by using the show processes command.

Remember, when you telnet into a remote device, you will not see console messages by default! For example, you will not see debugging output. To allow console messages to be sent to your Telnet session, use the terminal monitor command.

Using the *show processes* Command

As mentioned in the previous section, you've really got to be careful when using the debug command on your devices. If your router's CPU utilization is consistently at 50 percent or more, it's probably not a good idea to type in the debug all command unless you want to see what a router looks like when it crashes!

So what other approaches can you use? Well, the show processes (or show processes cpu) is a good tool for determining a given router's CPU utilization. Plus, it'll give you a list of active processes along with their corresponding process ID, priority, scheduler test (status), CPU time used, number of times invoked, and so on. Lots of great stuff! Plus, this command is super handy when you want to evaluate your router's performance and CPU utilization—for instance, when you find yourself otherwise tempted to reach for the debug command.

Okay—what do you see in the following output? The first line shows the CPU utilization output for the last 5 seconds, 1 minute, and 5 minutes. The output provides 2%/0% in front of the CPU utilization for the last 5 seconds. The first number equals the total utilization and the second one indicates the utilization due to interrupt routines:

```
Corp#sh processes
CPU utilization for five seconds: 2%/0%; one minute: 0%; five minutes: 0%
 PID QTy PC Runtime (ms)    Invoked   uSecs    Stacks TTY Process
```

```
  1 Cwe 8034470C    0       1       0 5804/6000   0 Chunk Manager
  2 Csp 80369A88    4    1856         2 2616/3000 0 Load Meter
  3 M*           0    112    14    800010656/12000  0 Exec
  5 Lst 8034FD9C  268246   52101 5148 5768/6000   0 Check heaps
  6 Cwe 80355E5C  20         3   6666 5704/6000   0 Pool Manager
  7 Mst 802AC3C4   0         2       0 5580/6000   0 Timers
[output cut]
```

So basically, the output from the `show processes` command shows that our router is happily able to process debugging commands without being overloaded.

Summary

In this chapter, you learned how Cisco routers are configured and how to manage those configurations.

This chapter covered the internal components of a router, which included ROM, RAM, NVRAM, and flash.

In addition, I covered what happens when a router boots and which files are loaded. The configuration register tells the router how to boot and where to find files, and you learned how to change and verify the configuration register settings for password recovery purposes.

Next, you learned how to back up and restore a Cisco IOS image as well as how to back up and restore the configuration of a Cisco router. I showed you how to manage these files using the CLI, and IFS.

Then you learned how to use CDP and Telnet to gather information about remote devices. Finally, the chapter covered how to resolve hostnames and use the `ping` and `trace` commands to test network connectivity as well as how to use the `debug` and `show processes` commands.

Exam Essentials

Define the Cisco Router components. Describe the functions of the bootstrap, POST, ROM monitor, mini-IOS, RAM, ROM, flash memory, NVRAM and the configuration register.

Identify the steps in the router boot sequence. The steps in the boot sequence are POST, loading the IOS, and copying the startup configuration from NVRAM to RAM.

Understand configuration register commands and settings. The 0x2102 setting is the default on all Cisco routers and tells the router to look in NVRAM for the boot sequence. 0x2101 tells the router to boot from ROM, and 0x2142 tells the router to not load the startup-config in NVRAM to provide password recovery.

Perform password recovery. The steps in the password recovery process are interrupt the router boot sequence, change the configuration register, reload the router and enter privileged mode, change/set the password, save the new configuration, reset the configuration register, and reload the router.

Back up an IOS image. By using the privileged-mode command `copy flash tftp`, you can back up a file from flash memory to a TFTP (network) server.

Restore or upgrade an IOS image. By using the privileged-mode command `copy tftp flash`, you can restore or upgrade a file from a TFTP (network) server to flash memory.

Describe best practices to prepare to back up an IOS image to a network server. Make sure that you can access the network server, ensure that the network server has adequate space for the code image, and verify the file naming and path requirement.

Save the configuration of a router. There are a couple of ways to do this, but the most common, as well as most tested, method is copy running-config startup-config.

Erase the configuration of a router. Type the privileged-mode command `erase startup-config` and reload the router.

Understand and use Cisco IFS file system management commands. The commands to use are `dir`, `copy`, `more`, `delete`, `erase` or `format`, `cd` and `pwd`, and `mkdir` and `rmdir`.

Describe the value of CDP. Cisco Discovery Protocol can be used to help you document as well as troubleshoot your network.

List the information provided by the output of the `show cdp neighbors` command. The `show cdp neighbors` command provides the following information: device ID, local interface, holdtime, capability, platform, and port ID (remote interface).

Understand how to establish a Telnet session with multiple routers simultaneously. If you telnet to a router or switch, you can end the connection by typing **`exit`** at any time. However, if you want to keep your connection to a remote device but still come back to your original router console, you can press the Ctrl+Shift+6 key combination, release it, and then press X.

Identify current Telnet sessions. The command `show sessions` will provide you with information about all the currently active sessions your router has with other routers.

Build a static host table on a router. By using the global configuration command `ip host` *`host_name ip_address`*, you can build a static host table on your router. You can apply multiple IP addresses against the same host entry.

Verify the host table on a router. You can verify the host table with the show hosts command.

Describe the function of the ping command. Packet Internet Groper (Ping) uses ICMP echo request and ICMP echo replies to verify an active IP address on a network.

Ping a valid host ID from the correct prompt. You can ping an IP address from a router's user mode or privileged mode but not from configuration mode. You must ping a valid address, such as 1.1.1.1.

Written Lab 7

In this section, you'll complete the following labs to make sure you've got the information and concepts contained within them fully dialed in:

Lab 7.1: IOS Management

Lab 7.2: Router Memory

(The answers to the written labs can be found following the answers to the review questions for this chapter.)

Written Lab 7.1

Write the answers to the following questions:

1. What is the command to copy a Cisco IOS to a TFTP server?
2. What is the command to copy a Cisco startup-config file to a TFTP server?
3. What is the command to copy the startup-config file to DRAM?
4. What is an older command that you can use to copy the startup-config file to DRAM?
5. What command can you use to see the neighbor router's IP address from your router prompt?
6. What command can you use to see the hostname, local interface, platform, and remote port of a neighbor router?
7. What keystrokes can you use to telnet into multiple devices simultaneously?
8. What command will show you your active Telnet connections to neighbor and remote devices?
9. What command can you use to upgrade a Cisco IOS?
10. What command can you use to merge a backup configuration with the configuration in RAM?

Written Lab 7.2

Identify the location in a router where each of the following files is stored by default.

1. Cisco IOS
2. Bootstrap
3. Startup configuration
4. POST routine
5. Running configuration
6. ARP cache
7. Mini IOS
8. ROM Monitor

9. Routing tables
10. Packet buffers

Hands-on Labs

To complete the labs in this section, you need at least one router (three would be best) and at least one PC running as a TFTP server. TFTP server software must be installed and running on the PC. For this lab, it is also assumed that your PC and the router(s) are connected together with a switch or hub and that all interfaces (PC NIC and router interfaces) are in the same subnet. You can alternately connect the PC directly to the router or connect the routers directly to one another (use a crossover cable in that case). Remember that the labs listed here were created for use with real routers but can easily be used with Cisco's Packet Tracer program.

Here is a list of the labs in this chapter:

Lab 7.1: Backing Up Your Router IOS

Lab 7.2: Upgrading or Restoring Your Router IOS

Lab 7.3: Backing Up the Router Configuration

Lab 7.4: Using the Cisco Discovery Protocol (CDP)

Lab 7.5: Using Telnet

Lab 7.6: Resolving Hostnames

Hands-on Lab 7.1: Backing Up Your Router IOS

1. Log into your router and go into privileged mode by typing **`en`** or **`enable`**.
2. Make sure you can connect to the TFTP server that is on your network by pinging the IP address from the router console.
3. Type **`show flash to see the contents of flash memory.`**
4. Type **`show version`** at the router privileged-mode prompt to get the name of the IOS currently running on the router. If there is only one file in flash memory, the `show flash` and `show version` commands show the same file. Remember that the `show version` command shows you the file that is currently running and the `show flash` command shows you all of the files in flash memory.
5. Once you know you have good Ethernet connectivity to the TFTP server and you also know the IOS filename, back up your IOS by typing **`copy flash tftp`**. This command tells the router to copy a specified file from flash memory (this is where the IOS is stored by default) to a TFTP server.
6. Enter the IP address of the TFTP server and the source IOS filename. The file is now copied and stored in the TFTP server's default directory.

Hands-on Lab 7.2: Upgrading or Restoring Your Router IOS

1. Log into your router and go into privileged mode by typing **en** or **enable**.
2. Make sure you can connect to the TFTP server by pinging the IP address of the server from the router console.
3. Once you know you have good Ethernet connectivity to the TFTP server, issue the **copy tftp flash** command.
4. Confirm that the router will not function during the restore or upgrade by following the prompts provided on the router console. It is possible this prompt may not occur.
5. Enter the IP address of the TFTP server.
6. Enter the name of the IOS filename you want to restore or upgrade.
7. Confirm that you understand that the contents of flash memory will be erased if there is not enough room in flash to store the new image.
8. Watch in amazement as your IOS is deleted out of flash memory and your new IOS is copied to flash memory.

If the file that was in flash memory is deleted but the new version wasn't copied to flash memory, the router will boot from ROM monitor mode. You'll need to figure out why the copy operation did not take place.

Hands-on Lab 7.3: Backing Up the Router Configuration

1. Log into your router and go into privileged mode by typing **en** or **enable**.
2. Ping the TFTP server to make sure you have IP connectivity.
3. From RouterB, type **copy run tftp**.
4. When prompted, type the IP address of the TFTP server (for example, `172.16.30.2`) and press Enter.
5. By default, the router will prompt you for a filename. The hostname of the router is followed by the suffix `-confg` (yes, I spelled that correctly). You can use any name you want.

   ```
   Name of configuration file to write [RouterB-confg]?
   ```

   Press Enter to accept the default name.

   ```
   Write file RouterB-confg on host 172.16.30.2? [confirm]
   ```

   Press Enter to confirm.

Hands-on Lab 7.4: Using the Cisco Discovery Protocol (CDP)

1. Log into your router and go into privileged mode by typing **en** or **enable**.
2. From the router, type **sh cdp** and press Enter. You should see that CDP packets are being sent out to all active interfaces every 60 seconds and the holdtime is 180 seconds (these are the defaults).
3. To change the CDP update frequency to 90 seconds, type **cdp timer 90** in global configuration mode.

```
RouterC#config t
Enter configuration commands, one per line.  End with
  CNTL/Z.
RouterC(config)#cdp timer ?
  <5-900>  Rate at which CDP packets are sent (in sec)
RouterC(config)#cdp timer 90
```

4. Verify that your CDP timer frequency has changed by using the command **show cdp** in privileged mode.

```
RouterC#sh cdp
Global CDP information:
Sending CDP packets every 90 seconds
Sending a holdtime value of 180 seconds
```

5. Now use CDP to gather information about neighbor routers. You can get the list of available commands by typing **sh cdp ?**.

```
RouterC#sh cdp ?
  entry      Information for specific neighbor entry
  interface  CDP interface status and configuration
  neighbors  CDP neighbor entries
  traffic    CDP statistics
  <cr>
```

6. Type **sh cdp int** to see the interface information plus the default encapsulation used by the interface. It also shows the CDP timer information.
7. Type **sh cdp entry *** to see complete CDP information received from all devices.
8. Type **show cdp neighbors** to gather information about all connected neighbors. (You should know the specific information output by this command.)
9. Type **show cdp neighbors detail**. Notice that it produces the same output as show cdp entry *.

Hands-on Lab 7.5: Using Telnet

1. Log into your router and go into privileged mode by typing **en** or **enable**.
2. From RouterA, telnet into your remote router (RouterB) by typing **telnet *ip_address*** from the command prompt. Type **exit** to disconnect.
3. Now type in RouterB's IP address from RouterA's command prompt. Notice that the router automatically tries to telnet to the IP address you specified. You can use the `telnet` command or just type in the IP address.
4. From RouterB, press Ctrl+Shift+6 and then X to return to RouterA's command prompt. Now telnet into your third router, RouterC. Press Ctrl+Shift+6 and then X to return to RouterA.
5. From RouterA, type **show sessions**. Notice your two sessions. You can press the number displayed to the left of the session and press Enter twice to return to that session. The asterisk shows the default session. You can press Enter twice to return to that session.
6. Go to the session for your RouterB. Type **show users**. This shows the console connection and the remote connection. You can use the `disconnect` command to clear the session or just type **exit** from the prompt to close your session with RouterB.
7. Go to RouterC's console port by typing **show sessions** on the first router and using the connection number to return to RouterC. Type **show user** and notice the connection to your first router, RouterA.
8. Type **clear line *line_number*** to disconnect the Telnet session.

Hands-on Lab 7.6: Resolving Hostnames

1. Log into your router and go into privileged mode by typing **en** or **enable**.
2. From RouterA, type **todd** and press Enter at the command prompt. Notice the error you receive and the delay. The router is trying to resolve the hostname to an IP address by looking for a DNS server. You can turn this feature off by using the `no ip domain-lookup` command from global configuration mode.
3. To build a host table, you use the `ip host` command. From RouterA, add a host table entry for RouterB and RouterC by entering the following commands:

```
ip host routerb ip_address
ip host routerc ip_address
```

   Here is an example:

```
ip host routerb 172.16.20.2
ip host routerc 172.16.40.2
```

4. Test your host table by typing **ping routerb** from the privileged mode prompt (not the config prompt).

```
RouterA#ping routerb
Type escape sequence to abort.
Sending 5, 100-byte ICMP Echos to 172.16.20.2, timeout
  is 2 seconds:
!!!!!
Success rate is 100 percent (5/5), round-trip
  min/avg/max = 4/4/4 ms
```

5. Test your host table by typing **ping routerc**.

```
RouterA#ping routerc
Type escape sequence to abort.
Sending 5, 100-byte ICMP Echos to 172.16.40.2, timeout
  is 2 seconds:
!!!!!
Success rate is 100 percent (5/5), round-trip
  min/avg/max = 4/6/8 ms
```

6. Telnet to RouterB and keep your session to RouterB open to RouterA by pressing Ctrl+Shift+6, then X.
7. Telnet to RouterC by typing **routerc** at the command prompt.
8. Return to RouterA and keep the session to RouterC open by pressing Ctrl+Shift+6, then X.
9. View the host table by typing **show hosts** and pressing Enter.

```
Default domain is not set
Name/address lookup uses domain service
Name servers are 255.255.255.255
Host                    Flags      Age Type   Address(es)
routerb               (perm, OK)  0    IP    172.16.20.2
routerc               (perm, OK)  0    IP    172.16.40.2
```

Review Questions

The following questions are designed to test your understanding of this chapter's material. For more information on how to get additional questions, please see this book's Introduction.

1. What does the command `confreg 0x2142` provide?
   - A. It is used to restart the router.
   - B. It is used to bypass the configuration in NVRAM.
   - C. It is used to enter ROM monitor mode.
   - D. It is used to view the lost password.
2. Which command will copy the IOS to a backup host on your network?
   - A. `transfer IOS to 172.16.10.1`
   - B. `copy run start`
   - C. `copy tftp flash`
   - D. `copy start tftp`
   - E. `copy flash tftp`
3. You are troubleshooting a connectivity problem in your corporate network and want to isolate the problem. You suspect that a router on the route to an unreachable network is at fault. What IOS user exec command should you issue?
   - A. `Router>ping`
   - B. `Router>trace`
   - C. `Router>show ip route`
   - D. `Router>show interface`
   - E. `Router>show cdp neighbors`
4. You copy a configuration from a network host to a router's RAM. The configuration looks correct, yet it is not working at all. What could the problem be?
   - A. You copied the wrong configuration into RAM.
   - B. You copied the configuration into flash memory instead.
   - C. The copy did not override the `shutdown` command in running-config.
   - D. The IOS became corrupted after the `copy` command was initiated.

5. A network administrator wants to upgrade the IOS of a router without removing the image currently installed. What command will display the amount of memory consumed by the current IOS image and indicate whether there is enough room available to hold both the current and new images?

   A. `show version`

   B. `show flash`

   C. `show memory`

   D. `show buffers`

   E. `show running-config`

6. The corporate office sends you a new router to connect, but upon connecting the console cable, you see that there is already a configuration on the router. What should be done before a new configuration is entered in the router?

   A. RAM should be erased and the router restarted.

   B. Flash should be erased and the router restarted.

   C. NVRAM should be erased and the router restarted.

   D. The new configuration should be entered and saved.

7. Which command loads a new version of the Cisco IOS into a router?

   A. `copy flash ftp`

   B. `copy ftp flash`

   C. `copy flash tftp`

   D. `copy tftp flash`

8. Which command will show you the IOS version running on your router?

   A. `sh IOS`

   B. `sh flash`

   C. `sh version`

   D. `sh running-config`

9. What should the configuration register value be after you successfully complete the password recovery procedure and return the router to normal operation?

   A. 0x2100

   B. 0x2101

   C. 0x2102

   D. 0x2142

10. You save the configuration on a router with the `copy running-config startup-config` command and reboot the router. The router, however, comes up with a blank configuration. What can the problem be?

    A. You didn't boot the router with the correct command.

    B. NVRAM is corrupted.

    C. The configuration register setting is incorrect.

    D. The newly upgraded IOS is not compatible with the hardware of the router.

    E. The configuration you save is not compatible with the hardware.

11. If you want to have more than one Telnet session open at the same time, what keystroke combination would you use?

    A. Tab+spacebar

    B. Ctrl+X, then 6

    C. Ctrl+Shift+X, then 6

    D. Ctrl+Shift+6, then X

12. You are unsuccessful in telnetting into a remote device, but you could telnet to the router earlier however, you can still ping the remote device. What could the problem be? (Choose two.)

    A. IP addresses are incorrect.

    B. Access control list is filtering Telnet.

    C. There is a defective serial cable.

    D. The VTY password is missing.

13. What information is displayed by the `show hosts` command? (Choose two.)

    A. Temporary DNS entries

    B. The names of the routers created using the `hostname` command

    C. The IP addresses of workstations allowed to access the router

    D. Permanent name-to-address mappings created using the `ip host` command

    E. The length of time a host has been connected to the router via Telnet

14. Which three commands can be used to check LAN connectivity problems on a router? (Choose three.)

    A. `show interfaces`

    B. `show ip route`

    C. `tracert`

    D. `ping`

    E. `dns lookups`

15. You telnet to a router and make your necessary changes; now you want to end the Telnet session. What command do you type in?

    A. `close`

    B. `disable`

    C. `disconnect`

    D. `exit`

16. You telnet into a remote device and type `debug ip rip`, but no output from the `debug` command is seen. What could the problem be?

    A. You must type the `show ip rip` command first.

    B. IP addressing on the network is incorrect.

    C. You must use the `terminal monitor` command.

    D. Debug output is sent only to the console.

17. Which command displays the configuration register setting?

    A. `show ip route`

    B. `show boot version`

    C. `show version`

    D. `show flash`

18. You need to gather the IP address of a remote switch that is located in Hawaii. What can you do to find the address?

    A. Fly to Hawaii, console into the switch, then relax and have a drink with an umbrella in it.

    B. Issue the `show ip route` command on the router connected to the switch.

    C. Issue the `show cdp neighbor` command on the router connected to the switch.

    D. Issue the `show ip arp` command on the router connected to the switch.

    E. Issue the `show cdp neighbors detail` command on the router connected to the switch.

19. You have your laptop directly connected into a router's Ethernet port. Which of the following are among the requirements for the `copy flash tftp` command to be successful? (Choose three.)

    A. TFTP server software must be running on the router.

    B. TFTP server software must be running on your laptop.

    C. The Ethernet cable connecting the laptop directly into the router's Ethernet port must be a straight-through cable.

    D. The laptop must be on the same subnet as the router's Ethernet interface.

    E. The `copy flash tftp` command must be supplied the IP address of the laptop.

    F. There must be enough room in the flash memory of the router to accommodate the file to be copied.

20. The configuration register setting of 0x2102 provides what function to a router?

A. Tells the router to boot into ROM monitor mode

B. Provides password recovery

C. Tells the router to look in NVRAM for the boot sequence

D. Boots the IOS from a TFTP server

E. Boots an IOS image stored in ROM

Answers to Review Questions

1. B. The default configuration setting is 0x2102, which tells the router to load the IOS from flash and the configuration from NVRAM. `0x2142` tells the router to bypass the configuration in NVRAM so that you can perform password recovery.

2. E. To copy the IOS to a backup host, which is stored in flash memory by default, use the `copy flash tftp` command.

3. B. The command `traceroute` (`trace` for short), which can be issued from user mode or privileged mode, is used to find the path a packet takes through an internetwork and will also show you where the packet stops because of an error on a router.

4. C. Since the configuration looks correct, you probably didn't screw up the copy job. However, when you perform a copy from a network host to a router, the interfaces are automatically shut down and need to be manually enabled with the `no shutdown` command.

5. B. The `show flash` command will provide you with the current IOS name and size and the size of flash memory.

6. C. Before you start to configure the router, you should erase the NVRAM with the `erase startup-config` command and then reload the router using the `reload` command.

7. D. The command `copy tftp flash` will allow you to copy a new IOS into flash memory on your router.

8. C. The best answer is `show version`, which shows you the IOS file running currently on your router. The `show flash` command shows you the contents of flash memory, not which file is running.

9. C. All Cisco routers have a default configuration register setting of 0x2102, which tells the router to load the IOS from flash memory and the configuration from NVRAM.

10. C. If you save a configuration and reload the router and it comes up either in setup mode or as a blank configuration, chances are you have the configuration register setting incorrect.

11. D. To keep open one or more Telnet sessions, use the Ctrl+Shift+6 and then X keystroke combination.

12. B, D. The best answers, the ones you need to remember, are that either an access control list is filtering the Telnet session or the VTY password is not set on the remote device.

13. A, D. The `show hosts` command provides information on temporary DNS entries and permanent name-to-address mappings created using the `ip host` command.

14. A, B, D. The `tracert` command is a Windows command and will not work on a router! A router uses the `traceroute` command.

15. D. Since the question never mentioned anything about a suspended session, you can assume that the Telnet session is still open, and you would just type **exit** to close the session.

16. C. To see console messages through your Telnet session, you must enter the `terminal monitor` command.

17. C. The `show version` command provides you with the current configuration register setting.

18. E. Although option A is certainly the "best" answer, unfortunately option E will work just fine and your boss would probably prefer you to use the `show cdp neighbors detail` command.

19. B, D, E. Before you back up an IOS image to a laptop directly connected to a router's Ethernet port, make sure the TFTP server software is running on your laptop, that the Ethernet cable is a "crossover," and that the laptop is in the same subnet as the router's Ethernet port, and then you can use the `copy flash tftp` command from your laptop.

20. C. The default configuration setting of 0x2102 tells the router to look in NVRAM for the boot sequence.

Answers to Written Lab 7

Written Lab 7.1

1. `copy flash tftp`
2. `copy start tftp`
3. `copy start run`
4. `config mem`
5. `show cdp neighbor detail` or `show cdp entry *`
6. `show cdp neighbor`
7. Ctrl+Shift+6, then X
8. `show sessions`
9. `copy tftp flash`
10. Either `copy tftp run` or `copy start run`

Written Lab 7.2

1. Flash memory
2. ROM
3. NVRAM
4. ROM
5. RAM
6. RAM
7. ROM
8. ROM
9. RAM
10. RAM

IP Routing

THE CCNA EXAM TOPICS COVERED IN THIS CHAPTER INCLUDE THE FOLLOWING:

✓ **Describe how a network works**

- Determine the path between two hosts across a network

✓ **Configure, verify, and troubleshoot basic router operation and routing on Cisco devices**

- Describe basic routing concepts (including: packet forwarding, router lookup process)
- Configure, verify, and troubleshoot RIPv2
- Access and utilize the router to set basic parameters (including: CLI/SDM)
- Connect, configure, and verify operation status of a device interface
- Verify device configuration and network connectivity using ping, traceroute, telnet, SSH. or other utilities
- Perform and verify routing configuration tasks for a static or default route given specific routing requirements
- Compare and contrast methods of routing and routing protocols
- Configure, verify, and troubleshoot OSPF
- Configure, verify, and troubleshoot EIGRP
- Verify network connectivity (including: using ping, traceroute, and telnet or SSH)
- Troubleshoot routing issues
- Verify router hardware and software operation using SHOW and DEBUG commands
- Implement basic router security

In this chapter, I'm going to discuss the IP routing process. This is an important subject to understand since it pertains to all routers and configurations that use IP. IP routing is the process of moving packets from one network to another network using routers. And as before, by routers I mean Cisco routers, of course!

But before you read this chapter, you must understand the difference between a routing protocol and a routed protocol. A *routing protocol* is used by routers to dynamically find all the networks in the internetwork and to ensure that all routers have the same routing table. Basically, a routing protocol determines the path of a packet through an internetwork. Examples of routing protocols are RIP, RIPv2, EIGRP, and OSPF.

Once all routers know about all networks, a *routed protocol* can be used to send user data (packets) through the established enterprise. Routed protocols are assigned to an interface and determine the method of packet delivery. Examples of routed protocols are IP and IPv6.

I'm pretty sure that I don't have to tell you that this is definitely important stuff to know. You most likely understand that from what I've said so far. IP routing is basically what Cisco routers do, and they do it very well. Again, this chapter is dealing with truly fundamental material—these are things you must know if you want to understand the objectives covered in this book!

In this chapter, I'm going to show you how to configure and verify IP routing with Cisco routers. I'll be covering the following:

- Routing basics
- The IP routing process
- Static routing
- Default routing
- Dynamic routing

In Chapter 9, "Enhanced IGRP (EIGRP) and Open Shortest Path First (OSPF)," I'll be moving into more advanced, dynamic routing with EIGRP and OSPF. But first, you've really got to nail down the basics of how packets actually move through an internetwork, so let's get started!

For up-to-the minute updates for this chapter, please see `www.lammle.com` and/or `www.sybex.com/go/ccna7e`.

Routing Basics

Once you create an internetwork by connecting your WANs and LANs to a router, you'll need to configure logical network addresses, such as IP addresses, to all hosts on the internetwork so that they can communicate across that internetwork.

The term *routing* refers to taking a packet from one device and sending it through the network to another device on a different network. Routers don't really care about hosts—they only care about networks and the best path to each network. The logical network address of the destination host is used to get packets to a network through a routed network, and then the hardware address of the host is used to deliver the packet from a router to the correct destination host.

If your network has no routers, then it should be apparent that you are not routing. Routers route traffic to all the networks in your internetwork. To be able to route packets, a router must know, at a minimum, the following:

- Destination address
- Neighbor routers from which it can learn about remote networks
- Possible routes to all remote networks
- The best route to each remote network
- How to maintain and verify routing information

The router learns about remote networks from neighboring routers or from an administrator. The router then builds a routing table (a map of the internetwork) that describes how to find the remote networks. If a network is directly connected, then the router already knows how to get to it.

If a network isn't directly connected to the router, the router must use one of two ways to learn how to get to the remote network: static routing, meaning that someone must hand-type all network locations into the routing table, or something called dynamic routing.

In *dynamic routing*, a protocol on one router communicates with the same protocol running on neighboring routers. The routers then update each other about all the networks they know about and place this information into the routing table. If a change occurs in the network, the dynamic routing protocols automatically inform all routers about the event. If *static routing* is used, the administrator is responsible for updating all changes by hand onto all routers. Typically, in a large network, a combination of both dynamic and static routing is used.

Before we jump into the IP routing process, let's take a look at a very simple example that demonstrates how a router uses the routing table to route packets out of an interface. We'll be going into a more detailed study of the process in the next section, but what I am showing now is called the "longest match rule," which means that IP will look through a routing table for the longest match compared to the destination address of a packet. Let's take a look.

Figure 8.1 shows a simple two-router network. Lab_A has one serial interface and three LAN interfaces.

Looking at Figure 8.1, can you see which interface Lab_A will use to forward an IP datagram to a host with an IP address of 10.10.10.10?

FIGURE 8.1 A simple routing example

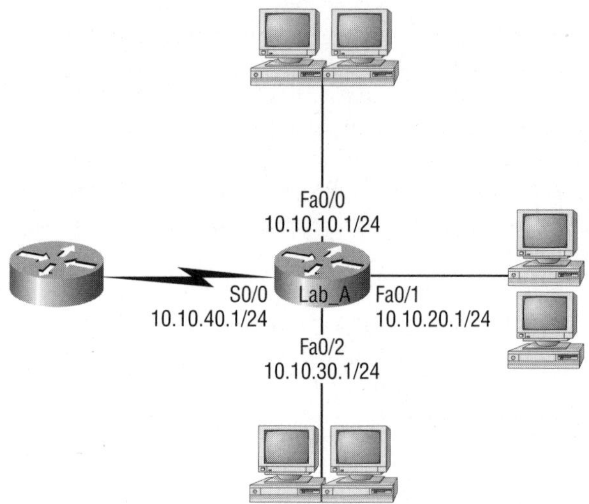

By using the command `show ip route`, we can see the routing table (map of the internetwork) that Lab_A uses to make forwarding decisions:

```
Lab_A#sh ip route
[output cut]
Gateway of last resort is not set
C       10.10.10.0/24 is directly connected, FastEthernet0/0
C       10.10.20.0/24 is directly connected, FastEthernet0/1
C       10.10.30.0/24 is directly connected, FastEthernet0/2
C       10.10.40.0/24 is directly connected, Serial 0/0
```

The `C` in the routing table output means that the networks listed are "directly connected," and until we add a routing protocol—something like RIP, EIGRP, etc.—to the routers in our internetwork (or use static routes), we'll have only directly connected networks in our routing table.

So let's get back to the original question: By looking at the figure and the output of the routing table, can you tell what IP will do with a received packet that has a destination IP address of 10.10.10.10? The router will packet-switch the packet to interface FastEthernet 0/0, and this interface will frame the packet and then send it out on the network segment. To reiterate on the longest match rule, IP would look for 10.10.10.10 in this example, and if that is not found in the table, then IP would search for 10.10.10.0, then 10.10.0.0, and so on until a route is found.

Because we can, let's do another example: Based on the output of the next routing table, which interface will a packet with a destination address of 10.10.10.14 be forwarded from?

```
Lab_A#sh ip route
[output cut]
```

```
Gateway of last resort is not set
C       10.10.10.16/28 is directly connected, FastEthernet0/0
C       10.10.10.8/29 is directly connected, FastEthernet0/1
C       10.10.10.4/30 is directly connected, FastEthernet0/2
C       10.10.10.0/30 is directly connected, Serial 0/0
```

First, you can see that the network is subnetted and each interface has a different mask. And I have to tell you—you just can't answer this question if you can't subnet! 10.10.10.14 would be a host in the 10.10.10.8/29 subnet connected to the FastEthernet0/1 interface. Don't freak out if you don't get it. Just go back and reread Chapter 4 if you're struggling, and this should make perfect sense to you afterward.

For everyone who's ready to move on, let's get into this process in more detail.

The IP Routing Process

The IP routing process is fairly simple and doesn't change, regardless of the size of your network. For an example, we'll use Figure 8.2 to describe step-by-step what happens when Host_A wants to communicate with Host_B on a different network.

FIGURE 8.2 IP routing example using two hosts and one router

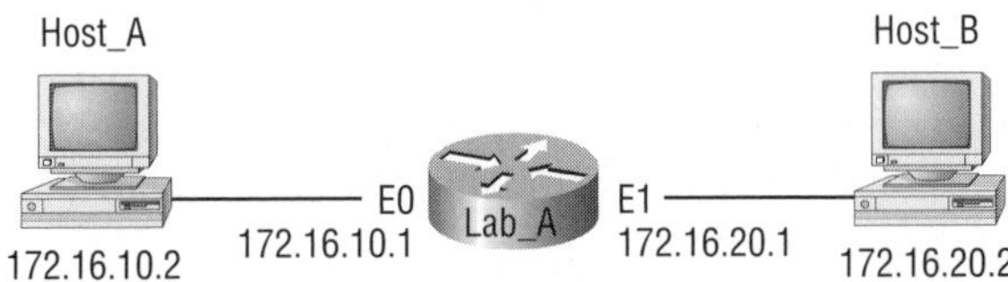

In this example, a user on Host_A pings Host_B's IP address. Routing doesn't get simpler than this, but it still involves a lot of steps. Let's work through them:

1. Internet Control Message Protocol (ICMP) creates an echo request payload (which is just the alphabet in the data field).
2. ICMP hands that payload to Internet Protocol (IP), which then creates a packet. At a minimum, this packet contains an IP source address, an IP destination address, and a Protocol field with 01h. (Remember that Cisco likes to use *0x* in front of hex characters, so this could look like 0x01.) All that tells the receiving host to whom it should hand the payload when the destination is reached—in this example, ICMP.
3. Once the packet is created, IP determines whether the destination IP address is on the local network or a remote one.
4. Since IP determines that this is a remote request, the packet needs to be sent to the default gateway so it can be routed to the remote network. The Registry in Windows is parsed to find the configured default gateway.

5. The default gateway of host 172.16.10.2 (Host_A) is configured to 172.16.10.1. For this packet to be sent to the default gateway, the hardware address of the router's interface Ethernet 0 (configured with the IP address of 172.16.10.1) must be known. Why? So the packet can be handed down to the Data Link layer, framed, and sent to the router's interface that's connected to the 172.16.10.0 network. Because hosts only communicate via hardware addresses on the local LAN, it's important to recognize that for Host_A to communicate to Host_B, it has to send packets to the Media Access Control (MAC) address of the default gateway on the local network.

MAC addresses are always local on the LAN and never go through and past a router.

6. Next, the Address Resolution Protocol (ARP) cache of the host is checked to see if the IP address of the default gateway has already been resolved to a hardware address:
   - If it has, the packet is then free to be handed to the Data Link layer for framing. (The hardware destination address is also handed down with that packet.) To view the ARP cache on your host, use the following command:

```
C:\>arp -a
Interface: 172.16.10.2 --- 0x3
  Internet Address      Physical Address      Type
  172.16.10.1          00-15-05-06-31-b0     dynamic
```

   - If the hardware address isn't already in the ARP cache of the host, an ARP broadcast is sent out onto the local network to search for the hardware address of 172.16.10.1. The router responds to the request and provides the hardware address of Ethernet 0, and the host caches this address.

7. Once the packet and destination hardware address are handed to the Data Link layer, the LAN driver is used to provide media access via the type of LAN being used (in this example, Ethernet). A frame is then generated, encapsulating the packet with control information. Within that frame are the hardware destination and source addresses plus, in this case, an Ether-Type field that describes the Network layer protocol that handed the packet to the Data Link layer—in this instance, IP. At the end of the frame is something called a Frame Check Sequence (FCS) field that houses the result of the cyclic redundancy check (CRC). The frame would look something like what I've detailed in Figure 8.3. It contains Host_A's hardware (MAC) address and the destination hardware address of the default gateway. It does not include the remote host's MAC address—remember that!

FIGURE 8.3 Frame used from Host_A to the Lab_A router when Host_B is pinged

Destination MAC (routers E0 MAC address)	Source MAC (Host_A MAC address)	Ether-Type field	Packet	FCS (CRC)

8. Once the frame is completed, it's handed down to the Physical layer to be put on the physical medium (in this example, twisted-pair wire) one bit at a time.
9. Every device in the collision domain receives these bits and builds the frame. They each run a CRC and check the answer in the FCS field. If the answers don't match, the frame is discarded.
   - If the CRC matches, then the hardware destination address is checked to see if it matches too (which, in this example, is the router's interface Ethernet 0).
   - If it's a match, then the Ether-Type field is checked to find the protocol used at the Network layer.
10. The packet is pulled from the frame, and what is left of the frame is discarded. The packet is handed to the protocol listed in the Ether-Type field—it's given to IP.
11. IP receives the packet and checks the IP destination address. Since the packet's destination address doesn't match any of the addresses configured on the receiving router itself, the router will look up the destination IP network address in its routing table.
12. The routing table must have an entry for the network 172.16.20.0 or the packet will be discarded immediately and an ICMP message will be sent back to the originating device with a destination network unreachable message.
13. If the router does find an entry for the destination network in its table, the packet is switched to the exit interface—in this example, interface Ethernet 1. The output below displays the Lab_A router's routing table. The `C` means "directly connected." No routing protocols are needed in this network since all networks (all two of them) are directly connected.

```
Lab_A>sh ip route
Codes:C - connected,S - static,I - IGRP,R - RIP,M - mobile,B -
[output cut]
Gateway of last resort is not set

     172.16.0.0/24 is subnetted, 2 subnets
C       172.16.10.0 is directly connected, Ethernet0
C       172.16.20.0 is directly connected, Ethernet1
```

14. The router packet-switches the packet to the Ethernet 1 buffer.
15. The Ethernet 1 buffer needs to know the hardware address of the destination host and first checks the ARP cache.
   - If the hardware address of Host_B has already been resolved and is in the router's ARP cache, then the packet and the hardware address are handed down to the Data Link layer to be framed. Let's take a look at the ARP cache on the Lab_A router by using the `show ip arp` command:

```
Lab_A#sh ip arp
Protocol  Address     Age(min) Hardware Addr  Type   Interface
```

```
Internet  172.16.20.1    -     00d0.58ad.05f4  ARPA   Ethernet1
Internet  172.16.20.2    3     0030.9492.a5dd  ARPA   Ethernet1
Internet  172.16.10.1    -     00d0.58ad.06aa  ARPA   Ethernet0
Internet  172.16.10.2   12     0030.9492.a4ac  ARPA   Ethernet0
```

The dash (-) means that this is the physical interface on the router. From the output above, we can see that the router knows the 172.16.10.2 (Host_A) and 172.16.20.2 (Host_B) hardware addresses. Cisco routers will keep an entry in the ARP table for 4 hours.

- If the hardware address has not already been resolved, the router sends an ARP request out E1 looking for the hardware address of 172.16.20.2. Host_B responds with its hardware address, and the packet and destination hardware addresses are both sent to the Data Link layer for framing.

16. The Data Link layer creates a frame with the destination and source hardware address, Ether-Type field, and FCS field at the end. The frame is handed to the Physical layer to be sent out on the physical medium one bit at a time.
17. Host_B receives the frame and immediately runs a CRC. If the result matches what's in the FCS field, the hardware destination address is then checked. If the host finds a match, the Ether-Type field is then checked to determine the protocol that the packet should be handed to at the Network layer—IP in this example.
18. At the Network layer, IP receives the packet and runs a CRC on the IP header. If that passes, IP then checks the destination address. Since there's finally a match made, the Protocol field is checked to find out to whom the payload should be given.
19. The payload is handed to ICMP, which understands that this is an echo request. ICMP responds to this by immediately discarding the packet and generating a new payload as an echo reply.
20. A packet is then created including the source and destination addresses, Protocol field, and payload. The destination device is now Host_A.
21. IP then checks to see whether the destination IP address is a device on the local LAN or on a remote network. Since the destination device is on a remote network, the packet needs to be sent to the default gateway.
22. The default gateway IP address is found in the Registry of the Windows device, and the ARP cache is checked to see if the hardware address has already been resolved from an IP address.
23. Once the hardware address of the default gateway is found, the packet and destination hardware addresses are handed down to the Data Link layer for framing.
24. The Data Link layer frames the packet of information and includes the following in the header:
    - The destination and source hardware addresses
    - The Ether-Type field with 0x0800 (IP) in it
    - The FCS field with the CRC result in tow

25. The frame is now handed down to the Physical layer to be sent out over the network medium one bit at a time.
26. The router's Ethernet 1 interface receives the bits and builds a frame. The CRC is run, and the FCS field is checked to make sure the answers match.
27. Once the CRC is found to be okay, the hardware destination address is checked. Since the router's interface is a match, the packet is pulled from the frame and the Ether-Type field is checked to see what protocol at the Network layer the packet should be delivered to.
28. The protocol is determined to be IP, so it gets the packet. IP runs a CRC check on the IP header first and then checks the destination IP address.

IP does not run a complete CRC as the Data Link layer does—it only checks the header for errors.

Since the IP destination address doesn't match any of the router's interfaces, the routing table is checked to see whether it has a route to 172.16.10.0. If it doesn't have a route over to the destination network, the packet will be discarded immediately. (This is the source point of confusion for a lot of administrators—when a ping fails, most people think the packet never reached the destination host. But as we see here, that's not *always* the case. All it takes is for just one of the remote routers to be lacking a route back to the originating host's network and—*poof!*—the packet is dropped on the *return trip*, not on its way to the host.)

Just a quick note to mention that when (if) the packet is lost on the way back to the originating host, you will typically see a request timed out message because it is an unknown error. If the error occurs because of a known issue, such as if a route is not in the routing table on the way to the destination device, you will see a destination unreachable message. This should help you determine if the problem occurred on the way to the destination or on the way back.

29. In this case, the router does know how to get to network 172.16.10.0—the exit interface is Ethernet 0—so the packet is switched to interface Ethernet 0.
30. The router checks the ARP cache to determine whether the hardware address for 172.16.10.2 has already been resolved.
31. Since the hardware address to 172.16.10.2 is already cached from the originating trip to Host_B, the hardware address and packet are handed to the Data Link layer.
32. The Data Link layer builds a frame with the destination hardware address and source hardware address and then puts IP in the Ether-Type field. A CRC is run on the frame and the result is placed in the FCS field.
33. The frame is then handed to the Physical layer to be sent out onto the local network one bit at a time.

34. The destination host receives the frame, runs a CRC, checks the destination hardware address, and looks in the Ether-Type field to find out to whom to hand the packet.
35. IP is the designated receiver, and after the packet is handed to IP at the Network layer, it checks the Protocol field for further direction. IP finds instructions to give the payload to ICMP, and ICMP determines the packet to be an ICMP echo reply.
36. ICMP acknowledges that it has received the reply by sending an exclamation point (!) to the user interface. ICMP then attempts to send four more echo requests to the destination host.

You've just experienced Todd's 36 easy steps to understanding IP routing. The key point to understand here is that if you had a much larger network, the process would be the *same*. In a really big internetwork, the packet just goes through more hops before it finds the destination host.

It's super-important to remember that when Host_A sends a packet to Host_B, the destination hardware address used is the default gateway's Ethernet interface. Why? Because frames can't be placed on remote networks—only local networks. So packets destined for remote networks must go through the default gateway.

Let's take a look at Host_A's ARP cache now:

```
C:\ >arp -a
Interface: 172.16.10.2 --- 0x3
  Internet Address      Physical Address      Type
  172.16.10.1           00-15-05-06-31-b0     dynamic
  172.16.20.1           00-15-05-06-31-b0     dynamic
```

Did you notice that the hardware (MAC) address that Host_A uses to get to Host_B is the Lab_A E0 interface? Hardware addresses are *always* local, and they never pass a router's interface. Understanding this process is as important as air to you, so carve this into your memory!

Testing Your IP Routing Understanding

I really want to make sure you understand IP routing because it's super-important. So I'm going to use this section to test your understanding of the IP routing process by having you look at a couple of figures and answer some very basic IP routing questions.

Figure 8.4 shows a LAN connected to RouterA, which is, in turn, connected via a WAN link to RouterB. RouterB has a LAN connected with an HTTP server attached.

The critical information you need to glean from this figure is exactly how IP routing will occur in this example. Okay—we'll cheat a bit. I'll give you the answer, but then you should go back over the figure and see if you can answer example 2 without looking at my answers.

1. The destination address of a frame, from HostA, will be the MAC address of the Fa0/0 interface of the RouterA router.
2. The destination address of a packet will be the IP address of the network interface card (NIC) of the HTTP server.
3. The destination port number in the segment header will have a value of 80.

FIGURE 8.4 IP routing example 1

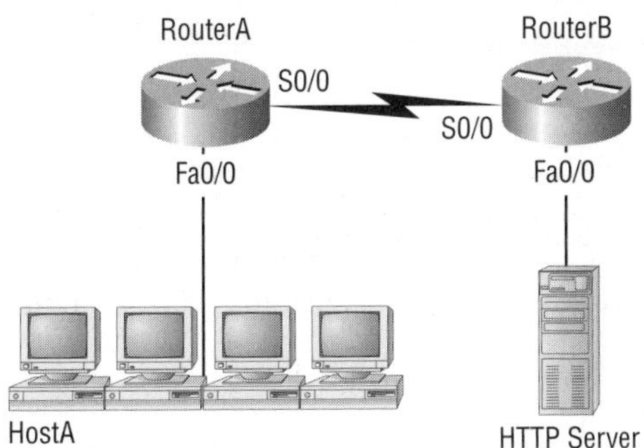

That example was a pretty simple one, and it was also very to the point. One thing to remember is that if multiple hosts are communicating to the server using HTTP, they must all use a different source port number. That is how the server keeps the data separated at the Transport layer.

Let's mix it up a little and add another internetworking device into the network and then see if you can find the answers. Figure 8.5 shows a network with only one router but two switches.

FIGURE 8.5 IP routing example 2

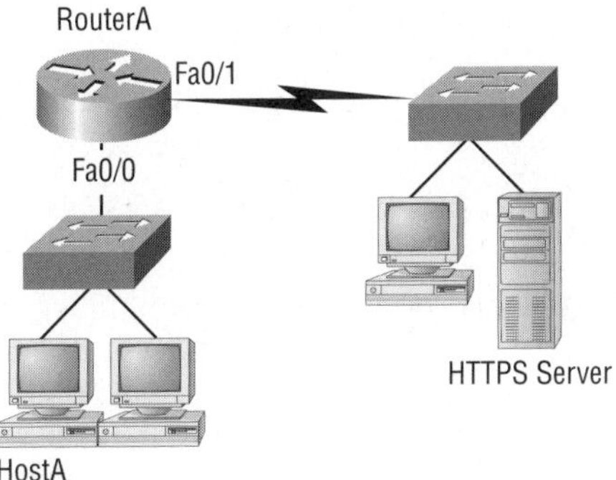

What you want to understand about the IP routing process here is what happens when HostA sends data to the HTTPS server:

1. The destination address of a frame, from HostA, will be the MAC address of the Fa0/0 interface of the RouterA router.
2. The destination address of a packet will be the IP address of the network interface card (NIC) of the HTTPS server.
3. The destination port number in the segment header will have a value of 443.

Notice that the switches weren't used as either a default gateway or another destination. That's because switches have nothing to do with routing. I wonder how many of you chose the switch as the default gateway (destination) MAC address for HostA? If you did, don't feel bad—just take another look with that fact in mind. It's very important to remember that the destination MAC address will always be the router's interface—if your packets are destined for outside the LAN, as they were in these last two examples.

Before we move into some of the more advanced aspects of IP routing, let's discuss ICMP in more detail, as well as how ICMP is used in an internetwork. Take a look at the network shown in Figure 8.6. Ask yourself what will happen if the LAN interface of Lab_C goes down.

FIGURE 8.6 ICMP error example

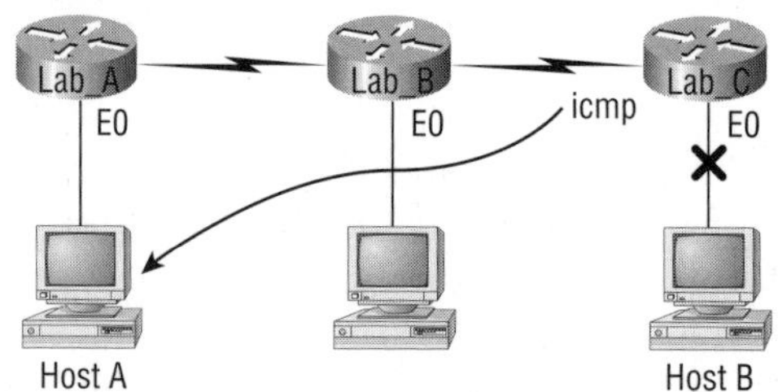

Lab_C will use ICMP to inform Host A that Host B can't be reached, and it will do this by sending an ICMP destination unreachable message. The point of this figure is to help you visualize how ICMP data is routed via IP back to the originating station.

Let's look at another problem: Look at the output of a corporate router's routing table:

```
Corp#sh ip route
[output cut]
R     192.168.215.0 [120/2] via 192.168.20.2, 00:00:23, Serial0/0
R     192.168.115.0 [120/1] via 192.168.20.2, 00:00:23, Serial0/0
R     192.168.30.0 [120/1] via 192.168.20.2, 00:00:23, Serial0/0
C     192.168.20.0 is directly connected, Serial0/0
C     192.168.214.0 is directly connected, FastEthernet0/0
```

What do we see here? If I were to tell you that the corporate router received an IP packet with a source IP address of 192.168.214.20 and a destination address of 192.168.22.3, what do you think the Corp router will do with this packet?

If you said, "The packet came in on the FastEthernet 0/0 interface, but since the routing table doesn't show a route to network 192.168.22.0 (or a default route), the router will discard the packet and send an ICMP destination unreachable message back out to interface FastEthernet 0/0," you're a genius! The reason it does this is because that's the source LAN where the packet originated from.

Now, let's check out another figure and talk about the frames and packets in detail. Really, we're not exactly chatting about anything new; I'm just making sure that you totally, completely, fully understand basic IP routing. That's because this book, and the exam objectives it's geared toward, are all about IP routing, which means you need to be all over this stuff! We'll use Figure 8.7 for the next few questions.

FIGURE 8.7 Basic IP routing using MAC and IP addresses

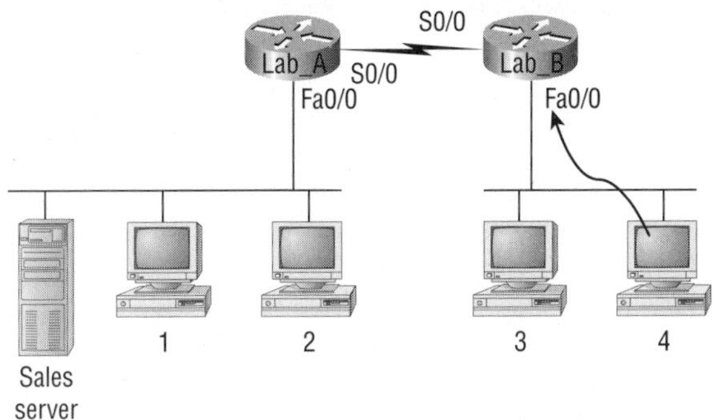

Referring to Figure 8.7, here's a list of all the questions you need the answers to emblazoned in your brain:

1. In order to begin communicating with the Sales server, Host 4 sends out an ARP request. How will the devices exhibited in the topology respond to this request?
2. Host 4 has received an ARP reply. Host 4 will now build a packet, then place this packet in the frame. What information will be placed in the header of the packet that leaves Host 4 if Host 4 is going to communicate to the Sales server?
3. At last, the Lab_A router has received the packet and will send it out Fa0/0 onto the LAN toward the server. What will the frame have in the header as the source and destination addresses?
4. Host 4 is displaying two web documents from the Sales server in two browser windows at the same time. How did the data find its way to the correct browser windows?

I probably should write the following in a teensy font and put them upside down in another part of the book so it would be really hard for you to cheat and peek, but since it's actually you who's going to lose out if you peek, here are your answers:

1. In order to begin communicating with the server, Host 4 sends out an ARP request. How will the devices exhibited in the topology respond to this request? Since MAC addresses must stay on the local network, the Lab_B router will respond with the MAC address of the Fa0/0 interface and Host 4 will send all frames to the MAC address of the Lab_B Fa0/0 interface when sending packets to the Sales server.
2. Host 4 has received an ARP reply. Host 4 will now build a packet, then place this packet in the frame. What information will be placed in the header of the packet that leaves Host 4 if Host 4 is going to communicate to the Sales server? Since we're now talking about packets, not frames, the source address will be the IP address of Host 4 and the destination address will be the IP address of the Sales server.

3. Finally, the Lab_A router has received the packet and will send it out Fa0/0 onto the LAN toward the server. What will the frame have in the header as the source and destination addresses? The source MAC address will be the Lab_A router's Fa0/0 interface, and the destination MAC address will be the Sales server's MAC address. (All MAC addresses must be local on the LAN.)
4. Host 4 is displaying two web documents from the Sales server in two different browser windows at the same time. How did the data find its way to the correct browser windows? TCP port numbers are used to direct the data to the correct application window.

Great! But we're not quite done yet. I've got a few more questions for you before you actually get to configure routing in a real network. Ready? Figure 8.8 shows a basic network, and Host 4 needs to get email. Which address will be placed in the destination address field of the frame when it leaves Host 4?

FIGURE 8.8 Testing basic routing knowledge

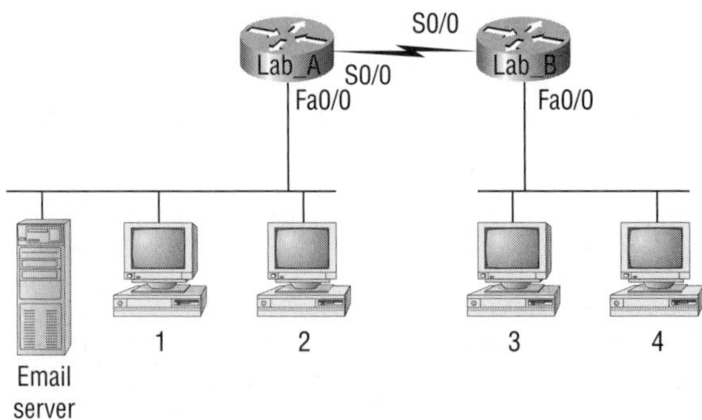

The answer is that Host 4 will use the destination MAC address of the Fa0/0 interface of the Lab_B router—which I'm so sure you knew, right? Look at Figure 8.8 again: Host 4 needs to communicate with Host 1. Which OSI layer 3 source address will be found in the packet header when it reaches Host 1?

Hopefully you know this: At layer 3, the source IP address will be Host 4 and the destination address in the packet will be the IP address of Host 1. Of course, the destination MAC address from Host 4 will always be the Fa0/0 address of the Lab_B router, right? And since we have more than one router, we'll need a routing protocol that communicates between both of them so that traffic can be forwarded in the right direction to reach the network in which Host 1 is attached.

Okay—one more question and you're on your way to being an IP routing genius! Again, using Figure 8.8., Host 4 is transferring a file to the email server connected to the Lab_A router. What would be the layer 2 destination address leaving Host 4? Yes, I've asked this question more than once. But not this one: What will be the source MAC address when the frame is received at the email server?

Hopefully, you answered that the layer 2 destination address leaving Host 4 will be the MAC address of the Fa0/0 interface of the Lab_B router and that the source layer 2 address that the email server will receive will be the Fa0/0 interface of the Lab_A router.

If you did, you're all set to get the skinny on how IP routing is handled in a larger network.

Configuring IP Routing

It's time to get serious and configure a real network! Figure 8.9 shows four routers: Corp, Remote1, Remote2, and Remote3. Remember that, by default, these routers only know about networks that are directly connected to them. I'll continue to use this figure and network throughout the rest of the chapters in this book.

FIGURE 8.9 Configuring IP routing

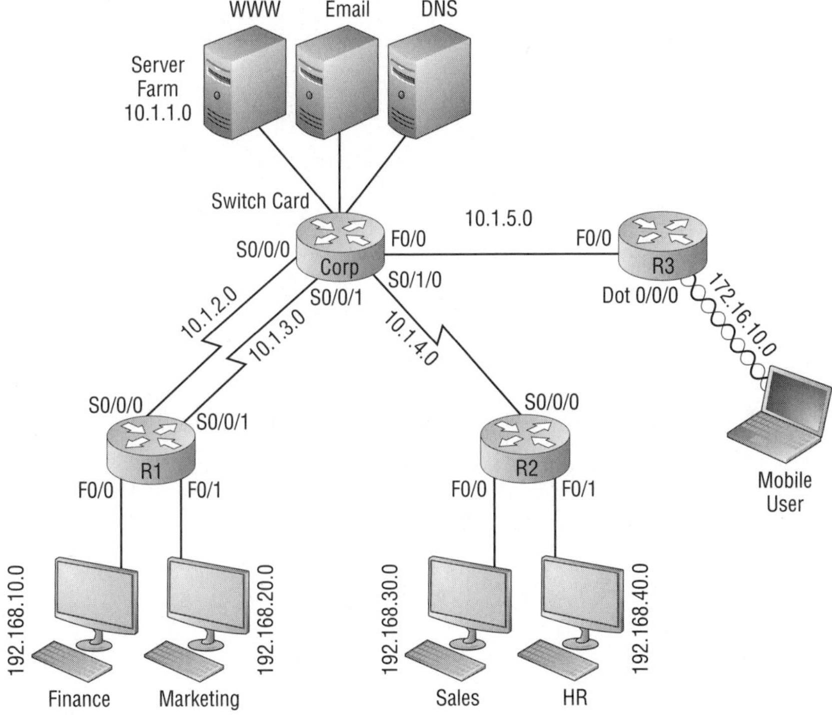

As you might guess, I've got quite a nice collection of routers for us to play with. The Corp router is a 2811 with four serial interfaces and a switch module, and remote routers 1 and 2 are 1841 routers. Remote 3 is another 2811 with a wireless interface card. I'm simply going to call the remote routers R1, R2, and R3. (Understand that you can still perform most of the commands I use in this book with older routers or with a router simulator)

The first step for this project is to correctly configure each router with an IP address on each interface. Table 8.1 shows the IP address scheme I'm going to use to configure the network. After we go over how the network is configured, I'll cover how to configure IP routing. Each network in the following table has a 24-bit subnet mask (255.255.255.0), which makes the interesting (subnet) octet the third one.

TABLE 8.1 Network addressing for the IP network

Router	Network Address	Interface	Address
CORP			
Corp	10.1.1.0	Vlan1 (switch card)	10.1.1.1
Corp	10.1.2.0	S0/0/0	10.1.2.1
Corp	10.1.3.0	S0/0/1(DCE)	10.1.3.1
Corp	10.1.4.0	S0/1/0	10.1.4.1
Corp	10.1.5.0	F0/0	10.1.5.1
R1			
R1	10.1.2.0	S0/0/0 (DCE)	10.1.2.2
R1	10.1.3.0	S0/0/1	10.1.3.2
R1	192.168.10.0	F0/0	192.168.10.1
R1	192.168.20.0	F0/1	192.168.20.1
R2			
R2	10.1.4.0	S0/0/0 (DCE)	10.1.4.2
R2	192.168.30.0	F0/0	192.168.30.1
R2	192.168.40.0	F0/1	192.168.40.1
R3			
R3	10.1.5.0	F0/0	10.1.5.2
R3	172.16.10.0	Dot11Radio0/0/0	172.16.10.1

The router configuration is really a pretty straightforward process since you just need to add IP addresses to your interfaces and then perform a `no shutdown` on those same interfaces. It gets a tad more complex later on, but for right now, let's configure the IP addresses in the network.

Corp Configuration

We need to configure five interfaces to configure the Corp router. And configuring the hostnames of each router will make identification much easier. While we're at it, why not set the interface descriptions, banner, and router passwords too? It's a really good idea to make a habit of configuring these commands on every router.

To get started, I performed an `erase startup-config` on the router and reloaded, so we'll start in setup mode. I choose no to entering setup mode, which will get us straight to the username prompt of the console. I'm going to configure all my routers this same way.

I need to mention one small issue before I configure the Corp router and that is the switch card configuration. The IP address is configured on a logical interface on a switch, not a physical interface, and that interface by default is named vlan 1. Also, unlike with standalone switches, the interfaces on my switch card installed in the router are not enabled by default, so you'll see that I enable the ports we are using in this lab.

Here's how I did all that:

```
        --- System Configuration Dialog ---

Would you like to enter the initial configuration dialog? [yes/no]: n

Press RETURN to get started!
Router>en
Router#config t
Enter configuration commands, one per line.  End with CNTL/Z.
Router(config)#hostname Corp
Corp(config)#enable secret todd
Corp(config)#interface vlan 1
Corp(config-if)#description Switch Card to Core Network
Corp(config-if)#ip address 10.1.1.1 255.255.255.0
Corp(config-if)#no shutdown
Corp(config-if)#int f1/0
Corp(config-if)#description Switch Port connection to WWW Server
Corp(config-if)#no shutdown
Corp(config-if)#int f1/1
Corp(config-if)#description Switch port connection to Email Server
Corp(config-if)#no shut
Corp(config-if)#int f1/2
Corp(config-if)#description Switch port connection to DNS Server
```

```
Corp(config-if)#no shut
Corp(config-if)#int s0/0/0
Corp(config-if)#description 1st Connection to R1
Corp(config-if)#ip address 10.1.2.1 255.255.255.0
Corp(config-if)#no shut
Corp(config-if)#int s0/0/1
Corp(config-if)#description 2nd Connection to R1
Corp(config-if)#ip address 10.1.3.1 255.255.255.0
Corp(config-if)#no shut
Corp(config-if)#int s0/1/0
Corp(config-if)#description Connection to R2
Corp(config-if)#ip address 10.1.4.1 255.255.255.0
Corp(config-if)#no shut
Corp(config-if)#int fa0/0
Corp(config-if)# description Connection to R3
Corp(config-if)# ip address 10.1.5.1 255.255.255.0
Corp(config-if)#no shut
Corp(config-if)#line con 0
Corp(config-line)#password console
Corp(config-line)#login
Corp(config-line)#logging synchronous
Corp(config-line)#exec-timeout 0 0
Corp(config-line)#line aux 0
Corp(config-line)#password aux
Corp(config-line)#login
Corp(config-line)#exit
Corp(config)#line vty 0 ?
  <1-15>  Last Line number
  <cr>
Corp(config)#line vty 0 15
Corp(config-line)#password telnet
Corp(config-line)#login
Corp(config-line)#exit
Corp(config)#no ip domain lookup
Corp(config)#banner motd # This is my Corp 2811 ISR Router #
Corp(config-if)#^Z
Corp#copy running-config startup-config
Destination filename [startup-config]?[enter]
Building configuration...
[OK]
Corp#
```

If you have a hard time understanding this configuration process, refer back to Chapter 6, "Cisco's Internetworking Operating System (IOS)."

To view the IP routing tables created on a Cisco router, use the command `show ip route`. The command output is shown as follows:

```
Corp#sh ip route
Codes: C - connected, S - static, R - RIP, M - mobile, B - BGP
       D - EIGRP, EX - EIGRP external, O - OSPF, IA - OSPF inter area
       N1 - OSPF NSSA external type 1, N2 - OSPF NSSA external type 2
       E1 - OSPF external type 1, E2 - OSPF external type 2
       i - IS-IS, su - IS-IS summary, L1 - IS-IS level-1, L2 - IS-IS
   level-2, ia - IS-IS inter area, * - candidate default, U - per-user
   static route, o - ODR, P - periodic downloaded static route

Gateway of last resort is not set

     10.0.0.0/24 is subnetted, 1 subnets
C       10.1.1.0 is directly connected, Vlan1
Corp#
```

It's important to remember that only configured, directly connected networks are going to show up in the routing table. So why is it that I only see the Vlan1 interface in the routing table? No worries—that's just because you won't see the serial interfaces come up until the other side of the links are operational. As soon as we configure our R1, R2, and R3 routers, all those interfaces should pop right up.

But did you notice the `C` on the left side of the output of the routing table? When you see that there, it means that the network is directly connected. The codes for each type of connection are listed at the top of the `show ip route` command, along with their descriptions.

In the interest of brevity, the codes will be cut in the rest of this chapter.

R1 Configuration

Now we're ready to configure the next router—R1. To make that happen correctly, keep in mind that we have four interfaces to deal with: serial 0/0/0, serial 0/0/1, FastEthernet 0/0, and FastEthernet 0/1. So let's make sure we don't forget to add the hostname, passwords, interface descriptions, and banner to the router configuration. As I did with the Corp router, I erased the configuration and reloaded.

Here's the configuration I used:

```
R1#erase start
% Incomplete command.
R1#erase startup-config
Erasing the nvram filesystem will remove all configuration files!
   Continue? [confirm][enter]
[OK]
Erase of nvram: complete
R1#reload
Proceed with reload? [confirm][enter]
[output cut]
%Error opening tftp://255.255.255.255/network-confg (Timed out)
%Error opening tftp://255.255.255.255/cisconet.cfg (Timed out)

         --- System Configuration Dialog ---

Would you like to enter the initial configuration dialog? [yes/no]: n
```

Before we move on, I really want to discuss the preceding output with you. First, notice that the new 12.4 ISR routers will no longer take the command `erase start`. The router has only one command after `erase` that starts with *s*, as shown here:

```
Router#erase s?
startup-config
```

I know, you'd think that the IOS would continue to accept the command, but nope—sorry! The second thing I want to point out is that the output tells us the router is looking for a TFTP host to see if it can download a configuration. When that fails, it goes straight into setup mode. This gives you a great picture of the Cisco router default boot sequence we talked about in Chapter 7.

Okay, let's get back to configuring our router:

```
Press RETURN to get started!
Router>en
Router#config t
Router(config)#hostname R1
R1(config)#enable secret todd
R1(config)#int s0/0/0
R1(config-if)#ip address 10.1.2.2 255.255.255.0
R1(config-if)#Description 1st Connection to Corp Router
R1(config-if)#no shut
R1(config-if)#int s0/0/1
```

```
R1(config-if)#ip address 10.1.3.2 255.255.255.0
R1(config-if)#no shut
R1(config-if)#description 2nd connection to Corp Router
R1(config-if)#int f0/0
R1(config-if)#ip address 192.168.10.1 255.255.255.0
R1(config-if)#description Connection to Finance PC
R1(config-if)#no shut
R1(config-if)#int f0/1
R1(config-if)#ip address 192.168.20.1 255.255.255.0
R1(config-if)#description Connection to Marketing PC
R1(config-if)#no shut
R1(config-if)#line con 0
R1(config-line)#password console
R1(config-line)#login
R1(config-line)#logging synchronous
R1(config-line)#exec-timeout 0 0
R1(config-line)#line aux 0
R1(config-line)#password aux
R1(config-line)#login
R1(config-line)#exit
R1(config)#line vty 0 ?
  <1-807>  Last Line number
  <cr>
R1(config)#line vty 0 807
R1(config-line)#password telnet
R1(config-line)#login
R1(config-line)#banner motd # This is my R1 Router #
R1(config)#no ip domain-lookup
R1(config)#exit
R1#copy run start
Destination filename [startup-config]?[enter]
Building configuration...
[OK]
R1#
```

Let's take a look at our configuration of the interfaces:

```
R1#sh run | begin interface
interface FastEthernet0/0
 description Connection to Finance PC
 ip address 192.168.10.1 255.255.255.0
```

```
 duplex auto
 speed auto
!
interface FastEthernet0/1
 description Connection to Marketing PC
 ip address 192.168.20.1 255.255.255.0
 duplex auto
 speed auto
!
interface Serial0/0/0
 description 1st Connection to Corp Router
 ip address 10.1.2.2 255.255.255.0
!
interface Serial0/0/1
 description 2nd connection to Corp Router
 ip address 10.1.3.2 255.255.255.0
!
```

The show ip route command displays the following:

```
R1#show ip route
     10.0.0.0/24 is subnetted, 4 subnets
C       10.1.3.0 is directly connected, Serial0/0/1
C       10.1.2.0 is directly connected, Serial0/0/0
C       192.168.20.0 is directly connected, FastEthernet0/1
C       192.168.10.0 is directly connected, FastEthernet0/0
R1#
```

Notice that router R1 knows how to get to networks 10.1.3.0, 10.1.2.0, 192.168.20.0, and 192.168.10.0. We can now ping to the Corp router from R1:

```
R1#10.1.2.1

Type escape sequence to abort.
Sending 5, 100-byte ICMP Echos to 10.1.2.1, timeout is 2 seconds:
!!!!!
Success rate is 100 percent (5/5), round-trip min/avg/max = 1/2/4 ms
R1#
```

Now let's go back to the Corp router and look at the routing table:

```
Corp#sh ip route
[output cut]
     10.0.0.0/24 is subnetted, 4 subnets
```

```
C       10.1.3.0 is directly connected, Serial0/0/1
C       10.1.2.0 is directly connected, Serial0/0/0
C       10.1.1.0 is directly connected, Vlan1
Corp#
```

The R1 serial interface 0/0/0 and 0/0/1 are DCE connections, which means a `clock rate` needs to be set on the interface. Remember that you don't need to use the `clock rate` command in production. Even though this is very true, it's still imperative that you know how/when you can use it and that you understand it really well when studying for your CCNA exam!

We can see our clocking with the `show controllers` command:

```
R1#sh controllers s0/0/1
Interface Serial0/0/1
Hardware is GT96K
DCE V.35, clock rate 2000000
```

One last thing before we get into configuring the other remote routers: Did you notice the clock rate is 2000000 under the serial interfaces of the R1 router? That's important because if you think back to when we were configuring the R1 router, you'll recall that I didn't set the clock rate. The reason I didn't is because ISR routers will auto-detect a DCE-type cable and automatically configure the clock rate—a really sweet feature!

Since the serial links are showing up, we can now see three networks in the Corp routing table. And once we configure R2 and R3, we'll see two more networks in the routing table of the Corp router. The Corp router can't see either the 192.168.10.0 or 192.168.20.0 networks because we don't have any routing configured yet—routers see only directly connected networks by default.

R2 Configuration

To configure R2, we're going to do pretty much the same thing we did with the other two routers. There are three interfaces: serial 0/0/0, FastEthernet 0/0, and FastEthernet 0/1 to deal with, and again, we'll be sure to add the hostname, passwords, interface descriptions, and a banner to the router configuration:

```
Router>en
Router#config t
Router(config)#hostname R2
R2(config)#enable secret todd
R2(config)#int s0/0/0
R2(config-if)#ip address 10.1.4.2 255.255.255.0
R2(config-if)#description Connection to Corp Router
R2(config-if)#no shut
R2(config-if)#int f0/0
R2(config-if)#ip address 192.168.30.1 255.255.255.0
```

```
R2(config-if)#description Connection to Sales PC
R2(config-if)#no shut
R2(config-if)#int f0/1
R2(config-if)#ip address 192.168.40.1 255.255.255.0
R2(config-if)#description Connection to HR PC
R2(config-if)#no shut
R2(config-if)#line con 0
R2(config-line)#password console
R2(config-line)#login
R2(config-line)#logging sync
R2(config-line)#exec-timeout 0 0
R2(config-line)#line aux 0
R2(config-line)#password aux
R2(config-line)#login
R2(config-line)#exit
R2(config)#line vty 0 ?
  <1-807>  Last Line number
  <cr>
R2(config)#line vty 0 807
R2(config-line)#password telnet
R2(config-line)#login
R2(config-line)#exit
R2(config)#banner motd # This is my R2 Router #
R2(config)#no ip domain-lookup
R2(config)#^Z
R2#copy run start
Destination filename [startup-config]?[enter]
Building configuration...
[OK]
R2#
```

Nice—everything was pretty straightforward. The output of the following `show ip route` command displays the directly connected networks of 192.168.30.0, and 192.168.40.0 and 10.1.4.0, as you can see here:

```
R2#sh ip route
     10.0.0.0/24 is subnetted, 3 subnets
C       192.168.30.0 is directly connected, FastEthernet0/0
C       192.168.40.0 is directly connected, FastEthernet0/1
C       10.1.4.0 is directly connected, Serial0/0/0
R2#
```

The Corp, R1, and R2 routers now have all their directly connected links up. But we still need to configure the R3 router.

R3 Configuration

To configure R3, we're going to do pretty much the same thing we did with the other routers. However, there are only two interfaces: FastEthernet 0/0, and Dot11Radio0/0/0 to deal with, and again, we'll be sure to add the hostname, passwords, interface descriptions, and a banner to the router configuration:

```
Router>en
Router#config t
Router(config)#hostname R3
R3(config)#enable secret todd
R3(config)#int f0/0
R3(config-if)#ip address 10.1.5.2 255.255.255.0
R3(config-if)#description Connection to Corp Router
R3(config-if)#no shut
R3(config-if)#int dot11radio0/0/0
R3(config-if)#ip address 172.16.10.1 255.255.255.0
R3(config-if)#description WLAN for Mobile User
R3(config-if)#no shut
R3(config-if)#ssid ADMIN
R3(config-if-ssid)#guest-mode
R3(config-if-ssid)#authentication open
R3(config-if-ssid)#infrastructure-ssid
R3(config-if-ssid)#exit
R3(config-line)#line con 0
R3(config-line)#password console
R3(config-line)#login
R3(config-line)#logging sync
R3(config-line)#exec-timeout 0 0
R3(config-line)#line aux 0
R3(config-line)#password aux
R3(config-line)#login
R3(config-line)#exit
R3(config)#line vty 0 ?
  <1-807>  Last Line number
  <cr>
R3(config)#line vty 0 807
R3(config-line)#password telnet
R3(config-line)#login
```

```
R3(config-line)#exit
R3(config)#banner motd # This is my R3 Router #
R3(config)#no ip domain-lookup
R3(config)#^Z
R3#copy run start
Destination filename [startup-config]?[enter]
Building configuration...
[OK]
R3#
```

Nice—everything again was pretty straightforward...except for that wireless interface. It's true, the wireless interface is really just another interface on a router, and it looks just like that in the routing table as well. But, in order to bring up the wireless interface, more configurations are needed than for a simple FastEthernet interface. So check out the following output, and then I'll tell you about the special configuration needs for this wireless interface:

```
R3(config-if)#int dot11radio0/0/0
R3(config-if)#ip address 172.16.10.1 255.255.255.0
R3(config-if)# description WLAN for Mobile User
R3(config-if)#no shut
R3(config-if)#ssid ADMIN
R3(config-if-ssid)#guest-mode
R3(config-if-ssid)#authentication open
R3(config-if-ssid)#infrastructure-ssid
```

So, what we see here is that everything is pretty commonplace until we get to the SSID configuration. This is the Service Set Identifier that creates a wireless network that hosts can connect to. Unlike access points, the interface on the R3 router is actually a routed interface, which is the reason the IP address is placed under the physical interface—typically, if this was an access point only and not a router, the IP address would be placed under the Bridge-Group Virtual Interface (BVI), which is a logical management interface.

That `guest-mode` line means that the interface will broadcast the SSID so wireless hosts will understand that they can connect to this interface. `Authentication open` means just that... no authentication. (Even so, you still have to type that command in at minimum to make the wireless interface work.) Last, the `infrastructure-ssid` indicates that this interface can be used to communicate to other access points, or other devices on the infrastructure—to the actual wired network itself.

Configuring DHCP on Our Router

But wait, we're not done yet—we still need to configure the DHCP pool for the wireless clients connecting to the Dot11Radio0/0/0 interface, so let's do that now:

```
R3#config t
R3(config)#ip dhcp pool Admin
```

```
R3(dhcp-config)#network 172.16.10.0 255.255.255.0
R3(dhcp-config)#default-router 172.16.10.1
R3(dhcp-config)#ip name-server 172.16.10.4
R3(dhcp-config)#exit
R3(config)#ip dhcp excluded-address 172.16.10.1 172.16.10.10
R3(config)#
```

Creating DHCP pools on a router is actually a pretty simple process, and this would be the same configuration for any router you need to add a DHCP pool to. To create the DHCP server on a router, you just create the pool name, add the network/subnet and the default gateway, and exclude any addresses you don't want handed out (like the default gateway address), and you'd usually add a DNS server as well. Don't forget to add your exclusions, addresses you don't want the DHCP server handing out as valid host IPs. These exclusions are configured from global config mode, not within the DHCP pool config. Notice, also, that you can exclude a range of addresses on one line—very convenient. In the preceding example, I excluded 172.16.10.1 through 172.16.10.10 from being assigned by the DHCP server as valid IP addresses to DHCP clients. You can verify the DHCP pool with the `show ip dhcp binding` command:

```
R3#sh ip dhcp binding
IP address       Client-ID/              Lease expiration        Type
                 Hardware address
172.16.10.11     0001.96AB.8538           --                     Automatic
R3#
```

And of course, you can verify the client with the `ipconfig` command.

```
PC>ipconfig /all

Physical Address................: 0001.96AB.8538
IP Address......................: 172.16.10.11
Subnet Mask.....................: 255.255.255.0
Default Gateway.................: 172.16.10.1
DNS Servers.....................: 172.16.10.2
```

Now that we did a basic WLAN configuration, our mobile user is connected to the wireless network. The user just can't get anywhere else yet in our internetwork! Let's fix that.

Wireless networks will be discussed in detail in Chapter 14, "Cisco's Wireless Technologies."

Configuring IP Routing in Our Network

Our network is good to go—right? After all, it's been correctly configured with IP addressing, administrative functions, and even clocking (automatically on the ISR routers). But how does a router send packets to remote networks when the only way it can send them is by looking at the routing table to find out how to get to the remote networks? Our configured routers only have information about directly connected networks in each routing table. And what happens when a router receives a packet for a network that isn't listed in the routing table? It doesn't send a broadcast looking for the remote network—the router just discards it. Period.

So we're not exactly ready to rock after all. But no worries—there are several ways to configure the routing tables to include all the networks in our little internetwork so that packets will be forwarded. And what's best for one network isn't necessarily what's best for another. Understanding the different types of routing will really help you come up with the best solution for your specific environment and business requirements.

You'll learn about the following types of routing in the following sections:

- Static routing
- Default routing
- Dynamic routing

I'm going to start off by describing and implementing static routing on our network because if you can implement static routing *and* make it work, it means you have a solid understanding of the internetwork. So let's get started.

Static Routing

Static routing occurs when you manually add routes in each router's routing table. There are pros and cons to static routing, but that's true for all routing processes.

Static routing has the following benefits:

- There is no overhead on the router CPU, which means you could possibly buy a cheaper router than you would use if you were using dynamic routing.
- There is no bandwidth usage between routers, which means you could possibly save money on WAN links.
- It adds security because the administrator can choose to allow routing access to certain networks only.

Static routing has the following disadvantages:

- The administrator must really understand the internetwork and how each router is connected in order to configure routes correctly.
- If a network is added to the internetwork, the administrator has to add a route to it on all routers—by hand.
- It's not feasible in large networks because maintaining it would be a full-time job in itself.

Okay—that said, here's the command syntax you use to add a static route to a routing table:

```
ip route [destination_network] [mask] [next-hop_address or
  exitinterface] [administrative_distance] [permanent]
```

This list describes each command in the string:

ip route The command used to create the static route.

destination_network The network you're placing in the routing table.

mask The subnet mask being used on the network.

next-hop_address The address of the next-hop router that will receive the packet and forward it to the remote network. This is the IP address of a router interface that's on a directly connected network. You must be able to ping the router interface before you can successfully add the route. If you type in the wrong next-hop address or the interface to that router is down, the static route will show up in the router's configuration but not in the routing table.

exitinterface Used in place of the next-hop address if you want, and shows up as a directly connected route.

administrative_distance By default, static routes have an administrative distance of 1 (or even 0 if you use an exit interface instead of a next-hop address). You can change the default value by adding an administrative weight at the end of the command. I'll talk a lot more about this subject later in the chapter when we get to the section on dynamic routing.

permanent If the interface is shut down or the router can't communicate to the next-hop router, the route will automatically be discarded from the routing table by default. Choosing the `permanent` option keeps the entry in the routing table no matter what happens.

Before we dive into configuring static routes, let's take a look at a sample static route and see what we can find out about it.

```
Router(config)#ip route 172.16.3.0 255.255.255.0 192.168.2.4
```

- The `ip route` command tells us simply that it is a static route.
- 172.16.3.0 is the remote network we want to send packets to.
- 255.255.255.0 is the mask of the remote network.
- 192.168.2.4 is the next hop, or router, we will send packets to.

However, suppose the static route looked like this:

```
Router(config)#ip route 172.16.3.0 255.255.255.0 192.168.2.4 150
```

The 150 at the end changes the default administrative distance (AD) of 1 to 150. No worries—I'll talk much more about AD when we get into dynamic routing. For now, just remember that the AD is the trustworthiness of a route, where 0 is best and 255 is worst.

One more example, then we'll start configuring:

```
Router(config)#ip route 172.16.3.0 255.255.255.0 s0/0/0
```

Instead of using a next-hop address, we can use an exit interface that will make the route show up as a directly connected network. Functionally, the next hop and exit interface work exactly the same.

To help you understand how static routes work, I'll demonstrate the configuration on the internetwork shown previously in Figure 8.9. I have shown this internetwork again here, in Figure 8.10, to save you from having to go back many pages to view the same figure when needed.

FIGURE 8.10 Our internetwork

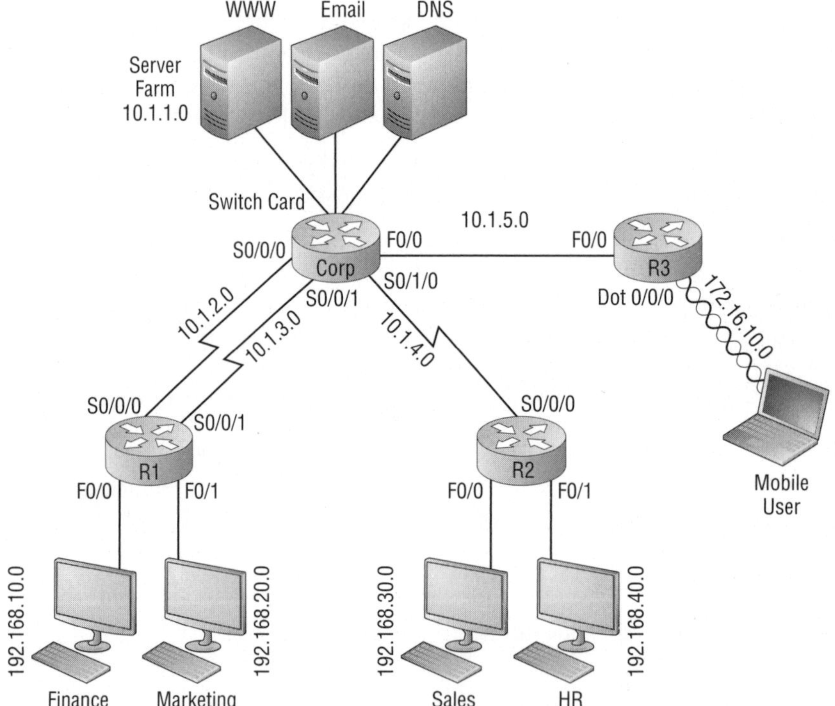

Corp

Each routing table automatically includes directly connected networks. To be able to route to all indirectly connected networks within the internetwork, the routing table must include information that describes where these other networks are located and how to get to them.

The Corp router is connected to five networks. For the Corp router to be able to route to all networks, the following networks have to be configured into its routing table:

- 192.168.10.0
- 192.168.20.0
- 192.168.30.0
- 192.168.40.0
- 172.16.10.0

The following router output shows the static routes on the Corp router and the routing table after the configuration. For the Corp router to find the remote networks, I had to place an entry into the routing table describing the remote network, the remote mask, and where to send the packets. I am going to add a 150 at the end of each line to raise the administrative distance. (When we get to dynamic routing, you'll see why I did it this way.)

```
Corp(config)#ip route 192.168.10.0 255.255.255.0 10.1.2.2 150
Corp(config)#ip route 192.168.20.0 255.255.255.0 10.1.3.2 150
Corp(config)#ip route 192.168.30.0 255.255.255.0 10.1.4.2 150
Corp(config)#ip route 192.168.40.0 255.255.255.0 10.1.4.2 150
Corp(config)#ip route 172.16.10.0 255.255.255.0 10.1.5.2 150
Corp(config)#do show run | begin ip route
ip route 192.168.10.0 255.255.255.0 10.1.2.2 150
ip route 192.168.20.0 255.255.255.0 10.1.3.2 150
ip route 192.168.30.0 255.255.255.0 10.1.4.2 150
ip route 192.168.40.0 255.255.255.0 10.1.4.2 150
ip route 172.16.10.0 255.255.255.0 10.1.5.2 150
```

For networks 192.168.10.0 and 192.168.20.0, I used a different path for each network, although I could have used just one. After the router is configured, you can type **show ip route** to see the static routes:

```
Corp(config)#do show ip route
10.0.0.0/24 is subnetted, 5 subnets
C       10.1.1.0 is directly connected, Vlan1
C       10.1.2.0 is directly connected, Serial0/0/0
C       10.1.3.0 is directly connected, Serial0/0/1
C       10.1.4.0 is directly connected, Serial0/1/0
C       10.1.5.0 is directly connected, FastEthernet0/0
     172.16.0.0/24 is subnetted, 1 subnets
S       172.16.10.0 [150/0] via 10.1.5.2
S    192.168.10.0/24 [150/0] via 10.1.2.2
S    192.168.20.0/24 [150/0] via 10.1.3.2
S    192.168.30.0/24 [150/0] via 10.1.4.2
S    192.168.40.0/24 [150/0] via 10.1.4.2
```

The Corp router is configured to route and know about all routes to all networks.

I want you to understand that if the routes don't appear in the routing table, it's because the router can't communicate with the next-hop address you've configured. You can use the `permanent` parameter to keep the route in the routing table even if the next-hop device can't be contacted.

The S in the preceding routing table entries means that the route is a static entry. The `[150/0]` is the administrative distance and metric (something we'll cover later) to the remote network.

Okay—we're good. The Corp router now has all the information it needs to communicate with the other remote networks. But keep in mind that if the R1, R2, and R3 routers aren't configured with all the same information, the packets will simply be discarded. We'll need to fix this by configuring static routes.

Don't stress about the 150 at the end of the static route configuration. I promise I will discuss the topic really soon in this chapter, not a later one! Be assured that you don't need to worry about it at this point.

R1

The R1 router is directly connected to the networks 10.1.2.0, 10.1.3.0, 192.168.10.0, and 192.168.20.0, so we've got to configure the following static routes on the R1 router:

- 10.1.1.0
- 10.1.4.0
- 10.1.5.0
- 192.168.30.0
- 192.168.40.0
- 172.16.10.0

Here's the configuration for the R1 router. Remember, we'll never create a static route to any network we're directly connected to, and we can use the next hop of either 10.1.2.1 or 10.1.3.1 since we have two links between the Corp and R1 router. I'll change between next hops so all data doesn't go down one link. It really doesn't matter which link I use at this point. Let's check out the commands:

```
R1(config)#ip route 10.1.1.0 255.255.255.0 10.1.2.1 150
R1(config)#ip route 10.1.4.0 255.255.255.0 10.1.3.1 150
R1(config)#ip route 10.1.5.0 255.255.255.0 10.1.2.1 150
R1(config)#ip route 192.168.30.0 255.255.255.0 10.1.3.1 150
R1(config)#ip route 192.168.40.0 255.255.255.0 10.1.2.1 150
R1(config)#ip route 172.16.10.0 255.255.255.0 10.1.3.1 150
R1(config)#do show run | begin ip route
ip route 10.1.1.0 255.255.255.0 10.1.2.1 150
```

```
ip route 10.1.4.0 255.255.255.0 10.1.3.1 150
ip route 10.1.5.0 255.255.255.0 10.1.2.1 150
ip route 192.168.30.0 255.255.255.0 10.1.3.1 150
ip route 192.168.40.0 255.255.255.0 10.1.2.1 150
ip route 172.16.10.0 255.255.255.0 10.1.3.1 150
```

By looking at the routing table, you can see that the R1 router now understands how to find each network:

```
R1(config)#do show ip route
      10.0.0.0/24 is subnetted, 5 subnets
S        10.1.1.0 [150/0] via 10.1.2.1
C        10.1.2.0 is directly connected, Serial0/0/0
C        10.1.3.0 is directly connected, Serial0/0/1
S        10.1.4.0 [150/0] via 10.1.3.1
S        10.1.5.0 [150/0] via 10.1.2.1
     172.16.0.0/24 is subnetted, 1 subnets
S        172.16.10.0 [150/0] via 10.1.3.1
C     192.168.10.0/24 is directly connected, FastEthernet0/0
C     192.168.20.0/24 is directly connected, FastEthernet0/1
S     192.168.30.0/24 [150/0] via 10.1.3.1
S     192.168.40.0/24 [150/0] via 10.1.2.1
```

The R1 router now has a complete routing table. As soon as the other routers in the internetwork have all the networks in their routing table, R1 will be able to communicate with all remote networks.

R2

The R2 router is directly connected to three networks 10.1.4.0, 192.168.30.0, and 192.168.40.0, so these are the routes that need to be added:

- 10.1.1.0
- 10.1.2.0
- 10.1.3.0
- 10.1.5.0
- 192.168.10.0
- 192.168.20.0
- 172.16.10.0

Here's the configuration for the R2 router:

```
R2(config)#ip route 10.1.1.0 255.255.255.0 10.1.4.1 150
R2(config)#ip route 10.1.2.0 255.255.255.0 10.1.4.1 150
```

```
R2(config)#ip route 10.1.3.0 255.255.255.0 10.1.4.1 150
R2(config)#ip route 10.1.5.0 255.255.255.0 10.1.4.1 150
R2(config)#ip route 192.168.10.0 255.255.255.0 10.1.4.1 150
R2(config)#ip route 192.168.20.0 255.255.255.0 10.1.4.1 150
R2(config)#ip route 172.16.10.0 255.255.255.0 10.1.4.1 150
R2(config)#do show run | begin ip route
ip route 10.1.1.0 255.255.255.0 10.1.4.1 150
ip route 10.1.2.0 255.255.255.0 10.1.4.1 150
ip route 10.1.3.0 255.255.255.0 10.1.4.1 150
ip route 10.1.5.0 255.255.255.0 10.1.4.1 150
ip route 192.168.10.0 255.255.255.0 10.1.4.1 150
ip route 192.168.20.0 255.255.255.0 10.1.4.1 150
ip route 172.16.10.0 255.255.255.0 10.1.4.1 150
```

The following output shows the routing table on the R2 router:

```
R2(config)#do show ip route
      10.0.0.0/24 is subnetted, 5 subnets
S        10.1.1.0 [150/0] via 10.1.4.1
S        10.1.2.0 [150/0] via 10.1.4.1
S        10.1.3.0 [150/0] via 10.1.4.1
C        10.1.4.0 is directly connected, Serial0/0/0
S        10.1.5.0 [150/0] via 10.1.4.1
     172.16.0.0/24 is subnetted, 1 subnets
S        172.16.10.0 [150/0] via 10.1.4.1
S     192.168.10.0/24 [150/0] via 10.1.4.1
S     192.168.20.0/24 [150/0] via 10.1.4.1
C     192.168.30.0/24 is directly connected, FastEthernet0/0
C     192.168.40.0/24 is directly connected, FastEthernet0/1
```

R2 now shows all 10 networks in the internetwork, so it too can now communicate with all routers and networks (that are configured so far).

R3

The R3 router is directly connected to networks 10.1.5.0 and 172.16.10.0, but we need to add all these routes, eight in total:

- 10.1.1.0
- 10.1.2.0
- 10.1.3.0
- 10.1.4.0
- 192.168.10.0

- 192.168.20.0
- 192.168.30.0
- 192.168.40.0

Here's the configuration for the R3 router; however, I am going to use the exit interface instead of the next hop address for this router:

```
R3#show run | begin ip route
R3(config)#ip route 10.1.1.0 255.255.255.0 fastethernet 0/0 150
R3(config)#ip route 10.1.2.0 255.255.255.0 fastethernet 0/0 150
R3(config)#ip route 10.1.3.0 255.255.255.0 fastethernet 0/0 150
R3(config)#ip route 10.1.4.0 255.255.255.0 fastethernet 0/0 150
R3(config)#ip route 192.168.10.0 255.255.255.0 fastethernet 0/0 150
R3(config)#ip route 192.168.20.0 255.255.255.0 fastethernet 0/0 150
R3(config)#ip route 192.168.30.0 255.255.255.0 fastethernet 0/0 150
R3(config)#ip route 192.168.40.0 255.255.255.0 fastethernet 0/0 150
R3#show ip route
       10.0.0.0/24 is subnetted, 5 subnets
S        10.1.1.0 is directly connected, FastEthernet0/0
S        10.1.2.0 is directly connected, FastEthernet0/0
S        10.1.3.0 is directly connected, FastEthernet0/0
S        10.1.4.0 is directly connected, FastEthernet0/0
C        10.1.5.0 is directly connected, FastEthernet0/0
     172.16.0.0/24 is subnetted, 1 subnets
C        172.16.10.0 is directly connected, Dot11Radio0/0/0
S     192.168.10.0/24 is directly connected, FastEthernet0/0
S     192.168.20.0/24 is directly connected, FastEthernet0/0
S     192.168.30.0/24 is directly connected, FastEthernet0/0
S     192.168.40.0/24 is directly connected, FastEthernet0/0
R3#
```

Looking at the `show ip route` command output, you can see that the static routes are listed as directly connected. Strange? Not really, because I used the exit interface instead of the next-hop address, and functionally, there's no difference, only how they display in the routing table. However, now that I showed you what using an exit interface displays in the routing table instead of using a next hop with static routing, let me show you an easier way for the R3 router.

Default Routing

For the R2 and R3 routers that I have connected to the Corp router, they are considered stub routers. A stub indicates that the networks in this design have only one way out to reach all other networks. I'll show you the configuration, verify the network in the next section, and then I'll discuss default routing in detail. Here's the configuration I could have done on the R3 router instead of typing in eight static routes due to its stub status:

```
R3(config)#no ip route 10.1.1.0 255.255.255.0 FastEthernet0/0 150
R3(config)#no ip route 10.1.2.0 255.255.255.0 FastEthernet0/0 150
R3(config)#no ip route 10.1.3.0 255.255.255.0 FastEthernet0/0 150
R3(config)#no ip route 10.1.4.0 255.255.255.0 FastEthernet0/0 150
R3(config)#no ip route 192.168.10.0 255.255.255.0 FastEthernet0/0 150
R3(config)#no ip route 192.168.20.0 255.255.255.0 FastEthernet0/0 150
R3(config)#no ip route 192.168.30.0 255.255.255.0 FastEthernet0/0 150
R3(config)#no ip route 192.168.40.0 255.255.255.0 FastEthernet0/0 150
R3(config)#ip route 0.0.0.0 0.0.0.0 10.1.5.1
R3(config)#ip classless
R3(config)#do show ip route
       10.0.0.0/24 is subnetted, 1 subnets
C        10.1.5.0 is directly connected, Vlan1
172.16.0.0/24 is subnetted, 1 subnets
C        172.16.10.0 is directly connected, Dot11Radio0
S*   0.0.0.0/0 [1/0] via 10.1.5.1
```

Okay—once I removed all the initial static routes I configured, this seems a lot easier than typing eight static routes, doesn't it? And it is, but there's a catch—you can't do things like this on all routers, only on stub routers. I could've used default routing on the R2 as well since that router is considered a stub, and I didn't add the 150 to this default route even though I easily could have. I didn't do that because it's just really simple to just remove the route if we need to when we get to dynamic routing later.

So we're there—we've done it! All the routers have the correct routing table, so all routers and hosts should be able to communicate without a hitch—for now. But if you add even one more network or another router to the internetwork, you'll have to update each and every router's routing tables by hand—yikes! This isn't a problem at all if you've got a small network, but it's obviously extremely time-consuming if you're dealing with a large internetwork!

Verifying Your Configuration

We're not done yet—once all the routers' routing tables are configured, they need to be verified. The best way to do this, besides using the `show ip route` command, is with the Ping program. I'll start by pinging from the R3 router to the R1 router.

Here's the output:

```
R3#ping 10.1.2.2
Type escape sequence to abort.
Sending 5, 100-byte ICMP Echos to 10.1.2.2, timeout is 2 seconds:
!!!!!
Success rate is 100 percent (5/5), round-trip min/avg/max = 1/2/4 ms
```

From router R3, a ping to the Corp backbone, the servers WWW, Email, and DNS would be a good test as well. Here's the router output:

```
R3#ping 10.1.1.1
Type escape sequence to abort.
Sending 5, 100-byte ICMP Echos to 10.1.1.1, timeout is 2 seconds:
!!!!!
Success rate is 100 percent (5/5), round-trip min/avg/max = 1/2/5 ms

R3#ping 10.1.1.2
Type escape sequence to abort.
Sending 5, 100-byte ICMP Echos to 10.1.1.2, timeout is 2 seconds:
!!!!!
Success rate is 100 percent (5/5), round-trip min/avg/max = 4/7/10 ms

R3# ping 10.1.1.3
Type escape sequence to abort.
Sending 5, 100-byte ICMP Echos to 10.1.1.3, timeout is 2 seconds:
!!!!!
Success rate is 100 percent (5/5), round-trip min/avg/max = 5/7/10 ms

R3#ping 10.1.1.4
Type escape sequence to abort.
Sending 5, 100-byte ICMP Echos to 10.1.1.4, timeout is 2 seconds:
!!!!!
Success rate is 100 percent (5/5), round-trip min/avg/max = 3/5/10 ms
```

Also, we can trace from the Mobile User wireless host to the Finance host connected to the R2 router to see the hops the packet takes to get to the Finance host, but first we have to make sure the Mobile User host received a DHCP server address from the R3 router:

```
PC>ipconfig

IP Address......................: 172.16.10.2
Subnet Mask.....................: 255.255.255.0
Default Gateway.................: 172.16.10.1

PC>ping 192.168.10.2
Pinging 192.168.10.2 with 32 bytes of data:
Reply from 192.168.10.2: bytes=32 time=17ms TTL=125
Reply from 192.168.10.2: bytes=32 time=21ms TTL=125
Reply from 192.168.10.2: bytes=32 time=19ms TTL=125
```

```
Reply from 192.168.10.2: bytes=32 time=17ms TTL=125

Ping statistics for 192.168.10.2:
    Packets: Sent = 4, Received = 4, Lost = 0 (0% loss),
Approximate round trip times in milli-seconds:
    Minimum = 17ms, Maximum = 21ms, Average = 18ms

PC>tracert 192.168.10.2
Tracing route to 192.168.10.2 over a maximum of 30 hops:

  1   15 ms     11 ms     14 ms     172.16.10.1
  2   13 ms     13 ms     8 ms      10.1.5.1
  3   12 ms     14 ms     15 ms     10.1.2.2
  4   16 ms     14 ms     15 ms     192.168.10.2
Trace complete.
```

Notice I used a "tracert" command because I am on a Windows host. Remember, `tracert` is not a valid Cisco command; we must use the command `traceroute` from a router prompt.

Okay, since we can communicate from end to end and to each host without a problem, our static and default route configurations have been a success!

Default Routing

We use *default routing* to send packets with a remote destination network not in the routing table to the next-hop router. You should only use default routing on stub networks—those with only one exit path out of the network, although there are exceptions to this statement, and default routing is configured on a case-by-case basis when a network is designed. This is a rule of thumb to keep in mind.

If you tried to put a default route on a router that isn't a stub, it is possible that packets wouldn't be forwarded to the correct networks because they have more than one interface routing to other routers. You can easily create loops with default routing, so be careful!

To configure a default route, you use wildcards in both the network address and mask locations of a static route (as I demonstrated in the R3 configuration). In fact, you can just think of a default route as a static route that uses wildcards instead of network and mask information.

By using a default route, you can just create one static route entry instead. This sure is easier then typing in all those routes!

```
R3(config)#ip route 0.0.0.0 0.0.0.0 10.1.5.1
R3(config)#ip classless
R3(config)#do show ip route
Gateway of last resort is 10.1.5.1 to network 0.0.0.0
     10.0.0.0/24 is subnetted, 1 subnets
```

```
C        10.1.5.0 is directly connected, FastEthernet0/0
     172.16.0.0/24 is subnetted, 1 subnets
C        172.16.10.0 is directly connected, Dot11Radio0/0/0
S*   0.0.0.0/0 [1/0] via 10.1.5.1
```

If you look at the routing table, you'll see only the two directly connected networks plus an S*, which indicates that this entry is a candidate for a default route. So instead of configuring eight static routes on R3, I could also have completed the default route command another way:

```
R3(config)#ip route 0.0.0.0 0.0.0.0 Fa0/0
```

What this is telling us is that if you don't have an entry for a network in the routing table, just forward it out Fa0/0. You can choose the IP address of the next-hop router or the exit interface—either way, it will work the same. Remember, I used the exit interface configuration with the R3 static route configs, which showed as directly connected in the router table. However, when I configured the default route on R3, I used the next-hop functionally; there is no difference.

Notice also on the first line in the routing table that the gateway of last resort is now set. Even so, there's one more command you must be aware of when using default routes: the `ip classless` command.

All Cisco routers are classful routers, meaning they expect a default subnet mask on each interface of the router. When a router receives a packet for a destination subnet that's not in the routing table, it will drop the packet by default. If you're using default routing, you must use the `ip classless` command because it is possible that no remote subnets will be in the routing table. Why? Because a configured default route will be ignored for subnets that are members of the same classful network as the other routes in the router's routing table and this command basically says, "Hey, IP! Before you discard that packet, check to see if a gateway of last resort is set!"

Since I have version 12.4 of the IOS on my routers, the `ip classless` command is on by default and it doesn't even show in the configuration. If you're using default routing and this command isn't in your configuration, you will need to add it if you have subnetted networks on your routers. The command is shown here:

```
R3(config)#ip classless
```

There's another command you can use to help you in your internetwork if you have configured a gateway of last resort—the `ip default-network` command, and I'll use this in a configuration example at the end of the chapter. Figure 8.11 shows a network that needs to have a gateway of last resort statement configured.

Here are three commands (all providing a default route solution) for adding a gateway of last resort on the router to the ISP.

```
Gateway(config)#ip route 0.0.0.0 0.0.0.0 217.124.6.1
```

```
Gateway(config)#ip route 0.0.0.0 0.0.0.0 s0/0
```

```
Gateway(config)#ip default-network network
```

FIGURE 8.11 Configuring a gateway of last resort

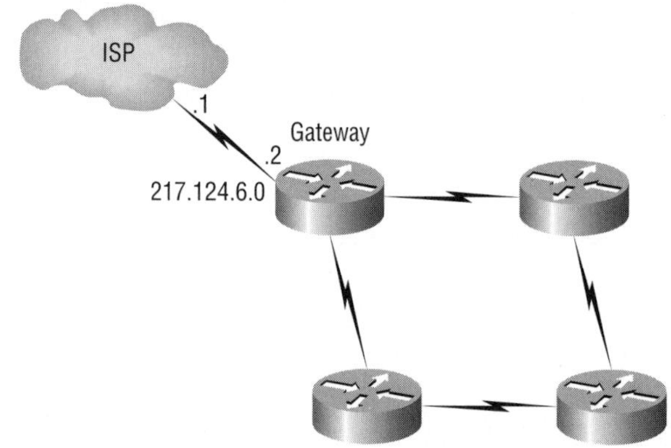

The first two are the same command—one just uses the next hop and one the exit interface. You will find no difference in this configuration, as I've already discussed. However, if you set them both for some reason, the exit interface would be used. Do you know why? Directly connected routes have an administrative distance of 0, but in this example, you'd see absolutely no functional difference between the two commands.

The `ip default-network` command would advertise the default network you configured on your border router when you configure an Interior Gateway Protocol (IGP), like RIP (like RIP) on the router. This is so other routers in your internetwork will receive this route as a default route automatically. Again, I'll configure this in our network at the end of the chapter, so now you have something pretty exciting to look forward to!

But what happens if you misconfigured a default route? Let's take a look at the output of a `show ip route` command and compare that to the network in Figure 8.12 and see if you can find a problem:

```
Router#sh ip route
[output cut]
Gateway of last resort is 172.19.22.2 to network 0.0.0.0

C       172.17.22.0 is directly connected, FastEthernet0/0
C       172.18.22.0  is directly connected, Serial0/0
S*      0.0.0.0/0 [1/0] via 172.19.22.2
```

Find anything? You can see by looking at the figure and the directly connected routes in the routing table that the WAN link is on network 172.18.22.0 and that the default route is forwarding all packets to the 172.19.22.0 network. This is just bad—it will never work, so the problem is a misconfigured static (default) route.

FIGURE 8.12 Misconfigured default route

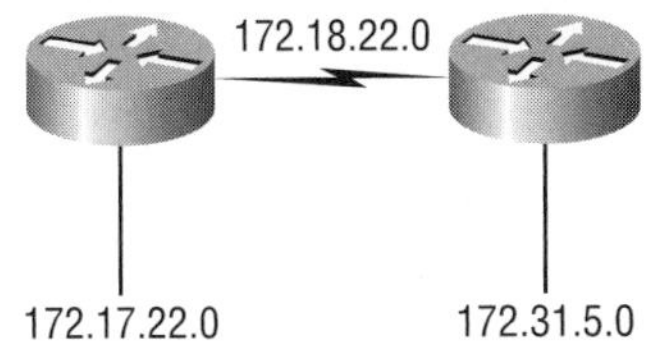

One last thing before moving on to dynamic routing: if you have the routing table output as shown in the following lines, what happens if the router receives a packet from 10.1.6.100 destined for host 10.1.8.5?

```
Router#sh ip route
[output cut]
Gateway of last resort is 10.1.5.5 to network 0.0.0.0

R     10.1.3.0 [120/1] via 101.2.2, 00:00:00, Serial 0/0
C     10.1.2.0  is directly connected, Serial0/0
C     10.1.5.0  is directly connected, Serial0/1
C     10.1.6.0  is directly connected, Fastethernet0/0
R*    0.0.0.0/0 [120/0] via 10.1.5.5, 00:00:00 Serial 0/1
```

This is a tad different than what I've shown you up until now because the default route is listed as `R*`, which means it's a RIP-injected route. This is because someone configured the `ip default-network` command on a remote router as well as configuring RIP, causing RIP to advertise this route through the internetwork as a default route. Since the destination address is 10.1.8.5 and there is no route to network 10.1.8.0, the router would use the default route and send the packet out serial 0/1.

Dynamic Routing

Dynamic routing is when protocols are used to find networks and update routing tables on routers. True, this is easier than using static or default routing, but it'll cost you in terms of router CPU processing and bandwidth on the network links. A routing protocol defines the set of rules used by a router when it communicates routing information between neighboring routers.

The routing protocol I'm going to talk about in this chapter is Routing Information Protocol (RIP) versions 1 and 2.

Two types of routing protocols are used in internetworks: interior gateway protocols (IGPs) and exterior gateway protocols (EGPs). IGPs are used to exchange routing information with routers in the same autonomous system (AS). An AS is a collection of networks under a common administrative domain, which basically means that all routers sharing the same routing table information are in the same AS. EGPs are used to communicate between ASes. An example of an EGP is Border Gateway Protocol (BGP), which is beyond the scope of this book.

Since routing protocols are so essential to dynamic routing, I'm going to give you the basic information you need to know about them next. Later on in this chapter, we'll focus on configuration.

Routing Protocol Basics

There are some important things you should know about routing protocols before getting deeper into RIP. Specifically, you need to understand administrative distances, the three different kinds of routing protocols, and routing loops. We will look at each of these in more detail in the following sections.

Administrative Distances

The *administrative distance (AD)* is used to rate the trustworthiness of routing information received on a router from a neighbor router. An administrative distance is an integer from 0 to 255, where 0 is the most trusted and 255 means no traffic will be passed via this route.

If a router receives two updates listing the same remote network, the first thing the router checks is the AD. If one of the advertised routes has a lower AD than the other, then the route with the lowest AD will be placed in the routing table.

If both advertised routes to the same network have the same AD, then routing protocol metrics (such as *hop count* or bandwidth of the lines) will be used to find the best path to the remote network. The advertised route with the lowest metric will be placed in the routing table. But if both advertised routes have the same AD as well as the same metrics, then the routing protocol will load-balance to the remote network (which means that it sends packets down each link).

Table 8.2 shows the default administrative distances that a Cisco router uses to decide which route to take to a remote network.

TABLE 8.2 Default administrative distances

Route Source	Default AD
Connected interface	0
Static route	1
EIGRP	90
IGRP	100
OSPF	110

Route Source	Default AD
RIP	120
External EIGRP	170
Unknown	255 (This route will never be used.)

If a network is directly connected, the router will always use the interface connected to the network. If you configure a static route, the router will then believe that route over any other learned routes. You can change the administrative distance of static routes, but by default, they have an AD of 1. In our previous static route configuration, the AD of each route is set at 150. This lets us configure routing protocols without having to remove the static routes. They'll be used as backup routes in case the routing protocol experiences a failure of some type.

For example, if you have a static route, a RIP-advertised route, and an EIGRP-advertised route listing the same network, then by default, the router will always use the static route unless you change the AD of the static route—which we did.

Routing Protocols

There are three classes of routing protocols:

Distance vector The *distance-vector protocols* in use today find the best path to a remote network by judging distance. For example, in the case of RIP routing, each time a packet goes through a router, that's called a *hop*. The route with the least number of hops to the network is determined to be the best route. The vector indicates the direction to the remote network. Both RIP and IGRP are distance-vector routing protocols. They periodically send the entire routing table to directly connected neighbors.

Link state In *link-state protocols*, also called *shortest-path-first protocols*, the routers each create three separate tables. One of these tables keeps track of directly attached neighbors, one determines the topology of the entire internetwork, and one is used as the routing table. Link-state routers know more about the internetwork than any distance-vector routing protocol. OSPF is an IP routing protocol that is completely link state. Link-state protocols send updates containing the state of their own links to all other directly connected routers on the network, which is then propagated to their neighbors.

Hybrid *Hybrid protocols* use aspects of both distance vector and link state—for example, EIGRP.

There's no set way of configuring routing protocols for use with every business. This is something you really have to do on a case-by-case basis. If you understand how the different routing protocols work, you can make good, solid decisions that truly meet the individual needs of any business.

Distance-Vector Routing Protocols

The distance-vector routing algorithm passes complete routing table contents to neighboring routers, which then combine the received routing table entries with their own routing tables to complete the router's routing table. This is called routing by rumor because a router receiving an update from a neighbor router believes the information about remote networks without actually finding out for itself.

It's possible to have a network that has multiple links to the same remote network, and if that's the case, the administrative distance of each received update is checked first. If the AD is the same, the protocol will have to use metrics to determine the best path to use to that remote network.

RIP uses only hop count to determine the best path to a network. If RIP finds more than one link with the same hop count to the same remote network, it will automatically perform a round-robin load balancing. RIP can perform load balancing for up to six equal-cost links (four by default).

However, a problem with this type of routing metric arises when the two links to a remote network are different bandwidths but the same hop count. Figure 8.13, for example, shows two links to remote network 172.16.10.0.

FIGURE 8.13 Pinhole congestion

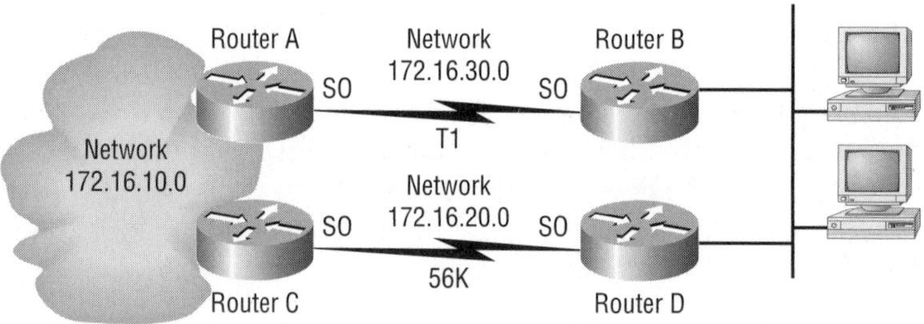

Since network 172.16.30.0 is a T1 link with a bandwidth of 1.544Mbps and network 172.16.20.0 is a 56K link, you'd want the router to choose the T1 over the 56K link, right? But because hop count is the only metric used with RIP routing, the two links would be seen as being of equal cost. This little snag is called *pinhole congestion*.

It's important to understand what a distance-vector routing protocol does when it starts up. In Figure 8.14, the four routers start off with only their directly connected networks in their routing tables. After a distance-vector routing protocol is started on each router, the routing tables are updated with all route information gathered from neighbor routers.

As shown in Figure 8.14, each router has only the directly connected networks in each routing table. Each router sends its complete routing table out to each active interface. The routing table of each router includes the network number, exit interface, and hop count to the network.

In Figure 8.15, the routing tables are complete because they include information about all the networks in the internetwork. They are considered *converged*. When the routers are converging, it is possible that no data will be passed. That's why fast convergence time is a serious plus. In fact, that's one of the problems with RIP—its slow convergence time.

The routing table in each router keeps information regarding the remote network number, the interface to which the router will send packets to reach that network, and the hop count or metric to the network.

FIGURE 8.14 The internetwork with distance-vector routing

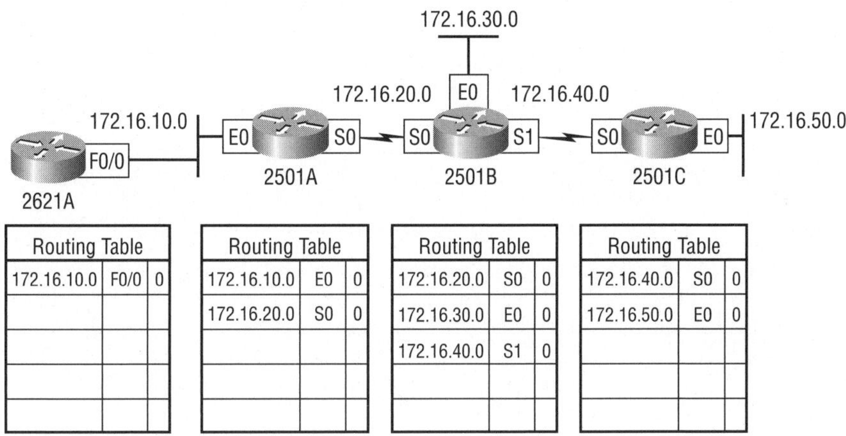

FIGURE 8.15 Converged routing tables

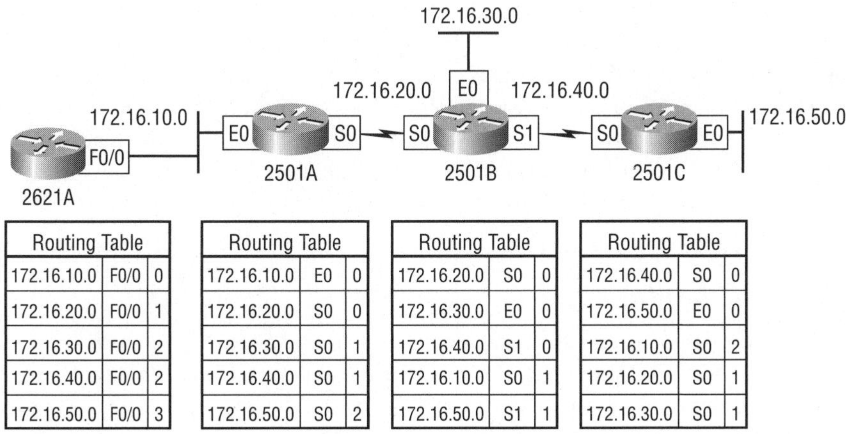

Routing Loops

Distance-vector routing protocols keep track of any changes to the internetwork by broadcasting periodic routing updates out all active interfaces. This broadcast includes the complete routing table. This works just fine, but it's expensive in terms of CPU processing and link bandwidth. And if a network outage happens, real problems can occur. Plus, the slow convergence of distance-vector routing protocols can result in inconsistent routing tables and routing loops.

Routing loops can occur because every router isn't updated simultaneously, or even close to it. Here's an example—let's say that the interface to Network 5 in Figure 8.16 fails. All routers know about Network 5 from RouterE. RouterA, in its tables, has a path to Network 5 through RouterB.

FIGURE 8.16 Routing loop example

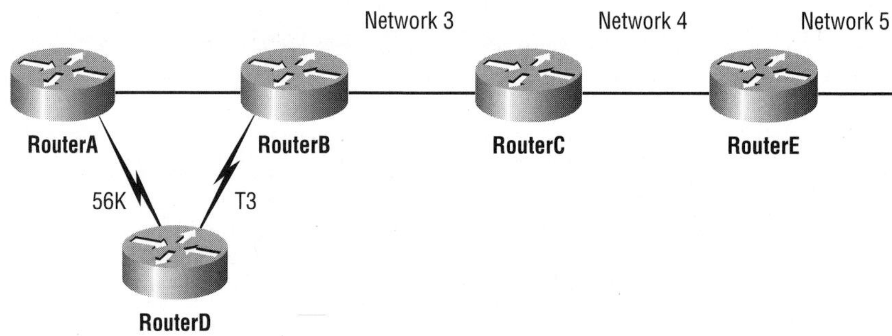

When Network 5 fails, RouterE tells RouterC. This causes RouterC to stop routing to Network 5 through RouterE. But routers A, B, and D don't know about Network 5 yet, so they keep sending out update information. RouterC will eventually send out its update and cause B to stop routing to Network 5, but routers A and D are still not updated. To them, it appears that Network 5 is still available through RouterB with a metric of 3.

The problem occurs when RouterA sends out its regular 30-second "Hello, I'm still here—these are the links I know about" message, which includes the ability to reach Network 5, and now routers B and D receive the wonderful news that Network 5 can be reached from RouterA, so routers B and D then send out the information that Network 5 is available. Any packet destined for Network 5 will go to RouterA, to RouterB, and then back to RouterA. This is a routing loop—how do you stop it?

Maximum Hop Count

The routing loop problem just described can create an issue called *counting to infinity*, and it's caused by gossip (broadcasts) and wrong information being communicated and propagated throughout the internetwork. Without some form of intervention, the hop count increases indefinitely each time a packet passes through a router.

One way of solving this problem is to define a *maximum hop count*. RIP permits a hop count of up to 15, so anything that requires 16 hops is deemed unreachable. In other words, after a loop of 15 hops, Network 5 will be considered down. Thus, the maximum hop count will control how long it takes for a routing table entry to become invalid or questionable.

Split Horizon

Another solution to the routing loop problem is called *split horizon*. This reduces incorrect routing information and routing overhead in a distance-vector network by enforcing the rule that routing information cannot be sent back in the direction from which it was received.

In other words, the routing protocol differentiates which interface a network route was learned on, and once this is determined, it won't advertise the route back out that same interface. This would have prevented RouterA from sending the update information it received from RouterB back to RouterB.

Route Poisoning

Another way to avoid problems caused by inconsistent updates and stop network loops is *route poisoning*. For example, when Network 5 goes down, RouterE initiates route poisoning by advertising Network 5 with a hop count of 16, or unreachable (sometimes referred to as *infinite*).

This poisoning of the route to Network 5 keeps RouterC from being susceptible to incorrect updates about the route to Network 5. When RouterC receives a route poisoning from RouterE, it sends an update, called a *poison reverse*, back to RouterE. This ensures that all routers on the segment have received the poisoned route information.

Holddowns

A *holddown* prevents regular update messages from reinstating a route that is going up and down (called *flapping*). Typically, this happens on a serial link that's losing connectivity and then coming back up. If there wasn't a way to stabilize this, the network would never converge and that one flapping interface could bring the entire network down!

Holddowns prevent routes from changing too rapidly by allowing time for either the downed route to come back up or the network to stabilize somewhat before changing to the next best route. These also tell routers to restrict, for a specific time period, changes that might affect recently removed routes. This prevents inoperative routes from being prematurely restored to other routers' tables.

Routing Information Protocol (RIP)

Routing Information Protocol (RIP) is a true distance-vector routing protocol. RIP sends the complete routing table out to all active interfaces every 30 seconds. RIP only uses hop count to determine the best way to a remote network, but it has a maximum allowable hop count of 15 by default, meaning that 16 is deemed unreachable. RIP works well in small networks, but it's inefficient on large networks with slow WAN links or on networks with a large number of routers installed.

RIP version 1 uses only *classful routing*, which means that all devices in the network must use the same subnet mask. This is because RIP version 1 doesn't send updates with subnet mask information in tow. RIP version 2 provides something called *prefix routing* and does send subnet mask information with the route updates. This is called *classless routing.*

In the following sections, we will discuss the RIP timers and then RIP configuration.

RIP Timers

RIP uses four different kinds of timers to regulate its performance:

Route update timer Sets the interval (typically 30 seconds) between periodic routing updates in which the router sends a complete copy of its routing table out to all neighbors.

Route invalid timer Determines the length of time that must elapse (180 seconds) before a router determines that a route has become invalid. It will come to this conclusion if it hasn't heard any updates about a particular route for that period. When that happens, the router will send out updates to all its neighbors letting them know that the route is invalid.

Holddown timer This sets the amount of time during which routing information is suppressed. Routes will enter into the holddown state when an update packet is received that indicates the route is unreachable. This continues either until an update packet is received with a better metric, the original route comes back up, or the holddown timer expires. The default is 180 seconds.

Route flush timer Sets the time between a route becoming invalid and its removal from the routing table (240 seconds). Before it's removed from the table, the router notifies its neighbors of that route's impending demise. The value of the route invalid timer must be less than that of the route flush timer. This gives the router enough time to tell its neighbors about the invalid route before the local routing table is updated.

Configuring RIP Routing

To configure RIP routing, just turn on the protocol with the `router rip` command and tell the RIP routing protocol which networks to advertise. That's it. Let's configure our four-router internetwork (Figure 8.10) with RIP routing.

Corp

RIP has an administrative distance of 120. Static routes have an administrative distance of 1 by default, and since we currently have static routes configured, the routing tables won't be populated with RIP information. However, because I added the 150 to the end of each static route, we're good to go.

You can add the RIP routing protocol by using the `router rip` command and the `network` command. The `network` command tells the routing protocol which classful network to advertise. By doing this process, you activate the RIP routing process on the interfaces whose addressing falls within the specified classful networks configured with the network command under the RIP routing process.

Look at the Corp router configuration and see how easy this is:

```
Corp#config t
Corp(config)#router rip
Corp(config-router)#network 10.0.0.0
```

That's it. Typically just two or three commands and you're done—sure makes your job a lot easier than when using static routes, doesn't it? However, keep in mind the extra router CPU process and bandwidth that you're consuming.

Notice I didn't type in subnets, only the classful network address (all subnet bits and host bits off!). It is the job of the routing protocol to find the subnets and populate the routing tables. Since we have no router buddies running RIP, we won't see any RIP routes in the routing table yet.

Remember that RIP uses the classful address when configuring the network address. Because of this, all subnet masks of any particular classful network must be the same on all devices in the network (this is called classful routing). To clarify this, let's say you're using a Class B network address of 172.16.0.0/24 with subnets 172.16.10.0, 172.16.20.0, and 172.16.30.0. You would only type in the classful network address of 172.16.0.0 and let RIP find the subnets and place them in the routing table.

R1

Let's configure our R1 router, which is connected to three networks, and we need to configure all directly connected classful network (not subnets) :

```
R1#config t
R1(config)#router rip
R1(config-router)#network 10.0.0.0
R1(config-router)#network 192.168.10.0
R1(config-router)#network 192.168.20.0
R1(config-router)#do show ip route

     10.0.0.0/24 is subnetted, 5 subnets
R       10.1.1.0 [120/1] via 10.1.2.1, 00:00:15, Serial0/0/0
                 [120/1] via 10.1.3.1, 00:00:15, Serial0/0/1
C       10.1.2.0 is directly connected, Serial0/0/0
C       10.1.3.0 is directly connected, Serial0/0/1
R       10.1.4.0 [120/1] via 10.1.2.1, 00:00:15, Serial0/0/0
                 [120/1] via 10.1.3.1, 00:00:15, Serial0/0/1
R       10.1.5.0 [120/1] via 10.1.2.1, 00:00:15, Serial0/0/0
                 [120/1] via 10.1.3.1, 00:00:15, Serial0/0/1
```

```
     172.16.0.0/24 is subnetted, 1 subnets
S       172.16.10.0 [150/0] via 10.1.3.1
C    192.168.10.0/24 is directly connected, FastEthernet0/0
C    192.168.20.0/24 is directly connected, FastEthernet0/1
S    192.168.30.0/24 [150/0] via 10.1.3.1
S    192.168.40.0/24 [150/0] via 10.1.2.1
R1(config-router)#
```

That was pretty straightforward. Let's talk about this routing table. Since we have one RIP buddy out there that we are exchanging routing tables with, we can see the RIP networks coming from the Corp router. (All the other routes still show up as static.) RIP also found both connections to the Corp router and will load-balance between them for each network that is advertised as a RIP injected route since the hop count is being advertised as 1 to each network. Luckily for us they are all the same bandwidth or we'd have pinhole congestion!

R2

Let's configure our R2 router with RIP:

```
R2#config t
R2(config)#router rip
R2(config-router)#network 10.0.0.0
R2(config-router)#network 192.168.30.0
R2(config-router)#network 192.168.40.0
R2(config-router)#do show ip route
     10.0.0.0/24 is subnetted, 5 subnets
R       10.1.1.0 [120/1] via 10.1.4.1, 00:00:17, Serial0/0/0
R       10.1.2.0 [120/1] via 10.1.4.1, 00:00:17, Serial0/0/0
R       10.1.3.0 [120/1] via 10.1.4.1, 00:00:17, Serial0/0/0
C       10.1.4.0 is directly connected, Serial0/0/0
R       10.1.5.0 [120/1] via 10.1.4.1, 00:00:17, Serial0/0/0
     172.16.0.0/24 is subnetted, 1 subnets
S       172.16.10.0 [150/0] via 10.1.4.1
R    192.168.10.0/24 [120/2] via 10.1.4.1, 00:00:17, Serial0/0/0
R    192.168.20.0/24 [120/2] via 10.1.4.1, 00:00:17, Serial0/0/0
C    192.168.30.0/24 is directly connected, FastEthernet0/0
C    192.168.40.0/24 is directly connected, FastEthernet0/1
R2(config-router)#
```

The routing table is growing Rs as we add RIP buddies! We can still see that all routes are in the routing table; only one is still a static route—just one more router to go.

R3

Let's configure our R3 router with RIP—here is the last router's RIP configuration:

```
R3#config t
R3(config)#router rip
R3(config-router)#network 10.0.0.0
R3(config-router)#network 172.16.0.0
R3(config-router)#do sh ip route
     10.0.0.0/24 is subnetted, 5 subnets
R       10.1.1.0 [120/1] via 10.1.5.1, 00:00:15, FastEthernet0/0
R       10.1.2.0 [120/1] via 10.1.5.1, 00:00:15, FastEthernet0/0
R       10.1.3.0 [120/1] via 10.1.5.1, 00:00:15, FastEthernet0/0
R       10.1.4.0 [120/1] via 10.1.5.1, 00:00:15, FastEthernet0/0
C       10.1.5.0 is directly connected, FastEthernet0/0
     172.16.0.0/24 is subnetted, 1 subnets
C       172.16.10.0 is directly connected, Dot11Radio0/0/0
R    192.168.10.0/24 [120/2] via 10.1.5.1, 00:00:15, FastEthernet0/0
R    192.168.20.0/24 [120/2] via 10.1.5.1, 00:00:15, FastEthernet0/0
R    192.168.30.0/24 [120/2] via 10.1.5.1, 00:00:15, FastEthernet0/0
R    192.168.40.0/24 [120/2] via 10.1.5.1, 00:00:15, FastEthernet0/0
R3#
```

Finally, all routes showing in the routing table are RIP injected routes. Notice that since we are configuring classful network statements that the WLAN network is 172.16.0.0, not 172.16.10.0!

It's also to important to remember administrative distances and why we needed to either remove the static routes before we added RIP routing or set them higher than 120 as we did.

By default, directly connected routes have an administrative distance of 0, static routes have an administrative distance of 1, and RIP has an administrative distance of 120. I call RIP the "gossip protocol" because it reminds me of junior high school, where if you hear a rumor (advertised route), it just has to be true without exception. And that pretty much sums up how RIP behaves on an internetwork—rumor mill as protocol!

Verifying the RIP Routing Tables

Each routing table should now have all directly connected routes as well as RIP-injected routes received from neighboring routers. Now we can go back to the Corp router and check it out.

This output shows us the contents of the Corp routing table:

```
     10.0.0.0/24 is subnetted, 5 subnets
C       10.1.1.0 is directly connected, Vlan1
```

```
C       10.1.2.0 is directly connected, Serial0/0/0
C       10.1.3.0 is directly connected, Serial0/0/1
C       10.1.4.0 is directly connected, Serial0/1/0
C       10.1.5.0 is directly connected, FastEthernet0/0
     172.16.0.0/16 is variably subnetted, 2 subnets, 2 masks
R       172.16.0.0/16 [120/1] via 10.1.5.2, 00:00:19, FastEthernet0/0
S       172.16.10.0/24 [150/0] via 10.1.5.2
R    192.168.10.0/24 [120/1] via 10.1.2.2, 00:00:19, Serial0/0/0
                     [120/1] via 10.1.3.2, 00:00:19, Serial0/0/1
R    192.168.20.0/24 [120/1] via 10.1.2.2, 00:00:19, Serial0/0/0
                     [120/1] via 10.1.3.2, 00:00:19, Serial0/0/1
R    192.168.30.0/24 [120/1] via 10.1.4.2, 00:00:19, Serial0/1/0
R    192.168.40.0/24 [120/1] via 10.1.4.2, 00:00:19, Serial0/1/0
Corp#
```

This output shows us basically the same routing table has the same entries that it had when we were using static routes—except for that R. The R means that the networks were added dynamically using the RIP routing protocol. The [120/1] is the administrative distance of the route (120) along with the number of hops to that remote network (1). From the Corp router, all networks are one hop away. There is one odd entry in this table, and you may have noticed this: The 172.16.10.0 network is listed twice, once as a /16 and once as a /24. One route is listed as a static route and one is listed as a RIP injected route. This route should not be in the table twice, especially since the static route even has [150/0], which is a high administrative distance.

Let's take a look at R2's routing table as well:

```
     10.0.0.0/24 is subnetted, 5 subnets
R       10.1.1.0 [120/1] via 10.1.4.1, 00:00:21, Serial0/0/0
R       10.1.2.0 [120/1] via 10.1.4.1, 00:00:21, Serial0/0/0
R       10.1.3.0 [120/1] via 10.1.4.1, 00:00:21, Serial0/0/0
C       10.1.4.0 is directly connected, Serial0/0/0
R       10.1.5.0 [120/1] via 10.1.4.1, 00:00:21, Serial0/0/0
     172.16.0.0/16 is variably subnetted, 2 subnets, 2 masks
R       172.16.0.0/16 [120/2] via 10.1.4.1, 00:00:21, Serial0/0/0
S       172.16.10.0/24 [150/0] via 10.1.4.1
R    192.168.10.0/24 [120/2] via 10.1.4.1, 00:00:21, Serial0/0/0
R    192.168.20.0/24 [120/2] via 10.1.4.1, 00:00:21, Serial0/0/0
C    192.168.30.0/24 is directly connected, FastEthernet0/0
C    192.168.40.0/24 is directly connected, FastEthernet0/1
R2#
```

Notice the same issue. RIPv1 doesn't work with discontiguous networks, and that is what we have here. Keep this thought in mind and I'll tell you why this is happening later in this chapter, and what must be done to fix it in Chapter 9.

So, while yes, it's true that RIP has worked in our little internetwork, it's not the solution for every enterprise. That's because this technique has a maximum hop count of only 15 (16 is deemed unreachable). Plus, it performs full routing-table updates every 30 seconds, which would bring a larger internetwork to a painful crawl pretty quick!

There's one more thing I want to show you about RIP routing tables and the parameters used to advertise remote networks. Notice, using as an example a different router on a different network for a second, that the following routing table shows `[120/15]` in the 10.1.3.0 network metric. This means that the administrative distance is 120, the default for RIP, but the hop count is 15. Remember that each time a router sends out an update to a neighbor router, it increments the hop count by one for each route.

```
Router#sh ip route
     10.0.0.0/24 is subnetted, 12 subnets
C       10.1.11.0 is directly connected, FastEthernet0/1
C       10.1.10.0 is directly connected, FastEthernet0/0
R       10.1.9.0 [120/2] via 10.1.5.1, 00:00:15, Serial0/0/1
R       10.1.8.0 [120/2] via 10.1.5.1, 00:00:15, Serial0/0/1
R       10.1.12.0 [120/1] via 10.1.11.2, 00:00:00, FastEthernet0/1
R       10.1.3.0 [120/15] via 10.1.5.1, 00:00:15, Serial0/0/1
R       10.1.2.0 [120/1] via 10.1.5.1, 00:00:15, Serial0/0/1
R       10.1.1.0 [120/1] via 10.1.5.1, 00:00:15, Serial0/0/1
R       10.1.7.0 [120/2] via 10.1.5.1, 00:00:15, Serial0/0/1
R       10.1.6.0 [120/2] via 10.1.5.1, 00:00:15, Serial0/0/1
C       10.1.5.0 is directly connected, Serial0/0/1
R       10.1.4.0 [120/1] via 10.1.5.1, 00:00:15, Serial0/0/1
```

So this `[120/15]` is really bad because the next router that receives the table from router R3 will just discard the route to network 10.1.3.0 since the hop count would then be 16, which is invalid.

If a router receives a routing update that contains a higher-cost path to a network that's already in its routing table, the update will be ignored.

Configuring RIP Routing Example 2

Before we move onto learning more about RIP configurations, let's take a look at Figure 8.17. In this example, we first will find and implement our subnets and then add the RIP configuration to the router.

For this configuration, we are going to assume that the Lab_B and Lab_C routers are already configured and we just need to configure the Lab_A router. We will use the network ID of 192.168.164.0/28. The s0/0 interface of Lab_A will use the last available IP address in the eighth subnet and the fa0/0 will use the last available IP address in the second subnet. Do not consider the zero subnet valid.

FIGURE 8.17 RIP routing example 2

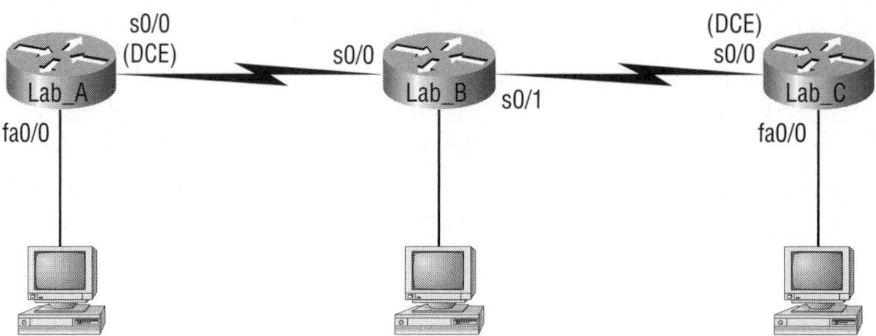

Before we start, you do know that /28 is a 255.255.255.240 mask, right? And that we have a block size of 16 in the fourth octet? It is very important that you know this, and if you need another review of Chapters 3 and 4, that's okay! Reviewing subnetting will never hurt you.

Since we have a block size of 16, our subnets are 16 (remember we are not starting at zero for this example), 32, 48, 64, 80, 96, 112, 128, 144, etc. The eighth subnet (which we will use for the s0/0 interface) is subnet 128. The valid host range for the 128 subnet is 129 through 142, and 143 is the broadcast address of the 128 subnet. The second subnet (which we will use for the fa0/0 interface) is the 32 subnet. The valid hosts are 33 through 46, and 47 is the broadcast address of the 32 subnet.

So, here is what our configuration on the Lab_A router will look like:

```
Lab_A(config)#interface s0/0
Lab_A(config-if)#ip address 192.168.164.142 255.255.255.240
Lab_A(config-if)#no shutdown
Lab_A(config-if)#interface fa0/0
Lab_A(config-if)#ip address 192.168.164.46 255.255.255.240
Lab_A(config-if)#no shutdown
Lab_A(config-if)#router rip
Lab_A(config-router)#network 192.168.164.0
Lab_A(config-router)#^Z
Lab_A#
```

Finding the subnets and configuring the last valid host should be pretty straightforward. If not, head back to Chapter 4. However, what I really want you to notice is that although we added two subnets to the Lab_A router, we only had one network statement under RIP. Sometimes it is hard to remember that you configure only the classful network statement, which means you turn all host bits off.

This was the real purpose of this second RIP configuration example—to remind you of classful network addressing. And it never hurts to practice subnetting, right?

Holding Down RIP Propagations

You probably don't want your RIP network advertised everywhere on your LAN and WAN. There's not a whole lot to be gained by advertising your RIP network to the Internet, now, is there?

There are a few different ways to stop unwanted RIP updates from propagating across your LANs and WANs, and the easiest one is through the `passive-interface` command. This command prevents RIP update broadcasts from being sent out a specified interface, yet that same interface can still receive RIP updates.

Here's an example of how to configure a `passive-interface` on a router using the CLI:

```
Lab_A#config t
Lab_A(config)#router rip
Lab_A(config-router)#network 192.168.10.0
Lab_A(config-router)#passive-interface serial 0/0
```

This command will stop RIP updates from being propagated out serial interface 0/0, but serial interface 0/0 can still receive RIP updates.

RIP Version 2 (RIPv2)

Let's spend a couple of minutes discussing RIPv2, and although I don't solve our little routing table mystery of two routes to the same network in the Corp and R2 routing table until Chapter 9, the answer lies within this section, and we'll advertise the routes on R3 to the other routers in the internetwork.

Real World Scenario

Should We Really Use RIP in an Internetwork?

You have been hired as a consultant to install a couple of Cisco routers into a growing network. They have a couple of old Unix routers that they want to keep in the network. These routers do not support any routing protocol except RIP. I guess this means you just have to run RIP on the entire network.

Well, yes and no. You can run RIP on a router connecting that old network, but you certainly don't need to run RIP throughout the whole internetwork!

You can do what is called *redistribution*, which is basically translating from one type of routing protocol to another. This means that you can support those old routers using RIP but use Enhanced IGRP, for example, on the rest of your network.

This will stop RIP routes from being sent all over the internetwork and eating up all that precious bandwidth.

RIP version 2 is mostly the same as RIP version 1. Both RIPv1 and RIPv2 are distance-vector protocols, which means that each router running RIP sends its complete routing table out all active interfaces at periodic time intervals. Also, the timers and loop-avoidance schemes are the same in both RIP versions (i.e., holddown timers and split horizon rule). Both RIPv1 and RIPv2 are configured using classful addressing (but RIPv2 is considered classless because subnet information is sent with each route update), and both have the same administrative distance (120).

But there are some important differences that make RIPv2 more scalable than RIPv1. And I've got to add a word of advice here before we move on: I'm definitely not advocating using RIP of either version in your network. But since RIP is an open standard, you can use it with any brand of router. You can also use OSPF (discussed in Chapter 9) since OSPF is an open standard as well. RIP just requires too much bandwidth, making it pretty intensive to use in your network. Why go there when you have other, more elegant options?

Table 8.3 discusses the differences between RIPv1 and RIPv2.

TABLE 8.3 RIPv1 vs. RIPv2

RIPv1	RIPv2
Distance vector	Distance vector
Maximum hop count of 15	Maximum hop count of 15
Classful	Classless
Broadcast based	Uses multicast 224.0.0.9
No support for VLSM	Supports VLSM networks
No authentication	Allows for MD5 authentication
No support for discontiguous networks	Supports discontiguous networks

RIPv2, unlike RIPv1, is a classless routing protocol (even though it is configured as classful, like RIPv1), which means that it sends subnet mask information along with the route updates. By sending the subnet mask information with the updates, RIPv2 can support Variable Length Subnet Masks (VLSMs) as well as the summarization of network boundaries, which cause more harm than good at times in our current network designs. In addition, RIPv2 can support discontiguous networking, which I'll go over more in Chapter 9 and finally solve our routing table mystery!

Configuring RIPv2 is pretty straightforward. Here's an example:

```
Lab_C(config)#router rip
Lab_C(config-router)#network 192.168.40.0
```

```
Lab_C(config-router)#network 192.168.50.0
Lab_C(config-router)#version 2
```

That's it; just add the command **`version 2`** under the `(config-router)#` prompt and you are now running RIPv2. I am going to go through the RIP verification commands and then configure RIPv2 on our internetwork.

RIPv2 is classless and supports VLSM and discontiguous networks.

Verifying Your Configurations

It's important to verify your configurations once you've completed them, or at least once you *think* you've completed them. The following list includes the commands you can use to verify the routed and routing protocols configured on your Cisco routers:

- `show ip route`
- `show ip protocols`
- `debug ip rip`

The first command was covered in the previous section—I'll go over the others in the sections that follow.

The *show ip protocols* Command

The `show ip protocols` command shows you the routing protocols that are configured on your router. Looking at the following output, you can see that RIP is running on the router and the timers that RIP uses:

```
Corp#sh ip protocols
Routing Protocol is "rip"
Sending updates every 30 seconds, next due in 23 seconds
Invalid after 180 seconds, hold down 180, flushed after 240
Outgoing update filter list for all interfaces is not set
Incoming update filter list for all interfaces is not set
Redistributing: rip
Default version control: send version 1, receive any version
  Interface            Send  Recv  Triggered RIP  Key-chain
  Vlan1                1     2 1
  FastEthernet0/0      1     2 1
  Serial0/0/0          1     2 1
```

```
  Serial0/0/1           1     2 1
  Serial0/1/0           1     2 1
Automatic network summarization is in effect
Maximum path: 4
Routing for Networks:
       10.0.0.0
Passive Interface(s):
Routing Information Sources:
       Gateway         Distance      Last Update
       10.1.5.2             120      00:00:28
       10.1.2.2             120      00:00:21
       10.1.3.2             120      00:00:21
       10.1.4.2             120      00:00:12
Distance: (default is 120)
```

Notice in this output that RIP is sending updates every 30 seconds, which is the default. The other timers used in distance vector are also shown.

Notice further down that RIP is routing for directly connected interfaces f0/0, S0/0/0, s0/0/1, and s0/1/0. The send and receive versions are listed to the right of the interfaces—RIPv1 and v2. This is an important troubleshooting section. If the interface you need is not listed in this section, you did not type the correct network statements in and this information can be found under the heading Routing for Networks.

Under the Gateway heading, the neighbors it found and the last entry is the default AD for RIP (120).

Troubleshooting with the *show ip protocols* Command

Let's use a sample router and use the `show ip protocols` command to see what we can determine about routing by looking at this output from a router on another network:

```
Router#sh ip protocols
Routing Protocol is "rip"
  Sending updates every 30 seconds, next due in 6 seconds
  Invalid after 180 seconds, hold down 180, flushed afteR340
  Outgoing update filter list for all interfaces is
  Incoming update filter list for all interfaces is
  Redistributing: rip
  Default version control: send version 1, receive any version
    Interface         Send  Recv   Key-chain
    Serial0/0          1     1 2
    Serial0/1          1     1 2
  Routing for Networks:
    10.0.0.0
```

```
Routing Information Sources:
  Gateway         Distance    Last Update
  10.168.11.14        120     00:00:21
Distance: (default is 120)
```

Let's also look at the `show ip interface brief` command from the same router and see what we find out:

```
Router#sh ip interface brief
Interface         IP-Address      OK?    Method Status
FastEthernet0/0   192.168.18.1    YES    manual  up
Serial0/0         10.168.11.17    YES    manual  up
FastEthernet0/1   unassigned      YES    NRAM    Administratively down
Serial0/1         192.168.11.21   YES    manual  up
```

Under the `show ip protocols` output, you can see that we're using RIP routing for network 10.0.0.0, which means our configuration would look like this:

```
Router(config)#router rip
Router(config-router)#network 10.0.0.0
```

Also, only serial 0/0 and serial 0/1 are participating in the RIP network. And last, our neighbor router is 10.168.11.14.

From the output of the `show ip interface brief` command, you can see that only serial 0/0 is in the 10.0.0.0 network. This means that the router will only send and receive routing updates with the 10.0.0.0 network and not advertise the 192.168.0.0 networks out any interface. To fix this, you would need to add the 192.168.11.0 and 192.168.18.0 networks under the `router rip` global command.

The *debug ip rip* Command

The `debug ip rip` command displays routing updates as they are sent and received on the router to the console session. If you are telnetted into the router, you'll need to use the `terminal monitor` command to be able to receive the output from the `debug` commands.

We can see in this output that RIP is both sending and receiving (the metric is the hop count):

```
R3#debug ip rip
RIP protocol debugging is on
RIP: received v1 update from 10.1.5.1 on FastEthernet0/0
      10.1.1.0 in 1 hops
      10.1.2.0 in 1 hops
      10.1.3.0 in 1 hops
      10.1.4.0 in 1 hops
```

```
      192.168.10.0 in 2 hops
      192.168.20.0 in 2 hops
      192.168.30.0 in 2 hops
      192.168.40.0 in 2 hops

RIP: sending  v1 update to 255.255.255.255 via Dot11Radio0/0/0(172.16.10.1)
RIP: build update entries
      network 10.0.0.0 metric 1
      network 192.168.10.0 metric 3
      network 192.168.20.0 metric 3
      network 192.168.30.0 metric 3
      network 192.168.40.0 metric 3

RIP: sending  v1 update to 255.255.255.255 via FastEthernet0/0 (10.1.5.2)
RIP: build update entries
      network 172.16.0.0 metric 1)
```

Let's talk about the output for a minute. First, R3 received all the routes that the Corp router has, and RIP is sending v1 packets to 255.255.255.255—an "all-hands" broadcast—out interface Dot11Radio0/0/0/0 via 172.16.10.1. This is where RIPv2 will come in handy. Why? Because RIPv2 doesn't send broadcasts; it used the multicast 224.0.0.9. So even though the RIP packets could be transmitted onto a network with no routers, all hosts would just ignore them, making RIPv2 a bit of an improvement over RIPv1.

Okay—now check out the fact that RIP is sending advertisements for all networks out Dot11Radio0/0/0/0, yet the last advertisement out FastEthernet 0/0 on R3 is only advertising 172.16.0.0. Why? If you answered the split horizon rule, you nailed it! The R3 router in this example will not advertise all those networks received from a neighbor router back to the same router.

If the metric of a route shows 16, this is a route poison, and the network being advertised is unreachable.

Troubleshooting with the *debug ip rip* Command

Now let's use the `debug ip rip` command to both discover a problem and figure out how RIP was configured on a router from a different sample network:

```
07:12:58: RIP: sending v1 update to 255.255.255.255 via
  FastEthernet0/0 (172.16.1.1)
07:12:58:  network 10.0.0.0, metric 1
07:12:58:  network 192.168.1.0, metric 2
07:12:58: RIP: sending v1 update to 255.255.255.255 via
  Serial0/0 (10.0.8.1)
```

```
07:12:58:  network 172.16.0.0, metric 1
07:12:58: RIP: Received v1 update from 10.0.15.2 n Serial0/0
07:12:58: 192.168.1.0 in one hop
07:12:58: 192.168.168.0 in 16 hops (inaccessible)
```

You can see from the updates that we're sending out information about networks 10.0.0.0, 192.168.1.0, and 172.16.0.0. But both the 10.0.0.0 network and the 172.16.0.0 network are being advertised with a hop count (metric) of 1, meaning that these networks are directly connected. The 192.168.1.0 is being advertised as a metric of 2, which means that it is not directly connected.

For this to be happening, our configuration would have to look like this:

```
Router(config)#router rip
Router(config-router)#network 10.0.0.0
Router(config-router)#network 172.16.0.0
```

And there's something else you can find out by looking at this: There are at least two routers participating in the RIP network because we're sending out two interfaces but only receiving RIP updates on one interface. Also, notice that the network 192.168.168.0 is being advertised as 16 hops away. RIP has a maximum hop count of 15, so 16 is considered unreachable, making this network inaccessible. So what will happen if you try to ping to a host on network 192.168.168.0? You just will not be successful, that's what! But if you try any pings to network 10.0.0.0, you should be successful.

I have one more output I want to show you—see if you can find the problem. Both a `debug ip rip` and a `show ip route` output are shown from our sample router:

```
07:12:56: RIP: received v1 update from 172.16.100.2 on Serial0/0
07:12:56:      172.16.10.0 in 1 hops
07:12:56:      172.16.20.0 in 1 hops
07:12:56:      172.16.30.0 in 1 hops

Router#sh ip route
[output cut]
Gateway of last resort is not set

   172.16.0.0/24 is subnetted, 8 subnets
C  172.16.150.0 is directly connected, FastEthernet0/0
C  172.16.220.0 is directly connected, Loopback2
R  172.16.210.0 is directly connected, Loopback1
R  172.16.200.0 is directly connected, Loopback0
R  172.16.30.0 [120/2] via 172.16.100.2, 00:00:04, Serial0/0
S  172.16.20.0 [120/2] via 172.16.150.15
R  172.16.10.0 [120/2] via 172.16.100.2, 00:00:04, Serial0/0
R  172.16.100.0 [120/2] is directly connected, Serial0/0
```

Looking at the two outputs, can you tell why users can't access 172.16.20.0?

The debug output shows that network 172.16.20.0 is one hop away and being received on serial0/0 from 172.16.100.2. By viewing the `show ip route` output, you can see that packets with a destination of 172.16.20.0 are being sent to 172.16.150.15 because of a static route entry. The output also shows that 172.16.150.0 is directly connected to FastEthernet 0/0 and network 172.16.20.0 is really out serial 0/0, so packets with a destination of 172.16.20.0 are being sent out the wrong interface because of a mis-configured static route.

Enabling RIPv2 on Our Internetwork

Before we move on to Chapter 9 and configure EIGRP and OSPF, I want to enable RIPv2 on our routers. It'll only take a second. Here are my configurations:

```
Corp#config t
Corp(config)#router rip
Corp(config-router)#version 2
Corp(config-router)#^Z

R1#config t
R1(config)#router rip
R1(config-router)#version 2
R1(config-router)#^Z

R2#config t
Enter configuration commands, one per line.  End with CNTL/Z.
R2(config)#router rip
R2(config-router)#version 2
R2(config-router)#^Z

R3#config t
R3#(config)#router rip
R3#(config-router)#version 2
R3#(config-router)#^Z
```

This was probably the easiest configuration we have done in the book so far. Let's see if we can find a difference in our routing tables. Here's the Corp router's routing table now:

```
  10.0.0.0/24 is subnetted, 5 subnets
C       10.1.1.0 is directly connected, Vlan1
C       10.1.2.0 is directly connected, Serial0/0/0
C       10.1.3.0 is directly connected, Serial0/0/1
C       10.1.4.0 is directly connected, Serial0/1/0
C       10.1.5.0 is directly connected, FastEthernet0/0
```

```
     172.16.0.0/16 is variably subnetted, 2 subnets, 2 masks
R       172.16.0.0/16 [120/1] via 10.1.5.2, 00:00:18, FastEthernet0/0
S       172.16.10.0/24 [150/0] via 10.1.5.2
R    192.168.10.0/24 [120/1] via 10.1.2.2, 00:00:04, Serial0/0/0
                     [120/1] via 10.1.3.2, 00:00:04, Serial0/0/1
R    192.168.20.0/24 [120/1] via 10.1.2.2, 00:00:04, Serial0/0/0
                     [120/1] via 10.1.3.2, 00:00:04, Serial0/0/1
R    192.168.30.0/24 [120/1] via 10.1.4.2, 00:00:06, Serial0/1/0
R    192.168.40.0/24 [120/1] via 10.1.4.2, 00:00:06, Serial0/1/0
Corp#
```

Well—looks the same to me, and it still didn't fix my double entry for the 172.16.0.0 network. I'm going to turn on debugging and see if that shows us anything new:

```
Corp#debug ip rip
RIP protocol debugging is on
Corp#RIP: sending  v2 update to 224.0.0.9 via Vlan1 (10.1.1.1)

RIP: build update entries
      10.1.2.0/24 via 0.0.0.0, metric 1, tag 0
      10.1.3.0/24 via 0.0.0.0, metric 1, tag 0
      10.1.4.0/24 via 0.0.0.0, metric 1, tag 0
      10.1.5.0/24 via 0.0.0.0, metric 1, tag 0
      172.16.0.0/16 via 0.0.0.0, metric 2, tag 0
      192.168.10.0/24 via 0.0.0.0, metric 2, tag 0
      192.168.20.0/24 via 0.0.0.0, metric 2, tag 0
      192.168.30.0/24 via 0.0.0.0, metric 2, tag 0
      192.168.40.0/24 via 0.0.0.0, metric 2, tag 0

RIP: sending  v2 update to 224.0.0.9 via FastEthernet0/0 (10.1.5.1)
[output cut]
```

Bingo! Look at that! The networks are still being advertised every 30 seconds, but they're now sending the advertisements as v2 and as a multicast address of 224.0.0.9. Let's take a look at the `show ip protocols` output:

```
Corp#sh ip protocols
Routing Protocol is "rip"
Sending updates every 30 seconds, next due in 20 seconds
Invalid after 180 seconds, hold down 180, flushed after 240
Outgoing update filter list for all interfaces is not set
Incoming update filter list for all interfaces is not set
Redistributing: rip
```

```
Default version control: send version 2, receive 2
  Interface             Send  Recv  Triggered RIP  Key-chain
  Vlan1                 2     2
  FastEthernet0/0       2     2
  Serial0/0/0           2     2
  Serial0/0/1           2     2
  Serial0/1/0           2     2
Automatic network summarization is in effect
Maximum path: 4
Routing for Networks:
       10.0.0.0
Passive Interface(s):
Routing Information Sources:
       Gateway         Distance         Last Update
       10.1.5.2             120         00:00:09
       10.1.2.2             120         00:00:20
       10.1.3.2             120         00:00:20
       10.1.4.2             120         00:00:23
Distance: (default is 120)
```

We are now sending and receiving RIPv2. Nice when things work out well, huh? However, I never did fix that double entry for the 172.16.0.0 network in the Corp and R2 routing tables, even though I could have using RIPv2, with an additional configuration entry, I want to save that example for EIGRP. But the answer for this problem was previously shown in Table 8.3.

Advertising a Default Route Using RIP

I want to show you how to advertise a way out of your autonomous system. Imagine that you were to look at our network diagram and that instead of having our wireless network connected to R3, we could use a serial interface and configure our little internetwork to the Internet from R3.

If we do add an Internet connection to R3, all routers in our AS need to know where to send packets that are destined for networks on the Internet, or they'll just drop the packets if they get a packet with a remote request. One solution would be to put a default route on every router and funnel the information to R3, which in turn would have a default route to the ISP. Most people do this type of configuration in small to medium size networks.

However, since I am running RIPv2 on all routers including R3, I'll just add a default route on R3 to the ISP, as I would normally, but then add another command to advertise my network to the other routers in the AS as the default route.

Here would be an example of my new R3 configuration:

```
R3(config)#interface s0/0
R3(config-if)#ip address 172.16.10.5 255.255.255.252
```

```
R3(config-if)#exit
R3(config)#ip route 0.0.0.0 0.0.0.0 s0/0
R3(config)#ip default-network 172.16.0.0
```

Now, let's see what the Corp and R2 routers' routing tables see:

```
Corp#
10.0.0.0/24 is subnetted, 5 subnets
C       10.1.1.0 is directly connected, Vlan1
C       10.1.2.0 is directly connected, Serial0/0/0
C       10.1.3.0 is directly connected, Serial0/0/1
C       10.1.4.0 is directly connected, Serial0/1/0
C       10.1.5.0 is directly connected, FastEthernet0/0
     172.16.0.0/16 is variably subnetted, 2 subnets, 2 masks
R       172.16.0.0/16 [120/1] via 10.1.5.2, 00:00:16, FastEthernet0/0
S       172.16.10.0/24 [150/0] via 10.1.5.2
R    192.168.10.0/24 [120/1] via 10.1.2.2, 00:00:16, Serial0/0/0
                     [120/1] via 10.1.3.2, 00:00:16, Serial0/0/1
R    192.168.20.0/24 [120/1] via 10.1.2.2, 00:00:16, Serial0/0/0
                     [120/1] via 10.1.3.2, 00:00:16, Serial0/0/1
R    192.168.30.0/24 [120/1] via 10.1.4.2, 00:00:02, Serial0/1/0
R    192.168.40.0/24 [120/1] via 10.1.4.2, 00:00:02, Serial0/1/0
R*   0.0.0.0/0 [120/1] via 10.1.5.2, 00:00:16, FastEthernet0/0
Corp#
```

Nice—look at the last entry: R3 is advertising to the Corp router that "Hey, I am the way to the Internet!" or "I am the way out of the AS!" Let's see if R2 can see this same entry:

```
R2#
 10.0.0.0/24 is subnetted, 5 subnets
R       10.1.1.0 [120/1] via 10.1.4.1, 00:00:29, Serial0/0/0
R       10.1.2.0 [120/1] via 10.1.4.1, 00:00:29, Serial0/0/0
R       10.1.3.0 [120/1] via 10.1.4.1, 00:00:29, Serial0/0/0
C       10.1.4.0 is directly connected, Serial0/0/0
R       10.1.5.0 [120/1] via 10.1.4.1, 00:00:29, Serial0/0/0
     172.16.0.0/16 is variably subnetted, 2 subnets, 2 masks
R       172.16.0.0/16 [120/2] via 10.1.4.1, 00:00:29, Serial0/0/0
S       172.16.10.0/24 [150/0] via 10.1.4.1
R    192.168.10.0/24 [120/2] via 10.1.4.1, 00:00:29, Serial0/0/0
R    192.168.20.0/24 [120/2] via 10.1.4.1, 00:00:29, Serial0/0/0
C    192.168.30.0/24 is directly connected, FastEthernet0/0
```

```
C     192.168.40.0/24 is directly connected, FastEthernet0/1
R*    0.0.0.0/0 [120/2] via 10.1.4.1, 00:00:29, Serial0/0/0
R2#
```

R2 is seeing it as well, so our `ip default-network` command is working and advertising with RIP, and in addition, I verified that R1 is receiving the default route as well. This command would work with either RIP or RIPv2.

You're ready now to move on to the next chapter!

Summary

This chapter covered IP routing in detail. It's extremely important that you really understand the basics we covered in this chapter because everything that's done on a Cisco router typically will have some type of IP routing configured and running.

You learned in this chapter how IP routing uses frames to transport packets between routers and to the destination host. From there, we configured static routing on our routers and discussed the administrative distance used by IP to determine the best route to a destination network. If you have a stub network, you can configure default routing, which sets the gateway of last resort on a router.

We then discussed dynamic routing in detail, specifically RIP and how it works on an internetwork (not well). We finished by verifying RIP and then adding RIPv2 to our little internetwork, and also advertising a default route throughout the AS.

In the next chapter, we'll continue on with dynamic routing by discussing EIGRP and OSPF.

Exam Essentials

Describe the basic IP routing process. You need to remember that the frame changes at each hop but that the packet is never changed or manipulated in any way until it reaches the destination device (the TTL field in the IP header is decremented for each hop, but that's it!).

List the information required by a router to successfully route packets. To be able to route packets, a router must know, at a minimum, the destination address, the location of neighboring routers through which it can reach remote networks, possible routes to all remote networks, the best route to each remote network, and how to maintain and verify routing information.

Describe how MAC addresses are used during the routing process. A MAC (hardware) address will only be used on a local LAN. It will never pass a router's interface. A frame uses MAC (hardware) addresses to send a packet on a LAN. The frame will take the packet to either a host on the LAN or a router's interface (if the packet is destined for a remote network). As packets move from one router to another, the MAC addresses used will change but normally the original source and destination IP addresses within the packet will not.

View and interpret the routing table of a router. Use the `show ip route` command to view the routing table. Each route will be listed along with the source of the routing information. A `C` to the left of the route will indicate directly connected routes, and other letters next to the route can also indicate a particular routing protocol that provided the information, such as, for example, `R` for RIP.

Differentiate the three types of routing. The three types of routing are static (in which routes are manually configured at the CLI), dynamic (in which the routers share routing information via a routing protocol), and default routing (in which a special route is configured for all traffic without a more specific destination network found in the table).

Compare and contrast static and dynamic routing. Static routing creates no routing update traffic and creates less overhead on the router and network links, but it must be configured manually and does not have the ability to react to link outages. Dynamic routing creates routing update traffic and uses more overhead on the router and network links, but it can both react to link outages and choose the best route when multiple routes exist to the same network.

Configure static routes at the CLI. The command syntax to add a route is `ip route [destination_network] [mask] [next-hop_address or exitinterface] [administrative_distance] [permanent]`.

Create a `default route`. To add a default route, use the command syntax `ip route 0.0.0.0 0.0.0.0` *`ip-address`* `or` *`exit interface type and number`*.

Understand administrative distance and its role in the selection of the best route. Administrative distance (AD) is used to rate the trustworthiness of routing information received on a router from a neighbor router. Administrative distance is an integer from 0 to 255, where 0 is the most trusted and 255 means no traffic will be passed via this route. All routing protocols are assigned a default AD, but it can be changed at the CLI.

Differentiate distance-vector, link-state and hybrid routing protocols. Distance-vector routing protocols make routing decisions based on hop count (think RIP), while link-state routing protocols are able to consider multiple factors such as bandwidth available and delay when selecting the best route. Hybrid routing protocols exhibit characteristics of both types.

List mechanisms used to prevent routing loops in the network. Maximum hop count, split horizon, route poisoning, and holddown counters all play roles in preventing routing loops.

Describe the counters used in the operation of RIP. The route update timer is the interval between routing updates, the route invalid timer determines the length of time that must elapse (180 seconds) before a router determines that a route has become invalid, the holddown timer sets the amount of time during which routing information is suppressed (when a link is lost), and the route flush timer sets the time between a route becoming invalid and its removal from the routing table (240 seconds).

Configure RIP routing. To configure RIP routing, first you must be in global configuration mode and then you type the command **`router rip`**. Then you add all directly connected networks, making sure to use the classful address.

Identify commands used to verify RIP routing. The `show ip route` command will provide you with the contents of the routing table. An `R` on the left side of the table indicates a RIP-found route. The `debug ip rip` command will show you RIP updates being sent and received on your router. If you see a route with a metric of 16, that route is considered down.

Describe the differences between RIPv1 and RIPv2. RIPv1 sends broadcasts every 30 seconds and has an AD of 120. RIPv2 sends multicasts (224.0.0.9) every 30 seconds and also has an AD of 120. RIPv2 sends subnet mask information with the route updates, which allows it to support classless networking and discontiguous networks. RIPv2 also supports authentication between routers and RIPv1 does not.

Written Lab 8

Write the answers to the following questions:

1. At the appropriate command prompt, create a static route to network 172.16.10.0/24 with a next-hop gateway of 172.16.20.1 and an administrative distance of 150.
2. When a PC sends a packet to another PC in a remote network, what destination IP address and MAC address will be in the frame that it sends to its default gateway?
3. At the appropriate command prompt, create a default route to 172.16.40.1.
4. If you are using default routing in a classless environment, what command must also be used?
5. On which type of network is a default route most beneficial?
6. At the appropriate command prompt, display the routing table on your router.
7. When creating a static or default route, you don't have to use the next-hop IP address; you can use the ________________.
8. True/False: To reach a destination host, you must know the MAC address of the remote host.
9. True/False: To reach a destination host, you must know the IP address of the remote host.
10. At the appropriate command prompt, execute the command required on a DCE serial interface that is not required on a DTE serial interface.
11. At the appropriate command prompt(s), enable RIP routing on the interface with the IP address 10.0.0.1/24.
12. At the appropriate command prompt(s), prevent a router from propagating RIP information out serial 1.
13. What routing loop prevention mechanism sends out a maximum hop count as soon as a link fails?

14. What routing loop prevention mechanism suppresses the resending of routing information to an interface through which it was received?
15. At the appropriate command prompt, display RIP routing updates as they are sent and received on the router to the console session.

(The answers to Written Lab 8 can be found following the answers to the review questions for this chapter.)

Hands-on Labs

In the following hands-on labs, you will configure a network with three routers. These exercises assume all the same setup requirements as the labs found in earlier chapters.

This chapter includes the following labs:

Lab 8.1: Creating Static Routes

Lab 8.2: Configuring RIP Routing

The internetwork shown in the following graphic will be used to configure all routers.

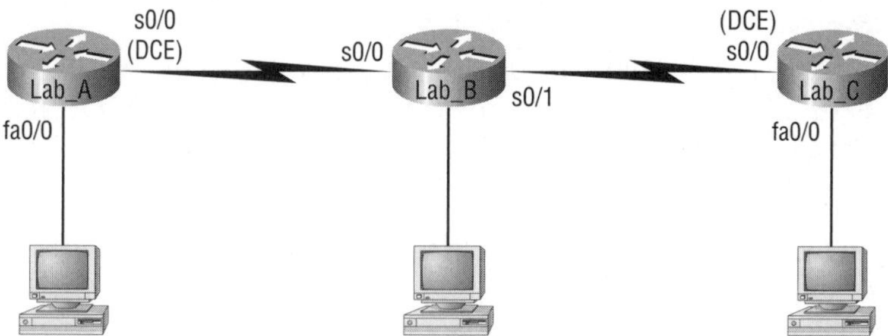

Table 8.4 shows our IP addresses for each router (each interface uses a /24 mask).

TABLE 8.4 Our IP addresses

Router	Interface	IP Address
Lab_A	F0/0	172.16.10.1
Lab_A	S0/0	172.16.20.1
Lab_B	S0/0	172.16.20.2
Lab_B	S0/1	172.16.30.1
Lab_C	S0/0	172.16.30.2
Lab_C	Fa0/0	172.16.40.1

These labs were written without using the LAN interface on the Lab_B router. You can choose to add that LAN into the labs if necessary.

Hands-on Lab 8.1: Creating Static Routes

In this lab, you will create a static route in all three routers so that the routers see all networks. Verify with the Ping program when complete.

1. The Lab_A router is connected to two networks, 172.16.10.0 and 172.16.20.0. You need to add routes to networks 172.16.30.0 and 172.16.40.0. Use the following commands to add the static routes.

```
Lab_A#config t
Lab_A(config)#ip route 172.16.30.0 255.255.255.0
  172.16.20.2
Lab_A(config)#ip route 172.16.40.0 255.255.255.0
  172.16.20.2
```

2. Save the current configuration for the Lab_A router by going to the privileged mode, typing **copy run start**, and pressing Enter.
3. On the Lab_B router, you have direct connections to networks 172.16.20.0 and 172.16.30.0. You need to add routes to networks 172.16.10.0 and 172.16.40.0. Use the following commands to add the static routes.

```
Lab_B#config t
Lab_B(config)#ip route 172.16.10.0 255.255.255.0
  172.16.20.1
Lab_B(config)#ip route 172.16.40.0 255.255.255.0
  172.16.30.2
```

4. Save the current configuration for router Lab_B by going to the enabled mode, typing **copy run start**, and pressing Enter.
5. On router Lab_C, create a static route to networks 172.16.10.0 and 172.16.20.0, which are not directly connected. Create static routes so that router Lab_C can see all networks, using the commands shown here:

```
Lab_C#config t
Lab_C(config)#ip route 172.16.10.0 255.255.255.0
  172.16.30.1
Lab_C(config)#ip route 172.16.20.0 255.255.255.0
  172.16.30.1
```

6. Save the current configuration for router Lab_C by going to the enable mode, typing **copy run start**, and pressing Enter.

7. Check your routing tables to make sure all four networks show up by executing the **show ip route** command.
8. Now ping from each router to your hosts and from each router to each router. If it is set up correctly, it will work.

Hands-on Lab 8.2: Configuring RIP Routing

In this lab, we will use the dynamic routing protocol RIP instead of static routing.

1. Remove any static routes or default routes configured on your routers by using the no ip route command. For example, here is how you would remove the static routes on the Lab_A router:

```
Lab_A#config t
Lab_A(config)#no ip route 172.16.30.0 255.255.255.0
  172.16.20.2
Lab_A(config)#no ip route 172.16.40.0 255.255.255.0
  172.16.20.2
```

   Do the same thing for routers Lab_B and Lab_C. Verify that only your directly connected networks are in the routing tables.
2. After your static and default routes are clear, go into configuration mode on router Lab_A by typing **config t**.
3. Tell your router to use RIP routing by typing **router rip** and pressing Enter, as shown here:

```
config t
router rip
```

4. Add the network number for the networks you want to advertise. Since router Lab_A has two interfaces that are in two different networks you must enter a network statement using the network ID of the network in which each interface resides. Alternately, you could use a summarization of these networks and use a single statement, minimizing the size of the routing table. Since the two networks are 172.16.10.0/24 and 172.16.20.0/24, the network summarization 172.16.0.0 would include both subnets. Do this by typing **network 172.16.0.0** and pressing Enter.
5. Press Ctrl+Z to get out of configuration mode.
6. The interfaces on Lab_B and Lab_C are in the 172.16.20.0/24 and 172.16.30.0/24 networks; therefore, the same summarized network statement will work there as well. Type the same commands, as shown here:

```
Config t
Router rip
network 172.16.0.0
```

7. Verify that RIP is running at each router by typing the following commands at each router:

   `show ip protocols`

   (Should indicate to you that RIP is present on the router.

   `show ip route`

   (Should have routes present with an *R* to the left of them)

   `show running-config or show run`

   (Should indicate that RIP is present and the networks are being advertised)

8. Save your configurations by typing **`copy run start`** or **`copy running-config startup-config`** and pressing Enter at each router.

9. Verify the network by pinging all remote networks and hosts.

Review Questions

The following questions are designed to test your understanding of this chapter's material. For more information on how to get additional questions, please see this book's Introduction.

1. The Acme Company uses a router named Gateway to connect to its ISP. The address of the ISP router is 206.143.5.2. Which commands could be configured on the Gateway router to allow Internet access to the entire network? (Choose two.)

   A. `Gateway(config)#`**`ip route 0.0.0.0 0.0.0.0 206.143.5.2`**

   B. `Gateway(config)#`**`router rip`**

   `Gateway(config-router)#`**`network 206.143.5.0`**

   C. `Gateway(config)#`**`router rip`**

   `Gateway(config-router)#`**`network 206.143.5.0 default`**

   D. `Gateway(config)#`**`ip route 206.143.5.0 255.255.255.0 default`**

   E. `Gateway(config)#`**`ip default-network 206.143.5.0`**

2. What command will prevent RIP routing updates from exiting an interface but will still allow the interface to receive RIP route updates?

   A. `Router(config-if)#`**`no routing`**

   B. `Router(config-if)#`**`passive-interface`**

   C. `Router(config-router)#`**`passive-interface s0`**

   D. `Router(config-router)#`**`no routing updates`**

3. Which of the following statements are true regarding the command `ip route 172.16.4.0 255.255.255.0 192.168.4.2`? (Choose two.)

   A. The command is used to establish a static route.

   B. The default administrative distance is used.

   C. The command is used to configure the default route.

   D. The subnet mask for the source address is 255.255.255.0.

   E. The command is used to establish a stub network.

4. What destination addresses will be used by HostA to send data to the HTTPS server as shown in the following network? (Choose two.)

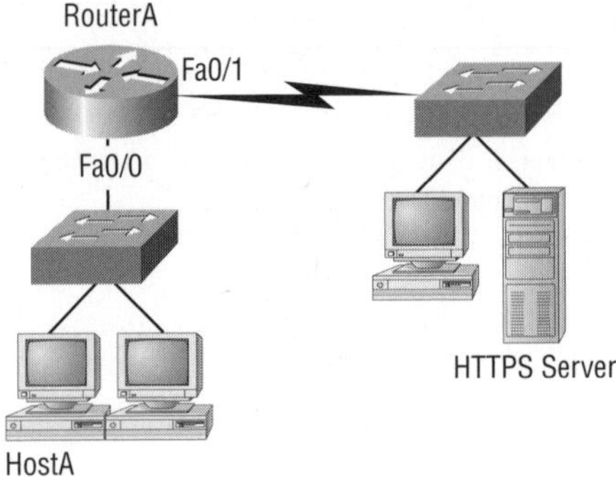

A. The IP address of the switch
B. The MAC address of the remote switch
C. The IP address of the HTTPS server
D. The MAC address of the HTTPS server
E. The IP address of RouterA's Fa0/0 interface
F. The MAC address of RouterA's Fa0/0 interface

5. Which of the following is true regarding the following output? (Choose two.)

```
04:06:16: RIP: received v1 update from 192.168.40.2 on Serial0/1
04:06:16:      192.168.50.0 in 16 hops (inaccessible)
04:06:40: RIP: sending v1 update to 255.255.255.255 via
   FastEthernet0/0 (192.168.30.1)
04:06:40: RIP: build update entries
04:06:40:       network 192.168.20.0 metric 1
04:06:40:       network 192.168.40.0 metric 1
04:06:40:       network 192.168.50.0 metric 16
04:06:40: RIP: sending v1 update to 255.255.255.255 via Serial0/1
   (192.168.40.1)
```

A. There are three interfaces on the router participating in this update.
B. A ping to 192.168.50.1 will be successful.
C. There are at least two routers exchanging information.
D. A ping to 192.168.40.2 will be successful.

6. Which of the following is the best description of the operation of split horizon?
   A. Information about a route should not be sent back in the direction from which the original update came.
   B. It splits the traffic when you have a large bus (horizon) physical network.
   C. It holds the regular updates from broadcasting to a downed link.
   D. It prevents regular update messages from reinstating a route that has gone down.

7. Which of the following would be true if HostA is trying to communicate to HostB and interface F0/0 of RouterC goes down, as shown in the following graphic? (Choose two.)

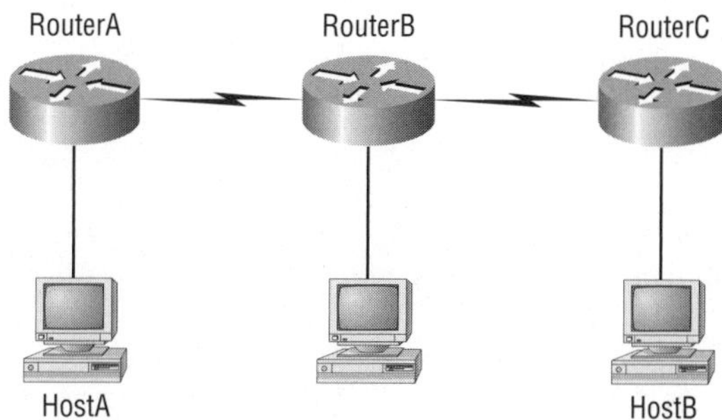

   A. RouterC will use an ICMP to inform HostA that HostB cannot be reached.
   B. RouterC will use ICMP to inform RouterB that HostB cannot be reached.
   C. RouterC will use ICMP to inform HostA, RouterA, and RouterB that HostB cannot be reached.
   D. RouterC will send a destination unreachable message type.
   E. RouterC will send a router selection message type.
   F. RouterC will send a source quench message type.

8. Which statement is true regarding classless routing protocols? (Choose two.)
   A. The use of discontiguous networks is not allowed.
   B. The use of Variable Length Subnet Masks is permitted.
   C. RIPv1 is a classless routing protocol.
   D. IGRP supports classless routing within the same autonomous system.
   E. RIPv2 supports classless routing.

9. Which two of the following are true regarding the distance-vector and link-state routing protocols?
   A. Link state sends its complete routing table out all active interfaces at periodic time intervals.
   B. Distance vector sends its complete routing table out all active interfaces at periodic time intervals.
   C. Link state sends updates containing the state of its own links to all routers in the internetwork.
   D. Distance vector sends updates containing the state of its own links to all routers in the internetwork.

10. Which command displays RIP routing updates?
    A. `show ip route`
    B. `debug ip rip`
    C. `show protocols`
    D. `debug ip route`

11. What does RIPv2 use to prevent routing loops? (Choose two.)
    A. CIDR
    B. Split horizon
    C. Authentication
    D. Classless masking
    E. Holddown timers

12. A network administrator views the output from the `show ip route` command. A network that is advertised by both RIP and EIGRP appears in the routing table flagged as an EIGRP route. Why is the RIP route to this network not used in the routing table?
    A. EIGRP has a faster update timer.
    B. EIGRP has a lower administrative distance.
    C. RIP has a higher metric value for that route.
    D. The EIGRP route has fewer hops.
    E. The RIP path has a routing loop.

13. You type **`debug ip rip`** on your router console and see that 172.16.10.0 is being advertised to you with a metric of 16. What does this mean?
    A. The route is 16 hops away.
    B. The route has a delay of 16 microseconds.
    C. The route is inaccessible.
    D. The route is queued at 16 messages a second.

14. What metric does RIPv2 use to find the best path to a remote network?
   A. Hop count
   B. MTU
   C. Cumulative interface delay
   D. Load
   E. Path bandwidth value

15. The Corporate router receives an IP packet with a source IP address of 192.168.214.20 and a destination address of 192.168.22.3. Looking at the output from the Corporate router, what will the router do with this packet?

```
Corp#sh ip route
[output cut]
R     192.168.215.0 [120/2] via 192.168.20.2, 00:00:23, Serial0/0
R     192.168.115.0 [120/1] via 192.168.20.2, 00:00:23, Serial0/0
R     192.168.30.0 [120/1] via 192.168.20.2, 00:00:23, Serial0/0
C     192.168.20.0 is directly connected, Serial0/0
C     192.168.214.0 is directly connected, FastEthernet0/0
```

   A. The packet will be discarded.
   B. The packet will be routed out the S0/0 interface.
   C. The router will broadcast looking for the destination.
   D. The packet will be routed out the Fa0/0 interface.

16. If your routing table has a static, a RIP, and an EIGRP route to the same network, which route will be used to route packets by default?
   A. Any available route
   B. RIP route
   C. Static route
   D. EIGRP route
   E. They will all load-balance.

17. You have the following routing table. Which of the following networks will not be placed in the neighbor routing table?

```
R    192.168.30.0/24 [120/1] via 192.168.40.1, 00:00:12, Serial0
C    192.168.40.0/24 is directly connected, Serial0
     172.16.0.0/24 is subnetted, 1 subnets
C       172.16.30.0 is directly connected, Loopback0
R    192.168.20.0/24 [120/1] via 192.168.40.1, 00:00:12, Serial0
R    10.0.0.0/8 [120/15] via 192.168.40.1, 00:00:07, Serial0
C    192.168.50.0/24 is directly connected, Ethernet0
```

A. 172.16.30.0

B. 192.168.30.0

C. 10.0.0.0

D. All of them will be placed in the neighbor routing table.

18. Two connected routers are configured only with RIP routing. What will be the result when a router receives a routing update that contains a higher-cost path to a network already in its routing table?

A. The updated information will be added to the existing routing table.

B. The update will be ignored and no further action will occur.

C. The updated information will replace the existing routing table entry.

D. The existing routing table entry will be deleted from the routing table and all routers will exchange routing updates to reach convergence.

19. Which of the following is true about route poisoning?

A. It sends back the protocol received from a router as a poison pill, which stops the regular updates.

B. It is information received from a router that can't be sent back to the originating router.

C. It prevents regular update messages from reinstating a route that has just come up.

D. It describes when a router sets the metric for a downed link to infinity.

20. Which of the following is true regarding RIPv2?

A. It has a lower administrative distance than RIPv1.

B. It converges faster than RIPv1.

C. It has the same timers as RIPv1.

D. It is harder to configure than RIPv1.

Answers to Review Questions

1. A, E. There are actually three different ways to configure the same default route, but only two are shown in the answer. First, you can set a default route with the 0.0.0.0 0.0.0.0 mask and then specify the next hop, as in option A. Or you can use 0.0.0.0 0.0.0.0 and use the exit interface instead of the next hop. Finally, you can use option E with the `ip default-network` command.

2. C. The `(config-router)#`**`passive-interface`** command stops updates from being sent out an interface, but route updates are still received. It is not executed in interface configuration mode, but in RIP configuration mode (accessed by typing **`router rip`**) and the interface is specified at the end of the command in the form *`interface_type number`*.

3. A, B. Although option D almost seems right, it is not; the mask is the mask used on the remote network, not the source network. Since there is no number at the end of the static route, it is using the default administrative distance of 1.

4. C, F. The switches are not used as either a default gateway or other destination. Switches have nothing to do with routing. It is very important to remember that the destination MAC address will always be the router's interface. The destination address of a frame, from HostA, will be the MAC address of the Fa0/0 interface of RouterA. The destination address of a packet will be the IP address of the network interface card (NIC) of the HTTPS server. The destination port number in the segment header will have a value of 443 (HTTPS).

5. C, D. The route to 192.168.50.0 is unreachable (a metric of 16 for RIP means the same thing) and only interfaces s0/1 and FastEthernet 0/0 are participating in the RIP update. Since a route update was received, at least two routers are participating in the RIP routing process. Since a route update for network 192.168.40.0 is being sent out Fa0/0 and a route was received from 192.168.40.2, we can assume a ping to that address will be successful.

6. A. A split horizon will not advertise a route back to the same router it learned the route from.

7. A, D. RouterC will use ICMP to inform HostA that HostB cannot be reached. It will perform this by sending a destination unreachable ICMP message type.

8. B, E. Classful routing means that all hosts in the internetwork use the same mask and that only default masks are in use. Classless routing means that you can use Variable Length Subnet Masks (VLSMs) and can also support discontiguous networking.

9. B, C. The distance-vector routing protocol sends its complete routing table out all active interfaces at periodic time intervals. Link-state routing protocols send updates containing the state of its own links to all routers in the internetwork.

10. B. `Debug ip rip` is used to show the Internet Protocol (IP) Routing Information Protocol (RIP) updates being sent and received on the router.

11. B, E. RIPv2 uses the same timers and loop-avoidance schemes as RIPv1. Split horizon is used to stop an update from being sent out the same interface it was received on. Holddown timers allow time for a network to become stable in the case of a flapping link.

12. B. RIP has an administrative distance (AD) of 120, while EIGRP has an administrative distance of 90, so the router will discard any route with a higher AD than 90 to that same network.

13. C. You cannot have 16 hops on a RIP network by default. If you receive a route advertised with a metric of 16, this means it is inaccessible.

14. A. RIPv1 and RIPv2 only use the lowest hop count to determine the best path to a remote network.

15. A. Since the routing table shows no route to the 192.168.22.0 network, the router will discard the packet and send an ICMP destination unreachable message out interface FastEthernet 0/0, which is the source LAN from which the packet originated.

16. C. Static routes have an administrative distance of 1 by default. Unless you change this, a static route will always be used over any other dynamically learned route. EIGRP has an administrative distance of 90, and RIP has an administrative distance of 120, by default.

17. C. The network 10.0.0.0 cannot be placed in the next router's routing table because it already is at 15 hops. One more hop would make the route 16 hops, and that is not valid in RIP networking.

18. B. When a routing update is received by a router, the router first checks the administrative distance (AD) and always chooses the route with the lowest AD. However, if two routes are received and they both have the same AD and differing metrics, then the router will choose the one route with the lowest metrics or, in RIP's case, hop count.

19. D. Another way to avoid problems caused by inconsistent updates and to stop network loops is route poisoning. When a network goes down, the distance-vector routing protocol initiates route poisoning by advertising the network with an unreachable metric of 16 (for RIP), sometimes referred to as *infinite*.

20. C. RIPv2 is pretty much just like RIPv1. It has the same administrative distance and timers and is configured similarly.

Answers to Written Lab 8

1. `router(config)#ip route 172.16.10.0 255.255.255.0 150`
2. It will use the gateway interface MAC at L2 and the actual destination IP at L3.
3. `router(config)#ip route 0.0.0.0 0.0.0.0 172.16.40.1`
4. `Router(config)#`**`ip classless`**
5. Stub network
6. `Router#`**`show ip route`**
7. Exit interface
8. False. The MAC address would be the router interface, not the remote host.
9. True
10. `Router(config-if)#`**`clock rate`** ***`speed`***
11. `router(config)#router rip`
    `routre(config-router)#network 10.0.0.0`
12. `router(config)#router rip`
    `router(config-router)#passive-interface S1`
13. Route poisoning
14. Split horizon
15. `debug ip rip`

Enhanced IGRP (EIGRP) and Open Shortest Path First (OSPF)

THE CCNA EXAM TOPICS COVERED IN THIS CHAPTER INCLUDE THE FOLLOWING:

✓ **Configure, verify, and troubleshoot basic router operation and routing on Cisco devices**

- Access and utilize the router to set basic parameters (including CLI/SDM)
- Connect, configure, and verify operation status of a device interface
- Verify device configuration and network connectivity using ping, traceroute, telnet, SSH, or other utilities
- Perform and verify routing configuration tasks for a static or default route given specific routing requirements
- Compare and contrast methods of routing and routing protocols
- Configure, verify, and troubleshoot OSPF
- Configure, verify, and troubleshoot EIGRP
- Verify network connectivity (including: using ping, traceroute, and telnet or SSH)
- Troubleshoot routing issues
- Verify router hardware and software operation using SHOW and DEBUG commands
- Implement basic router security

Enhanced Interior Gateway Routing Protocol (EIGRP) is a proprietary Cisco protocol that runs on Cisco routers. It is important for you to understand EIGRP because it is probably one of the two most popular routing protocols in use today. In this chapter, I'll show you the many features of EIGRP and describe how it works, with particular focus on the unique way it discovers, selects, and advertises routes.

I'm also going to introduce you to the Open Shortest Path First (OSPF) routing protocol, which is the other popular routing protocol in use today. You'll build a solid foundation for understanding OSPF by first becoming familiar with the terminology and internal operation of it and then learning about OSPF's advantages over RIP. Next, we'll explore the issues surrounding implementations of OSPF in broadcast and non-broadcast networks of various types. I'll explain how to implement single-area OSPF in different and specific networking environments and demonstrate how to verify that everything is running smoothly.

For up-to-the minute updates for this chapter, please see `www.lammle.com` and/or `www.sybex.com/go/ccna7e`.

EIGRP Features and Operation

Enhanced IGRP (EIGRP) is a classless, enhanced distance-vector protocol that uses the concept of an autonomous system to describe the set of contiguous routers that run the same routing protocol and share routing information. EIGRP includes the subnet mask in its route updates because it is considered classless. And as you now know, the advertisement of subnet information allows us to use Variable Length Subnet Masks (VLSMs) and manual summarization when designing our networks!

EIGRP is sometimes referred to as a *hybrid routing protocol* because it has characteristics of both distance-vector and link-state protocols. For example, EIGRP doesn't send link-state packets as OSPF does; instead, it sends traditional distance-vector updates containing information about networks plus the cost of reaching them from the perspective of the advertising router. And EIGRP has link-state characteristics as well—it synchronizes routing tables between neighbors at startup and then sends specific updates only when topology changes occur. This makes EIGRP suitable for very large networks. EIGRP has a maximum hop count of 255 (the default is set to 100). Don't get confused by what I just said. EIGRP does not use hop count as a metric as RIP does; what hop count means with EIGRP is how many routers an

EIGRP route update packet can go through before it is discarded. This limits the size of the AS and, again, has no bearing on how metrics are calculated.

There are a number of powerful features that make EIGRP a real standout from other protocols. The main ones are listed here:

- Support for IP and IPv6 (and some other useless routed protocols) via protocol-dependent modules
- Considered classless (same as RIPv2 and OSPF)
- Support for VLSM/CIDR
- Support for summaries and discontiguous networks
- Efficient neighbor discovery
- Communication via Reliable Transport Protocol (RTP)
- Best path selection via Diffusing Update Algorithm (DUAL)

Cisco calls EIGRP a distance-vector routing protocol or sometimes an advanced distance-vector or even a hybrid routing protocol.

Protocol-Dependent Modules

One of the most interesting features of EIGRP is that it provides routing support for multiple Network layer protocols: IP, IPX, AppleTalk, and now IPv6. (Obviously we won't use IPX and AppleTalk, but EIGRP does support them.) The only other routing protocol that comes close and supports multiple network layer protocols is *Intermediate System-to-Intermediate System (IS-IS)*.

EIGRP supports different Network layer protocols through the use of *protocol-dependent modules (PDMs)*. Each EIGRP PDM will maintain a separate series of tables containing the routing information that applies to a specific protocol. What this means to you is that there will be IP/EIGRP routing tables and IPv6/EIGRP routing tables, for example.

Neighbor Discovery

Before EIGRP routers are willing to exchange routes with each other, they must become neighbors. There are three conditions that must be met for neighborship establishment:

- Hellos received
- AS numbers match
- Identical metrics (K values)

Link-state protocols tend to use Hello messages to establish neighborship (also called adjacency) because they normally do not send out periodic route updates and there has to be some mechanism to help neighbors realize when a new peer has moved in or an old one has left or gone down. To maintain the neighborship relationship, EIGRP routers must also continue receiving Hellos from their neighbors.

EIGRP routers that belong to different autonomous systems (ASs) don't automatically share routing information and they don't become neighbors. This behavior can be a real benefit when used in larger networks to reduce the amount of route information propagated through a specific AS. The only catch is that you might have to take care of redistribution between the different ASs manually.

The only time EIGRP advertises its complete information is when it discovers a new neighbor and forms an adjacency with it through the exchange of Hello packets. When this happens, both neighbors advertise all their information to one another. After each has learned its neighbor's routes, only changes to the routing table are propagated from then on.

When EIGRP routers receive their neighbors' updates, they store them in a local topology table. This table contains all known routes from all known neighbors and serves as the raw material from which the best routes are selected and placed into the routing table.

Let's define some terms before we move on:

Feasible distance (FD) This is the best metric among all paths to a remote network, including the metric to the neighbor that is advertising that remote network. The route with the lowest FD is the route that you will find in the routing table because it is considered the best path. The metric of a feasible distance is the metric reported by the neighbor (called reported or advertised distance) plus the metric to the neighbor reporting the route.

Reported/advertised distance (AD) This is the metric of a remote network, as reported by a neighbor. It is also the routing table metric of the neighbor and is the same as the second number in parentheses as displayed in the topology table, the first number being the feasible distance.

Neighbor table Each router keeps state information about adjacent neighbors. When a newly discovered neighbor is learned, the address and interface of the neighbor are recorded, and this information is held in the neighbor table, stored in RAM. There is one neighbor table for each protocol-dependent module. Sequence numbers are used to match acknowledgments with update packets. The last sequence number received from the neighbor is recorded so that out-of-order packets can be detected.

Topology table The topology table is populated by the protocol-dependent modules and acted upon by the Diffusing Update Algorithm (DUAL). It contains all destinations advertised by neighboring routers, holding each destination address and a list of neighbors that have advertised the destination. For each neighbor, the advertised metric (distance), which comes only from the neighbor's routing table, is recorded as well as the FD. If the neighbor is advertising this destination, it must be using the route to forward packets.

The neighbor and topology tables are stored in RAM and maintained through the use of Hello and update packets. Yes, the routing table is also stored in RAM, but the information stored in the routing table is gathered only from the topology table.

Feasible successor A feasible successor is a path whose advertised distance is less than the feasible distance of the current successor, and it is considered a backup route. EIGRP will keep up to 16 feasible successors in the topology table. Only the one with the best metric (the successor) is copied and placed in the routing table. The `show ip eigrp topology` command will display all the EIGRP feasible successor routes known to a router.

A feasible successor is a backup route and is stored in the topology table. A successor route is stored in the topology table and is copied and placed in the routing table.

Successor A successor route (think successful!) is the best route to a remote network. A successor route is used by EIGRP to forward traffic to a destination and is stored in the routing table. It is backed up by a feasible successor route that is stored in the topology table—if one is available.

By using the successor, and having feasible successors in the topology table as backup links, the network can converge instantly, and updates to any neighbor make up the only traffic sent from EIGRP.

Reliable Transport Protocol (RTP)

EIGRP uses a proprietary protocol called *Reliable Transport Protocol (RTP)* to manage the communication of messages between EIGRP-speaking routers. And as the name suggests, reliability is a key concern of this protocol. Cisco has designed a mechanism that leverages multicasts and unicasts to deliver updates quickly and to track the receipt of the data.

When EIGRP sends multicast traffic, it uses the Class D address 224.0.0.10. As I said, each EIGRP router is aware of who its neighbors are, and for each multicast it sends out, it maintains a list of the neighbors who have replied. If EIGRP doesn't get a reply from a neighbor, it will switch to using unicasts to resend the same data. If it still doesn't get a reply after 16 unicast attempts, the neighbor is declared dead. People often refer to this process as *reliable multicast*.

Routers keep track of the information they send by assigning a sequence number to each packet. With this technique, it's possible for them to detect the arrival of old, redundant, or out-of-sequence information.

Being able to do these things is highly important because EIGRP is a quiet protocol. It depends upon its ability to synchronize routing databases at startup time and then maintain the consistency of databases over time by communicating only changes. So the permanent loss of any packets, or the out-of-order execution of packets, can result in corruption of the routing database.

Diffusing Update Algorithm (DUAL)

EIGRP uses *Diffusing Update Algorithm (DUAL)* for selecting and maintaining the best path to each remote network. This algorithm allows for the following:

- Backup route determination if one is available
- Support of VLSMs

- Dynamic route recoveries
- Queries for an alternate route if no feasible successor route can be found

DUAL provides EIGRP with possibly the fastest route convergence time among all protocols. The key to EIGRP's speedy convergence is twofold: First, EIGRP routers maintain a copy of all of their neighbors' routes, which they use to calculate their own cost to each remote network—if the best path goes down, it may be as simple as examining the contents of the topology table to select the best replacement route. Second, if there isn't a good alternative in the local topology table, EIGRP routers very quickly ask their neighbors for help finding one—they aren't afraid to ask directions! Relying on other routers and leveraging the information, they provide accounts for the "diffusing" character of DUAL.

And as I said, the whole idea of the Hello protocol is to enable the rapid detection of new or dead neighbors. RTP answers this call by providing a reliable mechanism for conveying and sequencing update, query, and query response messages. Building upon this solid foundation, DUAL is responsible for selecting and maintaining information about the best paths.

Using EIGRP to Support Large Networks

EIGRP includes a bunch of cool features that make it suitable for use in large networks:

- Support for multiple ASs on a single router
- Support for VLSM and summarization
- Route discovery and maintenance

Each of these capabilities adds one small piece to the complex puzzle of supporting a huge number of routers and multiple networks.

Multiple ASs

EIGRP uses autonomous system numbers to identify the collection of routers that share route information. Only routers that have the same autonomous system numbers share routes. In large networks, you can easily end up with really complicated topology and route tables, and that can markedly slow convergence during diffusing computation operations.

So what's an administrator to do to mitigate the impact of managing really big networks? Well, it's possible to divide the network into multiple distinct EIGRP autonomous systems, or ASs. Each AS is populated by a contiguous series of routers, and route information can be shared among the different ASs via redistribution.

The use of redistribution within EIGRP leads us to another interesting feature. Normally, the administrative distance (AD) of an EIGRP route is 90, but this is true only for what is known as an *internal EIGRP route*. These are routes originated within a specific autonomous system by EIGRP routers that are members of the same autonomous system. The other type of route is called an *external EIGRP route* and has an AD of 170, which is not so good. These routes appear within EIGRP route tables courtesy of manual redistribution, and they represent networks that originated outside of the EIGRP autonomous system. And it doesn't matter if the routes originated from another EIGRP autonomous system or from another routing protocol such as OSPF—they're all considered to be external routes when redistributed within EIGRP.

VLSM Support and Summarization

As one of the more sophisticated classless routing protocols, EIGRP supports the use of Variable Length Subnet Masks. This is really important because it allows for the conservation of address space through the use of subnet masks that more closely fit the host requirements, such as using 30-bit subnet masks for point-to-point networks. And because the subnet mask is propagated with every route update, EIGRP also supports the use of discontiguous subnets, something that gives us a lot more flexibility when designing the network's IP address plan.

What's a discontiguous network? I mentioned this term many times in Chapter 8 and it's now time to get to the answer! It's one internetwork that has two or more subnetworks of a classful network connected together by different classful networks. Sounds complicated, but it's not. Let's take a look. Figure 9.1 displays a typical discontiguous network.

FIGURE 9.1 A discontiguous network

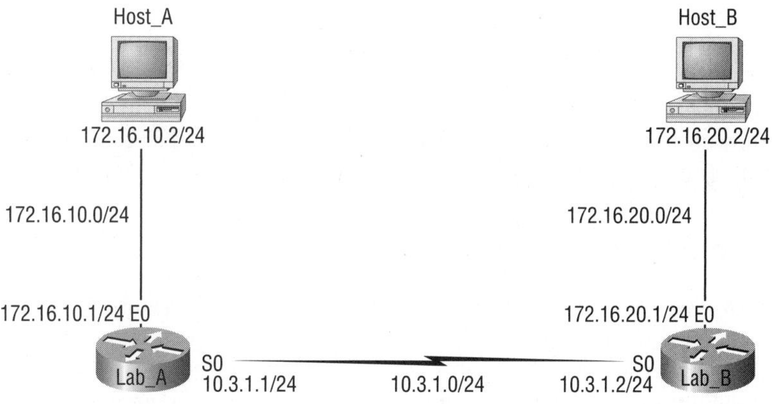

The subnets 172.16.10.0 and 172.16.20.0 are connected together with a 10.3.1.0 network. By default, for the purpose of route advertising, each router thinks it has the only 172.16.0.0 classful network.

It's important to understand that discontiguous networks just won't work with RIPv1 or Cisco's old IGRP at all. And they don't work by default on RIPv2 or EIGRP either, but discontiguous networks do work on OSPF networks by default because OSPF does not auto-summarize like EIGRP. Ah ha! So that must be the answer we've been looking for since Chapter 8. RIP, RIPv2, and EIGRP auto-summarize classful boundaries by default! But no worries—there are ways to make this work; it just doesn't work by default. I'll show you how to fix this when we configure EIGRP.

EIGRP also supports the manual creation of summaries at any and all EIGRP routers on a per-interface basis, which can substantially reduce the size of the routing table because EIGRP automatically summarizes networks at their classful boundaries. Figure 9.2 shows how a router running EIGRP would see the network plus the boundaries that it would auto-summarize.

FIGURE 9.2 EIGRP auto-summarization

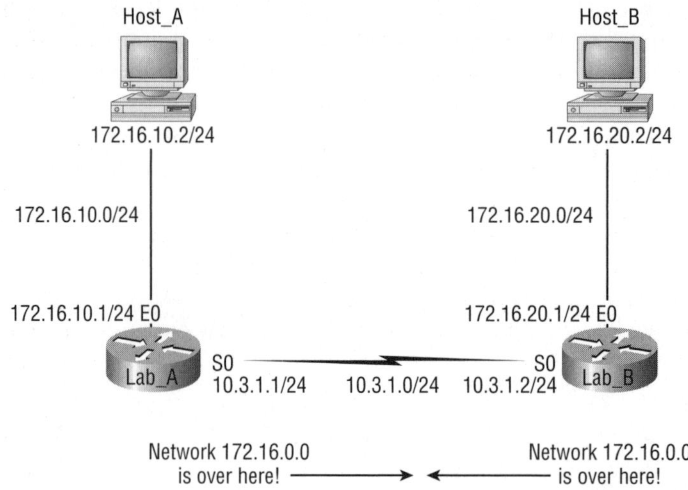

Obviously, this would never work by default! Make a note to yourself that RIPv1 and RIPv2 would also auto-summarize these same classful boundaries by default, but OSPF won't.

Route Discovery and Maintenance

The hybrid nature of EIGRP is fully revealed in its approach to route discovery and maintenance. Like many link-state protocols, EIGRP supports the concept of neighbors that are discovered via a Hello process and whose states are monitored. Like many distance-vector protocols, EIGRP uses the routing-by-rumor mechanism I talked about earlier that implies that many routers never hear about a route update firsthand. Instead, they hear about it from another router that may also have heard about it from another one, and so on.

Given the huge amount of information that EIGRP routers have to collect, it makes sense that they have a place to store it, right? Well they do—EIGRP uses a series of tables to store important information about its environment:

Neighborship table The *neighborship table* (usually referred to as the neighbor table) records information about routers with whom neighborship relationships have been formed.

Topology table The *topology table* stores the route advertisements received from each neighbor about every route in the internetwork.

Route table The *route table* stores the routes that are currently used to make routing decisions. There would be separate copies (instances) of each of these tables for each protocol that is actively being supported by EIGRP, whether it's IP or IPv6.

I am now going to discuss the EIGRP metrics and then move right into the *easy* configuration of EIGRP.

EIGRP Metrics

Another really sweet thing about EIGRP is that unlike many other protocols that use a single factor to compare routes and select the best possible path, EIGRP can use a combination of four, called a composite metric:

- *Bandwidth*
- *Delay*
- *Reliability*
- *Load*

EIGRP uses only bandwidth and delay of the line to determine the best path to a remote network by default. Cisco sometimes likes to call these *path bandwidth value* and *cumulative line delay*—go figure.

And it's worth noting that there's a fifth element, *maximum transmission unit (MTU)* size. This element has never been used in EIGRP calculations, but it's a required parameter in some EIGRP-related commands, especially those involving redistribution. The value of the MTU element represents the smallest MTU value encountered along the path to the destination network.

Maximum Paths and Hop Count

By default, EIGRP can provide equal-cost load balancing across up to 4 links (RIP does this as well). However, you can have EIGRP actually load-balance across up to 16 links (equal or unequal) by using the following command:

```
R1(config)#router eigrp 10
R1(config-router)#maximum-paths ?
  <1-16>  Number of paths
```

In addition, EIGRP has a default maximum hop count of 100, but it can be set up to 255. Chances are you wouldn't want to ever change this, but if you did, here is how you would do it:

```
R1(config)#router eigrp 10
R1(config-router)#metric maximum-hops ?
  <1-255>  Hop count
```

As you can see from this router output, EIGRP can be set to a maximum of 255 hops, and even though it doesn't use hop count in the path metric calculation, it still uses the maximum hop count to limit the scope of the AS.

Configuring EIGRP

Although EIGRP can be configured for IP, IPv6, IPX, and AppleTalk, as a future Cisco Certified Network Associate, you really only need to focus on the configuration of IP for now.

There are two modes from which EIGRP commands are entered: router configuration mode and interface configuration mode. Router configuration mode enables the protocol, determines which networks will run EIGRP, and sets global characteristics. Interface configuration mode allows customization of summaries and bandwidth.

To start an EIGRP session on a router, use the `router eigrp` command followed by the autonomous system number of your network. You then enter the network numbers connected to the router using the `network` command followed by the network number.

Let's look at an example of enabling EIGRP for autonomous system 20 on a router connected to two networks, with the network numbers being 10.3.1.0/24 and 172.16.10.0/24:

```
Router#config t
Router(config)#router eigrp 20
Router(config-router)#network 172.16.0.0
Router(config-router)#network 10.0.0.0
```

Remember—as with RIP, you use the classful network address, which is all subnet and host bits turned off. This is why EIGRP is so great—it has the complexity of a link-state protocol running in the background, with the same easy configuration of RIP.

Understand that the AS number is irrelevant—that is, as long as all routers use the same number! You can use any number from 1 to 65,535.

Say you need to stop EIGRP from working on a specific interface, such as a FastEthernet interface or a serial connection to the Internet. To do that, you would flag the interface as passive using the `passive-interface` *`interface`* command, as discussed in Chapter 8 with RIP. The following command shows you how to make interface serial 0/1 a passive interface:

```
Router(config)#router eigrp 20
Router(config-router)#passive-interface serial 0/1
```

Doing this will prohibit the interface from sending or receiving Hello packets and, as a result, stop it from forming adjacencies. This means that it won't send or receive route information on this interface.

Okay, let's configure the same network that we configured in the last chapter with RIP and RIPv2. It doesn't matter that RIPv2 (as well as our static routes) are already running—unless you're worried about bandwidth consumption and CPU cycles, of course, because EIGRP has an AD of 90. Remember that our static routes were changed to an AD of 150, and RIP is 120, so only EIGRP routes will populate the routing tables, even if RIP and static routing are enabled.

The impact of the `passive-interface` command depends upon the routing protocol under which the command is issued. For example, on an interface running RIP, the `passive-interface` command will prohibit the sending of route updates but allow their receipt. Thus, a RIP router with a passive interface will still learn about the networks advertised by other routers. This is different from EIGRP, where a `passive-interface` will neither send nor receive updates.

Figure 9.3 shows the network that we've been working with—the same one we're going to use to configure with EIGRP.

FIGURE 9.3 Our internetwork

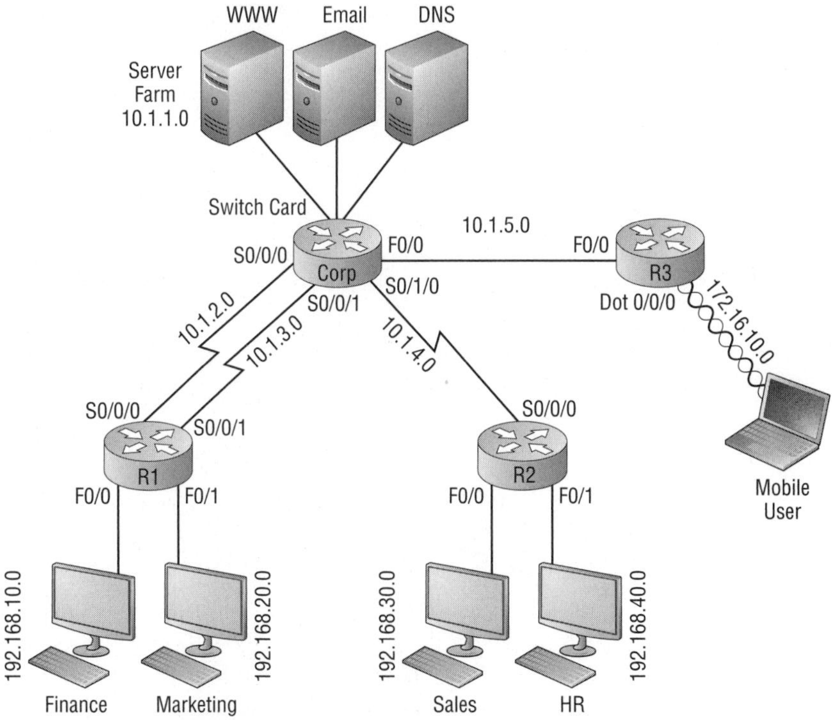

So you can use it as a reminder, Table 9.1 contains the IP addresses we've been using on each interface.

TABLE 9.1 Network addressing for the IP network

Router	Network Address	Interface	Address
CORP			
Corp	10.1.1.0	Vlan1 (switch card)	10.1.1.1
Corp	10.1.2.0	S0/0/0	10.1.2.1
Corp	10.1.3.0	S0/0/1(DCE)	10.1.3.1
Corp	10.1.4.0	S0/1/0	10.1.4.1
Corp	10.1.5.0	F0/0	10.1.5.1
R1			
R1	10.1.2.0	S0/0/0 (DCE)	10.1.2.2
R1	10.1.3.0	S0/0/1	10.1.3.2
R1	192.168.10.0	F0/0	192.168.10.1
R1	192.168.20.0	F0/1	192.168.20.1
R2			
R2	10.1.4.0	S0/0/0 (DCE)	10.1.4.2
R2	192.168.30.0	F0/0	192.168.30.1
R2	192.168.40.0	F0/1	192.168.40.1
R3			
R3	10.1.5.0	F0/0	10.1.5.2
R3	172.16.10.0	Dot11Radio0/0/0 (wireless)	172.16.10.1

It's actually really easy to add EIGRP to our internetwork—this is the beauty of EIGRP.

Corp

The AS number, as shown in the following router output, can be any number from 1 to 65,535. A router can be a member of as many ASs as you want it to be, but for this book's purposes, we're just going to configure a single AS:

```
Corp#config t
Corp(config)#router eigrp ?
  <1-65535>  Autonomous system number

Corp(config)#router eigrp 10
Corp(config-router)#network 10.0.0.0
```

The `router eigrp [as]` command turns EIGRP routing on in the router. As with RIPv1, you still need to add the classful network numbers you want to advertise. But unlike RIP, EIGRP uses classless routing—but you still configure it as classful. Classless, which I'm sure you remember, means that the subnet mask information is sent along with routing protocol updates (RIPv2 is classless).

R1

To configure the R1 router, all you need to do is turn on EIGRP routing using AS 10 and then add the network number like this:

```
R1#config t
Enter configuration commands, one per line.  End with CNTL/Z.
R1(config)#router eigrp 10
R1(config-router)#network 10.0.0.0
R1(config-router)#
%DUAL-5-NBRCHANGE: IP-EIGRP 10: Neighbor 10.1.2.1 (Serial0/0/0) is up:
new adjacency

%DUAL-5-NBRCHANGE: IP-EIGRP 10: Neighbor 10.1.3.1 (Serial0/0/1) is up:
new adjacency

R1(config-router)#network 192.168.10.0
R1(config-router)#network 192.168.20.0
```

The R1 router found the Corp neighbor—the two routers are adjacent! Notice that it found both links connected between the routers. This is a good thing.

R2

To configure the R2 router, all I need to do is again turn on EIGRP using AS 10:

```
R2#config t
Enter configuration commands, one per line.  End with CNTL/Z.
R2(config)#router eigrp 10
R2(config-router)#network 10.0.0.0
R2(config-router)#
%DUAL-5-NBRCHANGE: IP-EIGRP 10: Neighbor 10.1.4.1 (Serial0/0/0) is up:
new adjacency

R2(config-router)#network 192.168.30.0
R2(config-router)#network 192.168.40.0
```

That's it—really! Most routing protocols are pretty simple to set up, and EIGRP is no exception. But that's only for the basic configuration, of course.

R3

To configure the R3 router, all I need to do is turn on EIGRP using AS 10:

```
R3#config t
Enter configuration commands, one per line.  End with CNTL/Z.
R3(config)#router eigrp 10
R3(config-router)#network 10.0.0.0
R3(config-router)#
%DUAL-5-NBRCHANGE: IP-EIGRP 10: Neighbor 10.1.5.1 (FastEthernet0/0) is
up: new adjacency

R3(config-router)#network 172.16.0.0
```

That's it, done.

Our configuration seems pretty solid, but remember—only our directly connected and EIGRP routes are going to wind up in the routing table because EIGRP has the lowest AD. So by having RIP running in the background, we're not only using more memory and CPU cycles on the router, we're sucking up precious bandwidth across every one of our links! This is definitely not good, and it's something you'll really want to keep in mind.

Let's check out the Corp's routing table:

```
Corp#sh ip route
  10.0.0.0/24 is subnetted, 5 subnets
C       10.1.1.0 is directly connected, Vlan1
C       10.1.2.0 is directly connected, Serial0/0/0
C       10.1.3.0 is directly connected, Serial0/0/1
```

```
C        10.1.4.0 is directly connected, Serial0/1/0
C        10.1.5.0 is directly connected, FastEthernet0/0
     172.16.0.0/16 is variably subnetted, 2 subnets, 2 masks
D        172.16.0.0/16 [90/28160] via 10.1.5.2, 00:01:48, FastEthernet0/0
S        172.16.10.0/24 [150/0] via 10.1.5.2
D     192.168.10.0/24 [90/2172416] via 10.1.3.2, 00:05:07, Serial0/0/1
                      [90/2172416] via 10.1.2.2, 00:05:07, Serial0/0/0
D     192.168.20.0/24 [90/2172416] via 10.1.2.2, 00:05:04, Serial0/0/0
                      [90/2172416] via 10.1.3.2, 00:05:04, Serial0/0/1
D     192.168.30.0/24 [90/20514560] via 10.1.4.2, 00:03:32, Serial0/1/0
D     192.168.40.0/24 [90/20514560] via 10.1.4.2, 00:03:29, Serial0/1/0
Corp#
```

Okay, cool—all routes are showing up as "D" for DUAL. Let's take a look at R2's routing table:

```
R2#sh ip route
[output cut]
     10.0.0.0/8 is variably subnetted, 6 subnets, 2 masks
D        10.0.0.0/8 is a summary, 00:02:27, Null0
D        10.1.1.0/24 [90/27769856] via 10.1.4.1, 00:02:31, Serial0/0/0
D        10.1.2.0/24 [90/2681856] via 10.1.4.1, 00:02:31, Serial0/0/0
D        10.1.3.0/24 [90/2681856] via 10.1.4.1, 00:02:31, Serial0/0/0
C        10.1.4.0/24 is directly connected, Serial0/0/0
D        10.1.5.0/24 [90/2172416] via 10.1.4.1, 00:02:31, Serial0/0/0
     172.16.0.0/16 is variably subnetted, 2 subnets, 2 masks
D        172.16.0.0/16 [90/2172416] via 10.1.4.1, 00:00:42, Serial0/0/0
S        172.16.10.0/24 [150/0] via 10.1.4.1
D     192.168.10.0/24 [90/2684416] via 10.1.4.1, 00:02:31, Serial0/0/0
D     192.168.20.0/24 [90/2684416] via 10.1.4.1, 00:02:31, Serial0/0/0
C     192.168.30.0/24 is directly connected, FastEthernet0/0
C     192.168.40.0/24 is directly connected, FastEthernet0/1
R2#
```

We can see all the networks in the routing table, including our extra route to the 172.16.10.0 network still. Finally! Let's fix this!

Configuring Discontiguous Networks

There's one more configuration that you need to be aware of that has to do with auto-summarization. Remember Figure 9.2 and how it demonstrated how EIGRP would auto-summarize the boundaries on a discontiguous network? Take a look at that figure again, and then I'll provide a sample configuration on both routers with EIGRP.

In the Figure 9.1, the Lab_A router is connected to a 172.16.10.0/24 network and the 10.3.1.0/24 backbone. The Lab_B router is connected to the 172.16.20.0/24 network and the 10.3.1.0/24 backbone. Both routers, by default, would automatically summarize across classful boundaries and routing would not work. Here's the configuration that would make this network work:

```
Lab_A#config t
Lab_A(config)#router eigrp 100
Lab_A(config-router)#network 172.16.0.0
Lab_A(config-router)#network 10.0.0.0
Lab_A(config-router)#no auto-summary

Lab_B#config t
Lab_B(config)#router eigrp 100
Lab_B(config-router)#network 172.16.0.0
Lab_B(config-router)#network 10.0.0.0
Lab_B(config-router)#no auto-summary
```

Because I used the `no auto-summary` command, EIGRP will advertise all the subnets between the two routers. If the networks were larger, you could then provide manual summarization on these same boundaries.

So, with this in mind, why is our Corp router showing the extra route to 172.16.0.0 network? The configuration on R3 is this:

```
R3(config)#router eigrp 10
R3(config-router)#network 10.0.0.0
R3(config-router)#network 172.16.0.0
```

There are actually two answers to our 172.16.0.0 mystery. R3 has a pretty solid classful boundary from the 10.0.0.0 network to the 172.16.0.0 network and will auto-summarize. But so will our other routers in our internetwork. Take a look at R1:

```
R1#sh ip route
     10.0.0.0/8 is variably subnetted, 6 subnets, 2 masks
D       10.0.0.0/8 is a summary, 00:10:14, Null0
D       10.1.1.0/24 [90/27769856] via 10.1.2.1, 00:10:18, Serial0/0/0
                    [90/27769856] via 10.1.3.1, 00:10:18, Serial0/0/1
C       10.1.2.0/24 is directly connected, Serial0/0/0
C       10.1.3.0/24 is directly connected, Serial0/0/1
D       10.1.4.0/24 [90/21024000] via 10.1.2.1, 00:10:18, Serial0/0/0
                    [90/21024000] via 10.1.3.1, 00:10:18, Serial0/0/1
D       10.1.5.0/24 [90/2172416] via 10.1.2.1, 00:10:18, Serial0/0/0
                    [90/2172416] via 10.1.3.1, 00:10:18, Serial0/0/1
```

```
     172.16.0.0/16 is variably subnetted, 2 subnets, 2 masks
D       172.16.0.0/16 [90/2172416] via 10.1.3.1, 00:06:54, Serial0/0/1
                      [90/2172416] via 10.1.2.1, 00:06:54, Serial0/0/0
S       172.16.10.0/24 [150/0] via 10.1.3.1
C    192.168.10.0/24 is directly connected, FastEthernet0/0
C    192.168.20.0/24 is directly connected, FastEthernet0/1
D    192.168.30.0/24 [90/21026560] via 10.1.2.1, 00:08:38, Serial0/0/0
                     [90/21026560] via 10.1.3.1, 00:08:38, Serial0/0/1
D    192.168.40.0/24 [90/21026560] via 10.1.3.1, 00:08:35, Serial0/0/1
                     [90/21026560] via 10.1.2.1, 00:08:35, Serial0/0/0
R1#
```

Okay, we're still seeing the 172.16.0.0 issue, but the R1 router is summarizing the 10.0.0.0 network out the FastEthernet links, which isn't necessarily a problem as our internetwork does not have discontiguous networking, but let's turn off auto-summary on our network:

```
Corp#config t
Corp(config)#router eigrp 10
Corp(config-router)#no auto-summary

R1#config t
R1(config)#router eigrp 10
R1(config-router)#no auto-summary

R2#config t
R2(config)#router eigrp 10
R2(config-router)#no auto-summary

R3#config t
R3(config)#router eigrp 10
R3(config-router)#no auto-summary
```

Let's take a look at our routing Corp routing table now:

```
10.0.0.0/24 is subnetted, 5 subnets
C       10.1.1.0 is directly connected, Vlan1
C       10.1.2.0 is directly connected, Serial0/0/0
C       10.1.3.0 is directly connected, Serial0/0/1
C       10.1.4.0 is directly connected, Serial0/1/0
C       10.1.5.0 is directly connected, FastEthernet0/0
     172.16.0.0/24 is subnetted, 1 subnets
D       172.16.10.0 [90/28160] via 10.1.5.2, 00:03:18, FastEthernet0/0
```

```
D    192.168.10.0/24 [90/2172416] via 10.1.3.2, 00:03:19, Serial0/0/1
                     [90/2172416] via 10.1.2.2, 00:03:19, Serial0/0/0
D    192.168.20.0/24 [90/2172416] via 10.1.3.2, 00:03:19, Serial0/0/1
                     [90/2172416] via 10.1.2.2, 00:03:19, Serial0/0/0
D    192.168.30.0/24 [90/20514560] via 10.1.4.2, 00:03:19, Serial0/1/0
D    192.168.40.0/24 [90/20514560] via 10.1.4.2, 00:03:19, Serial0/1/0
Corp#
```

Notice that our mystery link is gone, and now let's take a look at our R1 table:

```
   10.0.0.0/24 is subnetted, 5 subnets
D       10.1.1.0 [90/27769856] via 10.1.3.1, 00:03:50, Serial0/0/1
                 [90/27769856] via 10.1.2.1, 00:03:50, Serial0/0/0
C       10.1.2.0 is directly connected, Serial0/0/0
C       10.1.3.0 is directly connected, Serial0/0/1
D       10.1.4.0 [90/21024000] via 10.1.3.1, 00:03:50, Serial0/0/1
                 [90/21024000] via 10.1.2.1, 00:03:50, Serial0/0/0
D       10.1.5.0 [90/2172416] via 10.1.3.1, 00:03:50, Serial0/0/1
                 [90/2172416] via 10.1.2.1, 00:03:50, Serial0/0/0
     172.16.0.0/24 is subnetted, 1 subnets
D       172.16.10.0 [90/2172416] via 10.1.3.1, 00:03:49, Serial0/0/1
                    [90/2172416] via 10.1.2.1, 00:03:49, Serial0/0/0
C    192.168.10.0/24 is directly connected, FastEthernet0/0
C    192.168.20.0/24 is directly connected, FastEthernet0/1
D    192.168.30.0/24 [90/21026560] via 10.1.2.1, 00:03:50, Serial0/0/0
                     [90/21026560] via 10.1.3.1, 00:03:50, Serial0/0/1
D    192.168.40.0/24 [90/21026560] via 10.1.2.1, 00:03:50, Serial0/0/0
                     [90/21026560] via 10.1.3.1, 00:03:50, Serial0/0/1
R1#
```

No more auto-summarizing the 10.0.0.0 network out for R1. Okay, if we don't have discontiguous networking, why did this solve our problem? Well, we didn't necessarily have a problem; we had a mystery route in our Corp router but our network was still working, and auto-summarizing in our network was fine as long as we didn't scale incorrectly in the future and create a discontiguous network. Remember back to the beginning of Chapter 8 where I discussed the longest match rule? Let's discuss this.

172.16.10.0 is a better match than 172.16.0.0, and the Corp, R1, and R2 each had a static route with an AD of 150 to R3, with the longest match of 172.16.10.0. However, R3 was advertising with a summary that 172.16.0.0 was directly connected, so the routing tables inserted both. Once auto-summary was turned off, the route of 172.16.10.0 with a lower AD was advertised and the static route disappeared from the routing table. If our internetwork had an actual discontiguous network, RIPv2 and EIGRP would not have worked at all until we used the `no auto-summary` command.

Load Balancing with EIGRP

You might know that by default, EIGRP can load-balance up to 4 equal-cost links. But did you remember that we can configure EIGRP to load-balance across up to 16 equal-/ unequal-cost links to a remote network? Well, we can, so let's take a look at the load balancing that our Corp and R1 routers have running. First, let's take a look at the R1 routing table and make sure that EIGRP has already found both links between the routers:

```
R1#sh ip route
     10.0.0.0/24 is subnetted, 5 subnets
D       10.1.1.0 [90/27769856] via 10.1.3.1, 00:21:30, Serial0/0/1
                 [90/27769856] via 10.1.2.1, 00:21:30, Serial0/0/0
C       10.1.2.0 is directly connected, Serial0/0/0
C       10.1.3.0 is directly connected, Serial0/0/1
D       10.1.4.0 [90/21024000] via 10.1.3.1, 00:21:30, Serial0/0/1
                 [90/21024000] via 10.1.2.1, 00:21:30, Serial0/0/0
D       10.1.5.0 [90/2172416] via 10.1.3.1, 00:21:30, Serial0/0/1
                 [90/2172416] via 10.1.2.1, 00:21:30, Serial0/0/0
     172.16.0.0/24 is subnetted, 1 subnets
D       172.16.10.0 [90/2172416] via 10.1.3.1, 00:21:29, Serial0/0/1
                    [90/2172416] via 10.1.2.1, 00:21:29, Serial0/0/0
C    192.168.10.0/24 is directly connected, FastEthernet0/0
C    192.168.20.0/24 is directly connected, FastEthernet0/1
D    192.168.30.0/24 [90/21026560] via 10.1.2.1, 00:21:30, Serial0/0/0
                     [90/21026560] via 10.1.3.1, 00:21:30, Serial0/0/1
D    192.168.40.0/24 [90/21026560] via 10.1.2.1, 00:21:30, Serial0/0/0
                     [90/21026560] via 10.1.3.1, 00:21:30, Serial0/0/1
R1#
```

You can see that we have two links to every remote route in our internetwork, and again, EIGRP will load-balance across the s0/0/0 and S0/0/1 links by default because they're the same metric.

EIGRP really does offer some pretty cool features, and one of them is automatic load balancing. But how about bundling links? Well, EIGRP can allow us to do this too—even with no extra configuration! Let me show you how this works. I'm going to configure the links between our Corp and R1 routers with the same subnet, meaning both links will have all interfaces within the same subnet.

Check out my configuration as I configure the s0/0/1 on each router to be in the 10.1.2.0 network, which will place these interfaces in the same subnet as the S0/0/0 interfaces of both routers:

```
Corp#config t
Corp(config)#int s0/0/1
```

```
Corp(config-if)#ip address 10.1.2.4 255.255.255.0

R1#config t
R1(config)#int s0/0/1
R1(config-if)#ip address 10.1.2.3 255.255.255.0
R1(config-if)#do show run | begin interface
interface Serial0/0/0
 description 1st Connection to Corp Router
 ip address 10.1.2.2 255.255.255.0
!
interface Serial0/0/1
 description 2nd connection to Corp Router
 ip address 10.1.2.3 255.255.255.0
```

Now both links have all four interfaces in the same subnet.

```
R1#sh ip route
     10.0.0.0/24 is subnetted, 5 subnets
D       10.1.1.0 [90/27769856] via 10.1.2.3, 00:21:30, Serial0/0/1
                 [90/27769856] via 10.1.2.1, 00:21:30, Serial0/0/0
C       10.1.2.0 is directly connected, Serial0/0/0
    is directly connected, Serial0/0/1
D       10.1.4.0 [90/21024000] via 10.1.2.3, 00:21:30, Serial0/0/1
                 [90/21024000] via 10.1.2.1, 00:21:30, Serial0/0/0
D       10.1.5.0 [90/2172416] via 10.1.2.3, 00:21:30, Serial0/0/1
                 [90/2172416] via 10.1.2.1, 00:21:30, Serial0/0/0
     172.16.0.0/24 is subnetted, 1 subnets
D       172.16.10.0 [90/2172416] via 10.1.2.3, 00:21:29, Serial0/0/1
                    [90/2172416] via 10.1.2.1, 00:21:29, Serial0/0/0
C    192.168.10.0/24 is directly connected, FastEthernet0/0
C    192.168.20.0/24 is directly connected, FastEthernet0/1
D    192.168.30.0/24 [90/21026560] via 10.1.2.1, 00:21:30, Serial0/0/0
                     [90/21026560] via 10.1.2.3, 00:21:30, Serial0/0/1
D    192.168.40.0/24 [90/21026560] via 10.1.2.1, 00:21:30, Serial0/0/0
                     [90/21026560] via 10.1.2.3, 00:21:30, Serial0/0/1
R1#
```

To make this fabulous configuration work, EIGRP positively must be enabled first. If not, you'll get an error on your router that the addresses overlap!

Did you notice there's a subtle change or two in the routing table now? Networks 10.1.2.0 and 10.1.3.0 used to show up as individual, directly connected interfaces, but not anymore. Now only the 10.1.2.0 network shows up as two directly connected interfaces, and the router now has a 3MB pipe through that line instead of just two 1.5Mbps T1 links. And just because these changes are subtle doesn't make them any less cool!

I am going to add subnet 10.1.3.0 back into the network so we can have some more fun with these dual links. I'll go to the Corp and R1 s0/0/1 interfaces and configure 10.1.3.1/24 and 10.1.3.2/24. Now 10.1.3.0 is being advertised again, but let's mix things up a bit and change the metric of the 10.1.3.0 link and see what happens:

```
R1#config t
R1(config)#int s0/0/1
R1(config-if)#bandwidth 256
R1(config-if)#delay 300000
Corp#config t
Corp(config)#int s0/0/1
Corp(config-if)#bandwidth 256
Corp(config-if)#delay 300000
```

Since by default EIGRP uses bandwidth and delay of the line to determine the best path to each network, I lowered the bandwidth and raised the delay of the s0/0/1 interfaces of the both the R1 and Corp routers. Now, let's verify EIGRP on our network, plus check out what our dual links are up to now between the R1 and Corp routers.

Verifying EIGRP

There are several commands that can be used on a router to help you troubleshoot and verify the EIGRP configuration. Table 9.2 contains all of the most important commands that are used in conjunction with verifying EIGRP operation and offers a brief description of what each command does.

TABLE 9.2 EIGRP troubleshooting commands

Command	Description/Function
`show ip route`	Shows the entire routing table
`show ip route eigrp`	Shows only EIGRP entries in the routing table
`show ip eigrp neighbors`	Shows all EIGRP neighbors
`show ip eigrp topology`	Shows entries in the EIGRP topology table

TABLE 9.2 EIGRP troubleshooting commands *(continued)*

Command	Description/Function
`show ip protocols`	Shows routing protocols configuration
`debug eigrp packet`	Shows Hello packets sent/received between adjacent routers
`debug ip eigrp events`	Shows EIGRP changes and updates as they occur on your network

Since EIGRP is pretty simple to configure, you'd be wise to study the verification and troubleshooting of EIGRP. I can't remind you enough throughout this book that the CCENT/CCNA is a routing and switching course and exam. Twenty-five percent of the objectives are routing and 25 percent of the objectives are switching, which we'll start working on in the next chapter. But we still have another 50 percent to cover: 25 percent is verification and troubleshooting routing, and the last 25 percent is verification and troubleshooting switching. So, with this in mind, let's concentrate hard on this next section.

I'll demonstrate how you would use the commands in Table 9.2 by using them on our internetwork.

The following router output is from the Corp router in our example:

```
Corp#sh ip route
     10.0.0.0/24 is subnetted, 5 subnets
C       10.1.1.0 is directly connected, Vlan1
C       10.1.2.0 is directly connected, Serial0/0/0
C       10.1.3.0 is directly connected, Serial0/0/1
C       10.1.4.0 is directly connected, Serial0/1/0
C       10.1.5.0 is directly connected, FastEthernet0/0
     172.16.0.0/24 is subnetted, 1 subnets
D       172.16.10.0 [90/28160] via 10.1.5.2, 01:00:11, FastEthernet0/0
D    192.168.10.0/24 [90/2172416] via 10.1.2.2, 01:00:12, Serial0/0/0
D    192.168.20.0/24 [90/2172416] via 10.1.2.2, 01:00:12, Serial0/0/0
D    192.168.30.0/24 [90/20514560] via 10.1.4.2, 01:00:12, Serial0/1/0
D    192.168.40.0/24 [90/20514560] via 10.1.4.2, 01:00:12, Serial0/1/0
Corp#
```

You can see that all routes are there in the routing table (10.1.3.0 shows that it's directly connected again) and we have only one link to each of the remote networks now! Notice that EIGRP routes are indicated with simply a *D* designation (DUAL) and that the default AD of these routes is 90. This represents internal EIGRP routes. Let's take a look at the R1 router table now that we've changed the metrics:

```
R1#sh ip route
     10.0.0.0/24 is subnetted, 5 subnets
D       10.1.1.0 [90/27769856] via 10.1.2.1, 00:59:38, Serial0/0/0
C       10.1.2.0 is directly connected, Serial0/0/0
C       10.1.3.0 is directly connected, Serial0/0/1
D       10.1.4.0 [90/21024000] via 10.1.2.1, 00:59:38, Serial0/0/0
D       10.1.5.0 [90/2172416] via 10.1.2.1, 00:59:38, Serial0/0/0
      172.16.0.0/24 is subnetted, 1 subnets
D       172.16.10.0 [90/2172416] via 10.1.2.1, 00:59:37, Serial0/0/0
C    192.168.10.0/24 is directly connected, FastEthernet0/0
C    192.168.20.0/24 is directly connected, FastEthernet0/1
D    192.168.30.0/24 [90/21026560] via 10.1.2.1, 00:59:38, Serial0/0/0
D    192.168.40.0/24 [90/21026560] via 10.1.2.1, 00:59:38, Serial0/0/0
R1#
```

Again, in the R1 router we have only one route to each remote network, and the 10.1.3.0 network is our backup link. Obviously, it would be better if we could use both links at the same time, but in my example, I made the 10.1.3.0 network a backup link.

Let's go back to the Corp router and see what it shows us in the neighbor table:

```
Corp#sh ip eigrp neighbors
IP-EIGRP neighbors for process 10
H   Address         Interface     Hold Uptime    SRTT   RTO   Q    Seq
                                  (sec)          (ms)         Cnt  Num
0   10.1.5.2        Fa0/0         14   01:02:00  40     1000  0    143
1   10.1.4.2        Se0/1/0       12   01:02:00  40     1000  0    114
2   10.1.2.2        Se0/0/0       11   01:02:00  40     1000  0    131
3   10.1.3.2        Se0/0/1       11   00:33:37  40     1000  0    132
```

We read the information in this output like this:

- The H field indicates the order in which the neighbor was discovered.
- The hold time is how long this router will wait for a Hello packet to arrive from a specific neighbor.
- The uptime indicates how long the neighborship has been established.
- The SRTT field is the smooth round-trip timer—an indication of the time it takes for a round-trip from this router to its neighbor and back. This value is used to determine how long to wait after a multicast for a reply from this neighbor. If a reply isn't received in time, the router will switch to using unicasts in an attempt to complete the communication. The time between multicast attempts is specified by:

- The Retransmission Time Out (RTO) field, which is the amount of time EIGRP waits before retransmitting a packet from the retransmission queue to a neighbor.
- The Q value, which indicates whether there are any outstanding messages in the queue—consistently large values would indicate a problem.
- The Seq field, which indicates the sequence number of the last update from that neighbor—something that's used to maintain synchronization and avoid duplicate or out-of-sequence processing of messages.

The show `ip eigrp neighbors` command allows you to check the IP addresses as well as the retransmit interval and queue counts for the neighbors that have established an adjacency—remember this.

Now let's see what's in the Corp topology table by using the `show ip eigrp topology` command—this should be interesting!

```
Corp#sh ip eigrp topology
IP-EIGRP Topology Table for AS 10

Codes: P - Passive, A - Active, U - Update, Q - Query, R - Reply,
       r - Reply status

P 10.1.1.0/24, 1 successors, FD is 25625600
        via Connected, Vlan1
P 10.1.5.0/24, 1 successors, FD is 28160
        via Connected, FastEthernet0/0
P 10.1.4.0/24, 1 successors, FD is 20512000
        via Connected, Serial0/1/0
P 10.1.3.0/24, 1 successors, FD is 76809984
        via Connected, Serial0/0/1
P 10.1.2.0/24, 1 successors, FD is 2169856
        via Connected, Serial0/0/0
P 192.168.10.0/24, 1 successors, FD is 2172416
        via 10.1.2.2 (2172416/28160), Serial0/0/0
        via 10.1.3.2 (76828160/28160), Serial0/0/1
P 192.168.20.0/24, 1 successors, FD is 2172416
        via 10.1.2.2 (2172416/28160), Serial0/0/0
        via 10.1.3.2 (76828160/28160), Serial0/0/1
P 192.168.30.0/24, 1 successors, FD is 20514560
        via 10.1.4.2 (20514560/28160), Serial0/1/0
P 192.168.40.0/24, 1 successors, FD is 20514560
```

```
        via 10.1.4.2 (20514560/28160), Serial0/1/0
P 172.16.10.0/24, 1 successors, FD is 28160
        via 10.1.5.2 (28160/25600), FastEthernet0/0
```

Notice that every route is preceded by a *P*. This means that the route is in the *passive state*, which is a good thing because routes in the *active state* (*A*) indicate that the router has lost its path to this network and is searching for a replacement. Each entry also indicates the feasible distance, or FD, to each remote network plus the next-hop neighbor through which packets will travel to their destination. Plus, each entry also has two numbers in parentheses. The first indicates the feasible distance (FD) and the second the advertised distance (AD) to a remote network.

Now here's where things get interesting—notice that under the 192.168.10.0 and 192.168.20.0 outputs there are two links to each network and that the feasible distance of each are different. What this means is that we have one successor to the networks and one feasible successor—a backup route! So very cool!

Let's take a closer look:

```
P 192.168.10.0/24, 1 successors, FD is 2172416
        via 10.1.2.2 (2172416/28160), Serial0/0/0
        via 10.1.3.2 (76828160/28160), Serial0/0/1
P 192.168.20.0/24, 1 successors, FD is 2172416
        via 10.1.2.2 (2172416/28160), Serial0/0/0
        via 10.1.3.2 (76828160/28160), Serial0/0/1
```

The FD is the feasible distance—the cost from the Corp router to get to that network. But we also need to look at the AD, or advertised distance. For the 192.168.10.0, we're seeing this in the table:

```
via 10.1.2.2 (2172416/28160), Serial0/0/0
via 10.1.3.2 (76828160/28160), Serial0/0/1
```

For the s0/0/0 link, we see (2172416/28160); the first number is the FD and the second number is the AD. The R1 router is advertising the same cost of 28160 to get to the 192.168.10.0 and 192.168.20.0 network. However, the Corp router needs to add the cost of what it will take to get to each network, and this is where we get our FD. Since the s0/0/1 link has a lower bandwidth and higher delay, we can see that the s0/0/0 has a lower FD and that is the path placed in the routing table.

You need to remember that even though both routes are in the topology table, only the successor route (the ones with the lowest metrics) will be copied and placed into the routing table.

In order for the route to be a feasible successor, its advertised distance must be less than the feasible distance of the successor route.

EIGRP will load-balance across both links automatically when they are of equal variance (equal cost), but EIGRP can load-balance across unequal-cost links as well if we use the `variance` command. The variance metric is set to 1 by default, meaning that only equal-cost links will load-balance. You can change the variance anywhere up to 128. Changing a variance value enables EIGRP to install multiple, loop-free routes with unequal cost in a local routing table.

So basically, if the variance is set to 1, only routes with the same metric as the successor will be installed in the local routing table. And, for example, if the variance is set to 2, any EIGRP-learned route with a metric less than or equal to two times the successor metric will be installed in the local routing table (if it is already a feasible successor). This is a complicated configuration and you need to be careful before you start configuring the `variance` command.

Let's check out one last `show` command before we look at a debugging output, the `show ip protocols` command. We can get information about all routing protocols configured on our router, but let's see what EIGRP shows us:

```
Corp#sh ip protocols

Routing Protocol is "eigrp  10 "
  Outgoing update filter list for all interfaces is not set
  Incoming update filter list for all interfaces is not set
  Default networks flagged in outgoing updates
  Default networks accepted from incoming updates
  EIGRP metric weight K1=1, K2=0, K3=1, K4=0, K5=0
  EIGRP maximum hopcount 100
  EIGRP maximum metric variance 1
Redistributing: eigrp 10
  Automatic network summarization is in effect
  Automatic address summarization:
  Maximum path: 4
  Routing for Networks:
     10.0.0.0
  Routing Information Sources:
    Gateway         Distance      Last Update
    10.1.5.2        90            40
    10.1.3.2        90            6867
    10.1.2.2        90            6916
    10.1.4.2        90            8722
  Distance: internal 90 external 170
Corp#
```

From the output of the `show ip protocols` command, we can see the AS number and the metric weights called the "k" values, where bandwidth and delay of the line are used and enabled by default. Also the maximum hop count for a route update packet is shown

(100 by default) as well as the variance, which is set to 1, meaning equal-cost load balancing. Maximum path 4 means that four equal-cost paths will load-balance by default.

Now's a great time for us to check out some debugging outputs. First, let's use the debug eigrp packet command that will show our Hello packets being sent between neighbor routers:

```
Corp#debug eigrp packet
EIGRP: Received HELLO on Serial0/1/0 nbr 10.1.4.2
  AS 10, Flags 0x0, Seq 115/0 idbQ 0/0
EIGRP: Sending HELLO on Serial0/0/0
  AS 10, Flags 0x0, Seq 148/0 idbQ 0/0 iidbQ un/rely 0/0
EIGRP: Received HELLO on Serial0/0/1 nbr 10.1.3.2
  AS 10, Flags 0x0, Seq 133/0 idbQ 0/0
EIGRP: Received HELLO on Serial0/0/0 nbr 10.1.2.2
  AS 10, Flags 0x0, Seq 133/0 idbQ 0/0
EIGRP: Received HELLO on FastEthernet0/0 nbr 10.1.5.2
  AS 10, Flags 0x0, Seq 144/0 idbQ 0/0
EIGRP: Sending HELLO on Serial0/1/0
  AS 10, Flags 0x0, Seq 148/0 idbQ 0/0 iidbQ un/rely 0/0
EIGRP: Sending HELLO on Serial0/0/1
  AS 10, Flags 0x0, Seq 148/0 idbQ 0/0 iidbQ un/rely 0/0
EIGRP: Sending HELLO on FastEthernet0/0
  AS 10, Flags 0x0, Seq 148/0 idbQ 0/0 iidbQ un/rely 0/0
EIGRP: Received HELLO on Serial0/1/0 nbr 10.1.4.2
  AS 10, Flags 0x0, Seq 115/0 idbQ 0/0
EIGRP: Sending HELLO on Vlan1
  AS 10, Flags 0x0, Seq 148/0 idbQ 0/0 iidbQ un/rely 0/0
EIGRP: Sending HELLO on Serial0/0/0
  AS 10, Flags 0x0, Seq 148/0 idbQ 0/0 iidbQ un/rely 0/0
```

Since my Corp router is connected to three EIGRP neighbors, and because the 224.0.0.10 multicast is sent out every 5 seconds, I didn't have any problem seeing the updates. The Hello packets are sent out every active interface as well as all the interfaces that we have neighbors connected to. Did you notice that the AS number is provided in the update? This is because if a neighbor doesn't have the same AS number, the Hello update would just be discarded.

I know you've learned a lot about EIGRP so far, but stick around because you're not done with this chapter just yet! It's now time to give you the skinny on OSPF!

Open Shortest Path First (OSPF) Basics

Open Shortest Path First (OSPF) is an open standard routing protocol that's been implemented by a wide variety of network vendors, including Cisco. If you have multiple routers and not all of them are Cisco (what!), then you can't use EIGRP, can you? So your remaining

CCNA objective options are basically RIP, RIPv2, and OSPF. If it's a large network, then, really, your only options are OSPF and something called route redistribution—a translation service between routing protocols.

OSPF works by using the Dijkstra algorithm. First, a shortest path tree is constructed, and then the routing table is populated with the resulting best paths. OSPF converges quickly, although perhaps not as quickly as EIGRP, and it supports multiple, equal-cost routes to the same destination. Like EIGRP, it does support both IP and IPv6 routed protocols.

OSPF provides the following features:

- Consists of areas and autonomous systems
- Minimizes routing update traffic
- Allows scalability
- Supports VLSM/CIDR
- Has unlimited hop count
- Allows multi-vendor deployment (open standard)

OSPF is the first link-state routing protocol that most people are introduced to, so it's useful to see how it compares to more traditional distance-vector protocols such as RIPv2 and RIPv1. Table 9.3 gives you a comparison of these three protocols.

TABLE 9.3 OSPF and RIP comparison

Characteristic	OSPF	RIPv2	RIPv1
Type of protocol	Link state	Distance vector	Distance vector
Classless support	Yes	Yes	No
VLSM support	Yes	Yes	No
Auto-summarization	No	Yes	Yes
Manual summarization	Yes	No	No
Discontiguous support	Yes	Yes	No
Route propagation	Multicast on change	Periodic multicast	Periodic broadcast
Path metric	Bandwidth	Hops	Hops
Hop count limit	None	15	15
Convergence	Fast	Slow	Slow
Peer authentication	Yes	Yes	No

Characteristic	OSPF	RIPv2	RIPv1
Hierarchical network requirement	Yes (using areas)	No (flat only)	No (flat only)
Updates	Event triggered	Route table updates	Route table updates
Route computation	Dijkstra	Bellman-Ford	Bellman-Ford

OSPF has many features beyond the few I've listed in Table 9.3, and all of them contribute to a fast, scalable, and robust protocol that can be actively deployed in thousands of production networks.

OSPF is supposed to be designed in a hierarchical fashion, which basically means that you can separate the larger internetwork into smaller internetworks called areas. This is the best design for OSPF.

The following are reasons for creating OSPF in a hierarchical design:

- To decrease routing overhead
- To speed up convergence
- To confine network instability to single areas of the network

This does not make configuring OSPF easier, but more elaborate and difficult.

Figure 9.4 shows a typical OSPF simple design. Notice how some routers connect to the backbone—called area 0, or the backbone area. OSPF must have an area 0, and all other areas should connect to this area. (Areas that do not connect directly to area 0 can be connected by using virtual links, which are beyond the scope of this book.) Routers that connect other areas to the backbone area within an AS are called Area Border Routers (ABRs). Still, at least one interface of the ABR must be in area 0.

FIGURE 9.4 OSPF design example

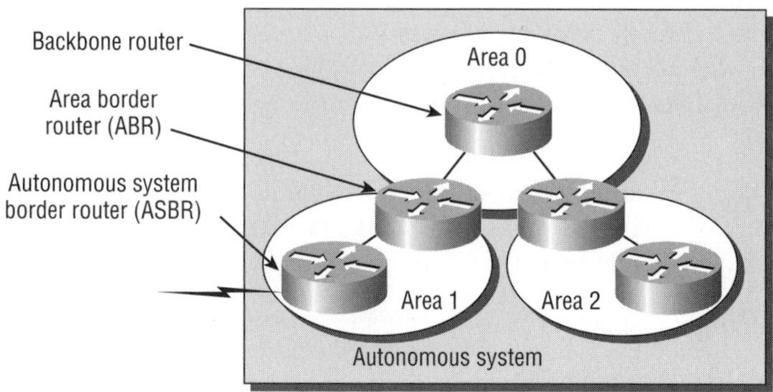

OSPF runs inside an autonomous system, but it can also connect multiple autonomous systems together. The router that connects these ASs is called an Autonomous System Boundary Router (ASBR).

Ideally, you would create other areas of networks to help keep route updates to a minimum in larger networks and to keep problems from propagating throughout the network, basically isolating them to a single area.

As in the sections on EIGRP, I'll first cover the essential terminology you need to understand OSPF.

OSPF Terminology

Imagine how challenging it would be if you were given a map and compass but had no knowledge of east or west, north or south, river or mountain, lake or desert. You'd probably not get very far putting your new tools to good use without knowing about this stuff. For this reason, you'll begin your exploration of OSPF with a long list of terms that will prevent you from getting lost in the later sections. The following are important OSPF terms to familiarize yourself with before you proceed:

Link A *link* is a network or router interface assigned to any given network. When an interface is added to the OSPF process, it's considered by OSPF to be a link. This link, or interface, will have state information associated with it (up or down) as well as one or more IP addresses.

Router ID The *Router ID (RID)* is an IP address used to identify the router. Cisco chooses the Router ID by using the highest IP address of all configured loopback interfaces. If no loopback interfaces are configured with addresses, OSPF will choose the highest IP address of all active physical interfaces.

Neighbor *Neighbors* are two or more routers that have an interface on a common network, such as two routers connected on a point-to-point serial link.

Adjacency An *adjacency* is a relationship between two OSPF routers that permits the direct exchange of route updates. OSPF is really picky about sharing routing information—unlike EIGRP, which directly shares routes with all of its neighbors. Instead, OSPF directly shares routes only with neighbors that have also established adjacencies. And not all neighbors will become adjacent—this depends upon both the type of network and the configuration of the routers.

Hello protocol The OSPF Hello protocol provides dynamic neighbor discovery and maintains neighbor relationships. Hello packets and Link State Advertisements (LSAs) build and maintain the topological database. Hello packets are addressed to multicast address 224.0.0.5.

Neighborship database The *neighborship database* is a list of all OSPF routers for which Hello packets have been seen. A variety of details, including the Router ID and state, are maintained on each router in the neighborship database.

Topological database The *topological database* contains information from all of the Link State Advertisement packets that have been received for an area. The router uses the information from the topology database as input into the Dijkstra algorithm that computes the shortest path to every network.

LSA packets are used to update and maintain the topological database.

Link State Advertisement A *Link State Advertisement (LSA)* is an OSPF data packet containing link-state and routing information that's shared among OSPF routers. There are different types of LSA packets, and I'll go into these shortly. An OSPF router will exchange LSA packets only with routers to which it has established adjacencies.

Designated router A *designated router (DR)* is elected whenever OSPF routers are connected to the same multi-access network. Cisco likes to call these "broadcast" networks, but really, they are networks that have multiple recipients. Try not to confuse multi-access with multipoint, which can be easy to do sometimes.

A prime example is an Ethernet LAN. To minimize the number of adjacencies formed, a DR is chosen (elected) to disseminate/receive routing information to/from the remaining routers on the broadcast network or link. This ensures that their topology tables are synchronized. All routers on the shared network will establish adjacencies with the DR and backup designated router (BDR)—I'll define this next. The election is won by the router with the highest priority, and the highest Router ID is used as a tiebreaker if the priority of more than one router turns out to be the same.

Backup designated router A *backup designated router (BDR)* is a hot standby for the DR on multi-access links (remember that Cisco sometimes likes to call these "broadcast" networks). The BDR receives all routing updates from OSPF adjacent routers but doesn't flood LSA updates.

OSPF areas An *OSPF area* is a grouping of contiguous networks and routers. All routers in the same area share a common Area ID. Because a router can be a member of more than one area at a time, the Area ID is associated with specific interfaces on the router. This would allow some interfaces to belong to area 1 while the remaining interfaces can belong to area 0. All of the routers within the same area have the same topology table. When configuring OSPF, you've got to remember that there must be an area 0 and that this is typically considered the backbone area. Areas also play a role in establishing a hierarchical network organization—something that really enhances the scalability of OSPF!

Broadcast (multi-access) *Broadcast (multi-access) networks* such as Ethernet allow multiple devices to connect to (or access) the same network as well as provide a *broadcast* ability in which a single packet is delivered to all nodes on the network. In OSPF, a DR and a BDR must be elected for each broadcast multi-access network.

Non-broadcast multi-access *Non-broadcast multi-access (NBMA) networks* are types such as Frame Relay, X.25, and Asynchronous Transfer Mode (ATM). These networks allow for multi-access but have no broadcast ability like Ethernet. So, NBMA networks require special OSPF configuration to function properly and neighbor relationships must be defined.

DR and BDR are elected on broadcast and non-broadcast multi-access networks. Elections are covered in detail later in this chapter.

Point-to-point *Point-to-point* refers to a type of network topology consisting of a direct connection between two routers that provides a single communication path. The point-to-point connection can be physical, as in a serial cable directly connecting two routers, or it can be logical, as in two routers that are thousands of miles apart yet connected by a circuit in a Frame Relay network. In either case, this type of configuration eliminates the need for DRs or BDRs—but neighbors are discovered automatically.

Point-to-multipoint *Point-to-multipoint* refers to a type of network topology consisting of a series of connections between a single interface on one router and multiple destination routers. All of the interfaces on all of the routers sharing the point-to-multipoint connection belong to the same network. As with point-to-point, no DRs or BDRs are needed.

All of these terms play an important part in understanding the operation of OSPF, so again, make sure you're familiar with each of them. Reading through the rest of this chapter will help you to place the terms within their proper context.

SPF Tree Calculation

Within an area, each router calculates the best/shortest path to every network in that same area. This calculation is based upon the information collected in the topology database and an algorithm called *shortest path first (SPF)*. Picture each router in an area constructing a tree—much like a family tree—where the router is the root and all other networks are arranged along the branches and leaves. This is the shortest path tree used by the router to insert OSPF routes into the routing table.

It's important to understand that this tree contains only networks that exist in the same area as the router itself does. If a router has interfaces in multiple areas, then separate trees will be constructed for each area. One of the key criteria considered during the route selection process of the SPF algorithm is the metric or cost of each potential path to a network. But this SPF calculation doesn't apply to routes from other areas.

OSPF uses a metric referred to as *cost*. A cost is associated with every outgoing interface included in an SPF tree. The cost of the entire path is the sum of the costs of the outgoing interfaces along the path. Because cost is an arbitrary value as defined in RFC 2338, Cisco had to implement its own method of calculating the cost for each OSPF-enabled interface. Cisco uses a simple equation of 10^8/bandwidth. The bandwidth is the configured bandwidth for the interface. Using this rule, a 100Mbps Fast Ethernet interface would have a default OSPF cost of 1 and a 10Mbps Ethernet interface would have a cost of 10.

An interface set with a bandwidth of 64,000 would have a default cost of 1,563.

This value may be overridden by using the `ip ospf cost` command. The cost is manipulated by changing the value to a number within the range of 1 to 65,535. Because the cost is assigned to each link, the value must be changed on the interface for which you want to change the cost.

Cisco bases link cost on bandwidth. Other vendors may use other metrics to calculate a given link's cost. When connecting links between routers from different vendors, you may have to adjust the cost to match another vendor's router. Both routers must assign the same cost to the link for OSPF to work properly.

Configuring OSPF

Configuring basic OSPF isn't as simple as configuring RIP and EIGRP, and it can get really complex once the many options that are allowed within OSPF are factored in. But that's okay—for your studies, you should be interested in the basic single-area OSPF configuration. The following sections describe how to configure single-area OSPF.

These two elements are the basic elements of OSPF configuration:

- Enabling OSPF
- Configuring OSPF areas

Enabling OSPF

The easiest and also least scalable way to configure OSPF is to just use a single area. Doing this requires a minimum of two commands.

The command you use to activate the OSPF routing process is as follows:

```
Router(config)#router ospf ?
<1-65535>
```

A value in the range from 1 to 65,535 identifies the OSPF Process ID. It's a unique number on this router that groups a series of OSPF configuration commands under a specific running process. Different OSPF routers don't have to use the same Process ID to communicate. It's purely a local value that essentially has little meaning, but it cannot start at 0; it has to start at a minimum of 1.

You can have more than one OSPF process running simultaneously on the same router if you want, but this isn't the same as running multi-area OSPF. The second process will maintain an entirely separate copy of its topology table and manage its communications independently of the first process. And because the CCNA objectives only cover single-area OSPF with each router running a single OSPF process, that's what I'm going to focus on in this book.

The OSPF Process ID is needed to identify a unique instance of an OSPF database and is locally significant.

Configuring OSPF Areas

After identifying the OSPF process, you need to identify the interfaces that you want to activate OSPF communications on as well as the area in which each resides. This will also configure the networks you're going to advertise to others. OSPF uses wildcards in the configuration—which are also used in access list configurations (covered in Chapter 13).

Here's an OSPF basic configuration example for you:

```
Router#config t
Router(config)#router ospf 1
Router(config-router)#network 10.0.0.0 0.255.255.255
 area ?
  <0-4294967295>  OSPF area ID as a decimal value
  A.B.C.D         OSPF area ID in IP address format
Router(config-router)#network 10.0.0.0 0.255.255.255
 area 0
```

The areas can be any number from 0 to 4.2 billion. Don't get these numbers confused with the Process ID, which is from 1 to 65,535.

Remember, the OSPF Process ID number is irrelevant. It can be the same on every router on the network, or it can be different—doesn't matter. It's locally significant and just enables the OSPF routing on the router.

The arguments of the `network` command are the network number (10.0.0.0) and the wildcard mask (0.255.255.255). The combination of these two numbers identifies the interfaces that OSPF will operate on and will also be included in its OSPF LSA advertisements. Based on my sample configuration, OSPF will use this command to find any interface on the router configured in the 10.0.0.0 network, and it will place any interface it finds into area 0. Notice that you can create about 4.2 billion areas. (A router wouldn't let you actually create that many, but you can certainly name them using the numbers up to 4.2 billion.) You can also label an area using an IP address format.

A quick explanation of wildcards: A 0 octet in the wildcard mask indicates that the corresponding octet in the network must match exactly. On the other hand, a 255 indicates that you don't care what the corresponding octet is in the network number. A network and wildcard mask combination of 1.1.1.1 0.0.0.0 would match an interface configured exactly with 1.1.1.1 only, and nothing else. This is really useful if you want to activate OSPF on a specific interface in a very clear and simple way. If you insist on matching a range of networks, the network and wildcard mask combination of 1.1.0.0 0.0.255.255 would match any interface in the range of 1.1.0.0 to 1.1.255.255. Because of this, it's simpler and safer to stick to using wildcard masks of 0.0.0.0 and identify each OSPF interface individually, but once configured, they function exactly the same—one way is not better than the other.

The final argument is the area number. It indicates the area to which the interfaces identified in the network and wildcard mask portion belong. Remember that OSPF routers will become neighbors only if their interfaces share a network that's configured to belong to the same area number. The format of the area number is either a decimal value from the range 1 to 4,294,967,295 or a value represented in standard dotted-decimal notation. For example, area 0.0.0.0 is a legitimate area and is identical to area 0.

Wildcard Example

Before getting down to configuring our network, let's take a quick peek at a harder OSPF network configuration to find out what our OSPF network statements would be if we were using subnets and wildcards.

You have a router with these four subnets connected to four different interfaces:

- 192.168.10.64/28
- 192.168.10.80/28
- 192.168.10.96/28
- 192.168.10.8/30

All interfaces need to be in area 0. Seems to me, the easiest configuration would be this:

```
Test#config t
Test(config)#router ospf 1
Test(config-router)#network 192.168.10.0 0.0.0.255 area 0
```

The preceding example is pretty simple, but easy isn't always best, so although this example is an easy way to configure OSPF, what fun is that? And worse yet, the CCNA objectives are not likely to cover something so simple for you! So let's create a separate network statement for each interface using the subnet numbers and wildcards. That would look something like this:

```
Test#config t
Test(config)#router ospf 1
Test(config-router)#network 192.168.10.64 0.0.0.15 area 0
Test(config-router)#network 192.168.10.80 0.0.0.15 area 0
Test(config-router)#network 192.168.10.96 0.0.0.15 area 0
Test(config-router)#network 192.168.10.8 0.0.0.3 area 0
```

Wow, now that's a different looking config! Truthfully, OSPF would work exactly the same way as in the easy configuration I showed you first—but unlike the easy configuration, this one covers the CCNA objectives!

Although this looks complicated, trust me, it is not. All you need to do is understand your block sizes! So all you have to do is just remember when configuring wildcards that they're always one less than the block size. A /28 is a block size of 16, so we'd add our network statement using the subnet number and then add a wildcard of 15 in the interesting octet. For the /30, which is a block size of 4, we'd use a wildcard of 3. Once you practice this a few times, it's pretty simple, and we'll see them again when we get to access lists.

Let's use Figure 9.5 as an example and configure that network with OSPF using wildcards to make sure you have a solid grip on this. Figure 9.5 shows a three-router network with the IP addresses of each interface.

FIGURE 9.5 Sample OSPF wildcard configuration

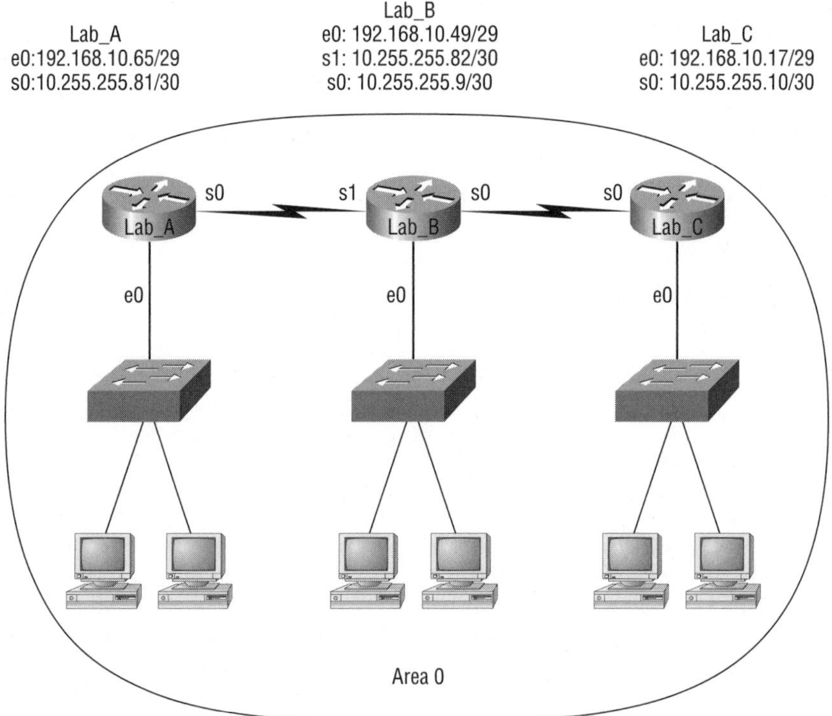

The very first thing you need to be able to do is to look at each interface and determine the subnet that the addresses are in. Hold on, I know what you're thinking: "Why don't I just use the exact IP addresses of the interface with the 0.0.0.0 wildcard?" Well, you can, but we're paying attention to CCNA objectives here, not just what's easiest, remember?

The IP addresses for each interface are shown in the figure. The Lab_A router has two directly connected subnets: 192.168.10.64/29 and 10.255.255.80/30. Here's the OSPF configuration using wildcards:

```
Lab_A#config t
Lab_A(config)#router ospf 1
```

```
Lab_A(config-router)#network 192.168.10.64 0.0.0.7 area 0
Lab_A(config-router)#network 10.255.255.80 0.0.0.3 area 0
```

The Lab_A router is using a /29, or 255.255.255.248, mask on the ethernet0 interface. This is a block size of 8, which is a wildcard of 7. The s0 interface is a mask of 255.255.255.252—block size of 4, with a wildcard of 3. You can't configure OSPF this way if you can't look at the IP address and slash notation and then figure out the subnet, mask, and wildcard, can you? So don't take your exam until you can do this.

Here are our other two configurations to help you practice:

```
Lab_B#config t
Lab_B(config)#router ospf 1
Lab_B(config-router)#network 192.168.10.48 0.0.0.7 area 0
Lab_B(config-router)#network 10.255.255.80 0.0.0.3 area 0
Lab_B(config-router)#network 10.255.255.8 0.0.0.3 area 0

Lab_C#config t
Lab_C(config)#router ospf 1
Lab_C(config-router)#network 192.168.10.16 0.0.0.7 area 0
Lab_C(config-router)#network 10.255.255.8 0.0.0.3 area 0
```

As I mentioned with the Lab_A configuration, you've got to be able to determine the subnet, mask, and wildcard just by looking at the IP address and mask of an interface. If you can't do that, you won't be able to configure OSPF using wildcards as I just demonstrated. So go over this until you're really comfortable with it!

Configuring Our Network with OSPF

Okay—now we get to have some fun! Let's configure our internetwork with OSPF using just area 0. Before we do that, we've got to remove EIGRP because OSPF has an administrative distance of 110. (EIGRP is 90—but you already knew that, right?). Let's remove RIP while we're at it, just because I don't want you to get in the habit of having RIP running on your network.

There's a bunch of different ways to configure OSPF, and as I said, the simplest and easiest is to use the wildcard mask of 0.0.0.0. But I want to demonstrate that we can configure each router differently with OSPF and still come up with the exact same result. This is one reason why OSPF is more fun than other routing protocols—it gives us all a lot more ways to screw things up, which provides a troubleshooting opportunity! We'll use our network as shown in Figure 9.3 to configure OSPF.

Corp

Here's the Corp router's configuration:

```
Corp#config t
Corp(config)#no router eigrp 10
```

```
Corp(config)#no router rip
Corp(config)#router ospf 132
Corp(config-router)#network 10.1.1.1 0.0.0.0 area 0
Corp(config-router)#network 10.1.2.1 0.0.0.0 area 0
Corp(config-router)#network 10.1.3.1 0.0.0.0 area 0
Corp(config-router)#network 10.1.4.1 0.0.0.0 area 0
Corp(config-router)#network 10.1.5.1 0.0.0.0 area 0
```

Hmmmm—it seems we have a few things to discuss here. First, I removed EIGRP and RIP and then added OSPF. So why did I use OSPF 132? It really doesn't matter—the number is irrelevant. I guess it just felt good to use 132!

The network commands are pretty straightforward. I typed in the IP address of each interface and used the wildcard mask of 0.0.0.0, which means that the IP address must match each octet exactly. But if this is one of those times where easier is better—just do this:

```
Corp(config)#router ospf 132
Corp(config-router)#network 10.1.0.0 0.0.255.255 area 0
```

One line instead of five! I really want you to understand that no matter which way you configure the network statement, OSPF will work the same here. Now, let's move on to R1. To keep things simple, we're going to use our same sample configuration.

R1

The R1 router has four directly connected networks. Instead of typing in each interface, I can use the one network command example and still make it work exactly the same:

```
R1#config t
R1(config)#no router eigrp 10
R1(config)#no router rip
R1(config)#router ospf 1
R1(config-router)#network 10.1.0.0 0.0.255.255 area0
                                                  ^

% Invalid input detected at '^' marker.

R1(config-router)#network 10.1.0.0 0.0.255.255 area 0
R1(config-router)#
14:12:39: %OSPF-5-ADJCHG: Process 1, Nbr 10.1.5.1 on Serial0/0/0
from LOADING to FULL, Loading Done

R1(config-router)#
14:12:43: %OSPF-5-ADJCHG: Process 1, Nbr 10.1.5.1 on Serial0/0/1
from LOADING to FULL, Loading Done
R1(config-router)#network 192.168.0.0 0.0.255.255 area 0
```

Okay—other than my little typo, where I forgot to place a space between the area command and the area number, this is truly a fast and efficient configuration.

All I did was to first disable EIGRP, and then I turned on OSPF routing process 1 and added the network command 10.1.0.0 with a wildcard of 0.0.255.255. What this did is basically say, "Find any interface that starts with 10.1, and place those interfaces into area 0." Last, I added both 192.168.10.0 and 192.168.20.0 with one configuration line. Quick, easy, and slick!

R2

Let's give the R2 router that's directly connected to three networks some attention:

```
R2#config t
R2(config)#no router eigrp 10
R2(config)#no router rip
R2(config)#router ospf 45678
R2(config-router)#network 10.0.0.0 0.0.0.255 area 0
R2(config-router)#network 192.168.30.1 0.0.0.0 area 0
R2(config-router)#network 192.168.40.1 0.0.0.0 area
```

I can use any process ID I want—as long as it's a value from 1 to 65,535. And notice I used the 10.0.0.0 with wildcard 0.255.255.255 and then I used the 0.0.0.0 wildcard configuration for my 192.168.30 and 40.0 networks. This works well too.

R3

Finally, our last router! For the R3 router, we need to turn off RIP and EIGRP, and then configure OSPF.

```
R3(config)#no router eigrp 10
R3(config)#no router rip
R3(config)#router ospf 1
R3(config-router)#network 10.1.5.1 0.0.0.0 area 0
R3(config-router)#network 172.16.10.0 0.0.0.255 area 0
```

Cool! Now that we've configured all the routers with OSPF, what's next? Miller Time? Nope—not yet. It's that verification thing again. We still have to make sure that OSPF is really working. That's exactly what we're going to do next.

Verifying OSPF Configuration

There are several ways to verify proper OSPF configuration and operation, and in the following sections I'll show you the OSPF `show` commands you need to know in order to do this. We're going to start by taking a quick look at the routing table of the Corp router.

So, let's issue a `show ip route` command on the Corp router see if there is a troubleshooting opportunity for us:

```
     10.0.0.0/24 is subnetted, 5 subnets
C       10.1.1.0 is directly connected, Vlan1
C       10.1.2.0 is directly connected, Serial0/0/0
C       10.1.3.0 is directly connected, Serial0/0/1
C       10.1.4.0 is directly connected, Serial0/1/0
C       10.1.5.0 is directly connected, FastEthernet0/0
     172.16.0.0/24 is subnetted, 1 subnets
S       172.16.10.0 [150/0] via 10.1.5.2
O    192.168.10.0/24 [110/65] via 10.1.2.2, 00:01:55, Serial0/0/0
O    192.168.20.0/24 [110/65] via 10.1.2.2, 00:01:55, Serial0/0/0
S    192.168.30.0/24 [150/0] via 10.1.4.2
S    192.168.40.0/24 [150/0] via 10.1.4.2
```

The Corp router shows only two dynamic routes for internetwork, with the *O* representing OSPF internal routes (the Cs are obviously our directly connected networks), but what's with the *S* in the routing table?

So, unlike EIGRP, our little internetwork just didn't "work" the first time I configured the routers. Let's look at the problems and fix them. Let's start with the 192.168.30.0 and 40.0; those should not be showing up as static. Let's run over to R2 and take a look at what the configuration is:

```
!
router ospf 45678
 log-adjacency-changes
 network 10.0.0.0 0.0.0.255 area 0
 network 192.168.30.1 0.0.0.0 area 0
 network 192.168.40.1 0.0.0.0 area 0
!
```

The 192.168.30.0 and 40.0 looks correct, but I see a mistake in my first line for the 10.0.0.0 network. Do you see it? That's right, my wildcards are telling OSPF to match the first three octets exactly, and I don't have any interface that starts with 10.0.0, so I need to redo that network statement:

```
R2(config)#router ospf 45678
R2(config-router)#no  network 10.0.0.0 0.0.0.255 area 0
R2(config-router)#network 10.1.4.0 0.0.0.255 area 0
```

So, I took out the wrong statement and then configured a correct network statement. Let's take a look at the Corp routing table now:

```
     10.0.0.0/24 is subnetted, 5 subnets
C       10.1.1.0 is directly connected, Vlan1
```

```
C       10.1.2.0 is directly connected, Serial0/0/0
C       10.1.3.0 is directly connected, Serial0/0/1
C       10.1.4.0 is directly connected, Serial0/1/0
C       10.1.5.0 is directly connected, FastEthernet0/0
     172.16.0.0/24 is subnetted, 1 subnets
S       172.16.10.0 [150/0] via 10.1.5.2
O    192.168.10.0/24 [110/65] via 10.1.2.2, 00:09:50, Serial0/0/0
O    192.168.20.0/24 [110/65] via 10.1.2.2, 00:09:50, Serial0/0/0
O    192.168.30.0/24 [110/782] via 10.1.4.2, 00:00:02, Serial0/1/0
O    192.168.40.0/24 [110/782] via 10.1.4.2, 00:00:02, Serial0/1/0
Corp#
```

Okay, that's better...but we're still seeing that mystery 172.16.0.0 network that's been popping in and out of our Corp routing table. Let's take a look at R3 and see what I did wrong with the configuration:

```
router ospf 1
 log-adjacency-changes
 network 10.1.5.1 0.0.0.0 area 0
 network 172.16.10.0 0.0.0.255 area 0
```

Ah, another typo. See how easy this is to do with OSPF? Do you see my error? Typing `show ip interface brief` should help you see it:

```
R3#sh ip int brief
Interface              IP-Address      OK? Method Status          Protocol
FastEthernet0/0        10.1.5.2        YES manual up                    up
Dot11Radio0/0/0        172.16.10.1     YES manual up                    up
```

You should see that my FastEthernet is 10.1.5.2, not the 10.1.5.1 that is in my OSPF configuration. Remember, in your network statements always type in your directly connected interfaces or networks, not the remote router's networks. Here's how I'll fix it and then we should be up:

```
R3(config)#router ospf 1
R3(config-router)#no network 10.1.5.1 0.0.0.0 area 0
R3(config-router)#network 10.1.5.2 0.0.0.0 area 0
```

Now let's take a last look at our Corp routing table. We should be good to go now:

```
     10.0.0.0/24 is subnetted, 5 subnets
C       10.1.1.0 is directly connected, Vlan1
C       10.1.2.0 is directly connected, Serial0/0/0
C       10.1.3.0 is directly connected, Serial0/0/1
C       10.1.4.0 is directly connected, Serial0/1/0
```

```
C       10.1.5.0 is directly connected, FastEthernet0/0
     172.16.0.0/24 is subnetted, 1 subnets
O       172.16.10.0 [110/2] via 10.1.5.2, 00:00:28, FastEthernet0/0
O    192.168.10.0/24 [110/65] via 10.1.2.2, 00:15:34, Serial0/0/0
O    192.168.20.0/24 [110/65] via 10.1.2.2, 00:15:34, Serial0/0/0
O    192.168.30.0/24 [110/782] via 10.1.4.2, 00:05:47, Serial0/1/0
O    192.168.40.0/24 [110/782] via 10.1.4.2, 00:05:47, Serial0/1/0
```

Now that's a nice-looking OSPF routing table. It is important that you can troubleshoot and fix an OSPF network as I showed in my example here. It is very easy to make little mistakes with OSPF, so watch for the little details.

It's time to show you all the OSPF verification commands that you need to know.

The *show ip ospf* Command

The `show ip ospf` command is used to display OSPF information for one or all OSPF processes running on the router. Information contained therein includes the Router ID, area information, SPF statistics, and LSA timer information. Let's check out the output from the Corp router:

```
Corp#sh ip ospf
 Routing Process "ospf 132" with ID 10.1.5.1
 Supports only single TOS(TOS0) routes
 Supports opaque LSA
 SPF schedule delay 5 secs, Hold time between two SPFs 10 secs
 Minimum LSA interval 5 secs. Minimum LSA arrival 1 secs
 Number of external LSA 0. Checksum Sum 0x000000
 Number of opaque AS LSA 0. Checksum Sum 0x000000
 Number of DCbitless external and opaque AS LSA 0
 Number of DoNotAge external and opaque AS LSA 0
 Number of areas in this router is 1. 1 normal 0 stub 0 nssa
 External flood list length 0
    Area BACKBONE(0)
        Number of interfaces in this area is 5
        Area has no authentication
        SPF algorithm executed 5 times
        Area ranges are
        Number of LSA 5. Checksum Sum 0x0283f4
        Number of opaque link LSA 0. Checksum Sum 0x000000
        Number of DCbitless LSA 0
        Number of indication LSA 0
        Number of DoNotAge LSA 0
        Flood list length 0
```

Notice the Router ID (RID) of 10.1.5.1, which is the highest IP address configured on the router.

The *show ip ospf database* Command

Using the `show ip ospf database` command will give you information about the number of routers in the internetwork (AS) plus the neighboring router's ID (this is the topology database I mentioned earlier). Unlike the `show ip eigrp topology` command, this command shows the OSPF routers, not each and every link in the AS as EIGRP does.

The output is broken down by area. Here's a sample output, again from Corp:

```
Corp#sh ip ospf database

            OSPF Router with ID (10.1.5.1) (Process ID 132)

                Router Link States (Area 0)

Link ID         ADV Router      Age         Seq#       Checksum Link count
192.168.20.1    192.168.20.1    1585        0x80000006 0x00ae08 6
192.168.40.1    192.168.40.1    1005        0x80000005 0x0069c7 4
10.1.5.1        10.1.5.1        688         0x80000009 0x008108 8
172.16.10.1     172.16.10.1     688         0x80000004 0x0021a6 2

                Net Link States (Area 0)
Link ID         ADV Router      Age         Seq#       Checksum
10.1.5.1        10.1.5.1        688         0x80000001 0x00c977
```

You can see all four routers and the RID of each router (the highest IP address on each router). The router output shows the link ID—remember that an interface is also a link—and the RID of the router on that link under the ADV router, or advertising router.

The *show ip ospf interface* Command

The `show ip ospf interface` command displays all interface-related OSPF information. Data is displayed about OSPF information for all OSPF-enabled interfaces or for specified interfaces. (I'll bold some of the important things.)

```
Corp#sh ip ospf int f0/0
FastEthernet0/0 is up, line protocol is up
  Internet address is 10.1.5.1/24, Area 0
  Process ID 132, Router ID 10.1.5.1, Network Type BROADCAST, Cost: 1
  Transmit Delay is 1 sec, State DR, Priority 1
  Designated Router (ID) 10.1.5.1, Interface address 10.1.5.1
  Backup Designated Router (ID) 172.16.10.1, Interface address 10.1.5.2
```

```
Timer intervals configured, Hello 10, Dead 40, Wait 40, Retransmit 5
  Hello due in 00:00:04
Index 5/5, flood queue length 0
Next 0x0(0)/0x0(0)
Last flood scan length is 1, maximum is 1
Last flood scan time is 0 msec, maximum is 0 msec
Neighbor Count is 1, Adjacent neighbor count is 1
  Adjacent with neighbor 172.16.10.1  (Backup Designated Router)
Suppress hello for 0 neighbor(s)
```

The following information is displayed by this command:

- Interface IP address
- Area assignment
- Process ID
- Router ID
- Network type
- Cost
- Priority
- DR/BDR election information (if applicable)
- Hello and Dead timer intervals
- Adjacent neighbor information

The reason I used the `show ip ospf interface f0/0` command is because I knew that there would be a designated router elected on the FastEthernet broadcast multi-access network between our Corp and R3 routers. We'll get into DR and BDR elections in detail in a minute, as well as the other information that I bolded—all very important! We'll especially come back to the timers shown in the `show ip ospf interface` command output later.

Okay, so as an example you type in the `show ip ospf interface` command and receive this response:

```
Corp#sh ip ospf int f0/0
%OSPF: OSPF not enabled on FastEthernet0/0
```

This error occurs when OSPF is enabled on the router, but not the interface. You need to check your network statements because the interface you are trying to verify is not in your OSPF process.

The *show ip ospf neighbor* Command

The `show ip ospf neighbor` command is super-useful because it summarizes the pertinent OSPF information regarding neighbors and the adjacency state. If a DR or BDR exists, that information will also be displayed. Here's a sample:

```
Corp#sh ip ospf neighbor
```

```
Neighbor ID     Pri   State      Dead Time   Address       Interface
172.16.10.1       1   FULL/DR     00:00:39    10.1.5.2    FastEthernet0/0
192.168.20.1      0   FULL/  -    00:00:38    10.1.2.2    Serial0/0/0
192.168.20.1      0   FULL/  -    00:00:38    10.1.3.2    Serial0/0/1
192.168.40.1      0   FULL/  -    00:00:36    10.1.4.2    Serial0/1/0
```

This is a super-important command to understand because it's extremely useful in production networks. Let's take a look at the R3 router output:

```
R3#sh ip ospf neighbor
Neighbor ID     Pri   State        Dead Time   Address     Interface
10.1.5.1          1   FULL/BDR     00:00:31    10.1.5.1    FastEthernet0/0
```

Since there's an Ethernet link (broadcast multi-access) on the link between the R3 and the Corp router, there's going to be an election to determine who will be the designated router (DR) and who will be the backup designated router (BDR). We can see that the R3 became the designated router, and it won because it had the highest IP address on the network. You can change this, but that's the default.

The reason that the Corp connections to R1 and R2 don't have a DR or BDR listed in the output is that by default, elections don't happen on point-to-point links and they show FULL/ - .But we can see that the Corp router is fully adjacent to all three routers from its output.

The *show ip protocols* Command

The `show ip protocols` command is also useful, whether you're running OSPF, EIGRP, IGRP, RIP, BGP, IS-IS, or any other routing protocol that can be configured on your router. It provides an excellent overview of the actual operation of all currently running protocols.

Check out the output from the Corp router:

```
Corp#sh ip protocols
Routing Protocol is "ospf 132"
  Outgoing update filter list for all interfaces is not set
  Incoming update filter list for all interfaces is not set
  Router ID 10.1.5.1
  Number of areas in this router is 1. 1 normal 0 stub 0 nssa
  Maximum path: 4
  Routing for Networks:
    10.1.1.1 0.0.0.0 area 0
    10.1.2.1 0.0.0.0 area 0
    10.1.3.1 0.0.0.0 area 0
    10.1.4.1 0.0.0.0 area 0
    10.1.5.1 0.0.0.0 area 0
  Routing Information Sources:
```

```
    Gateway         Distance      Last Update
    10.1.5.1             110      00:05:16
    172.16.10.1          110      00:05:16
    192.168.20.1         110      00:16:36
    192.168.40.1         110      00:06:55
  Distance: (default is 110)
```

From looking at this output, you can determine the OSPF Process ID, OSPF Router ID, type of OSPF area, networks and areas configured for OSPF, and the OSPF Router IDs of neighbors—that's a lot. Read efficient! And hold on a second. Did you notice the absence of timers like the ones we were shown before in the RIP outputs from this command? That's because link-state routing protocols don't use timers to keep the network stable like distance-vector routing algorithms do.

Debugging OSPF

Debugging is a great tool for any protocol, so let's take a look in Table 9.4 at a few debugging commands for troubleshooting OSPF.

TABLE 9.4 Debugging commands for troubleshooting OSPF

Command	Description/Function
`debug ip ospf packet`	Shows Hello packets being sent on your router.
`debug ip ospf hello`	Shows Hello packets being sent and received on your router. Shows more detail than the `debug ip ospf packet` output.
`debug ip ospf adj`	Shows DR and BDR elections on a broadcast or non-broadcast multi-access network.

I'll start by showing you the output from the Corp router I got using the `debug ip ospf packet` command:

```
Corp#debug ip ospf packet
OSPF packet debugging is on
*Mar 23 01:20:45.507: OSPF: rcv. v:2 t:1 l:48 rid:10.1.2.2
      aid:0.0.0.0 chk:8076 aut:0 auk: from Serial0/0/0
*Mar 23 01:20:45.531: OSPF: rcv. v:2 t:1 l:48 rid: 10.1.4.2
      aid:0.0.0.0 chk:8076 aut:0 auk: from Serial0/1/0
*Mar 23 01:20:45.531: OSPF: rcv. v:2 t:1 l:48 rid: 10.1.5.2
      aid:0.0.0.0 chk:8074 aut:0 auk: from FastEthernet0/0
```

In the preceding output, we can see that our router is receiving Hello packets from neighbor (adjacent) routers. OSPF sends Hello packets every 10 seconds.

The next debug command I'm going show you is the `debug ip ospf adj` command that will show us elections as they occur on broadcast and non-broadcast multi-access networks, an important command for our next section. To get output, I'll shut down F0/0 on R3 and then enable it again:

```
Corp#debug ip ospf adj
OSPF adjacency events debugging is on
05:32:12: %OSPF-5-ADJCHG: Process 132, Nbr 172.16.10.1 on
FastEthernet0/0 from FULL to DOWN, Neighbor Down: Interface down or detached

05:32:12: OSPF: Build router LSA for area 0, router ID 10.1.5.1, seq 0x80000016
05:32:12: OSPF: DR/BDR election on FastEthernet0/0
05:32:12: OSPF: Elect BDR 0.0.0.0
05:32:12: OSPF: Elect DR 0.0.0.0
05:32:12: OSPF: Elect BDR 0.0.0.0
05:32:12: OSPF: Elect DR 0.0.0.0
05:32:12:        DR: none   BDR: none
05:32:12: OSPF: Build router LSA for area 0, router ID 10.1.5.1, seq 0x80000017
05:32:12: OSPF: Build router LSA for area 0, router ID 10.1.5.1, seq 0x80000017

Corp#
%LINEPROTO-5-UPDOWN: Line protocol on Interface FastEthernet0/0,
changed state to up
05:33:57: OSPF: end of Wait on interface FastEthernet0/0
05:33:57: OSPF: DR/BDR election on FastEthernet0/0
05:33:57: OSPF: Elect BDR 172.16.10.1
05:33:57: OSPF: Elect DR 172.16.10.1
05:33:57:        DR: 172.16.10.1 (Id)   BDR: 172.16.10.1 (Id)
05:33:57: OSPF: Send DBD to 172.16.10.1 on FastEthernet0/0 seq 0x2d9e
opt 0x00 flag 0x7 len 32
05:33:57: OSPF: Build router LSA for area 0, router ID 10.1.5.1, seq 0x80000018
05:33:57: OSPF: DR/BDR election on FastEthernet0/0
05:33:57: OSPF: Elect BDR 10.1.5.1
05:33:57: OSPF: Elect DR 172.16.10.1
05:33:57: OSPF: Elect BDR 10.1.5.1
05:33:57: OSPF: Elect DR 172.16.10.1
05:33:57:        DR: 172.16.10.1 (Id)   BDR: 10.1.5.1 (Id)
05:33:57: OSPF: Build router LSA for area 0, router ID 10.1.5.1, seq 0x80000018
```

All right—let's move on and discover how elections occur in an OSPF network.

OSPF DR and BDR Elections

In this chapter, I have discussed OSPF in detail; however, I need to expand the section on designated routers and backup designated routers that I've only briefly touched on so far. I'm also going to delve deeper into verifying the election process as well as provide you with a hands-on lab at the end of the chapter to help you understand that process even better.

To start with, I need to make sure you fully understand the terms *neighbors* and *adjacencies* again because they're really crucial to the DR and BDR election process. The election process happens when a broadcast or non-broadcast multi-access network is connected to a router and the link comes up. (Think Ethernet or Frame Relay.)

Neighbors

Routers that share a common segment become neighbors on that segment. These neighbors are elected via the Hello protocol. Hello packets are sent periodically out of each interface using IP multicast.

Two routers won't become neighbors unless they agree on the following:

Area ID The idea here is that the two routers' interfaces have to belong to the same area on a particular segment. And of course, those interfaces have to belong to the same subnet.

Authentication OSPF allows for the configuration of a password for a specific area. Although authentication between routers isn't required, you have the option to set it if you need to do so. Also, keep in mind that in order for routers to become neighbors, they need to have the same password on a segment if you're using authentication.

Hello and Dead intervals OSPF exchanges Hello packets on each segment. This is a keepalive system used by routers to acknowledge their existence on a segment and for electing a designated router (DR) and backup designated router on both broadcast and non-broadcast multi-access segments.

The Hello interval specifies the number of seconds between Hello packets. The Dead interval is the number of seconds that a router's Hello packets can go without being seen before its neighbors declare the OSPF router dead (down). OSPF requires these intervals to be exactly the same between two neighbors. If either of these intervals is different, the routers won't become neighbors on that segment. You can see these timers with the `show ip ospf interface` command.

Adjacencies

In the election process, adjacency is the next step after the neighboring process. Adjacent routers are routers that go beyond the simple Hello exchange and proceed into the database exchange process. In order to minimize the amount of information exchanged on a particular segment, OSPF elects one router to be a designated router (DR) and one router to be a backup designated router (BDR) on each multi-access segment.

The BDR is elected as a backup router in case the DR goes down. The idea behind this is that routers have a central point of contact for information exchange. Instead of each router exchanging updates with every other router on the segment, every router sends its information to the DR and BDR. The DR then relays the information to everybody else.

DR and BDR Elections

DR and BDR election is accomplished via the Hello protocol. Hello packets are exchanged via IP multicast packets on each segment. However, only segments that are broadcast and non-broadcast multi-access networks (such as Ethernet and Frame Relay) will perform DR and BDR elections. Point-to-point links, like a serial WAN for example, will not have a DR/BDR election process.

On a broadcast or non-broadcast multi-access network, the router with the highest OSPF priority on a segment will become the DR for that segment. This priority is shown with the `show ip ospf interface` command and is set to 1 by default. If all routers have the default priority set, the router with the highest Router ID (RID) will win.

As you know, the RID is determined by the highest IP address on any interface at the moment of OSPF startup. This can be overridden with a loopback (logical) interface, which I'll talk about in the next section.

If you set a router's interface to a priority value of zero, that router won't participate in the DR or BDR election on that interface. The state of the interface with priority zero will then be DROTHER.

Now let's play with the RID on an OSPF router.

OSPF and Loopback Interfaces

Configuring loopback interfaces when using the OSPF routing protocol is important, and Cisco suggests using them whenever you configure OSPF on a router.

Loopback interfaces are logical interfaces, which are virtual, software-only interfaces; they are not real router interfaces. Using loopback interfaces with your OSPF configuration ensures that an interface is always active for OSPF processes.

They can be used for diagnostic purposes as well as OSPF configuration. The reason you want to configure a loopback interface on a router is because if you don't, the highest active IP address on a router at the time of bootup will become that router's RID. The RID is used to advertise the routes as well as elect the DR and BDR.

By default, OSPF uses the highest IP address on any active interface at the moment of OSPF startup. However, this can be overridden by a logical interface. The highest IP address of any logical interface will always become a router's RID.

In the following sections, you will see how to configure loopback interfaces and how to verify loopback addresses and RIDs.

Configuring Loopback Interfaces

Configuring loopback interfaces rocks mostly because it's the easiest part of OSPF configuration, and we all need a break about now—right? So hang on—we're in the home stretch!

First, let's see what the RID is on the Corp router with the `show ip ospf` command:

```
Corp#sh ip ospf
 Routing Process "ospf 132" with ID 10.1.5.1
[output cut]
```

We can see that the RID is 10.1.5.1, or the FastEthernet0/0 interface of the router. So let's configure a loopback interface using a completely different IP addressing scheme:

```
Corp(config)#int loopback 0
*Mar 22 01:23:14.206: %LINEPROTO-5-UPDOWN: Line protocol on Interface
   Loopback0, changed state to up
Corp(config-if)#ip address 172.31.1.1 255.255.255.255
```

The IP scheme really doesn't matter here, but each has to be in a separate subnet. By using the /32 mask, we can use any IP address we want as long as the addresses are never the same on any two routers.

Let's configure the other routers:

```
R1#config t
R1(config)#int loopback 0
*Mar 22 01:25:11.206: %LINEPROTO-5-UPDOWN: Line protocol on Interface
   Loopback0, changed state to up
R1(config-if)#ip address 172.31.1.2 255.255.255.255
```

Here's the configuration of the loopback interface on R2:

```
R2#config t
R2(config)#int loopback 0
*Mar 22 02:21:59.686: %LINEPROTO-5-UPDOWN: Line protocol on Interface
   Loopback0, changed state to up
R2(config-if)#ip address 172.31.1.3 255.255.255.255
```

Here's the configuration of the loopback interface on R3. I am going to use a different IP and I'll explain why in a second:

```
R3#config t
R3(config)#int loopback 0
*Mar 22 02:01:49.686: %LINEPROTO-5-UPDOWN: Line protocol on Interface
   Loopback0, changed state to up
R3(config-if)#ip address 172.31.100.4 255.255.255.255
```

I'm pretty sure you're wondering what the IP address mask of 255.255.255.255 (/32) means and why we don't just use 255.255.255.0 instead. Well, either mask works, but the /32 mask is called a host mask and works fine for loopback interfaces, and it allows us to save subnets. Notice how I was able to use 172.31.1.1, .2, .3, and .4? If I didn't use the /32, I'd have to use a separate subnet for each and every router!

Now, before we move on, did we actually change the RIDs of our router by setting the loopback interfaces? Let's check into that by taking a look at the Corp's RID:

```
Corp#sh ip ospf
 Routing Process "ospf 132" with ID 10.1.5.1
```

What happened? You'd think that because we set logical interfaces, the IP addresses under the logical interfaces automatically become the RID of the router, right? Well, sort of—but only if you do one of two things: either reboot the router or delete OSPF and re-create the database on your router. And neither is really that great an option.

I'm going with rebooting the Corp router because it's the easier of the two.

Now let's look and see what our RID is:

```
Corp#sh ip ospf
 Routing Process "ospf 132" with ID 172.31.1.1
```

Okay, that did it. The Corp router now has a new RID! So I guess I'll just go ahead and reboot all my routers to get their RIDs reset to our logical addresses.

Or not—there is *one* other way. What would you say about adding a new RID for the router right under the `router ospf process-id` command instead? I'd say let's give it a shot! Here's an example of doing that on the R3 router:

```
R3#sh ip ospf
 Routing Process "ospf 1" with ID 10.1.12.1
R3#config t
R3(config)#router ospf 1
R3(config-router)#router-id 172.31.1.4
R3(config-router)#Reload or use "clear ip ospf process" command, for
this to take effect
R3(config-router)#do clear ip ospf process
Reset ALL OSPF processes? [no]: yes

20:16:35: %OSPF-5-ADJCHG: Process 1, Nbr 10.1.5.1 on FastEthernet0/0
from FULL to DOWN, Neighbor Down: Adjacency forced to reset

20:16:35: %OSPF-5-ADJCHG: Process 1, Nbr 10.1.5.1 on FastEthernet0/0
from FULL to DOWN, Neighbor Down: Interface down or detached
R3(config-router)#do sh ip ospf
 Routing Process "ospf 1" with ID 172.31.1.4
```

Take a look at that—it worked! We changed the RID without reloading the router! But wait—remember, we set a loopback (logical interface) earlier. So does the loopback interface win over the `router-id` command? Well, we can see our answer. A logical (loopback) interface will *not* override the `router-id` command, and we don't have to reboot the router to make it take effect as the RID.

So it goes in this order:

1. Highest active interface by default.
2. Highest logical interface overrides a physical interface.
3. The `router-id` overrides the interface and loopback interface.

The only thing left now is to decide whether you want to advertise the loopback interfaces under OSPF. There are pros and cons to using an address that won't be advertised versus using an address that will be. Using an unadvertised address saves on real IP address space, but the address won't appear in the OSPF table, which means you can't ping it.

So basically, what you're faced with here is a choice that equals a trade-off between the ease of debugging the network and conservation of address space—what to do? A really tight strategy is to use a private IP address scheme as I did. Do this, and all will be well!

OSPF Interface Priorities

Another way to configure DRs and BDRs in OSPF is to "fix" elections instead of using loopback interfaces. We can do this by configuring interfaces on our router to gain a better priority over another router when elections occur. In other words, we can use priorities instead of logical addresses to force a certain router to become the DR or BDR in a network.

Let's use Figure 9.6 as an example. Looking at Figure 9.6, what options would you use to ensure that the R2 router will be elected the designated router (DR) for the LAN (broadcast multi-access) segment? The first thing you'd need to do is determine what the RID is of each router and which router is the default DR for the 172.16.1.0 LAN.

At this point, we can see that R3 will be the DR by default because it has the highest RID of 192.168.11.254. That gives us three options to ensure that R2 will be elected the DR for the LAN segment 172.16.1.0/24:

- Configure the priority value of the Fa0/0 interface of the R2 router to a higher value than any other interface on the Ethernet network.
- Configure a loopback interface on the R2 with an IP address higher than any IP address on the other routers.
- Change the priority value of the Fa0/0 interface of R1 and R3 to zero.

If we set a priority of zero (0) on the R1 and R3 routers, they wouldn't be allowed to participate in the election process. But that may not be the best way to go—we might just be better off choosing options one and two.

Since you already know how to configure a loopback (logical) interface, here's how to set a priority on the Fa0/0 interface on the R2 router:

```
R2#config t
R2(config)#int f0/0
```

```
R2(config-if)#ip ospf priority ?
  <0-255>  Priority
R2(config-if)#ip ospf priority 2
```

FIGURE 9.6 Ensuring your designated router

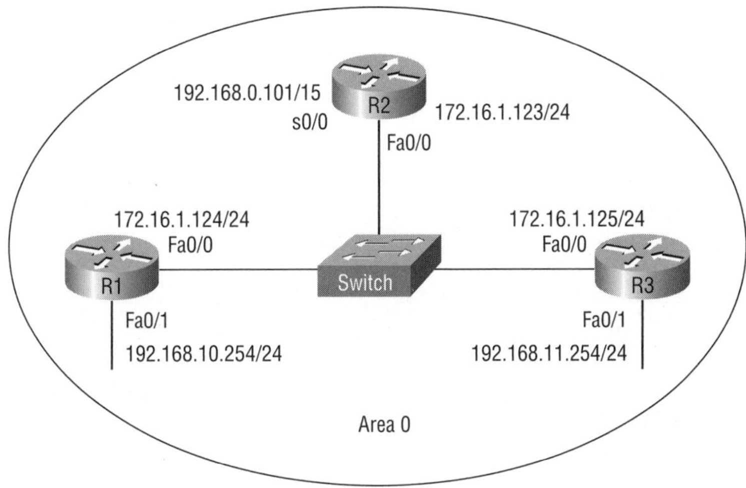

What options can you configure that will ensure that R2 will be the DR of the LAN segment?

That's it! All router interfaces default to a priority of 1, so by setting this interface to 2, I've ensured that it will automatically become the DR of the LAN segment. Setting an interface to 255 means that no one can beat your router!

Hold on though. Even if you change the priority of the interface, the router will not become the DR of the LAN segment until both the existing DR and the BDR are shut down. Once an election occurs, that's all she wrote, and the election won't happen again until the DR and BDR are reloaded and/or shut down. Just having a router with a better RID come up on your network doesn't mean your DR or BDR will change!

You can see your priority with the `show ip ospf interface` command:

```
R2(config-if)#do show ip ospf int f0/0
FastEthernet0/0 is up, line protocol is up
  Internet Address 10.1.13.1/24, Area 0
  Process ID 132, Router ID 172.16.30.1, Network Type BROADCAST,Cost:1
  Transmit Delay is 1 sec, State UP, Priority 2
```

Remember, you can see the elections occur on a broadcast or non-broadcast multi-access network with the `debug ip ospf adj` command.

Troubleshooting OSPF

This section will have you verify sample OSPF configurations and configuration outputs in order to troubleshoot, maintain, and fix OSPF-related issues.

If you see a configuration as shown here, you must know that there is no way a router will accept this input because the wildcard is incorrect:

```
Router(config)#router ospf 1
Router(config-router)#network 10.0.0.0 255.0.0.0 area 0
```

This would be the correct statement:

```
Router(config)#router ospf 1
Router(config-router)#network 10.0.0.0 0.255.255.255 area 0
```

Next, let's take a look at a figure and see if we can determine which of the routers will become the designated router of the area. Figure 9.7 shows a network with six routers connected by two switches and a WAN link.

FIGURE 9.7 Designated router example

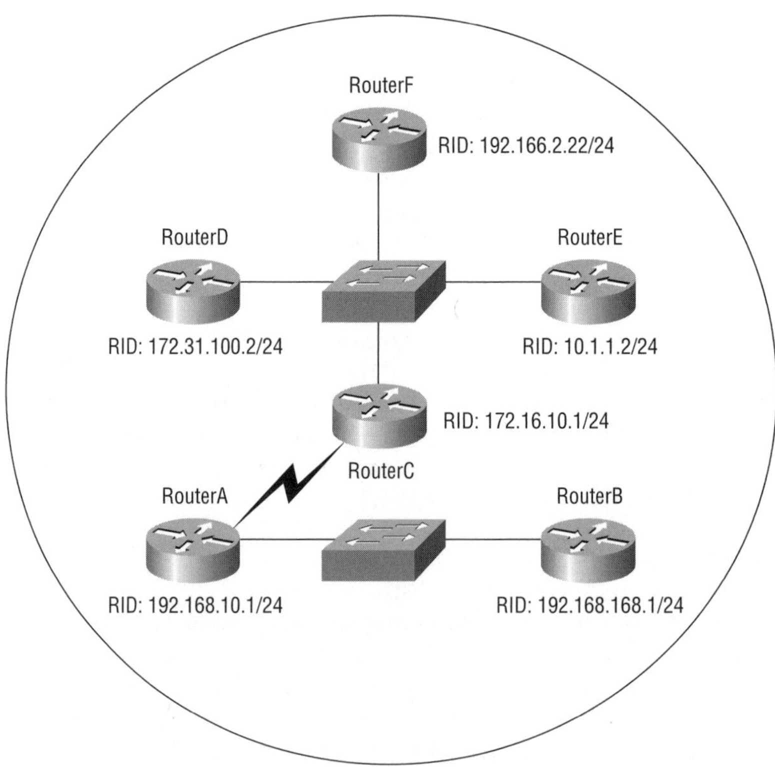

Looking at Figure 9.7, which routers are likely to be elected as a designated router (DR)? All the router OSPF priorities are at the default.

Notice the RIDs of each router. The routers with the highest RIDs are routers A and B, since they have the highest IP addresses. RouterB should be the DR and RouterA should be the BDR. Okay, now here's the thing: Since elections do not occur on point-to-point links by default, the top LAN would have its own election. But since you're reading this because you're studying for the CCNA exam objectives, RouterB is the best answer.

Let's use another command to verify an OSPF configuration: the `show ip ospf interface` command. Look at the following output for routers A and B and see if you can determine why the two directly connected routers cannot establish an adjacency:

```
RouterA#sh ip ospf interface e0/0
Ethernet0/0 is up, line protocol is up
  Internet Address 172.16.1.2/16, Area 0
  Process ID 2, Router ID 172.126.1.1, Network Type BROADCAST, Cost: 10
  Transmit Delay is 1 sec, State DR, Priority 1
  Designated Router (ID) 172.16.1.2, interface address 172.16.1.1
  No backup designated router on this network
  Timer intervals configured, Hello 5, Dead 20, Wait 20, Retransmit 5

RouterB#sh ip ospf interface e0/0
Ethernet0/0 is up, line protocol is up
  Internet Address 172.16.1.1/16, Area 0
  Process ID 2, Router ID 172.126.1.2, Network Type BROADCAST, Cost: 10
  Transmit Delay is 1 sec, State DR, Priority 1
  Designated Router (ID) 172.16.1.1, interface address 172.16.1.2
  No backup designated router on this network
  Timer intervals configured, Hello 10, Dead 40, Wait 40, Retransmit 5
```

Everything in the two outputs looks pretty good, except that the Hello and Dead timers are not the same. RouterA has Hello and Dead timers of 5 and 20, and RouterB has Hello and Dead timers of 10 and 40, which are the default timers for OSPF. If two directly connected routers do not have the timers set the same, they will not form an adjacency. Notice also that the `show ip ospf interface` command will show you who the designated and backup designated routers (DR/BDR) are for your area.

Take a look at the network shown in Figure 9.8 with four routers and two different routing protocols.

If all parameters are set to default and redistribution is not configured, which path do you think RouterA will use to reach RouterD? Since Cisco's old and defunct IGRP routing protocol has an AD of 100 and OSPF has an AD of 110, RouterA will send packets to RouterD through RouterC.

Study Figure 9.9 carefully. You are running OSPF on the routers as shown and an ISDN link provides connectivity to the Remote Office LAN.

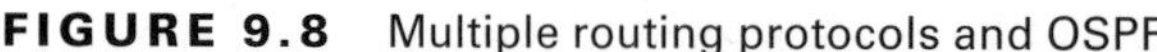

FIGURE 9.8 Multiple routing protocols and OSPF

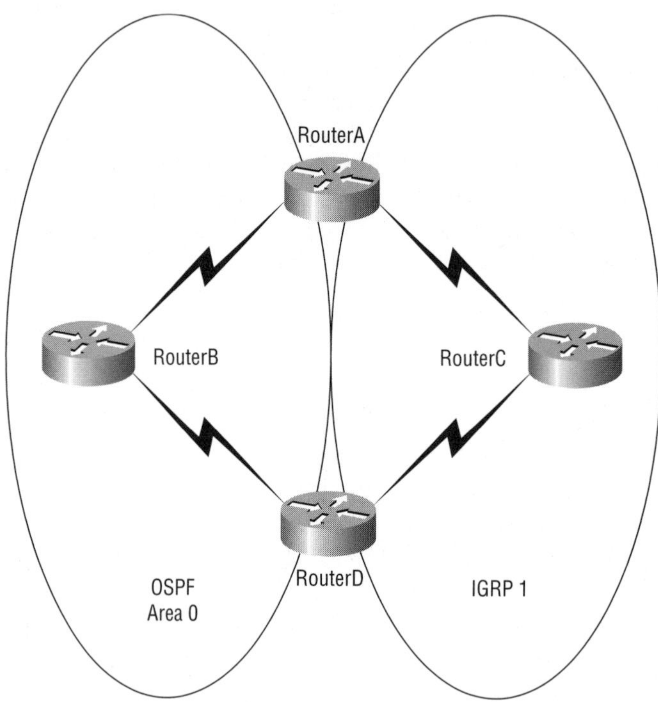

FIGURE 9.9 OSPF and ISDN connectivity

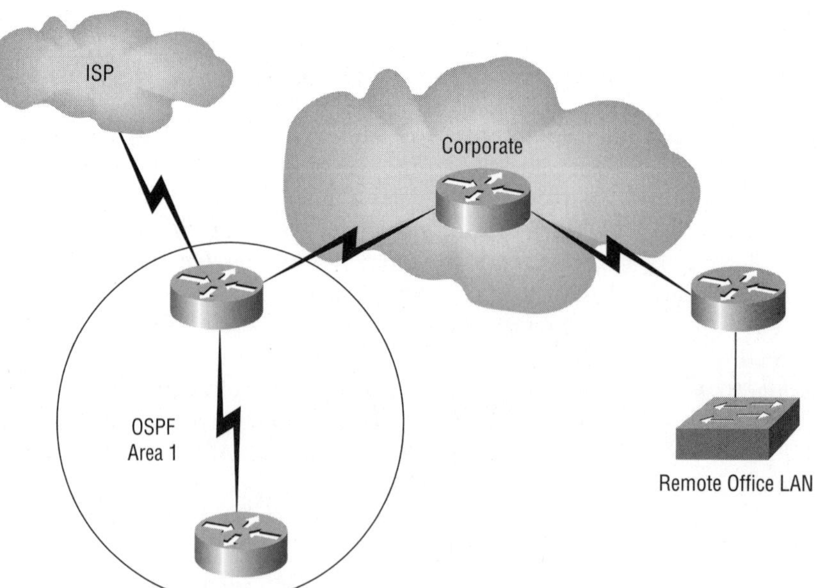

What type of route should be configured on the Corporate router to connect to the sales office's remote network while minimizing network overhead on the ISDN link as shown in Figure 9.9?

The best solution to this problem is to dump the ISDN link and connect a broadband link from the remote office to the Internet and then create a VPN from the Corporate office to the remote office through the Internet. Yeah, well, wouldn't that be nice? Anyway, the question asks how we can make this work with the ISDN link and minimize network overhead. The only way we can do that is to create a static route on the Corporate router to connect to the remote network; anything else would be too bandwidth intensive.

Configuring EIGRP and OSPF Summary Routes

This section will provide you with the commands to summarize both EIGRP and OSPF. Although OSPF can be summarized a few different ways, I'll provide the most common OSPF summary command, which summarizes multiple-area OSPF networks into area 0.

You learned in Chapter 5 how to determine summary routes for a network. This section will have you apply the summary routes to a router's configuration.

Figure 9.10 shows a contiguous network design—yes, contiguous networks do not happen by accident; they have to be planned! Figure 9.10 shows six networks with four block sizes of 4 (WAN links) and two block sizes of 8 (LAN connections). This network design fits nicely into a block size of 32. The network address used is 192.168.10.64, and with a block size of 32, the mask would be 255.255.255.224—because as you know, 224 provides a block size of 32.

FIGURE 9.10 Contiguous network design

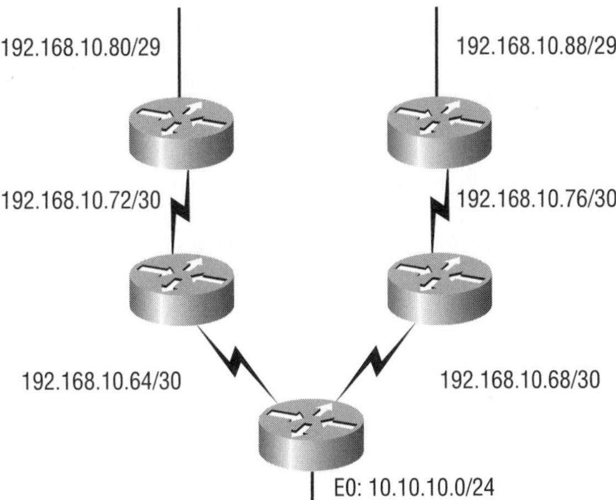

On the core (backbone connection) router, for EIGRP we'll place the summary route on Ethernet0, which will advertise our summary route out to the backbone network (10.10.10.0 network). This will stop all six of our networks from being advertised individually and instead advertise them as one route to the other routers in the internetwork. However, it is imperative that no other router outside our contiguous network have a subnet in this advertised block behind it, which would allow it to advertise conflicting routes.

Here is the complete configuration of EIGRP on the core router:

```
Core#config t
Core(config)#router eigrp 10
Core(config-router)#network 192.168.10.0
Core(config-router)#network 10.0.0.0
Core(config-router)#no auto-summary
Core(config-router)#interface ethernet 0
Core(config-if)#ip summary-address eigrp 10 192.168.10.64 255.255.255.224
```

The preceding EIGRP configuration for autonomous system 10 advertises directly connected networks 192.168.10.0/24 and 10.10.10.0/24. Since EIGRP auto-summarizes at classful boundaries, you must use the `no auto-summary` command as well. The summary route we will advertise to the backbone network is placed on the interface connected to the backbone, not under the routing process. This summary route tells EIGRP to find all networks in the 192.168.10.64 network with a block size of 32 and advertise them as one route out interface E0. This means, basically, that any packet with a destination IP address of 192.168.10.64 through 192.168.10.95 will be forwarded via this summary route.

To summarize the contiguous network with OSPF we used with the EIGRP example, we need to configure OSPF into multiple areas, as shown in Figure 9.11.

FIGURE 9.11 OSPF multiple area design

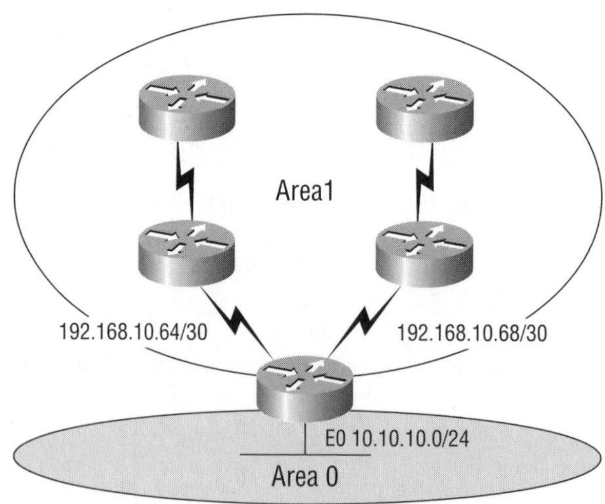

To summarize area 1 into the area 0 backbone, use the following command under the OSPF Process ID. Here is the complete OSPF configuration for the Core (backbone) router:

```
Core#config t
Core(config)#router ospf 1
Core(config-router)#network 192.168.10.64 0.0.0.3 area 1
Core(config-router)#network 192.168.10.68 0.0.0.3 area 1
Core(config-router)#network 10.10.10.0 0.0.0.255 area 0
Core(config-router)#area 1 range 192.168.10.64 255.255.255.224
```

The `no auto-summary` command is not needed since OSPF does not summarize at any boundary by default. The preceding OSPF configuration will summarize all the networks from area 1 to the backbone area as one entry of 192.168.10.64/27.

Summary

I know—this chapter has been, you could say, a touch on the extensive side. But it's really important! EIGRP, the main focus of the chapter, is a hybrid of link-state routing and distance-vector protocols. It allows for unequal-cost load balancing, controlled routing updates, and formal neighbor adjacencies.

EIGRP uses the capabilities of the Reliable Transport Protocol (RTP) to communicate between neighbors and utilizes the Diffusing Update Algorithm (DUAL) to compute the best path to each remote network.

EIGRP also supports large networks through features such as support for VLSM, discontiguous networks, and summarization. The ability to configure EIGRP behavior over NBMA networks also makes it a really hot protocol for large networks.

I also went over the configuration of EIGRP and explored a number of troubleshooting commands.

This chapter also provided you with a great deal of information about OSPF. It's really difficult to include everything about OSPF because so much of it falls outside the scope of this chapter and book, but I've given you a few tips here and there, so you're good to go—as long as you make sure you've got what I presented to you dialed in, that is!

I talked about a lot of OSPF topics, including terminology, operations, and configuration as well as verification and monitoring.

Each of these topics encompasses quite a bit of information—the terminology section just scratched the surface of OSPF. But you've got the goods for your studies—things like configuring single-area OSPF, VLSM implementation, and summarizing contiguous boundaries. Finally, I gave you a tight survey of commands useful in observing the operation of OSPF so you can verify that things are moving along as they should. So eat it all up, and you're set!

Exam Essentials

Know EIGRP features. EIGRP is a classless, advanced distance-vector protocol that supports IP, IPX, AppleTalk, and now IPv6. EIGRP uses a unique algorithm, called DUAL, to maintain route information and uses RTP to communicate with other EIGRP routers reliably.

Know how to configure EIGRP. Be able to configure basic EIGRP. This is configured the same as RIP with classful addresses.

Know how to verify EIGRP operation. Know all of the EIGRP `show` commands and be familiar with their output and the interpretation of the main components of their output.

Compare OSPF and RIPv1. OSPF is a link-state protocol that supports VLSM and classless routing; RIPv1 is a distance-vector protocol that does not support VLSM and supports only classful routing.

Know how OSPF routers become neighbors and/or adjacent. OSPF routers become neighbors when each router sees the other's Hello packets.

Be able to configure single-area OSPF. A minimal single-area configuration involves only two commands: `router ospf` *`process-id`* and `network` *`x.x.x.x y.y.y.y area Z`*.

Be able to verify the operation of OSPF. There are many `show` commands that provide useful details on OSPF, and it is useful to be completely familiar with the output of each: `show ip ospf`, `show ip ospf database`, `show ip ospf interface`, `show ip ospf neighbor`, and `show ip protocols`.

Written Lab 9

1. What four routed protocols are supported by EIGRP?
2. When is redistribution required for EIGRP?
3. What command would be used to enable EIGRP with an autonomous system number of 300?
4. What command will tell EIGRP that it is connected to network 172.10.0.0?
5. What type of EIGRP interface will neither send nor receive Hello packets?
6. Write the command that will enable OSPF process 101 on a router.
7. Write the command that will display details of all OSPF routing processes enabled on a router.
8. Write the command that will display interface-specific OSPF information.

9. Write the command that will display all OSPF neighbors.
10. Write the command that will display all different OSPF route types that are currently known by the router.

(The answers to Written Lab 9 can be found following the answers to the review questions for this chapter.)

Hands-on Labs

In this section, you will use the following network and add EIGRP and OSPF routing.

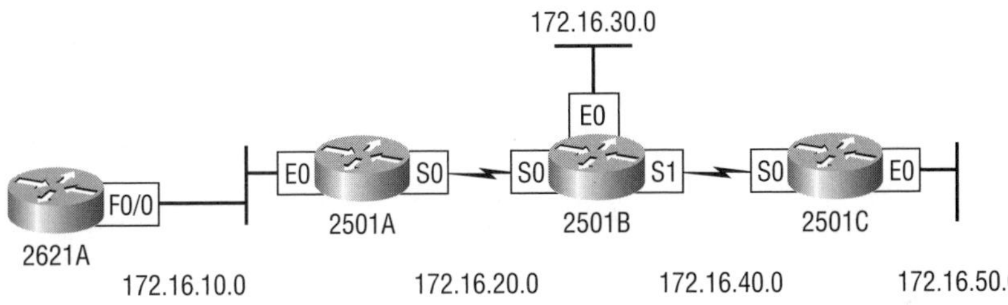

The first lab (Lab 9.1) requires you to configure four routers for EIGRP and then view the configuration. In the last four labs, you will be asked to enable OSPF routing on the same network. Note that the labs in this chapter were written to be used with real equipment—real cheap equipment that is. I wrote these labs with the cheapest, oldest routers I had lying around so you can see that you don't need expensive gear to get through some of the hardest labs in this book.

You must remove EIGRP before starting Labs 9.2 through 9.4 because this routing protocol has a lower administrative distance than OSPF.

The labs in this chapter are as follows:

Lab 9.1: Configuring and Verifying EIGRP

Lab 9.2: Enabling the OSPF Process

Lab 9.3 Configuring OSPF Interfaces

Lab 9.4: Verifying OSPF Operation

Lab 9.5: OSPF DR and BDR Elections

Table 9.5 shows our IP addresses for each router (each interface uses a /24 mask).

TABLE 9.5 Our IP addresses

Router	Interface	IP address
2621A	F0/0	172.16.10.1
2501A	E0	172.16.10.2
2501A	S0	172.16.20.1
2501B	E0	172.16.30.1
2501B	S0	172.16.20.2
2501B	S1	172.16.40.1
2501C	S0	172.16.40.2
2501C	E0	172.16.50.1

Hands-on Lab 9.1: Configuring and Verifying EIGRP

1. Implement EIGRP on 2621A:

```
2621A#conf t
Enter configuration commands, one per line.
  End with CNTL/Z.
2621A(config)#router eigrp 100
2621A(config-router)#network 172.16.0.0
2621A(config-router)#^Z
2621A#
```

2. Implement EIGRP on 2501A:

```
2501A#conf t
Enter configuration commands, one per line.
  End with CNTL/Z.
2501A(config)#router eigrp 100
2501A(config-router)#network 172.16.0.0
2501A(config-router)#exit
2501A#
```

3. Implement EIGRP on 2501B:

```
2501B#conf t
Enter configuration commands, one per line.
  End with CNTL/Z.
2501B(config)#router eigrp 100
2501B(config-router)#network 172.16.0.0
2501B(config-router)#^Z
2501B#
```

4. Implement EIGRP on 2501C:

```
2501C#conf t
Enter configuration commands, one per line.
  End with CNTL/Z.
2501C(config)#router eigrp 100
2501C(config-router)#network 172.16.0.0
2501C(config-router)#^Z
2501C#
```

5. Display the topology table for 2501B:

```
2501B#show ip eigrp topology
```

6. Display the routing table on the 2501B router:

```
2501B#show ip route
```

7. Display the neighbor table on the 2501B router:

```
2501B#show ip eigrp neighbor
```

Hands-on Lab 9.2: Enabling the OSPF Process

1. Enable OSPF process 100 on 2621A:

```
2621A#conf t
Enter configuration commands, one per line.
  End with CNTL/Z.
2621A(config)#router ospf 100
2621A(config-router)#^Z
```

2. Enable OSPF process 101 on 2501A:

```
2501A#conf t
Enter configuration commands, one per line.
  End with CNTL/Z.
2501A(config)#router ospf 101
2501A(config-router)#^Z
```

3. Enable OSPF process 102 on 2501B:

```
2501B#conf t
Enter configuration commands, one per line.
  End with CNTL/Z.
2501B(config)#router ospf 102
2501B(config-router)#^Z
```

4. Enable OSPF process 103 on 2501C:

```
2501C#conf t
Enter configuration commands, one per line.
  End with CNTL/Z.
Router(config)#router ospf 103
2501C(config-router)#^Z
```

Hands-on Lab 9.3: Configuring OSPF Interfaces

1. Configure the network between 2621A and 2501A. Assign it to area 0:

```
2621A#conf t
Enter configuration commands, one per line.
  End with CNTL/Z.
2621A(config)#router ospf 100
2621A(config-router)#network 172.16.10.1 0.0.0.0 area 0
2621A(config-router)#^Z
2621A#
```

2. Configure the networks on the 2501A router. Assign them to area 0:

```
2501A#conf t
Enter configuration commands, one per line.
  End with CNTL/Z.
2501A(config)#router ospf 101
2501A(config-router)#network 172.16.10.2 0.0.0.0 area 0
2501A(config-router)#network 172.16.20.1 0.0.0.0
  area 0
2501A(config-router)#^Z
2501A#
```

3. Configure the networks on the 2501B router. Assign them to area 0:

```
2501B#conf t
Enter configuration commands, one per line.
  End with CNTL/Z.
2501B(config)#router ospf 102
2501B(config-router)#network 172.16.20.2 0.0.0.0 area 0
2501B(config-router)#network 172.16.30.1 0.0.0.0 area 0
2501B(config-router)#network 172.16.40.1 0.0.0.0 area 0
2501B(config-router)#^Z
2501B#
```

4. Configure the networks on the 2501C router. Assign them to area 0:

```
2501C#conf t
Enter configuration commands, one per line.
  End with CNTL/Z.
2501C(config)#router ospf 103
2501C(config-router)#network 172.16.40.2 0.0.0.0 area 0
2501C(config-router)#network 172.16.50.1 0.0.0.0 area 0
2501C(config-router)#^Z
2501C#
```

Hands-on Lab 9.4: Verifying OSPF Operation

1. Execute a `show ip ospf neighbors` command from the 2621 router and view the results:

```
2621A#sho ip ospf neig
```

2. Execute a `show ip route` command to verify that all other routers are learning all routes:

```
2621A#sho ip route
```

If EIGRP is still enabled on the routers, you will not see any OSPF routes.

Hands-on Lab 9.5: OSPF DR and BDR Elections

In this lab, you'll watch the DR and BDR elections on your test network by forcing and verifying the election process. You're going to start by using the following diagram to build your network. The more routers you have, the better, but you need at least three routers connected via a LAN segment to complete this lab.

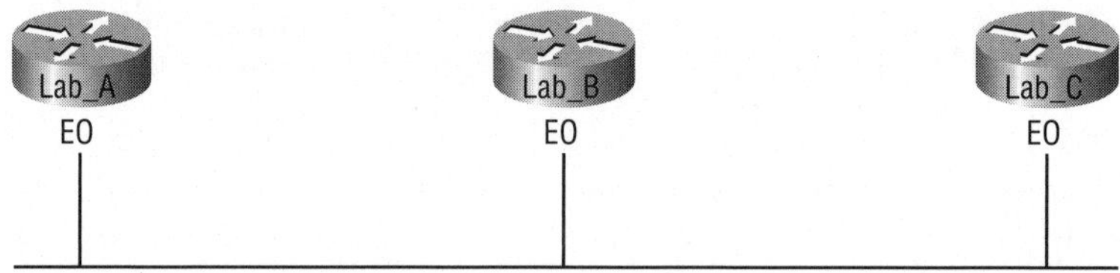

In this lab, I am using cheap 2500 series routers, but you can use any type of router with any type of LAN interface. Or you can use the Cisco Packet Tracer simulator program if you have it.

1. First, connect the network together as shown in the diagram. Create an IP scheme for the network—something simple like 10.1.1.1/24, 10.1.1.2/24, and 10.1.1.3/24 will work great.
2. Now configure OSPF, and place all routers into area 0. Only the Ethernet LAN interface needs to be configured in this lab because, as you know, elections don't take place on serial connections.
3. Next, type **`show ip ospf interface e0`** on each router to verify Area ID, DR, BDR information and the Hello and Dead timers of the interface connected to the LAN network.
4. By looking at the `show ip ospf interface e0` output, determine which router is the DR and which router is the BDR.
5. Now verify the network type of your router. Because the connection is on an Ethernet LAN, the network type is BROADCAST. If you were viewing a serial connection, you'd see a point-to-point network.
6. Here you have to set the priority for the router. The priority of all routers, by default, is 1. If you were to change the priority to 0, the router would never participate in the election process for the LAN. (Remember that elections do not occur on serial point-to-point links.)

7. Now you need to decide which router will be the new DR.
8. Next, enable the debugging process that allows you to see the DR and BDR election take place. Type **debug ip ospf adj** on all your routers.

Try to open more than one console connection by telnetting into the other routers. Remember to use the `terminal monitor` command on the Telnet session or you won't see any debugging output.

9. Here, set the priority of the new DR Ethernet 0 interface to 3 by typing **ip ospf priority 3**.
10. Next, shut down the Ethernet interface of the DR router and bring it back up with the `no shutdown` command. Obviously, if you're telnetted into that router, you'll lose your session at this point.
11. Here's where the election should take place and the router you picked to be the DR should now actually be the BDR. For the router to be the DR, you need to shut down the DR and BDR.
12. Finally, type **show ip ospf interface e0** to verify the DR and BDR information on each router. You can also type **show ip ospf neighbor** to see this information.

The priority of a router's interface can be set all the way up to 255, which means it will always be the DR of the area. You can then set a router in your test network with a higher priority and see that the priority takes precedence over a high RID on a router, even if you are using a loopback (logical) interface.

Review Questions

The following questions are designed to test your understanding of this chapter's material. For more information on how to get additional questions, please see this book's Introduction.

1. There are three possible routes for a router to reach a destination network. The first route is from OSPF with a metric of 782. The second route is from RIPv2 with a metric of 4. The third is from EIGRP with a composite metric of 20514560. Which route will be installed by the router in its routing table?
   A. RIPv2
   B. EIGRP
   C. OSPF
   D. All three

2. Which EIGRP information is held in RAM and maintained through the use of Hello and update packets? (Choose two.)
   A. Neighbor table
   B. STP table
   C. Topology table
   D. DUAL table

3. Which of the following describe the process identifier that is used to run OSPF on a router? (Choose two.)
   A. It is locally significant.
   B. It is globally significant.
   C. It is needed to identify a unique instance of an OSPF database.
   D. It is an optional parameter required only if multiple OSPF processes are running on the router.
   E. All routes in the same OSPF area must have the same Process ID if they are to exchange routing information.

4. Where are EIGRP successor routes stored?
   A. In the routing table only
   B. In the neighbor table only
   C. In the topology table only
   D. In the routing table and neighbor table
   E. In the routing table and the topology table
   F. In the topology table and the neighbor table

5. Which command will display all the EIGRP feasible successor routes known to a router?
   A. `show ip routes *`
   B. `show ip eigrp summary`
   C. `show ip eigrp topology`
   D. `show ip eigrp adjacencies`
   E. `show ip eigrp neighbors detail`

6. You get a call from a network administrator who tells you that he typed the following into his router:

```
Router(config)#router ospf 1
Router(config-router)#network 10.0.0.0 255.0.0.0 area 0
```

   He tells you he still can't see any routes in the routing table. What configuration error did the administrator make?
   A. The wildcard mask is incorrect.
   B. The OSPF area is wrong.
   C. The OSPF Process ID is incorrect.
   D. The AS configuration is wrong.

7. Which of the following protocols support VLSM, summarization, and discontiguous networking? (Choose three.)
   A. RIPv1
   B. IGRP
   C. EIGRP
   D. OSPF
   E. RIPv2

8. Which of the following are true regarding OSPF areas? (Choose three.)
   A. You must have separate loopback interfaces configured in each area.
   B. The numbers you can assign an area go up to 65,535.
   C. The backbone area is also called area 0.
   D. If your design is hierarchical, then you don't need multiple areas.
   E. All areas must connect to area 0.
   F. If you have only one area, it must be called area 1.

9. Which of the following network types have a designated router and a backup designated router assigned? (Choose two.)

   A. Broadcast

   B. Point-to-point

   C. NBMA

   D. NBMA point-to-point

   E. NBMA point-to-multipoint

10. A network administrator needs to configure a router with a distance-vector protocol that allows classless routing. Which of the following satisfies those requirements?

   A. IGRP

   B. OSPF

   C. RIPv1

   D. EIGRP

   E. IS-IS

11. You need the IP address of the devices with which the router has established an adjacency. Also, the retransmit interval and the queue counts for the adjacent routers need to be checked. What command will display the required information?

   A. `show ip eigrp adjacency`

   B. `show ip eigrp topology`

   C. `show ip eigrp interfaces`

   D. `show ip eigrp neighbors`

12. For some reason, you cannot establish an adjacency relationship on a common Ethernet link between two routers. Looking at the output below, what is the cause of the problem?

```
RouterA#
Ethernet0/0 is up, line protocol is up
  Internet Address 172.16.1.2/16, Area 0
  Process ID 2, Router ID 172.126.1.2, Network Type BROADCAST, Cost: 10
  Transmit Delay is 1 sec, State DR, Priority 1
  Designated Router (ID) 172.16.1.2, interface address 172.16.1.1
  No backup designated router on this network
  Timer intervals configured, Hello 5, Dead 20, Wait 20, Retransmit 5

RouterB#
```

```
Ethernet0/0 is up, line protocol is up
  Internet Address 172.16.1.1/16, Area 0
  Process ID 2, Router ID 172.126.1.1, Network Type BROADCAST, Cost: 10
  Transmit Delay is 1 sec, State DR, Priority 1
  Designated Router (ID) 172.16.1.1, interface address 172.16.1.2
  No backup designated router on this network
  Timer intervals configured, Hello 10, Dead 40, Wait 40, Retransmit 5
```

A. The OSPF area is not configured properly.

B. The priority on RouterA should be set higher.

C. The cost on RouterA should be set higher.

D. The Hello and Dead timers are not configured properly.

E. A backup designated router needs to be added to the network.

F. The OSPF Process ID numbers must match.

13. Which is true regarding EIGRP successor routes? (Choose two.)

A. A successor route is used by EIGRP to forward traffic to a destination.

B. Successor routes are saved in the topology table to be used if the primary route fails.

C. Successor routes are flagged as "active" in the routing table.

D. A successor route may be backed up by a feasible successor route.

E. Successor routes are stored in the neighbor table following the discovery process.

14. Which type of OSPF network will elect a backup designated router? (Choose two.)

A. Broadcast multi-access

B. Non-broadcast multi-access

C. Point-to-point

D. Broadcast multipoint

15. Which two of the following commands will place network 10.2.3.0/24 into area 0? (Choose two.)

A. `router eigrp 10`

B. `router ospf 10`

C. `router rip`

D. `network 10.0.0.0`

E. `network 10.2.3.0 255.255.255.0 area 0`

F. `network 10.2.3.0 0.0.0.255 area0`

G. `network 10.2.3.0 0.0.0.255 area 0`

16. With which network type will OSPF establish router adjacencies but not perform the DR/BDR election process?

A. Point-to-point

B. Backbone area 0

C. Broadcast multi-access

D. Non-broadcast multi-access

17. What are three reasons for creating OSPF in a hierarchical design? (Choose three.)

A. To decrease routing overhead

B. To speed up convergence

C. To confine network instability to single areas of the network

D. To make configuring OSPF easier

18. What is the administrative distance of OSPF?

A. 90

B. 100

C. 110

D. 120

19. You have an internetwork as shown in the following illustration. However, the two networks are not sharing routing table route entries. Which command is needed to fix the problem?

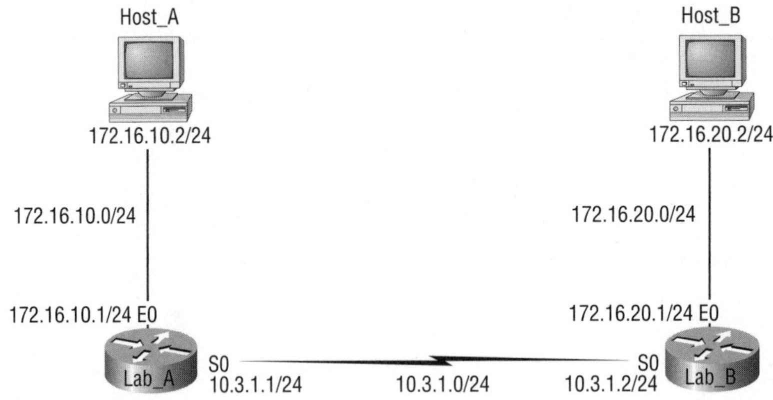

A. `version 2`

B. `no auto-summary`

C. `redistribute eigrp 10`

D. `default-information originate`

20. If routers in a single area are configured with the same priority value, what value does a router use for the OSPF Router ID in the absence of a loopback interface?

   A. The lowest IP address of any physical interface

   B. The highest IP address of any physical interface

   C. The lowest IP address of any logical interface

   D. The highest IP address of any logical interface

Answers to Review Questions

1. B. Only the EIGRP routes will be placed in the routing table because it has the lowest administrative distance (AD), and that is always used before metrics.

2. A, C. EIGRP maintains three tables in RAM: neighbor, topology, and routing. The neighbor and topology tables are built and maintained with the use of Hello and update packets.

3. A, C. The Process ID for OSPF on a router is only locally significant and you can use the same number on each router, or each router can have a different number—it just doesn't matter. The numbers you can use are from 1 to 65,535. Don't get this confused with area numbers, which can be from 0 to 4.2 billion.

4. E. Successor routes are going to be in the routing table since they are the best path to a remote network. However, the topology table has a link to each and every network, so the best answer is topology table and routing table. Any secondary route to a remote network is considered a feasible successor, and those routes are found only in the topology table and used as backup routes in case of primary route failure.

5. C. Any secondary route to a remote network is considered a feasible successor, and those routes are found only in the topology table and used as backup routes in case of primary route failure. You can see the topology table with the `show ip eigrp topology` command.

6. A. The administrator typed in the wrong wildcard mask configuration. The wildcard should have been 0.0.0.255 or even 0.255.255.255.

7. C, D, E. RIPv1 and IGRP are true distance-vector routing protocols and can't do much, really—except build and maintain routing tables and use a lot of bandwidth! RIPv2, EIGRP, and OSPF build and maintain routing tables, but they also provide classless routing, which allows for VLSM, summarization, and discontiguous networking.

8. C, D, E. Loopback interfaces are created on a router, and the highest IP address on a loopback (logical) interface becomes the RID of the router but has nothing to do with areas and is optional, so option A is wrong. The numbers you can create an area with are from 0 to 4,294,967,295—option B is wrong. The backbone area is called area 0, so option C is correct. All areas must connect to area 0, so option E is correct. If you have only one area, it must be called area 0, so option F is incorrect. This leaves option D, which must be correct; it doesn't make much sense, but it is the best answer.

9. A, C. No DR is assigned on any type of point-to-point link. No DR/BDR is assigned on the NBMA point-to-multipoint due to the hub/spoke topology. DR and BDR are elected on broadcast and non-broadcast multi-access networks. Frame Relay is a non-broadcast multi-access (NBMA) network by default.

10. D. In this question, we're calling EIGRP just plain old distance vector. EIGRP is an advanced distance-vector routing protocol, sometimes called a hybrid routing protocol because it uses the characteristics of both distance-vector and link-state routing protocols.

11. D. The `show ip eigrp neighbors` command allows you to check the IP addresses as well as the retransmit interval and queue counts for the neighbors that have established an adjacency.

12. D. The Hello and Dead timers must be set the same on two routers on the same link or they will not form an adjacency (relationship). The default timers for OSPF are 10 seconds for the Hello timer and 40 seconds for the Dead timer.

13. A, D. Successor routes are the routes picked from the topology table as the best route to a remote network, so these are the routes that IP uses in the routing table to forward traffic to a remote destination. The topology table contains any route that is not as good as the successor route and is considered a feasible successor, or backup route. Remember that all routes are in the topology table, even successor routes.

14. A, B. DR and BDR are elected on broadcast and non-broadcast multi-access networks. Frame Relay is a non-broadcast multi-access (NBMA) network by default. No DR is assigned on any type of point-to-point link. No DR/BDR is assigned on the NBMA point-to-multipoint due to the hub/spoke topology.

15. B, G. To enable OSPF, you must first start OSPF using a Process ID. The number is irrelevant; just choose a number from 1 to 65,535 and you're good to go. After you start the OSPF process, you must configure interfaces on which to activate OSPF using the network command with wildcards and specification of an area. Option F is wrong because there must be a space after the parameter area and before you list the area number.

16. A. No DR is assigned on any type of point-to-point link. No DR/BDR is assigned on the NBMA point-to-multipoint due to the hub/spoke topology. DR and BDR are elected on broadcast and non-broadcast multi-access networks. Frame Relay is a non-broadcast multi-access (NBMA) network by default.

17. A, B, C. OSPF is created in a hierarchical design, not a flat design like RIP. This decreases routing overhead, speeds up convergence, and confines network instability to a single area of the network.

18. C. The administrative distance (AD) is a very important parameter in a routing protocol. The lower the AD, the more trusted the route. If you have IGRP and OSPF running, by default IGRP routes would be placed in the routing table because IGRP has a lower AD of 100. OSPF has an AD of 110. RIPv1 and RIPv2 both have an AD of 120, and EIGRP is the lowest, at 90.

19. B. The network in the diagram is considered a discontiguous network because you have one classful address subnetted and separated by another classful address. Only RIPv2, OSPF, and EIGRP can work with discontiguous networks, but RIPv2 and EIGRP won't work by default. You must use the `no auto-summary` command under the routing protocol configuration.

20. B. At the moment of OSPF process startup, the highest IP address on any active interface will be the Router ID (RID) of the router. If you have a loopback interface configured (logical interface), then that will override the interface IP address and become the RID of the router automatically.

Answers to Written Lab 9

1. The four routed protocols supported by EIGRP are IP, IPv6, IPX, and AppleTalk.
2. Redistribution is required when more than one EIGRP session or process is running and they are identified with different ASNs. Redistribution shares topology information between EIGRP sessions.
3. `router eigrp 300`
4. `network 172.10.0.0`
5. Passive interface
6. `router ospf 101`
7. `show ip ospf`
8. `show ip ospf interface`
9. `show ip ospf neighbor`
10. `show ip route ospf`

Layer 2 Switching and Spanning Tree Protocol (STP)

THE CCNA EXAM TOPICS COVERED IN THIS CHAPTER INCLUDE THE FOLLOWING:

- ✓ **Configure, verify, and troubleshoot a switch with VLANs and interswitch communications**
- ✓ **Configure, verify, and troubleshoot basic router operation and routing on Cisco devices**
  - Select the appropriate media, cables, ports, and connectors to connect switches to other network devices and hosts
  - Explain the technology and media access control method for Ethernet networks
  - Explain network segmentation and basic traffic management concepts
  - Explain basic switching concepts and the operation of Cisco switches
  - Perform and verify initial switch configuration tasks including remote access management
  - Verify network status and switch operation using basic utilities (including: ping, traceroute, telnet, SSH, arp, ipconfig), SHOW and DEBUG commands
  - Identify, prescribe, and resolve common switched network media issues, configuration issues, auto negotiation, and switch hardware failures

When folks at Cisco discuss switching for the CCENT or CCNA objectives, they're talking about layer 2 switching unless they say otherwise. Layer 2 switching is the process of using the hardware address of devices on a LAN to segment a network. Since you've got the basic ideas down, I'm now going to focus on the particulars of layer 2 switching and nail down how it works.

You know that switching breaks up large collision domains into smaller ones and that a collision domain is a network segment with two or more devices sharing the same bandwidth. A hub network is a typical example of this type of technology. But since each port on a switch is actually its own collision domain, you can make a much better Ethernet LAN network just by replacing your hubs with switches!

Switches truly have changed the way networks are designed and implemented. If a pure switched design is properly implemented, it absolutely will result in a clean, cost-effective, and resilient internetwork. In this chapter, we'll survey and compare how networks were designed before and after switching technologies were introduced.

Routing protocols (such as RIP, which you learned about in Chapter 8, "IP Routing") have processes for stopping network loops from occurring at the Network layer. However, if you have redundant physical links between your switches, routing protocols won't do a thing to stop loops from occurring at the Data Link layer. That's exactly the reason Spanning Tree Protocol (STP) was developed—to put a stop to loops in a layer 2 switched network. The essentials of this vital protocol, as well as how it works within a switched network, are also important subjects that we'll cover thoroughly in this chapter.

I'll be using three switches to start our configuration of a switched network, and we'll actually continue with their configuration in Chapter 11, "Virtual LANs (VLANs)."

For up-to-the minute updates for this chapter, please see `www.lammle.com` and/or `www.sybex.com/go/ccna7e`.

Before Layer 2 Switching

Let's go back in time a bit and take a look at the condition of networks before switches and how switches have helped segment the corporate LAN. Before LAN switching, the typical network design looked like the network in Figure 10.1.

FIGURE 10.1 Before switching

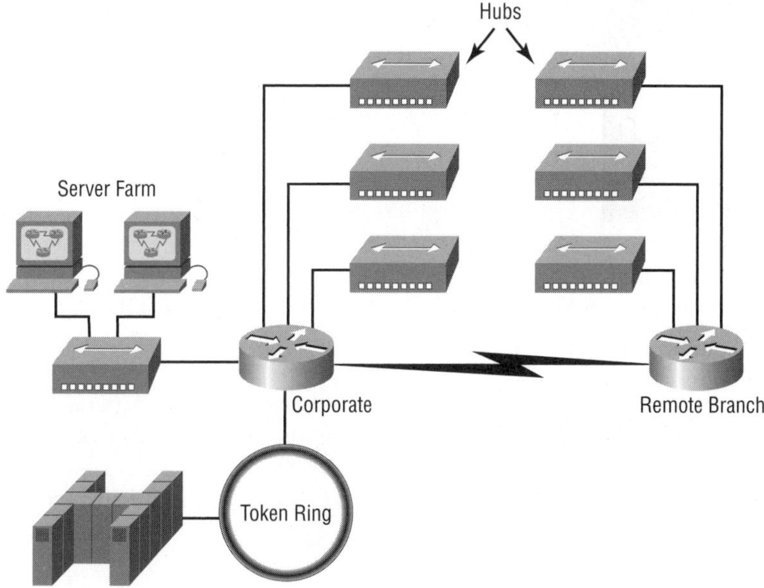

The design in Figure 10.1 was called a collapsed backbone because all hosts would need to go to the corporate backbone to reach any network services—both LAN and mainframe.

Going back even further, before networks like the one shown in Figure 10.1 had physical segmentation devices such as routers and hubs, there was the mainframe network. This network included the mainframe (IBM, Honeywell, Sperry, DEC, etc.), controllers, and dumb terminals that connected into the controllers. Any remote sites were connected to the mainframe with bridges.

And then the PC began its rise to stardom and the mainframe was connected to the Ethernet or to a Token Ring LAN where the servers were installed. These servers were usually OS/2 or LAN Manager because this was "pre-NT." Each floor of a building ran either coax or twisted-pair wiring to the corporate backbone and was then connected to a router. PCs ran an emulating software program that allowed them to connect to the mainframe services, giving those PCs the ability to access services from the mainframe and LAN simultaneously. Eventually the PC became robust enough to allow application developers to port applications more effectively than they could ever before—an advance that markedly reduced networking prices and enabled businesses to grow at a much faster rate.

When Novell became more popular in the late 1980s and early 1990s, OS/2 and LAN Manager servers were by and large replaced with NetWare servers. This made the Ethernet network even more popular because that's what Novell 3.*x* servers used to communicate with client/server software.

So that's the story about how the network in Figure 10.1 came into being. There was only one problem—the corporate backbone grew and grew, and as it grew, network services became slower. A big reason for this was that, at the same time this huge burst in growth was taking place, LAN services needed even faster service and the network was becoming totally saturated. Everyone was dumping the Macs and dumb terminals used for the mainframe service in favor of those slick new PCs so they could more easily connect to the corporate backbone and network services.

All this was taking place before the Internet's momentous popularity, so everyone in the company needed to access the corporate network's services. Why? Because without the Internet, all network services were internal—exclusive to the company network. This created a screaming need to segment that one humongous and plodding corporate network, connected with sluggish old routers. At first, Cisco just created faster routers (no doubt about that), but more segmentation was needed, especially on the Ethernet LANs. The invention of FastEthernet was a very good and helpful thing, too, but it didn't address that network segmentation need at all.

But devices called bridges did, and they were first used in the network to break up collision domains. Bridges were sorely limited by the number of ports and other network services they could provide, and that's when layer 2 switches came to the rescue. These switches saved the day by breaking up collision domains on each and every port—like a bridge—and switches could provide hundreds of ports! This early, switched LAN looked like the network pictured in Figure 10.2.

FIGURE 10.2 The first switched LAN

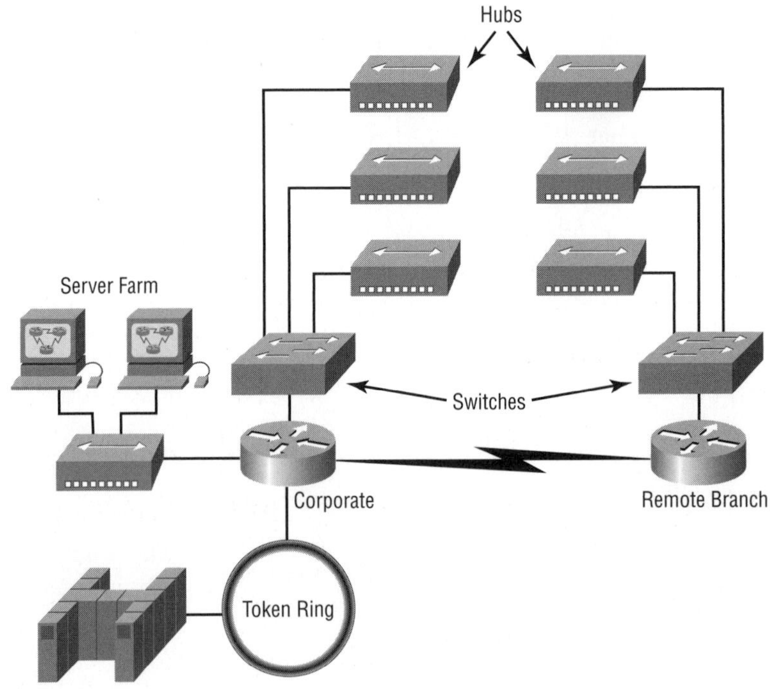

Each hub was placed into a switch port, an innovation that vastly improved the network. Now, instead of each building being crammed into the same collision domain, each hub became its own separate collision domain. But there was a catch—switch ports were still very new, hence unbelievably expensive. Because of that, simply adding a switch into each floor of the building just wasn't going to happen—at least not yet. Thanks to whomever you choose to thank for these things, the price has dropped dramatically, so now having every one of your users plugged into a switch port is both good and feasible.

So there it is—if you're going to create a network design and implement it, including switching services is a must. A typical, simple contemporary network design would look something like Figure 10.3, a complete switched network design and implementation.

FIGURE 10.3 The typical switched network design

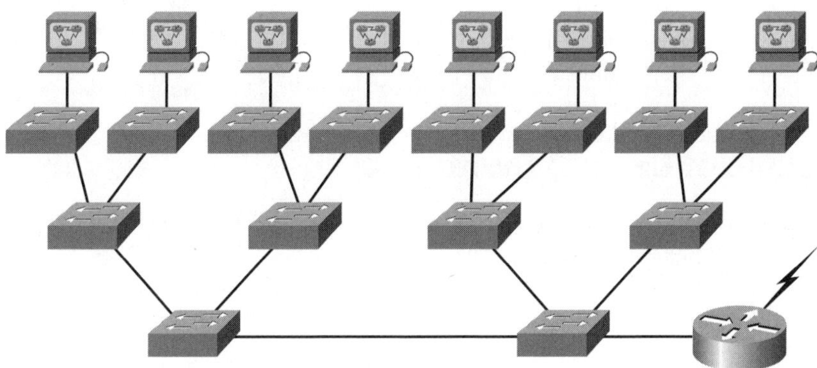

"But I still see a router in there," you say! Yes, it's not a mirage—there *is* a router in there. But its job has changed. Instead of performing just logical segmentation, it now creates and handles both logical and physical segmentation. Those logical segments are called VLANs, and I promise I'll explain them thoroughly—both in the duration of this chapter and in Chapter 11, where they'll be given a starring role.

Switching Services

Unlike bridges, which use software to create and manage a filter table, switches use application-specific integrated circuits (ASICs) to build and maintain their filter tables. But it's still okay to think of a layer 2 switch as a multiport bridge because their basic reason for being is the same: to break up collision domains.

Layer 2 switches and bridges are faster than routers because they don't take up time looking at the Network layer header information. Instead, they look at the frame's hardware addresses before deciding to either forward, flood, or drop the frame.

Switches create private, dedicated collision domains and provide independent bandwidth on each port, unlike hubs.

Layer 2 switching provides the following:

- Hardware-based bridging (ASICs)
- Wire speed
- Low latency
- Low cost

What makes layer 2 switching so efficient is that no modification to the data packet takes place. The device only reads the frame encapsulating the packet, which makes the switching process considerably faster and less error prone than routing processes are.

And if you use layer 2 switching for both workgroup connectivity and network segmentation (breaking up collision domains), you can create more network segments than you can with traditional routed networks.

Plus, layer 2 switching increases bandwidth for each user because, again, each connection (interface) into the switch is its own collision domain.

In the following sections, I will dive deeper into the layer 2 switching technology.

Limitations of Layer 2 Switching

Since we commonly stick layer 2 switching into the same category as bridged networks, we also tend to think it has the same hang-ups and issues that bridged networks do. Keep in mind that bridges are good and helpful things if we design the network correctly, keeping their features as well as their limitations in mind. And to design well with bridges, these are the two most important considerations:

- We absolutely must break up the collision domains correctly.
- The right way to create a functional bridged network is to make sure that its users spend 80 percent of their time on the local segment.

Bridged networks break up collision domains, but remember, that network is still one large broadcast domain. Neither layer 2 switches nor bridges break up broadcast domains by default—something that not only limits your network's size and growth potential, but also can reduce its overall performance.

Broadcasts and multicasts, along with the slow convergence time of legacy spanning trees, can give you some major grief as your network grows. These are the big reasons layer 2 switches cannot completely replace routers (layer 3 devices) in the internetwork.

Bridging vs. LAN Switching

It's true—layer 2 switches really are pretty much just bridges that give us a lot more ports, but there are some important differences you should always keep in mind:

- Bridges are software based, while switches are hardware based because they use ASIC chips to help make filtering decisions.
- A switch can be viewed as a multiport bridge.

- There can be only one spanning-tree instance per bridge, while switches can have many. (I'm going to tell you all about spanning trees in a bit.)
- Most switches have a higher number of ports than most bridges.
- Both bridges and switches flood layer 2 broadcasts.
- Bridges and switches learn MAC addresses by examining the source address of each frame received.
- Both bridges and switches make forwarding decisions based on layer 2 addresses.

Three Switch Functions at Layer 2

There are three distinct functions of layer 2 switching (you need to remember these!): *address learning*, *forward/filter decisions*, and *loop avoidance*.

Address learning Layer 2 switches and bridges remember the source hardware address of each frame received on an interface, and they enter this information into a MAC database called a forward/filter table.

Forward/filter decisions When a frame is received on an interface, the switch looks at the destination hardware address and finds the exit interface in the MAC database. The frame is only forwarded out an appropriate destination port.

Loop avoidance If multiple connections between switches are created for redundancy purposes, network loops can occur. Spanning Tree Protocol (STP) is used to stop network loops while still permitting redundancy.

I'm going to talk about address learning, forward/filtering decisions, and loop avoidance in detail in the next sections.

Address Learning

When a switch is first powered on, the MAC forward/filter table is empty, as shown in Figure 10.4.

When a device transmits and an interface receives a frame, the switch places the frame's source address in the MAC forward/filter table, allowing it to remember which interface the sending device is located on. The switch then has no choice but to flood the network with this frame out of every port except the source port because it has no idea where the destination device is actually located.

If a device answers this flooded frame and sends a frame back, then the switch will take the source address from that frame and place that MAC address in its database as well, associating this address with the interface that received the frame. Since the switch now has both of the relevant MAC addresses in its filtering table, the two devices can now make a point-to-point connection. The switch doesn't need to flood the frame as it did the first time because now the frames can and will be forwarded only between the two devices. This is exactly the thing that makes layer 2 switches better than hubs. In a hub network, all frames are forwarded out all ports every time—no matter what. Figure 10.5 shows the processes involved in building a MAC database.

FIGURE 10.4 Empty forward/filter table on a switch

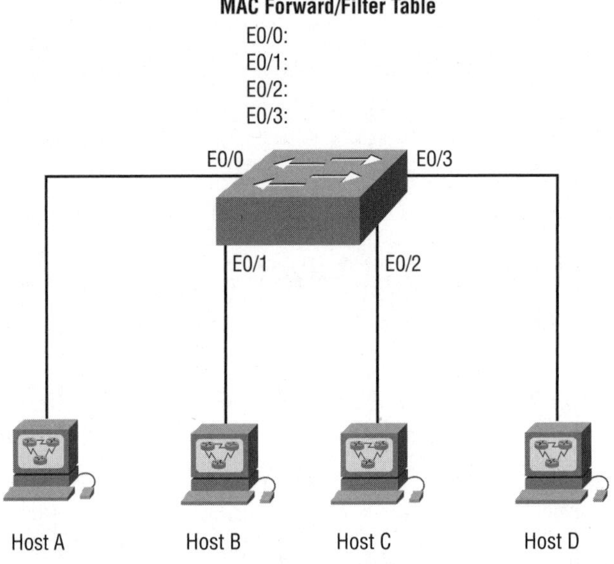

FIGURE 10.5 How switches learn hosts' locations

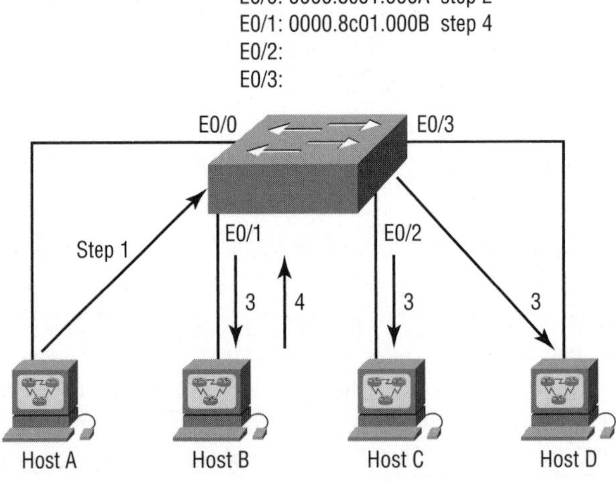

In this figure, you can see four hosts attached to a switch. When the switch is powered on, it has nothing in its MAC address forward/filter table, just as in Figure 10.4. But when the hosts start communicating, the switch places the source hardware address of each frame in the table along with the port that the frame's source address corresponds to.

Let me give you an example of how a forward/filter table is populated using Figure 10.5:

1. Host A sends a frame to Host B. Host A's MAC address is 0000.8c01.000A; Host B's MAC address is 0000.8c01.000B.
2. The switch receives the frame on the E0/0 interface and places the source address in the MAC address table.
3. Since the destination address is not in the MAC database, the frame is forwarded out all interfaces—except the source port.
4. Host B receives the frame and responds to Host A. The switch receives this frame on interface E0/1 and places the source hardware address in the MAC database.
5. Host A and Host B can now make a point-to-point connection and only the two devices will receive the frames. Hosts C and D will not see the frames, nor are their MAC addresses found in the database because they haven't yet sent a frame to the switch.

If Host A and Host B don't communicate to the switch again within a certain amount of time, the switch will flush their entries from the database to keep it as current as possible.

Forward/Filter Decisions

When a frame arrives at a switch interface, the destination hardware address is compared to the forward/filter MAC database. If the destination hardware address is known and listed in the database, the frame is only sent out the correct exit interface. The switch doesn't transmit the frame out any interface except for the destination interface. This preserves bandwidth on the other network segments and is called *frame filtering*.

But if the destination hardware address is not listed in the MAC database, then the frame is flooded out all active interfaces except the interface the frame was received on. If a device answers the flooded frame, the MAC database is updated with the device's location (interface).

If a host or server sends a broadcast on the LAN, the switch will flood the frame out all active ports except the source port by default. Remember, the switch creates smaller collision domains, but it's always still one large broadcast domain by default.

In Figure 10.6, Host A sends a data frame to Host D. What will the switch do when it receives the frame from Host A?

FIGURE 10.6 Forward/filter table

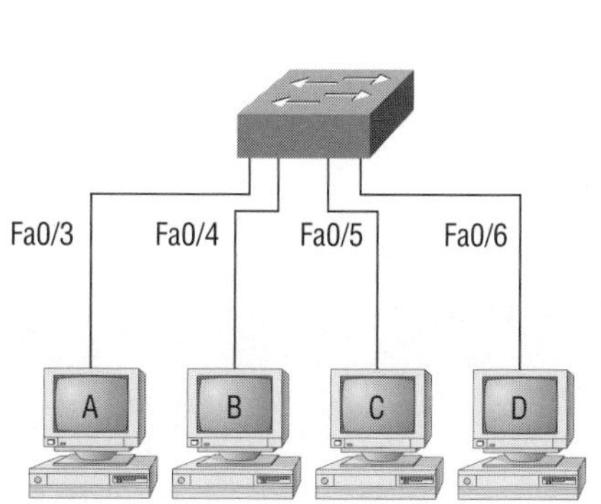


```
Switch#sh mac address-table
Vlan    Mac Address       Ports
----    -----------       -----
   1    0005.dccb.d74b    Fa0/4
   1    000a.f467.9e80    Fa0/5
   1    000a.f467.9e8b    Fa0/6
```

Since Host A's MAC address is not in the forward/filter table, the switch will add the source address and port to the MAC address table and then forward the frame to Host D. If Host D's MAC address was not in the forward/filter table, the switch would have flooded the frame out all ports except for port Fa0/3.

Now let's take a look at the output of a `show mac address-table`:

```
Switch#sh mac address-table
Vlan    Mac Address       Type        Ports
----    -----------       --------    -----
   1    0005.dccb.d74b    DYNAMIC     Fa0/1
   1    000a.f467.9e80    DYNAMIC     Fa0/3
   1    000a.f467.9e8b    DYNAMIC     Fa0/4
   1    000a.f467.9e8c    DYNAMIC     Fa0/3
   1    0010.7b7f.c2b0    DYNAMIC     Fa0/3
   1    0030.80dc.460b    DYNAMIC     Fa0/3
   1    0030.9492.a5dd    DYNAMIC     Fa0/1
   1    00d0.58ad.05f4    DYNAMIC     Fa0/1
```

Suppose the preceding switch received a frame with the following MAC addresses:

Source MAC: **0005.dccb.d74b**

Destination MAC: **000a.f467.9e8c**

How will the switch handle this frame? Answer: The destination MAC address will be found in the MAC address table and the frame will be forwarded out Fa0/3 only. Remember that if the destination MAC address is not found in the forward/filter table, it will forward the frame out all ports of the switch, except for the port it originated on, looking for the destination device. Now that we can see the MAC address table and how switches add host addresses to the forward filter table, how can we secure it from unauthorized users?

Port Security

So just how do you stop someone from simply plugging a host into one of your switch ports—or worse, adding a hub, switch, or access point into the Ethernet jack in their office? By default, MAC addresses will just dynamically appear in your MAC forward/filter database. You can stop them in their tracks by using port security. Here are your options:

```
Switch#config t
Switch(config)#int f0/1
Switch(config-if)#switchport mode access
Switch(config-if)#switchport port-security ?
  aging          Port-security aging commands
  mac-address    Secure mac address
  maximum        Max secure addresses
  violation      Security violation mode
  <cr>
```

Since all Cisco's latest switches ship with the ports in desirable mode (the port desires to trunk if it senses another switch just connected), we must first change the port from desirable mode to access port or we cannot configure port security. Once that is done, we can continue on with our `port-security` commands.

You can see clearly in the preceding output that the `switchport port-security` command can be used with four options. Personally, I like the `port-security` command because it allows me to easily control users on my network. You can use the `switchport port-security mac-address` *`mac-address`* command to assign individual MAC addresses to each switch port, but if you choose to go there, you'd better have a lot of time on your hands!

If you want to set up a switch port to allow only one host per port, and to shut down the port if this rule is violated, use the following commands:

```
Switch(config-if)#switchport port-security maximum 1
Switch(config-if)#switchport port-security violation shutdown
```

These commands are probably the most popular because they prevent random users from connecting to a switch or access point that's in their office. The `maximum` setting of 1 (which is the port security default) means only one MAC address can be used on that port; if the user tries to add another host on that segment, the switch port will shut down. If that happens, you'd have to manually go into the switch and enable the port by cycling it with a `shutdown` and then a `no shutdown` command.

Probably one of my favorite commands is the `sticky` command. Not only does it perform a cool function, it's got a cool name! You can find this command under the `mac-address` command:

```
Switch(config-if)#switchport port-security mac-address sticky
Switch(config-if)#switchport port-security maximum 2
Switch(config-if)#switchport port-security violation shutdown
```

Basically, what this does is provide static MAC address security without having to type in everyone's MAC address on the network. As I said—cool!

In the preceding example, the first two MAC addresses into the port "stick" as static addresses and will stay that way for however long you set the aging command. Why did I set it to 2? Well, I needed one for the PC/data and one for telephony/phone. I'll cover this type of configuration more in the next chapter, which is about VLANs.

I'll be going over port security again in the configuration examples later in this chapter.

Loop Avoidance

Redundant links between switches are a good idea because they help prevent irrecoverable network failures in the event one link stops working.

Sounds great, but even though redundant links can be extremely helpful, they often cause more problems than they solve. This is because frames can be flooded down all redundant links simultaneously, creating network loops as well as other evils. Here's a list of some of the ugliest problems:

- If no loop avoidance schemes are put in place, the switches will flood broadcasts endlessly throughout the internetwork. This is sometimes referred to as a *broadcast storm*. (But most of the time it's referred to in ways we're not permitted to repeat in print!) Figure 10.7 illustrates how a broadcast can be propagated throughout the network. Observe how a frame is continually being flooded through the internetwork's physical network media.

FIGURE 10.7 Broadcast storm

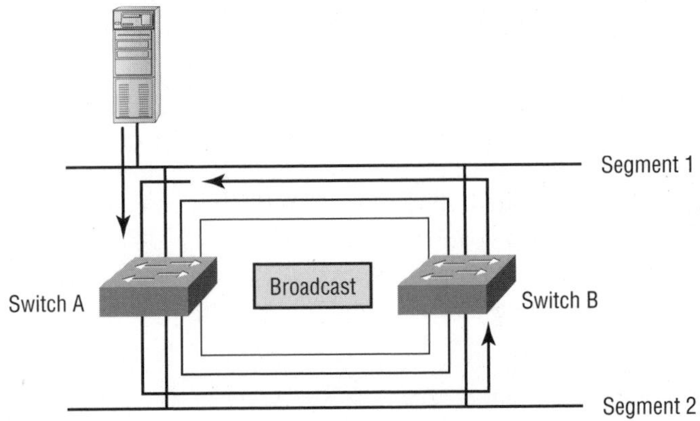

- A device can receive multiple copies of the same frame since that frame can arrive from different segments at the same time. Figure 10.8 demonstrates how a whole bunch of frames can arrive from multiple segments simultaneously. The server in the figure sends a unicast frame to Router C. Since it's a unicast frame, Switch A forwards the frame and Switch B provides the same service—it forwards the unicast. This is bad because it means that Router C receives that unicast frame twice, causing additional overhead on the network.
- You may have thought of this one: The MAC address filter table could be totally confused about the source device's location because the switch can receive the frame from more than one link. And what's more, the bewildered switch could get so caught up in constantly updating the MAC filter table with source hardware address locations that it will fail to forward a frame! This is called thrashing the MAC table.
- One of the nastiest things that can happen is multiple loops generating throughout a network. This means that loops can occur within other loops, and if a broadcast storm were to also occur, the network wouldn't be able to perform frame switching—period!

FIGURE 10.8 Multiple frame copies

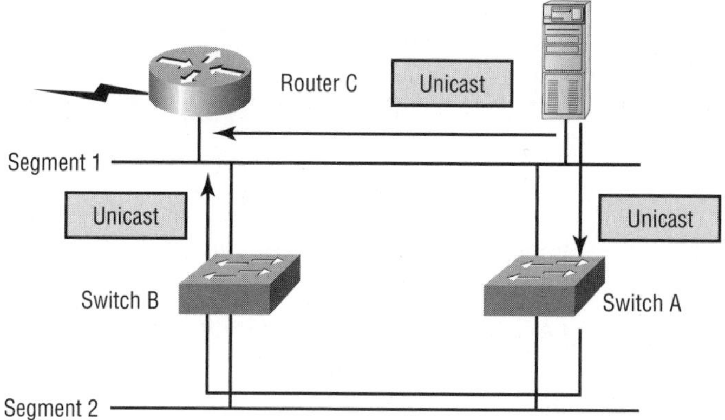

All of these problems spell disaster (or at least close to it) and are decidedly evil situations that must be avoided, or at least fixed somehow. That's where the Spanning Tree Protocol comes into the game. It was developed to solve each and every one of the problems I just told you about.

Spanning Tree Protocol (STP)

Once upon a time a company called Digital Equipment Corporation (DEC) was purchased and renamed Compaq. But 30 years before that happened, DEC created the original version of *Spanning Tree Protocol*, or *STP*. The IEEE later created its own version of STP called 802.1D. Cisco has moved toward another industry standard in its newer switches called 802.1w. I'll cover that STP version in this section as well, but first, let's define some important STP basics.

STP's main task is to stop network loops from occurring on your layer 2 network (bridges or switches). It vigilantly monitors the network to find all links, making sure that no loops occur by shutting down any redundant links. STP uses the spanning-tree algorithm (STA) to first create a topology database and then search out and disable redundant links. With STP running, frames will be forwarded only on the premium, STP-picked links.

In the following sections, I am going to hit the nitty-gritty of the Spanning Tree Protocol.

STP is a layer 2 protocol that is used to maintain a loop-free switched network.

The Spanning Tree Protocol is necessary in networks such as the one shown in Figure 10.9.

FIGURE 10.9 A switched network with switching loops

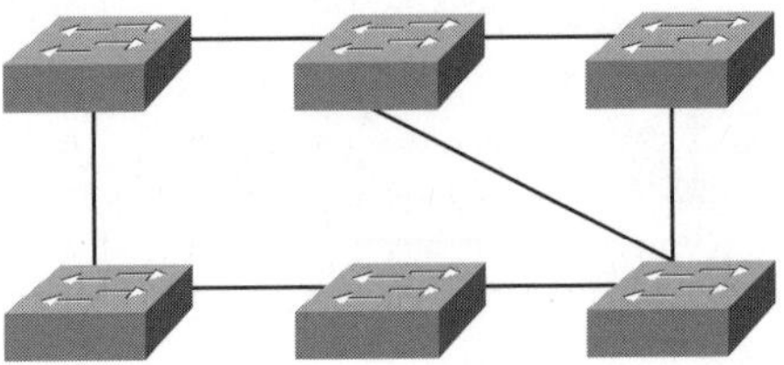

In Figure 10.9, we have a switched network with a redundant topology (switching loops). Without some type of layer 2 mechanism to stop the network loop, we would have the problems we discussed previously: broadcast storms, multiple frame copies, and thrashing of the MAC table.

Understand that the network in Figure 10.9 without STP enabled would actually sort of work, albeit extremely slowly. This clearly demonstrates the danger of switching loops. And to make matters worse, it can be super hard to find this problem once it starts!

Spanning Tree Terms

Before I get into describing the details of how STP works in the network, you need to understand some basic ideas and terms and how they relate within the layer 2 switched network:

Root bridge The *root bridge* is the bridge with the best bridge ID. With STP, the key is for all the switches in the network to elect a root bridge that becomes the focal point in the network. All other decisions in the network—such as which port is to be blocked and which port is to be put in forwarding mode—are made from the perspective of this root bridge. Once a root bridge is elected on the network, all other bridges must make a single path to this root bridge. The port with the best path to the root bridge is called the root port.

BPDU All the switches exchange information to use in the selection of the root switch as well as in subsequent configuration of the network. Each switch compares the parameters in the *Bridge Protocol Data Unit (BPDU)* that it sends to one neighbor with the ones that it receives from other neighbors.

Bridge ID The bridge ID is how STP keeps track of all the switches in the network. It is determined by a combination of the bridge priority (32,768 by default on all Cisco switches) and the base MAC address. The bridge with the lowest bridge ID becomes the root bridge in the network.

Nonroot bridges These are all bridges that are not the root bridge. Nonroot bridges exchange BPDUs with all bridges and update the STP topology database on all switches, preventing loops and providing a measure of defense against link failures.

Port cost Port cost determines the best path when multiple links are used between two switches. The cost of a link is determined by the bandwidth of a link.

Root port The root port is always the link directly connected to the root bridge, or the lowest path cost to the root bridge. If more than one link connects to the root bridge, then a port cost is determined by checking the bandwidth of each link. The lowest-cost port becomes the root port. If multiple upstream switches have the same cost, the bridge with the lower advertising bridge ID is used. When multiple links connect to the same device, the port connected to the lowest port number on the upstream switch will be used.

Designated port A *designated port* is one that has been determined as having the best (lowest) cost to the root bridge via its root port. A designated port will be marked as a forwarding port.

Nondesignated port A *nondesignated port* is one with a higher cost than the designated port. They are what's left over after the root ports and designated ports have been determined. Nondesignated ports are put in blocking mode—they are not forwarding ports.

Forwarding port A forwarding port forwards frames and can be a root port or a designated port.

Blocked port A blocked port is the port that, in order to prevent loops, will not forward frames. However, a blocked port will always listen to BPDU frames but drop any and all other frames.

Spanning Tree Operations

As I've said before, STP's job is to find all links in the network and shut down any redundant ones, thereby preventing network loops from occurring.

STP accomplishes this by first electing a root bridge that will forward through all ports and act as a point of reference for all other devices in the STP domain. Once all switches agree on who the root bridge is, every bridge must find its one and only allotted root port. Each and every link between two switches must have one, and only one, designated port—the port on that link that provides the highest bandwidth toward the root. It's really important to remember that a bridge can go through many other bridges to get to the root, meaning that it's not always the shortest path but the fastest (highest bandwidth) path that will be the one used.

Obviously, every port on the root bridge is a designated port (forwarding port for a segment), as you can get no closer to the root than being the root. After the dust settles, any port that is not either a root port or a designated port—which means it is a nonroot, nondesignated port—is placed in the blocking state, thus breaking the switching loop.

Things tend to go a lot more smoothly when you don't have more than one person making a navigational decision, so similarly there can be only one root bridge in any given network. I'll discuss the root bridge election process more completely in the next section.

Selecting the Root Bridge

The bridge ID is used to elect the root bridge in the STP domain and to determine the root port for each of the remaining devices in the STP domain when there are multiple candidate root ports available and path costs are equal. This ID is 8 bytes long and includes both the priority and the MAC address of the device. The default priority on all devices running the IEEE STP version is 32,768.

To determine the root bridge, you combine the priority of each bridge with its MAC address. If two switches or bridges happen to have the same priority value, the MAC address becomes the tiebreaker for figuring out which one has the lowest (best) ID. It's like this: If two switches—I'll name them A and B—both use the default priority of 32,768, then the MAC address will be used instead. If Switch A's MAC address is 0000.0c00.1111 and Switch B's MAC address is 0000.0c00.2222, then Switch A would become the root bridge. Just remember that the lower value is the better one when it comes to electing a root bridge.

By default, prior to election of the root bridge, BPDUs are sent every two seconds out all active ports on a bridge/switch—again, the bridge with the lowest (best) bridge ID is elected the root bridge. You can change the bridge's ID by lowering its priority so that it will become a root bridge automatically. Being able to do that is important in a large switched network—it ensures that the best paths are chosen. Efficiency is what you're after here!

Figure 10.10 shows a typical switched network with redundant switched paths. First, let's find out which switch is the root; then we can have the nonroot bridge become the root by changing the priority of the switch.

FIGURE 10.10 A switched network with redundant switched paths

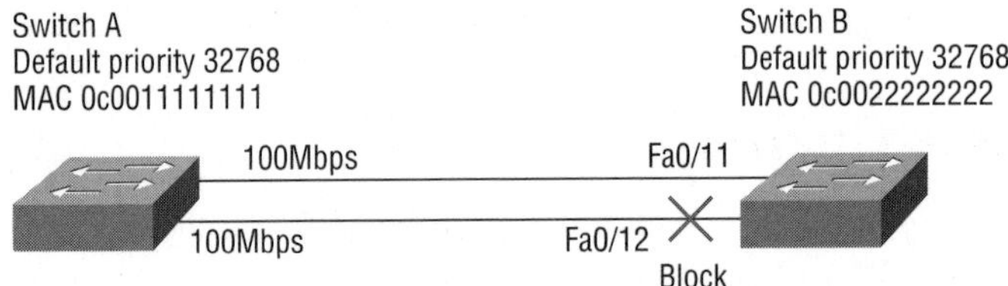

By looking at Figure 10.10, you can tell that Switch A is the root bridge because it's the one with the lowest bridge ID. Switch B must shut down one of its ports connected to Switch A to prevent a switching loop from occurring. Remember that even though Switch B won't transmit out the blocked port, it will still receive BPDUs.

To determine which port STP will shut down on Switch B, it will first check each link's amount of bandwidth and then shut down the link with the lowest bandwidth value. Since both links between Switch A and Switch B are 100Mbps, STP will typically shut down the higher of the port numbers. In this example, 12 is higher than 11, so port 12 would be put into blocking mode.

Changing the default priority is the best way to choose a root bridge. This is important because you want the switch closest to the center of your network to be the root bridge in your network so STP will converge quickly.

Let's have some fun and make Switch B the root in our network. Here's the output from Switch B that shows the default priority. We'll use the `show spanning-tree` command:

```
Switch B(config)#do show spanning-tree
VLAN0001
```

```
  Spanning tree enabled protocol ieee
  Root ID    Priority    32769
             Address     0005.74ae.aa40
             Cost        19
             Port        1 (FastEthernet0/1)
             Hello Time   2 sec  Max Age 20 sec  Forward Delay 15 sec

  Bridge ID  Priority    32769  (priority 32768 sys-id-ext 1)
             Address     0012.7f52.0280
             Hello Time   2 sec  Max Age 20 sec  Forward Delay 15 sec
             Aging Time 300
[output cut]
```

There are two things to notice right off the bat here: Switch B is running the IEEE 802.1d protocol (the output just says "ieee"), and the first output (Root ID) is the root bridge information for the switched network. But it's not Switch B. Switch B's port (called root port) to the root bridge is port 1. The Bridge ID is the actual spanning tree bridge ID information for Switch B and for VLAN 1, listed as VLAN0001—each VLAN can have a different root bridge. Switch B's MAC address is listed as well, and you can see that it's different than the root bridge's MAC address.

Switch B's priority is 32,768—the default for every switch. You see it listed as 32769, but the actual VLAN ID is added, so in this case it shows up as 32769 for VLAN 1. VLAN 2 would be 32770, and so on.

As I said, you can change the priority to force a switch to become the root of your STP network, so let's do that now for Switch B. Use the following command to change a bridge priority on a Catalyst switch:

```
Switch B(config)#spanning-tree vlan 1 priority ?
  <0-61440>  bridge priority in increments of 4096
Switch B(config)#spanning-tree vlan 1 priority 4096
```

You can set the priority to any value from 0 through 61440. Setting it to zero (0) means that the switch will always be a root bridge (assuming it also has a lower MAC than another switch that also has its bridge ID set to 0), and the bridge priority is set in increments of 4096. If you want to set a switch to be the root bridge for every VLAN in your network, then you have to change the priority for each VLAN, with 0 being the lowest priority you can use. It would not be advantageous to set all switches to a priority of 0.

Check out the following output—now that we've changed the priority of Switch B for VLAN 1 to 4096, we've successfully forced this switch to become the root:

```
Switch B(config)#do show spanning-tree
VLAN0001
  Spanning tree enabled protocol ieee
  Root ID    Priority    4097
```

```
                Address     0012.7f52.0280
                This bridge is the root
                Hello Time   2 sec  Max Age 20 sec  Forward Delay 15 sec

  Bridge ID  Priority    4097   (priority 4096 sys-id-ext 1)
                Address     0012.7f52.0280
                Hello Time   2 sec  Max Age 20 sec  Forward Delay 15 sec
                Aging Time 15
[output cut]
```

Both the root's MAC address and the bridge priority of Switch B are now the same, meaning that Switch B is now the root bridge, and it tells us so. Knowing the `show spanning-tree` command is a very important thing; we'll use it again toward the end of this chapter.

Believe it or not, there's yet another command that you can use to set your root bridge, and I promise to tell you all about it when I show you my switch configuration examples later in this chapter.

Spanning-Tree Port States

The ports on a bridge or switch running IEEE 802.1d STP can transition through five different states:

Blocking A blocked port won't forward frames; it just listens to BPDUs. The purpose of the blocking state is to prevent the use of looped paths. All ports are in blocking state by default when the switch is powered up.

Listening The port listens to BPDUs to make sure no loops occur on the network before passing data frames. A port in listening state prepares to forward data frames without populating the MAC address table.

Learning The switch port listens to BPDUs and learns all the paths in the switched network. A port in learning state populates the MAC address table but still doesn't forward data frames. Forward delay means the time it takes to transition a port from listening to learning mode (or from learning to forwarding mode), which is set to 15 seconds by default and can be seen in the `show spanning-tree` output.

Forwarding The port sends and receives all data frames on the bridged port. If the port is still a designated or root port at the end of the learning state, it enters the forwarding state.

Disabled (technically not a transition state) A port in the disabled state (administratively) does not participate in the frame forwarding or STP. A port in the disabled state is virtually nonoperational.

Switches populate the MAC address table in learning and forwarding modes only.

Switch ports are most often in either the blocking or forwarding state. A forwarding port is typically one that has been determined to have the lowest (best) cost to the root bridge. But when and if the network experiences a topology change (because of a failed link or because someone adds in a new switch), you'll find the ports on a switch transitioning through listening and learning states.

As I mentioned, blocking ports is a strategy for preventing network loops. Once a switch determines the best path to the root bridge for its root port as well as any designated ports, all other redundant ports will be in blocking mode. Blocked ports can still receive BPDUs—they just don't send out any frames.

If a switch determines that a blocked port should now be the designated or root port because of a topology change, it will go into listening mode and check all BPDUs it receives to make sure it won't create a loop once the port goes to forwarding mode.

Convergence

Convergence occurs when all ports on bridges and switches have transitioned to either forwarding or blocking modes. No data will be forwarded until convergence is complete. Yes—you read that right: When STP is converging, all host data stops transmitting! So if you want to remain on speaking terms with your network's users (or remain employed for any length of time), you positively must make sure that your switched network is physically designed really well so that STP can converge quickly.

Figure 10.11 shows you some really great considerations for designing and implementing your switched network so that STP converges efficiently.

FIGURE 10.11 An optimal hierarchical switch design

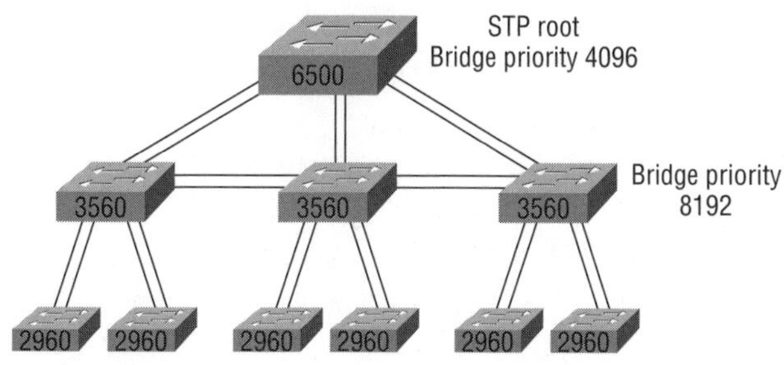

Convergence is truly important because it ensures that all devices have a coherent database. But as I've drilled into you, it does cost you some time. It usually takes 50 seconds to go from blocking to forwarding mode, and I don't recommend changing the default STP timers. (But you can adjust those timers if necessary and have a large network.) By creating your physical switch design in a hierarchical manner, as shown in Figure 10.11, you can make your Core switch the STP root, which will then make STP convergence time nice and quick.

Because the typical spanning-tree topology's time to convergence from blocking to forwarding on a switch port is 50 seconds, this could create time-out problems on your servers or hosts—for example, when you reboot them. To address this hitch, you can disable spanning tree on individual ports using PortFast.

Spanning Tree PortFast

If you have a server or other devices connected into your switch that you're totally sure won't create a switching loop if STP is disabled, you can use something called `portfast` on these ports. Using it means the port won't spend the usual 50 seconds to come up into forwarding mode while STP is converging.

Here are the commands—they're pretty simple:

```
Switch(config-if)#spanning-tree portfast ?
  disable  Disable portfast for this interface
  trunk    Enable portfast on the interface even in trunk mode
  <cr>
```

We haven't discussed trunk ports yet, but basically, these are used to connect switches together and pass VLAN information between them. You have to specifically tell `portfast` if you want to enable it on a trunk port. This isn't a typical configuration because ports between switches should usually run STP. So let's take a look at the message I get when I turn on portfast on an interface:

```
Switch(config-if)#spanning-tree portfast
%Warning: portfast should only be enabled on ports connected to a
   single host. Connecting hubs, concentrators, switches, bridges,
   etc... to this interface  when portfast is enabled, can cause
   temporary bridging loops.
 Use with CAUTION
%Portfast has been configured on FastEthernet0/1 but will only
 have effect when the interface is in a non-trunking mode.
Switch(config-if)#
```

Portfast is enabled on port F0/1, but notice that you get a pretty long message telling you to be careful. One last helpful interface command I want to tell you about is the `range` command, which you can use on switches to help you configure multiple ports at the same time. Here's an example:

```
Switch(config)#int range fastEthernet 0/1 - 12
Switch(config-if-range)#spanning-tree portfast
```

The preceding `range` command allows me to set all 12 of my switch ports into `portfast` mode by typing in one command and then simply pressing the Enter key. Sure hope I didn't create any loops! Again, just be super careful with the `portfast` command. I also want you to know that the `interface range` command can be used in conjunction with any command. I just used it with the `portfast` command as an example.

Spanning Tree UplinkFast

UplinkFast is a Cisco-specific feature that improves the convergence time of STP in case of a link failure. And beware, just as with the `portfast` command, you've got to be really careful where you use this command! The UplinkFast feature is designed to run in a switched environment when the switch has at least one alternate/backup root port (a port in blocking state). This is why Cisco recommends that UplinkFast be enabled only for switches with blocked ports and, typically, at the Access layer.

UplinkFast allows a switch to find alternate paths to the root bridge before the primary link fails. This means that if the primary link fails, the secondary link would come up more quickly—the port wouldn't wait for the normal STP convergence time of 50 seconds. So if you're running the 802.1d STP and you have redundant links on your Access layer switches, you definitely want to turn on UplinkFast. But don't use it on switches without the implied topology knowledge of an alternative/backup root link that's typically used for distribution and Core switches in Cisco multilayer design.

Spanning Tree BackboneFast

Unlike UplinkFast, which is used to determine and quickly fix link failures on the local switch, another Cisco-proprietary STP extension called BackboneFast is used for speeding up convergence when a link that's not directly connected to the switch fails. If a switch running BackboneFast receives an inferior BPDU from its designated bridge, it knows that a link on the path to the root has failed. Just to make sure you're clear on this, an inferior BPDU is one that lists the same switch for the root bridge and the designated bridge.

And again, unlike UplinkFast, which is only configured on Access layer switches or switches with redundant links and at least one link in blocking mode, BackboneFast should be enabled on all Catalyst switches to allow for detection of indirect link failures. Enabling BackboneFast is also beneficial because it starts the spanning tree reconfiguration more quickly—it can save 20 seconds on the default 50-second STP convergence time.

Rapid Spanning Tree Protocol (RSTP) 802.1w

How would you like to have a good STP configuration running on your switched network (regardless of the brand of switches) and have all the features we just discussed built in and enabled on every switch? Absolutely—yes! Well then, welcome to the world of Rapid Spanning Tree Protocol (RSTP).

Cisco created PortFast, UplinkFast, and BackboneFast to "fix" the holes and liabilities the IEEE 802.1d standard presented. The drawbacks to these enhancements are only that they are Cisco proprietary and need additional configuration. But the new 802.1w standard (RSTP) addresses all these "issues" in one tight package—just turn on RSTP and you're good to go. It's important that you make sure all the switches in your network are running the 802.1w protocol for 802.1w to work properly!

It might come as a surprise, but RSTP actually can interoperate with legacy STP protocols. Just know that the inherently fast convergence ability of 802.1w is lost when it interacts with legacy bridges.

RSTP was not designed to be a "brand-new" protocol, but more of an evolution of the 802.1d standard, with faster convergence time when a topology change occurs. Backward compatibility was a must when 802.1w was created.

The 802.1w is defined in these different port states:

Disabled = Discarding

Blocking = Discarding

Listening = Discarding

Learning = Learning

Forwarding = Forwarding

Figuring out what your root bridge, root ports, and designated ports are has not changed; however, you need to understand the cost of each link to make this determination. Table 10.1 shows the IEEE costs based on bandwidth that STP and RSTP use to determine the best path to the root bridge.

TABLE 10.1 IEEE costs

Link Speed	Cost (Revised IEEE Specification)	Cost (Previous IEEE Specification)
10Gb/s	2	1
1Gb/s	4	1
100Mb/s	19	10
10Mb/s	100	100

Let's take a look at an example in Figure 10.12 on how to determine our ports using the revised IEEE cost specifications.

In Figure 10.12, which is your root bridge and which are your root ports and designated ports?

SwitchC has the lowest MAC address, so SwitchC becomes our root bridge and all ports are forwarding designated ports on a root bridge, so that is the easy part. Now, what is the root port for SwitchA? If the path between SwitchA and SwitchB were both Gigabit, then that cost would only be 4, but they are a FastEthernet link, so the cost on the link between SwitchA and SwitchB is 19. Looking at the cost of the link between SwitchB and SwitchD, we can see that this is a cost of 4 since that is Gigabit link; however, the cost between SwitchD and SwitchC is 19 since that is a FastEthernet link, same for the link between SwitchA and SwitchB. The full cost from SwitchA to SwitchC through SwitchB and D is 19+4+19 = 42. We can get a lower cost if we go from SwitchA directly to SwitchC with a cost of 19, so Fa0/1 on SwitchA is our root port. For SwitchB, the best path is through SwitchD with a cost of 4+19 = 23, so Gi0/1 is the root port of SwitchB and Gi0/2 is the root port of SwitchD. We just need a forwarding port on the link between SwitchA and B, and since SwitchA has the lowest bridge ID, Fa0/2 on SwitchA would be a forwarding port. Any port not listed here would go into blocking mode (nondesignated) to stop any loops.

FIGURE 10.12 RSTP example 1

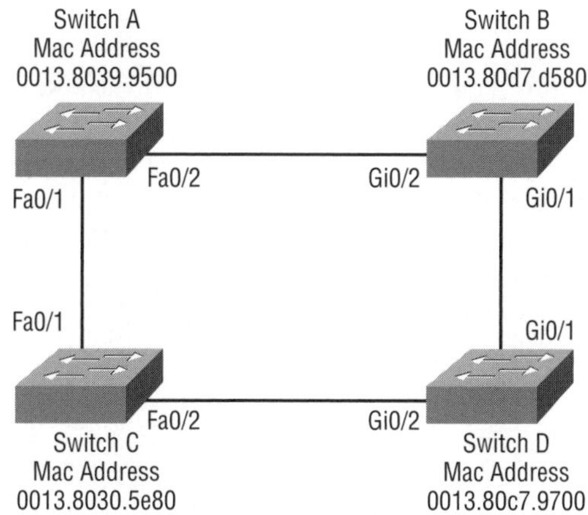

If this seems confusing, know that you just need to find your root bridge, and then determine your root ports, then your designated ports. The best way to understand this is to practice, so let's take a look at another example with Figure 10.13.

FIGURE 10.13 RSTP example 2

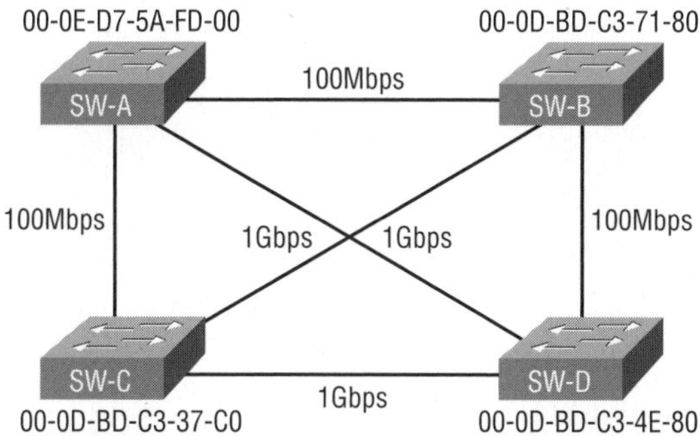

Which bridge is your root bridge? Since all priorities are assumed default, SW-C would be the root bridge because it has the lowest MAC address. We can quickly see that SW-D has a direct Gigabit port to SW-C, so that would be the root port for SW-D with a cost of 4. SW-B's best path would also be the direct Gigabit port to SW-C with a cost of 4, but what about SW-A? The root port for SW-A would not be the direct 100Mbps port with a cost of 19, but the Gigabit port to SW-D and then the Gigabit port to SW-C with a total cost of only 8.

I'll show you how to configure RSTP later in this chapter. It's pretty easy, actually.

EtherChannel

Instead of having redundant links and allowing STP to put one of the links in BLK (blocked) mode, we can bundle the links and create a logical aggregation so that our multiple links will then appear as a single one. Since doing this would still provide the same redundancy as STP, why wouldn't we want to bundle our redundant links?

Well, as usual, there's the Cisco version of EtherChannel and the IEEE version of port channel negation protocols to choose from—take your pick. Cisco's version is called Port Aggregation Protocol (PAgP) and the IEEE 802.3ad standard is called Link Aggregation Control Protocol (LACP). Both versions work equally well, but how you configure each is different. I'm going to bundle some links toward the end of this chapter to demonstrate this just for fun. And no worries—I'm also going to cover all configurations for the STP extensions coming right up in the next section.

Configuring Catalyst Switches

Cisco Catalyst switches come in many flavors—some run 10Mbps, and some jam all the way up to 10Gbps switched ports with a combination of twisted-pair and fiber. These newer switches (specifically the 2960s and 3560s) have more intelligence, so they can give you data fast—video and voice services, too.

It's time to get down to it—I'm going to show you how to start up and configure a Cisco Catalyst switch using the command-line interface (CLI). After you get the basic commands down in this chapter, in the next chapter I'll show you how to configure virtual LANs (VLANs) plus Inter-Switch Link (ISL), 802.1q trunking, and Cisco's Virtual Trunk Protocol (VTP).

Here's a list of the basic tasks we'll be covering in the following sections:

- Administrative functions
- Configuring the IP address and subnet mask
- Setting the IP default gateway
- Setting port security
- Setting PortFast
- Enabling BPDUGuard and BPDUFilter
- Enabling UplinkFast
- Enabling BackboneFast
- Enabling RSTP (802.1w)
- Enabling EtherChannel
- Configuring an STP root switch

You can learn all about the Cisco family of Catalyst switches at www.ciscos.com/en/US/products/hw/switches/index.html.

Catalyst Switch Configuration

Just as we did with the routers we configured in Chapters 8 and 9, we'll use a diagram and switch setup to configure in this chapter as well as in Chapter 11. Figure 10.14 shows the switched network we'll be working on.

FIGURE 10.14 Our switched network

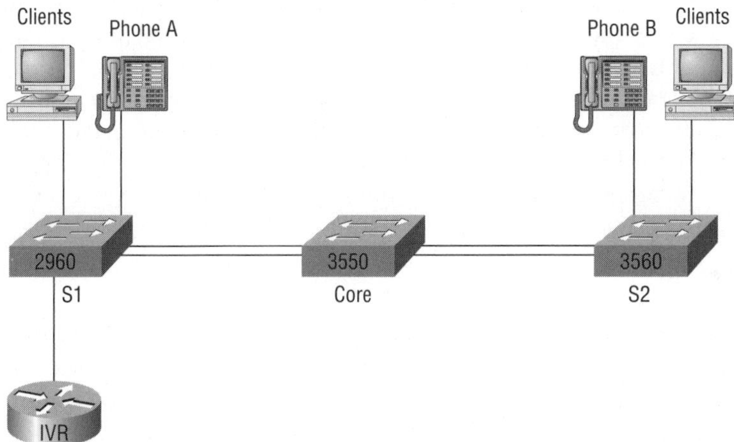

I'm going to use a new 3560, a 2960, and a 3550 switch. Keep in mind that the hosts, phones, and router shown in the network will become more important later when we get to Chapter 11.

But before we actually get into configuring one of the Catalyst switches, I've got to fill you in regarding the bootup process of these switches, just as I did with the routers in Chapter 7. Figure 10.15 shows the detail of a typical Cisco Catalyst switch, and I need to tell you about the different interfaces and features of this product.

FIGURE 10.15 A Cisco Catalyst switch

System LED

PoE

The first thing I want you to know is that the console port for the Catalyst switches are typically located on the back of the switch. But on a smaller switch like the 3560 shown in the figure, the console is right in the front to make it easier to use. (The eight-port 2960 looks exactly the same.) If the POST completes successfully, the system LED turns green; if the POST fails, it will turn amber. And seeing the amber glow is a very bad thing—typically fatal. So you may just want to keep a spare switch around—especially in case it happens to be a production switch that's croaked! The bottom button is used to show you which lights are providing Power over Ethernet (PoE). You can see this by pressing the Mode button. The PoE is a very nice feature of these switches. It allows me to power my access point and phone by just connecting them into the switch with an Ethernet cable! Sweet.

Now if we connect our switches to each other, as shown in Figure 10.14, remember that first we'll need a crossover cable between the switches. My 2960 and 3560 switches autodetect the connection type, so I was able to use straight-through cables. But a 2950 or 3550 switch won't autodetect the cable type. Different switches have different needs and abilities, so just keep this in mind when connecting your various switches together.

When you first connect the switch ports to each other, the link lights are amber and then turn green indicating normal operation. This is spanning-tree converging, and as you already know, this process takes around 50 seconds with no extensions enabled. But if you connect into a switch port and the switch port LED is alternating green and amber, this means the port is experiencing errors. If this happens, check the host NIC card or the cabling.

S1

Okay—let's start our configuration by connecting into each switch and setting the administrative functions. We'll also assign an IP address to each switch, but this isn't really necessary to make our network function. The only reason we're going to do that is so we can manage/administer it remotely, via telnet for example. Let's use a simple IP scheme like 192.168.10.16/28. This mask should be familiar to you! Check out the following output:

```
Switch>en
Switch#config t
Enter configuration commands, one per line.  End with CNTL/Z.
Switch(config)#hostname S1
S1(config)#enable secret todd
S1(config)#int f0/1
S1(config-if)#description 1st Connection to Core Switch
S1(config-if)#int f0/2
S1(config-if)#description 2nd Connection to Core Switch
S1(config-if)#int f0/3
S1(config-if)#description Connection to HostA
S1(config-if)#int f0/4
S1(config-if)#description Connection to PhoneA
S1(config-if)#int f0/8
S1(config-if)#description Connection to IVR
```

```
S1(config-if)#line console 0
S1(config-line)#password console
S1(config-line)#login
S1(config-line)#exit
S1(config)#line vty 0 ?
  <1-15>  Last Line number
  <cr>
S1(config)#line vty 0 15
S1(config-line)#password telnet
S1(config-line)#login
S1(config-line)#int vlan 1
S1(config-if)#ip address 192.168.10.17 255.255.255.240
S1(config-if)#no shut
S1(config-if)#exit
S1(config)#banner motd # This is the S1 switch #
S1(config)#exit
S1#copy run start
Destination filename [startup-config]? [enter]
Building configuration...
[OK]
S1#
```

The first thing to notice about this is that there's no IP address configured on the switch's physical interfaces. Since all ports on a switch are enabled by default, there's not so much to configure. The IP address is configured under a logical interface, called a management domain or VLAN. You would typically use the default VLAN 1 to manage a switched network just as we're doing here. The rest of the configuration is basically the same as the process you go through for router configuration. Remember, no IP addresses on physical switch interfaces, no routing protocols, and so on. We're performing layer 2 switching at this point, not routing! Also, note that there is no aux port on Cisco switches.

S2

Here is the S2 configuration:

```
Switch#config t
Switch(config)#hostname S2
S2(config)#enable secret todd
S2(config)#int fa0/1
2(config-if)#description 1st Connection to Core
S2(config-if)#int fa0/2
S2(config-if)#description 2nd Connection to Core
S2(config-if)#int fa0/3
S2(config-if)#description Connection to HostB
```

```
S2(config-if)#int fa0/4
S2(config-if)#description Connection to PhoneB
S2(config-if)#line con 0
S2(config-line)#password console
S2(config-line)#login
S2(config-line)#exit
S2(config)#line vty 0 ?
  <1-15>  Last Line number
  <cr>
S2(config)#line vty 0 15
S2(config-line)#password telnet
S2(config-line)#login
S2(config-line)#int vlan 1
S2(config-if)#ip address 192.168.10.18 255.255.255.240
S2(config-if)#no shut
S2(config-if)#exit
S2(config)#banner motd # This is my S2 Switch #
S2(config)#exit
S2#copy run start
Destination filename [startup-config]?[enter]
Building configuration...
[OK]
S2#
```

We should now be able to ping from S2 to S1. Let's try it:

```
S2#ping 192.168.10.17

Type escape sequence to abort.
Sending 5, 100-byte ICMP Echos to 192.168.10.17, timeout is 2 seconds:
.!!!!
Success rate is 80 percent (4/5), round-trip min/avg/max = 1/1/1 ms
S2#
```

I have two questions for you: How can I ping through the Core switch if I haven't configured it yet, and why did I get only four pings to work instead of five? (The first period [.] is a time-out; the exclamation point [!] is a success.)

Both are good questions. Here's why: First, you don't need the switch configured to make it work. All ports are enabled by default, so by just turning it on you should be able to communicate between connected hosts. Second, the first ping didn't work because of the time that ARP takes to resolve the IP address to its corresponding hardware MAC address.

Core

Here is the Core switch configuration:

```
Switch>en
Switch#config t
Switch(config)#hostname Core
Core(config)#enable secret todd
Core(config)#int f0/5
Core(config-if)#description 1st Connection to S2
Core(config-if)#int fa0/5
Core(config-if)#description 2nd Connection to S2
Core(config-if)#int f0/7
Core(config-if)#desc 1st Connection to S1
Core(config-if)#int f0/8
Core(config-if)#desc 2nd Connection to S1
Core(config-if)#line con 0
Core(config-line)#password console
Core(config-line)#login
Core(config-line)#line vty 0 15
Core(config-line)#password telnet
Core(config-line)#login
Core(config-line)#int vlan 1
Core(config-if)#ip address 192.168.10.19 255.255.255.240
Core(config-if)#no shut
Core(config-if)#exit
Core(config)#banner motd # This is the Core Switch #
Core(config)#exit
Core#copy run start
Destination filename [startup-config]?[enter]
Building configuration...
[OK]
Core#
```

Now let's ping to S1 and S2 from the Core switch and see what happens:

```
Core#ping 192.168.10.17
Type escape sequence to abort.
Sending 5, 100-byte ICMP Echos to 192.168.10.17, timeout is 2 seconds:
.!!!!
Success rate is 80 percent (4/5), round-trip min/avg/max = 1/1/1 ms
Core#ping 192.168.10.18
```

```
Type escape sequence to abort.
Sending 5, 100-byte ICMP Echos to 192.168.10.18, timeout is 2 seconds:
.!!!!
Success rate is 80 percent (4/5), round-trip min/avg/max = 1/1/1 ms
Core#sh ip arp
Protocol  Address          Age (min)  Hardware Addr   Type   Interface
Internet  192.168.10.18           0   001a.e2ce.ff40  ARPA   Vlan1
Internet  192.168.10.19           -   000d.29bd.4b80  ARPA   Vlan1
Internet  192.168.10.17           0   001b.2b55.7540  ARPA   Vlan1
Core#
```

Now, before we move on to verifying the switch configurations, there's one more command you need to know about, even though we don't need it in our current network because we don't have a router involved. It's the `ip default-gateway` command. If you want to manage your switches from outside your LAN, you need to set a default gateway on the switches, just as you would with a host. You do this from global config. Here's an example where we introduce our router with an IP address using the last IP address in our subnet range (we'll use the router in our next chapter, on VLANs):

```
Core#config t
Enter configuration commands, one per line.  End with CNTL/Z.
Core(config)#ip default-gateway 192.168.10.30
Core(config)#exit
Core#
```

Now that we have all three switches basically configured, let's have some fun with them.

Port Security

As I said earlier in the chapter, it's usually not a good thing to have your switches available for anyone to just plug into and play around with. I mean, you demand wireless security, so why wouldn't you want switch security just as much?

The answer is, you do, and by using port security, you can limit the number of MAC addresses that can be assigned dynamically to a port, set static MAC addresses, and—here's my favorite part—set penalties for users who abuse your policy. Personally, I like to have the port shut down when the security policy is violated and then make the abusers bring me a memo from their boss explaining to me why they violated the security policy before I'll enable their port again. That usually really helps them remember to behave!

A secured switch port can associate anywhere from 1 to 8,192 MAC addresses, but the '50 series can support only 132, which seems like enough to me. You can choose to allow the switch to learn these values dynamically, or you can set static addresses for each port using the `switchport port-security mac-address` *`mac-address`* command.

So let's set port security on our S1 switch now. Ports fa0/3 and fa0/4 have only one device connected in our lab. By using port security, we can know for certain that no other device can connect once our host in port Fa0/3 and the phone in Fa0/4 are connected. Here's how we'll do that:

```
S1#config t
Enter configuration commands, one per line.  End with CNTL/Z.
S1(config)#int range fa0/3 - 4
S1(config-if-range)#switchport mode access
S1(config-if-range)#switchport port-security
S1(config-if-range)#switchport port-security maximum ?
  <1-8192>  Maximum addresses
S1(config-if-range)#switchport port-security maximum 1
S1(config-if-range)#switchport port-security mac-address sticky
S1(config-if-range)#switchport port-security violation ?
  protect   Security violation protect mode
  restrict  Security violation restrict mode
  shutdown  Security violation shutdown mode
S1(config-if-range)#switchport port-security violation shutdown
S1(config-if-range)#exit
```

The first commands I typed in set the mode of the ports to "access" ports, as they are set to "desirable" by default, meaning they "desire" to trunk if they find they are connected to another switch. You can't set port security on a port while in desirable mode. After enabling port security on the ports, I set the port security on port fa0/3 and fa0/4 to allow a maximum association of one MAC address, and only the first MAC address associated to the port will be able to send frames through the switch. If a second device with a different MAC address were to try to send a frame into the switch, the port would be shut down because of our `violation` command. I used the `sticky` command because I am way too lazy to type in all the MAC addresses of each device by hand!

Now, let's verify the port security on one of the ports by using the `show port-security interface` command:

```
S1#sh port-security interface f0/3
Port Security              : Enabled
Port Status                : Secure-down
Violation Mode             : shutdown
Aging Time                 : 2 mins
Aging Type                 : Inactivity
SecureStatic Address Aging : Disabled
Maximum MAC Addresses      : 1
Total MAC Addresses        : 0
Configured MAC Addresses   : 0
Sticky MAC Addresses       : 0
```

```
Last Source Address:Vlan    : 0000.0000.0000:0
Security Violation Count    : 0
```

There are two other modes you can use instead of just shutting down the port. The protect mode means that another host can connect but its frames will just be dropped. Restrict mode is also pretty cool—it alerts you via SNMP that a violation has occurred on a port. You can then call the abuser and tell them they're so busted—you can see them, you know what they did, and they're in big-time trouble!

In our connection between switches we have redundant links, so it's best to let STP run on those links (for now). But on our S1 and S2 switches, we also have hosts connected to port fa0/3 and fa0/4 (not the Core). So let's turn STP off on those ports.

Understand that hosts can directly connect physically to the back of phones since phones typically will have an Ethernet jack. So we really need only one port on the switch for both devices. I'll go over that in depth in the telephony section of Chapter 11.

PortFast

If we use the `portfast` command on our switches, we prevent the problem of our hosts possibly being unable to receive a DHCP address because STP takes way too long to converge and the host's DHCP request times out. So I'm going to use PortFast on port fa0/3 and fa0/4 on both the S1 and S2 switches:

```
S1#config t
S1(config)#int range f0/3 - 4
S1(config-if-range)#spanning-tree portfast ?
  disable  Disable portfast for this interface
  trunk    Enable portfast on the interface even in trunk mode
  <cr>
S1(config-if-range)#spanning-tree portfast
%Warning: portfast should only be enabled on ports connected to a
   single host. Connecting hubs, concentrators, switches, bridges,
   etc... to this interface when portfast is enabled, can cause
   temporary bridging loops.
 Use with CAUTION

%Portfast will be configured in 2 interfaces due to the range command
 but will only have effect when the interfaces are in a non-trunking mode.
S1(config-if-range)#
```

Now that I have configured S1, I won't show you the next output, but I'm going over to S2 to enable PortFast on fa0/3-4 as well. Again, just a reminder to be careful when using PortFast—you definitely do not want to create a network loop! Why? Because if you let this happen, even though the network may still work (well, kind of), data will pass super slowly, and worse, it could take you a really long time to find the source of the problem, making you very unpopular. So proceed carefully.

It would be good to know that there are some safeguard commands you can use when using PortFast in case someone accidentally causes a loop in a port that's configured with PortFast enabled. Here they are.

BPDUGuard

I talked about this a bit earlier: If you turn on PortFast for a switch port, turning on BPDUGuard is a really good idea. If a switch port that has BPDUGuard enabled receives a BPDU on that port, it will place the port into error disabled state. This stops an administrator from accidentally connecting another switch or hub port into a switch port configured with PortFast. Basically, you're preventing (guarding) this from happening and bringing down, or at least severely crippling, your network. You'd only configure this command on your Access layer switches—switches where users are directly connected—so we wouldn't configure this on our Core switch.

BPDUFilter

Another helpful command to use with PortFast is BPDUFilter. Since a switch port that has PortFast enabled will still receive BPDUs by default, you can use BPDUFilter to completely stop BPDUs from coming to or going from that port. BPDUFilter filtering will immediately take a port out of PortFast if it receives a BPDU and force the port to be part of the STP topology again. Unlike BPDUGuard, which places the port into error disabled state, the BPDUFilter will keep a port up, but without PortFast running. There's just no reason to have BPDUs received on an interface configured with PortFast. To be perfectly honest, I have no idea why BPDUGuard or BPDUFilter are not enabled by default when PortFast is enabled.

So let's configure our S1 and S2 interfaces that are already configured with PortFast with both the BPDUGuard and BPDUFilter now—it's easy:

```
S1(config-if-range)#spanning-tree bpduguard ?
  disable  Disable BPDU guard for this interface
  enable   Enable BPDU guard for this interface
S1(config-if-range)#spanning-tree bpduguard enable
S1(config-if-range)#spanning-tree bpdufilter ?
  disable  Disable BPDU filtering for this interface
  enable   Enable BPDU filtering for this interface
S1(config-if-range)#spanning-tree bpdufilter enable

S2(config-if-range)#spanning-tree bpduguard enable
S2(config-if-range)#spanning-tree bpdufilter enable
```

Understand that you typically would use either the bpduguard command or the bpdufilter command, because although the IOS will allow it, applying both commands to the same interface would seem inherently at odds with each other. Whereas bpdufilter would transition to non-portfast status upon receipt of a BPDU, bpduguard would err-disable the port upon receipt of a BPDU—so configuring both commands is somewhat overkill. We're also going to configure a couple more STP 802.1d extensions that you can use when configuring STP.

UplinkFast

Here's how to configure UplinkFast on our Access layer switches (S1 and S2):

```
S1#config t
S1(config)#spanning-tree uplinkfast

S2#config t
S2(config)#spanning-tree uplinkfast
S1(config)#do show spanning-tree uplinkfast
UplinkFast is enabled

Station update rate set to 150 packets/sec.

UplinkFast statistics
-----------------------
Number of transitions via uplinkFast (all VLANs)            : 1
Number of proxy multicast addresses transmitted (all VLANs) : 8

Name                 Interface List
-------------------- ------------------------------------
VLAN0001             Fa0/1(fwd), Fa0/2
S1(config)#
```

The uplinkfast command is a global command and it's enabled on every port.

BackboneFast

Here's how you would configure BackboneFast on a switch:

```
S1(config)#spanning-tree backbonefast
S2(config)#spanning-tree backbonefast
Core(config)#spanning-tree backbonefast
S2(config)#do show spanning-tree backbonefast
BackboneFast is enabled
```

```
BackboneFast statistics
-----------------------
Number of transition via backboneFast (all VLANs)            : 0
Number of inferior BPDUs received (all VLANs)                : 2
Number of RLQ request PDUs received (all VLANs)              : 0
Number of RLQ response PDUs received (all VLANs)             : 1
Number of RLQ request PDUs sent (all VLANs)                  : 1
Number of RLQ response PDUs sent (all VLANs)                 : 0
S2(config)#
```

Notice that unlike what I did with UplinkFast, I configured BackboneFast on all switches in the network, not just the Access layer switches. Remember, BackboneFast is used to determine indirectly connected root path link failures on a remote switch, unlike UplinkFast, which is used to both determine and quickly fix link failures on the local switch.

RSTP (802.1w)

Configuring RSTP actually is as easy as configuring any of our other 802.1d extensions. Considering how much better it is than 802.1d, you'd think the configuration would be more complex, but we're in luck—it's not. So let's turn it on in the Core switch now and see what happens:

```
Core#config t
Core(config)#spanning-tree mode ?
  mst         Multiple spanning tree mode
  pvst        Per-Vlan spanning tree mode
  rapid-pvst  Per-Vlan rapid spanning tree mode
Core(config)#spanning-tree mode rapid-pvst
Core(config)#
1d02h: %LINEPROTO-5-UPDOWN: Line protocol on Interface Vlan1,
 changed state to down
1d02h: %LINEPROTO-5-UPDOWN: Line protocol on Interface Vlan1,
 changed state to up
```

Sweet! The Core switch is now running the 802.1w STP. Let's verify that:

```
Core(config)#do show spanning-tree
VLAN0001
  Spanning tree enabled protocol rstp
  Root ID    Priority    32769
             Address     000d.29bd.4b80
             This bridge is the root
             Hello Time   2 sec  Max Age 20 sec  Forward Delay 15 sec
```

```
  Bridge ID  Priority    32769  (priority 32768 sys-id-ext 1)
             Address     000d.29bd.4b80
             Hello Time   2 sec  Max Age 20 sec  Forward Delay 15 sec
             Aging Time 300

Interface        Role Sts Cost      Prio.Nbr Type
---------------- ---- --- --------- -------- ------------
Fa0/5            Desg FWD 19        128.5    P2p Peer(STP)
Fa0/6            Desg FWD 19        128.6    P2p Peer(STP)
Fa0/7            Desg FWD 19        128.7    P2p Peer(STP)
Fa0/8            Desg FWD 19        128.8    P2p Peer(STP)
```

Interesting…it looks like nothing really happened. I can see on my two other switches that all ports have converged. Once everything was up, everything looked the same. 802.1d and 802.1w seem to be cohabiting with no problem.

But, if we were to look under the hood more closely, we'd see that the 802.1w switch has changed from 802.1w BPDUs to 802.1d BPDUs on the ports connecting to the other switches running 802.1d (which is all of them).

The S1 and S2 switches believe that the Core switch is actually running 802.1d because the Core reverted back to 802.1d BPDUs just for them. And even though the S1 and S2 switches receive the 802.1w BPDUs, they don't understand them, so they simply drop them. However, the Core does receive the 802.1d BPDUs and accepts them from the S1 and S2 switches, now knowing which ports to run 802.1d on. In other words, turning 802.1w on for just one switch didn't really help our network at all!

One small annoying issue is that once the Core switch knows to send 802.1d BPDUs out the ports connected to S1 and S2, it won't change this automatically if the S1 and S2 switches were later configured with 802.1w—we'd still need to reboot the Core switch to stop the 802.1d BPDUs.

EtherChannel

The easiest way to configure EtherChannel is through the Cisco Network Assistant (CNA). Just search Cisco's website for a free download of the GUI software. However, I'm going with the CLI because you need to know CLI commands, plus I'm a CLI guy, especially in smaller networks.

Remember, there are two versions of EtherChannel negotiation protocols, the Cisco version and the IEEE version. I'm going to use the Cisco version and bundle the links between the S1 switch and the Core.

I'll use the `interface port-channel` global command and the `channel-group` and the `channel-protocol` interface commands on the S1 and Core switches. Here's what that looks like:

```
S1#config t
S1(config)#int port-channel 1
S1(config-if)#int range f0/1-2
```

```
S1(config-if-range)#switchport mode trunk
1d03h: %SPANTREE_FAST-7-PORT_FWD_UPLINK: VLAN0001 FastEthernet0/2
 moved to Forwarding (UplinkFast).
S1(config-if-range)#switchport nonegotiate
S1(config-if-range)#channel-group 1 mode desirable
S1(config-if-range)#do sh int fa0/1 etherchannel
Port state    = Up Sngl-port-Bndl Mstr Not-in-Bndl
Channel group = 1      Mode = Desirable-Sl    Gcchange = 0
Port-channel  = null   GC   = 0x00010001   Pseudo port-channel = Po1
Port index    = 0      Load = 0x00         Protocol =   PAgP
[output cut]

Core#config t
Core(config)#int port-channel 1
Core(config-if)#int range f0/7-8
Core(config-if-range)#switchport trunk encap dot1q
Core(config-if-range)#switchport mode trunk
1d03h: %SPANTREE_FAST-7-PORT_FWD_UPLINK: VLAN0001 FastEthernet0/2
 moved to Forwarding (UplinkFast).
Core(config-if-range)#switchport nonegotiate
Core(config-if-range)#channel-group 1 mode desirable
1d04h: %SPANTREE_FAST-7-PORT_FWD_UPLINK: VLAN0001 FastEthernet0/2
 moved to Forwarding (UplinkFast).
1d04h: %SPANTREE_FAST-7-PORT_FWD_UPLINK: VLAN0001 FastEthernet0/2
 moved to Forwarding (UplinkFast).
1d04h: %LINK-3-UPDOWN: Interface Port-channel1, changed state to up
1d04h: %LINEPROTO-5-UPDOWN: Line protocol on Interface
Port-channel1, changed state to up
Core(config-if-range)#do show int port-channel 1
Port-channel1 is up, line protocol is up (connected)
  Hardware is EtherChannel, address is 001b.2b55.7501 (bia 001b.2b55.7501)
  MTU 1500 bytes, BW 200000 Kbit, DLY 100 usec,
     reliability 255/255, txload 1/255, rxload 1/255
  Encapsulation ARPA, loopback not set
  Full-duplex, 100Mb/s, link type is auto, media type is unknown
[output cut]
```

I added the `switchport nonegotiate` interface command to stop the switches from trying to autodetect the link types and also to automatically set up trunking; instead, I statically configured my trunk links. The two links between the S1 and the Core are now bundled using the Cisco EtherChannel version of PAgP.

Okay—but wait, we still need to verify our switch configurations and play with our root bridge before we can learn about Virtual LANs (VLANs) in the next chapter.

Verifying Cisco Catalyst Switches

The first thing I like to do with any router or switch is to run through the configurations with a `show running-config` command. Why? Because doing this gives me a really great headshot of each device. However, it's time consuming, and showing you all the configs would take up a whole bunch of pages in this book. Besides, we can run other commands that will still stock us with really good information.

For example, to verify the IP address set on a switch, we can use the `show interface` command. Here is the output:

```
S1#sh int vlan 1
Vlan1 is up, line protocol is up
  Hardware is EtherSVI, address is 001b.2b55.7540 (bia 001b.2b55.7540)
  Internet address is 192.168.10.17/28
  MTU 1500 bytes, BW 1000000 Kbit, DLY 10 usec,
     reliability 255/255, txload 1/255, rxload 1/255
  Encapsulation ARPA, loopback not set, reliability 255/255,
txload 1/255, rxload 1/255
  [output cut]
```

Remember that IP addresses aren't needed on a switch to operate. The only reason we would set an IP address, mask, and default gateway is for management purposes.

show mac address-table

I'm sure you remember being shown this command earlier in the chapter. Using it displays the forward filter table, also called a content addressable memory (CAM) table. Here's the output from the S1 switch:

```
S1#sh mac address-table
          Mac Address Table
-------------------------------------------
Vlan    Mac Address       Type        Ports
----    -----------       --------    -----
 All    0100.0ccc.cccc    STATIC      CPU
 All    ffff.ffff.ffff    STATIC      CPU
[output cut]
   1    0002.1762.b235    DYNAMIC     Po1
   1    0009.b79f.c080    DYNAMIC     Po1
```

```
   1    000d.29bd.4b87    DYNAMIC     Po1
   1    000d.29bd.4b88    DYNAMIC     Po1
   1    0016.4662.52b4    DYNAMIC     Fa0/4
   1    0016.4677.5eab    DYNAMIC     Po1
   1    001a.2f52.49d8    DYNAMIC     Po1
   1    001a.2fe7.4170    DYNAMIC     Fa0/8
   1    001a.e2ce.ff40    DYNAMIC     Po1
   1    0050.0f02.642a    DYNAMIC     Fa0/3
Total Mac Addresses for this criterion: 31
S1#
```

The switches use what are called base MAC addresses that are assigned to the CPU, and the 2960s use 20. From the preceding output, you can see that we have seven MAC addresses dynamically assigned to EtherChannel port 1. Ports Fa0/3, Fa0/8, and Fa0/4 only have one MAC address assigned, and all ports are assigned to VLAN 1.

Let's take a look at the S2 switch CAM and see what we can find. Keep in mind that the S2 switch doesn't have EtherChannel configured as the S1 switch does, so STP will shut down one of the redundant links to the Core switch:

```
S2#sh mac address-table
          Mac Address Table
-------------------------------------------


Vlan    Mac Address       Type        Ports
----    -----------       --------    -----
 All    0008.205a.85c0    STATIC      CPU
 All    0100.0ccc.cccc    STATIC      CPU
 All    0100.0ccc.cccd    STATIC      CPU
 All    0100.0cdd.dddd    STATIC      CPU
[output cut]
   1    0002.1762.b235    DYNAMIC     Fa0/3
   1    000d.29bd.4b80    DYNAMIC     Fa0/1
   1    000d.29bd.4b85    DYNAMIC     Fa0/1
   1    0016.4662.52b4    DYNAMIC     Fa0/1
   1    0016.4677.5eab    DYNAMIC     Fa0/4
   1    001b.2b55.7540    DYNAMIC     Fa0/1
Total Mac Addresses for this criterion: 26
S2#
```

We can see in the preceding output that we have four MAC addresses assigned to Fa0/1. And of course, we can also see that we have one connection for each host on ports 3 and 4. But where's port 2? Since port 2 is a redundant link, STP placed Fa0/2 into blocking mode. I'll get into more about this again in a minute.

Assigning Static MAC Addresses

You can set a static MAC address in the MAC address table, but like setting static MAC port security, it's a ton of work. But in case you want to do it, here's how it's done:

```
S1#config t
S1(config)#mac-address-table static aaaa.bbbb.cccc vlan 1 int fa0/5
S1(config)#do show mac address-table
          Mac Address Table
-------------------------------------------

Vlan    Mac Address       Type        Ports
----    -----------       --------    -----
 All    0100.0ccc.cccc    STATIC      CPU
[output cut]
   1    0002.1762.b235    DYNAMIC     Po1
   1    0009.b79f.c080    DYNAMIC     Po1
   1    000d.29bd.4b87    DYNAMIC     Po1
   1    000d.29bd.4b88    DYNAMIC     Po1
   1    0016.4662.52b4    DYNAMIC     Fa0/4
   1    0016.4677.5eab    DYNAMIC     Po1
   1    001a.2f52.49d8    DYNAMIC     Po1
   1    001a.2fe7.4170    DYNAMIC     Fa0/8
   1    001a.e2ce.ff40    DYNAMIC     Po1
   1    0050.0f02.642a    DYNAMIC     Fa0/3
   1    aaaa.bbbb.cccc    STATIC      Fa0/5
Total Mac Addresses for this criterion: 31
S1(config)#
```

You can see that a static MAC address is now assigned permanently to interface Fa0/5 and that it's also assigned to VLAN 1 only as shown on the left side of the output.

show spanning-tree

By this time you know that the `show spanning-tree` command is important. With it, you can see who the root bridge is and what our priorities are set to for each VLAN.

Understand that by default Cisco switches run what is called Per-VLAN Spanning Tree (PVST), which basically means that each VLAN runs its own instance of the STP protocol. If we typed **`show spanning-tree`**, we'd receive information for each VLAN, starting with VLAN 1. So, say we've got multiple VLANs and we want to see what's up with VLAN 2—we'd use the command **`show spanning-tree vlan 2`**.

Here is an output from the `show spanning-tree` command from switch S1. Since we are only using VLAN 1, we don't need to add the VLAN number to the command:

```
S1#sh spanning-tree
VLAN0001
```

```
Spanning tree enabled protocol ieee
Root ID     Priority     32769
            Address      000d.29bd.4b80
            Cost         3012
            Port         56 (Port-channel1)
            Hello Time    2 sec  Max Age 20 sec  Forward Delay 15 sec

Bridge ID   Priority     49153  (priority 49152 sys-id-ext 1)
            Address      001b.2b55.7500
            Hello Time    2 sec  Max Age 20 sec  Forward Delay 15 sec
            Aging Time 15
Uplinkfast enabled

Interface        Role Sts Cost      Prio.Nbr Type
---------------- ---- --- --------- -------- ----------
Fa0/3            Desg FWD 3100      128.3    Edge Shr
Fa0/4            Desg FWD 3019      128.4    Edge P2p
Fa0/8            Desg FWD 3019      128.8    P2p
Po1              Root FWD 3012      128.56   P2p
```

Since we only have VLAN 1 configured, there's no more output for this command, but if we had more, we would get another page for each VLAN configured on the switch. The default priority is 32768, but there's something called the system ID extension (sys-id-ext), which is the VLAN identifier. The Bridge ID priority is incremented by the number of that VLAN. And since we only have VLAN 1, we increment by one to 32769. But understand, by default, BackboneFast raises the default priority to 49152 to prevent that bridge from becoming the root.

The top of the output shows us who the root bridge is:

```
VLAN0001
    Root ID  Priority     32769
             Address      000d.29bd.4b80
             Cost         3012
             Port         56 (Port-channel1)
             Hello Time    2 sec  Max Age 20 sec  Forward Delay 15 sec
```

EtherChannel Port 1 is our root port, which means that it's our chosen path to the root bridge, and it has an identifier of 000d.29bd.4b80. That can only be either the Core switch or S2, and we'll find out which one it is in a minute.

The last output from the command displays the ports that are running STP and have a connection to another device. Because we're running EtherChannel, we have no blocked ports. One way to determine if your bridge is not the root is to look to see whether there are any Altn BLK ports (meaning blocked ports that are alternates). A root bridge would never have a blocked port on any interface, but all our ports on S1 show forwarding (FWD) because of our EtherChannel configuration.

Determining Our Root Bridge

To determine our root bridge, we would obviously use the `show spanning-tree` command. Let's take a look at our other two switches and see which switch is the default root bridge. Make a mental note of the Bridge ID MAC address as well as the priority of the S1 switch. Here's the S2 output:

```
S2#sh spanning-tree

VLAN0001
  Spanning tree enabled protocol ieee
  Root ID    Priority    32769
             Address     000d.29bd.4b80
             Cost        3019
             Port        2 (FastEthernet0/1)
             Hello Time   2 sec  Max Age 20 sec  Forward Delay 15 sec

  Bridge ID  Priority    49153  (priority 49152 sys-id-ext 1)
             Address     001a.e2ce.ff00
             Hello Time   2 sec  Max Age 20 sec  Forward Delay 15 sec
             Aging Time 300
  Uplinkfast enabled

Interface        Role Sts Cost      Prio.Nbr Type
---------------- ---- --- --------- -------- ------------
Fa0/1            Root FWD 3019      128.2    P2p
Fa0/2            Altn BLK 3019      128.3    P2p
Fa0/3            Desg FWD 3100      128.4    Edge Shr
Fa0/4            Desg FWD 3019      128.5    Edge P2p
S2#
```

We can see that port Fa0/2 is blocked, so this switch cannot be our root bridge. A root bridge cannot have blocked ports. Again, pay special attention to the Bridge ID MAC address and the priority on the top of the output, which provides our root bridge information. Here's the output from the Core switch:

```
Core#sh spanning-tree
VLAN0001
  Spanning tree enabled protocol rstp
  Root ID    Priority    32769
             Address     000d.29bd.4b80
```

```
           This bridge is the root
           Hello Time   2 sec  Max Age 20 sec  Forward Delay 15 sec

  Bridge ID  Priority    32769  (priority 32768 sys-id-ext 1)
             Address     000d.29bd.4b80
             Hello Time   2 sec  Max Age 20 sec  Forward Delay 15 sec
             Aging Time 300

Interface        Role Sts Cost      Prio.Nbr Type
---------------- ---- --- --------- -------- --------------
Fa0/5            Desg FWD 19        128.5    P2p Peer(STP)
Fa0/6            Desg FWD 19        128.6    P2p Peer(STP)
Po1              Desg FWD 12        128.66   P2p Peer(STP)
```

Well there you have it— "This bridge is the root" listed on the top of the output.

But think about this—why does the Core switch just have the default of 32768 and not 49152 like the other switches? Because it's running the 802.1w version of STP, and BackboneFast is disabled by default.

Let's take a look at the bridge MAC address of each switch:

- *S1 address:* 001b.2b55.7500
- *S2 address:* 001a.e2ce.ff00
- *Core address:* 000d.29bd.4b80

By checking out the MAC addresses, and if all switches are set to the default priority, which switch do you think will be the root switch? Start reading the MAC addresses from the left, moving toward the right. Core is obviously the lowest MAC address, and by looking at the output of the `show spanning-tree` command, we can see that it is, indeed, our root bridge (even if all switches had the same priority). It's good practice to figure out the potential root bridge by comparing the MAC addresses of the switches once in awhile.

Setting Our Root Bridge

It's kind of convenient that the Core switch is our root bridge by default because that's right where I'd typically choose to set the root. But just for fun, let's change it. Here's how we'll do that:

```
S1#config t
S1(config)#spanning-tree vlan 1 priority ?
  <0-61440>  bridge priority in increments of 4096
S1(config)#spanning-tree vlan 1 priority 16384
S1(config)#do show spanning-tree
VLAN0001
Spanning tree enabled protocol ieee
  Root ID    Priority    16385
```

```
             Address     001b.2b55.7500
             This bridge is the root
             Hello Time   2 sec  Max Age 20 sec  Forward Delay 15 sec

  Bridge ID  Priority    16385  (priority 16384 sys-id-ext 1)
             Address     001b.2b55.7500
             Hello Time   2 sec  Max Age 20 sec  Forward Delay 15 sec
             Aging Time 300

Interface        Role Sts Cost      Prio.Nbr Type
---------------- ---- --- --------- -------- -----------
Fa0/3            Desg FWD 100       128.3    Edge Shr
Fa0/4            Desg FWD 19        128.4    Edge P2p
Fa0/8            Desg FWD 19        128.8    P2p
Po1              Desg FWD 12        128.56   P2p
```

When you lower the S1 priority to 16384, the S1 switch immediately became the root bridge. You can set your priorities all the way from 0 to 61440. Zero (0) means that the switch will always be the root bridge (unless another switch with its bridge priority also set to 0 happens to have a lower MAC address), and 61440 means the switch will never be a root.

There's one last command I want to tell you about, if you want to skip all this verification and configuration of the root bridge stuff—and no, you don't get to skip all that if you want to pass the Cisco exams! Here's a simple command you can run on a switch to set it as a root bridge:

```
S1(config)#spanning-tree vlan 1 root ?
  primary    Configure this switch as primary root for this spanning tree
  secondary  Configure switch as secondary root
S1(config)#spanning-tree vlan 1 root primary
```

Oh, and did I mention that you would have to configure this per VLAN, and that you can also set a primary and secondary switch as roots? Yep, you can, and it's certainly a whole lot easier than how we've done it in this chapter! But this is, first and foremost, a guide to prepare you for the CCNA exam—something you definitely want to pass. So make sure you know how to do it like we did even though it really is the hard way!

Now admit it—even though this was a huge chapter, you really did learn a lot, and well, maybe you even had a little fun along the way! You've now configured and verified all switches, set port security, and navigated STP extensions as well as set your root bridge. That means you're now ready to learn all about virtual LANs! I'm going to save all our switch configurations so we'll be able to start right from here in Chapter 11, "Virtual LANs (VLANs)."

Summary

In this chapter, I talked about the differences between switches and bridges and how they both work at layer 2 and create a MAC address forward/filter table in order to make decisions on whether to forward or flood a frame.

I also discussed problems that can occur if you have multiple links between bridges (switches) and how to solve these problems by using the Spanning Tree Protocol (STP).

Finally, I covered detailed configuration of Cisco's Catalyst switches, including verifying the configuration, setting the Cisco STP extensions, and changing the root bridge by setting a bridge priority.

Exam Essentials

Remember the three switch functions. Address learning, forward/filter decisions, and loop avoidance are the functions of a switch.

Remember the command `show mac address-table`. The command `show mac address-table` will show you the forward/filter table used on the LAN switch.

Understand the main purpose of the Spanning Tree Protocol in a switched LAN. The main purpose of STP is to prevent switching loops in a network with redundant switched paths.

Remember the states of STP. The purpose of the blocking state is to prevent the use of looped paths. A port in listening state prepares to forward data frames without populating the MAC address table. A port in learning state populates the MAC address table but doesn't forward data frames. A port in forwarding state sends and receives all data frames on the bridged port. Last, a port in the disabled state is virtually nonoperational.

Remember the command `show spanning-tree`. You must be familiar with the command `show spanning-tree` and how to determine who the root bridge is.

Written Lab 10

Write the answers to the following questions:

1. What command will show you the forward/filter table?
2. If a destination MAC address is not in the forward/filter table, what will the switch do with the frame?
3. What are the three switch functions at layer 2?

4. If a frame is received on a switch port and the source MAC address is not in the forward/filter table, what will the switch do?
5. Which proprietary Cisco STP extension would put a switch port into err-disabled if a BPDU is received on this port?
6. 802.1w is also called what?
7. When is STP considered to be converged?
8. Switches break up _________ domains.
9. What is used to prevent switching loops in a network with redundant switched paths?
10. Which Cisco 802.1d extension stops BPDU from being transmitted out a port?

(The answers to Written Lab 10 can be found following the review questions for this chapter.)

Review Questions

The following questions are designed to test your understanding of this chapter's material. For more information on how to get additional questions, please see this book's Introduction.

1. Which of the following is a layer 2 protocol used to maintain a loop-free network?
   A. VTP
   B. STP
   C. RIP
   D. CDP
2. What command will display the forward/filter table?
   A. `show mac filter`
   B. `show run`
   C. `show mac address-table`
   D. `show mac filter-table`
3. What is the result of segmenting a network with a bridge (switch)? (Choose two.)
   A. It increases the number of collision domains.
   B. It decreases the number of collision domains.
   C. It increases the number of broadcast domains.
   D. It decreases the number of broadcast domains.
   E. It makes smaller collision domains.
   F. It makes larger collision domains.
4. Which statement describes a spanning-tree network that has converged?
   A. All switch and bridge ports are in the forwarding state.
   B. All switch and bridge ports are assigned as either root or designated ports.
   C. All switch and bridge ports are in either the forwarding or blocking state.
   D. All switch and bridge ports are either blocking or looping.
5. What is the purpose of Spanning Tree Protocol in a switched LAN?
   A. To provide a mechanism for network monitoring in switched environments
   B. To prevent routing loops in networks with redundant paths
   C. To prevent switching loops in networks with redundant switched paths
   D. To manage the VLAN database across multiple switches
   E. To create collision domains

6. What are the three distinct functions of layer 2 switching that increase available bandwidth on the network? (Choose three.)
   A. Address learning
   B. Routing
   C. Forwarding and filtering
   D. Creating network loops
   E. Loop avoidance
   F. IP addressing

7. Your switch has a port status LED that is alternating between green and amber. What could this indicate?
   A. The port is experiencing errors.
   B. The port is shut down.
   C. The port is in STP blocking mode.
   D. Nothing; this is normal.

8. Which of the following statements is true?
   A. A switch creates a single collision domain and a single broadcast domain. A router creates a single collision domain.
   B. A switch creates separate collision domains but one broadcast domain. A router provides a separate broadcast domain.
   C. A switch creates a single collision domain and separate broadcast domains. A router provides a separate broadcast domain as well.
   D. A switch creates separate collision domains and separate broadcast domains. A router provides separate collision domains.

9. You need to configure a Catalyst switch so it can be managed remotely. Which of the following would you use to accomplish this task?
   A.
   ```
   Switch(config)#int fa0/1
   Switch(config-if)#ip address 192.168.10.252 255.255.255.0
   Switch(config-if)#no shut
   ```
   B.
   ```
   Switch(config)#int vlan 1
   Switch(config-if)#ip address 192.168.10.252 255.255.255.0
   Switch(config-if)#ip default-gateway 192.168.10.254 255.255.255.0
   ```
   C.
   ```
   Switch(config)#ip default-gateway 192.168.10.254
   Switch(config)#int vlan 1
   Switch(config-if)#ip address 192.168.10.252 255.255.255.0
   Switch(config-if)#no shut
   ```
   D.
   ```
   Switch(config)#ip default-network 192.168.10.254
   Switch(config)#int vlan 1
   Switch(config-if)#ip address 192.168.10.252 255.255.255.0
   Switch(config-if)#no shut
   ```

10. What does a switch do when a frame is received on an interface and the destination hardware address is unknown or not in the filter table?

    A. Forwards the switch to the first available link

    B. Drops the frame

    C. Floods the network with the frame looking for the device

    D. Sends back a message to the originating station asking for a name resolution

11. If a switch receives a frame and the source MAC address is not in the MAC address table but the destination address is, what will the switch do with the frame?

    A. Discard it and send an error message back to the originating host

    B. Flood the network with the frame

    C. Add the source address and port to the MAC address table and forward the frame out the destination port

    D. Add the destination to the MAC address table and then forward the frame

12. You want to run the new 802.1w on your switches. Which of the following would enable this protocol?

    A. `Switch(config)#spanning-tree mode rapid-pvst`

    B. `Switch#spanning-tree mode rapid-pvst`

    C. `Switch(config)#spanning-tree mode 802.1w`

    D. `Switch#spanning-tree mode 802.1w`

13. In which circumstance are multiple copies of the same unicast frame likely to be transmitted in a switched LAN?

    A. During high-traffic periods

    B. After broken links are reestablished

    C. When upper-layer protocols require high reliability

    D. In an improperly implemented redundant topology

14. Which command was used to produce the following output:

```
Vlan    Mac Address       Type        Ports
----    -----------       --------    -----
   1    0005.dccb.d74b    DYNAMIC     Fa0/1
   1    000a.f467.9e80    DYNAMIC     Fa0/3
   1    000a.f467.9e8b    DYNAMIC     Fa0/4
   1    000a.f467.9e8c    DYNAMIC     Fa0/3
   1    0010.7b7f.c2b0    DYNAMIC     Fa0/3
   1    0030.80dc.460b    DYNAMIC     Fa0/3
```

    A. `show vlan`

    B. `show ip route`

    C. `show mac address-table`

    D. `show mac address-filter`

15. If you want to disable STP on a port connected to a server, which command would you use?

    A. `disable spanning-tree`

    B. `spanning-tree off`

    C. `spanning-tree security`

    D. `spanning-tree portfast`

16. Refer to the diagram. Why does the switch have two MAC addresses assigned to the FastEthernet 0/1 port in the switch address table?

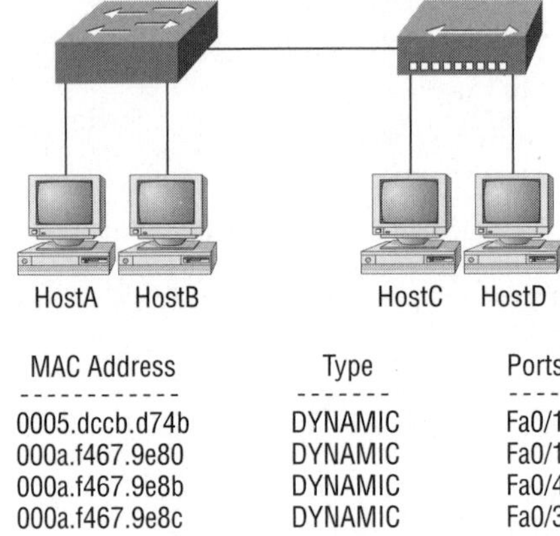

MAC Address	Type	Ports
0005.dccb.d74b	DYNAMIC	Fa0/1
000a.f467.9e80	DYNAMIC	Fa0/1
000a.f467.9e8b	DYNAMIC	Fa0/4
000a.f467.9e8c	DYNAMIC	Fa0/3

    A. Data from HostC and HostD has been received by the switch port FastEthernet 0/1.

    B. Data from two of the devices connected to the switch has been forwarded out to HostD.

    C. HostC and HostD had their NIC replaced.

    D. HostC and HostD are on different VLANs.

17. Layer 2 switching provides which of the following? (Choose four.)

    A. Hardware-based bridging (ASIC)

    B. Wire speed

    C. Low latency

    D. Low cost

    E. Routing

    F. WAN services

18. You type **show mac address-table** and receive the following output:

```
Switch#sh mac address-table
Vlan    Mac Address       Type        Ports
----    -----------       --------    -----
   1    0005.dccb.d74b    DYNAMIC     Fa0/1
   1    000a.f467.9e80    DYNAMIC     Fa0/3
   1    000a.f467.9e8b    DYNAMIC     Fa0/4
   1    000a.f467.9e8c    DYNAMIC     Fa0/3
   1    0010.7b7f.c2b0    DYNAMIC     Fa0/3
   1    0030.80dc.460b    DYNAMIC     Fa0/3
```

Suppose the above switch received a frame with the following MAC addresses:

- Source MAC: 0005.dccb.d74b
- Destination MAC: 000a.f467.9e8c

What will it do?

A. It will discard the frame.

B. It will forward the frame out port Fa0/3 only.

C. It will forward it out Fa0/1 only.

D. It will send it out all ports except Fa0/1.

19. You need to allow one host to be permitted to attach dynamically to each switch interface. Which two commands must you configure on your Catalyst switch to meet this policy? (Choose two.)

A. `Switch(config-if)#ip access-group 10`

B. `Switch(config-if)#switchport port-security maximum 1`

C. `Switch(config)#access-list 10 permit ip host 1`

D. `Switch(config-if)#switchport port-security violation shutdown`

E. `Switch(config)#mac-address-table secure`

20. You have two switches connected together with two crossover cables for redundancy, and STP is disabled. Which of the following will happen between the switches?

A. The routing tables on the switches will not update.

B. The MAC forward/filter table will not update on the switch.

C. Broadcast storms will occur on the switched network.

D. The switches will automatically load-balance between the two links.

Answers to Review Questions

1. B. The Spanning Tree Protocol is used to stop switching loops in a switched network with redundant paths.

2. C. The command `show mac address-table` displays the forward/filter table on the switch.

3. A, E. Bridges break up collision domains, which would increase the number of collision domains in a network and also make smaller collision domains.

4. C. Convergence occurs when all ports on bridges and switches have transitioned to either the forwarding or blocking states. No data is forwarded until convergence is complete. Before data can be forwarded again, all devices must be updated.

5. C. The Spanning Tree Protocol (STP) was designed to stop layer 2 loops. All Cisco switches have the STP on by default.

6. A, C, E. Layer 2 features include address learning, forwarding and filtering of the network, and loop avoidance.

7. A. When you connect to a switch port, at first the link lights are orange/amber, and then they turn green, indicating normal operation. If the link light is blinking, you have a problem.

8. B. Switches break up collision domains, and routers break up broadcast domains.

9. C. To manage a switch remotely, you must set an IP address under the management VLAN, which is, by default, interface vlan 1. Then, from global configuration mode, you set the default gateway with the `ip default-gateway` command. Option C enables the management interface, which makes it correct over option B.

10. C. Switches flood all frames that have an unknown destination address. If a device answers the frame, the switch will update the MAC address table to reflect the location of the device.

11. C. Since the source MAC address is not in the MAC address table, the switch will add the source address and the port it is connected to into the MAC address table and then forward the frame to the outgoing port.

12. A. 802.1w is the also called Rapid Spanning Tree Protocol. It is not enabled by default on Cisco switches, but it is a better STP to run since it has all the fixes that the Cisco extensions provide with 802.1d.

13. D. If the Spanning Tree Protocol is not running on your switches and you connect them together with redundant links, you will have broadcast storms and multiple frame copies.

14. C. The command `show mac address-table` will display the forward/filter table, also called a CAM table, on a switch.

15. D. If you have a server or other devices connected into your switch that you're totally sure won't create a switching loop if STP is disabled, you can use something called `portfast` on these ports. Using it means the port won't spend the usual 50 seconds to come up while STP is converging.

16. A. A switch can have multiple MAC addresses associated with a port. In the diagram, a hub is connected to port Fa0/1, which has two hosts connected.

17. A, B, C, D. Switches, unlike bridges, are hardware based. Cisco says its switches are wire speed and provide low latency, and I guess they are low cost compared to their prices in the 1990s.

18. B. Since the destination MAC address is in the MAC address table (forward/filter table), it will send it out port Fa0/3 only.

19. B, D. `switchport port-security` is an important command, and it's super easy with the CNA; however, from the CLI you can set the maximum number of MAC addresses allowed into the port and then set the penalty if this maximum has been passed.

20. C. If spanning tree is disabled on a switch and you have redundant links to another switch, broadcast storms will occur, among other possible problems.

Answers to Written Lab 10

1. `show mac address-table`
2. Flood the frame out all ports except the port on which it was received
3. Address learning, forward/filter decisions, and loop avoidance
4. It will add the source MAC address in the forward/filter table and associate it with the port on which the frame was received.
5. BPDUGuard
6. Rapid Spanning Tree Protocol (RSTP)
7. When all ports are in either the blocking or the forwarding mode
8. Collision
9. Spanning Tree Protocol (STP)
10. PortFast

Virtual LANs (VLANs)

THE CCNA EXAM TOPICS COVERED IN THIS CHAPTER INCLUDE THE FOLLOWING:

✓ **Describe how a network works**

- Describe the impact of applications (Voice Over IP and Video Over IP) on a network

✓ **Configure, verify, and troubleshoot a switch with VLANs and interswitch communications**

- Verify network status and switch operation using basic utilities (including: ping, traceroute, telnet, SSH, arp, ipconfig), SHOW and DEBUG commands
- Identify, prescribe, and resolve common switched network media issues, configuration issues, auto negotiation, and switch hardware failures
- Describe enhanced switching technologies (including: VTP, RSTP, VLAN, PVSTP, 802.1q)
- Describe how VLANs create logically separate networks and the need for routing between them
- Configure, verify, and troubleshoot VLANs
- Configure, verify, and troubleshoot trunking on Cisco switches
- Configure, verify, and troubleshoot interVLAN routing
- Configure, verify, and troubleshoot VTP
- Configure, verify, and troubleshoot RSTP operation
- Interpret the output of various show and debug commands to verify the operational status of a Cisco switched network
- Implement basic switch security (including: port security, trunk access, management vlan other than vlan1, etc.)

I know I keep telling you this, but I've got to be sure you never forget it, so here I go, one last time: By default, switches break up collision domains and routers break up broadcast domains. Okay, I feel better! Now we can move on.

In contrast to the networks of yesterday that were based on collapsed backbones, today's network design is characterized by a flatter architecture—thanks to switches. So now what? How do we break up broadcast domains in a pure switched internetwork? By creating virtual local area network (VLANs). A VLAN is a logical grouping of network users and resources connected to administratively defined ports on a switch. When you create VLANs, you're given the ability to create smaller broadcast domains within a layer 2 switched internetwork by assigning different ports on the switch to service different subnetworks. A VLAN is treated like its own subnet or broadcast domain, meaning that frames broadcast onto the network are only switched between the ports logically grouped within the same VLAN.

So, does this mean we no longer need routers? Maybe yes; maybe no. It really depends on what you want or what your needs are. By default, hosts in a specific VLAN cannot communicate with hosts that are members of another VLAN, so if you want inter-VLAN communication, the answer is that you still need a router.

In this chapter, you're going to learn, in detail, exactly what a VLAN is and how VLAN memberships are used in a switched network. Also, I'm going to tell you all about how VLAN Trunk Protocol (VTP) is used to update switch databases with VLAN information and how trunking is used to send information from all VLANs across a single link. I'll wrap things up by demonstrating how you can make inter-VLAN communication happen by introducing a router into a switched network.

Of course, we'll configure our switched network with VLANs, VTP, and inter-VLAN routing.

For up-to-the-minute updates to this chapter, please see `www.lammle.com` and/or `www.sybex.com/go/ccna7e`.

VLAN Basics

Figure 11.1 shows how layer 2 switched networks are typically designed—as flat networks. With this configuration, every broadcast packet transmitted is seen by every device on the network regardless of whether the device needs to receive that data or not.

FIGURE 11.1 Flat network structure

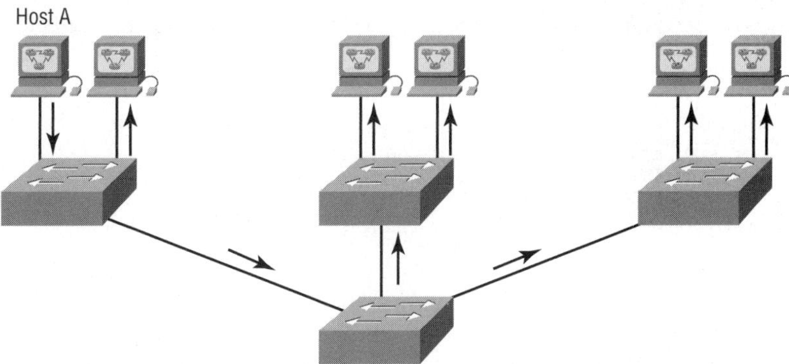

By default, routers allow broadcasts to occur only within the originating network, while switches forward broadcasts to all segments. Oh, and by the way, the reason it's called a *flat network* is because it's one *broadcast domain*, not because the actual design is physically flat. In Figure 11.1 we see Host A sending out a broadcast and all ports on all switches forwarding it—all except the port that originally received it.

Now check out Figure 11.2. It pictures a switched network and shows Host A sending a frame with Host D as its destination. What's important is that, as you can see, that frame is only forwarded out the port where Host D is located. This is a huge improvement over the old hub networks, unless having one *collision domain* by default is what you really want. (Probably not!)

Now you already know that the largest benefit you gain by having a layer 2 switched network is that it creates individual collision domain segments for each device plugged into each port on the switch. This scenario frees us from the Ethernet density constraints, so now larger networks can be built. But often, each new advance comes with new issues. For instance, the larger the number of users and devices, the more broadcasts and packets each switch must handle.

FIGURE 11.2 The benefit of a switched network

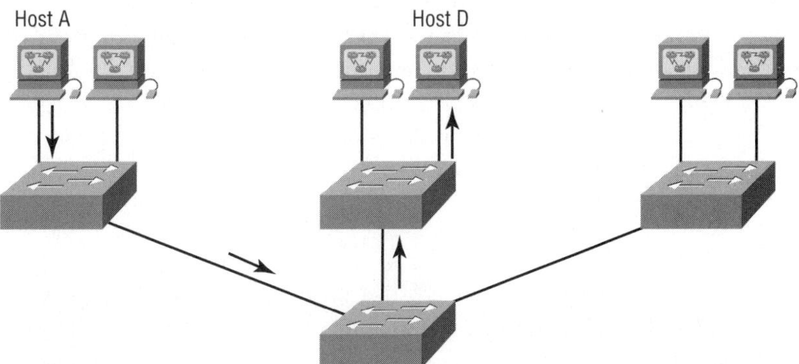

And here's another issue: security! This one's real trouble because within the typical layer 2 switched internetwork, all users can see all devices by default. And you can't stop devices from broadcasting, plus you can't stop users from trying to respond to broadcasts. This means your security options are dismally limited to placing passwords on your servers and other devices.

But wait—there's hope! That is, if you create a *virtual LAN (VLAN)*. You can solve many of the problems associated with layer 2 switching with VLANs, as you'll soon see.

Here's a short list of ways VLANs simplify network management:

- Network adds, moves, and changes are achieved with ease by just configuring a port into the appropriate VLAN.
- A group of users that need an unusually high level of security can be put into its own VLAN so that users outside of the VLAN can't communicate with them.
- As a logical grouping of users by function, VLANs can be considered independent from their physical or geographic locations.
- VLANs greatly enhance network security.
- VLANs increase the number of broadcast domains while decreasing their size.

Coming up, I'm going to tell you all about switching characteristics and thoroughly describe how switches provide us with better network services than hubs can in our networks today.

Broadcast Control

Broadcasts occur in every protocol, but how often they occur depends upon three things:

- The type of protocol
- The application(s) running on the internetwork
- How these services are used

Some older applications have been rewritten to reduce their bandwidth appetites, but there's a new generation of applications that are incredibly bandwidth greedy that will consume any and all they can find. These bandwidth gluttons are multimedia applications that use both broadcasts and multicasts extensively. And faulty equipment, inadequate segmentation, and poorly designed firewalls seriously compound the problems that these broadcast-intensive applications create. All of this has added a major new dimension to network design and presents a bunch of new challenges for an administrator. Positively making sure your network is properly segmented so you can quickly isolate a single segment's problems to prevent them from propagating throughout your entire internetwork is imperative! And the most effective way to do that is through strategic switching and routing.

Since switches have become more affordable lately, a lot of companies are replacing their flat hub networks with pure switched network and VLAN environments. All devices within a VLAN are members of the same broadcast domain and receive all broadcasts. By default, these broadcasts are filtered from all ports on a switch that aren't members of the same VLAN. This is great because you get all the benefits you would with a switched design without getting hit with all the problems you'd have if all your users were in the same broadcast domain—sweet!

Security

Okay, I know. There's always a catch, though, right? Time to get back to those security issues. A flat internetwork's security used to be tackled by connecting hubs and switches together with routers. So it was basically the router's job to maintain security. This arrangement was pretty ineffective for several reasons. First, anyone connecting to the physical network could access the network resources located on that particular physical LAN. Second, all anyone had to do to observe any and all traffic happening in that network was to simply plug a network analyzer into the hub. And similar to that last ugly fact, users could join a workgroup by just plugging their workstations into the existing hub. That's about as secure as an open barrel of honey in a bear enclosure!

But that's exactly what makes VLANs so cool. If you build them and create multiple broadcast groups, you can have total control over each port and user! So the days when anyone could just plug their workstations into any switch port and gain access to network resources are history because now you get to control each port, plus whatever resources that port can access.

And it doesn't end there my friends, because VLANs can be created in accordance with the network resources a given user requires, plus switches can be configured to inform a network management station of any unauthorized access to network resources. And if you need inter-VLAN communication, you can implement restrictions on a router to make sure that happens securely. You can also place restrictions on hardware addresses, protocols, and applications. *Now* we're talking security—the honey barrel is now sealed, shrouded in razor wire, and made of solid titanium!

Flexibility and Scalability

If you were paying attention to what you've read so far, you know that layer 2 switches only read frames for filtering—they don't look at the Network layer protocol. And by default, switches forward broadcasts to all ports. But if you create and implement VLANs, you're essentially creating smaller broadcast domains at layer 2.

What this means is that broadcasts sent out from a node in one VLAN won't be forwarded to ports configured to belong to a different VLAN. So by assigning switch ports or users to VLAN groups on a switch or group of connected switches, you gain the flexibility to add only the users you want into that broadcast domain regardless of their physical location. This setup can also work to block broadcast storms caused by a faulty network interface card (NIC) as well as prevent an intermediate device from propagating broadcast storms throughout the entire internetwork. Those evils can still happen on the VLAN where the problem originated, but the disease will instead be quarantined to that one ailing VLAN.

Another advantage is that when a VLAN gets too big, you can create more VLANs to keep the broadcasts from consuming too much bandwidth—the fewer users in a VLAN, the fewer users affected by broadcasts. This is all well and good, but you seriously need to keep network services in mind and understand how the users connect to these services when you create your VLAN. It's a good move to try to keep all services, except for the email and Internet access that everyone needs, local to all users whenever possible.

To understand how a VLAN looks to a switch, it's helpful to begin by first looking at a traditional network. Figure 11.3 shows how a network was created by using hubs to connect physical LANs to a router.

FIGURE 11.3 Physical LANs connected to a router

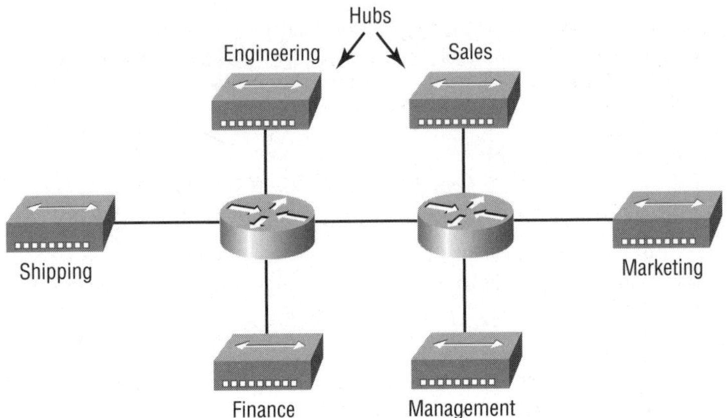

Here you can see that each network is attached with a hub port to the router (each segment also has its own logical network number even though this isn't obvious looking at the figure). Each node attached to a particular physical network has to match that network's number in order to be able to communicate on the internetwork. Notice that each department has its own LAN, so if you needed to add new users to, let's say, Sales, you would just plug them into the Sales LAN and they would automatically be part of the Sales collision and broadcast domain. This design really did work well for many years.

But there was one major flaw: What happens if the hub for Sales is full and we need to add another user to the Sales LAN? Or, what do we do if there's no more physical space where the Sales team is located for this new employee? Well, let's say there just happens to be plenty of room in the Finance section of the building. That new Sales team member will just have to sit on the same side of the building as the Finance people, and we'll just plug the poor soul into the hub for Finance.

Doing this obviously makes the new user part of the Finance LAN, which is very bad for many reasons. First and foremost, we now have a major security issue. Because the new Sales employee is a member of the Finance broadcast domain, the newbie can see all the same servers and access all network services that the Finance folks can. Second, for this user to access the Sales network services they need to get their job done, they would have to go through the router to log in to the Sales server—not exactly efficient!

Now let's look at what a switch accomplishes for us. Figure 11.4 demonstrates how switches come to the rescue by removing the physical boundary to solve our problem. It also shows how six VLANs (numbered 2 through 7) are used to create a broadcast domain for each department. Each switch port is then administratively assigned a VLAN membership, depending on the host and which broadcast domain it's to be placed in.

FIGURE 11.4 Switches removing the physical boundary

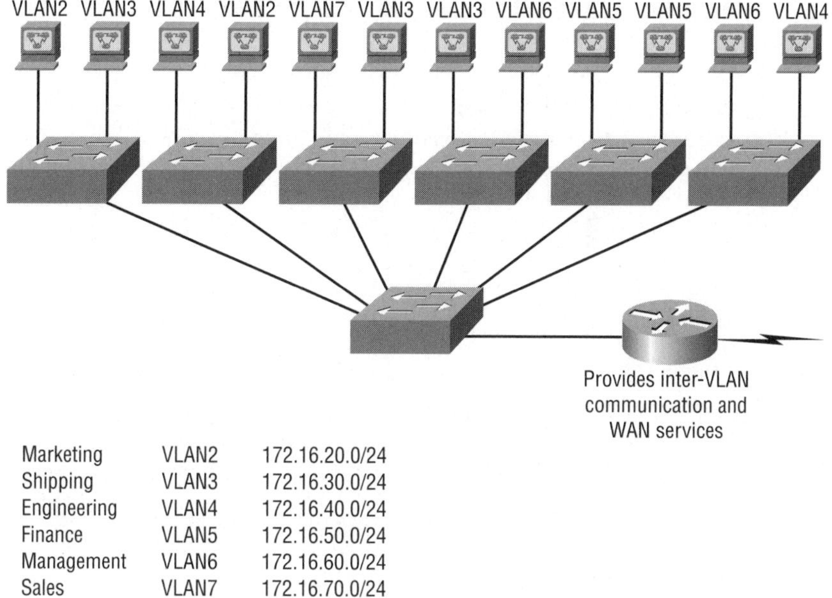

So now, if we needed to add another user to the Sales VLAN (VLAN 7), we could just assign the port to VLAN 7 regardless of where the new Sales team member is physically located—nice! This illustrates one of the sweetest advantages to designing your network with VLANs over the old collapsed backbone design. Now, cleanly and simply, each host that needs to be in the Sales VLAN is merely connected to a port assigned to VLAN 7.

Notice that I started assigning VLANs with VLAN number 2. The number is irrelevant, but you might be wondering what happened to VLAN 1? Well that VLAN is an administrative VLAN, and even though it can be used for a workgroup, Cisco recommends that you use it for administrative purposes only. You can't delete or change the name of VLAN 1, and by default, all ports on a switch are members of VLAN 1 until you change them.

Since each VLAN is considered a broadcast domain, it's got to also have its own subnet number (refer again to Figure 11.4). And if you're also using IPv6, then each VLAN must also be assigned its own IPv6 network number. So you don't get confused, just keep thinking of VLANs as separate subnets or networks.

Now let's get back to that "because of switches, we don't need routers anymore" misconception. Looking at Figure 11.4, notice that there are seven VLANs, or broadcast domains, counting VLAN 1. The nodes within each VLAN can communicate with each other but not with anything in a different VLAN because the nodes in any given VLAN "think" that they're actually in a collapsed backbone, as illustrated in Figure 11.3.

So what handy little tool do we need to enable the hosts in Figure 11.4 to communicate to a node or host on a different VLAN? You guessed it—a router! Those nodes positively need to go through a router, or some other layer 3 device, just as when they're configured for internetwork communication (as shown in Figure 11.3). It works the same way it would if we were trying to connect different physical networks. Communication between VLANs must go through a layer 3 device. So don't expect mass router extinction anytime soon!

We'll use both a router and the 3560 switch to provide inter-VLAN routing on our switched network toward the end of this chapter. We could actually employ the 3560 to also be a layer 3 switch, acting just like a router.

VLAN Memberships

Most of the time, VLANs are created by a sys admin who proceeds to assign switch ports to each VLAN. VLANs of this type are known as *static VLANs*. If you don't mind doing a little more work when you begin this process, assign all the host devices' hardware addresses into a database so your switches can be configured to assign VLANs dynamically anytime you plug a host into a switch. I hate saying things like "obviously," but obviously, this type of VLAN is known as a *dynamic VLAN*. I'll be covering both static and dynamic VLANs in the next couple of sections.

Static VLANs

Creating static VLANs is the most common way to create a VLAN, and one of the reasons for that is because static VLANs are the most secure. This security stems from the fact that any switch port you've assigned a VLAN association to will always maintain that association unless you change the port assignment manually.

Static VLAN configuration is pretty easy to set up and supervise, and it works really well in a networking environment where any user movement within the network needs to be controlled. It can be helpful to use network management software to configure the ports, but you don't have to use it if you don't want to.

In Figure 11.4, each switch port was configured manually with a VLAN membership based upon which VLAN the host needed to be a member of—remember, the device's actual physical location doesn't matter a bit. Which broadcast domain your hosts become members of is purely up to you. And again, remember that each host also has to have the correct IP address information. For instance, you must configure each host in VLAN 2 into the 172.16.20.0/24 network for it to become a member of that VLAN. It's also a good idea to keep in mind that if you plug a host into a switch, you have to verify the VLAN membership of that port. If the membership is different than what's needed for that host (given its IP address configuration), the host won't be able to gain access to the network services that it needs, such as a workgroup server.

Static access ports are either manually assigned to a VLAN or assigned through a RADIUS server for use with IEEE 802.1x.

Dynamic VLANs

On the other hand, a dynamic VLAN determines a node's VLAN assignment automatically. Using intelligent management software, you can base VLAN assignments on hardware (MAC) addresses, protocols, or even applications that create dynamic VLANs.

For example, let's say MAC addresses have been entered into a centralized VLAN management application and you hook up a new node. If you attached it to a switch port designated as a dynamic VLAN port, the VLAN management database can look up the hardware address and both assign and configure the switch port into the correct VLAN. Needless to say, this makes management and configuration much easier because if a user moves, the switch will simply assign them to the correct VLAN automatically. But here again, there's a catch: You've got to do a lot more work initially setting up the database. It can be very worthwhile though!

And here's some good news: You can use the VLAN Management Policy Server (VMPS) service to set up a database of MAC addresses to be used for the dynamic addressing of your VLANs. The VMPS database maps MAC addresses to VLANs.

A dynamic-access port can belong to one VLAN (VLAN ID 1 all the way up to 4094) and, as I said, is dynamically assigned by the VMPS. The Catalyst 2960 switch can be a VMPS client only. You can have dynamic-access ports and trunk ports on the same switch, but you have to connect the dynamic-access port to an end station or hub—*not* to another switch!

Identifying VLANs

Know that switch ports are layer 2–only interfaces that are associated with a physical port. A switch port can belong to only one VLAN if it is an access port or all VLANs if it is a trunk port. You can manually configure a port as an access or trunk port, or you can let the Dynamic Trunking Protocol (DTP) operate on a per-port basis to set the switchport mode. DTP does this by negotiating with the port on the other end of the link.

Switches are definitely pretty busy devices. As frames are switched throughout the network, they've got to be able to keep track of all the different types plus understand what to do with them depending on the hardware address. And remember—frames are handled differently according to the type of link they're traversing.

There are two different types of ports in a switched environment:

Access ports An access port belongs to and carries the traffic of only one VLAN. Traffic is both received and sent in native formats with no VLAN tagging whatsoever. Anything arriving on an access port is simply assumed to belong to the VLAN assigned to the port. So, what do you think will happen if an access port receives a tagged packet, like IEEE 802.1Q tagged? Right—that packet would simply be dropped. But why? Well, because an access port doesn't look at the source address, so tagged traffic can be forwarded and received only on trunk ports.

With an access link, this can be referred to as the *configured VLAN* of the port. Any device attached to an *access link* is unaware of a VLAN membership—the device just assumes it's part of some broadcast domain, but it doesn't have the big picture, so it doesn't understand the physical network topology at all.

Another good bit of information to know is that switches remove any VLAN information from the frame before it's forwarded out to an access-link device. Remember that access-link devices can't communicate with devices outside their VLAN unless the packet is routed. And you can only create a switch port to be either an access port or a trunk port—not both. So you've got to choose one or the other and know that if you make it an access port, that port can be assigned to one VLAN only.

Voice access ports Not to confuse you, but all that I just said about the fact that an access port can be assigned to only one VLAN is really only sort of true. Nowadays, most switches will allow you to add a second VLAN to an access port on a switch port for your voice traffic; it's called the voice VLAN. The voice VLAN used to be called the auxiliary VLAN, which allowed it to be overlaid on top of the data VLAN, enabling both types of traffic through the same port. Even though this is technically considered to be a different type of link, it's still just an access port that can be configured for both data and voice VLANs. This allows you to connect both a phone and a PC device to one switch port but still have each device in a separate VLAN. I'll go into voice VLANs in detail and clear all this up for you in the section "Telephony: Configuring Voice VLANs" later in this chapter.

Trunk Ports Believe it or not, the term *trunk port* was inspired by the telephone system trunks that carry multiple telephone conversations at a time. So it follows that trunk ports can similarly carry multiple VLANs at a time.

A *trunk link* is a 100- or 1000Mbps point-to-point link between two switches, between a switch and router, or even between a switch and server, and it carries the traffic of multiple VLANs—from 1 to 4,094 at a time (though it's really only up to 1,005 unless you're going with extended VLANs).

Trunking can be a real advantage because with it, you get to make a single port part of a whole bunch of different VLANs at the same time. This is a great feature because you can actually set ports up to have a server in two separate broadcast domains simultaneously so your users won't have to cross a layer 3 device (router) to log in and access it. Another benefit to trunking comes into play when you're connecting switches. Trunk links can carry the frames of various VLANs across the link, but by default, if the links between your switches aren't trunked, only information from the configured access VLAN will be switched across that link.

It's also good to know that all VLANs send information on a trunked link unless you clear each VLAN by hand, and no worries, I'll show you how to clear individual VLANs from a trunk in a bit.

Check out Figure 11.5. It shows how the different links are used in a switched network. All hosts connected to the switches can communicate to all ports in their VLAN because of the trunk link between them. Remember, if we used an access link between the switches, this would allow only one VLAN to communicate across the switches. As you can see, these hosts are using access links to connect to the switch, so they're communicating in one VLAN only. That means that without a router, no host can communicate outside its own VLAN, but they can send data over trunked links to hosts on another switch configured in their same VLAN.

FIGURE 11.5 Access and trunk links in a switched network

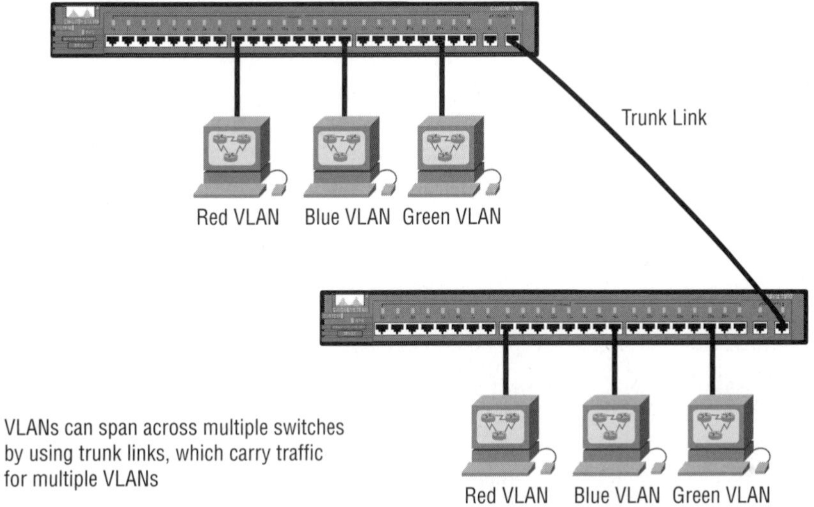

Okay—it's finally time to tell you about frame tagging and the VLAN identification methods used in it.

Frame Tagging

As you now know, you can set up your VLANs to span more than one connected switch. You can see that going on in Figure 11.4, which depicts hosts from various VLANs spread across a bunch of switches. This flexible, power-packed capability is probably the main advantage to implementing VLANs.

But it can get kind of complicated—even for a switch—so there needs to be a way for each one to keep track of all the users and frames as they travel the switch fabric and VLANs. When I say "switch fabric," I'm just referring to a group of switches that share the same VLAN information. And this just happens to be where *frame tagging* enters the scene. This frame identification method uniquely assigns a user-defined VLAN ID to each frame. Sometimes people refer to it as a VLAN ID or even VLAN color.

Here's how it works: Once within the switch fabric, each switch that the frame reaches must first identify the VLAN ID from the frame tag. It then finds out what to do with the frame by looking at the information in what's known as the filter table. If the frame reaches a switch that has another trunked link, the frame will be forwarded out the trunk-link port.

Once the frame reaches an exit that's determined by the forward/filter table to be an access link matching the frame's VLAN ID, the switch will remove the VLAN identifier. This is so the destination device can receive the frames without being required to understand their VLAN identification information.

Another thing about trunk ports is that they will support tagged and untagged traffic simultaneously (if you are using 802.1Q trunking, which we will talk about later). The trunk port is assigned a default port VLAN ID (PVID) for a VLAN on which all untagged traffic will travel. This VLAN is also called the native VLAN and is always VLAN 1 by default (but it can be changed to any VLAN number).

Similarly, any untagged or tagged traffic with a NULL (unassigned) VLAN ID is assumed to belong to the VLAN with the port default PVID (again, VLAN 1 by default). A packet with a VLAN ID equal to the outgoing port native VLAN is sent untagged and can only communicate to hosts or devices in that same VLAN. All other VLAN traffic has to be sent with a VLAN tag to communicate within a particular VLAN that corresponds with that tag.

VLAN Identification Methods

VLAN identification is what switches use to keep track of all those frames as they're traversing a switch fabric. It's how switches identify which frames belong to which VLANs, and there's more than one trunking method.

Inter-Switch Link (ISL)

Inter-Switch Link (ISL) is a way of explicitly tagging VLAN information onto an Ethernet frame. This tagging information allows VLANs to be multiplexed over a trunk link through an external encapsulation method (ISL), which allows the switch to identify the VLAN membership of a frame received over the trunked link.

By running ISL, you can interconnect multiple switches and still maintain VLAN information as traffic travels between switches on trunk links. ISL functions at layer 2 by encapsulating a data frame with a new header and a new cyclic redundancy check (CRC).

Of note is that this is proprietary to Cisco switches, and it's used for FastEthernet and Gigabit Ethernet links only. *ISL routing* is pretty versatile and can be used on a switch port, router interfaces, and server interface cards to trunk a server.

IEEE 802.1Q

Created by the IEEE as a standard method of frame tagging, IEEE 802.1Q actually inserts a field into the frame to identify the VLAN. If you're trunking between a Cisco switched link and a different brand of switch, you've got to use 802.1Q for the trunk to work.

It works like this: You first designate each port that is going to be a trunk with 802.1Q encapsulation. The ports must be assigned a specific VLAN ID, in order for them to communicate. (VLAN 1 is the default native VLAN and all traffic for a native VLAN when using 801.q is untagged.) The ports that populate the same trunk create a group with this native VLAN, and each port gets tagged with an identification number reflecting that, again the default being VLAN 1. The native VLAN allows the trunks to accept information that was received without any VLAN identification or frame tag.

The 2960s support only the IEEE 802.1Q trunking protocol, but the 3560s will support both the ISL and IEEE methods.

The basic purpose of ISL and 802.1Q frame-tagging methods is to provide inter-switch VLAN communication. Also, remember that any ISL or 802.1Q frame tagging is removed if a frame is forwarded out an access link—tagging is used internally and across trunk links only!

VLAN Trunking Protocol (VTP)

Cisco created this one too. The basic goals of *VLAN Trunking Protocol (VTP)* are to manage all configured VLANs across a switched internetwork and to maintain consistency throughout that network. VTP allows you to add, delete, and rename VLANs—information that is then propagated to all other switches in the VTP domain.

Here's a list of some of the cool features VTP has to offer:

- Consistent VLAN configuration across all switches in the network
- VLAN trunking over mixed networks, such as Ethernet to ATM LANE or even FDDI
- Accurate tracking and monitoring of VLANs
- Dynamic reporting of added VLANs to all switches in the VTP domain
- Adding VLANs using Plug and Play

Very nice, but before you can get VTP to manage your VLANs across the network, you have to create a VTP server (really, you don't need to even do that since all switches default to VTP server mode, but just make sure you have a server). All servers that need to share VLAN information must use the same domain name, and a switch can be in only one domain at a time. So basically, this means that a switch can share VTP domain information with other switches only if they're configured into the same VTP domain. You can use a VTP domain if you have more than one switch connected in a network, but if you've got all your switches in only one VLAN, you just don't need to use VTP. Do keep in mind that VTP information is sent between switches only via a trunk port.

Switches advertise VTP management domain information as well as a configuration revision number and all known VLANs with any specific parameters. But there's also something called *VTP transparent mode*. In it, you can configure switches to forward VTP information through trunk ports but not to accept information updates or update their VTP databases.

If you've got sneaky users adding switches to your VTP domain behind your back, you can include passwords, but don't forget—every switch must be set up with the same password. And as you can imagine, this little snag can be a real hassle administratively!

Switches detect any added VLANs within a VTP advertisement and then prepare to send information on their trunk ports with the newly defined VLAN in tow. Updates are sent out as revision numbers that consist of summary advertisements. Anytime a switch sees a higher revision number, it knows the information it's getting is more current, so it will overwrite the existing VLAN database with the latest information.

You should know these three requirements for VTP to communicate VLAN information between switches:

- The VTP management domain name of both switches must be set the same.
- One of the switches has to be configured as a VTP server.
- Set a VTP password if used.

No router is necessary and is not a requirement. Now that you've got that down, we're going to delve deeper into the world of VTP with VTP modes and VTP pruning.

VTP Modes of Operation

Figure 11.6 shows you all three different modes of operation within a VTP domain:

FIGURE 11.6 VTP modes

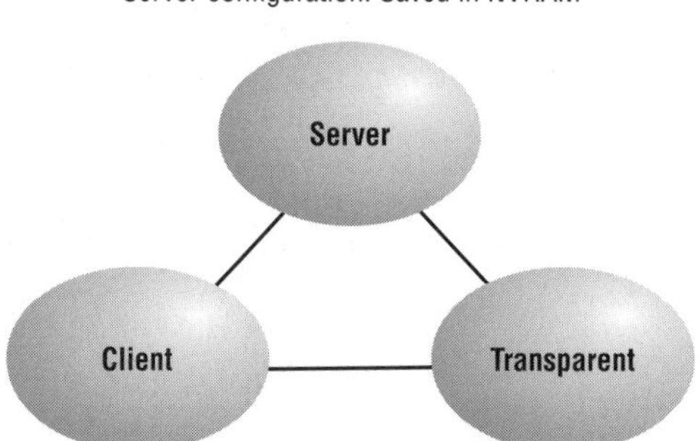

Server This is the default mode for all Catalyst switches. You need at least one server in your VTP domain to propagate VLAN information throughout that domain. Also important: The switch must be in server mode to be able to create, add, and delete VLANs in a VTP domain. VLAN information has to be changed in server mode, and any change made to VLANs on a switch in server mode will be advertised to the entire VTP domain. In VTP server mode, VLAN configurations are saved in NVRAM on the switch.

Client In client mode, switches receive information from VTP servers, but they also receive and forward updates, so in this way, they behave like VTP servers. The difference is that they can't create, change, or delete VLANs. Plus, none of the ports on a client switch can be added to a new VLAN before the VTP server notifies the client switch of the new VLAN and the

VLAN exists in the client's VLAN database. Also good to know is that VLAN information sent from a VTP server isn't stored in NVRAM, which is important because it means that if the switch is reset or reloaded, the VLAN information will be deleted. Here's a hint: If you want a switch to become a server, first make it a client so it receives all the correct VLAN information, then change it to a server—so much easier!

So basically, a switch in VTP client mode will forward VTP summary advertisements and process them. This switch will learn about but won't save the VTP configuration in the running configuration, and it won't save it in NVRAM. Switches that are in VTP client mode will only learn about and pass along VTP information—that's it!

Real World Scenario

So, When Do I Need to Consider Using VTP?

Here's a scenario for you. Bob, a senior network administrator at Acme Corporation in San Francisco, has about 25 switches all connected together, and he wants to configure VLANs to break up broadcast domains. When do you think he should start to consider using VTP?

If you answered that he should have used VTP the moment he had more than one switch and multiple VLANs, you're right. If you have only one switch, then VTP is irrelevant. It also isn't a player if you're not configuring VLANs in your network. But if you do have multiple switches that use multiple VLANs, you'd better configure your VTP server and clients, and you better do it right!

When you first bring up your switched network, verify that your main switch is a VTP server and that all the other ones are VTP clients. When you create VLANs on the main VTP server, all switches will receive the VLAN database.

If you have an existing switched network and you want to add a new switch, make sure to configure it as a VTP client before you install it. If you don't, it's possible—okay, highly probable—that your new little beauty will send out a new VTP database to all your other switches, effectively wiping out all your existing VLANs like a nuclear blast. No one needs that!

Transparent Switches in transparent mode don't participate in the VTP domain or share its VLAN database, but they'll still forward VTP advertisements through any configured trunk links. They can create, modify, and delete VLANs because they keep their own database—one they keep secret from the other switches. Despite being kept in NVRAM, the VLAN database in transparent mode is actually only locally significant. The whole purpose of transparent mode is to allow remote switches to receive the VLAN database from a VTP server-configured switch through a switch that is not participating in the same VLAN assignments.

VTP only learns about normal-range VLANs, with VLAN IDs 1 to 1005; VLANs with IDs greater than 1005 are called extended-range VLANs and they're not stored in the VLAN database. The switch must be in VTP transparent mode when you create VLAN IDs from 1006 to 4094, so it would be pretty rare that you'd ever use these VLANs. One other thing: VLAN IDs 1 and 1002 to 1005 are automatically created on all switches and can't be removed.

VTP Pruning

VTP gives you a way to preserve bandwidth by configuring it to reduce the amount of broadcasts, multicasts, and unicast packets. This is called *pruning*. Switches enabled for VTP pruning send broadcasts only to trunk links that actually must have the information.

Here's what this means: If Switch A doesn't have any ports configured for VLAN 5 and a broadcast is sent throughout VLAN 5, that broadcast wouldn't traverse the trunk link to Switch A. By default, VTP pruning is disabled on all switches. Seems to me this would be a good default parameter. When you enable pruning on a VTP server, you enable it for the entire domain. By default, VLANs 2 through 1001 are pruning eligible, but VLAN 1 can never be pruned because it's an administrative VLAN. VTP pruning is supported with both VTP version 1 and version 2.

By using the `show interface trunk` command, we can see that all VLANs are allowed across a trunked link by default:

```
S1#sh int trunk

Port        Mode         Encapsulation  Status        Native vlan
Fa0/1       auto         802.1q         trunking      1
Fa0/2       auto         802.1q         trunking      1

Port        Vlans allowed on trunk
Fa0/1       1-4094
Fa0/2       1-4094

Port        Vlans allowed and active in management domain
Fa0/1       1
Fa0/2       1

Port        Vlans in spanning tree forwarding state and not pruned
Fa0/1       1
Fa0/2       none
S1#
```

Looking at the preceding output, you can see that VTP pruning is disabled by default. I'm going to go ahead and enable pruning. It only takes one command and it is enabled on your entire switched network for the listed VLANs. Let's see what happens:

```
S1#config t
S1(config)#int f0/1
S1(config-if)#switchport trunk ?
  allowed  Set allowed VLAN characteristics when interface is
  in trunking mode
  native   Set trunking native characteristics when interface
  is in trunking mode
  pruning  Set pruning VLAN characteristics when interface is
  in trunking mode
S1(config-if)#switchport trunk pruning ?
  vlan  Set VLANs enabled for pruning when interface is in
  trunking mode
S1(config-if)#switchport trunk pruning vlan 3-4
```

The valid VLANs that can be pruned are 2 to 1001. Extended-range VLANs (VLAN IDs 1006 to 4094) can't be pruned, and these pruning-ineligible VLANs can receive a flood of traffic.

It is imperative that you go through this VTP section more than once, and it is extremely important for the CCNA objectives that you go through the VTP configuration section later in this chapter. To become a CCNA, you must have a very clear fundamental understanding of VTP.

Routing between VLANs

Hosts in a VLAN live in their own broadcast domain and can communicate freely. VLANs create network partitioning and traffic separation at layer 2 of the OSI, and as I said when I told you why we still need routers, if you want hosts or any other IP-addressable device to communicate between VLANs, you just have to have a layer 3 device to provide routing—period.

For this, you can use a router that has an interface for each VLAN or a router that supports ISL or 802.1Q routing. The least expensive router that supports ISL or 802.1Q routing is the 2600 series router. (You'd have to buy that from a used-equipment reseller, because they are end of life, or EOL.) The 1600, 1700, and 2500 series don't support ISL or 802.1Q routing. I'd recommend at least a 2800 as a bare minimum, and that only supports 802.1Q—Cisco is really moving away from ISL, so you probably should only be using 802.1Q anyway. (Some IOSs on the 2800 may support both ISL and 802.1Q—I just have never seen it supported.)

As shown in Figure 11.7, if you had only a few VLANs (two or three), you could get by with a router equipped with two or three FastEthernet connections. And 10BaseT is okay for home use, and I mean only for home use, but for anything else I'd honestly recommend FastEthernet or Gigabit interfaces for something serious under the hood.

FIGURE 11.7 Router with individual VLAN associations

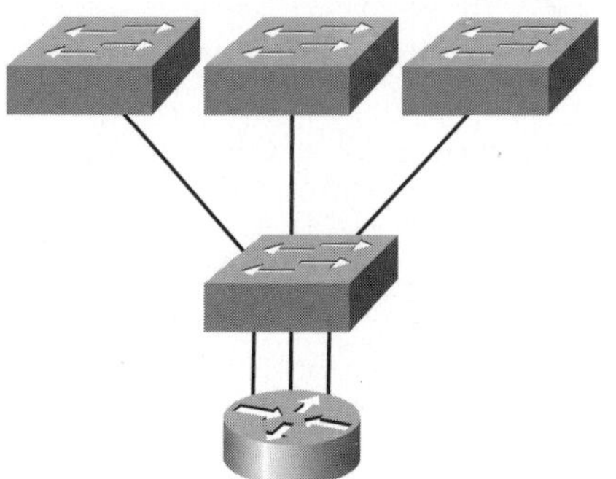

Router connecting three VLANs together for inter-VLAN communication, one interface for each VLAN.

What we see in Figure 11.7 is that each router interface is plugged into an access link. This means that each of the routers' interface IP addresses would then become the default gateway address for each host in each respective VLAN.

If you have more VLANs available than router interfaces, you can configure trunking on one FastEthernet interface or buy a layer 3 switch, like the Cisco 3560 or a higher-end switch like a 6500.

Instead of using a router interface for each VLAN, you can use one FastEthernet interface and run ISL or 802.1Q trunking. Figure 11.8 shows how a FastEthernet interface on a router will look when configured with ISL or 802.1Q trunking. This allows all VLANs to communicate through one interface. Cisco calls this a "router on a stick."

I need to point out that this creates a potential bottleneck, as well as a single point of failure, so your host/VLAN count is limited. How many? That depends on your traffic level. To really make things really right, you'd be better off using a higher-end switch and routing on the backplane, but if you just happen to have a router sitting around, configuring this method is free, right?

Configuring VLANs

It may come as a surprise to you, but configuring VLANs is actually pretty easy. Figuring out which users you want in each VLAN is not; it's extremely time consuming. But once you've decided on the number of VLANs you want to create and established which users you want to belong to each one, it's time to bring your first VLAN into the world.

FIGURE 11.8 "Router on a stick"

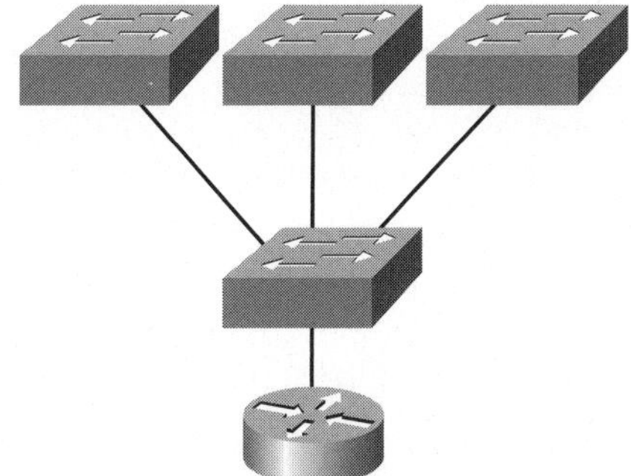

Router connecting all VLANs together allowing for inter-VLAN communication, using only one router interface (router on a stick).

To configure VLANs on a Cisco Catalyst switch, use the global config `vlan` command. In the following example, I'm going to demonstrate how to configure VLANs on the S1 switch by creating three VLANs for three different departments—again, remember that VLAN 1 is the native and administrative VLAN by default:

```
S1#config t
S1(config)#vlan ?
  WORD      ISL VLAN IDs 1-4094
  internal  internal VLAN
S1(config)#vlan 2
S1(config-vlan)#name Sales
S1(config-vlan)#vlan 3
S1(config-vlan)#name Marketing
S1(config-vlan)#vlan 4
S1(config-vlan)#name Accounting
S1(config-vlan)#^Z
S1#
```

From the preceding commands, you can see that you can create VLANs from 2 to 4094. This is only mostly true. As I said, VLANs can really only be created up to 1005, and you can't use, change, rename, or delete VLANs 1 and 1002 through 1005 because they're reserved. The VLAN numbers above 1005 are called extended VLANs and won't be saved in the database unless your switch is set to VTP transparent mode. You won't see these VLAN numbers used too often in production. Here's an example of attempting to set my S1 switch to VLAN 4000 when my switch is set to VTP server mode (the default VTP mode):

```
S1#config t
S1(config)#vlan 4000
```

```
S1(config-vlan)#^Z
% Failed to create VLANs 4000
Extended VLAN(s) not allowed in current VTP mode.
%Failed to commit extended VLAN(s) changes.
```

After you create the VLANs that you want, you can use the `show vlan` command to check them out. But notice that, by default, all ports on the switch are in VLAN 1. To change the VLAN associated with a port, you need to go to each interface and tell it which VLAN to be a part of.

Remember that a created VLAN is unused until it is assigned to a switch port or ports and that all ports are always assigned in VLAN 1 unless set otherwise.

Once the VLANs are created, verify your configuration with the `show vlan` command (`sh vlan` for short):

```
S1#sh vlan

VLAN Name                     Status    Ports
---- ----------------------------------------------------------
1    default                   active    Fa0/3, Fa0/4, Fa0/5, Fa0/6
                                         Fa0/7, Fa0/8, Gi0/1
2    Sales                     active
3    Marketing                 active
4    Accounting                active
 [output cut]
```

This may seem repetitive, but it's important, and I want you to remember it: You can't change, delete, or rename VLAN 1 because it's the default VLAN and you just can't change that—period. It's also the native VLAN of all switches by default, and Cisco recommends that you use it as your administrative VLAN. Basically, any ports that aren't specifically assigned to a different VLAN will be sent down to the native VLAN (VLAN 1).

In the preceding S1 output, you can see that ports Fa0/3 through Fa0/8 and the Gi0/1 uplink are all in VLAN 1, but where are ports 1 and 2? Remember that in the previous chapter I trunked and created an EtherChannel bundle. Any port that is a trunk port won't show up in the VLAN database. You have to use the `show interface trunk` command to see your trunked ports.

Now that we can see the VLANs created, we can assign switch ports to specific ones. Each port can be part of only one VLAN, with the exception of our voice access ports. With the trunking we went over earlier, you can make a port available to traffic from all VLANs. I'll cover that next.

Assigning Switch Ports to VLANs

You configure a port to belong to a VLAN by assigning a membership mode that specifies the kind of traffic the port carries, plus the number of VLANs to which it can belong. You can configure each port on a switch to be in a specific VLAN (access port) by using the interface `switchport` command. You can also configure multiple ports at the same time with the `interface range` command we talked about in Chapter 8.

Remember that you can configure either static or dynamic memberships on a port. For this book's purpose, I'm only going to cover the static flavor. In the following example, I'll configure interface Fa0/3 to VLAN 3. This is the connection from the S1 switch to the HostA device:

```
S1#config t
S1(config)#int fa0/3
S1(config-if)#switchport ?
  access         Set access mode characteristics of the interface
  backup         Set backup for the interface
  block          Disable forwarding of unknown uni/multi cast addresses
  host           Set port host
  mode           Set trunking mode of the interface
  nonegotiate    Device will not engage in negotiation protocol on this
                 interface
  port-security  Security related command
  priority       Set appliance 802.1p priority
  protected      Configure an interface to be a protected port
  trunk          Set trunking characteristics of the interface
  voice          Voice appliance attributes
```

Well now, what do we have here? There's some new stuff showing up in the preceding output. We can see various commands—some that I've already covered, but no worries; I'm going to cover the `access`, `mode`, `nonegotiate`, `trunk`, and `voice` commands very soon in this chapter. Let's start with setting an access port on S1, which is probably the most widely used type of port on production switches that have VLANs configured:

```
S1(config-if)#switchport mode ?
  access   Set trunking mode to ACCESS unconditionally
  dynamic  Set trunking mode to dynamically negotiate access or
  trunk mode
  trunk    Set trunking mode to TRUNK unconditionally

S1(config-if)#switchport mode access
S1(config-if)#switchport access vlan 3
```

By starting with the `switchport mode access` command, you're telling the switch that this is a nontrunking layer 2 port. You can then assign a VLAN to the port with the `switchport access` command. Remember, you can choose many ports to configure at the same time if you use the `interface range` command.

That's it. Well, sort of. If you plugged devices into each VLAN port, they can only talk to other devices in the same VLAN. We want to enable inter-VLAN communication and we're going to do that, but first you need to learn a bit more about trunking.

Configuring Trunk Ports

The 2960 switch only runs the IEEE 802.1Q encapsulation method. To configure trunking on a FastEthernet port, use the interface command `switchport mode trunk`. It's a tad different on the 3560 switch, and I'll show you that in the next section.

The following switch output shows the trunk configuration on interface fa0/8 as set to `trunk`:

```
S1#config t
S1(config)#int fa0/8
S1(config-if)#switchport mode trunk
```

The following list describes the different options available when configuring a switch interface:

`switchport mode access` I discussed this in the previous section, but this puts the interface (access port) into permanent nontrunking mode and negotiates to convert the link into a nontrunk link. The interface becomes a nontrunk interface regardless of whether the neighboring interface is a trunk interface. The port would be a dedicated layer 2 access port.

`switchport mode dynamic auto` This mode makes the interface able to convert the link to a trunk link. The interface becomes a trunk interface if the neighboring interface is set to trunk or desirable mode. The default is dynamic auto now.

`switchport mode dynamic desirable` This one makes the interface actively attempt to convert the link to a trunk link. The interface becomes a trunk interface if the neighboring interface is set to trunk, desirable, or auto mode. I used to see this mode as the default on some switches, but not any longer. This is now the default switchport mode for all Ethernet interfaces on all new Cisco switches.

`switchport mode trunk` Puts the interface into permanent trunking mode and negotiates to convert the neighboring link into a trunk link. The interface becomes a trunk interface even if the neighboring interface isn't a trunk interface.

`switchport nonegotiate` Prevents the interface from generating DTP frames. You can use this command only when the interface switchport mode is access or trunk. You must manually configure the neighboring interface as a trunk interface to establish a trunk link.

Dynamic Trunking Protocol (DTP) is used for negotiating trunking on a link between two devices, as well as negotiating the encapsulation type of either 802.1Q or ISL. I use the `nonegotiate` command when I want dedicated trunk ports no questions asked.

To disable trunking on an interface, use the `switchport mode access` command, which sets the port back to a dedicated layer 2 access switch port.

Trunking with the Cisco Catalyst 3560 switch

Okay, let's take a look at one more switch—the Cisco Catalyst 3560. The configuration is pretty much the same as it is for a 2960, with the exception that the 3560 can provide layer 3 services and the 2960 can't. Plus, the 3560 can run both the ISL and the IEEE 802.1Q trunking encapsulation methods—the 2960 can only run 802.1Q. With all this in mind, let's take a quick look at the VLAN encapsulation difference regarding the 3560 switch.

The 3560 has the `encapsulation` command, which the 2960 switch doesn't:

```
Core(config-if)#switchport trunk encapsulation ?
  dot1q      Interface uses only 802.1q trunking encapsulation
 when trunking
  isl        Interface uses only ISL trunking encapsulation
 when trunking
  negotiate  Device will negotiate trunking encapsulation with peer on
             interface
Core(config-if)#switchport trunk encapsulation dot1q
Core(config-if)#switchport mode trunk
```

As you can see, we've got the option to add either the IEEE 802.1Q (`dot1q`) encapsulation or the ISL encapsulation to the 3560 switch port. After you set the encapsulation, you still have to set the interface mode to trunk. Honestly, it's pretty rare that you'd continue to use the ISL encapsulation method. Cisco is moving away from ISL—its new routers don't even support it.

Defining the Allowed VLANs on a Trunk

As I've mentioned, trunk ports send and receive information from all VLANs by default, and if a frame is untagged, it's sent to the management VLAN. This applies to the extended range VLANs as well.

But we can remove VLANs from the allowed list to prevent traffic from certain VLANs from traversing a trunked link. Here's how you'd do that:

```
S1#config t
S1(config)#int f0/1
S1(config-if)#switchport trunk allowed vlan ?
```

```
  WORD    VLAN IDs of the allowed VLANs when this port is in
  trunking mode
  add     add VLANs to the current list
  all     all VLANs
  except  all VLANs except the following
  none    no VLANs
  remove  remove VLANs from the current list
S1(config-if)#switchport trunk allowed vlan remove ?
  WORD  VLAN IDs of disallowed VLANS when this port is in trunking mode
S1(config-if)#switchport trunk allowed vlan remove 4
```

The preceding command affected the trunk link configured on S1 port f0/1, causing it to drop all traffic sent and received for VLAN 4. You can try to remove VLAN 1 on a trunk link, but it will still send and receive management like CDP, PAgP, LACP, DTP, and VTP, so what's the point?

To remove a range of VLANs, just use the hyphen:

```
S1(config-if)#switchport trunk allowed vlan remove 4-8
```

If by chance someone has removed some VLANs from a trunk link and you want to set the trunk back to default, just use this command:

```
S1(config-if)#switchport trunk allowed vlan all
```

Or this command to accomplish the same thing:

```
S1(config-if)#no switchport trunk allowed vlan
```

Next, I want to show you how to configure a native VLAN for a trunk before we start routing between VLANs.

Changing or Modifying the Trunk Native VLAN

You really don't want to change the trunk port native VLAN from VLAN 1, but you can, and some people do it for security reasons. To change the native VLAN, use the following command:

```
S1#config t
S1(config)#int f0/1
S1(config-if)#switchport trunk ?
  allowed  Set allowed VLAN characteristics when interface is
  in trunking mode
  native   Set trunking native characteristics when interface
  is in trunking mode
  pruning  Set pruning VLAN characteristics when interface is
  in trunking mode
```

```
S1(config-if)#switchport trunk native ?
  vlan  Set native VLAN when interface is in trunking mode
S1(config-if)#switchport trunk native vlan ?
  <1-4094>  VLAN ID of the native VLAN when this port is in
  trunking mode
S1(config-if)#switchport trunk native vlan 40
S1(config-if)#^Z
```

So we've changed our native VLAN on our trunk link to 40, and by using the `show running-config` command, I can see the configuration under the trunk link:

```
!
interface FastEthernet0/1
 switchport trunk native vlan 40
 switchport trunk allowed vlan 1-3,9-4094
 switchport trunk pruning vlan 3,4
!
```

Hold on there partner! You didn't think it would be this easy and would just start working, did you? Sure you didn't. Here's the rub: If all switches don't have the same native VLAN configured on the given trunk links, then we'll start to receive this error:

```
19:23:29: %CDP-4-NATIVE_VLAN_MISMATCH: Native VLAN mismatch
discovered on FastEthernet0/1 (40), with Core FastEthernet0/7 (1).
19:24:29: %CDP-4-NATIVE_VLAN_MISMATCH: Native VLAN mismatch
discovered on FastEthernet0/1 (40), with Core FastEthernet0/7 (1).
```

Actually, this is a good, noncryptic error, so either we go to the other end of our trunk link(s) and change the native VLAN or we set the native VLAN back to the default. Here's how we'd do that:

```
S1(config-if)#no switchport trunk native vlan
```

Now our trunk link is using the default VLAN 1 as the native VLAN. Just remember that all switches on a given trunk must use the same native VLAN or you'll have some serious problems. Now, let's mix it up by connecting a router into our switched network and configuring inter-VLAN communication.

Configuring Inter-VLAN Routing

By default, only hosts that are members of the same VLAN can communicate. To change this and allow inter-VLAN communication, you need a router or a layer 3 switch. I'm going to start with the router approach.

To support ISL or 802.1Q routing on a FastEthernet interface, the router's interface is divided into logical interfaces—one for each VLAN. These are called *subinterfaces*.

From a FastEthernet or Gigabit interface, you can set the interface to trunk with the `encapsulation` command:

```
ISR#config t
ISR(config)#int f0/0.1
ISR(config-subif)#encapsulation ?
  dot1Q  IEEE 802.1Q Virtual LAN
ISR(config-subif)#encapsulation dot1Q ?
  <1-4094>  IEEE 802.1Q VLAN ID
```

Notice that my 2811 router (named ISR) only supports 802.1Q. We'd need an older-model router to run the ISL encapsulation, but why bother?

The subinterface number is only locally significant, so it doesn't matter which subinterface numbers are configured on the router. Most of the time, I'll configure a subinterface with the same number as the VLAN I want to route. It's easy to remember that way since the subinterface number is used only for administrative purposes.

It's really important that you understand that each VLAN is a separate subnet. True, I know—they don't *have* to be. But it really is a good idea to configure your VLANs as separate subnets, so just do that.

Now, I need to make sure you're fully prepared to configure inter-VLAN routing as well as determine the IP addresses of hosts connected in a switched VLAN environment. And as always, it's also a good idea to be able to fix any problems that may arise. To set you up for success, let me give you few examples.

First, start by looking at Figure 11.9, and read the router and switch configuration within it. By this point in the book, you should be able to determine the IP address, masks, and default gateways of each of the hosts in the VLANs.

FIGURE 11.9 Configuring Inter-VLAN example 1

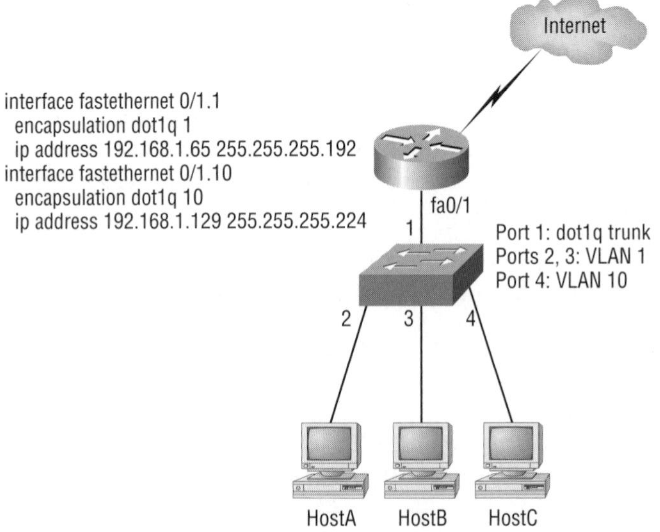

The next step after that is to figure out which subnets are being used. By looking at the router configuration in the figure, you can see that we're using 192.168.1.64/26 with VLAN 1 and 192.168.1.128/27 with VLAN 10. And by looking at the switch configuration, you can see that ports 2 and 3 are in VLAN 1 and port 4 is in VLAN 10. This means that HostA and HostB are in VLAN 1 and HostC is in VLAN 10.

Here's what the hosts' IP addresses should be:

HostA: 192.168.1.66, 255.255.255.192, default gateway 192.168.1.65

HostB: 192.168.1.67, 255.255.255.192, default gateway 192.168.1.65

HostC: 192.168.1.130, 255.255.255.224, default gateway 192.168.1.129

The hosts could be any address in the range—I just chose the first available IP address after the default gateway address. That wasn't so hard, was it?

Now, again using Figure 11.9, let's go through the commands necessary to configure switch port 1 to establish a link with the router and provide inter-VLAN communication using the IEEE version for encapsulation. Keep in mind that the commands can vary slightly depending on what type of switch you're dealing with.

For a 2960 switch, use the following:

```
2960#config t
2960(config)#interface fa0/1
2960(config-if)#switchport mode trunk
```

As you already know, the 2960 switch can only run the 802.1Q encapsulation, so there's no need to specify it. You can't anyway! For a 3560, it's basically the same, but since it can run ISL and 802.1Q, you have to specify the trunking protocol you're going to use.

Remember that when you create a trunked link, all VLANs are allowed to pass data by default.

Let's take a look at Figure 11.10 and see what we can learn from it. This figure shows three VLANs, with two hosts in each of them.

The router in Figure 11.10 is connected to the fa0/1 switch port, and VLAN 2 is configured on port F0/6.

Looking at the diagram, these are the things that Cisco expects you to know:

- The router is connected to the switch using subinterfaces.
- The switch port connecting to the router is a trunk port.
- The switch ports connecting to the clients and the hub are access ports, not trunk ports.

The configuration of the switch would look something like this:

```
2960#config t
2960(config)#int f0/1
2960(config-if)#switchport mode trunk
2960(config-if)#int f0/2
```

```
2960(config-if)#switchport access vlan 1
2960(config-if)#int f0/3
2960(config-if)#switchport access vlan 1
2960(config-if)#int f0/4
2960(config-if)#switchport access vlan 3
2960(config-if)#int f0/5
2960(config-if)#switchport access vlan 3
2960(config-if)#int f0/6
2960(config-if)#switchport access vlan 2
```

FIGURE 11.10 Inter-VLAN example 2

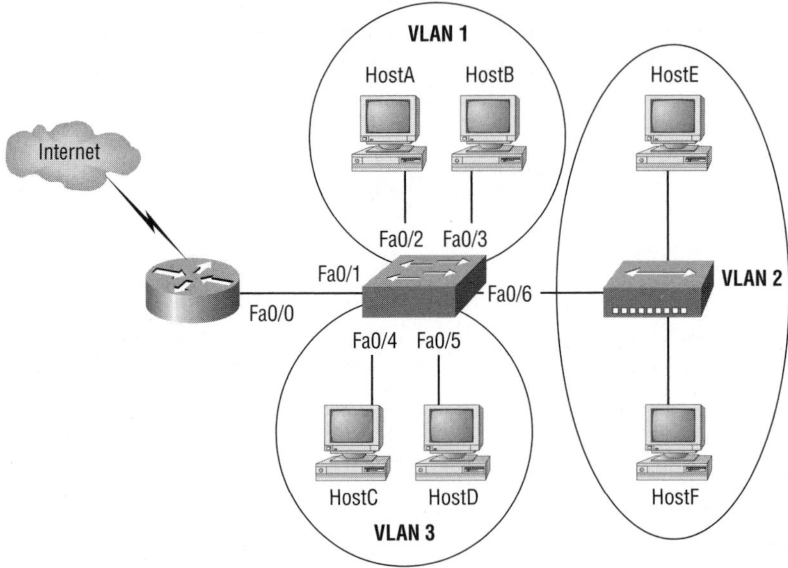

Before we configure the router, we need to design our logical network:

VLAN 1: 192.168.10.16/28

VLAN 2: 192.168.10.32/28

VLAN 3: 192.168.10.48/28

The configuration of the router would then look like this:

```
ISR#config t
ISR(config)#int Fa0/0
ISR(config-if)#no ip address
ISR(config-if)#no shutdown
ISR(config-if)#int f0/0.1
```

```
ISR(config-subif)#encapsulation dotlq 1
ISR(config-subif)#ip address 192.168.10.17 255.255.255.240
ISR(config-subif)#int f0/0.2
ISR(config-subif)#encapsulation dotlq 2
ISR(config-subif)#ip address 192.168.10.33 255.255.255.240
ISR(config-subif)#int f0/0.3
ISR(config-subif)#encapsulation dotlq 3
ISR(config-subif)#ip address 192.168.10.49 255.255.255.240
```

The hosts in each VLAN would be assigned an address from their subnet range, and the default gateway would be the IP address assigned to the router's subinterface in that VLAN.

Now, let's take a look at another figure and see if you can determine the switch and router configurations without looking at the answer—no cheating! Figure 11.11 shows a router connected to a 2960 switch with two VLANs. One host in each VLAN is assigned an IP address. What are your router and switch configurations based on these IP addresses?

FIGURE 11.11 Inter-VLAN example 3

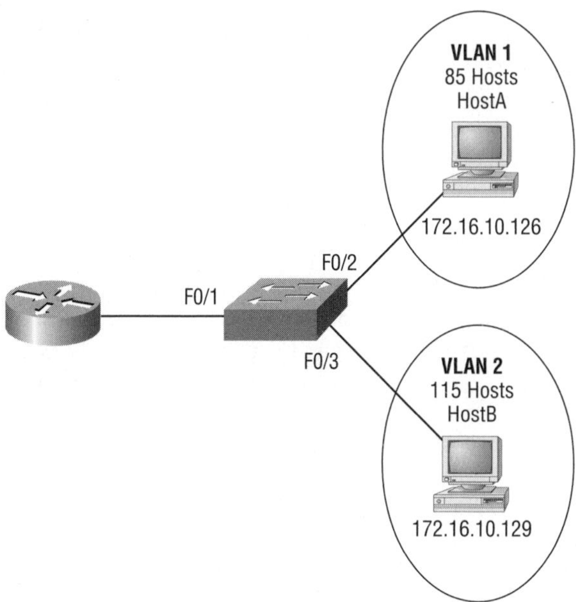

Since the hosts don't list a subnet mask, you have to look for the number of hosts used in each VLAN to figure out the block size. VLAN 1 has 85 hosts and VLAN 2 has 115 hosts. Each of these will fit in a block size of 128, which is a /25 mask, or 255.255.255.128.

You should know by now that the subnets are 0 and 128; the 0 subnet (VLAN 1) has a host range of 1–126, and the 128 subnet (VLAN 2) has a range of 129–254. You can almost be fooled since HostA has an IP address of 126, which makes it *almost* seem that HostA and

B are in the same subnet. But they're not, and you're way too smart by now to be fooled by this one!

Here is the switch configuration:

```
2960#config t
2960(config)#int f0/1
2960(config-if)#switchport mode trunk
2960(config-if)#int f0/2
2960(config-if)#switchport access vlan 1
2960(config-if)#int f0/3
2960(config-if)#switchport access vlan 2
```

Here is the router configuration:

```
ISR#config t
ISR(config)#int f0/0
ISR(config-if)#no ip address
ISR(config-if)#no shutdown
ISR(config-if)#int f0/0.1
ISR(config-subif)#encapsulation dotlq 1
ISR(config-subif)#ip address 172.16.10.1 255.255.255.128
ISR(config-subif)#int f0/0.2
ISR(config-subif)#encapsulation dotlq 2
ISR(config-subif)#ip address 172.16.10.254 255.255.255.128
```

I used the first address in the host range for VLAN 1 and the last address in the range for VLAN 2, but any address in the range would work. You just have to configure the host's default gateway to whatever you make the router's address.

Now, before we go on to the next example, I need to make sure you know how to set the IP address on the switch. Since VLAN 1 is typically the administrative VLAN, we'll use an IP address from that pool of addresses. Here's how to set the IP address of the switch (I'm not nagging, but you really should already know this!):

```
2960#config t
2960(config)#int vlan 1
2960(config-if)#ip address 172.16.10.2 255.255.255.128
2960(config-if)#no shutdown
```

Yes, you have to do a `no shutdown` on the VLAN interface.

One more example, and then we'll move on to VTP—another important subject that you definitely don't want to miss! In Figure 11.12 there are two VLANs. By looking at the router configuration, what's the IP address, mask, and default gateway of HostA? Use the last IP address in the range for HostA's address.

FIGURE 11.12 Inter-VLAN example 4

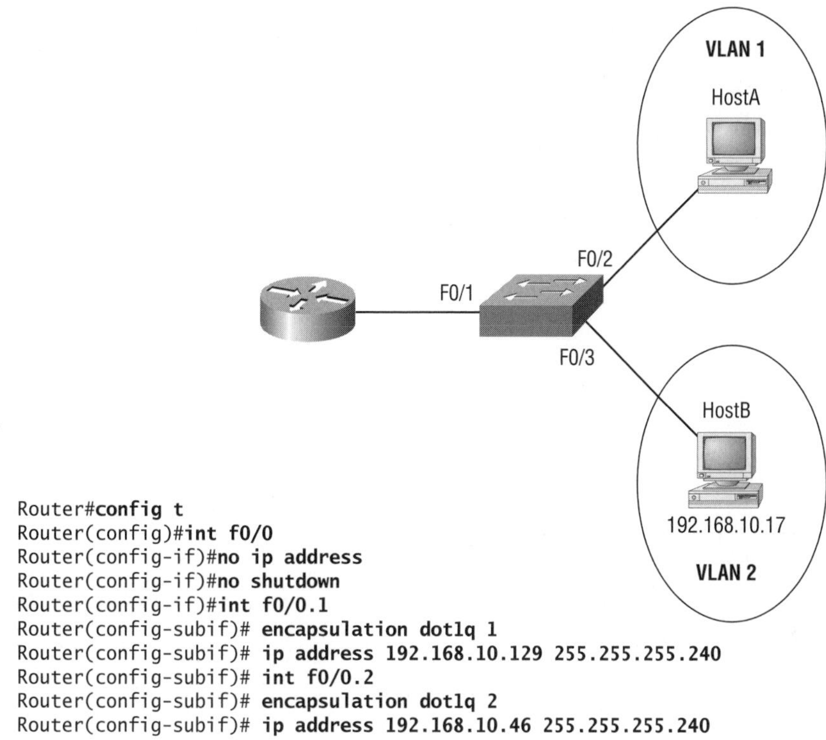

VLAN 1
HostA
F0/2
F0/1
F0/3
HostB
192.168.10.17
VLAN 2
Router#config t
Router(config)#int f0/0
Router(config-if)#no ip address
Router(config-if)#no shutdown
Router(config-if)#int f0/0.1
Router(config-subif)# encapsulation dotlq 1
Router(config-subif)# ip address 192.168.10.129 255.255.255.240
Router(config-subif)# int f0/0.2
Router(config-subif)# encapsulation dotlq 2
Router(config-subif)# ip address 192.168.10.46 255.255.255.240

If you really look carefully at the router configuration (the hostname in this figure is just Router), there is a simple and quick answer. Both subnets are using a /28, which is a 255.255.255.240 mask. This is a block size of 16. The router's address for VLAN 1 is in subnet 128. The next subnet is 144, so the broadcast address of VLAN 1 is 143 and the valid host range is 129–142. So the host address would be this:

IP Address: 192.168.10.142

Mask: 255.255.255.240

Default Gateway: 192.168.10.129

Configuring VTP

All Cisco switches are configured to be VTP servers by default. To configure VTP, first you have to configure the domain name you want to use. And of course, once you configure the VTP information on a switch, you need to verify it.

When you create the VTP domain, you have a few options, including setting the domain name, password, operating mode, and pruning capabilities of the switch. Use the vtp global configuration mode command to set all this information. In the following example, I'll set the S1 switch to vtp server, the VTP domain to Lammle, and the VTP password to todd, using the layout we used in Figure 10.14:

```
S1#config t
S1#(config)#vtp mode server
Device mode already VTP SERVER.
S1(config)#vtp domain Lammle
Changing VTP domain name from null to Lammle
S1(config)#vtp password todd
Setting device VLAN database password to todd
S1(config)#do show vtp password
VTP Password: todd
S1(config)#do show vtp status
VTP Version                     : 2
Configuration Revision          : 0
Maximum VLANs supported locally : 255
Number of existing VLANs        : 8
VTP Operating Mode              : Server
VTP Domain Name                 : Lammle
VTP Pruning Mode                : Disabled
VTP V2 Mode                     : Disabled
VTP Traps Generation            : Disabled
MD5 digest                      : 0x15 0x54 0x88 0xF2 0x50 0xD9 0x03 0x07
Configuration last modified by 192.168.24.6 at 3-14-93 15:47:32
Local updater ID is 192.168.24.6 on interface Vl1 (lowest numbered VLAN
interface found)
```

Please make sure you remember that all switches are set to VTP server mode by default, and if you want to change and distribute any VLAN information on a switch, you absolutely must be in VTP server mode. After you configure the VTP information, you can verify it with the show vtp command as shown in the preceding output. The preceding switch output shows the VTP domain, the VTP password, and the switch's mode.

Before we move onward to examples of configuring switches with VTP information, take a minute to reflect on the fact that the show vtp status output shows that the maximum number of VLANs supported locally is only 255. Since you can create over 1,000 VLANs on a switch, this seems like it would definitely be a problem if you have more than 255 VLANs and you're using VTP. And, well, yes, it is problem—if you are trying to configure the 256th VLAN on a switch, you'll get a nice little error message stating that there are not enough hardware resources available, and then it will shut down the VLAN and the 256th VLAN will show up in suspended state in the output of the show vlan command. Not so good!

You must remember that the show vtp status command will show you how many VLANs are supported on a switch!

Let's go to the Core and S2 switches and set them into the Lammle VTP domain. It is very important to remember that the VTP domain name is case sensitive! VTP is not forgiving—one teeny small mistake and it just won't work.

```
Core#config t
Core(config)#vtp mode client
Setting device to VTP CLIENT mode.
Core(config)#vtp domain Lammle
Changing VTP domain name from null to Lammle
Core(config)#vtp password todd
Setting device VLAN database password to todd
Core(config)#do show vtp status
VTP Version                     : 2
Configuration Revision          : 0
Maximum VLANs supported locally : 1005
Number of existing VLANs        : 5
VTP Operating Mode              : Server
VTP Domain Name                 : Lammle
VTP Pruning Mode                : Disabled
VTP V2 Mode                     : Disabled
VTP Traps Generation            : Disabled
MD5 digest                      : 0x2A 0x6B 0x22 0x17 0x04 0x4F 0xB8 0xC2
Configuration last modified by 192.168.10.19 at 3-1-93 03:13:16
Local updater ID is 192.168.24.7 on interface Vl1 (first interface found)
S2#config t
S2(config)#vtp mode client
Setting device to VTP CLIENT mode.
S2(config)#vtp domain Lammle
Changing VTP domain name from null to Lammle
S2(config)#vtp password todd
Setting device VLAN database password to todd
S2(config)#do show vtp status
VTP Version                     : 2
Configuration Revision          : 0
Maximum VLANs supported locally : 1005
Number of existing VLANs        : 5
VTP Operating Mode              : Client
VTP Domain Name                 : Lammle
```

```
VTP Pruning Mode                : Disabled
VTP V2 Mode                     : Disabled
VTP Traps Generation            : Disabled
MD5 digest                      : 0x02 0x11 0x18 0x4B 0x36 0xC5 0xF4 0x1F
Configuration last modified by 0.0.0.0 at 0-0-00 00:00:00
```

Nice—now that all our switches are set to the same VTP domain and password, the VLANs I created earlier on the S1 switch should be advertised to the Core and S2 VTP client switches. Let's take a look using the `show vlan brief` command on the Core and S2 switch:

```
Core#sh vlan brief
VLAN Name                 Status    Ports
---- ------------------ --------- ---------------------
1    default              active    Fa0/1,Fa0/2,Fa0/3,Fa0/4
                                    Fa0/9,Fa0/10,Fa0/11,Fa0/12
                                    Fa0/13,Fa0/14,Fa0/15,
                                    Fa0/16,Fa0/17, Fa0/18, Fa0/19,
                                    Fa0/20,Fa0/21, Fa0/22, Fa0/23,
                                    Fa0/24, Gi0/1, Gi0/2
2    Sales                 active
3    Marketing             active
4    Accounting            active
[output cut]

S2#sh vlan bri
VLAN Name                     Status    Ports
---- ---------------------- --------- ---------------------
1    default                  active    Fa0/3, Fa0/4, Fa0/5, Fa0/6
                                        Fa0/7, Fa0/8, Gi0/1
2    Sales                    active
3    Marketing                active
4    Accounting               active
[output cut]
```

The VLAN database that I created on the S1 (2960) switch earlier in this chapter was uploaded to the Core and S2 switch via VTP advertisements. VTP is a great way to keep VLAN naming consistent across the switched network. We can now assign VLANs to the ports on the Core, S1, and S2 switches, and they'll communicate with the hosts in the same VLANs on the other switches across the trunked ports between switches.

It's imperative that you can assign a VTP domain name, set the switch to VTP server mode, and create a VLAN!

Troubleshooting VTP

You connect your switches with crossover cables, the lights go green on both ends, and you're up and running! Yeah—in a perfect world, right? Don't you wish it was that easy? Well, actually, it pretty much is—without VLANs, of course. But if you're using VLANs—and you definitely should be—then you need to use VTP if you have multiple VLANs configured in your switched network.

But here there be monsters: If VTP is not configured correctly, it (surprise!) will not work, so you absolutely must be capable of troubleshooting VTP. Let's take a look at a couple of configurations and solve the problems. Study the output from the two following switches:

```
SwitchA#sh vtp status
VTP Version                     : 2
Configuration Revision          : 0
Maximum VLANs supported locally : 64
Number of existing VLANs        : 7
VTP Operating Mode              : Server
VTP Domain Name                 : RouterSim
VTP Pruning Mode                : Disabled
VTP V2 Mode                     : Disabled
VTP Traps Generation            : Disabled

SwitchB#sh vtp status
VTP Version                     : 2
Configuration Revision          : 1
Maximum VLANs supported locally : 64
Number of existing VLANs        : 7
VTP Operating Mode              : Server
VTP Domain Name                 : GlobalNet
VTP Pruning Mode                : Disabled
VTP V2 Mode                     : Disabled
VTP Traps Generation            : Disabled
```

So what's happening with these two switches? Why won't they share VLAN information? At first glance, it seems that both servers are in VTP server mode, but that's not the problem. Servers in VTP server mode will share VLAN information using VTP. The problem is that they're in two different VTP *domains*. SwitchA is in VTP domain RouterSim and SwitchB is in VTP domain GlobalNet. They will never share VTP information because the VTP domain names are configured differently.

Now that you know how to look for common VTP domain configuration errors in your switches, let's take a look at another switch configuration:

```
SwitchC#sh vtp status
VTP Version                     : 2
```

```
Configuration Revision          : 1
Maximum VLANs supported locally : 64
Number of existing VLANs        : 7
VTP Operating Mode              : Client
VTP Domain Name                 : Todd
VTP Pruning Mode                : Disabled
VTP V2 Mode                     : Disabled
VTP Traps Generation            : Disabled
```

There you are just trying to create a new VLAN on SwitchC and what do you get for your trouble? A loathsome error! Why can't you create a VLAN on SwitchC? Well, the VTP domain name isn't the important thing in this example. What is critical here is the VTP *mode*. The VTP mode is client, and a VTP client cannot create, delete, or change VLANs, remember? VTP clients only keep the VTP database in RAM, and that's not saved to NVRAM. So, in order to create a VLAN on this switch, you've got to make the switch a VTP server first.

Here's what will happen when you have the preceding VTP configuration:

```
SwitchC(config)#vlan 50
VTP VLAN configuration not allowed when device is in CLIENT mode.
```

So to fix this problem, here's what you need to do:

```
SwitchC(config)#vtp mode server
Setting device to VTP SERVER mode
SwitchC(config)#vlan 50
SwitchC(config-vlan)#
```

Wait, we're not done. Now take a look at the output from these two switches and determine why SwitchB is not receiving VLAN information from SwitchA:

```
SwitchA#sh vtp status
VTP Version                     : 2
Configuration Revision          : 4
Maximum VLANs supported locally : 64
Number of existing VLANs        : 7
VTP Operating Mode              : Server
VTP Domain Name                 : GlobalNet
VTP Pruning Mode                : Disabled
VTP V2 Mode                     : Disabled
VTP Traps Generation            : Disabled

SwitchB#sh vtp status
VTP Version                     : 2
Configuration Revision          : 14
Maximum VLANs supported locally : 64
```

```
Number of existing VLANs        : 7
VTP Operating Mode              : Server
VTP Domain Name                 : GlobalNet
VTP Pruning Mode                : Disabled
VTP V2 Mode                     : Disabled
VTP Traps Generation            : Disabled
```

You may be tempted to say it's because they're both VTP servers, but that is not the problem. All your switches can be servers and they can still share VLAN information. As a matter of fact, Cisco actually suggests that all switches stay VTP servers and that you just make sure the switch you want to advertise VTP VLAN information has the highest revision number. If all switches are VTP servers, then all of the switches will save the VLAN database. But SwitchB isn't receiving VLAN information from SwitchA because SwitchB has a higher revision number than SwitchA. It's very important that you can recognize this problem.

There are a couple ways to go about resolving this issue. The first thing you could do is to change the VTP domain name on SwitchB to another name, then set it back to GlobalNet, which will reset the revision number to zero (0) on SwitchB. The second approach would be to create or delete VLANs on SwitchA until the revision number passes the revision number on SwitchB. I didn't say the second way was better; I just said it's another way to fix it!

Where Did You Get Your VLAN Database?

One last thing you must be able to understand. Where did your switch receive the VLAN database? If you type `show vlan` on your switch and see a VLAN database, did your switch receive the VLAN database from the `vlan.dat` file in flash memory? Possibly. Is it a server and does it have the highest revision number of all servers in your network? Then yes. However, you can find out exactly where you received the VLAN database by using the `show vtp status` command:

```
Core#do show vtp status
VTP Version                     : 2
Configuration Revision          : 0
Maximum VLANs supported locally : 1005
Number of existing VLANs        : 5
VTP Operating Mode              : Client
VTP Domain Name                 : Lammle
VTP Pruning Mode                : Disabled
VTP V2 Mode                     : Disabled
VTP Traps Generation            : Disabled
MD5 digest                      : 0x02 0x11 0x18 0x4B 0x36 0xC5 0xF4 0x1F
Local updater ID is 192.168.24.7 on interface Vl1 (first interface found)
```

The last line in the output tells us where we received the VLAN database we are using. If our switch management IP address is 192.168.24.7, then we used our database from `vlan.dat`. However, if that is not the switch's IP address, then we can just do a `show cdp neighbors detail` and find out which switch is 192.168.24.7.

Telephony: Configuring Voice VLANs

If you do yoga, meditate, chain smoke, or consume mass quantities of comfort food when stressed, take a little break and do that now because, and I'm going to be honest, this isn't the easiest part of the chapter—or even the book, for that matter. But I promise that I'll do my best to make this as painless for you as possible.

The voice VLAN feature enables access ports to carry IP voice traffic from an IP phone. When a switch is connected to a Cisco IP phone, the IP phone sends voice traffic with layer 3 IP precedence and layer 2 class of service (CoS) values, which are both set to 5 for voice traffic; all other traffic defaults to 0.

Because the sound quality of an IP phone call can deteriorate if the data is unevenly sent, the switch supports quality of service (QoS) based on IEEE 802.1p CoS. (802.1p provides a mechanism for implementing QoS at the Data Link level.) The 802.1p field is carried in the 802.1Q trunk header. If you look at the fields in an 802.1Q tag, you will see a field called the priority field; this is where the 802.1p information goes. QoS uses classification and scheduling to send network traffic from the switch in an organized, predictable manner.

The Cisco IP phone is a configurable device, and you can configure it to forward traffic with an IEEE 802.1p priority. You can also configure the switch to either trust or override the traffic priority assigned by an IP phone—which is exactly what we're going to do. The Cisco phone basically has a three-port switch: one to connect to the Cisco switch, one to a PC device, and one to the actual phone, which is internal.

You can also configure an access port with an attached Cisco IP phone to use one VLAN for voice traffic and another VLAN for data traffic from a device attached to the phone—such as a PC. You can configure access ports on the switch to send Cisco Discovery Protocol (CDP) packets that instruct an attached Cisco IP phone to send voice traffic to the switch in any of these ways:

- In the voice VLAN tagged with a layer 2 CoS priority value
- In the access VLAN tagged with a layer 2 CoS priority value
- In the access VLAN, untagged (no layer 2 CoS priority value)

The switch can also process tagged data traffic (traffic in IEEE 802.1Q or IEEE 802.1p frame types) from the device attached to the access port on the Cisco IP phone. You can configure layer 2 access ports on the switch to send CDP packets that instruct the attached Cisco IP phone to configure the IP phone PC access port in one of these modes:

- In trusted mode, all traffic received through the access port on the Cisco IP phone passes through the IP phone unchanged.
- In untrusted mode, all traffic in IEEE 802.1Q or IEEE 802.1p frames received through the access port on the IP phone receive a configured layer 2 CoS value. The default layer 2 CoS value is 0. Untrusted mode is the default.

Configuring the Voice VLAN

By default, the voice VLAN feature is disabled; you enable it by using the interface command `switchport voice vlan`. When the voice VLAN feature is enabled, all untagged traffic is sent according to the default CoS priority of the port. The CoS value is not trusted for IEEE 802.1p or IEEE 802.1Q tagged traffic.

These are the voice VLAN configuration guidelines:

- You should configure a voice VLAN on switch access ports; voice VLAN isn't supported on trunk ports, even though you can actually configure it!
- The voice VLAN should be present and active on the switch for the IP phone to correctly communicate on it. Use the `show vlan` privileged EXEC command to see if the voice VLAN is present--if it is, it'll be listed in the display.
- Before you enable the voice VLAN, it's recommend that you enable QoS on the switch by entering the `mls qos` global configuration command and set the port trust state to trust by entering the `mls qos trust cos` interface configuration command.
- You must make sure that CDP is enabled on the switch port connected to the Cisco IP phone to send the configuration. This is on by default, so unless you disabled it, you shouldn't have a problem.
- The PortFast feature is automatically enabled when the voice VLAN is configured, but when you disable the voice VLAN, the PortFast feature isn't automatically disabled.
- To return the port to its default setting, use the `no switchport voice vlan` interface configuration command.

Configuring IP Phone Voice Traffic

You can configure a port connected to the Cisco IP phone to send CDP packets to the phone in order to configure how the phone sends voice traffic. The phone can carry voice traffic in IEEE 802.1Q frames for a specified voice VLAN with a layer 2 CoS value. It can use IEEE 802.1p priority tagging to give voice traffic a higher priority as well as forward all voice traffic through the access VLAN instead of the native (access) VLAN. The IP phone can also send untagged voice traffic or use its own configuration to send voice traffic in the access VLAN. In all configurations, the voice traffic carries a layer 3 IP precedence value—again, for voice the setting is usually 5.

I think it's about time to give you some actual examples to make this clear to you. This example shows you how to configure four things:

1. How to configure a port connected to an IP phone to use the CoS value for classifying incoming traffic
2. How to configure the port to use IEEE 802.1p priority tagging for voice traffic
3. How to configure it to use the Voice VLAN (10) to carry all voice traffic

4. And last, how to configure VLAN 3 to carry PC data

```
Switch#configure t
Switch(config)#mls qos
Switch(config)#interface f0/1
Switch(config-if)#switchport priority extend ?
  cos    Override 802.1p priority of devices on appliance
  trust  Trust 802.1p priorities of devices on appliance
Switch(config-if)#switchport priority extend trust
Switch(config-if)#mls qos trust cos
Switch(config-if)#switchport voice vlan dot1p
Switch(config-if)#switchport mode access
Switch(config-if)#switchport access vlan 3
Switch(config-if)#switchport voice vlan 10
```

The command **mls qos trust cos** will configure the interface to classify incoming traffic packets by using the packet CoS value. For untagged packets, the port's default CoS value will be used. But before configuring the port trust state, you must first globally enable QoS by using the `mls qos` global configuration command.

Notice how I added two access VLANs to the same port? I can only do this if I have one for a data VLAN and another one for a voice VLAN.

This section was probably the hardest part of this entire book, and I honestly created the simplest configuration you should use to get you through it!

Summary

This chapter introduced you to the world of virtual LANs and described how Cisco switches can use them. We talked about how VLANs break up broadcast domains in a switched internetwork—a very important, necessary thing because layer 2 switches only break up collision domains and, by default, all switches make up one large broadcast domain. I also described access links to you, and we went over how trunked VLANs work across a FastEthernet or faster link.

Trunking is a crucial technology to understand well when you're dealing with a network populated by multiple switches that are running several VLANs. I also talked at length about VLAN Trunk Protocol (VTP), which, in reality, has nothing to do with trunking. You learned that it does send VLAN information down a trunked link but that the trunk configuration in and of itself isn't part of VTP.

This chapter also provided important troubleshooting and configuration examples of VTP, trunking, and VLAN configurations,

And then there was the telephony gauntlet—something you may want to forget, but if you want to succeed, you'll make sure you've got it down even if it means going through it all again!

Exam Essentials

Understand the term *frame tagging*. *Frame tagging* refers to VLAN identification; this is what switches use to keep track of all those frames as they're traversing a switch fabric. It's how switches identify which frames belong to which VLANs.

Understand the ISL VLAN identification method. Inter-Switch Link (ISL) is a way of explicitly tagging VLAN information onto an Ethernet frame. This tagging information allows VLANs to be multiplexed over a trunk link through an external encapsulation method, which allows the switch to identify the VLAN membership of a frame over the link. ISL is a Cisco-proprietary frame-tagging method that can be used only with Cisco switches and routers.

Understand the 802.1Q VLAN identification method. This is a nonproprietary IEEE method of frame tagging. If you're trunking between a Cisco switched link and a different brand of switch, you have to use 802.1Q for the trunk to work.

Remember how to set a trunk port on a 2960 switch. To set a port to trunking on a 2960, use the `switchport mode trunk` command.

Remember to check a switch port's VLAN assignment when plugging in a new host. If you plug a new host into a switch, then you must verify the VLAN membership of that port. If the membership is different than what is needed for that host, the host will not be able to reach the needed network services, such as a workgroup server.

Understand the purpose and configuration of VTP. VTP provides propagation of the VLAN database throughout your switched network. All switches must be in the same VTP domain in order to exchange this information.

Remember how to create a Cisco "router on a stick" to provide inter-VLAN communication. You can use a Cisco FastEthernet or Gigabit Ethernet interface to provide inter-VLAN routing. The switch port connected to the router must be a trunk port; then you must create virtual interfaces (subinterfaces) on the router port for each VLAN connecting to it. The hosts in each VLAN will use this subinterface address as their default gateway address.

Written Lab 11

In this section, write the answers to the following questions:

1. What VTP mode can only accept VLAN information and not change it?
2. What command will show us where we received our VLAN database from?
3. VLANs break up _______ domains.
4. Switches, by default, only break up _______ domains.

5. What is the default VTP mode?
6. What does trunking provide?
7. What is frame tagging?
8. True/False: The ISL encapsulation is removed from the frame if the frame is forwarded out an access link.
9. What type of link on a switch is a member of only one VLAN?
10. What type of Cisco tagging information allows VLANs to be multiplexed over a trunk link through an external encapsulation method?

(The answers to Written Lab 11 can be found following the answers to the review questions for this chapter.)

Review Questions

The following questions are designed to test your understanding of this chapter's material. For more information on how to get additional questions, please see this book's Introduction.

1. Which of the following is true regarding VLANs?
   - A. You must have at least two VLANs defined in every Cisco switched network.
   - B. All VLANs are configured at the fastest switch and, by default, propagate this information to all other switches.
   - C. You should not have more than 10 switches in the same VTP domain.
   - D. VTP is used to send VLAN information to switches in a configured VTP domain.
2. According to the following diagram, which of the following describes the router port configuration and the switch port configuration as shown in the topology? (Choose three.)

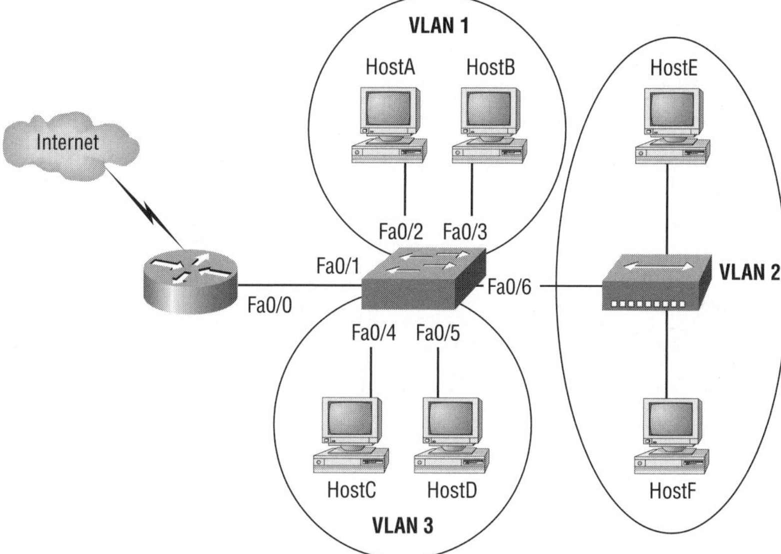

   - A. The router WAN port is configured as a trunk port.
   - B. The router port connected to the switch is configured using subinterfaces.
   - C. The router port connected to the switch is configured at 10Mbps.
   - D. The switch port connected to the hub is configured as full duplex.
   - E. The switch port connected to the router is configured as a trunking port.
   - F. The switch ports connected to the hosts are configured as access ports.

3. A switch has been configured for three different VLANs: VLAN2, VLAN3, and VLAN4. A router has been added to provide communication between the VLANs. What minimum type of interface is necessary on the router if only one connection is to be made between the router and the switch?

   A. 10Mbps Ethernet

   B. 56Kbps Serial

   C. 100Mbps Ethernet

   D. 1Gbps Ethernet

4. You want to improve network performance by increasing the bandwidth available to hosts and limit the size of the broadcast domains. Which of the following options will achieve this goal?

   A. Managed hubs

   B. Bridges

   C. Switches

   D. Switches configured with VLANs

5. Which of the following protocols are used to configure trunking on a switch? (Choose two.)

   A. VLAN Trunk Protocol

   B. VLAN

   C. 802.1Q

   D. ISL

6. When a new trunk link is configured on an IOS-based switch, which VLANs are allowed over the link?

   A. By default, all VLANs are allowed on the trunk.

   B. No VLANs are allowed; you must configure each VLAN by hand

   C. Only configured VLANs are allowed on the link.

   D. Only extended VLANs are allowed by default.

7. Which switching technology reduces the size of a broadcast domain?

   A. ISL

   B. 802.1Q

   C. VLANs

   D. STP

8. What VTP mode allows you to change VLAN information on the switch?

   A. Client

   B. STP

   C. Server

   D. 802.1q

9. Which command will configure a switch port to use the IEEE standard method of inserting VLAN membership information into Ethernet frames?
   A. `Switch(config)#switchport trunk encapsulation isl`
   B. `Switch(config)#switchport trunk encapsulation ietf`
   C. `Switch(config)#switchport trunk encapsulation dot1q`
   D. `Switch(config-if)#switchport trunk encapsulation isl`
   E. `Switch(config-if)#switchport trunk encapsulation ietf`
   F. `Switch(config-if)#switchport trunk encapsulation dot1q`

10. Which of the following is true regarding VTP?
    A. All switches are VTP servers by default.
    B. All switches are VTP transparent by default.
    C. VTP is on by default with a domain name of Cisco on all Cisco switches.
    D. All switches are VTP clients by default.

11. Which protocol reduces administrative overhead in a switched network by allowing the configuration of a new VLAN to be distributed to all the switches in a domain?
    A. STP
    B. VTP
    C. DHCP
    D. ISL

12. Which of the following commands sets a trunk port on a 2960 switch?
    A. `trunk on`
    B. `trunk all`
    C. `switchport trunk on`
    D. `switchport mode trunk`

13. Which of the following is an IEEE standard for frame tagging?
    A. ISL
    B. 802.3Z
    C. 802.1Q
    D. 802.3U

14. You connect a host to a switch port, but the new host cannot log into the server that is plugged into the same switch. What could the problem be? (Choose the most likely answer.)
    A. The router is not configured for the new host.
    B. The VTP configuration on the switch is not updated for the new host.
    C. The host has an invalid MAC address.
    D. The switch port the host is connected to is not configured with the correct VLAN membership.

15. According to the diagram, which three commands can be used to establish a link with the router's FastEthernet interface using the IEEE version of frame tagging? (Choose three.)

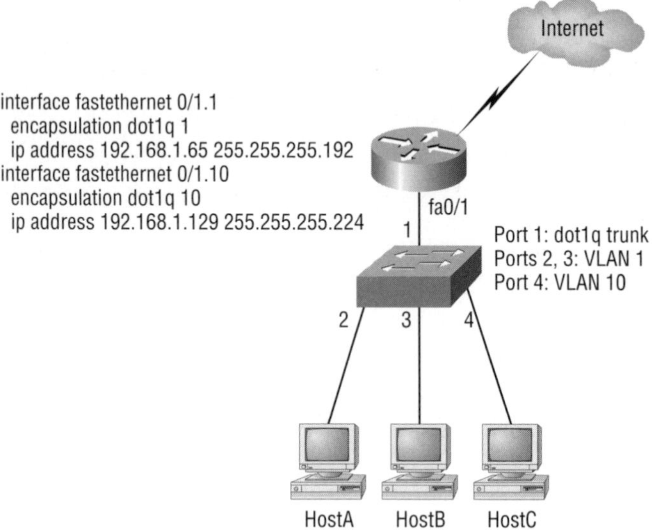

A. `Switch(config)#interface fastethernet 0/1`

B. `Switch(config-if)#switchport mode access`

C. `Switch(config-if)#switchport mode trunk`

D. `Switch(config-if)#switchport access vlan 1`

E. `Switch(config-if)#switchport trunk encapsulation isl`

F. `Switch(config-if)#switchport trunk encapsulation dot1q`

16. These two switches are not sharing VLAN information. From the following output, what is the reason these switches are not sharing VTP messages?

```
SwitchA#sh vtp status
VTP Version                     : 2
Configuration Revision          : 0
Maximum VLANs supported locally : 64
Number of existing VLANs        : 7
VTP Operating Mode              : Server
VTP Domain Name                 : RouterSim
VTP Pruning Mode                : Disabled

SwitchB#sh vtp status
VTP Version                     : 2
Configuration Revision          : 1
Maximum VLANs supported locally : 64
Number of existing VLANs        : 7
```

```
VTP Operating Mode                 : Server
VTP Domain Name                    : GlobalNet
VTP Pruning Mode                   : Disabled
```

A. One of the switches needs to be set to VTP version 1.
B. Both switches are set to VTP server and one must be set to client.
C. The VTP domain names are not configured correctly.
D. VTP pruning is disabled.

17. Which of the following provide multi-VLAN inter-switch communications? (Choose two.)
    A. ISL
    B. VTP
    C. 802.1Q
    D. 802.3Z

18. To configure the VLAN Trunking Protocol to communicate VLAN information between two switches, what two requirements must be met? (Choose two.)
    A. Each end of the trunk link must be set to the IEEE 802.1e encapsulation.
    B. The VTP management domain name of both switches must be set the same.
    C. All ports on both the switches must be set as access ports.
    D. One of the two switches must be configured as a VTP server.
    E. A rollover cable is required to connect the two switches together.
    F. A router must be used to forward VTP traffic between VLANs.

19. Which of the following are benefits of VLANs? (Choose three.)
    A. They increase the size of collision domains.
    B. They allow logical grouping of users by function.
    C. They can enhance network security.
    D. They increase the size of broadcast domains while decreasing the number of collision domains.
    E. They simplify switch administration.
    F. They increase the number of broadcast domains while decreasing the size of the broadcast domains.

20. Which of the following modes are valid when a switch port is used as a VLAN trunk? (Choose three.)
    A. Blocking
    B. Dynamic auto
    C. Dynamic desirable
    D. Nonegotiate
    E. Access
    F. Learning

Answers to Review Questions

1. D. Switches do not propagate VLAN information by default; you must configure the VTP domain. VLAN Trunk Protocol (VTP) is used to propagate VLAN information across a trunked link.

2. B, E, F. A router connected to a switch that provides inter-VLAN communication is configured using subinterfaces. The switch port connected to the router must be using either ISL or 802.1Q trunking protocol, and the hosts are all connected as access ports, which is the default on all switch ports.

3. C. Although you can use either 100Mbps or 1Gbps Ethernet, the 100Mbps is necessary at a minimum and is the best answer to this question. You need to trunk the link from the switch to the router to make this connection work with inter-VLAN communication.

4. D. By creating and implementing VLANs in your switched network, you can break up broadcast domains at layer 2. For hosts on different VLANs to communicate, you must have a router or layer 3 switch.

5. C, D. Cisco has a proprietary trunking protocol called ISL. The IEEE version is 802.1Q.

6. A. By default, all VLANs are allowed on the trunk link and you must remove by hand each VLAN that you don't want traversing the trunked link.

7. C. Virtual LANs break up broadcast domains in layer 2 switched internetworks.

8. C. Only in server mode can you change VLAN information on a switch.

9. F. If you are on a 2950 switch, then the interface command is just `switchport mode trunk` since the 2950 can only run the IEEE 802.1Q version. However, a 3550 can run both ISL and 802.1Q, so you must also use the `encapsulation` command. The argument to choose 802.1Q for a trunking protocol is `dot1q`.

10. A. All Cisco switches are VTP servers by default. No other VTP information is configured on a Cisco switch by default. You must set the VTP domain name on all switches to be the same domain name or they will not share the VTP database.

11. B. Virtual Trunk Protocol (VTP) is used to pass a VLAN database to any or all switches in the switched network. The three VTP modes are server, client, and transparent.

12. D. To set a switch port to trunk mode, which allows the data of all VLAN information to pass down the link, use the `switchport mode trunk` command.

13. C. 802.1Q was created to allow trunked links between disparate switches.

14. D. This question is a little vague, but the best answer is that the VLAN membership for the port is not configured.

15. A, C, F. To create a trunked link on a switch port, you first need to go to the interface—in this question, interface FastEthernet 0/1. Then you choose your trunking command, either `switchport mode trunk` for the 2950/2960 switch (IEEE 802.1Q is the only version the 2950/2960 switch runs) or `switchport trunk encapsulation dot1q` for a 3560 switch.

16. C. Although one of the switches can be set to client, that would not stop them from sharing VLAN information through VTP. However, they will not share VLAN information through VTP if the domain names are not set the same.

17. A, C. ISL is a Cisco-proprietary frame-tagging method. IEEE 802.1Q is the nonproprietary version of frame tagging.

18. B, D. You must have the same VTP domain name on all switches in order to share VLAN information between the switches. At least one of the switches must be a VTP server; the other switches should be set to VTP client mode.

19. B, C, F. VLANs break up broadcast domains in a switched layer 2 network, which means smaller broadcast domains. They allow configuration by logical function instead of physical location and can create some security if configured correctly.

20. B, C, D. The valid modes of a VLAN trunk on a switch are dynamic auto, dynamic desirable, trunk (on), and nonegotiate.

Answers to Written Lab 11

1. Client
2. `show vtp status`
3. Broadcast
4. Collision
5. Server
6. Trunking allows you to make a single port part of multiple VLANs at the same time.
7. Frame identification (frame tagging) uniquely assigns a user-defined ID to each frame. This is sometimes referred to as a VLAN ID or color.
8. True
9. Access link
10. Inter-Switch Link (ISL)

Security

THE CCNA EXAM TOPICS COVERED IN THIS CHAPTER INCLUDE THE FOLLOWING:

✓ **Identify security threats to a network and describe general methods to mitigate those threats**

- Describe today's increasing network security threats and explain the need to implement a comprehensive security policy to mitigate the threats
- Explain general methods to mitigate common security threats to network devices, hosts, and applications
- Describe the functions of common security appliances and applications
- Describe security recommended practices including initial steps to secure network devices

✓ **Configure, verify, and troubleshoot basic router operation and routing on Cisco devices**

- Implement basic router security

✓ **Implement, verify, and troubleshoot NAT and ACLs in a medium-size Enterprise branch office network**

- Describe the purpose and types of ACLs
- Configure and apply ACLs based on network filtering requirements (including CLI/SDM)
- Configure and apply an ACLs to limit telnet and SSH access to the router using (including SDM/CLI)
- Verify and monitor ACLs in a network environment
- Troubleshoot ACL issues

If you're a sys admin, it's my guess that shielding sensitive, critical data, as well as your network's resources, from every possible evil exploit is a top priority of yours. Right? Good to know you're on the right page—Cisco has some really effective security solutions that will arm you with the tools you need to make this happen.

Access control lists (ACLs) are an integral part of Cisco's security solution, and in addition to showing you the keys to both simple and advanced access lists that will equip you with the ability to ensure internetwork security, I'll show you how to mitigate most security-oriented network threats.

The proper use and configuration of access lists is a vital part of router configuration because access lists are such versatile networking accessories. Contributing mightily to the efficiency and operation of your network, access lists give network managers a huge amount of control over traffic flow throughout the enterprise. With access lists, managers can gather basic statistics on packet flow and security policies can be implemented. Sensitive devices can also be protected from unauthorized access.

In this chapter, we'll discuss access lists for TCP/IP as well as cover some of the tools available to test and monitor the functionality of applied access lists.

Although virtual private networks (VPNs) can be an important part of your corporate security, I'll cover VPNs in Chapter 16, "Wide Area Networks."

For up-to-the minute updates for this chapter, please see `www.lammle.com` and/or `www.sybex.com/go/ccna7e`.

Perimeter, Firewall, and Internal Routers

You see this a lot—typically, in medium to large enterprise networks, the various strategies for security are based on some recipe of internal and perimeter routers plus firewall devices. Internal routers provide additional security by screening traffic to various parts of the protected corporate network, and they do this using access lists. You can see where each of these types of devices are found in Figure 12.1.

I'll use the terms *trusted network* and *untrusted network* throughout this chapter and in Chapter 13, "Network Address Translation (NAT)," so it's important that you can see where they are found in a typical secured network. The demilitarized zone (DMZ) can be global (real) Internet addresses or private addresses, depending on how you configure your firewall, but this is typically where you'll find the HTTP, DNS, email, and other Internet-type corporate servers.

FIGURE 12.1 A typical secured network

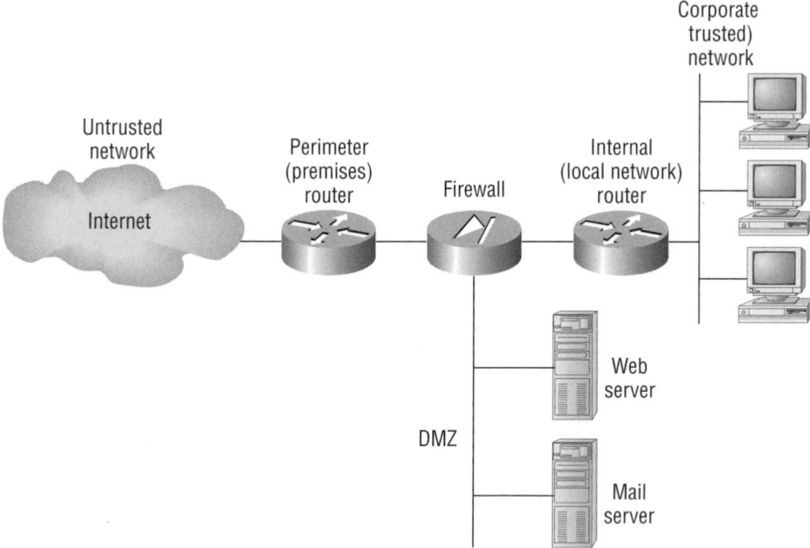

Instead of having routers, we can (as you already know) use virtual local area networks (VLANs) with switches on the inside trusted network. Multilayer switches containing their own security features can sometimes replace internal (LAN) routers to provide higher performance in VLAN architectures.

Let's look at some ways of protecting the internetwork using access lists.

Introduction to Access Lists

An *access list* is essentially a list of conditions that categorize packets. They can be really helpful when you need to exercise control over network traffic. An access list would be your tool of choice for decision making in these situations.

One of the most common and easiest-to-understand uses of access lists is filtering unwanted packets when implementing security policies. For example, you can set them up to make very specific decisions about regulating traffic patterns so that they'll allow only certain hosts to access web resources on the Internet while restricting others. With the right combination of access lists, network managers arm themselves with the power to enforce nearly any security policy they can invent.

Creating access lists is really a lot like programming a series of `if-then` statements—if a given condition is met, then a given action is taken. If the specific condition isn't met, nothing happens and the next statement is evaluated. Access-list statements are basically packet filters that packets are compared against, categorized by, and acted upon accordingly. Once the lists are built, they can be applied to either inbound or outbound traffic on any interface. Applying an access list causes the router to analyze every packet crossing that interface in the specified direction and take the appropriate action.

There are a few important rules that a packet follows when it's being compared with an access list:

- It's always compared with each line of the access list in sequential order—that is, it'll always start with the first line of the access list, then go to line 2, then line 3, and so on.
- It's compared with lines of the access list only until a match is made. Once the packet matches the condition on a line of the access list, the packet is acted upon and no further comparisons take place.
- There is an implicit "deny" at the end of each access list—this means that if a packet doesn't match the condition on any of the lines in the access list, the packet will be discarded.

Each of these rules has some powerful implications when filtering IP packets with access lists, so keep in mind that creating effective access lists truly takes some practice.

There are two main types of access lists:

Standard access lists These use only the source IP address in an IP packet as the condition test. All decisions are made based on the source IP address. This means that standard access lists basically permit or deny an entire suite of protocols. They don't distinguish between any of the many types of IP traffic such as Web, Telnet, UDP, and so on.

Extended access lists Extended access lists can evaluate many of the other fields in the layer 3 and layer 4 headers of an IP packet. They can evaluate source and destination IP addresses, the Protocol field in the Network layer header, and the port number at the Transport layer header. This gives extended access lists the ability to make much more granular decisions when controlling traffic.

Named access lists Hey, wait a minute—I said there were two types of access lists but listed three! Well, technically there really are only two since *named access lists* are either standard or extended and not actually a new type. I'm just distinguishing them because they're created and referred to differently than standard and extended access lists, but they're functionally the same.

We will look at these types of access lists in more depth later in the chapter.

Once you create an access list, it's not really going to do anything until you apply it. Yes, they're there on the router, but they're inactive until you tell that router what to do with them. To use an access list as a packet filter, you need to apply it to an interface on the router where you want the traffic filtered. And you've got to specify which direction of traffic you want the access list applied to. There's a good reason for this—you may want different controls in place for traffic leaving your enterprise destined for the Internet than you'd want for traffic coming into your enterprise from the Internet. So, by specifying the direction of traffic, you can—and frequently you'll need to—use different access lists for inbound and outbound traffic on a single interface:

Inbound access lists When an access list is applied to inbound packets on an interface, those packets are processed through the access list before being routed to the outbound interface. Any packets that are denied won't be routed because they're discarded before the routing process is invoked.

Outbound access lists When an access list is applied to outbound packets on an interface, packets are routed to the outbound interface and then processed through the access list before being queued.

There are some general access-list guidelines that should be followed when you're creating and implementing access lists on a router:

- You can assign only one access list per interface per protocol per direction. This means that when applying IP access lists, you can have only one inbound access list and one outbound access list per interface.

When you consider the implications of the implicit deny at the end of any access list, it makes sense that you can't have multiple access lists applied on the same interface in the same direction for the same protocol. That's because any packets that don't match some condition in the first access list would be denied and there wouldn't be any packets left over to compare against a second access list.

- Organize your access lists so that the more specific tests are at the top.
- Any time a new entry is added to the access list, it will be placed at the bottom of the list. Using a text editor for access lists is highly suggested.
- You cannot remove one line from an access list. If you try to do this, you will remove the entire list. It is best to copy the access list to a text editor before trying to edit the list. The only exception is when using named access lists.

You can edit, add, or delete a single line from a named access list. I'll show this to you shortly.

- Unless your access list ends with a `permit` any command, all packets will be discarded if they do not meet any of the list's tests. Every list should have at least one `permit` statement or it will deny all traffic.
- Create access lists and then apply them to an interface. Any access list applied to an interface without access list test statements present will not filter traffic.

- Access lists are designed to filter traffic going through the router. They will not filter traffic that has originated from the router.
- Place IP standard access lists as close to the destination as possible. This is the reason we don't really want to use standard access lists in our networks. You cannot put a standard access list close to the source host or network because you can only filter based on source address and all destinations would be affected.
- Place IP extended access lists as close to the source as possible. Since extended access lists can filter on very specific addresses and protocols, you don't want your traffic to traverse the entire network and then be denied. By placing this list as close to the source address as possible, you can filter traffic before it uses up your precious bandwidth.

Before I move on to how to configure basic and extended access lists, let's discuss how ACLs can be used to mitigate the security threats I discussed earlier in this chapter.

Mitigating Security Issues with ACLs

Here's a list of the many security threats you can mitigate with ACLs:

- IP address spoofing, inbound
- IP address spoofing, outbound
- Denial of service (DoS) TCP SYN attacks, blocking external attacks
- DoS TCP SYN attacks, using TCP Intercept
- DoS smurf attacks
- Denying/Filtering ICMP messages, inbound
- Denying/Filtering ICMP messages, outbound
- Denying/Filtering traceroute

This is not an introduction to security book, so you may have to research some of the preceding terms if you do not understand them.

It's generally wise not to allow into a private network any external IP packets that contain the source address of any internal hosts or networks—just don't do it!

Here's a list of rules to live by when configuring ACLs from the Internet to your production network to mitigate security problems:

- Deny any source addresses from your internal networks.
- Deny any local host addresses (127.0.0.0/8).
- Deny any reserved private addresses (RFC 1918).
- Deny any addresses in the IP multicast address range (224.0.0.0/4).

None of these source addresses should be allowed to enter your internetwork. Okay, finally, let's get to work on configuring some basic and advanced access lists.

Standard Access Lists

Standard IP access lists filter network traffic by examining the source IP address in a packet. You create a *standard IP access list* by using the access-list numbers 1–99 or 1300–1999 (expanded range). Access-list types are generally differentiated using a number. Based on the number used when the access list is created, the router knows which type of syntax to expect as the list is entered. By using numbers 1–99 or 1300–1999, you're telling the router that you want to create a standard IP access list, so the router will expect syntax specifying only the source IP address in the test lines.

The following is an example of the many access-list number ranges that you can use to filter traffic on your network (the protocols for which you can specify access lists depend on your IOS version):

```
Corp(config)#access-list ?
  <1-99>            IP standard access list
  <100-199>         IP extended access list
  <1100-1199>       Extended 48-bit MAC address access list
  <1300-1999>       IP standard access list (expanded range)
  <200-299>         Protocol type-code access list
  <2000-2699>       IP extended access list (expanded range)
  <700-799>         48-bit MAC address access list
  compiled          Enable IP access-list compilation
  dynamic-extended  Extend the dynamic ACL absolute timer
  rate-limit        Simple rate-limit specific access list
```

Let's take a look at the syntax used when creating a standard access list:

```
Corp(config)#access-list 10 ?
  deny    Specify packets to reject
  permit  Specify packets to forward
  remark  Access list entry comment
```

As I said, by using the access-list numbers 1–99 or 1300–1999, you're telling the router that you want to create a standard IP access list.

After you choose the access-list number, you need to decide whether you're creating a `permit` or deny statement. For this example, you will create a deny statement:

```
Corp(config)#access-list 10 deny ?
  Hostname or A.B.C.D  Address to match
  any                  Any source host
  host                 A single host address
```

The next step requires a more detailed explanation. There are three options available. You can use the any parameter to permit or deny any source host or network, you can use an IP address to specify either a single host or a range of them, or you can use the host command to specify a specific host only. The any command is pretty obvious—any source address matches the statement, so every packet compared against this line will match. The host command is relatively simple. Here's an example using it:

```
Corp(config)#access-list 10 deny host ?
  Hostname or A.B.C.D  Host address
Corp(config)#access-list 10 deny host 172.16.30.2
```

This tells the list to deny any packets from host 172.16.30.2. The default parameter is host. In other words, if you type **access-list 10 deny 172.16.30.2**, the router assumes you mean host 172.16.30.2 and that is how it will show in your running-config.

But there's another way to specify either a particular host or a range of hosts—you can use wildcard masking. In fact, to specify any range of hosts, you have to use wildcard masking in the access list.

What's wildcard masking? You'll learn all about it using a standard access list example, as well as how to control access to a virtual terminal, in the following sections. However, the good news is that we're going to be using the same wildcard masks we used in our OSPF section of Chapter 9.

Wildcard Masking

Wildcards are used with access lists to specify an individual host, a network, or a certain range of a network or networks. To understand a *wildcard*, you need to understand what a *block size* is; it's used to specify a range of addresses. Some of the different block sizes available are 64, 32, 16, 8, and 4.

When you need to specify a range of addresses, you choose the next-largest block size for your needs. For example, if you need to specify 34 networks, you need a block size of 64. If you want to specify 18 hosts, you need a block size of 32. If you specify only 2 networks, then a block size of 4 would work.

Wildcards are used with the host or network address to tell the router a range of available addresses to filter. To specify a host, the address would look like this:

```
172.16.30.5 0.0.0.0
```

The four zeros represent each octet of the address. Whenever a zero is present, it means that octet in the address must match the corresponding reference octet exactly. To specify that an octet can be any value, the value of 255 is used. As an example, here's how a /24 subnet is specified with a wildcard mask:

```
172.16.30.0 0.0.0.255
```

This tells the router to match up the first three octets exactly, but the fourth octet can be any value.

Now, that was the easy part. What if you want to specify only a small range of subnets? This is where the block sizes come in. You have to specify the range of values in a block size.

In other words, you can't choose to specify 20 networks. You can only specify the exact amount as the block size value. For example, the range would have to be either 16 or 32, but not 20.

Let's say that you want to block access to part of the network that is in the range from 172.16.8.0 through 172.16.15.0. That is a block size of 8. Your network number would be 172.16.8.0, and the wildcard would be 0.0.7.255. Whoa! What is that? The 7.255 is what the router uses to determine the block size. The network and wildcard tell the router to start at 172.16.8.0 and go up a block size of eight addresses to network 172.16.15.0.

Seriously, it really is easier than it looks—really! I could certainly go through the binary math for you, but no one needs that. Actually, all you have to do is remember that the wildcard is always one number less than the block size. So, in our example, the wildcard would be 7 since our block size is 8. If you used a block size of 16, the wildcard would be 15. Easy, huh?

But just in case, we'll go through some examples to help you nail it. The following example tells the router to match the first three octets exactly but that the fourth octet can be anything:

```
Corp(config)#access-list 10 deny 172.16.10.0 0.0.0.255
```

The next example tells the router to match the first two octets and that the last two octets can be any value:

```
Corp(config)#access-list 10 deny 172.16.0.0 0.0.255.255
```

Try to figure out this next line:

```
Corp(config)#access-list 10 deny 172.16.16.0 0.0.3.255
```

This configuration tells the router to start at network 172.16.16.0 and use a block size of 4. The range would then be 172.16.16.0 through 172.16.19.255 (the Cisco objectives like this one).

Okay, let's keep practicing; what about this next one?

```
Corp(config)#access-list 10 deny 172.16.16.0 0.0.7.255
```

This example shows an access list starting at 172.16.16.0 and going up a block size of 8 to 172.16.23.255.

We've got more practice to do in order to nail this process. What is the range of this one?

```
Corp(config)#access-list 10 deny 172.16.32.0 0.0.15.255
```

This example starts at network 172.16.32.0 and goes up a block size of 16 to 172.16.47.255.

Almost done practicing, and then we'll configure some real ACLs.

```
Corp(config)#access-list 10 deny 172.16.64.0 0.0.63.255
```

This example starts at network 172.16.64.0 and goes up a block size of 64 to 172.16.127.255.

What about my last example? Take a look:

```
Corp(config)#access-list 10 deny 192.168.160.0 0.0.31.255
```

The last example starts at network 192.168.160.0 and goes up a block size of 32 to 192.168.191.255.

Here are two more things to keep in mind when working with block sizes and wildcards:

- Each block size must start at 0 or a multiple of the block size. For example, you can't say that you want a block size of 8 and then start at 12. You must use 0–7, 8–15, 16–23, etc. For a block size of 32, the ranges are 0–31, 32–63, 64–95, etc.
- The command any is the same thing as writing out the wildcard 0.0.0.0 255.255.255.255.

Wildcard masking is a crucial skill to master when creating IP access lists. It's used identically when creating standard and extended IP access lists.

Standard Access List Example

In this section, you'll learn how to use a standard access list to stop specific users from gaining access to the Finance department LAN.

In Figure 12.2, a router has three LAN connections and one WAN connection to the Internet. Users on the Sales LAN should not have access to the Finance LAN, but they should be able to access the Internet and the marketing department files. The Marketing LAN needs to access the Finance LAN for application services.

On the router in the figure, the following standard IP access list is configured:

```
Lab_A#config t
Lab_A(config)#access-list 10 deny 172.16.40.0 0.0.0.255
Lab_A(config)#access-list 10 permit any
```

FIGURE 12.2 IP access list example with three LANs and a WAN connection

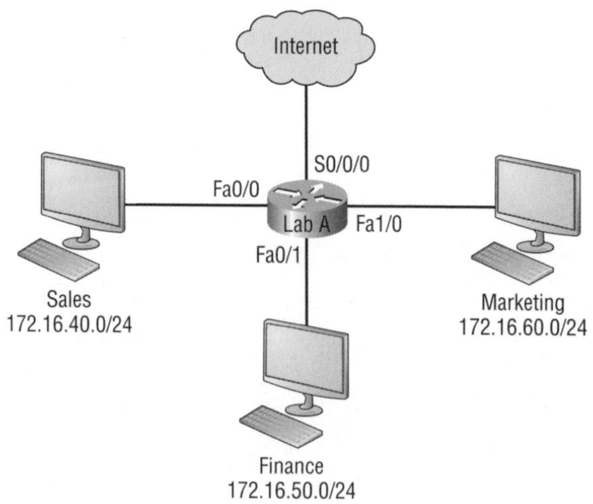

It's very important to know that the any command is the same thing as saying the following using wildcard masking:

```
Lab_A(config)#access-list 10 permit 0.0.0.0 255.255.255.255
```

Since the wildcard mask says that none of the octets are to be evaluated, every address matches the test condition. So this is functionally the same as using the any keyword.

At this point, the access list is configured to deny source addresses from the Sales LAN the Finance LAN and still allow everyone else. But remember, no action will be taken until the access list is applied on an interface in a specific direction.

But where should this access list be placed? If you place it as an incoming access list on fa0/0, you might as well shut down the FastEthernet interface because all of the Sales LAN devices will be denied access to all networks attached to the router. The best place to apply this access list is on the fa0/1 interface as an outbound list:

```
Lab_A(config)#int fa0/1
Lab_A(config-if)#ip access-group 10 out
```

This completely stops traffic from 172.16.40.0 from getting out FastEthernet0/1. It has no effect on the hosts from the Sales LAN accessing the Marketing LAN and the Internet since traffic to those destinations doesn't go through interface fa0/1. Any packet trying to exit out fa0/1 will have to go through the access list first. If there were an inbound list placed on f0/0, then any packet trying to enter interface f0/0 would have to go through the access list before being routed to an exit interface.

Let's take a look at another example of a standard access list. Figure 12.3 shows an internetwork of two routers with three LANs and one serial WAN connection.

FIGURE 12.3 IP standard access list example 2

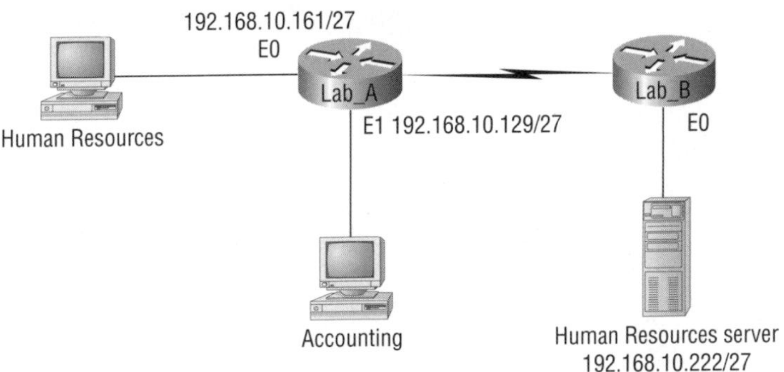

Using a standard ACL, you want to stop the Accounting users from accessing the Human Resources server attached to the Lab_B router but allow all other users access to that LAN. What standard access list would you create and where would you place it?

The real answer is that you should use an extended access list and place it closest to the source, but the question specifies that you should use a standard access list. Standard access lists, by rule of thumb, are placed closest to the destination—in this example, Ethernet 0 outbound on the Lab_B router. Here is the access list that should be placed on the Lab_B router:

```
Lab_B#config t
Lab_B(config)#access-list 10 deny 192.168.10.128 0.0.0.31
Lab_B(config)#access-list 10 permit any
Lab_B(config)#interface Ethernet 0
Lab_B(config-if)#ip access-group 10 out
```

To answer the question, you must understand subnetting, wildcard masks, and how to configure and implement ACLs. I think we need to practice this process again.

With that in mind, before we move on to restricting Telnet access on a router, let's take a look at one more standard access list example, but it will require some thought. In Figure 12.4 you have a router with four LAN connections and one WAN connection to the Internet.

You need to write an access list that will stop access from each of the four LANs shown in the diagram to the Internet. Each of the LANs shows a single host's IP address, and from that you need to determine the subnet and wildcards of each LAN to configure the access list.

FIGURE 12.4 IP standard access list example 3

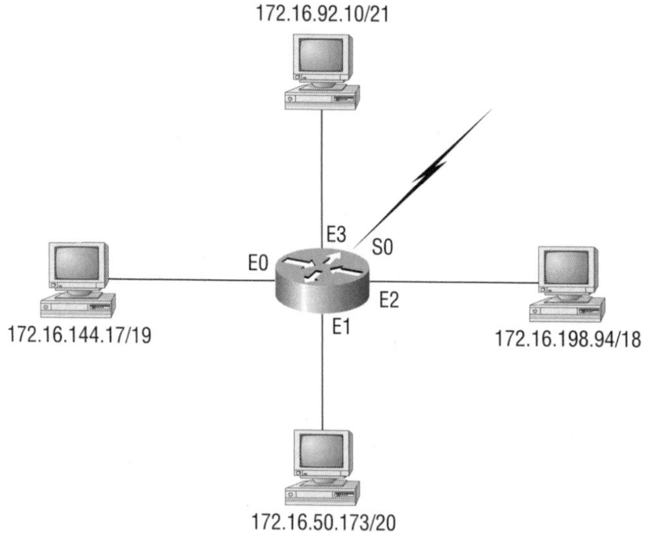

Here is an example of what your answer should look like (starting with the network on E0 and working through to E3):

```
Router(config)#access-list 1 deny 172.16.128.0 0.0.31.255
Router(config)#access-list 1 deny 172.16.48.0 0.0.15.255
Router(config)#access-list 1 deny 172.16.192.0 0.0.63.255
Router(config)#access-list 1 deny 172.16.88.0 0.0.7.255
```

```
Router(config)#access-list 1 permit any
Router(config)#interface serial 0
Router(config-if)#ip access-group 1 out
```

Sure, you could have done this with one line:

```
Router(config)#access-list 1 deny 172.16.0.0 0.0.255.255
```

But what fun is that?

Okay, what then is the purpose of creating this list? If you actually applied this access list on the router, you'd effectively shut down access to the Internet, so why even have an Internet connection? I wrote this exercise so you can practice how to use block sizes with access lists, which is critical for your success when studying the CCNA objectives.

Controlling VTY (Telnet/SSH) Access

You'll probably have a difficult time trying to stop users from telnetting or trying to SSH to a large router because any active interface on a router is fair game for VTY access. You could try to create an extended IP access list that limits access to every IP address on the router. But if you did that, you'd have to apply it inbound on every interface, and that really wouldn't scale well to a large router with dozens, even hundreds, of interfaces, would it? Plus, think of all the latency you would create on your network as every router looked at every packet just in case the packet was trying to access your VTY lines.

Here's a much better solution: Use a standard IP access list to control access to the VTY lines themselves.

Why does this work? Because when you apply an access list to the VTY lines, you don't need to specify the protocol since access to the VTY implies terminal access via the Telnet or SSH protocols. You also don't need to specify a destination address since it really doesn't matter which interface address the user used as a target for the Telnet session. You really only need to control where the user is coming from—their source IP address.

To perform this function, follow these steps:

1. Create a standard IP access list that permits only the host or hosts you want to be able to telnet into the routers.
2. Apply the access list to the VTY line with the `access-class in` command.

Here is an example of allowing only host 172.16.10.3 to telnet into a router:

```
Lab_A(config)#access-list 50 permit host 172.16.10.3
Lab_A(config)#line vty 0 4
Lab_A(config-line)#access-class 50 in
```

Because of the implied `deny any` at the end of the list, the access list stops any host from telnetting into the router except the host 172.16.10.3, regardless of which individual IP address on the router is used as a target. You may want to include an admin subnet address as the source instead of a single host, but I was just providing an example of how to create security on your VTY lines without adding latency to your router.

Real World Scenario

Should You Secure Your VTY Lines on a Router?

You're monitoring your network and notice that someone has telnetted into your core router by using the `show users` command. You use the `disconnect` command and they are disconnected from the router, but you notice that they are back into the router a few minutes later. You are thinking about putting an access list on the router interfaces, but you don't want to add a lot of latency on each interface since your router is already pushing a lot of packets. You are considering putting an access list on the VTY lines themselves, but not having done this before, you are not sure if this is a safe alternative to putting an access list on each interface. Is putting an access list on the VTY lines a good idea for this network?

Yes, absolutely, and the `access-class` command illustrated in this chapter is the way to do this. Why? Because it doesn't use an access list that just sits on an interface looking at every arriving packet that is coming and going. This can cause overhead on the packets trying to be routed.

When you put the `access-class in` command on the VTY lines, only packets trying to telnet into the router will be looked at and compared. This provides nice, easy-to-configure security for your router.

Cisco recommends that you use Secure Shell (SSH) instead of Telnet on the VTY lines of a router. See Chapter 6 for more information on SSH and how to configure SSH on your routers and switches.

Extended Access Lists

In the standard IP access list example earlier, you had to block all access from the Sales LAN to the finance department. What if you needed Sales to gain access to a certain server on the Finance LAN but not to other network services, for security reasons? With a standard IP access list, you can't allow users to get to one network service and not another. Said another way, a standard access list won't allow you to make decisions based on both source and destination addresses because it makes decisions based only on source address.

But an *extended access list* will hook you up. That's because extended access lists allow you to specify source and destination addresses as well as the protocol and port number that identify the upper-layer protocol or application. By using extended access lists, you can effectively allow users access to a physical LAN and stop them from accessing specific hosts—or even specific services on those hosts.

Here's an example of an extended IP access list:

```
Corp(config)#access-list ?
  <1-99>            IP standard access list
  <100-199>         IP extended access list
  <1100-1199>       Extended 48-bit MAC address access list
  <1300-1999>       IP standard access list (expanded range)
  <200-299>         Protocol type-code access list
  <2000-2699>       IP extended access list (expanded range)
  <700-799>         48-bit MAC address access list
  compiled          Enable IP access-list compilation
  dynamic-extended  Extend the dynamic ACL absolute timer
  rate-limit        Simple rate-limit specific access list
```

The first command shows the access-list numbers available. You'll use the extended access-list range from 100 to 199. Be sure to notice that the range 2000–2699 is also available for extended IP access lists.

At this point, you need to decide what type of list entry you are making. For this example, you'll choose a deny list entry:

```
Corp(config)#access-list 110 ?
  deny     Specify packets to reject
  dynamic  Specify a DYNAMIC list of PERMITs or DENYs
  permit   Specify packets to forward
  remark   Access list entry comment
```

Once you choose the access-list type, you need to select a protocol field entry:

```
Corp(config)#access-list 110 deny ?
  <0-255>  An IP protocol number
  ahp      Authentication Header Protocol
  eigrp    Cisco's EIGRP routing protocol
  esp      Encapsulation Security Payload
  gre      Cisco's GRE tunneling
  icmp     Internet Control Message Protocol
  igmp     Internet Gateway Message Protocol
  ip       Any Internet Protocol
  ipinip   IP in IP tunneling
  nos      KA9Q NOS compatible IP over IP tunneling
  ospf     OSPF routing protocol
  pcp      Payload Compression Protocol
  pim      Protocol Independent Multicast
  tcp      Transmission Control Protocol
  udp      User Datagram Protocol
```

If you want to filter by Application layer protocol, you have to choose the appropriate layer 4 transport protocol after the permit or deny statement. For example, to filter Telnet or FTP, you choose TCP since both Telnet and FTP use TCP at the Transport layer. If you were to choose IP, you wouldn't be allowed to specify a specific application protocol later and could only filter on source and destination address.

Here, you'll choose to filter an Application layer protocol that uses TCP by selecting TCP as the protocol. You'll specify the specific TCP port later. Next, you will be prompted for the source IP address of the host or network (you can choose the any command to allow any source address):

```
Corp(config)#access-list 110 deny tcp ?
  A.B.C.D  Source address
  any      Any source host
  host     A single source host
```

After the source address is selected, the destination address can be chosen:

```
Corp(config)#access-list 110 deny tcp any ?
  A.B.C.D  Destination address
  any      Any destination host
  eq       Match only packets on a given port number
  gt       Match only packets with a greater port number
  host     A single destination host
  lt       Match only packets with a lower port number
  neq      Match only packets not on a given port number
  range    Match only packets in the range of port numbers
```

In the following example, any source IP address that has a destination IP address of 172.16.30.2 has been denied:

```
Corp(config)#access-list 110 deny tcp any host 172.16.30.2 ?
  ack          Match on the ACK bit
  dscp         Match packets with given dscp value
  eq           Match only packets on a given port number
  established  Match established connections
  fin          Match on the FIN bit
  fragments    Check non-initial fragments
  gt           Match only packets with a greater port number
  log          Log matches against this entry
  log-input    Log matches against this entry, including input interface
  lt           Match only packets with a lower port number
  neq          Match only packets not on a given port number
```

```
  precedence   Match packets with given precedence value
  psh          Match on the PSH bit
  range        Match only packets in the range of port numbers
  rst          Match on the RST bit
  syn          Match on the SYN bit
  time-range   Specify a time-range
  tos          Match packets with given TOS value
  urg          Match on the URG bit
  <cr>
```

Once we have the destination host addresses in place, just specify the type of service you are denying using the `equal to` command, which we'd just type in as `eq`. The following help screen shows you the available options. You can choose a port number or use the application name:

```
Corp(config)#access-list 110 deny tcp any host 172.16.30.2 eq ?
  <0-65535>    Port number
  bgp          Border Gateway Protocol (179)
  chargen      Character generator (19)
  cmd          Remote commands (rcmd, 514)
  daytime      Daytime (13)
  discard      Discard (9)
  domain       Domain Name Service (53)
  drip         Dynamic Routing Information Protocol (3949)
  echo         Echo (7)
  exec         Exec (rsh, 512)
  finger       Finger (79)
  ftp          File Transfer Protocol (21)
  ftp-data     FTP data connections (20)
  gopher       Gopher (70)
  hostname     NIC hostname server (101)
  ident        Ident Protocol (113)
  irc          Internet Relay Chat (194)
  klogin       Kerberos login (543)
  kshell       Kerberos shell (544)
  login        Login (rlogin, 513)
  lpd          Printer service (515)
  nntp         Network News Transport Protocol (119)
  pim-auto-rp  PIM Auto-RP (496)
  pop2         Post Office Protocol v2 (109)
  pop3         Post Office Protocol v3 (110)
  smtp         Simple Mail Transport Protocol (25)
  sunrpc       Sun Remote Procedure Call (111)
```

```
syslog        Syslog (514)
tacacs        TAC Access Control System (49)
talk          Talk (517)
telnet        Telnet (23)
time          Time (37)
uucp          Unix-to-Unix Copy Program (540)
whois         Nicname (43)
www           World Wide Web (HTTP, 80)
```

At this point, let's block Telnet (port 23) to host 172.16.30.2 only. If the users want to FTP, fine—that's allowed. The `log` command is used to log messages every time the access list entry is hit. This can be an extremely cool way to monitor inappropriate access attempts, but only in a nonproduction network because it would overload your console with messages in a production network.

Here is how we ended up:

```
Corp(config)#access-list 110 deny tcp any host 172.16.30.2 eq 23 log
```

You need to keep in mind that the next line is an implicit `deny any` by default. If you apply this access list to an interface, you might as well just shut the interface down since by default there is an implicit `deny all` at the end of every access list. You've got to follow up the access list with the following command:

```
Corp(config)#access-list 110 permit ip any any
```

Remember, the `0.0.0.0 255.255.255.255` is the same command as `any`, so the command could also look like this:

```
Corp(config)#access-list 110 permit ip 0.0.0.0 255.255.255.255
0.0.0.0 255.255.255.255
```

However, if you did this, when you looked at the running-config the commands would be replaced with the `any any`. I use the `any` command because it is less typing.

Once the access list is created, you need to apply it to an interface (it's the same command as the IP standard list):

```
Corp(config-if)#ip access-group 110 in
```

Or this:

```
Corp(config-if)#ip access-group 110 out
```

In the following section, we'll look at some examples of how to use an extended access list.

Extended Access List Example 1

Using Figure 12.2 from the IP standard access list example earlier, let's use the same network and deny access to a host at 172.16.50.5 on the finance department LAN for both

Telnet and FTP services. All other services on this and all other hosts are acceptable for the sales and marketing departments to access.

The following access list should be created:

```
Lab_A#config t
Lab_A(config)#access-list 110 deny tcp any host 172.16.50.5 eq 21
Lab_A(config)#access-list 110 deny tcp any host 172.16.50.5 eq 23
Lab_A(config)#access-list 110 permit ip any any
```

The access-list 110 tells the router you are creating an extended IP access list. The tcp is the protocol field in the Network layer header. If the list doesn't say tcp here, you cannot filter by TCP port numbers 21 and 23 as shown in the example. (These are FTP and Telnet, and they both use TCP for connection-oriented services.) The any command is the source, which means any source IP address, and the host is the destination IP address. This ACL says specifically that all IP traffic except FTP and Telnet is permitted to host 172.16.50.5 from any source.

Remember that instead of the host 172.16.50.5 command when we created the extended access list, we could have entered 172.16.50.5 0.0.0.0 and there would be no difference in the result—other than the router would change the command to host 172.16.50.5 in the running-config.

After the list is created, it needs to be applied to the FastEthernet 0/1 interface outbound because we are blocking all traffic from getting to host 172.16.50.5 and performing FTP and telnet. However, if this list was created to block access only from the Sales LAN to host 172.16.50.5, then we'd have put this list closer to the source, or on FastEthernet 0/0. So, in that situation, we'd apply the list to inbound traffic. You must look at each situation carefully before creating and applying ACLs.

Let's go ahead and apply the list to interface F0/1 and block all outside FTP and Telnet access to the host 172.16.50.5:

```
Lab_A(config)#int fa0/1
Lab_A(config-if)#ip access-group 110 out
```

Extended Access List Example 2

In this example, we'll again use Figure 12.4, which has four LANs and a serial connection. What we need to do is stop Telnet access to the networks attached to the E1 and E2 interfaces.

The configuration on the router would look something like this, although the answer can vary:

```
Router(config)#access-list 110 deny tcp any 172.16.48.0 0.0.15.255
eq 23
Router(config)#access-list 110 deny tcp any 172.16.192.0 0.0.63.255
```

```
eq 23
Router(config)#access-list 110 permit ip any any
Router(config)#interface Ethernet 1
Router(config-if)#ip access-group 110 out
Router(config-if)#interface Ethernet 2
Router(config-if)#ip access-group 110 out
```

The important information that you need to understand from this list is as follows: First, you need to verify that the number range is correct for the type of access list you are creating—in this example it's extended, so the range must be 100–199. Second, you need to verify that the protocol field matches the upper-layer process or application—in this example, TCP port 23 (Telnet).

The protocol parameter must be TCP since Telnet uses TCP. If the question stated to use TFTP, for example, then the protocol parameter would have to be UDP since TFTP uses UDP. Third, verify that the destination port number matches the application you are filtering for—in this case, port 23 matches Telnet, which is correct, but understand that you can type in **telnet** at the end of the line instead of 23. Finally, the test statement `permit ip any any` is important to have at the end of the list to enable all packets other than Telnet packets destined for the LANs connected to Ethernet 1 and Ethernet 2.

Extended Access List Example 3

We need another extended ACL example before we move onto named ACLs. Figure 12.5 shows us the network we will use in this example:

FIGURE 12.5 Extended ACL example 3

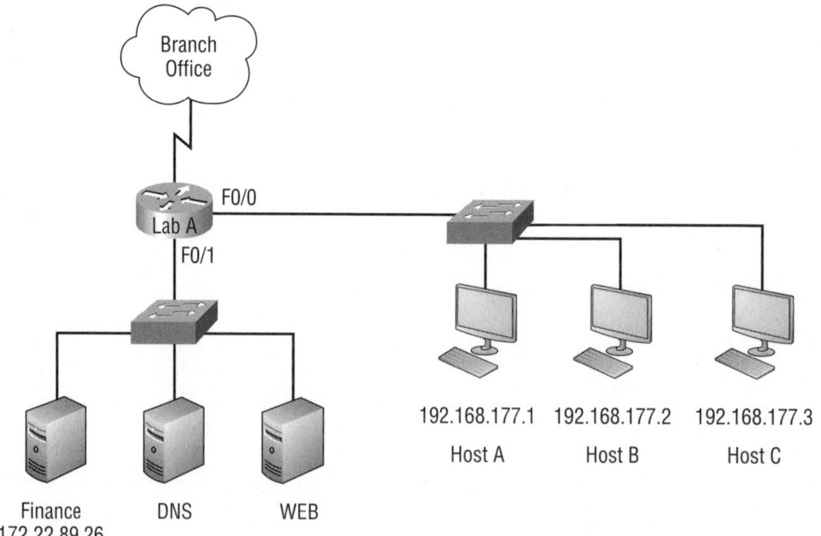

In this example, we will allow HTTP access to the Finance server from source Host B only. All other traffic is permitted. We need to be able to configure this in only three test statements, and then we'll need to add the interface configuration.

Let's take what we've learned and knock this out.

```
Lab_A#config t
Lab_A(config)#access-list 110 permit tcp host 192.168.177.2 host 172.22.89.26 eq 80
Lab_A(config)#access-list 110 deny tcp any host 172.22.89.26 eq 80
Lab_A(config)#access-list 110 permit ip any any
```

This is pretty simple actually. First we need to permit Host B HTTP access to the Finance server. However, since all other traffic must be allowed, we must be detailed in who cannot HTTP to the Finance server, so the second test statement denies anyone else from performing HTTP on the Finance server. Finally, now that Host B can HTTP to the Finance server and everyone else cannot, let's permit all other traffic with our third test statement.

Okay, really not bad. It just takes some thought. But wait—we're not done. We need to apply this to an interface. Since extended access lists are typically applied closest to the source, we should place this inbound on F0/0, right? Well, this is one example where we do not follow the rule of thumb. The example said to allow only HTTP traffic to the Finance server from Host B. If we apply the ACL inbound on F0/0, then the branch office would be able to access the Finance server and perform HTTP. In this example, we need to place the ACL closest to the destination:

```
Lab_A(config)#interface fastethernet 0/1
Lab_A(config-if)#ip access-group 110 out
```

Okay, let's take a look at creating ACLs using names.

Named ACLs

As I said earlier, named access lists are just another way to create standard and extended access lists. In medium to large enterprises, management of access lists can become, well, a real hassle over time. For example, when you need to make a change to an access list, a frequent practice is to copy the access list to a text editor, edit the list, then paste the new list back into the router.

This would work pretty well if it weren't for what I call "pack rat" mentality. The question becomes, what do I do with the old access list? Delete it? Or should I save it in case I find a problem with the new list and need to back out of the change? What happens is that over time—through this and countless other scenarios—you can end up with a whole bunch of unapplied access lists building up on a router. What were they for? Are they important? Do I need them? All good questions, and named access lists could be your answer.

This can also apply to access lists that are up and running. Let's say you come into an existing network and are looking at access lists on a router. Suppose you find an access list 177 (which is an extended access list) that is 33 lines long. This could cause you much needless existential questioning—what is it for? Why is it here? Instead, wouldn't it be easier to identify an access list called, say, FinanceLAN than one that's named 177?

Named access lists allow you to use names to both create and apply either standard or extended access lists. There is nothing new or different about these access lists aside from being able to refer to them in a way that makes sense to humans. But there are some subtle changes to the syntax, so let's re-create the standard access list we created earlier for our test network in Figure 12.2 using a named access list:

```
Lab_A#config t
Enter configuration commands, one per line.  End with CNTL/Z.
Lab_A(config)#ip access-list ?
  extended  Extended Acc
  logging   Control access list logging
  standard  Standard Access List
```

Notice that I started by typing **ip access-list**, not **access-list**. This allows me to enter a named access list. Next, I'll need to specify that it's to be a standard access list:

```
Lab_A(config)#ip access-list standard ?
  <1-99>  Standard IP access-list number
  WORD    Access-list name

Lab_A(config)#ip access-list standard BlockSales
Lab_A(config-std-nacl)#
```

I've specified a standard access list, then added a name: BlockSales. Notice that I could've used a number for a standard access list, but instead, I chose to use a descriptive name. Also, notice that after entering the name, I pressed Enter and the router prompt changed. I'm now in named access list configuration mode and entering the named access list:

```
Lab_A(config-std-nacl)#?
Standard Access List configuration commands:
  default  Set a command to its defaults
  deny     Specify packets to reject
  exit     Exit from access-list configuration mode
  no       Negate a command or set its defaults
  permit   Specify packets to forward

Lab_A(config-std-nacl)#deny 172.16.40.0 0.0.0.255
Lab_A(config-std-nacl)#permit any
Lab_A(config-std-nacl)#exit
Lab_A(config)#^Z
Lab_A#
```

I enter the access list, and then exit out of configuration mode. Next, I'll take a look at the running configuration to verify that the access list is indeed in the router:

```
Lab_A#show running-config

!
ip access-list standard BlockSales
 deny   172.16.40.0 0.0.0.255
 permit any
!
```

The BlockSales access list has truly been created and is in the running-config of the router. Next, I'll need to apply the access list to the correct interface:

```
Lab_A#config t
Lab_A(config)#int fa0/1
Lab_A(config-if)#ip access-group BlockSales out
Lab_A(config-if)#^Z
Lab_A#
```

All right! At this point, we've re-created the work done earlier using a named access list.

Remarks

The `remark` keyword is really important because it arms you with the ability to include comments, or rather remarks, regarding the entries you've made in both your IP standard and extended ACLs. Remarks are very cool because they efficiently increase your ability to examine and understand your ACLs to the superhero level. Without them, you'd be caught in a quagmire of potentially meaningless numbers without anything to help you recall what those numbers mean.

Even though you have the option of placing your remarks either before or after a `permit` or `deny` statement, I totally recommend that you chose to position them consistently so you don't get confused about which remark is relevant to which one of your `permit` or `deny` statements.

To get this going for both standard and extended ACLs, just use the `access-list` *`access-list number`* `remark` **`remark global configuration`** command. And if you want to get rid of a remark, just use the command's `no` form.

Let's take a look at an example of how to use the `remark` command:

```
R2#config t
R2(config)#access-list 110 remark Permit Bob from Sales Only To Finance
R2(config)#access-list 110 permit ip host 172.16.40.1 172.16.50.0 0.0.0.255
R2(config)#access-list 110 deny ip 172.16.40.0 0.0.0.255 172.16.50.0 0.0.0.255
R2(config)#ip access-list extended No_Telnet
```

```
R2(config-ext-nacl)#remark Deny all of Sales from Telnetting
to Marketing
R2(config-ext-nacl)#deny tcp 172.16.40.0 0.0.0.255 172.16.60.0 0.0.0.255 eq 23
R2(config-ext-nacl)#permit ip any any
R2(config-ext-nacl)#do show run
[output cut]
!
ip access-list extended No_Telnet
 remark Stop all of Sales from Telnetting to Marketing
 deny   tcp 172.16.40.0 0.0.0.255 172.16.60.0 0.0.0.255 eq telnet
 permit ip any any
!
access-list 110 remark Permit Bob from Sales Only To Finance
access-list 110 permit ip host 172.16.40.1 172.16.50.0 0.0.0.255
access-list 110 deny   ip 172.16.40.0 0.0.0.255 172.16.50.0 0.0.0.255
access-list 110 permit ip any any
!
```

I was able to add a `remark` to both an extended list and a named access list. However, you cannot see these remarks in the output of the `show access-list` command, only in the running-config.

Turning Off and Configuring Network Services

By default, the Cisco IOS runs some services that are unnecessary to its normal operation, and if you don't disable them, they can be easy targets for denial of service (DoS) attacks and break-in attempts.

DoS attacks are the most common attacks because they are the easiest to perform. Using software and/or hardware tools such as Intrusion Detection System (IDS) and Intrusion Prevention System (IPS) can both warn and stop these simple, but harmful, attacks. However, if we can't implement IDS/IPS, there are some basic commands we can use on our router to make them more safe, but nothing will make you completely safe in today's networks.

Let's take a look at the basic services we should disable on our routers.

Blocking SNMP Packets

The Cisco IOS default configurations permit remote access from any source, so unless you're either way too trusting or insane, it should be totally obvious to you that those configurations need a bit of attention. You've got to restrict them. If you don't, the router will be a pretty easy target for an attacker who wants to log in to it. This is where access lists come into the game—they can really protect you.

If you place the following command on the serial0/0 interface of the perimeter router, it'll stop any SNMP packets from entering the router or the DMZ. (You'd also need to have a `permit` command along with this list to really make it work, but this is just an example.)

```
Lab_B(config)#access-list 110 deny udp any any eq snmp
Lab_B(config)#interface s0/0
Lab_B(config-if)#access-group 110 in
```

Disabling Echo

In case you don't know this already, small services are servers (daemons) running in the router that are quite useful for diagnostics. And here we go again—by default, the Cisco router has a series of diagnostic ports enabled for certain UDP and TCP services, including echo, chargen, and discard.

When a host attaches to those ports, a small amount of CPU is consumed to service these requests. All a single attacking device needs to do is send a whole slew of requests with different, random, phony source IP addresses to overwhelm the router, making it slow down or even fail. You can use the `no` version of these commands to stop a chargen attack:

```
Lab_B(config)#no service tcp-small-servers
Lab_B(config)#no service udp-small-servers
```

Finger is a utility program designed to allow users of Unix hosts on the Internet to get information about each other:

```
Lab_B(config)#no service finger
```

This matters because the `finger` command can be used to find information about all users on the network and/or the router. It's also why you should disable it. The `finger` command is the remote equivalent to issuing the `show users` command on the router.

Here are the TCP small services:

- Echo: Echoes back whatever you type. Type the command `telnet` *`x.x.x.x`* `echo ?` to see the options.
- Chargen: Generates a stream of ASCII data. Type the command `telnet` *`x.x.x.x`* `chargen ?` to see the options.
- Discard: Throws away whatever you type. Type the command `telnet` *`x.x.x.x`* `discard ?` to see the options.
- Daytime: Returns the system date and time, if correct. It is correct if you are running NTP or have set the date and time manually from the EXEC level. Type the command `telnet` *`x.x.x.x`* `daytime ?` to see the options.

The UDP small services are as follows:

- Echo: Echoes the payload of the datagram you send
- Discard: Silently pitches the datagram you send
- Chargen: Pitches the datagram you send and responds with a 72-character string of ASCII characters terminated with a CR+LF

Turning off BootP and Auto-Config

Again, by default, the Cisco router also offers async line BootP service as well as remote auto-configuration. To disable these functions on your Cisco router, use the following commands:

```
Lab_B(config)#no ip boot server
Lab_B(config)#no service config
```

Disabling the HTTP Interface

The `ip http server` command may be useful for configuring and monitoring the router, but the cleartext nature of HTTP can obviously be a security risk. To disable the HTTP process on your router, use the following command:

```
Lab_B(config)#no ip http server
```

To enable an HTTP server on a router for AAA, use the global configuration command `ip http server`.

Disabling IP Source Routing

The IP header source-route option allows the source IP host to set a packet's route through the IP network. With IP source routing enabled, packets containing the source-route option are forwarded to the router addresses specified in the header. Use the following command to disable any processing of packets with source-routing header options:

```
Lab_B(config)#no ip source-route
```

Disabling Proxy ARP

Proxy ARP is the technique in which one host—usually a router—answers ARP requests intended for another machine. By "faking" its identity, the router accepts responsibility for getting those packets to the "real" destination. Proxy ARP can help machines on a subnet reach remote subnets without configuring routing or a default gateway. The following command disables proxy ARP:

```
Lab_B(config)#interface fa0/0
Lab_B(config-if)#no ip proxy-arp
```

Apply this command to all your router's LAN interfaces.

Disabling Redirect Messages

ICMP redirect messages are used by routers to notify hosts on the data link that a better route is available for a particular destination. To disable the redirect messages so bad people can't draw out your network topology with this information, use the following command:

```
Lab_B(config)#interface s0/0
Lab_B(config-if)#no ip redirects
```

Apply this command to all your router's interfaces. However, just understand that if this is configured, legitimate user traffic may end up taking a suboptimal route. Use caution when disabling this command.

Disabling the Generation of ICMP Unreachable Messages

The `no ip unreachables` command prevents the perimeter router from divulging topology information by telling external hosts which subnets are not configured. This command is used on a router's interface that is connected to an outside network:

```
Lab_B(config)#interface s0/0
Lab_B(config-if)#no ip unreachables
```

Again, apply this to all the interfaces of your router that connect to the outside world.

Disabling Multicast Route Caching

The multicast route cache lists multicast routing cache entries. These packets can be read, and so they create a security problem. To disable the multicast route caching, use the following command:

```
Lab_B(config)#interface s0/0
Lab_B(config-if)#no ip mroute-cache
```

Apply this command to all the interfaces of the router. However, use caution when disabling this command because it may slow legitimate multicast traffic.

Disabling the Maintenance Operation Protocol (MOP)

The Maintenance Operation Protocol (MOP) works at the Data Link and Network layers in the DECnet protocol suite and is used for utility services like uploading and downloading system software, remote testing, and problem diagnosis. So, who uses DECnet? Anyone with their hands up? I didn't think so. To disable this service, use the following command:

```
Lab_B(config)#interface s0/0
Lab_B(config-if)#no mop enabled
```

Apply this command to all the interfaces of the router.

Turning Off the X.25 PAD Service

Packet assembler/disassembler (PAD) connects asynchronous devices like terminals and computers to public/private X.25 networks. Since every computer in the world is pretty much IP savvy, and X.25 has gone the way of the dodo bird, there is no reason to leave this service running. Use the following command to disable the PAD service:

```
Lab_B(config)#no service pad
```

Enabling the Nagle TCP Congestion Algorithm

The Nagle TCP congestion algorithm is useful for small packet congestion, but if you're using a higher setting than the default MTU of 1,500 bytes, it can create an above-average traffic load. To enable this service, use the following command:

```
Lab_B(config)#service nagle
```

It is important to understand that the Nagle congestion service can break XWindow connections to an Xserver, so don't use it if you're using XWindow.

Logging Every Event

Used as a Syslog server, the Cisco ACS server can log events for you to verify. Use the `logging trap debugging` or `logging trap` *`level`* command and the `logging` *`ip_address`* command to turn this feature on:

```
Lab_B(config)#logging trap debugging
Lab_B(config)#logging 192.168.254.251
Lab_B(config)#exit
Lab_B#sh logging
Syslog logging: enabled (0 messages dropped, 0 flushes, 0 overruns)
    Console logging: level debugging, 15 messages logged
    Monitor logging: level debugging, 0 messages logged
    Buffer logging: disabled
    Trap logging: level debugging, 19 message lines logged
        Logging to 192.168.254.251, 1 message lines logged
```

The `show logging` command provides you with statistics of the logging configuration on the router.

Disabling Cisco Discovery Protocol

Cisco Discovery Protocol (CDP) does just that—it's a Cisco proprietary protocol that discovers directly connected Cisco devices on the network. But because it's a Data Link layer protocol, it can't find Cisco devices on the other side of a router. Plus, by default, Cisco switches don't forward CDP packets, so you can't see Cisco devices attached to any other port on a switch.

When you are bringing up your network for the first time, CDP can be a really helpful protocol for verifying it. But since you're going to be thorough and document your network, you don't need the CDP after that. And because CDP does discover Cisco routers and switches on your network, you should disable it. You do that in global configuration mode, which turns off CDP completely for your router or switch:

```
Lab_B(config)#no cdp run
```

Or, you can turn off CDP on each individual interface using the following command:

```
Lab_B(config-if)#no cdp enable
```

Disabling the Default Forwarded UDP Protocols

When you use the `ip helper-address` command as follows on an interface, your router will forward UDP broadcasts to the listed server or servers:

```
Lab_B(config)#interface f0/0
Lab_B(config-if)#ip helper-address 192.168.254.251
```

You would generally use the `ip helper-address` command when you want to forward DHCP client requests to a DHCP server. The problem is that not only does this forward port 67 (BOOTP server request), it forwards seven other ports by default as well. To disable the unused ports, use the following commands:

```
Lab_B(config)#no ip forward-protocol udp 69
Lab_B(config)#no ip forward-protocol udp 53
Lab_B(config)#no ip forward-protocol udp 37
Lab_B(config)#no ip forward-protocol udp 137
Lab_B(config)#no ip forward-protocol udp 138
Lab_B(config)#no ip forward-protocol udp 68
Lab_B(config)#no ip forward-protocol udp 49
```

Now, only the BOOTP server request (67) will be forwarded to the DHCP server. If you want to forward a certain port—say, TACACS+, for example—use the following command:

```
Lab_B(config)#ip forward-protocol udp 49
```

Cisco's Auto Secure

Okay, so ACLs seem like a lot of work and so does turning off all those services I just discussed. But you do want to secure you router with ACLs, especially on your interface connected to the Internet. However, you are just not sure what the best approach should be, or maybe you just don't want to miss happy hour with your buddies because you're creating ACLs and turning off default services all night long.

Either way, Cisco has a solution that is a good start, and it's darn easy to implement. The command is called `auto secure`, and you just run it from privileged mode as shown:

```
R1#auto secure
                --- AutoSecure Configuration ---

*** AutoSecure configuration enhances the security of
the router, but it will not make it absolutely resistant
to all security attacks ***

AutoSecure will modify the configuration of your device.
All configuration changes will be shown. For a detailed
explanation of how the configuration changes enhance
security and any possible side effects, please refer to Cisco.com
for Autosecure documentation.
At any prompt you may enter '?' for help.
Use ctrl-c to abort this session at any prompt.

Gathering information about the router for AutoSecure
Is this router connected to internet? [no]: yes
Enter the number of interfaces facing the internet [1]: [enter]
Interface              IP-Address      OK? Method Status                Protocol
FastEthernet0/0        10.10.10.1      YES NVRAM  up                    up
Serial0/0              1.1.1.1         YES NVRAM  down                  down
FastEthernet0/1        unassigned      YES NVRAM  administratively down down
Serial0/1              unassigned      YES NVRAM  administratively down down
Enter the interface name that is facing the internet: serial0/0

Securing Management plane services...
```

```
Disabling service finger
Disabling service pad
Disabling udp & tcp small servers
Enabling service password encryption
Enabling service tcp-keepalives-in
Enabling service tcp-keepalives-out
Disabling the cdp protocol

Disabling the bootp server
Disabling the http server
Disabling the finger service
Disabling source routing
Disabling gratuitous arp

Here is a sample Security Banner to be shown
at every access to device. Modify it to suit your
enterprise requirements.

Authorized Access only
  This system is the property of So-&-So-Enterprise.
  UNAUTHORIZED ACCESS TO THIS DEVICE IS PROHIBITED.
  You must have explicit permission to access this
  device. All activities performed on this device
  are logged. Any violations of access policy will result
  in disciplinary action.

Enter the security banner {Put the banner between
k and k, where k is any character}:
#
If you are not part of the www.globalnettc.com domain, disconnect now!
#
Enable secret is either not configured or
 is the same as enable password
Enter the new enable secret: [password not shown]
% Password too short - must be at least 6 characters. Password configuration
failed
Enter the new enable secret: [password not shown]
Confirm the enable secret : [password not shown]
Enter the new enable password: [password not shown]
Confirm the enable password: [password not shown]
```

```
Configuration of local user database
Enter the username: Todd
Enter the password: [password not shown]
Confirm the password: [password not shown]
Configuring AAA local authentication
Configuring Console, Aux and VTY lines for
local authentication, exec-timeout, and transport
Securing device against Login Attacks
Configure the following parameters
Blocking Period when Login Attack detected: ?
% A decimal number between 1 and 32767.
Blocking Period when Login Attack detected: 100
Maximum Login failures with the device: 5
Maximum time period for crossing the failed login attempts: 10
Configure SSH server? [yes]: [enter to take default of yes]
Enter the domain-name: lammle.com
Configuring interface specific AutoSecure services
Disabling the following ip services on all interfaces:

 no ip redirects
 no ip proxy-arp
 no ip unreachables
 no ip directed-broadcast
 no ip mask-reply
Disabling mop on Ethernet interfaces

Securing Forwarding plane services...

Enabling CEF (This might impact the memory requirements for your platform)
Enabling unicast rpf on all interfaces connected
to internet

Configure CBAC Firewall feature? [yes/no]:
Configure CBAC Firewall feature? [yes/no]: no
Tcp intercept feature is used prevent tcp syn attack
on the servers in the network. Create autosec_tcp_intercept_list
to form the list of servers to which the tcp traffic is to
be observed

Enable tcp intercept feature? [yes/no]: yes
```

And that's it—all the services I mentioned earlier are disabled, plus some! By saving the configuration that the `auto secure` command created, you can then take a look at your running-config to see your new configuration. It's a long one!

Although it is tempting to run out to happy hour right now, you still need to verify your security and add your internal access-list configurations to your intranet.

Speaking of ACLs, I still need to show you how to monitor and verify your ACLs. This is an important topic, so let's take a look.

Monitoring Access Lists

Again, it's always good to be able to verify a router's configuration. Table 12.1 lists the commands that can be used to verify the configuration.

TABLE 12.1 Commands used to verify access-list configuration

Command	Effect
`show access-list`	Displays all access lists and their parameters configured on the router. This command does not show you which interface the list is set on.
`show access-list 110`	Shows only the parameters for the access list 110. This command does not show you the interface the list is set on.
`show ip access-list`	Shows only the IP access lists configured on the router.
`show ip interface`	Shows which interfaces have access lists set.
`show running-config`	Shows the access lists and which interfaces have access lists set.

We've already used the `show running-config` command to verify that a named access list was in the router, so now let's take a look at the output from some of the other commands.

The `show access-list` command will list all access lists on the router, whether they're applied to an interface or not:

```
Lab_A#show access-list
Standard IP access list 10
    deny   172.16.40.0, wildcard bits 0.0.0.255
    permit any
Standard IP access list BlockSales
    deny   172.16.40.0, wildcard bits 0.0.0.255
```

```
    permit any
Extended IP access list 110
    deny tcp any host 172.16.30.5 eq ftp
    deny tcp any host 172.16.30.5 eq telnet
    permit ip any any
Lab_A#
```

First, notice that both access list 10 and our named access list appear on this list. Second, notice that even though I entered actual numbers for TCP ports in access list 110, the show command gives us the protocol names rather than TCP ports for readability. (Hey, not everyone has them all memorized!)

Here's the output of the `show ip interface` command:

```
Lab_A#show ip interface fa0/1
FastEthernet0/1 is up, line protocol is up
  Internet address is 172.16.30.1/24
  Broadcast address is 255.255.255.255
  Address determined by non-volatile memory
  MTU is 1500 bytes
  Helper address is not set
  Directed broadcast forwarding is disabled
  Outgoing access list is BlockSales
  Inbound access list is not set
  Proxy ARP is enabled
  Security level is default
  Split horizon is enabled
  ICMP redirects are always sent
  ICMP unreachables are always sent
  ICMP mask replies are never sent
  IP fast switching is disabled
  IP fast switching on the same interface is disabled
  IP Null turbo vector
  IP multicast fast switching is disabled
  IP multicast distributed fast switching is disabled
  Router Discovery is disabled
  IP output packet accounting is disabled
  IP access violation accounting is disabled
  TCP/IP header compression is disabled
  RTP/IP header compression is disabled
  Probe proxy name replies are disabled
  Policy routing is disabled
  Network address translation is disabled
```

```
  Web Cache Redirect is disabled
  BGP Policy Mapping is disabled
Lab_A#
```

Be sure to notice the bold line indicating that the outgoing list on this interface is BlockSales, but the inbound access list isn't set. As I've already mentioned, you can use the `show running-config` command to see any and all access lists.

Summary

In this chapter I covered how to configure standard access lists to properly filter IP traffic. You learned what a standard access list is and how to apply it to a Cisco router to add security to your network. You also learned how to configure extended access lists to further filter IP traffic. And I discussed the differences between standard and extended access lists as well as how to apply them to Cisco routers.

I then moved on to show you how to configure named access lists and apply them to interfaces on the router. Named access lists offer the advantage of being readily identifiable and, therefore, a whole lot easier to manage than access lists that are simply referred to by obscure numbers.

This chapter had a fun section in it: turning off default services. I have always found performing this administration task fun, and the `auto secure` command can help us configure basic, and well-needed, security on our routers.

We then covered how to monitor and verify selected access-list configurations on a router.

Exam Essentials

Remember the standard and extended IP access-list number ranges. The number ranges you can use to configure a standard IP access list are 1–99 and 1300–1999. The number ranges for an extended IP access list are 100–199 and 2000–2699.

Understand the term *implicit deny*. At the end of every access list is an implicit deny. What this means is that if a packet does not match any of the lines in the access list, it will be discarded. Also, if you have nothing but `deny` statements in your list, the list will not permit any packets.

Understand the standard IP access-list configuration command. To configure a standard IP access list, use the access-list numbers 1–99 or 1300–1999 in global configuration mode. Choose `permit` or `deny`, then choose the source IP address you want to filter on using one of the three techniques covered in this chapter.

Understand the extended IP access-list configuration command. To configure an extended IP access list, use the access-list numbers 100–199 or 2000–2699 in global configuration mode. Choose `permit` or `deny`, the Network layer protocol field, the source IP address you want to filter on, the destination address you want to filter on, and finally the Transport layer port number if TCP or UDP has been specified as the protocol.

Remember the command to verify an access list on a router interface. To see whether an access list is set on an interface and in which direction it is filtering, use the `show ip interface` command. This command will not show you the contents of the access list, merely which access lists are applied on the interface.

Remember the command to verify the access-list configuration. To see the configured access lists on your router, use the `show access-list` command. This command will not show you which interfaces have an access list set.

Written Lab 12

In this section, write the answers to the following questions:

1. What command would you use to configure a standard IP access list to prevent all machines on network 172.16.0.0/16 from accessing your Ethernet network?
2. What command would you use to apply the access list you created in question 1 to an Ethernet interface out?
3. What command would you use to create an access list that denies host 192.168.15.5 access to an Ethernet network?
4. Which command verifies that you've entered the access list correctly?
5. What two tools can help notify and prevent DoS attacks?
6. What command would you use to create an extended access list that stops host 172.16.10.1 from telnetting to host 172.16.30.5?
7. What command would you use to set an access list on a VTY line?
8. From question 1, write the same standard IP access list you wrote in question 1 but this time as a named access list.
9. From question 8, write the command to apply the named access list you created to an ethernet interface out.
10. Which command verifies the placement and direction of an access list?

(The answers to Written Lab 12 can be found following the answers to the review questions for this chapter.)

Hands-on Labs

In this section, you will complete two labs. To complete these labs, you will need at least three routers. You can easily perform these labs with the Cisco Packet Tracer program. If you are studying to take your CCNA exam, you really need to do these labs and more!

Lab 12.1: Standard IP Access Lists

Lab 12.2: Extended IP Access Lists

All of the labs will use the following diagram for configuring the routers.

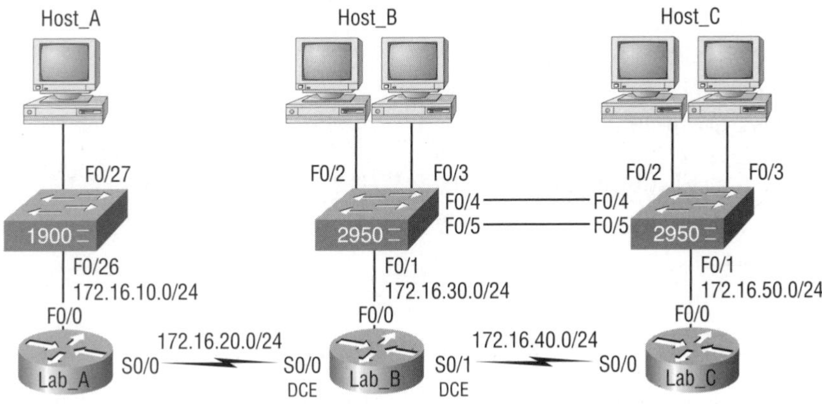

Hands-on Lab 12.1: Standard IP Access Lists

In this lab, you will allow only packets from Host_B on network 172.16.30.0 to enter network 172.16.10.0.

1. Go to Lab_A and enter global configuration mode by typing **config t**.
2. From global configuration mode, type **access-list ?** to get a list of all the different access lists available.
3. Choose an access-list number that will allow you to create an IP standard access list. This is a number between 1 and 99 or 1300 and 1399.
4. Choose to permit host 172.16.30.2, which is Host B's address:

```
Lab_A(config)#access-list 10 permit 172.16.30.2 ?
  A.B.C.D  Wildcard bits
  <cr>
```

   To specify only host 172.16.30.2, use the wildcards 0.0.0.0:

```
Lab_A(config)#access-list 10 permit 172.16.30.2
  0.0.0.0
```

5. Now that the access list is created, you must apply it to an interface to make it work:

```
Lab_A(config)#int f0/0
Lab_A(config-if)#ip access-group 10 out
```

6. Verify your access list with the following commands:

```
Lab_A#sh access-list
Standard IP access list 10
    permit 172.16.30.2
Lab_A#sh run
[output cut]
interface FastEthernet0/0
 ip address 172.16.10.1 255.255.255.0
 ip access-group 10 out
```

7. Test your access list by pinging from Host B (172.16.30.2) to Host A (172.16.10.2).
8. Ping from Lab_B and Lab_C to Host A (172.16.10.2); these should fail if your access list is correct.

Hands-on Lab 12.2: Extended IP Access Lists

In this lab, you will use an extended IP access list to stop host 172.16.10.2 from creating a Telnet session to router Lab_B (172.16.20.2). However, the host still should be able to ping the Lab_B router. IP extended lists should be placed close to the source, so add the extended list on router Lab_A.

1. Remove any access lists on Lab_A and add an extended list to Lab_A.
2. Choose a number to create an extended IP list. The IP extended lists use 100–199 or 2000–2699.
3. Use a `deny` statement. (You'll add a `permit` statement in step 7 to allow other traffic to still work.)

```
Lab_A(config)#access-list 110 deny ?
  <0-255>  An IP protocol number
  ahp      Authentication Header Protocol
  eigrp    Cisco's EIGRP routing protocol
  esp      Encapsulation Security Payload
  gre      Cisco's GRE tunneling
  icmp     Internet Control Message Protocol
  igmp     Internet Gateway Message Protocol
  igrp     Cisco's IGRP routing protocol
  ip       Any Internet Protocol
  ipinip   IP in IP tunneling
```

```
  nos       KA9Q NOS compatible IP over IP tunneling
  ospf      OSPF routing protocol
  pcp       Payload Compression Protocol
  tcp       Transmission Control Protocol
  udp       User Datagram Protocol
```

4. Since you are going to deny Telnet, you must choose TCP as a Transport layer protocol:

```
Lab_A(config)#access-list 110 deny tcp ?
  A.B.C.D   Source address
  any       Any source host
  host      A single source host
```

5. Add the source IP address you want to filter on, then add the destination host IP address. Use the `host` command instead of wildcard bits.

```
Lab_A(config)#access-list 110 deny tcp host
  172.16.10.2 host 172.16.20.2 ?
  ack           Match on the ACK bit
  eq            Match only packets on a given port
                number
  established   Match established connections
  fin           Match on the FIN bit
  fragments     Check fragments
  gt            Match only packets with a greater
                port number
  log           Log matches against this entry
  log-input     Log matches against this entry,
                including input interface
  lt            Match only packets with a lower port
                number
  neq           Match only packets not on a given
                port number
  precedence    Match packets with given precedence
                value
  psh           Match on the PSH bit
  range         Match only packets in the range of
                port numbers
  rst           Match on the RST bit
  syn           Match on the SYN bit
  tos           Match packets with given TOS value
  urg           Match on the URG bit
  <cr>
```

6. At this point, you can add the `eq telnet` command to filter host 172.16.10.2 from telnetting to 172.16.20.2. The `log` command can also be used at the end of the command so that whenever the access-list line is hit, a log will be generated on the console.

```
Lab_A(config)#access-list 110 deny tcp host
  172.16.10.2 host 172.16.20.2 eq telnet log
```

7. It is important to add this line next to create a `permit` statement. (Remember that 0.0.0.0 255.255.255.255 is the same as the `any` command.)

```
Lab_A(config)#access-list 110 permit ip any 0.0.0.0
  255.255.255.255
```

You must create a `permit` statement; if you just add a `deny` statement, nothing will be permitted at all. Please see the sections earlier in this chapter for more detailed information on the `deny any` command implied at the end of every ACL.

8. Apply the access list to the FastEthernet0/0 on Lab_A to stop the Telnet traffic as soon as it hits the first router interface.

```
Lab_A(config)#int f0/0
Lab_A(config-if)#ip access-group 110 in
Lab_A(config-if)#^Z
```

9. Try telnetting from host 172.16.10.2 to Lab_A using the destination IP address of 172.16.20.2. The following messages should be generated on Lab_A's console; however, the `ping` command should work:

```
From host 172.16.10.2: C:\>telnet 172.16.20.2
```

On Lab_A's console, this should appear as follows:

```
01:11:48: %SEC-6-IPACCESSLOGP: list 110 denied tcp
  172.16.10.2(1030) -> 172.16.20.2(23), 1 packet
01:13:04: %SEC-6-IPACCESSLOGP: list 110 denied tcp
  172.16.10.2(1030) -> 172.16.20.2(23), 3 packets
```

Review Questions

The following questions are designed to test your understanding of this chapter's material. For more information on how to get additional questions, please see this book's Introduction.

1. Which of the following is an example of a standard IP access list?
   A. `access-list 110 permit host 1.1.1.1`
   B. `access-list 1 deny 172.16.10.1 0.0.0.0`
   C. `access-list 1 permit 172.16.10.1 255.255.0.0`
   D. `access-list standard 1.1.1.1`
2. You need to create an access list that will prevent hosts in the network range of 192.168.160.0 to 192.168.191.0. Which of the following lists will you use?
   A. `access-list 10 deny 192.168.160.0 255.255.224.0`
   B. `access-list 10 deny 192.168.160.0 0.0.191.255`
   C. `access-list 10 deny 192.168.160.0 0.0.31.255`
   D. `access-list 10 deny 192.168.0.0 0.0.31.255`
3. You have created a named access list called Blocksales. Which of the following is a valid command for applying this to packets trying to enter interface s0 of your router?
   A. `(config)#ip access-group 110 in`
   B. `(config-if)#ip access-group 110 in`
   C. `(config-if)#ip access-group Blocksales in`
   D. `(config-if)#Blocksales ip access-list in`
4. Which of the following are valid ways to refer only to host 172.16.30.55 in an IP access list? (Choose two.)
   A. `172.16.30.55 0.0.0.255`
   B. `172.16.30.55 0.0.0.0`
   C. `any 172.16.30.55`
   D. `host 172.16.30.55`
   E. `0.0.0.0 172.16.30.55`
   F. `ip any 172.16.30.55`

5. Which of the following access lists will allow only HTTP traffic into network 196.15.7.0?
   - A. `access-list 100 permit tcp any 196.15.7.0 0.0.0.255 eq www`
   - B. `access-list 10 deny tcp any 196.15.7.0 eq www`
   - C. `access-list 100 permit 196.15.7.0 0.0.0.255 eq www`
   - D. `access-list 110 permit ip any 196.15.7.0 0.0.0.255`
   - E. `access-list 110 permit www 196.15.7.0 0.0.0.255`
6. What router command allows you to determine whether an IP access list is enabled on a particular interface?
   - A. `show ip port`
   - B. `show access-lists`
   - C. `show ip interface`
   - D. `show access-lists interface`
7. Which router command allows you to view the entire contents of all access lists?
   - A. `Router#`**`show interface`**
   - B. `Router>`**`show ip interface`**
   - C. `Router#`**`show access-lists`**
   - D. `Router>`**`show all access-lists`**
8. If you wanted to deny all Telnet connections to only network 192.168.10.0, which command could you use?
   - A. `access-list 100 deny tcp 192.168.10.0 255.255.255.0 eq telnet`
   - B. `access-list 100 deny tcp 192.168.10.0 0.255.255.255 eq telnet`
   - C. `access-list 100 deny tcp any 192.168.10.0 0.0.0.255 eq 23`
   - D. `access-list 100 deny 192.168.10.0 0.0.0.255 any eq 23`
9. If you wanted to deny FTP access from network 200.200.10.0 to network 200.199.11.0 but allow everything else, which of the following command strings is valid?
   - A. `access-list 110 deny 200.200.10.0 to network 200.199.11.0 eq ftp`

     `access-list 111 permit ip any 0.0.0.0 255.255.255.255`
   - B. `access-list 1 deny ftp 200.200.10.0 200.199.11.0 any any`
   - C. `access-list 100 deny tcp 200.200.10.0 0.0.0.255 200.199.11.0 0.0.0.255 eq ftp`
   - D. `access-list 198 deny tcp 200.200.10.0 0.0.0.255 200.199.11.0 0.0.0.255 eq ftp`

     `access-list 198 permit ip any 0.0.0.0 255.255.255.255`

10. You want to create a standard access list that denies the subnet of the following host: 172.16.50.172/20. Which of the following would you start your list with?

    A. `access-list 10 deny 172.16.48.0 255.255.240.0`

    B. `access-list 10 deny 172.16.0.0 0.0.255.255`

    C. `access-list 10 deny 172.16.64.0 0.0.31.255`

    D. `access-list 10 deny 172.16.48.0 0.0.15.255`

11. Which command would you use to apply an access list to a router interface?

    A. `ip access-list 101 out`

    B. `access-list ip 101 in`

    C. `ip access-group 101 in`

    D. `access-group ip 101 in`

12. You want to create a standard access list that denies the subnet of the following host: 172.16.198.94/19. Which of the following would you start your list with?

    A. `access-list 10 deny 172.16.192.0 0.0.31.255`

    B. `access-list 10 deny 172.16.0.0 0.0.255.255`

    C. `access-list 10 deny 172.16.172.0 0.0.31.255`

    D. `access-list 10 deny 172.16.188.0 0.0.15.255`

13. You want to create a standard access list that denies the subnet of the following host: 172.16.144.17/21. Which of the following would you start your list with?

    A. `access-list 10 deny 172.16.48.0 255.255.240.0`

    B. `access-list 10 deny 172.16.144.0 0.0.7.255`

    C. `access-list 10 deny 172.16.64.0 0.0.31.255`

    D. `access-list 10 deny 172.16.136.0 0.0.15.255`

14. Which of the following commands connect access list 110 inbound to interface ethernet0?

    A. `Router(config)#`**`ip access-group 110 in`**

    B. `Router(config)#`**`ip access-list 110 in`**

    C. `Router(config-if)#`**`ip access-group 110 in`**

    D. `Router(config-if)#`**`ip access-list 110 in`**

15. What command will permit SMTP mail to only host 1.1.1.1?

    A. `access-list 10 permit smtp host 1.1.1.1`

    B. `access-list 110 permit ip smtp host 1.1.1.1`

    C. `access-list 10 permit tcp any host 1.1.1.1 eq smtp`

    D. `access-list 110 permit tcp any host 1.1.1.1 eq smtp`

16. You configure the following access list:

```
access-list 110 deny tcp 10.1.1.128 0.0.0.63 any eq smtp
access-list 110 deny tcp any any eq 23
int ethernet 0
ip access-group 110 out
```

What will the result of this access list be?

A. Email and Telnet will be allowed out E0.

B. Email and Telnet will be allowed in E0.

C. Everything but email and Telnet will be allowed out E0.

D. No IP traffic will be allowed out E0.

17. Which of the following series of commands will restrict Telnet access to the router?

A. Lab_A(config)#**access-list 10 permit 172.16.1.1**
Lab_A(config)#**line con 0**
Lab_A(config-line)#**ip access-group 10 in**

B. Lab_A(config)#**access-list 10 permit 172.16.1.1**
Lab_A(config)#**line vty 0 4**
Lab_A(config-line)#**access-class 10 out**

C. Lab_A(config)#**access-list 10 permit 172.16.1.1**
Lab_A(config)#**line vty 0 4**
Lab_A(config-line)#**access-class 10 in**

D. Lab_A(config)#**access-list 10 permit 172.16.1.1**
Lab_A(config)#**line vty 0 4**
Lab_A(config-line)#**ip access-group 10 in**

18. Which of the following is true regarding access lists applied to an interface?

A. You can place as many access lists as you want on any interface until you run out of memory.

B. You can apply only one access list on any interface.

C. One access list may be configured, per direction, for each layer 3 protocol configured on an interface.

D. You can apply two access lists to any interface.

19. What is the most common attack on a network today?

A. Lock picking

B. Naggle

C. DoS

D. `auto secure`

20. You need to stop DoS attacks in real time and have a log of anyone who has tried to attack your network. What should you do your network?

    A. Add more routers

    B. Use the `auto secure` command

    C. Implement IDS/IPS

    D. Configure Naggle

Answers to Review Questions

1. B. Standard IP access lists use the numbers 1–99 and 1300–1999 and filter based on source IP address only. Option C is incorrect because the mask must be in wildcard format.

2. C. The range of 192.168.160.0 to 192.168.191.0 is a block size of 32. The network address is 192.168.160.0 and the mask would be 255.255.224.0, which for an access list must be a wildcard format of 0.0.31.255. The 31 is used for a block size of 32. The wildcard is always one less than the block size.

3. C. Using a named access list just replaces the number used when applying the list to the router's interface. `ip access-group Blocksales in` is correct.

4. B, D. The wildcard `0.0.0.0` tells the router to match all four octets. This wildcard format alone can be replaced with the `host` command.

5. A. The first thing to check in a question like this is the access-list number. Right away, you can see that the second option is wrong because it is using a standard IP access-list number. The second thing to check is the protocol. If you are filtering by upper-layer protocol, then you must be using either UDP or TCP; this eliminates the fourth option. The third and last answers have the wrong syntax.

6. C. Of the available choices only the `show ip interface` command will tell you which interfaces have access lists applied. `show access-lists` will not show you which interfaces have an access list applied.

7. C. The `show access-lists` command will allow you to view the entire contents of all access lists, but it will not show you the interfaces to which the access lists are applied.

8. C. The extended access list ranges are 100–199 and 2000–2699, so the access-list number of 100 is valid. Telnet uses TCP, so the protocol TCP is valid. Now you just need to look for the source and destination address. Only the third option has the correct sequence of parameters. Option B may work, but the question specifically states "only" to network 192.168.10.0, and the wildcard in option B is too broad.

9. D. Extended IP access lists use numbers 100–199 and 2000–2699 and filter based on source and destination IP address, protocol number, and port number. The last option is correct because of the second line that specifies `permit ip any any`. (I used `0.0.0.0 255.255.255.255`, which is the same as the `any` option.) The third option does not have this, so it would deny access but not allow everything else.

10. D. First, you must know that a /20 is 255.255.240.0, which is a block size of 16 in the third octet. Counting by 16s, this makes our subnet 48 in the third octet, and the wildcard for the third octet would be 15 since the wildcard is always one less than the block size.

11. C. To apply an access list, the proper command is `ip access-group 101 in`.

12. A. First, you must know that a /19 is 255.255.224.0, which is a block size of 32 in the third octet. Counting by 32, this makes our subnet 192 in the third octet, and the wildcard for the third octet would be 31 since the wildcard is always one less than the block size.

13. B. First, you must know that a /21 is 255.255.248.0, which is a block size of 8 in the third octet. Counting by eight, this makes our subnet 144 in the third octet, and the wildcard for the third octet would be 7 since the wildcard is always one less than the block size.

14. C. To place an access list on an interface, use the `ip access-group` command in interface configuration mode.

15. D. When trying to find the best answer to an access-list question, always check the access-list number and then the protocol. When filtering to an upper-layer protocol, you must use an extended list, numbers 100–199 and 2000–2699. Also, when you filter to the port of an upper-layer protocol, you must use either `tcp` or `udp` in the ACL protocol field. If it says `ip` in the protocol field, you cannot filter on the port number of an upper-layer protocol. SMTP uses TCP.

16. D. If you add an access list to an interface and you do not have at least one `permit` statement, then you will effectively shut down the interface because of the implicit `deny any` at the end of every list.

17. C. Telnet access to the router is restricted by using either a standard or extended IP access list inbound on the VTY lines of the router. The command `access-class` is used to apply the access list to the VTY lines.

18. C. A Cisco router has rules regarding the placement of access lists on a router interface. You can place one access list per direction for each layer 3 protocol configured on an interface.

19. C. The most common attack on a network today is a denial of service (DoS) because they are the easiest attack to achieve.

20. C. Implementing Intrusion Detection Service and Intrusion Prevention Service (IDS/IPS) will help notify you and stop attacks in real time.

Answers to Written Lab 12

1. access-list 10 deny 172.16.0.0 0.0.255.255

   access-list 10 permit any
2. ip access-group 10 out
3. access-list 10 deny host 192.168.15.5

   access-list 10 permit any
4. show access-lists
5. IDS, IPS
6. access-list 110 deny tcp host

   172.16.10.1 host 172.16.30.5 eq 23

   access-list 110 permit ip any any
7. line vty 0 4

   access-class 110 in
8. ip access-list standard No172Net

   deny 172.16.0.0 0.0.255.255

   permit any
9. ip access-group No172Net out
10. show ip interfaces

Network Address Translation (NAT)

THE CCNA EXAM TOPICS COVERED IN THIS CHAPTER INCLUDE THE FOLLOWING:

✓ **Implement, verify, and troubleshoot NAT and ACLs in a medium-size Enterprise branch office network**

- Explain the basic operation of NAT.
- Configure NAT for given network requirements (including CLI/SDM).
- Troubleshoot NAT issues.

In this chapter, I am going to give you the skinny on Network Address Translation (NAT), Dynamic NAT, and Port Address Translation (PAT), also known as NAT Overload. Of course, I'll demonstrate all the NAT commands. I also wrote some fantastic hands-on labs for you to configure at the end of this chapter.

It would be helpful for you to read Chapter 12 before reading this chapter since we need to use access lists in our NAT configurations.

For up-to-the minute updates for this chapter, please see `www.lammle.com` and/or `www.sybex.com/go/ccna7e`.

When Do We Use NAT?

NAT is similar to Classless Inter-Domain Routing (CIDR) in that the original intention for NAT was to slow the depletion of available IP address space by allowing many private IP addresses to be represented by some smaller number of public IP addresses.

Since then, it's been discovered that NAT is also a useful tool for network migrations and mergers, server load sharing, and creating "virtual servers." So in this chapter, I'm going to describe the basics of NAT functionality and the terminology common to NAT.

At times, NAT really decreases the overwhelming amount of public IP addresses required in your networking environment. And NAT comes in really handy when two companies that have duplicate internal addressing schemes merge. NAT is also great to have around when an organization changes its Internet service provider (ISP) and the networking manager doesn't want the hassle of changing the internal address scheme.

Here's a list of situations in which it's best to have NAT on your side:

- You need to connect to the Internet and your hosts don't have globally unique IP addresses.
- You change to a new ISP that requires you to renumber your network.
- You need to merge two intranets with duplicate addresses.

You typically use NAT on a border router. For example, in Figure 13.1, NAT is used on the Corporate router connected to the Internet.

Now you may be thinking, "NAT's totally cool. It's the grooviest, greatest network gadget and I just gotta have it." Well, hang on a minute. There are truly some serious snags related to NAT use. Don't get me wrong: It really can save you sometimes, but there's a dark side you need to know about too. For the pros and cons linked to using NAT, check out Table 13.1.

FIGURE 13.1 Where to configure NAT

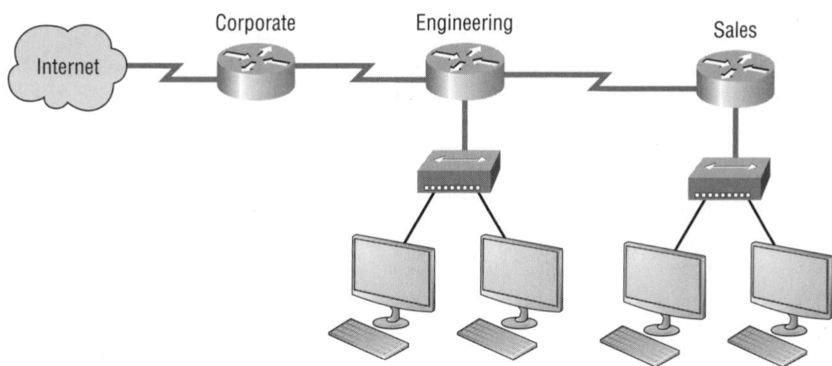

TABLE 13.1 Advantages and disadvantages of implementing NAT

Advantages	Disadvantages
Conserves legally registered addresses.	Translation introduces switching path delays.
Remedies address overlap occurrence.	Causes loss of end-to-end IP traceability.
Increases flexibility when connecting to Internet.	Certain applications will not function with NAT enabled.
Eliminates address renumbering as network changes.	

The most obvious advantage associated with NAT is that it allows you to conserve your legally registered address scheme. This is why we haven't run out of IPv4 addresses—yet.

Types of Network Address Translation

In this section, I'm going to go over the three types of NAT with you:

Static NAT This type of NAT is designed to allow one-to-one mapping between local and global addresses. Keep in mind that the static version requires you to have one real Internet IP address for every host on your network.

Dynamic NAT This version gives you the ability to map an unregistered IP address to a registered IP address from out of a pool of registered IP addresses. You don't have to statically configure your router to map each inside address to an individual outside address as you would using static NAT, but you do have to have enough real, bona-fide IP addresses for everyone who's going to be sending packets to and receiving them from the Internet at the same time.

Overloading This is the most popular type of NAT configuration. Understand that overloading really is a form of dynamic NAT that maps multiple unregistered IP addresses to a single registered IP address (many-to-one) by using different source ports. Now, why is this so special? Well, because it's also known as *Port Address Translation (PAT)*. And by using PAT (NAT Overload), you get to have thousands of users connect to the Internet using only one real global IP address—pretty slick, yeah? Seriously, NAT Overload is the real reason we haven't run out of valid IP address on the Internet. Really—I'm not joking.

Don't worry, I'll show you how to configure all three types of NAT at the end of this chapter with the hands-on labs.

NAT Names

The names we use to describe the addresses used with NAT are pretty simple. Addresses used after NAT translations are called *global* addresses. These are usually the public addresses used on the Internet, but remember, you don't need public addresses if you aren't going on the Internet.

Local addresses are the ones we use before NAT translation. So, the inside local address is actually the private address of the sending host that's trying to get to the Internet, while the outside local address typically would be your router interface connected to your ISP. The latter is usually a public address and is how the packet begins its journey.

After translation, the inside local address is then called the *inside global address* and the outside global address then becomes the address of the destination host. Check out Table 13.2, which lists all this terminology, for a clear picture of the various names used with NAT.

TABLE 13.2 NAT terms

Names	Meaning
Inside local	Name of inside source address before translation
Outside local	Name of destination host after translation
Inside global	Name of inside host after translation
Outside global	Name of outside destination host before translation

How NAT Works

Okay, now it's time to look at how this whole NAT thing works. I'm going to start by using Figure 13.2 to describe the basic translation of NAT.

FIGURE 13.2 Basic NAT translation

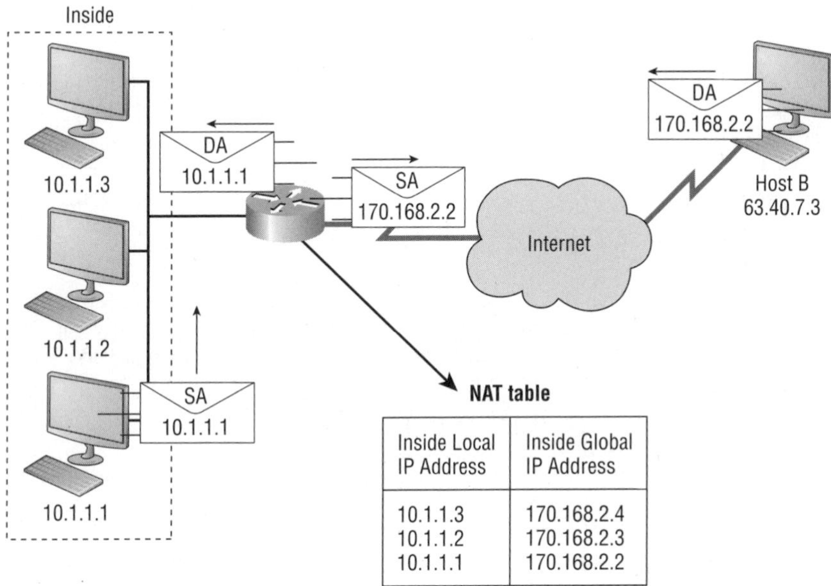

In the example shown in Figure 13.2, host 10.1.1.1 sends an outbound packet to the border router configured with NAT. The router identifies the source IP address as an inside local IP address destined for an outside network, translates the source address, and documents the translation in the NAT table.

The packet is sent to the outside interface with the new translated source address. The external host returns the packet to the destination host and the NAT router translates the inside global IP address back to the inside local IP address using the NAT table. This is as simple as it gets.

Let's take a look at a more complex configuration using overloading, or what is also referred to as Port Address Translation (PAT). I'll use Figure 13.3 to demonstrate how PAT works.

With overloading, all inside hosts get translated to one single IP address, hence the term *overloading*. Again, the reason we have not run out of available IP addresses on the Internet is because of overloading (PAT).

Take a look at the NAT table in Figure 13.3 again. In addition to the inside local IP address and outside global IP address, we now have port numbers. These port numbers help the router identify which host should receive the return traffic.

FIGURE 13.3 NAT overloading example (PAT)

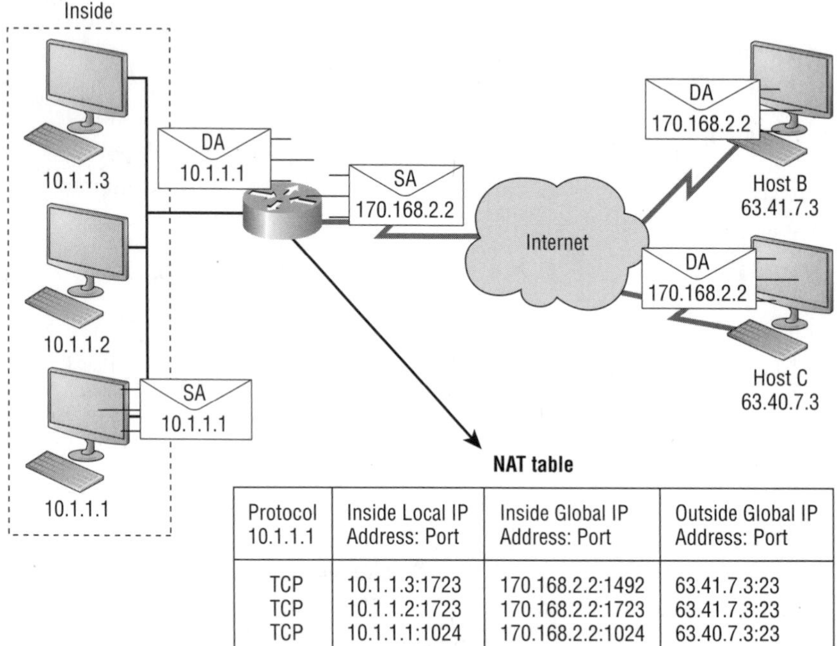

Protocol 10.1.1.1	Inside Local IP Address: Port	Inside Global IP Address: Port	Outside Global IP Address: Port
TCP	10.1.1.3:1723	170.168.2.2:1492	63.41.7.3:23
TCP	10.1.1.2:1723	170.168.2.2:1723	63.41.7.3:23
TCP	10.1.1.1:1024	170.168.2.2:1024	63.40.7.3:23

Port numbers are used at the Transport layer to identify the local host in this example. If we had to use registered IP addresses to identify the source hosts, that would be called *static NAT* and we would run out of addresses. PAT allows us to use the Transport layer to identify the hosts, which in turn allows us to use (theoretically) up to about 65,000 hosts with one real IP address.

Static NAT Configuration

Let's take a look at a simple basic static NAT configuration:

```
ip nat inside source static 10.1.1.1 170.46.2.2
!
interface Ethernet0
 ip address 10.1.1.10 255.255.255.0
 ip nat inside
!
interface Serial0
 ip address 170.46.2.1 255.255.255.0
 ip nat outside
!
```

In the preceding router output, the `ip nat inside source` command identifies which IP addresses will be translated. In this configuration example, the `ip nat inside source` command configures a static translation between the inside local IP address 10.1.1.1 to the outside global IP address 170.46.2.2.

If we look farther down in the configuration, we see that we have an `ip nat` command under each interface. The `ip nat inside` command identifies that interface as the inside interface. The `ip nat outside` command identifies that interface as the outside interface. When you look back at the `ip nat inside source` command, you see that the command is referencing the inside interface as the source or starting point of the translation. The command could also be used like this—`ip nat outside source`—which is referencing the interface you designated as the outside interface to be the source or starting point for the translation.

Dynamic NAT Configuration

Dynamic NAT means that we have a pool of addresses that we will use to provide real IP addresses to a group of users on the inside. We do not use port numbers, so we have to have real IP addresses for every user trying to get outside the local network at the same time.

Here is a sample output of a dynamic NAT configuration:

```
ip nat pool todd 170.168.2.3 170.168.2.254
    netmask 255.255.255.0
ip nat inside source list 1 pool todd
!
interface Ethernet0
 ip address 10.1.1.10 255.255.255.0
 ip nat inside
!
interface Serial0
 ip address 170.168.2.1 255.255.255.0
 ip nat outside
!
access-list 1 permit 10.1.1.0 0.0.0.255
!
```

The `ip nat inside source list 1 pool todd` command tells the router to translate IP addresses that match `access-list 1` to an address found in the IP NAT pool named `todd`. The access list in this case is not being used to permit or deny traffic as we would use it for security reasons to filter traffic. It is being used in this case to select or designate what we often call interesting traffic. When interesting traffic has been matched with the access list, it is pulled into the NAT process to be translated. This is a common use for access lists; they don't always have the dull job of just blocking traffic at an interface.

The `ip nat pool todd 170.168.2.3 192.168.2.254 netmask 255.255.255.0` command creates a pool of addresses that will be distributed to those hosts that require global addresses.

PAT (Overloading) Configuration

This last example shows how to configure inside global address overloading. This is the typical NAT that we would use today. It is rare that we would use static or dynamic NAT unless we were statically mapping a server, for example.

Here is a sample output of a PAT configuration:

```
ip nat pool globalnet 170.168.2.1 170.168.2.1 netmask 255.255.255.0
ip nat inside source list 1 pool globalnet overload


!
interface Ethernet0/0
 ip address 10.1.1.10 255.255.255.0
 ip nat inside
!
interface Serial0/0
 ip address 170.168.2.1 255.255.255.0
 ip nat outside
!
access-list 1 permit 10.1.1.0 0.0.0.255
```

The nice thing about PAT is that the only differences between this configuration and the previous dynamic NAT configuration is that our pool of addresses has shrunk to only one IP address and at the end of our `ip nat inside source` command we included the `overload` keyword.

Notice in the example that the one IP address that is in the pool for us to use is the IP address of the outside interface. This is perfect if you are configuring NAT Overload for yourself at home or for a small office that only has one IP address from your ISP. You could, however, use an additional address such as 170.168.2.2 if you had that address available to you. This could be helpful in a very large implementation where you may have so many simultaneously active internal users that you have to have more than one overloaded IP address on the outside.

Simple Verification of NAT

Once you have configured the type of NAT you are going to use, typically overload (PAT), you need to be able to verify the configuration.

To see basic IP address translation information, use the following command:

```
Router#show ip nat translations
```

When looking at the IP NAT translations, you may see many translations from the same host to the same host at the destination. This is typical of many connections to the same server.

In addition, you can verify your NAT configuration with the `debug ip nat` command. This output will show the sending address, the translation, and the destination address on each debug line:

```
Router#debug ip nat
```

How do you clear your NAT entries from the translation table? Use the `clear ip nat translation` command. To clear all entries from the NAT table, use an asterisk (*) at the end of the command.

Testing and Troubleshooting NAT

Cisco's NAT gives you some serious power—and without too much effort, because the configurations are really pretty simple. But we all know nothing's perfect, so in case something goes wrong, you can figure out some of the more common causes by going through this list of possible snags:

- Check the dynamic pools. Are they composed of the right scope of addresses?
- Check to see if any dynamic pools overlap.
- Check to see if the addresses used for static mapping and those in the dynamic pools overlap.
- Ensure that your access lists specify the correct addresses for translation.
- Make sure there aren't any addresses left out that need to be there, and ensure that none are included that shouldn't be.
- Check to make sure you've got both the inside and outside interfaces delimited properly.

One thing to keep in mind is that one of the most common problems with a new NAT configuration isn't specific to NAT at all—it usually involves a routing blooper. So, make sure that, because you're changing a source or destination address in a packet, your router knows what to do with the new address after the translation!

The first command you should typically use is the show ip nat translations command. Here an example:

```
Router#show ip nat trans
Pro     Inside global  Inside local   Outside local Outside global
---     192.2.2.1      10.1.1.1       ---      ---
---     192.2.2.2      10.1.1.2       ---      ---
```

From the above output can you tell me if the configuration on the router is static or dynamic NAT? The answer is "yes," static or dynamic NAT is configured because there is a one-to-one translation from the inside local to the inside global. Let's take a look at another output:

```
Router#sh ip nat trans
Pro Inside global      Inside local       Outside local      Outside global
```

```
tcp 170.168.2.1:11003  10.1.1.1:11003     172.40.2.2:23     172.40.2.2:23
tcp 170.168.2.1:1067   10.1.1.1:1067      172.40.2.3:23     172.40.2.3:23
```

Okay, you can easily see that the above output is using NAT overload or PAT. The protocol in this output is TCP and the inside global address is the same for both entries.

Supposedly the sky's the limit regarding the number of mappings the NAT table can hold. In reality, however, it comes down to things like memory and CPU or the boundaries set in place by the scope of available addresses or ports that do, in fact, cause there to be limitations placed on the number of entries possible. You see, each NAT mapping devours about 160 bytes of memory. And sometimes—but not very often—the amount of entries has to be limited for the sake of performance or because of policy restrictions. In situations like these, just use the `ip nat translation max-entries` command for help.

Another handy command for troubleshooting is `show ip nat statistics`. Deploying this gives you a summary of the NAT configuration, and it will count the number of active translation types. Also counted are hits to an existing mapping as well any misses—the latter will result in an attempt to create a mapping. This command will also reveal expired translations. If you want to check into dynamic pools, their types, the total available addresses, how many addresses have been allocated and how many failed, plus the number of translations that have occurred, just use the `pool` keyword.

Here is an example of the basic NAT debugging command:

```
Router#debug ip nat
NAT: s=10.1.1.1->192.168.2.1, d=172.16.2.2 [0]
NAT: s=172.16.2.2, d=192.168.2.1->10.1.1.1 [0]
NAT: s=10.1.1.1->192.168.2.1, d=172.16.2.2 [1]
NAT: s=10.1.1.1->192.168.2.1, d=172.16.2.2 [2]
NAT: s=10.1.1.1->192.168.2.1, d=172.16.2.2 [3]
NAT*: s=172.16.2.2, d=192.168.2.1->10.1.1.1 [1]
```

Notice the last line in the output and how the NAT at the beginning of the line has an asterisk (*). This means the packet was translated and fast switched to the destination. I know what you're thinking: what is fast switched? I'll explain it briefly. Fast switching has gone by many names; it is also called cache based switching and a good descriptive name, "route one switch many." The fast switching process is used on Cisco routers to create a cache of layer 3 routing information to be accessed at layer 2, in order to quickly forward packets through a router without having to parse the routing table for every packet. As packets are processed switched (looked up in the routing table), this information is stored in the cache for later use if needed for faster routing processing.

Okay, continuing on with our verification of NAT, did you know you can manually clear dynamic NAT entries from the NAT table? Doing this can come in pretty handy if you need to get rid of a specific rotten entry without sitting around waiting for the timeout to expire. A manual clear also is really useful when you want to clear the whole NAT table to reconfigure a pool of addresses.

You also need to know that the Cisco IOS software just won't allow you to change or delete address pools if any of that pool's addresses are mapped in the NAT table. The `clear ip nat` `translations` command clears entries—you can indicate a single entry via the global and local address and through TCP and UDP translations (including ports), or you can just type in an asterisk (*) to wipe out the entire table. But know that if you do that, only dynamic entries will be cleared because this command does not remove static entries.

Oh, and there's more—any outside device's packet destination address that happens to be responding to any inside device is known as the inside global (IG) address. This means that the initial mapping has to be held in the NAT table so that all packets arriving from a specific connection get translated consistently. Holding entries in the NAT table also cuts down on repeated translation operations happening each time the same inside machine sends packets to the same outside destinations on a regular basis.

Here's what I mean: When an entry is placed into the NAT table the first time, a timer begins ticking; the duration of that timer is known as the `translation timeout`. Each time a packet for a given entry translates through the router, the timer gets reset. If the timer expires, the entry will be unceremoniously removed from the NAT table and the dynamically assigned address will then be returned to the pool. Cisco's default translation time-out is 86,400 seconds (24 hours), but you can change that with the command `ip nat translation timeout`.

Before we move on to the configuration section and actually use the commands I just talked about, let's go through a couple of NAT examples and see if you can figure out the configuration that needs to be used. To start, look at Figure 13.4 and ask yourself two things: Where would you implement NAT in this design, and what type of NAT would you configure?

FIGURE 13.4 NAT example

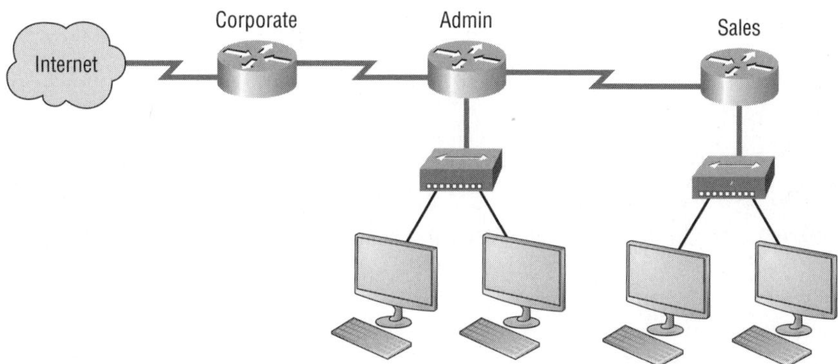

In Figure 13.4, the NAT configuration would be placed on the Corporate router and the configuration would be dynamic NAT with overload (PAT). In this NAT example, what type of NAT is being used?

```
ip nat pool todd-nat 170.168.10.10 170.168.10.20 netmask 255.255.255.0
ip nat inside source list 1 pool todd-nat
```

The preceding command uses dynamic NAT without PAT. The `pool` in the command gives the answer away, plus there is more than one address in the pool and there is no `overload` command at the end of our `ip nat inside source` command, which means we are not using PAT.

In the next NAT example, we'll use Figure 13.5 to see if we can figure out the configuration needed.

FIGURE 13.5 Another NAT example

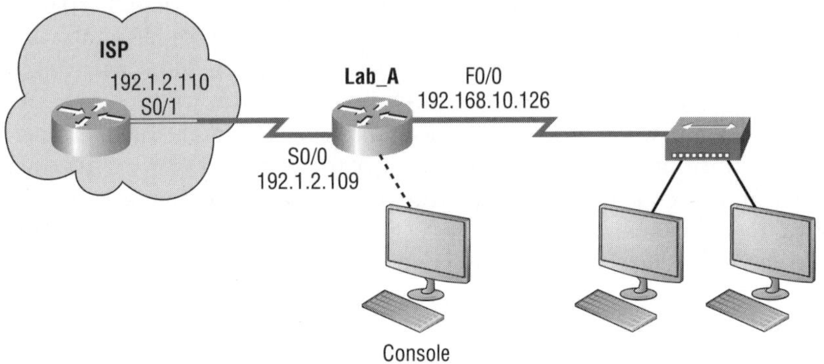

The example in Figure 13.5 shows a border router that needs to be configured with NAT and allow the use of six public IP addresses to the inside locals, 192.1.2.109 through 192.1.2.114. However, on the inside network, you have 62 hosts that use the private addresses of 192.168.10.65 through 192.168.10.126. What would your NAT configuration be on the border router?

Two different answers would work here, but the following would be my first choice:

```
ip nat pool Todd 192.1.2.109 192.1.2.109 netmask 255.255.255.248
access-list 1 permit 192.168.10.64 0.0.0.63
ip nat inside source list 1 pool Todd overload
```

The command `ip nat pool Todd 192.1.2.109 192.1.2.109 netmask 255.255.255.248` sets the pool name as Todd and creates a dynamic pool of only one address using NAT address 192.1.2.109. Instead of the `netmask` command, you can use the `prefix-length 29` statement. (And I know what you're thinking, but no, you cannot do this on router interfaces as well.) Plus, is this really less typing to use this full command?

The second answer would end up with the exact same result of having only 192.1.2.109 as your inside global, but you can type this in and have it work too: `ip nat pool Todd 192.1.2.109 192.1.2.114 netmask 255.255.255.248`. This is a waste because the second through sixth addresses would only be used if there was a conflict with a TCP port number. You would use something as shown in this example if you literally had about ten thousand hosts with one Internet connection. This would be used to help with the TCP-Reset issue (meaning two hosts are trying to use the same source port number and NAK'd). But in our example of only up to 62 hosts connecting to the Internet at the same time, having more than one inside global provides you nothing.

If you do not understand the second line where the access-list is set, please see Chapter 12, "Security." However, what you should easily see in this access-list list line is the *network number* and *wildcard* used with that command. I always say "every question is a subnet question" and this is no exception. The inside locals in this example were 192.168.10.65-126, which is a block of 64, or 255.255.255.192 mask. As I've said in pretty much every chapter, you must be able to subnet quickly!

The command `ip nat inside source list 1 pool Todd overload` sets the dynamic pool to use Port Address Translation (PAT) by using the `overload` command.

Be sure to add the `ip nat inside` and `ip nat outside` statements on the appropriate interfaces.

Be sure and configure the hands-on labs I wrote for this chapter.

Okay, one more example, and then you are off to the written lab, hands-on labs, and review questions.

The network in Figure 13.6 is already configured with IP addresses as shown in the figure, and there is only one configured host. However, you need to add 25 more hosts to the LAN. Now, all 26 hosts must be able to get to the Internet at the same time.

FIGURE 13.6 Last NAT example

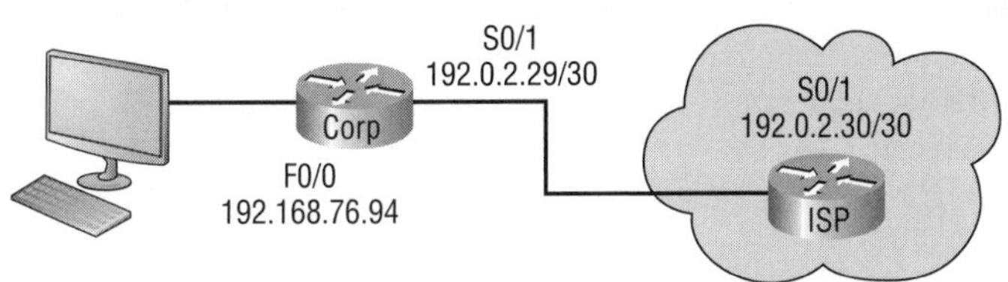

By looking at the configured network, use only the following inside addresses to configure NAT on the Corp router to allow all hosts to reach the Internet:

- Inside globals: 198.18.41.129 through 198.18.41.134
- Inside locals: 192.168.76.65 through 192.168.76.94

This one will take some thought because all we have is the inside globals and the inside locals; however, armed with that information as well as the IP addresses of the router interfaces shown in the figure, we can configure this.

We must first start by understanding what our block sizes are so we can get our subnet mask for our NAT pool as well as configure the wildcard for the access list.

You should easily be able to see that the block size of the inside globals is 8, and the block size of the inside locals is 32. It is critical that you do not stumble on this foundational information.

Okay, so we can configure NAT now that we have our block sizes:

```
ip nat pool Corp 198.18.41.129 198.18.41.134 netmask 255.255.255.248
ip nat inside source list 1 pool Corp overload
access-list 1 permit 192.168.76.64 0.0.0.31
```

Since we had a block of only 8 for our pool, we had to use the `overload` command to make sure all 26 hosts can get to the Internet at the same time.

There is one other simple way to configure NAT, and I use this command at my home office to connect my T1. One command line and it's done; here it is:

```
ip nat inside source list 1 int s0/0/0 overload
```

Wow! One line and it's Miller Time, and yes, this works! This single line just says, "Use my outside local as my inside global and overload it." Nice. Of course you must still create ACL 1 and add the inside and outside interface commands to the configuration, but this is a nice, fast way to configure NAT if you don't have a pool of addresses to use.

Summary

Now this really was a fun chapter. Come on—admit it! You learned a lot about Network Address Translation (NAT) and how it's configured with static, dynamic, and Port Address Translation (PAT), also called NAT Overload.

I also described how each flavor of NAT is used in a network as well as how each type is configured on a network.

I also went through some verification and troubleshooting commands.

Exam Essentials

Understand the term NAT. This may come as news to you, because I didn't—okay, failed to—mention it earlier, but NAT has a few nicknames. In the industry, it's referred to as network masquerading, IP-masquerading, and for those who are besieged with OCD and compelled to spell everything out, Network Address Translation. Whatever you want to dub it, basically, they all refer to the process of rewriting the source/destination addresses of IP packets when they go through a router or firewall. Just focus on the process that's occurring and your understanding of it (i.e., the important part) and you're on it for sure!

Remember the three methods of NAT. The three methods are static, dynamic, and overloading; the latter is also called Port Address Translation (PAT).

Understand static NAT. This type of NAT is designed to allow one-to-one mapping between local and global addresses.

Understand dynamic NAT. This version gives you the ability to map a range of unregistered IP addresses to a registered IP address from out of a pool of registered IP addresses.

Understand overloading. Overloading really is a form of dynamic NAT that maps multiple unregistered IP addresses to a single registered IP address (many-to-one) by using different ports. It's also known as *Port Address Translation (PAT)*.

Written Lab 13

In this section, write the answers to the following questions:

1. What type of address translation can use only one address to allow thousands of hosts to be translated globally?
2. What command can you use to show the NAT translations as they occur on your router?
3. What command will show you the translation table?
4. What command will clear all your NAT entries from the translation table?
5. An inside local is before or after translation?
6. An inside global is before or after translation?
7. Which command can be used for troubleshooting and displays a summary of the NAT configuration as well as counts of active translation types and hits to an existing mapping
8. What commands must be used on your router interfaces before NAT will translate addresses?
9. In the following output, what type of NAT is being used?

   ```
   ip nat pool todd-nat 170.168.10.10 170.168.10.20 netmask 255.255.255.0
   ```

10. Instead of the `netmask` command, you can use the __________ statement.

Hands-on Labs

I am going to use some basic routers for these labs, but really, almost any Cisco router will work.

Here is a list of the labs in this chapter:

Lab 13.1: Preparing for NAT

Lab 13.2: Configuring Dynamic NAT

Lab 13.3: Configuring PAT

I am going to use the network shown in the following diagram for our hands-on labs. I highly recommend you connect up some routers and run through these labs. You will configure NAT on router Lab_A to translate the private IP address of 192.168.10.0 to a public address of 171.16.10.0.

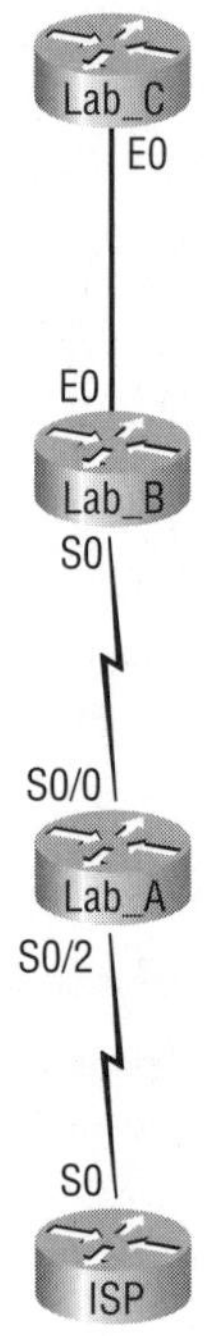

Table 13.3 shows the commands we will use and the purpose of each command.

TABLE 13.3 Command summary for NAT/PAT hands-on labs

Command	Purpose
`ip nat inside source list` *acl* `pool` *name*	Translates IPs that match the ACL to the pool
`ip nat inside source static` *inside_addr outside_addr*	Statically maps an inside local address to an outside global address
`ip nat pool` *name*	Creates an address pool
`ip nat inside`	Sets an interface to be an inside interface
`ip nat outside`	Sets an interface to be an outside interface
`show ip nat translations`	Shows current NAT translations

Lab 13.1: Preparing for NAT

In this lab, you'll set up your routers with IP addresses and RIP routing.

1. Configure the routers with the IP addresses listed in Table 13.4.

TABLE 13.4 Router IP address scheme

Router	Interface	IP Address
ISP	S0	171.16.10.1/24
Lab_A	S0/2	171.16.10.2/24
Lab_A	S0/0	192.168.20.1/24
Lab_B	S0	192.168.20.2/24
Lab_B	E0	192.168.30.1/24
Lab_C	E0	192.168.30.2/24

After you configure IP addresses on the routers, you should be able to ping from router to router, but since we do not have a routing protocol running until the next step, you can verify only from one router to another but not through the network until RIP is set up. You can use any routing protocol you wish; I am just using RIP for simplicity's sake to get this up and running.

2. On Lab_A, configure RIP routing, set a passive interface, and configure the default network.

```
Lab_A#config t
Lab_A(config)#router rip
Lab_A(config-router)#network 192.168.20.0
Lab_A(config-router)#network 171.16.0.0
Lab_A(config-router)#passive-interface s0/2
Lab_A(config-router)#exit
Lab_A(config)#ip default-network 171.16.10.1
```

The `passive-interface` command stops RIP updates from being sent to the ISP and the `ip default-network` command advertises a default network to the other routers so they know how to get to the Internet.

3. On Lab_B, configure RIP routing:

```
Lab_B#config t
Lab_B(config)#router rip
Lab_B(config-router)#network 192.168.30.0
Lab_B(config-router)#network 192.168.20.0
```

4. On Lab_C, configure RIP routing:

```
Lab_C#config t
Lab_C(config)#router rip
Lab_C(config-router)#network 192.168.30.0
```

5. On the ISP router, configure a default route to the corporate network:

```
ISP#config t
ISP(config)#ip route 0.0.0.0 0.0.0.0 s0
```

6. Configure the ISP router so you can telnet into the router without being prompted for a password:

```
ISP#config t
ISP(config)#line vty 0 4
ISP(config-line)#no login
```

7. Verify that you can ping from the ISP router to the Lab_C router and from the Lab_C router to the ISP router. If you cannot, troubleshoot your network.

Lab 13.2: Configuring Dynamic NAT

In this lab, you'll configure dynamic NAT on the Lab_A router.

1. Create a pool of addresses called GlobalNet on the Lab_A router. The pool should contain a range of addresses of 171.16.10.50 through 171.16.10.55.

```
Lab_A(config)#ip nat pool GlobalNet 171.16.10.50 171.16.10.55
net 255.255.255.0
```

2. Create access list 1. This list permits traffic from the 192.168.20.0 and 192.168.30.0 network to be translated.

```
Lab_A(config)#access-list 1 permit 192.168.20.0 0.0.0.255
Lab_A(config)#access-list 1 permit 192.168.30.0 0.0.0.255
```

3. Map the access list to the pool that was created.

```
Lab_A(config)#ip nat inside source list 1 pool GlobalNet
```

4. Configure serial 0/0 as an inside NAT interface.

```
Lab_A(config)#int s0/0
Lab_A(config-if)#ip nat inside
```

5. Configure serial 0/2 as an outside NAT interface.

```
Lab_A(config-if)#int s0/2
Lab_A(config-if)#ip nat outside
```

6. Move the console connection to the Lab_C router. Log in to the Lab_C router. Telnet from the Lab_C router to the ISP router.

```
Lab_C#telnet 171.16.10.1
```

7. Move the console connection to the Lab_B router. Log in to the Lab_B router. Telnet from the Lab_B router to the ISP router.

```
Lab_B#telnet 171.16.10.1
```

8. Execute the command **show users** from the ISP router. (This shows who is accessing the VTY lines.)

```
ISP#show users
```

   a. What does it show as your source IP address?________________

   b. What is your real source IP address?__________________

   The `show users` output should look something like this:

```
ISP>sh users
    Line       User       Host(s)              Idle       Location
   0 con 0                idle                 00:03:32
   2 vty 0                idle                 00:01:33 171.16.10.50
*  3 vty 1                idle                 00:00:09 171.16.10.51
  Interface  User        Mode                   Idle Peer Address
ISP>
```

Notice that there is a one-to-one translation. This means you must have a real IP address for every host that wants to get to the Internet, which is not always possible.

9. Leave the session open on the ISP router and connect to Lab_A. (Use **Ctrl+Shift+6**, let go, and then press **X**.)

10. Log in to your Lab_A router and view your current translations by entering the `show ip nat translations` command. You should see something like this:

```
Lab_A#sh ip nat translations
Pro Inside global       Inside local       Outside local      Outside global
--- 171.16.10.50        192.168.30.2       ---                ---
--- 171.16.10.51        192.168.20.2       ---                ---
Lab_A#
```

11. If you turn on `debug ip nat` on the Lab_A router and then ping through the router, you will see the actual NAT process take place, which will look something like this:

```
00:32:47: NAT*: s=192.168.30.2->171.16.10.50, d=171.16.10.1 [5]
00:32:47: NAT*: s=171.16.10.1, d=171.16.10.50->192.168.30.2
```

Lab 13.3: Configuring PAT

In this lab, you'll configure Port Address Translation (PAT) on the Lab_A router. We will use PAT because we don't want a one-to-one translation, which uses just one IP address for every user on the network.

1. On the Lab_A router, delete the translation table and remove the dynamic NAT pool.

```
Lab_A#clear ip nat translations *
Lab_A#config t
Lab_A(config)#no ip nat pool GlobalNet 171.16.10.50
171.16.10.55 netmask 255.255.255.0
Lab_A(config)#no ip nat inside source list 1 pool GlobalNet
```

2. On the Lab_A router, create a NAT pool with one address called Lammle. The pool should contain a single address 171.16.10.100. Enter the following command:

```
Lab_A#config t
Lab_A(config)#ip nat pool Lammle 171.16.10.100 171.16.10.100
net 255.255.255.0
```

3. Create access list 2. It should permit networks 192.168.20.0 and 192.168.30.0 to be translated.

```
Lab_A(config)#access-list 2 permit 192.168.20.0 0.0.0.255
Lab_A(config)#access-list 2 permit 192.168.30.0 0.0.0.255
```

4. Map access list 2 to the new pool, allowing PAT to occur by using the `overload` command.

```
Lab_A(config)#ip nat inside source list 2 pool Lammle overload
```

5. Log in to the Lab_C router and telnet to the ISP router; also, log in to the Lab_B router and telnet to the ISP router.
6. From the ISP router, use the `show users` command. The output should look like this:

```
ISP>sh users
    Line       User       Host(s)              Idle       Location
*  0 con 0                idle                 00:00:00
   2 vty 0                idle                 00:00:39 171.16.10.100
   4 vty 2                idle                 00:00:37 171.16.10.100

  Interface  User      Mode                 Idle Peer Address

ISP>
```

7. From the Lab_A router, use the show `ip nat translations` command.

```
Lab_A#sh ip nat translations
Pro Inside global  Inside local  Outside local Outside global
tcp 171.16.10.100:11001 192.168.20.2:11001 171.16.10.1:23    171.16.10.1:23
tcp 171.16.10.100:11002 192.168.30.2:11002 171.16.10.1:23    171.16.10.1:23
```

8. Also make sure the `debug ip nat` command is on for the Lab_A router. If you ping from the Lab_C router to the ISP router, the output will look like this:

```
01:12:36: NAT: s=192.168.30.2->171.16.10.100, d=171.16.10.1 [35]
01:12:36: NAT*: s=171.16.10.1, d=171.16.10.100->192.168.30.2 [35]
01:12:36: NAT*: s=192.168.30.2->171.16.10.100, d=171.16.10.1 [36]
01:12:36: NAT*: s=171.16.10.1, d=171.16.10.100->192.168.30.2 [36]
01:12:36: NAT*: s=192.168.30.2->171.16.10.100, d=171.16.10.1 [37]
01:12:36: NAT*: s=171.16.10.1, d=171.16.10.100->192.168.30.2 [37]
01:12:36: NAT*: s=192.168.30.2->171.16.10.100, d=171.16.10.1 [38]
01:12:36: NAT*: s=171.16.10.1, d=171.16.10.100->192.168.30.2 [38]
01:12:37: NAT*: s=192.168.30.2->171.16.10.100, d=171.16.10.1 [39]
01:12:37: NAT*: s=171.16.10.1, d=171.16.10.100->192.168.30.2 [39]
```

Review Questions

The following questions are designed to test your understanding of this chapter's material. For more information on how to get additional questions, please see this book's Introduction.

1. Which of the following are disadvantages of using NAT? (Choose three.)
   A. Translation introduces switching path delays.
   B. Conserves legally registered addresses.
   C. Causes loss of end-to-end IP traceability.
   D. Increases flexibility when connecting to the Internet.
   E. Certain applications will not function with NAT enabled.
   F. Reduces address overlap occurrence.

2. Which of the following are advantages of using NAT? (Choose three.)
   A. Translation introduces switching path delays.
   B. Conserves legally registered addresses.
   C. Causes loss of end-to-end IP traceability.
   D. Increases flexibility when connecting to the Internet.
   E. Certain applications will not function with NAT enabled.
   F. Remedies address overlap occurrence.

3. Which command will allow you to see real-time translations on your router?
   A. `show ip nat translations`
   B. `show ip nat statistics`
   C. `debug ip nat`
   D. `clear ip nat translations *`

4. Which command will show you all the translations active on your router?
   A. `show ip nat translations`
   B. `show ip nat statistics`
   C. `debug ip nat`
   D. `clear ip nat translations *`

5. Which command will clear all the translations active on your router?
   A. `show ip nat translations`
   B. `show ip nat statistics`
   C. `debug ip nat`
   D. `clear ip nat translations *`

6. Which command will show you the summary of the NAT configuration?
   - A. `show ip nat translations`
   - B. `show ip nat statistics`
   - C. `debug ip nat`
   - D. `clear ip nat translations *`
7. Which command will create a dynamic pool named Todd that will provide you with 30 global addresses?
   - A. `ip nat pool Todd 171.16.10.65 171.16.10.94 net 255.255.255.240`
   - B. `ip nat pool Todd 171.16.10.65 171.16.10.94 net 255.255.255.224`
   - C. `ip nat pool todd 171.16.10.65 171.16.10.94 net 255.255.255.224`
   - D. `ip nat pool Todd 171.16.10.1 171.16.10.254 net 255.255.255.0`
8. Which of the following are methods of NAT? (Choose three.)
   - A. Static
   - B. IP NAT pool
   - C. Dynamic
   - D. NAT double-translation
   - E. Overload
9. When creating a pool of global addresses, which of the following can be used instead of the `netmask` command?
   - A. / (slash notation)
   - B. `prefix-length`
   - C. `no mask`
   - D. `block-size`
10. Which of the following would be a good starting point for troubleshooting if your router is not translating?
    - A. Reboot.
    - B. Call Cisco.
    - C. Check your interfaces for the correct configuration.
    - D. Run the `debug all` command.
11. Which of the following would be good reasons to run NAT? (Choose three.)
    - A. You need to connect to the Internet and your hosts don't have globally unique IP addresses.
    - B. You change to a new ISP that requires you to renumber your network.
    - C. You don't want any hosts connecting to the Internet.
    - D. You require two intranets with duplicate addresses to merge.

12. Which of the following is considered to be the inside hosts address after translation?
    A. Inside local
    B. Outside local
    C. Inside global
    D. Outside global

13. Which of the following is considered to be the inside hosts address before translation?
    A. Inside local
    B. Outside local
    C. Inside global
    D. Outside global

14. By looking at the following output, which of the following commands would allow dynamic translations?

```
Router#show ip nat trans
Pro Inside global  Inside local   Outside local Outside global
--- 1.1.128.1      10.1.1.1       ---     ---
--- 1.1.130.178    10.1.1.2       ---     ---
--- 1.1.129.174    10.1.1.10      ---     ---
--- 1.1.130.101    10.1.1.89      ---     ---
--- 1.1.134.169    10.1.1.100     ---     ---
--- 1.1.135.174    10.1.1.200     ---     ---
```

    A. `ip nat inside source pool todd 1.1.128.1 1.1.135.254 prefix-length 19`
    B. `ip nat pool todd 1.1.128.1 1.1.135.254 prefix-length 19`
    C. `ip nat pool todd 1.1.128.1 1.1.135.254 prefix-length 18`
    D. `ip nat pool todd 1.1.128.1 1.1.135.254 prefix-length 21`

15. Your inside locals are not being translated to the inside global addresses. Which of the following commands will show you if your inside globals are allowed to use the NAT pool?

```
ip nat pool Corp 198.18.41.129 198.18.41.134 netmask 255.255.255.248
ip nat inside source list 100 int pool Corp overload
```

    A. `debug ip nat`
    B. `show access-list`
    C. `show ip nat translation`
    D. `show ip nat statistics`

16. Which command would you place on the interface of a private network?
    A. `ip nat inside`
    B. `ip nat outside`
    C. `ip outside global`
    D. `ip inside local`

17. Which command would you place on an interface connected to the Internet?

A. `ip nat inside`

B. `ip nat outside`

C. `ip outside global`

D. `ip inside local`

18. Pat Address Translation is also called what?

A. NAT Fast

B. NAT Static

C. NAT Overload

D. Overloading Static

19. What does the asterisk (*) represent in the following output?

```
NAT*: s=172.16.2.2, d=192.168.2.1->10.1.1.1 [1]
```

A. The packet was destined for a local interface on the router.

B. The packet was translated and fast switched to the destination.

C. The packet attempted to be translated but failed.

D. The packet was translated but there was no response from the remote host.

20. Which of the following needs to be added to the configuration to enable PAT?

```
ip nat pool Corp 198.18.41.129 198.18.41.134 netmask 255.255.255.248
access-list 1 permit 192.168.76.64 0.0.0.31
```

A. `ip nat pool inside overload`

B. `ip nat inside source list 1 pool Corp overload`

C. `ip nat pool outside overload`

D. `ip nat pool Corp 198.41.129 net 255.255.255.0 overload`

Answers to Review Questions

1. A, C, E. NAT is not perfect and can cause some issues in some networks, but most networks work just fine. NAT can cause delays and troubleshooting problems, and some applications just won't work.

2. B, D, F. NAT is not perfect, but there are some advantages. It conserves global addresses, which allow us to add millions of hosts to the Internet without "real" IP addresses. This provides flexibility in our corporate networks. NAT can also allow you to use the same subnet more than once in the same network without overlapping networks.

3. C. The command `debug ip nat` will show you in real time the translations occurring on your router.

4. A. The command `show ip nat translations` will show you the translation table containing all the active NAT entries.

5. D. The command `clear ip nat translations *` will clear all the active NAT entries in your translation table.

6. B. The `show ip nat statistics` command displays a summary of the NAT configuration as well as counts of active translation types, hits to an existing mapping, misses (causing an attempt to create a mapping), and expired translations.

7. B. The command `ip nat pool` *`name`* creates the pool that hosts can use to get onto the global Internet. What makes option B correct is that the range 171.16.10.65 through 171.16.10.94 includes 30 hosts, but the mask has to match 30 hosts as well, and that mask is 255.255.255.224. Option C is wrong because there is a lowercase *t* in the pool name. Pool names are case sensitive.

8. A, C, E. You can configure NAT three ways on a Cisco router: static, dynamic, and NAT Overload (PAT).

9. B. Instead of the `netmask` command, you can use the `prefix-length` *`length`* statement.

10. C. In order for NAT to provide translation services, you must have `ip nat inside` and `ip nat outside` configured on your router's interfaces.

11. A, B, D. The most popular use of NAT is if you want to connect to the Internet and you don't want hosts to have global (real) IP addresses, but options B and D are correct as well.

12. C. An inside global address is considered to be the IP address of the host on the private network after translation.

13. A. An inside local address is considered to be the IP address of the host on the private network before translation.

14. D. What we need to figure out for this question is only the inside global pool. Basically we start at 1.1.128.1 and end at 1.1.135.174; our block size is 8 in the third octet, or /21. Always look for your block size and the interesting octet and you can find your answer every time.

15. B. Once you create your pool, the command `ip nat inside source` must be used to say which inside locals are allowed to use the pool. In this question we need to see if access-list 100 is configured correctly, if at all, so `show access-list` is the best answer.

16. A. You must configure your interfaces before NAT will provide any translations. On the inside network interfaces, you would use the command `ip nat inside`. On the outside network interfaces, you will use the command `ip nat outside`.

17. B. You must configure your interfaces before NAT will provide any translations. On the inside networks you would use the command `ip nat inside`. On the outside network interfaces, you will use the command `ip nat outside`.

18. C. Another term for Port Address Translation is NAT Overload because that is the keyword used to enable port address translation.

19. B. Fast switching is used on Cisco routers to create a type of route cache in order to quickly forward packets through a router without having to parse the routing table for every packet. As packets are processed switched (looked up in the routing table), this information is stored in the cache for later use if needed for faster routing processing.

20. B. Once you create a pool for the inside locals to use to get out to the global Internet, you must configure the command to allow them access to the pool. The `ip nat inside source list` *`number pool-name`* `overload` command is the correct sequence for this question.

Answers to Written Lab 13

1. Port Address Translation (PAT), also called NAT Overload
2. `debug ip nat`
3. `show ip nat translations`
4. `clear ip nat translations *`
5. Before
6. After
7. `show ip nat statistics`
8. The `ip nat inside` and `ip nat outside` commands
9. Dynamic NAT
10. `prefix-length`

Cisco's Wireless Technologies

THE CCNA EXAM TOPICS COVERED IN THIS CHAPTER INCLUDE THE FOLLOWING:

✓ **Explain and select the appropriate administrative tasks required for a WLAN**

- Describe standards associated with wireless media (including: IEEE WI-FI Alliance, ITU/FCC)
- Identify and describe the purpose of the components in a small wireless network (including: SSID, BSS, ESS)
- Identify the basic parameters to configure on a wireless network to ensure that devices connect to the correct access point
- Compare and contrast wireless security features and capabilities of WPA security (including: open, WEP, WPA-1 and 2)
- Identify common issues with implementing wireless networks (including: Interface, misconfiguration)

Sipping coffee at a café or hanging out in an airport until they finally fix the plane you're waiting to board no longer requires reading actual papers and magazines to avoid mind-numbing boredom. Now it's easy to connect to the local wireless network and catch up on your emails and blog, do a little gaming—maybe even get some work done! It's come to the point that many of us wouldn't even think of checking into a hotel that doesn't offer this important amenity. So clearly, those of us already in or wishing to enter the IT field better have our chops down regarding wireless network components and their associated installation factors, right? (Answer: A resounding YES!).

With that established, we've come to a great starting point: If you want to understand the basic wireless LANs (WLANs) most commonly still in use today, just think 10BaseT Ethernet with hubs, except the wireless devices we connect into are called access points (APs). This means that our WLANs run half-duplex communication—everyone is sharing the same bandwidth, and only one device is communicating at a time per channel.

This isn't necessarily bad; it's just not good enough. Because most people rely upon wireless networks today, it's critical that they evolve faster than greased lightning to keep up with our rapidly escalating needs. The good news is that this is actually happening—and it even works securely!

In this chapter, I am going talk about the various types of wireless networks and then discuss the minimum devices needed to create a simple wireless network. I'll then show you some basic wireless topologies, give you a high overview of Wireless VoIP (WVoIP), and finish with wireless security.

For up-to-the-minute updates on the topics covered in this chapter, please see `www.lammle.com` and/or `www.sybex.com/go/ccna7e`.

Introduction to Wireless Technology

Wireless networks come in many different forms, cover various distances, and provide a range of low to high bandwidth depending on the type installed. The typical wireless network today is an extension of an Ethernet LAN, and wireless hosts use MAC addresses, IP addresses, and so on, just as any host would on a wired LAN. Figure 14.1 shows how the simple, typical wireless LAN looks today.

FIGURE 14.1 Wireless LANs are an extension of our existing LANs.

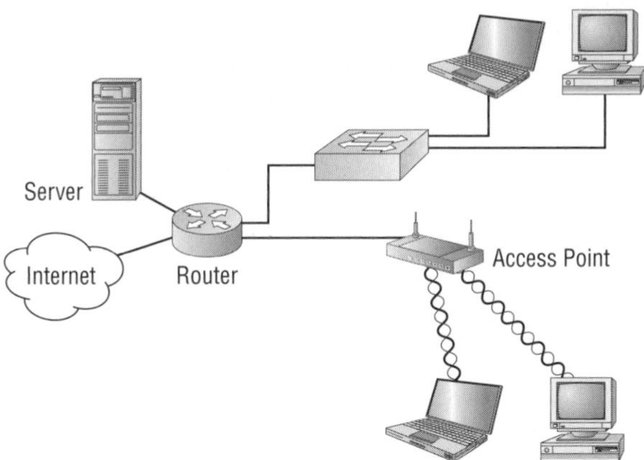

But wireless networks are more than just run-of-the-mill LANs because—you guessed it—they're wireless. And as I mentioned, they cover a range of distances, from short-range personal area networks all the way to wide area networks (WANs) that really go the distance. Figure 14.2 illustrates how different types of wireless networks look and the related distances they'll provide coverage for in today's world.

FIGURE 14.2 Today's wireless networks

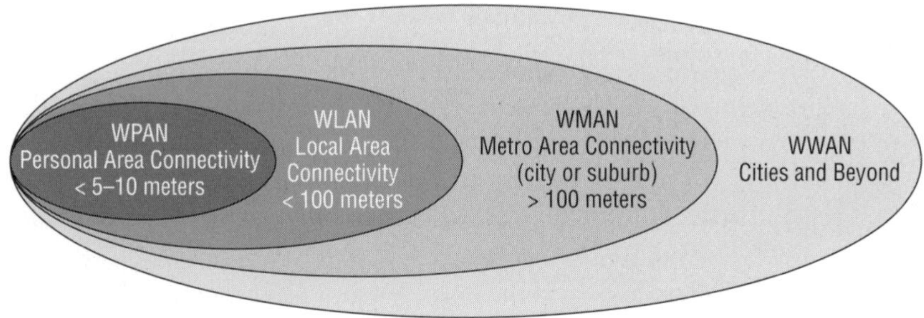

Okay, now that you've got the big picture, let's talk about the typical wireless devices you'll find in today's WLANs.

Basic Wireless Devices

Though it might not seem this way to you right now, *simple* wireless networks (WLANs) are less complex than their wired cousins because they require fewer components. To make a basic wireless network work properly, all you really need are two main devices: a wireless access point and a wireless NIC. This also makes it a lot easier to install a wireless network, because basically, you just need an understanding of these two components in order to do so. Obviously, wireless networks are getting more and more advanced and complicated by the day, but let's not worry about that right now.

Wireless Access Points

In the vast majority of wired networks, you'll find a central component such as a switch that's there to connect hosts together and allow them to communicate with each other. It's the same thing with wireless networks; they also have a component that connects all wireless devices together, only that device is known as a wireless *access point* (*AP*) instead. Wireless access points have at least one antenna. Usually there's two for better reception (referred to as *diversity*) and an Ethernet port to connect them to a wired network.

Access point devices have the following characteristics:

- APs function as a central junction point for the wireless stations much like a switch or hub does within a wired network. Due to the half-duplex nature of wireless networking, the hub comparison is more accurate, even though hubs are rarely found in the wired world anymore.
- APs have at least one antenna—most likely two or more.
- APs function as a bridge to the wired network, giving the wireless station access to the wired network and/or the Internet.
- Small office/home office (SOHO) APs come in two flavors—the stand-alone AP and the wireless router. They can and usually do include functions like NAT and DHCP.

Even though it's not a perfect analogy, you can compare an AP to a hub because it doesn't create collision domains for each connection as a switch does, but APs are definitely smarter than hubs. An AP is really a portal device that can either direct network traffic to the wired backbone or back out into the wireless realm. The connection back to the wired network is called the distribution system (DS), and the AP also maintains MAC address information found within the wireless frames.

Wireless Network Interface Card (WNIC)

Every host you want to connect to a wireless network needs a *wireless network interface card* (*WNIC*) to do so. Basically, a wireless NIC does the same job as a traditional Ethernet NIC, only instead of having a socket/port to plug a cable into, the wireless NIC has a radio antenna.

It would be difficult to buy a laptop today without a wireless card already built in.

Wireless Antennas

Wireless antennas work with both transmitters and receivers. There are two broad classes of antennas on the market today: *omnidirectional* (or point-to-multipoint) and *directional* (or point-to-point).

Yagi antennas usually provide greater range than Omni antennas of equivalent gain. Why? Because Yagis focus all their power in a single direction. Omnis must disperse the same amount of power in all directions at the same time, like a large donut.

A downside to using a directional antenna is that you've got to be much more precise when aligning communication points. It's also why most APs use Omnis, because often, clients and other APs can be located in any direction at any given moment, but every office/home/business has different needs, and the placement of various antennas may need to be carefully thought out before installing a wireless network.

To get a picture of this Omni antenna, think of the antenna on your car. Yes, it's a non-networking example, but it's still a good one because it clarifies the fact that your car's particular orientation doesn't affect the signal reception of whatever radio station you happen to be listening to. Well, most of the time, anyway. If you're in the boonies, you're out of range—something that also applies to the networking version of Omnis.

When setting up an AP in an office, keep the antenna away from devices that contain metal to avoid blocking or reflecting the signal.

Wireless Regulations

Most wireless networks use the Industrial, Scientific, and Medical (ISM) band. But being able to use a band, or "range of frequencies," doesn't mean you get to use it in any way you want. To get wireless devices to communicate together, these hosts need to understand the various modulation technique to use, how a frame should be coded, what type of headers need to be in that frame, what the physical transmission mechanism should be, and so on. Plus, they've all got to be accurately defined or machines just won't be capable of communicating with each other effectively. And all these elements just happen to be specified by the IEEE.

The IEEE's communication committee defined several network communication areas, which were then further divided into working groups. This is why most network protocols today start with 802—80 stands for the year 1980 and the 2 stands for February. The lion's share of all vendors follow the IEEE 802.11 family of protocol specifications when building wireless devices, so today, whenever a wireless device is used, its layer 1 and layer 2 functions are defined by an IEEE 802.11 series protocol.

IEEE 802.11 Transmission

Transmitting a signal using the typical 802.11 specifications works a lot like it does with a basic Ethernet hub: They're both two-way forms of communication, and they both use the same frequency to transmit and receive, but they can only transmit or receive one at a time; this is often referred to as half-duplex, as I mentioned in Chapter 14's intro.

Of course, we can also increase the transmitting power to gain a greater transmitting distance, but since doing this can create some pretty ugly distortion, you've got to do it really carefully! You can use the higher frequencies to attain higher data rates, but unfortunately, it will cost you because going this way will result in decreased transmitting distances. Opt for the lower-frequency approach and you'll get to transmit further but at lower data rates. This is just one factor that should begin to tune you into just how important it is to be highly knowledgeable about all the various types of WLANs you can implement. To come up with the best LAN solution—the one that most effectively meets the specific requirements of the unique situation you're faced with—can be real challenge!

Also important to note is the fact that the 802.11 specifications were developed to avoid licensing requirements in most countries, so you get to enjoy the freedom to install and operate without being socked with any licensing or operating fee surprises, which is nice. It also means that any manufacturer can create wireless networking products and sell them at a local computer store or pretty much wherever and that all our computers should be able to communicate wirelessly without configuring much of anything at all.

There are several agencies that have been around for a surprisingly long time to help govern the use of wireless devices, frequencies, standards, and how the frequency spectrum is used. Table 14.1 gives you the current agencies involved in this endeavor to help create, maintain, and even enforce wireless standards worldwide

TABLE 14.1 Wireless agencies and standards

Agency	Purpose	Web Site
Institute of Electrical and Electronics Engineers (IEEE)	Creates and maintains operational standards	`www.ieee.org`
Federal Communications Commission (FCC)	Regulates the use of wireless devices in the U.S.	`www.fcc.gov`
European Telecommunications Standards Institute (ETSi)	Chartered to produce common standards in Europe	`www.etsi.org`
Wi-Fi Alliance	Promotes and tests for WLAN interoperability	`www.wi-fi.com`

Because WLANs transmit over radio frequencies, they're regulated by the same laws used to govern devices like AM/FM radios, and in the U.S., the Federal Communications Commission (FCC) regulates the use of wireless LAN devices. The IEEE takes it from there and creates standards based upon the frequencies the FCC releases for public use.

Unlicensed Bands

To date, the FCC has released three unlicensed bands for public use—900MHz, 2.4GHz, and 5GHz—although there is talk about releasing a few more bands in the very near future. The 900MHz and 2.4GHz bands are referred to as the Industrial, Scientific, and Medical (ISM) bands, and the 5GHz band is known as the Unlicensed National Information Infrastructure (UNII) band. Figure 14.3 shows where the unlicensed bands sit within the RF spectrum.

FIGURE 14.3 Unlicensed frequencies

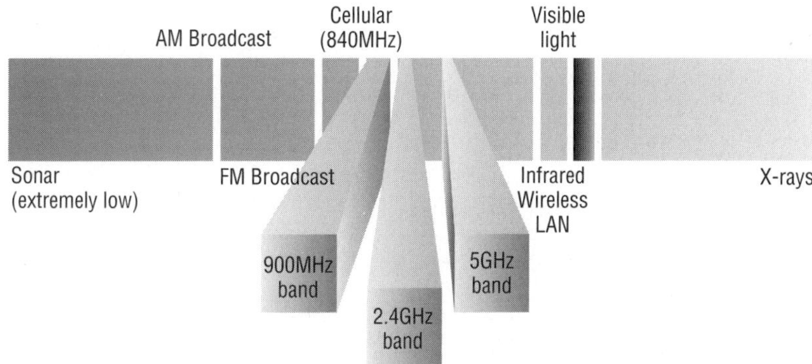

This is all good, but what if you want you to deploy wireless in a range outside of the three public bands shown in Figure 14.3? For that, you need to get permission in the form of a specific license from the FCC. Predictably, as soon as the FCC opened up the previously mentioned three frequency ranges to the public, manufacturers began offering a full menu of products that flooded the market, with 802.11b/g leading the way as the most widely used wireless network found today.

The 802.11 Standards

The wireless standards group starts with 802.11, and there's some other up-and-coming standards groups as well, such as, for example, 802.16 and 802.20. And if you use a cell phone and/or watch TV, you know that even cellular networks are becoming huge players in our wireless experience. For now though, we're going to concentrate on the 802.11 standards committee and subcommittees.

IEEE 802.11 was the first, original standardized WLAN at 1 and 2Mbps, and it runs in the 2.4GHz radio frequency range. It was ratified in 1997, although we didn't see a whole lot of products pop up until around 1999 when 802.11b was formally introduced. All the committees listed in Table 14.2 made amendments to the original 802.11 standard except for 802.11F and 802.11T, which produced stand-alone documents. Here's a great table to refer to—maybe even commit to memory.

TABLE 14.2 802.11 Committees and subcommittees

Committee	Purpose
IEEE 802.11a	54Mbps, 5GHz standard
IEEE 802.11b	Enhancements to 802.11 to support 5.5 and 11Mbps
IEEE 802.11c	Bridge operation procedures; included in the IEEE 802.1D standard
IEEE 802.11d	International roaming extensions
IEEE 802.11e	Quality of service
IEEE 802.11F	Inter-Access Point Protocol
IEEE 802.11g	54Mbps, 2.4GHz standard (backward compatible with 802.11b)
IEEE 802.11h	Dynamic Frequency Selection (DFS) and Transmit Power Control (TPC) at 5Ghz
IEEE 802.11i	Enhanced security
IEEE 802.11j	Extensions for Japan and U.S. public safety
IEEE 802.11k	Radio resource measurement enhancements
IEEE 802.11m	Maintenance of the standard; odds and ends
IEEE 802.11n	Higher throughput improvements using MIMO (multiple input, multiple output antennas)
IEEE 802.11p	Wireless Access for the Vehicular Environment (WAVE)
IEEE 802.11r	Fast roaming
IEEE 802.11s	Extended service set (ESS) Mesh Networking
IEEE 802.11T	Wireless Performance Prediction (WPP)
IEEE 802.11u	Internetworking with non-802 networks (cellular, for example)
IEEE 802.11v	Wireless network management
IEEE 802.11w	Protected management frames
IEEE 802.11y	3650–3700 MHz operation in the U.S.

Okay, now let's discuss some important specifics of the most popular 802.11 WLANs.

2.4GHz (802.11b)

First on the menu to really be deployed in home and corporate is the 802.11b standard. It used to be the most widely deployed wireless standard, and it operates in the 2.4GHz unlicensed radio band that delivers a maximum data rate of 11Mbps.

The 802.11b standard has been widely adopted by both vendors and customers who found that its 11Mbps data rate worked pretty well for most applications. But now that 802.11b has a big brother (802.11g), no one goes out and just buys an 802.11b card or access point anymore, because why would you buy a 10Mbps Ethernet card when you can score a 10/100 Ethernet card for the same price?

An interesting thing about all Cisco 802.11 WLAN products is that they have the ability to data-rate-shift while moving. This allows the person operating at 11Mbps to shift to 5.5Mbps, 2Mbps, and finally still communicate farthest from the access point at 1Mbps. And furthermore, this rate shifting happens without losing connection and with no interaction from the user. Rate shifting also occurs on a transmission-by-transmission basis. This is important because it means that the access point can support multiple clients at varying speeds depending upon the location of each client.

The problem with 802.11b lies in how the Data Link layer is dealt with. In order to solve problems in the RF spectrum, a variation of Ethernet collision detection was created called CSMA/CA, or Carrier Sense Multiple Access with Collision Avoidance. Check this out in Figure 14.4.

FIGURE 14.4 802.11b CSMA/CA

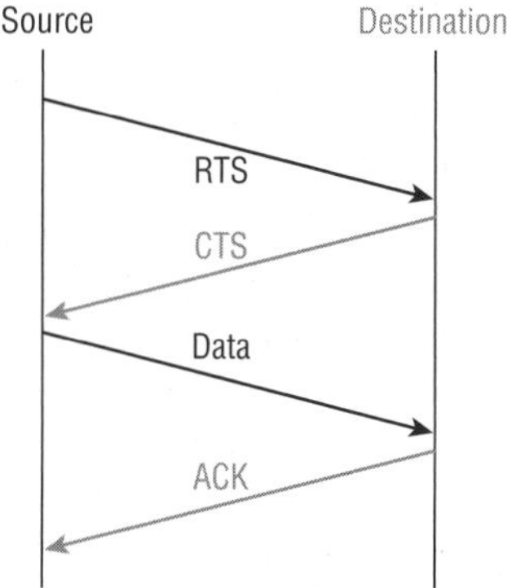

CSMA/CA is also called a *Request to Send, Clear to Send (RTS/CTS)* because of the way it requires hosts to communicate to the access point (AP). For every packet sent, an RTS/CTS *and* acknowledgment must be received, which doesn't exactly meet present-day networking demands efficiently!

Cordless phones and microwave ovens can cause interference in the 2.4Ghz range

Now there are 11 channels available we can configure in the United States within the 2.4GHz range. However, only 3 of these channels are considered non-overlapping: 1, 6, and 11.

Figure 14.5 shows the 14 different channels (each 22MHz wide) that the FCC released within the 2.4GHz range.

FIGURE 14.5 ISM 2.4GHz channels

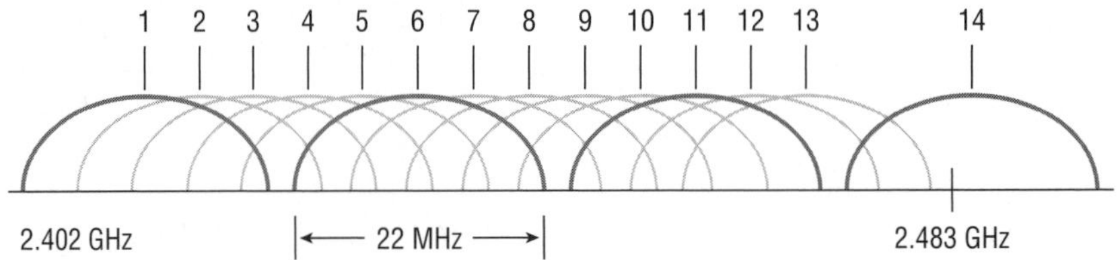

Since we've got three channels (1, 6, and 11) that don't overlap, we get to have three access points in the same general area without experiencing interference. Setting the AP channel is one of the most important first steps you should take when configuring an AP.

2.4GHz (802.11g)

The 802.11g standard was ratified in June 2003 and is backward compatible with 802.11b. The 802.11g standard delivers the same 54Mbps maximum data rate as 802.11a but runs in the 2.4GHz range—the same as 802.11b.

Because 802.11b/g operates in the same 2.4GHz unlicensed band, migrating to 802.11g is an affordable choice for organizations with existing 802.11b wireless infrastructures. Just keep in mind that 802.11b products can't be "software upgraded" to 802.11g. This limitation is because 802.11g radios use a different chipset in order to deliver the higher data rate.

But still, much like Ethernet and FastEthernet, 802.11g products can be commingled with 802.11b products in the same network. Yet, for example, completely unlike Ethernet, if you have four users running 802.11g and one user starts using an 802.11b card, everyone connected to the same access point is then forced to run the 802.11b CSMA/CA method—an ugly fact that really makes throughput suffer. So to optimize performance, it's recommended that you disable the 802.11b-only modes on all your access points.

To explain this further, 802.11b uses a modulation technique called Direct Sequence Spread Spectrum (DSSS) that's just not as robust as the Orthogonal Frequency Division Multiplexing (OFDM) modulation used by both 802.11g and 802.11a. 802.11g clients using OFDM enjoy much better performance at the same ranges as 802.11b clients do, but—and remember this—when 802.11g clients are operating at the 802.11b rates (11, 5.5, 2, and 1Mbps), they're actually using the same modulation 802.11b does.

Real World Scenario

You Won't Use 802.11b in *My* Network!

By now you should get the idea that we really shouldn't be using IEEE 802.11b clients or APs in our wireless networks, and since most laptops and other wireless devices all run a/b/g, we should be able to disable the 802.11b capabilities on our APs.

A few years back when I was installing a wireless network at a client, I disabled all the 802.11b capabilities on all access points. The next day a woman working in sales came up to me and said her wireless laptop stopped working. She had an older laptop with an external PCMIA wireless card, so I pretty much figured out the problem right away. Once I pulled the card out, I showed her that it was old and defective and that she needs to get a new wireless card. (It really wasn't defective, but it was defective in my network!) The next day she came back with a new wireless card in hand. Since it is impossible these days to buy an 802.11b card, except maybe a used one from eBay, I wasn't worried that the card was a "b only" card. However, after looking at the card, sure enough, it was a brand-new 802.11b card. I was stunned! Where would she get a brand-new 802.11b card? She said that CompUSA was going out of business and she found this new card for only four bucks in a clearance bin! Perfect.

5GHz (802.11a)

The IEEE ratified the 802.11a standard in 1999, but the first 802.11a products didn't begin appearing on the market until late 2001. And boy could these hot new commodities seriously set you back! The 802.11a standard delivers a maximum data rate of 54Mbps with up to 28 non-overlapping frequency channels—a whopping 23 of them available in the U.S.

Another 802.11a benefit is that when operating in the 5GHz radio band, it's immune to interference from devices that operate in the 2.4GHz band, like microwave ovens, cordless phones, and Bluetooth devices. As you probably guessed, 802.11a isn't backward compatible with 802.11b because they operate at different frequencies, so you don't get to just "upgrade" pieces and parts of your network and expect everything to sing in perfect harmony. But no worries—there are plenty of dual-radio devices that will work in both types of networks. Oh, and another definite plus for 802.11a is that it can work in the same physical environment without having to take measures to avoid interference from 802.11b users.

Like 802.11b radios, all 802.11a products also have the ability to data-rate-shift while moving. The difference being that 802.11a products allow someone moving at 54Mbps to shift to 48Mbps, 36Mbps, 24Mbps, 18Mbps, 12Mbps, and 9Mbps, and finally still communicate farthest from the AP way down at 6Mbps.

2.4GHz/5GHz (802.11n)

802.11n builds on previous 802.11 standards by adding *Multiple-Input Multiple-Output (MIMO)*, which uses multiple transmitters and receiver antennas to increase data throughput and range. 802.11n can allow up to eight antennas, but most of today's APs use only four to six. This setup permits considerably higher data rates than 802.11a/b/g does.

The following three vital items are combined in 802.11n to enhance performance:

- At the Physical layer, the way a signal is sent is changed, enabling reflections and interferences to become an advantage instead of a source of degradation.
- Two 20Mhz-wide channels are combined to increase throughput.
- At the MAC layer, a different way of managing packet transmission is used.

It's important to know is that 802.11n isn't truly compatible with 802.11b, 802.11g, or even 802.11a, but it is designed to be backward compatible with them. How 802.11n achieves backward compatibility is by changing the way frames are sent so they can be understood by 802.11a/b/g.

Here's a list of some of the primary components of 802.11n that together sum up why people claim 802.11n is more reliable and predictable:

40Mhz channels 802.11g and 802.11a use 20Mhz channels and employs tones on the sides of each channel that are not used in order to protect the main carrier. This means that 11Mbps go unused and are basically wasted. 802.11n aggregates two carriers to double the speed from 54Mbps to more than 108. Add in those wasted 11Mbps rescued from the side tones and you get a grand total of 119Mbps!

MAC efficiency 802.11 protocols require acknowledgment of each and every frame. 802.11n can pass many packets before an acknowledgment is required, which saves you a huge amount of overhead. This is called *block acknowledgment*.

Multiple-Input Multiple-Output (MIMO) Several frames are sent by several antennae over several paths and are then recombined by another set of antennae to optimize throughput and multipath resistance. This is called *spatial multiplexing*.

Okay—now that you've nailed down our a/b/g/n networks, it's time to move on and get into some detail about how wireless frames are actually sent, about frame shapes and speeds, and about the management frame used to discover and connect to the wireless network.

For more-detailed information about wireless networking, please see my book *CCNA Wireless Study Guide* (Sybex, 2010).

Comparing 802.11

Figure 14.6 lists the year each IEEE standard in use today was ratified along with its frequency, the number of non-overlapping channels, the Physical layer transmission techniques, and the data rates.

FIGURE 14.6 Standards for spectrums and speeds

	802.11	802.11b	802.11a	802.11g		802.11n
Ratified	1997	1999	1999	2003		2010
Frequency Band	2.4GHz	2.4GHz	5GHz	2.4GHz		2.4GHz, 5GHz
No. of Channels	3	3	Up to 23	3		Varies
Transmission	IR, FHSS, DSSS	DSSS	OFDM	DSSS	OFDM	DSSS, CCK, OFDM
Data Rates (Mbps)	1, 2	1, 2, 5.5, 11	6, 9, 12, 18, 24, 36, 48, 54	1, 2, 5.5, 11	6, 9, 12, 18, 24, 36, 48, 54	100+

Okay—now that you've have an understanding of our a/b/g/n networks, it's time to move on and get into some detail about the typical wireless topologies.

Wireless Topologies

Now that I've discussed the very basics of wireless devices used in today's simple networks, I want to describe the different types of networks you'll run across or design and implement as your wireless networks grow.

These include the following:

- IBSS
- BSS
- ESS

Let's take a look at these networks in more detail.

Independent Basic Service Set (Ad Hoc)

Using an ad hoc network is the easiest way to install wireless 802.11 devices. In this mode, the wireless NICs (or other devices) can communicate directly without the need for an AP. A good example of this is two laptops with wireless NICs installed. If both cards were set up to operate in ad hoc mode, they could connect and transfer files as long as the other network settings, like the IP protocols, were set up to enable this as well.

To create an *independent basic service set (IBSS)*, all you need is two or more wireless-capable devices. Once you've placed them within a range of 20 to 40 meters of each other, they'll "see" each other and be able to connect—assuming they share some basic configuration parameters. One computer may be able to share its Internet connection with the rest of them in your group. Figure 14.7 shows an example of an ad hoc wireless network. Notice that there's no access point!

FIGURE 14.7 A wireless network in ad hoc mode

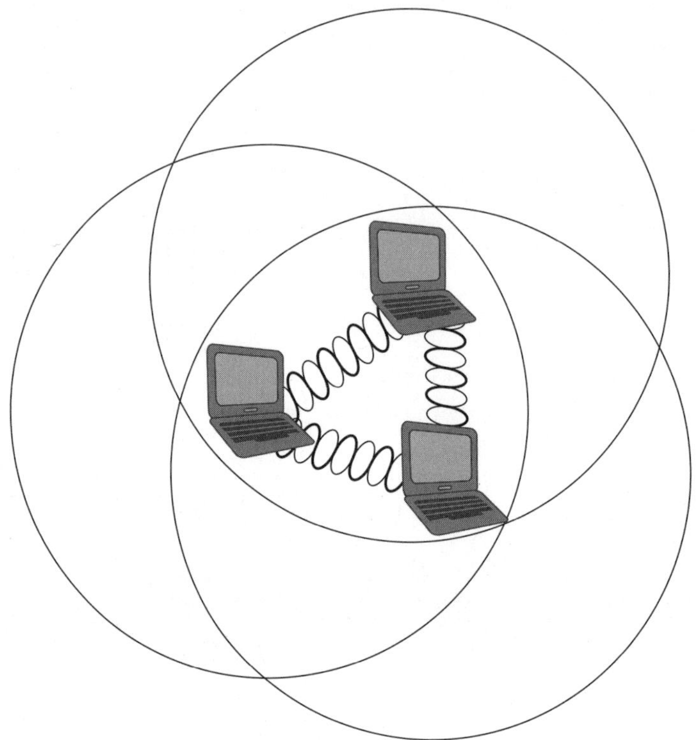

An ad hoc network, also referred to as peer to peer, doesn't scale well, and I wouldn't recommend it due to collision and organization issues in today's corporate networks. With the low cost of APs, you don't need this kind of network anymore, except for perhaps in your home, but maybe not even there.

Additionally, ad hoc networks are fairly insecure, and care should be taken to have the AdHoc setting turned off on your host prior to connecting to your wireless network.

Basic Service Set (BSS)

A basic service set (BSS) is the area, or cell, defined by the wireless signal served by the AP. It can also be called a basic service area (BSA) and the two terms, *BSS* and *BSA*, can be interchangeable. Even so, *BSS* is the term most commonly used to define the cell area. Figure 14.8 shows an AP providing a BSS for hosts in the area and the basic service area (cell) that's covered by the AP.

FIGURE 14.8 Basic service set/basic service area

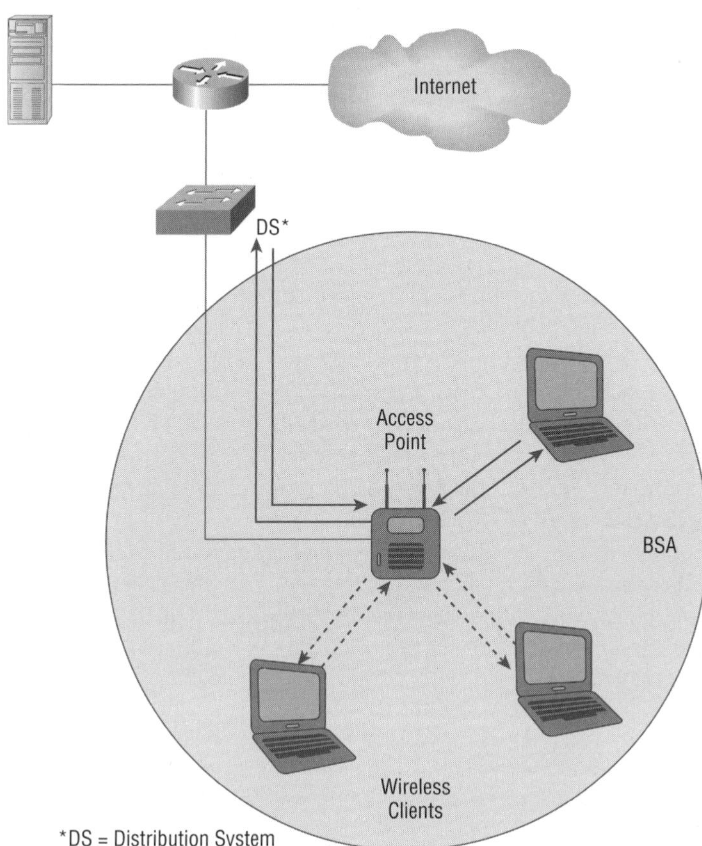

The AP provides management of wireless frames so the hosts can communicate. Unlike the ad hoc network, this network will scale better, and more hosts can communicate in this network because the AP manages all network connections.

Infrastructure Basic Service Set

In infrastructure mode, wireless NICs only communicate with an access point instead of directly with each other as they do when they're in ad hoc mode. All communication between hosts, as well as any wired portion of the network, must go through the access point. An important fact to remember is that in this mode, wireless clients appear to the rest of the network as though they were standard, wired hosts.

Figure 14.8 shows a typical infrastructure mode wireless network. Pay special attention to the access point and the fact that it's also connected to the wired network. This connection from the access point to the wired network is called the *distribution system (DS)* and this is how the APs communicate to each other about hosts in the BSA. APs do not communicate with each other via the wireless network, only through the DS.

When you configure a client to operate in wireless infrastructure mode, you need to understand what is called the SSID. The *service set identifier (SSID)* refers to the unique 32-character identifier that represents a particular wireless network and defines the BSS. (By the way, a lot of people use the terms *SSID* and *BSS* interchangeably, so don't let that confuse you!) All devices involved in a particular wireless network may be configured with the same SSID. Sometimes access points may even have multiple SSIDs configured. Let's talk about that in a little more detail.

Service Set ID

SSID is a basic name that defines the BSA transmitted from the AP. A good example of this is Linksys. You've probably seen that name pop up on your host when looking for a wireless network. This is the name the AP transmits out to identify which WLAN the client station can associate with. The SSID can be up to 32 characters long. It normally consists of human-readable ASCII characters, but the standard doesn't require this. The SSID is defined as a sequence of 1 to 32 octets, each of which may take any value.

The SSID is configured on the AP and can be either broadcasted to the outside world or hidden. If the SSID is broadcasted, when wireless stations use their client software to scan for wireless networks, the network will appear in a list identified by its SSID. But if it's hidden, it either won't appear in the list at all or it will show up as an "unknown network," depending on the client's operating system.

You should always change the default SSID name on an AP, and change the administrator password too while you're at it!

Either way, a hidden SSID will require that the client station be configured with a wireless profile, including the SSID, in order to connect. This requirement is above and beyond any other normal authentication steps or security essentials.

Extended Service Set

A good thing to know is that if you set all your access points to the same SSID, mobile wireless clients can roam around freely within the same network. This is the most common wireless network design you'll find in today's corporate settings.

Doing this creates something called an extended service set (ESS), which provides more coverage than a single access point and allows users to roam from one AP to another without having their host disconnected from the network. This design creates the ability to move more or less seamlessly from one AP to another. Figure 14.9 shows two APs configured with the same SSIDs in an office, thereby creating the ESS network.

For users to be able to roam throughout the wireless network—from AP to AP without losing their connection to the network—all APs must overlap by at least 10 to 20 percent of their signal to their neighbors' cells. To make this happen, be sure the channels (frequency) on each AP are set differently.

FIGURE 14.9 Extended service set (ESS)

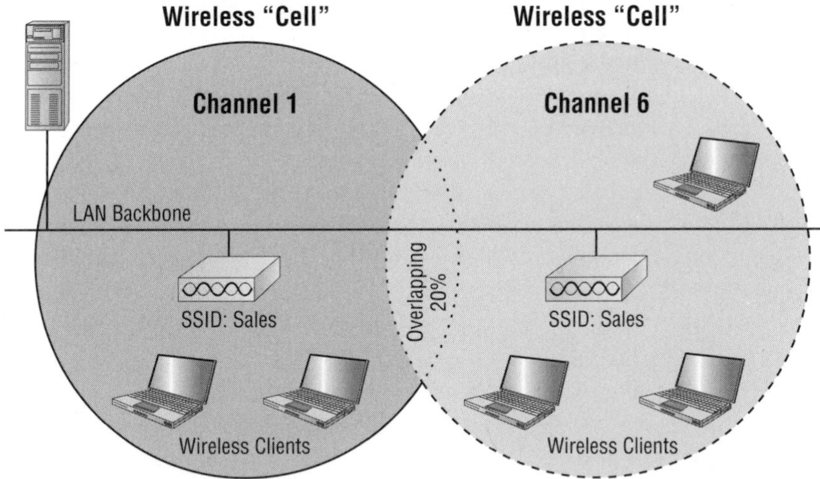

Adding Voice over IP (VoIP) in our WLANs

VoIP is an integral part of our world today, and it's only going to keep growing. Understanding the effects a VoIP network will have on our wired and wireless networks is important.

The actual configuration and detailed information is way beyond the CCENT and CCNA objectives, so I'll just discuss the requirements we need to remember.

So, what we must understand for our VoIP phone requirements in our network is this:

- VoIP traffic has special requirements (such as bandwidth, priority, and having small delay).
- Configure separate VLANs for IP telephony traffic and data traffic to avoid conflict. I discussed the voice VLAN in Chapter 11.
- Cisco IP phones are often implemented with PoE, and you must make sure you acquire the correct switches for your network.
- WLAN design must take into consideration the implementation of VoIP devices and the bandwidth requirements.
- QoS on our WLAN VLANs is necessary when adding VoIP.

LANs and WLANs consist of many network devices, and we cannot forget about our VoIP devices. Network administrators must take VoIP-specific parameters into consideration, such as bandwidth, priority, small delay, separate VLANs with QoS for VoIP, and power requirements, when designing a WLAN today.

Wireless Security

By default, wireless security is nonexistent on access points and clients. The original 802.11 committee just didn't imagine that wireless hosts would one day outnumber bounded media hosts, but that's truly where we're headed. Also, and unfortunately, just as with the IPv4 routed protocol, engineers and scientists didn't add security standards that are robust enough to work in a corporate environment. So we're left with proprietary solution add-ons to aid us in our quest to create a secure wireless network. And no—I'm not just sitting here bashing the standards committees, because the security problems we're experiencing were also created by the U.S. government because of export issues with its own security standards. Our world is a complicated place, so it follows that our security solutions are going to be as well.

A good place to start is by discussing the standard basic security that was added into the original 802.11 standards and why those standards are way too flimsy and incomplete to enable us to create a secure wireless network relevant to today's challenges.

Open Access

All Wi-Fi Certified wireless LAN products are shipped in "open-access" mode, with their security features turned off. While open access or no security may be appropriate and acceptable for public hot spots such as coffee shops, college campuses, and maybe airports, it's definitely not an option for an enterprise organization, and likely not even adequate for your private home network.

Security needs to be enabled on wireless devices during their installation in enterprise environments. It may come as quite a shock, but some companies actually don't enable any WLAN security features. Obviously, the companies that do this are exposing their networks to tremendous risk!

The reason that these products are shipped in open access mode is so that anyone—even someone without any IT knowledge, can just buy an access point, plug it into their cable or DSL modem, and voilà —they're up and running. It's marketing, plain and simple, and simplicity sells. But that doesn't mean you should leave it like that—unless you want to allow that network to be open to the public, you definitely shouldn't!

SSIDs, WEP, and MAC Address Authentication

What the original designers of 802.11 did to create basic security was include the use of service set identifiers (SSIDs), open or shared-key authentication, static Wired Equivalency Privacy (WEP), and optional Media Access Control (MAC) authentication. Sounds like a lot, but none of these really offer any type of serious security solution—all they may be close to adequate for is use on a common home network. But we'll go over them anyway.

SSID is a common network name for the devices in a WLAN system that create the wireless LAN. An SSID prevents access by any client device that doesn't have the SSID. The thing is, by default, an access point broadcasts its SSID in its beacon many times a second. And even if SSID broadcasting is turned off, a bad guy can discover the SSID by monitoring the network and just waiting for a client response to the access point. Why? Because, believe it or not, that information, as regulated in the original 802.11 specifications, must be sent in the clear—how secure!

Two types of authentication were specified by the IEEE 802.11 committee: open authentication and shared-key authentication. Open authentication involves little more than supplying the correct SSID—but it's the most common method in use today. With shared-key authentication, the access point sends the client device a challenge-text packet that the client must then encrypt with the correct Wired Equivalency Privacy (WEP) key and return to the access point. Without the correct key, authentication will fail and the client won't be allowed to associate with the access point. But shared-key authentication is still not considered secure because all an intruder has to do to get around this is detect both the cleartext challenge and the same challenge encrypted with a WEP key and then decipher the WEP key. Surprise—shared key isn't used in today's WLANs because of cleartext challenge, which presents vulnerability to a known-plain-text cryptographic attack.

With open authentication, even if a client can complete authentication and associate with an access point, the use of WEP prevents the client from sending and receiving data from the access point unless the client has the correct WEP key. A WEP key is composed of either 40 or 128 bits and, in its basic form, is usually statically defined by the network administrator on the access point and all clients that communicate with that access point. When static WEP keys are used, a network administrator must perform the time-consuming task of entering the same keys on every device in the WLAN. Obviously, we now have fixes for this because this would be administratively impossible in today's huge corporate wireless networks!

Last, client MAC addresses can be statically typed into each access point, and any of them that show up without that MAC addresses in the filter table would be denied access. Sounds good, but of course all MAC layer information must be sent in the clear—anyone equipped with a free wireless sniffer can just read the client packets sent to the access point and spoof their MAC address.

WEP can actually work if administered correctly in nonsecure areas. But basic static WEP keys are no longer a viable option in today's corporate networks without some of the proprietary fixes that run on top of it.

Encryption Methods

There are two basic types of encryption methods used in most wireless networks today: TKIP and AES. We'll cover TKIP first.

Temporal Key Integrity Protocol (TKIP)

Put up a fence, and it's only a matter of time until bad guys find a way over, around, or through it. And true to form, they indeed found ways to get through WEP's defenses, leaving our Wi-Fi networks vulnerable—stripped of their Data Link layer security! So someone had to come to the rescue. In this case, it happened to be the IEEE 802.11i task group and the Wi-Fi Alliance, joining forces for the cause. They came up with the solution called Temporal Key Integrity Protocol (TKIP) which is based on the RC4 encryption algorithm. TKIP first gained respect in the WLAN world due to the protections it affords the authentication process, but it is also used after that completes to encrypt the data traffic thereafter. The Wi-Fi Alliance unveiled it back in late 2002 and introduced it as Wi-Fi Protected Access (WPA). This little beauty even saved us lots of money because TKIP—say this like, "tee kip"—didn't make us upgrade all our legacy hardware equipment in order to use it. Then, in the summer of 2004, the IEEE put its seal of approval on its final version and added even more defensive muscle with goodies like 802.1X and AES-CCMP (AES-Counter Mode CBC-MAC Protocol) Upon publishing IEEE 802.11i-2004, the Wi-Fi Alliance responded positively by embracing the now-complete specification and dubbing it WPA2 for marketing purposes.

A big reason that new hardware wasn't required to run TKIP is that it really just kind of a wraps around the preexisting WEP RC4 encryption cipher, which was way too short, and upgrades it to a much more impenetrable 128-bit encryption. Another reason for TKIP's innate compatibility is that both its encryption mechanism and the RC4 algorithm used to power and define WEP, respectively, remained the same.

AES

Both WPA/2 and the 802.11i standard call for the use of 128-bit Advanced Encryption Standard (AES) for data encryption. It's widely considered the best encryption available today and has been approved by the National Institute of Standards and Technology (NIST). It's also referred to as AES-CCMP, or AES Counter Mode with CBC-MAC authentication.

The only shortcoming of AES is that due to the computational requirements, you need a cryptographic processor to run it. Still, compared to RC4, it's a lot more efficient while at the same time seriously augmenting security over what you get with RC4.

Wi-Fi Protected Access (WPA)

So how can we implement both authentication and encryption easily and effectively? Well, this used to be a hard process, that is until WPA. First, I would like to define the differences between personal and enterprise modes. The terms *personal* and *enterprise* are not from a specific standard; they're more marketing terms. The difference between personal and enterprise is defined by the authentication method used. Personal mode uses only pre-shared key for authentication, and enterprise mode uses 802.1x and EAP methods of authentication. Many people associate these terms as small business and large business, respectively, but that only depends on the implementation requirements.

Wi-Fi Protected Access (WPA) is a standard testing specification developed in 2003 by the Wi-Fi Alliance, formerly known as the Wireless Ethernet Compatibility Alliance (WECA). WPA provides a standard for authentication and encryption of WLANs that's intended to solve known security problems existing up to and including the year 2003. This takes into account the well-publicized AirSnort and man-in-the-middle WLAN attacks.

WPA is a step toward the IEEE 802.11i standard and uses many of the same components, with the exception of encryption—802.11i uses AES encryption. WPA's mechanisms are designed to be implementable by current WEP-oriented hardware vendors, meaning that users should be able to implement WPA on their systems with only a firmware/software modification. WPA addressed the inherit weaknesses found in WEP by adding a stronger encryption algorithm (although it still uses RC4, which isn't that great), and per frame sequence counters.

WPA or WPA2 Pre-Shared Key

Okay, now we're getting somewhere. Although this is another form of basic security that's really just an add-on to the specifications, WPA or WPA2 Pre-Shared Key (PSK) is a better form of wireless security than any other basic wireless security method mentioned so far. I did say basic.

The PSK verifies users via a password or identifying code (also called a passphrase) on both the client machine and the access point. A client gains access to the network only if its password matches the access point's password. The PSK also provides keying material that TKIP (WPA) or CCMP (AES) uses to generate an encryption key for each packet of transmitted data. While more secure than static WEP, PSK still has a lot in common with static WEP in that the PSK is stored on the client station and can be compromised if the client station is lost or stolen, even though finding this key isn't all that easy to do. It's a definite recommendation to use a strong PSK passphrase that includes a mixture of letters, numbers, and nonalphanumeric characters.

WPA or WPA2 Enterprise

WPA and WPA2 support an enterprise authentication method. This is called Extensible Authentication Protocol (EAP). Understand that EAP isn't a single method, but a framework that enhances the existing 802.1x framework. This framework describes a basic set of actions that will take place, and each EAP type differs in the specifics of how it operates within the framework. These variables include things like whether they use passwords or certificates and the ultimate level of security provided.

Most EAPs comprise three components:

- The authenticator
- The supplicant
- The authentication server

Since the authentication server will typically be a RADIUS server, let me explain RADIUS. Remote Authentication Dial-In User Service (RADIUS) is a networking protocol that offers us several nice security benefits:

- Authorization.
- Centralized access.

Accounting supervision of the users and/or computers that connect to and access our network's services. Once RADIUS has been authenticated, it allows us to specify the type of rights a specific user or workstation has.

- Control over what a device or user can do within the network.
- Creation of a record of all access attempts and actions.

The provision of Authentication, Authorization, and Accounting is called AAA, or Triple A.

The various types of EAPs that can be used in today's networks are as follows:

Local EAP EAP normally uses a RADIUS server as the authentication server in the process, but the AP can be configured as both the authenticator and the authentication server. This process is an arrangement called Local EAP. The user database that's checked to authenticate the users can be local to the AP or it can be an LDAP server like Active Directory.

LEAP Lightweight EAP (LEAP) is a method developed by Cisco early on in the wireless game, back in 2000. It's available in many non-Cisco devices through licensing from Cisco, and it uses only a username and password.

PEAP Whereas EAP-TLS requires certificates on both the server and the stations and EAP-FAST requires certificates on neither, protected EAP, or PEAP, requires one on the server but none on the stations. This EAP method was developed in a rare moment of enlightened cooperation between Microsoft, Cisco, and RSA security.

EAP-TLS EAP-TLS, or EAP Transport Layer Security, is the most secure method, but it's also the most difficult to configure and maintain. To use EAP-TLS, a certificate must be installed on both the authentication server and the client.

EAP-FAST EAP-FAST stands for EAP-Flexible Authentication via Secure Tunneling. EAP-FAST is designed to provide the same level of security as EAP-TLS without the difficulty of managing certificates.

The IEEE 802.11i standard has been sanctioned by the Wi-Fi Alliance and is termed WPA version 2.

802.11i

Although WPA2 was built with the upcoming 802.11i standard in mind, there were some features added when the standard was ratified:

- A list of EAP methods that can be used with the standard.
- AES/CCMP for encryption instead of RC4.
- Better key management. The master key can be cached, permitting a faster reconnect time for the station.

All good—we've got WPA, WPA2, and now 802.11i covered. But how do they compare? Table 14.3 breaks them down:

TABLE 14.3 WPA/WPA/802.11i summary

WPA	WPA2	802.11i
SOHO	Enterprise	Enterprise
802.1x authentication/PSK	802.1x authentication/PSK	802.1x authentication
128-bit RC4 w/TKIP encryption	128-bit AES encryption	128-bit AES encryption
Ad hoc not supported	Ad hoc not supported	Allows ad hoc

Lastly, I want to summarize the implementation techniques we discussed and what authentication and encryption methods each uses. Table 14.4 shows use the implementation methods:

TABLE 14.4 Wireless Security Implementations

Implementation	Authentication	Encryption
WEP	Open or Shared Key	RC4
WPA	PSK	TKIP
WPA2	PSK or 802.1x	TKIP or AES
802.11i	PSK or 802.1x	AES

Summary

Like rock 'n' roll, wireless technologies are here to stay, and for those of us who have come to depend on wireless technologies, it's actually pretty hard to imagine a world without wireless networks—what did we do before cell phones?

So we began this chapter by exploring the essentials and fundamentals of how wireless networks function.

Springing off that foundation, I then introduced you to the basics of wireless RF and the IEEE standards. We discussed 802.11 from its inception through its evolution to current and near future standards and talked about the subcommittees who create them.

All of this leads into a discussion of wireless security—or rather, non-security for the most part, which logically directed us towards the WPA and WPA2 standards, using PSK and 802.1x authentication, and TKIP and AES encryption methods.

Exam Essentials

Understand the IEEE 802.11a specification. 802.11a runs in the 5GHz spectrum, and if you use the 802.11h extensions, you have 23 non-overlapping channels. 802.11a can run up to 54Mbps, but only if you are less than 50 feet from an access point.

Understand the IEEE 802.11b specification. IEEE 802.11b runs in the 2.4GHz range and has three non-overlapping channels. It can handle long distances, but with a maximum data rate of up to 11Mpbs.

Understand the IEEE 802.11g specification. IEEE 802.11g is 802.11b's big brother and runs in the same 2.4GHz range, but it has a higher data rate of 54Mbps if you are less than 100 feet from an access point.

Understand the IEEE 802.11n components. 802.11n uses 40Mhz wide channels to provide more bandwidth, provides MAC efficiency with block acknowledgements, and uses MIMO to allow better throughput and distance at high speeds.

Understand the WVoIP requirements. Wireless VoIP has special requirements and this means we need to create separate VLANs for our data and voice traffic, provide switches with PoE, determine bandwidth needs, and configure QoS.

Written Lab 14

In this section, write the answers to the following questions:

1. What is the maximum data rate of IEEE 802.11b?
2. What is the maximum data rate of IEEE 802.11g?
3. True/False: The TKIP encryption is based on the RC4 algorithm.
4. What is the frequency range of IEEE 802.11b?
5. What is the frequency range of IEEE 802.11g?
6. What is the frequency range of IEEE 802.11a?
7. Which feature of 802.11n provides MAC efficiency?
8. WPA2 uses which encryption method?
9. Which IEEE committee has been sanctioned by WPA and is called WPA2?
10. What device must be on your wired network when running an enterprise EAP solution?

(The answers to Written Lab 14 can be found following the answers to the review questions for this chapter.)

Review Questions

The following questions are designed to test your understanding of this chapter's material. For more information on how to get additional questions, please see this book's Introduction.

1. Which three of the following are EAP types that allow us to use wireless LANs in enterprise networks? (Choose three.)
   A. PEAP
   B. SLEAP
   C. EAP-FAST
   D. Local-EAP
   E. Global-EAP

2. What is the frequency range of the IEEE 802.11b standard?
   A. 2.4Gbps
   B. 5Gbps
   C. 2.4GHz
   D. 5GHz

3. What is the frequency range of the IEEE 802.11a standard?
   A. 2.4Gbps
   B. 5Gbps
   C. 2.4GHz
   D. 5GHz

4. What is the frequency range of the IEEE 802.11g standard?
   A. 2.4Gbps
   B. 5Gbps
   C. 2.4GHz
   D. 5GHz

5. You have finished physically installing an access point on the ceiling of your office. At a minimum, which parameter must be configured on the access point in order to allow a wireless client to operate on it?

   A. AES

   B. PSK

   C. SSID

   D. TKIP

   E. WEP

   F. 802.11i

6. Which encryption type does WPA2 use?

   A. AES-CCMP

   B. PPK via IV

   C. PSK

   D. TKIP/MIC

7. How many non-overlapping channels are available with 802.11b?

   A. 3

   B. 12

   C. 23

   D. 40

8. A single 802.11g access point has been configured and installed in the center of a square-shaped office. A few wireless users are experiencing slow performance and drops while most users are operating at peak efficiency. In the following list, what are three likely causes of this problem? (Choose three.)

   A. Mismatched TKIP encryption

   B. Null SSID

   C. Cordless phones

   D. Mismatched SSID

   E. Metal file cabinets

   F. Antenna type or direction

9. What is the maximum data rate for the 802.11a standard?

   A. 6Mbps

   B. 11Mbps

   C. 22Mbps

   D. 54Mbps

10. What is the maximum data rate for the 802.11g standard?
    A. 6Mbps
    B. 11Mbps
    C. 22Mbps
    D. 54Mbps

11. What is the maximum data rate for the 802.11b standard?
    A. 6Mbps
    B. 11Mbps
    C. 22Mbps
    D. 54Mbps

12. Which two practices help secure the configuration utilities on wireless access points from unauthorized access? (Choose two.)
    A. Assigning a private IP address to the AP
    B. Changing the default SSID value
    C. Configuring a new administrator password
    D. Changing the mixed mode setting to single mode
    E. Configuring traffic filtering

13. A wireless client cannot connect to an 802.11b/g BSS with a b/g wireless card. The client section of the access point does not list any active WLAN clients. What is a possible reason for this?
    A. The incorrect channel is configured on the client.
    B. The client's IP address is on the wrong subnet.
    C. The client has an incorrect pre-shared key.
    D. The SSID is configured incorrectly on the client.

14. Which two features did WPA add to address the inherent weaknesses found in WEP? (Choose two.)
    A. A stronger encryption algorithm
    B. Key mixing using temporal keys
    C. Shared key authentication
    D. A shorter initialization vector
    E. Per frame sequence counter

15. Which two wireless encryption methods are based on the RC4 encryption algorithm? (Choose two.)
    A. WEP
    B. CCKM
    C. AES
    D. TKIP
    E. CCMP

16. Two workers have established wireless communication directly between their wireless laptops. What type of wireless topology has been created by these employees?
    A. BSS
    B. SSID
    C. IBSS
    D. ESS

17. Which two of the following describe the wireless security standard that WPA defines? (choose two)
    A. It specifies the use of dynamic encryption keys that change throughout the users connection time.
    B. It requires that all devices must use the same encryption key.
    C. It can use PSK authentication.
    D. Static keys must be used.

18. Which wireless LAN design ensures that a mobile wireless client will not lose connectivity when moving from one access point to another?
    A. Using adapters and access points manufactured by the same company
    B. Overlapping the wireless cell coverage by at least 10%
    C. Configuring all access points to use the same channel
    D. Utilizing MAC address filtering to allow the client MAC address to authenticate with the surrounding APs

19. You are connecting your access point and it is set to root. What does extended service set ID mean?
    A. That you have more than one access point and they are in the same SSID connected by a distribution system
    B. That you have more than one access point and they are in separate SSIDs connected by a distribution system
    C. That you have multiple access points, but they are placed physically in different buildings
    D. That you have multiple access points, but one is a repeater access point

20. What are three basic parameters to configure on a wireless access point? (Choose three.)
    A. Authentication method
    B. RF Channel
    C. RTS/CTS
    D. SSID
    E. Microwave interference resistance

Answers to Review Questions

1. A, C, D. There are some various flavors of EAP; some are easier to implement than others. The EAP protocols that are correct are PEAP, EAP-FAST, and Local-EAP
2. C. The IEEE 802.11b and IEEE 802.11g standards both run in the 2.4GHz RF range.
3. D. The IEEE 802.11a standard runs in the 5GHz RF range.
4. C. The IEEE 802.11b and IEEE 802.11g standards both run in the 2.4GHz RF range.
5. C. The minimum parameter configured on an AP for a simple WLAN installation is the SSID, although you should set the channel and authentication method as well.
6. A. WPA2 uses AES-CCMP for encryption. WPA uses TKIP.
7. A. The IEEE 802.11b standard provides three non-overlapping channels.
8. C, E, F. Cordless phone interference, antenna type or orientation, and metal filing cabinet reflection of the RF signal can all give rise to connectivity issues.
9. D. The IEEE 802.11a standard provides a maximum data rate of up to 54Mbps.
10. D. The IEEE 802.11g standard provides a maximum data rate of up to 54Mbps.
11. B. The IEEE 802.11b standard provides a maximum data rate of up to 11Mbps.
12. B, C. When setting up an AP, always change the default SSID and administrator password.
13. D. Although this question is cryptic at best, the only possible answer is option D. If the SSID is not being broadcast (which we must assume in this question), the client must be configured with the correct SSID in order to associate to the AP.
14. B, E. WPA uses Temporal Key Integrity Protocol (TKIP), which includes both broadcast key rotation (dynamic keys that change) and sequencing of frames.
15. A, D. Both WEP and TKIP (WPA) use the RC4 algorithm. It is advised to use WPA2 which uses the AES encryption.
16. C. Two wireless hosts directly connected wirelessly is no different then two hosts connecting with a crossover cable. They are both ad-hoc networks, but in wireless, we call this an Independent Basic Service Set (IBSS).
17. A, C. WPA, although using the same RC4 encryption that WEP uses, provides enhancements to the WEP protocol by using dynamic keys that change constantly, as well as providing a Pre-Shared Key method of authentication.
18. B. To create an Extended Service Set (ESS), you need to overlap the wireless BSA from each AP by at least 15% in order to not have a gap in coverage so users do not lose their connection when roaming between APs.

19. A. Extended service set ID means that you have more than one access point and they all are set to the same SSID and all are connected together in the same VLAN or distribution system so users can roam.

20. A, B, D. The three basic parameters to configure when setting up an access point are the SSID, the RF channel, and the authentication method.

Answers to Written Lab 14

1. 11Mbps
2. 54Mbps
3. True
4. 2.4GHz
5. 2.4GHz
6. 5GHz
7. Block acknowledgments
8. AES-CCMP
9. The IEEE 802.11i standard has been sanctioned by WPA and is termed WPA version 2.
10. RADIUS Server

Internet Protocol Version 6 (IPv6)

THE CCNA EXAM TOPICS COVERED IN THIS CHAPTER INCLUDE THE FOLLOWING:

✓ **Implement an IP addressing scheme and IP services to meet network requirements in a medium-size Enterprise branch office network**

- Describe the technological requirements for running IPv6 in conjunction with IPv4 (including: protocols, dual stack, tunneling, etc.)
- Describe IPv6 addresses

I hope you're ready to learn about the nuts and bolts of Internet Protocol version 6 (IPv6), because you're going to get the rub on it in this chapter!

You should have a solid hold on IPv4 by now, but if you think you could use a refresher, just page back to the TCP/IP and subnetting chapters. And if you're not crystal clear on the address problems inherent to IPv4, you really should review Chapter 13, "Network Address Translation (NAT)."

People refer to IPv6 as "the next-generation Internet protocol," and it was originally created as the answer to IPv4's inevitable, looming address-exhaustion crisis. Though you've probably heard a thing or two about IPv6 already, it has been improved even further in the quest to bring us the flexibility, efficiency, capability, and optimized functionality that can truly meet our ever-increasing needs. The capacity of its predecessor, IPv4, pales in comparison—and that's the reason it will eventually fade into history completely.

The IPv6 header and address structure has been completely overhauled, and many of the features that were basically just afterthoughts and addendums in IPv4 are now included as full-blown standards in IPv6. It's seriously well equipped, poised, and ready to manage the mind-blowing demands of the Internet to come.

I promise—really—to make this chapter pretty painless. In fact, you might even find yourself actually enjoying it—I definitely did! Because IPv6 is so complex yet elegant, innovative and chock-full of features, it fascinates me like some weird combination of a brand-new Lamborghini and a riveting futuristic novel. Hopefully you'll experience this chapter as the cool ride that I did writing it!

For up-to-the-minute updates for this chapter, please see `www.lammle.com` and/or `www.sybex.com/go/ccna7e`.

Why Do We Need IPv6?

Well, the short answer is because we need to communicate and our current system isn't really cutting it anymore—kind of like how the Pony Express can't compete with airmail. Just look at how much time and effort we've invested in coming up with slick new ways to conserve bandwidth and IP addresses. We've even come up with Variable Length Subnet Masks (VLSMs) in our struggle to overcome the worsening address drought.

It's reality—the number of people and devices that connect to networks increases each and every day. That's not a bad thing at all—we're finding new and exciting ways to communicate to more people all the time, and that's a good thing. In fact, it's a basic human need. But the forecast isn't exactly blue skies and sunshine because, as I alluded to in this chapter's introduction, IPv4, upon which our ability to communicate is presently dependent, is going to run out of addresses for us to use. IPv4 has only about 4.3 billion addresses available, in theory, and we know that we don't even get to use all of those. Sure, the use of Classless Inter-Domain Routing (CIDR) and Network Address Translation (NAT) has helped to extend the inevitable dearth of addresses, but we will run out of them, and it's going to happen within a few years. China is barely online, and we know there's a huge population of people and corporations there that surely want to be. There are a lot of reports that give us all kinds of numbers, but all you really need to think about to convince yourself that I'm not just being an alarmist is the fact that there are about 6.8 billion people in the world today, and it's estimated that just over 10 percent of that population is connected to the Internet—wow!

That statistic is basically screaming at us the ugly truth that based on IPv4's capacity, every person can't even have a computer—let alone all the other IP devices we use with them. I have more than one computer, and it's pretty likely you do too. And I'm not even including in the mix phones, laptops, game consoles, fax machines, routers, switches, and a mother lode of other devices we use every day! So I think I've made it pretty clear that we've got to do something before we run out of addresses and lose the ability to connect with each other as we know it. And that "something" just happens to be implementing IPv6.

The Benefits and Uses of IPv6

So what's so fabulous about IPv6? Is it really the answer to our coming dilemma? Is it really worth it to upgrade from IPv4? All good questions—you may even think of a few more. Of course, there's going to be that group of people with the time-tested and well-known "resistance to change syndrome," but don't listen to them. If we had done that years ago, we'd still be waiting weeks, even months for our mail to arrive via horseback. Instead, just know that the answer is a resounding YES! Not only does IPv6 give us lots of addresses (3.4×10^{38} = definitely enough), but there are many other features built into this version that make it well worth the cost, time, and effort required to migrate to it. Later in the chapter I'll talk about all that effort in the section called "Migrating to IPv6." In it, I'll cover some of the transition types available to move from version 4 to version 6, and I promise you'll discover that the huge benefits of migrating will vastly outweigh any associated cons.

Today's networks, as well as the Internet, have a ton of unforeseen requirements that simply were not considerations when IPv4 was created. We've tried to compensate with a collection of add-ons that can actually make implementing them more difficult than they would be if they were required by a standard. By default, IPv6 has improved upon and included many of those features as standard and mandatory. One of these sweet new standards is IPSec—a feature that provides end-to-end security and that I'll cover in Chapter 16, "Wide Area Networks."

Another little beauty is known as mobility, and as its name suggests, it allows a device to roam from one network to another without dropping connections.

But it's the efficiency features that are really going to rock the house! For starters, the headers in an IPv6 packet have half the fields, and they are aligned to 64 bits, which gives us some seriously souped-up processing speed—compared to IPv4, lookups happen at light speed! Most of the information that used to be bound into the IPv4 header was taken out, and now you can choose to put it, or parts of it, back into the header in the form of optional extension headers that follow the basic header fields.

And of course there's that whole new universe of addresses (3.4×10^{38}) we talked about already. But where did we get them? Did that Criss Angel Mindfreak dude just show up and, blammo? I mean, that huge proliferation of addresses had to come from somewhere! Well it just so happens that IPv6 gives us a substantially larger address space, meaning the address is a whole lot bigger—four times bigger as a matter of fact! An IPv6 address is actually 128 bits in length, and no worries—I'm going to break down the address piece by piece and show you exactly what it looks like coming up in the section "IPv6 Addressing and Expressions." For now, let me just say that all that additional room permits more levels of hierarchy inside the address space and a more flexible addressing architecture. It also makes routing much more efficient and scalable because the addresses can be aggregated a lot more effectively. And IPv6 also allows multiple addresses for hosts and networks. This is especially important for enterprises jonesing for enhanced availability. Plus, the new version of IP now includes an expanded use of multicast communication (one device sending to many hosts or to a select group), which will also join in to boost efficiency on networks because communications will be more specific.

IPv4 uses broadcasts quite prolifically, causing a bunch of problems, the worst of which is of course the dreaded broadcast storm—an uncontrolled deluge of forwarded broadcast traffic that can bring an entire network to its knees and devour every last bit of bandwidth. Another nasty thing about broadcast traffic is that it interrupts each and every device on the network. When a broadcast is sent out, every machine has to stop what it's doing and respond to the traffic whether the broadcast is meant for it or not.

But smile everyone: There is no such thing as a broadcast in IPv6 because it uses multicast traffic instead. And there are two other types of communication as well: unicast, which is the same as it is in IPv4, and a new type called anycast. Anycast communication allows the same address to be placed on more than one device so that when traffic is sent to the device service addressed in this way, it is routed to the nearest host that shares the same address. This is just the beginning—we'll get more into the various types of communication in the section called "Address Types."

IPv6 Addressing and Expressions

Just as understanding how IP addresses are structured and used is critical with IPv4 addressing, it's also vital when it comes to IPv6. You've already read about the fact that at 128 bits, an IPv6 address is much larger than an IPv4 address. Because of this, as well as the new ways the addresses can be used, you've probably guessed that IPv6 will be more complicated to manage. But no worries! As I said, I'll break down the basics and show you what the address looks like, how you can write it, and what many of its common uses are. It's going to be a little weird at first, but before you know it, you'll have it nailed!

So let's take a look at Figure 15.1, which has a sample IPv6 address broken down into sections.

FIGURE 15.1 IPv6 address example

```
2001:0db8:3c4d:0012:0000:0000:1234:56ab
_____________|____|__________________
Global prefix   Subnet        Interface ID
```

As you can now see, the address is truly much larger—but what else is different? Well, first, notice that it has eight groups of numbers instead of four and also that those groups are separated by colons instead of periods. And hey wait a second... there are letters in that address! Yep, the address is expressed in hexadecimal just like a MAC address is, so you could say this address has eight 16-bit hexadecimal colon-delimited blocks. That's already quite a mouthful, and you probably haven't even tried to say the address out loud yet!

One other thing I want to point out is for when you set up your test network to play with IPv6, because I know you're going to want to do that. When you use a web browser to make an HTTP connection to an IPv6 device, you have to type the address into the browser with brackets around the literal address. Why? Well, a colon is already being used by the browser for specifying a port number. So basically, if you don't enclose the address in brackets, the browser will have no way to identify the information.

Here's an example of how this looks:

```
http://[2001:0db8:3c4d:0012:0000:0000:1234:56ab]/default.html
```

Now obviously if you can, you would rather use names to specify a destination (like www.lammle.com), but even though it's definitely going to be a pain in the rear, we just have to accept the fact that sometimes we have to bite the bullet and type in the address number. So it should be pretty clear that DNS is going to remain extremely important when implementing IPv6.

There are four hexadecimal characters (16 bits) in each IPv6 field, separated by colons.

Shortened Expression

The good news is there are a few tricks to help rescue us when writing these monster addresses. For one thing, you can actually leave out parts of the address to abbreviate it, but to get away with doing that you have to follow a couple of rules. First, you can drop any leading zeros in each of the individual blocks. After you do that, the sample address from earlier would then look like this:

```
2001:db8:3c4d:12:0:0:1234:56ab
```

Okay, that's a definite improvement—at least we don't have to write all of those extra zeros! But what about whole blocks that don't have anything in them except zeros? Well, we can kind of lose those too—at least some of them. Again referring to our sample address, we can remove the two consecutive blocks of zeros by replacing them with a doubled colon, like this:

```
2001:db8:3c4d:12::1234:56ab
```

Cool—we replaced the blocks of all zeros with a doubled colon. The rule you have to follow to get away with this is that you can replace only one contiguous block of such zeros in an address. So if my address has four blocks of zeros and each of them were separated, I just don't get to replace them all; remember, the rule is that you can replace only one contiguous block with a doubled colon. Check out this example:

```
2001:0000:0000:0012:0000:0000:1234:56ab
```

And just know that you *can't* do this:

```
2001::12::1234:56ab
```

Instead, this is the best that you can do:

```
2001::12:0:0:1234:56ab
```

The reason the preceding example is our best shot is that if we remove two sets of zeros, the device looking at the address will have no way of knowing where the zeros go back in. Basically, the router would look at the incorrect address and say, "Well, do I place two blocks into the first set of doubled colons and two into the second set, or do I place three blocks into the first set and one block into the second set?" And on and on it would go because the information the router needs just isn't there.

Address Types

We're all familiar with IPv4's unicast, broadcast, and multicast addresses that basically define who or at least how many other devices we're talking to. But as I mentioned, IPv6 modifies that trio and introduces the anycast. Broadcasts, as we know them, have been eliminated in IPv6 because of their cumbersome inefficiency.

So let's find out what each of these types of IPv6 addressing and communication methods do for us:

Unicast Packets addressed to a unicast address are delivered to a single interface. For load balancing, multiple interfaces across several devices can use the same address, but we'll call that an anycast address. There are a few different types of unicast addresses, but we don't need to get into that here.

Global unicast addresses These are your typical publicly routable addresses, and they're the same as they are in IPv4. Global addresses start at 2000::/3.

Link-local addresses These are like the private addresses in IPv4 in that they're not meant to be routed and they start with FE80::/10. Think of them as a handy tool that gives you the ability to throw a temporary LAN together for meetings or to create a small LAN that's not going to be routed but still needs to share and access files and services locally.

Unique local addresses These addresses are also intended for non-routing purposes over the Internet, but they are nearly globally unique, so it's unlikely you'll ever have one of them overlap. Unique local addresses were designed to replace site-local addresses, so they basically do almost exactly what IPv4 private addresses do—allow communication throughout a site while being routable to multiple local networks. Site-local addresses were denounced as of September 2004.

Multicast Again, same as in IPv4, packets addressed to a multicast address are delivered to all interfaces tuned into the multicast address. Sometimes people call them one-to-many addresses. It's really easy to spot a multicast address in IPv6 because they always start with *FF*. I'll get into greater detail about multicast operation in the section "How IPv6 Works in an Internetwork."

Anycast Like multicast addresses, an anycast address identifies multiple interfaces on multiple devices, but there's a big difference: The anycast packet is delivered to only one device—actually, to the closest one it finds defined in terms of routing distance. And again, this address is special because you can apply a single address to more than one interface. These are referred to as "one-to-nearest" addresses.

You're probably wondering if there are any special, reserved addresses in IPv6 because you know they're there in IPv4. Well there are—plenty of them! Let's go over them now.

Special Addresses

I'm going to list some of the addresses and address ranges that you should definitely make a point to remember because you'll eventually use them. They're all special or reserved for specific use, but unlike IPv4, IPv6 gives us a galaxy of addresses, so reserving a few here and there doesn't hurt a thing!

0:0:0:0:0:0:0:0 Equals ::. This is the equivalent of IPv4's 0.0.0.0 and is typically the source address of a host when you're using DHCP-driven stateful configuration.

0:0:0:0:0:0:0:1 Equals ::1. The equivalent of 127.0.0.1 in IPv4.

0:0:0:0:0:0:192.168.100.1 This is how an IPv4 address would be written in a mixed IPv6/IPv4 network environment.

2000::/3 The global unicast address range.

FC00::/7 The unique local unicast range.

FE80::/10 The link-local unicast range.

FF00::/8 The multicast range.

3FFF:FFFF::/32 Reserved for examples and documentation.

2001:0DB8::/32 Also reserved for examples and documentation.

2002::/16 Used with 6to4 tunneling, which is an IPv4-to-IPv6 transition system—the structure allows IPv6 packets to be transmitted over an IPv4 network without the need to configure explicit tunnels.

We'll get more into this later in "Migrating to IPv6," but for now let me show you how IPv6 actually works in an internetwork. We all know how IPv4 works, so let's see what's new.

How IPv6 Works in an Internetwork

It's time to explore the finer points of IPv6. A great place to start is by showing you how to address a host and what gives it the ability to find other hosts and resources on a network.

I'll also demonstrate a device's ability to automatically address itself—something called stateless autoconfiguration—plus another type of autoconfiguration known as stateful. Keep in mind that stateful autoconfiguration uses a DHCP server in a very similar way to how it's used in an IPv4 configuration. I'll also show you how Internet Control Message Protocol (ICMP) and multicasting works for us on an IPv6 network.

Autoconfiguration

Autoconfiguration is an incredibly useful solution because it allows devices on a network to address themselves with a link-local unicast address as well as a global unicast address. This process happens through first learning the prefix information from the router and then appending the device's own interface address as the interface ID. But where does it get that interface ID? Well, you know every device on an Ethernet network has a physical MAC address, and that's exactly what's used for the interface ID. But since the interface ID in an IPv6 address is 64 bits in length and a MAC address is only 48 bits, where do the extra 16 bits come from? The MAC address is padded in the middle with the extra bits—it's padded with FFFE.

For example, let's say I have a device with a MAC address that looks like this: 0060:d673:1987. After it's been padded, it would look like this: 0260:d6FF:FE73:1987.

So where did that 2 in the beginning of the address come from? Another good question. You see, part of the process of padding, called modified eui-64 (extended unique identifier) format, changes a bit to specify if the address is locally unique or globally unique. And the bit that gets changed is the seventh bit in the address. A bit value of 1 means globally unique, and a bit value of 0 means locally unique, so looking at this example, would you say that this address is globally or locally unique? If you answered that it's a globally unique address, you're right! Trust me, this is going to save you time in addressing your host machines because they communicate with the router to make this happen.

To perform autoconfiguration, a host goes through a basic two-step process:

1. First, the host needs the prefix information (similar to the network portion of an IPv4 address) to configure its interface, so it sends a router solicitation (RS) request for it. This RS is then sent out as a multicast to all routers. The actual information being sent is a type of ICMP message, and like everything in networking, this ICMP message has a number that identifies it. The RS message is ICMP type 133.
2. The router answers back with the required prefix information via a router advertisement (RA). An RA message also happens to be a multicast packet that's sent to the all-nodes multicast address and is ICMP type 134. RA messages are sent on a periodic basis, but the host sends the RS for an immediate response so it doesn't have to wait until the next scheduled RA to get what it needs.

These two steps are shown in Figure 15.2.

FIGURE 15.2 Two steps to IPv6 autoconfiguration

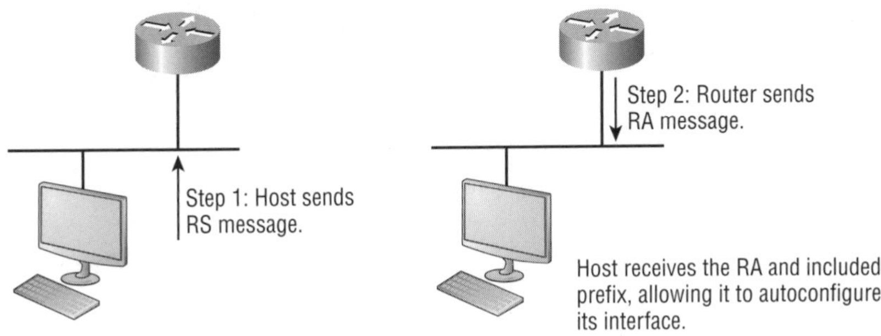
Step 1: Host sends RS message.
Step 2: Router sends RA message.
Host receives the RA and included prefix, allowing it to autoconfigure its interface.

By the way, this type of autoconfiguration is also known as stateless autoconfiguration because it doesn't contact or connect and receive any further information from the other device. We'll get to stateful configuration when we talk about DHCPv6 in a minute.

Now let's take a look at how to configure Cisco routers with IPv6.

Configuring Cisco Routers with IPv6

In order to enable IPv6 on a router, you have to use the `ipv6 unicast-routing` global configuration command:

```
Corp(config)#ipv6 unicast-routing
```

By default, IPv6 traffic forwarding is disabled, so using this command enables it. Also, as you've probably guessed, IPv6 isn't enabled by default on any interfaces either, so we have to go to each interface individually and enable it.

There are a few different ways to do this, but a really easy way is to just add an address to the interface. You use the interface configuration command `ipv6 address <ipv6prefix>/<prefix-length> [eui-64]`to get this done.

Here's an example:

```
Corp(config-if)#ipv6 address 2001:db8:3c4d:1:0260:d6FF.FE73:1987/64
```

You can specify the entire 128-bit global IPv6 address (as shown in the preceding command), or you can use the eui-64 option. Remember, the eui-64 format allows the device to use its MAC address and pad it to make the interface ID. Check it out:

```
Corp(config-if)#ipv6 address 2001:db8:3c4d:1::/64 eui-64
```

As an alternative to typing in an IPv6 address on a router, you can enable the interface instead to permit the application of an automatic link-local address.

Remember, if you only have a link-local address, you will only be able to communicate on that local subnet.

To configure a router so that it uses only link-local addresses, use the `ipv6 enable` interface configuration command:

```
Corp(config-if)#ipv6 enable
```

Okay, now let's dive into stateful IPv6 by configuring a DHCP server for IPv6 use.

DHCPv6

DHCPv6 works pretty much the same way DHCP does in v4, with the obvious difference that it supports the new addressing scheme for IPv6. And it might come as a surprise, but there are a couple of other options that DHCP still provides for us that autoconfiguration doesn't. I'm serious— in autoconfiguration, there's absolutely no mention of DNS servers, domain names, or many of the other options that DHCP has always provided for us via IPv4. This is a big reason it's likely we'll still be using DHCP in IPv6 most of the time.

Upon booting up in IPv4, a client sends out a DHCP discover message looking for a server to give it the information it needs. But remember, in IPv6, the RS and RA process happens first. If there's a DHCPv6 server on the network, the RA that comes back to the client will tell it if DHCP is available for use. If a router isn't found, the client will respond by sending out a DHCP solicit message—a solicit message that's actually a multicast message addressed with a destination of ff02::1:2, meaning all DHCP agents, both servers and relays.

It's good to know that there's some support for DHCPv6 in the Cisco IOS. But it's limited to a stateless DHCP server, meaning it doesn't offer any address management of the pool, plus the options available for configuring that address pool are limited to the DNS, domain name, default gateway, and SIP servers only.

This means that you're definitely going to need some other server around that can supply and dispense all the additional, required information as well as manage the address assignment, if needed.

ICMPv6

IPv4 used ICMP for many things, such as error messages like destination unreachable and troubleshooting functions like Ping and Traceroute. ICMPv6 still does those things for us, but unlike its predecessor, the v6 flavor isn't implemented as a separate layer 3 protocol. It's an integrated part of IPv6 and is carried after the basic IPv6 header information as an extension header. And ICMPv6 adds another cool feature—by default, it prevents IPv6 from doing any fragmentation through an ICMPv6 process called path MTU discovery.

This is how it works: The source node of a connection will send a packet that's equal to the MTU size of its local link's MTU. As this packet traverses the path toward its destination, any link that has an MTU smaller than the size of the current packet will force the intermediate router to send a "packet too big" message back to the source machine. This message tells the source node what the maximum size is that the restrictive link will allow and asks the source to send a new scaled-down packet that can pass through. This process will continue until the destination is finally reached, with the source node now sporting the new path's MTU. So now, when the rest of the data packets are transmitted, they'll be protected from fragmentation.

ICMPv6 now takes over the task of finding the address of other devices on the local link. Address Resolution Protocol used to perform this function for IPv4, but that's been renamed Neighbor Discovery in ICMPv6. This process is accomplished by using a multicast address called the solicited node address, and all hosts join this multicast group when they connect to the network. Part of their IPv6 address (the 24 bits farthest to the right) is added to the end of the multicast address FF02:0:0:0:0:1:FF/104. When this address is queried, the corresponding host will send back its layer 2 address. Devices can find and keep track of other neighbor devices on the network in pretty much the same way. When I talked about RA and RS messages earlier and told you that they use multicast traffic to request and send address information, that too was this function of ICMPv6—specifically, neighbor discovery.

In IPv4, the protocol IGMP was used to allow a host device to tell its local router that it was joining a multicast group and would like to receive the traffic for that group. This IGMP function has been replaced by ICMPv6, and the process has been renamed multicast listener discovery.

IPv6 Routing Protocols

All of the routing protocols we've already discussed have been upgraded for use in IPv6 networks. Also, many of the functions and configurations that we've already learned will be used in almost the same way as they're used now. Knowing that broadcasts have been eliminated in IPv6, it follows that any protocols that use entirely broadcast traffic will go the way of the dodo—but unlike with the dodo, it'll be good to say goodbye to these bandwidth-hogging, performance-annihilating little gremlins!

The routing protocols that we'll still use in IPv6 have new names and a facelift. Let's talk about a few of them now.

First on the list is RIPng (next generation). Those of you who have been in IT for awhile know that RIP has worked very well for us on smaller networks, which happens to be the very reason it didn't get whacked and will still be around in IPv6. And we still have EIGRPv6 because it already had protocol-dependent modules and all we had to do was add a new one to it for the IPv6 protocol. Rounding out our group of protocol survivors is OSPFv3—that's not a typo, it really is v3. OSPF for IPv4 was actually v2, so when it got its upgrade to IPv6, it became OSPFv3.

RIPng

To be honest, the primary features of RIPng are the same as they were with RIPv2. It is still a distance-vector protocol, has a max hop count of 15, and uses split horizon, poison reverse, and other loop avoidance mechanisms, but it now uses UDP port 521 instead of UDP 520.

And it still uses multicast to send its updates too, but in IPv6, it uses FF02::9 for the transport address. This is actually kind of cool since in RIPv2, the multicast address was 224.0.0.9, so the address still has a 9 at the end in the new IPv6 multicast range. In fact, most routing protocols got to keep a little bit of their IPv4 identities like that.

But of course there are differences in the new version or it wouldn't be a new version, would it? We know that routers keep the next-hop addresses of their neighbor routers for every destination network in their routing table. The difference is that with RIPng, the router keeps track of this next-hop address using the link-local address, not a global address.

Probably one of the biggest changes with RIPng (and all of the IPv6 routing protocols for that matter) is the fact that you configure or enable the advertisement of a network from interface configuration mode instead of with a network command in router configuration mode. So in RIPng's case, if you enable it directly on an interface without going into router configuration mode and starting a RIPng process, a new RIPng process will simply be started for you. It will look something like this:

```
Router1(config-if)#ipv6 rip 1 enable
```

That 1 you see in this command is a tag (that can also be named rather than numbered) that identifies the process of RIPng that's running, and as I said, this will start a process of RIPng so you don't have to go into router configuration mode.

But if you need to go to router configuration mode to configure something else like redistribution, you still can. If you do that, it will look like this on your router:

```
Router1(config)#ipv6 router rip 1
Router1(config-rtr)#
```

So just remember that RIPng will pretty much work the same way as with IPv4, with the biggest difference being that it uses the router interface itself instead of using the network command you used to use to enable the interface in order to route the connected network.

EIGRPv6

As with RIPng, EIGRPv6 works much the same as its IPv4 predecessor does—most of the features that EIGRP provided before EIGRPv6 will still be available.

EIGRPv6 is still an advanced distance-vector protocol that has some link-state features. The neighbor discovery process using Hellos still happens, and it still provides reliable communication with Reliable Transport Protocol (RTP) that gives us loop-free fast convergence using the Diffusing Update Algorithm (DUAL).

Hello packets and updates are sent using multicast transmission, and as with RIPng, EIGRPv6's multicast address stayed almost the same. In IPv4 it was 224.0.0.10; in IPv6, it's FF02::A (A = 10 in hexadecimal notation).

But obviously, there are differences between the two versions. Most notably, and just as with RIPng, the use of the network command is gone, and the network and interface to be advertised must be enabled from interface configuration mode. But you still have to use the router configuration mode to enable the routing protocol in EIGRPv6 because the routing process must be literally turned on like an interface with the `no shutdown` command—interesting!

The configuration for EIGRPv6 is going to look like this:

```
Router1(config)#ipv6 router eigrp 10
```

The 10 in this case is still the autonomous system (AS) number. The prompt changes to `(config-rtr)`, and from here you must perform a `no shutdown`:

```
Router1(config-rtr)#no shutdown
```

Other options also can be configured in this mode, such as redistribution.

So now, let's go to the interface and enable IPv6:

```
Router1(config-if)#ipv6 eigrp 10
```

The 10 in the interface command again references the AS number that was enabled in the configuration mode.

Last to check out in our group is what OSPF looks like in the IPv6 routing protocol.

OSPFv3

The new version of OSPF continues the trend of the routing protocols having many similarities with their IPv4 versions.

The foundation of OSPF remains the same—it is still a link-state routing protocol that divides an entire internetwork or autonomous system into areas, making a hierarchy. And just trust me—be really thankful that multi-area OSPF is out of scope for the CCNA objectives—at least, for now! But a few of the options we discussed in Chapter 9, "Enhanced IGRP (EIGRP) and Open Shortest Path First (OSPF)," are going to be a bit different.

In OSPF version 2, the router ID (RID) is determined by the highest IP addresses assigned to the router (or you could assign it). In version 3, you assign the RID and area ID, which are both still 32-bit values but are not found using the IP address anymore because an IPv6 address is 128 bits. Changes regarding how these values are assigned, along with the removal of the IP address information from OSPF packet headers, makes the new version of OSPF capable of being used over almost any Network layer protocol—cool!

Adjacencies and next-hop attributes now use link-local addresses, and OSPFv3 still uses multicast traffic to send its updates and acknowledgments, with the addresses FF02::5 for OSPF routers and FF02::6 for OSPF-designated routers. These new addresses are the replacements for 224.0.0.5 and 224.0.0.6, respectively.

Other, less-flexible IPv4 protocols don't give us the ability that OSPFv2 does to assign specific networks and interfaces into the OSPF process—however, this is something that is still configured under the router configuration process. And with OSPFv3, just as with the other IPv6 routing protocols we've talked about, the interfaces and therefore the networks attached to them are configured directly on the interface in interface configuration mode.

The configuration of OSPFv3 is going to look like this:

```
Router1(config)#ipv6 router osfp 10
Router1(config-rtr)#router-id 1.1.1.1
```

You get to perform some configurations from router configuration mode like summarization and redistribution, but we don't even need to configure OSPFv3 from this prompt if we configure OSPFv3 from the interface.

When the interface configuration is completed, the router configuration process is added automatically and the interface configuration looks like this:

```
Router1(config-if)#ipv6 ospf 10 area 0.0.0.0
```

So, if we just go to each interface and assign a process ID and area—poof, we're done!

With all that behind you, it's now time to move on and learn about how to migrate to IPv6 from IPv4.

Migrating to IPv6

We certainly have talked a lot about how IPv6 works and how we can configure it to work on our networks, but what is doing that going to cost us? And how much work is it really going to take? Good questions for sure, but the answers to them won't be the same for everyone. This is because how much you are going to end up having to pony up is highly dependent upon what you've got going on already in terms of your infrastructure. Obviously, if you've been making your really old routers and switches "last" and therefore have to upgrade every one of them so that they're IPv6 compliant, that could very well turn out to be a good-sized chunk of change! Oh, and that sum doesn't even include server and computer operating systems (OSs) and the blood, sweat, and maybe even tears spent on making all your applications compliant. So, my friend, it could cost you quite a bit! The good news is that unless you've really let things go, many OSs and network devices have been IPv6 compliant for a few years—we just haven't been using all their features until now.

Then there's that other question about the amount of work and time. Straight up—this one could still be pretty intense. No matter what, it's going to take you some time to get all of your systems moved over and make sure that things are working correctly. And if you're talking about a huge network with tons of devices, well, it could take a really long time! But don't panic—that's why migration strategies have been created to allow for a gradual integration. I'm going to show you three of the primary transition strategies available to us. The first is called dual stacking, which allows a device to have both the IPv4 and IPv6 protocol stacks running so it's capable of continuing on with its existing communications and simultaneously run newer IPv6 communications as they're implemented. The next strategy is the 6to4 tunneling approach; this is your choice if you have an all IPv6 network that must communicate over an IPv4 network to reach another IPv6 network. I'll surprise you with the third one just for fun!

Dual Stacking

This is the most common type of migration strategy because, well, it's the easiest on us—it allows our devices to communicate using either IPv4 or IPv6. Dual stacking lets you upgrade your devices and applications on the network one at a time. As more and more hosts and devices on the network are upgraded, more of your communication will happen over IPv6, and after you've arrived—everything's running on IPv6, and you get to remove all the old IPv4 protocol stacks you no longer need.

Plus, configuring dual stacking on a Cisco router is amazingly easy—all you have to do is enable IPv6 forwarding and apply an address to the interfaces already configured with IPv4. It'll look something like this:

```
Corp(config)#ipv6 unicast-routing
Corp(config)#interface fastethernet 0/0
Corp(config-if)#ipv6 address 2001:db8:3c4d:1::/64 eui-64
Corp(config-if)#ip address 192.168.255.1 255.255.255.0
```

But to be honest, it's really a good idea to understand the various tunneling techniques because it'll probably be awhile before we all start running IPv6 as a solo routed protocol.

6to4 Tunneling

6to4 tunneling is really useful for carrying IPv6 packets over a network that's still running IPv4. It's quite possible that you'll have IPv6 subnets or other portions of your network that are all IPv6, and those networks will have to communicate with each other. Not so complicated, but when you consider that you might find this happening over a WAN or some other network that you don't control, well, that could be a bit ugly. So what do we do about this if we don't control the whole tamale? Create a tunnel that will carry the IPv6 traffic for us across the IPv4 network, that's what.

The whole idea of tunneling isn't a difficult concept, and creating tunnels really isn't as hard as you might think. All it really comes down to is snatching the IPv6 packet that's happily traveling across the network and sticking an IPv4 header onto the front of it. Kind of like catch and release fishing, except the fish doesn't get something plastered on its face before being thrown back into the stream.

To get a picture of this, take a look at Figure 15.3.

FIGURE 15.3 Creating a 6to4 tunnel

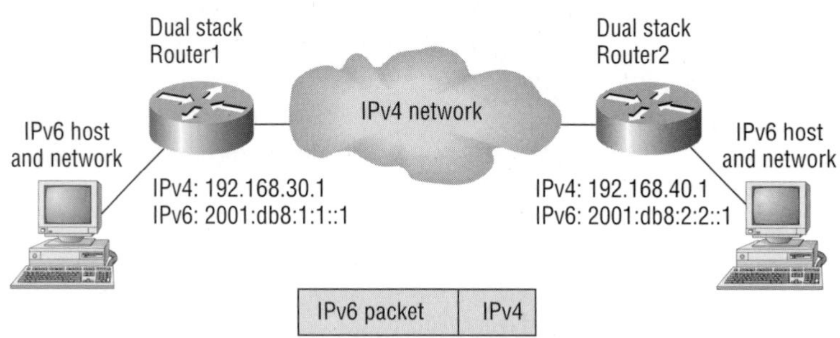

Nice—but to make this happen, we're going to need a couple of dual-stacked routers, which I just demonstrated for you, so you should be good to go. Now we have to add a little configuration to place a tunnel between those routers. Tunnels are pretty simple—we just have to tell each router where the tunnel begins and where we want it to end up. Referring again to Figure 15.3, we'll configure the tunnel on each router:

```
Router1(config)#int tunnel 0
Router1(config-if)#ipv6 address 2001:db8:1:1::1/64
Router1(config-if)#tunnel source 192.168.30.1
Router1(config-if)#tunnel destination 192.168.40.1
Router1(config-if)#tunnel mode ipv6ip

Router2(config)#int tunnel 0
Router2(config-if)#ipv6 address 2001:db8:2:2::1/64
Router2(config-if)#tunnel source 192.168.40.1
Router2(config-if)#tunnel destination 192.168.30.1
Router2(config-if)#tunnel mode ipv6ip
```

With this in place, our IPv6 networks can now communicate over the IPv4 network. Now, I've got to tell you that this is not meant to be a permanent configuration; your goal should still be to run a total, complete IPv6 network end to end.

One important note here—if the IPv4 network that you're traversing in this situation has a NAT translation point, it would absolutely break the tunnel encapsulation we've just created! Over the years, NAT has been upgraded a lot so that it can handle specific protocols and dynamic connections, and without one of these upgrades, NAT likes to demolish most connections. And since this transition strategy isn't present in most NAT implementations, that means trouble.

But there is a way around this little problem, and it's called Teredo, which allows all your tunnel traffic to be placed in UDP packets. NAT doesn't blast away at UDP packets, so they won't get broken as other protocols packets do. So with Teredo in place and your packets disguised under their UDP cloak, the packets will easily slip by NAT alive and well!

NAT-PT

You've probably heard that IPv6 doesn't have any NAT in it, and you've heard correctly—sort of. By itself, IPv6 doesn't have a NAT implementation. But that's only a technicality because there is a transition strategy known as NAT protocol translation (NAT-PT). Just know that you really only use this approach as a last resort because it's not that great of a solution. With it, your IPv4 hosts can communicate only with other IPv4 hosts, and those that are native IPv6, with other IPv6 hosts. What do I mean by that? Well, with a tunneling approach we took IPv6 packets and disguised them as IPv4 packets. With NAT-PT there is no encapsulation—the data of the source packet is removed from one IP type and repackaged as the new destination IP type. Even though being able to configure NAT-PT is beyond the scope of the CCNA objectives, I still want to explain it to you. And just as it is with NAT for IPv4, there are a couple of ways to implement it.

Static NAT-PT provides a one-to-one mapping of a single IPv4 address to a single IPv6 address (sounds like static NAT). There is also Dynamic NAT-PT, which uses a pool of IPv4 addresses to provide a one-to-one mapping with an IPv6 address (sounding kind of familiar). Finally, there is Network Address Port Translation protocol translation (NAPT-PT), which provides a many-to-one mapping of multiple IPv6 addresses to one IPv4 address and a unique port number (well, glad we have that cleared up from NAT).

As you can see, we are not using NAT-PT and NAPT-PT to translate a public and private IPv6 address as we did with IPv4 NAT, but rather between IPv4 and IPv6. Again, this should be used as an absolute last resort. In most cases a tunneling approach will work much better and without the headache of this configuration and system overhead.

Summary

Holy output! Now that is what I call a fun chapter. I really hope you found this chapter as rewarding and interesting as I did. The best thing you can do to learn IPv6 is to nick some routers and just have a go at it!

In this chapter, I covered the very basics of IPv6 and how to make IPv6 work within a Cisco internetwork. As you now know by reading this chapter, even when discussing and configuring the basics, there is a lot to understand—and we just scratched the surface. But trust me when I say this—you now know more than you'll need to meet the CCNA objectives.

I began by talking about why we need IPv6 and the benefits associated with it. I followed that up by covering addressing with IPv6 as well as how to use the shortened expressions. And during the talk on addressing with IPv6, I showed you the different address types, plus the special addresses reserved in IPv6.

IPv6 will mostly be deployed automatically, meaning hosts will use autoconfiguration, so I discussed how IPv6 uses autoconfiguration and how it comes into play when configuring a Cisco router. And as with IPv4, we can use a DHCP server to the router to provide options to hosts—not necessarily IPv6 addresses, but options like a DNS server address.

ICMP is extremely important with IPv6, and I discussed in detail how ICMP works with IPv6, followed by how to configure RIP, EIGRP, and OSPF with IPv6.

Migrating to IPv6 is no small matter either, and I went over the pros and cons of doing this. I told you about three migration strategies—dual stacking, tunneling using both IPv4 and IPv6, and a third approach, NAT-PT, to be used only as a last resort.

Exam Essentials

Understand why we need IPv6. Without IPv6, the world would be depleted of IP addresses.

Understand link-local. Link-local is like an IPv4 private IP address, but it can't be routed at all, not even in your organization.

Understand unique local. This, like link-local, is like a private IP address in IPv4 and cannot be routed to the Internet. However, the difference between link-local and unique local is that unique local can be routed within your organization or company.

Remember IPv6 addressing. IPv6 addressing is not like IPv4 addressing. IPv6 addressing has much more address space and is 128 bits long, and represented in hexadecimal, unlike IPv4, which is only 32 bits long and represented in decimal.

Written Lab 15

In this section, write the answers to the following IPv6 questions:

1. Which type of packet is addressed and delivered to only a single interface?
2. Which type of address is used just like a regular public routable address in IPv4?
3. Which type of address is not meant to be routed?
4. Which type of address is not meant to be routed to the Internet but is still globally unique?
5. Which type of address is meant to be delivered to multiple interfaces?
6. Which type of address identifies multiple interfaces, but packets are delivered only to the first address it finds?

7. Which routing protocol uses multicast address FF02::5?
8. IPv4 had a loopback address of 127.0.0.1. What is the IPv6 loopback address?
9. What does a link-local address always start with?
10. What does a unique local unicast range start with?

(The answers to Written Lab 15 can be found following the answers to the review questions for this chapter.)

Review Questions

The following questions are designed to test your understanding of this chapter's material. For more information on how to get additional questions, please see this book's Introduction.

1. Which of the following is true when describing a global unicast address?
   A. Packets addressed to a unicast address are delivered to a single interface.
   B. These are your typical publicly routable addresses, just like a regular publicly routable address in IPv4.
   C. These are like private addresses in IPv4 in that they are not meant to be routed over the Internet.
   D. These addresses are meant for nonrouting purposes, but they are almost globally unique, so it is unlikely they will have an address overlap.
2. Which of the following is true when describing a unicast address?
   A. Packets addressed to a unicast address are delivered to a single interface.
   B. These are your typical publicly routable addresses, just like a regular publicly routable address in IPv4.
   C. These are like private addresses in IPv4 in that they are not meant to be routed.
   D. These addresses are meant for nonrouting purposes, but they are almost globally unique, so it is unlikely they will have an address overlap.
3. Which of the following is true when describing a link-local address?
   A. Packets addressed to a broadcast address are delivered to a single interface.
   B. These are your typical publicly routable addresses, just like a regular publicly routable address in IPv4.
   C. These are like private addresses in IPv4 in that they are not meant to be routed over the Internet.
   D. These addresses are meant for nonrouting purposes, but they are almost globally unique, so it is unlikely they will have an address overlap.
4. Which of the following is true when describing a unique local address?
   A. Packets addressed to a unique local address are delivered to a single interface.
   B. These are your typical publicly routable addresses, just like a regular publicly routable address in IPv4.
   C. These are like private addresses in IPv4 in that they are not meant to be routed.
   D. These addresses are not meant for Internet routing purposes, but they are unique, so it is unlikely they will have an address overlap.

5. Which of the following is true when describing a multicast address?
   A. Packets addressed to a multicast address are delivered to a single interface.
   B. Packets are delivered to all interfaces identified with the address. This is also called a one-to-many address.
   C. A multicast address identifies multiple interfaces and is delivered to only one address. This address can also be called one-to-one-of-many.
   D. These addresses are meant for nonrouting purposes, but they are almost globally unique, so it is unlikely they will have an address overlap.

6. Which of the following is true when describing an anycast address?
   A. Packets addressed to an anycast address are delivered to a single interface.
   B. Packets are delivered to all interfaces identified by the address. This is also called a one-to-many address.
   C. This address identifies multiple interfaces and the anycast packet is only delivered to one device. This address can also be called one-to-one-of-many.
   D. These addresses are meant for nonrouting purposes, but they are almost globally unique, so it is unlikely they will have an address overlap.

7. You want to ping the loopback address of your IPv6 local host. What will you type?
   A. `ping 127.0.0.1`
   B. `ping 0.0.0.0`
   C. `ping ::1`
   D. `trace 0.0.::1`

8. What two multicast addresses does OSPFv3 use? (Choose two.)
   A. FF02::A
   B. FF02::9
   C. FF02::5
   D. FF02::6

9. What multicast addresses does RIPng use?
   A. FF02::A
   B. FF02::9
   C. FF02::5
   D. FF02::6

10. What multicast addresses does EIGRPv6 use?
   A. FF02::A
   B. FF02::9
   C. FF02::5
   D. FF02::6

11. To enable RIPng, which of the following would you use?
    A. `Router1(config-if)# ipv6 ospf 10 area 0.0.0.0`
    B. `Router1(config-if)#ipv6 router rip 1`
    C. `Router1(config)# ipv6 router eigrp 10`
    D. `Router1(config-rtr)#no shutdown`
    E. `Router1(config-if)#ipv6 eigrp 10`
12. To enable EIGRP, which three of the following would you use? (Choose three.)
    A. `Router1(config-if)# ipv6 ospf 10 area 0.0.0.0`
    B. `Router1(config-if)#ipv6 router rip 1`
    C. `Router1(config)# ipv6 router eigrp 10`
    D. `Router1(config-rtr)#no shutdown`
    E. `Router1(config-if)#ipv6 eigrp 10`
13. To enable OSPFv3, which of the following would you use?
    A. `Router1(config-if)# ipv6 ospf 10 area 0.0.0.0`
    B. `Router1(config-if)#ipv6 router rip 1`
    C. `Router1(config)# ipv6 router eigrp 10`
    D. `Router1(config-rtr)#no shutdown`
    E. `Router1(config-if)#ospf ipv6 10 area 0`
14. Which of the following statements about IPv6 addresses are true? (Choose two.)
    A. Leading zeros are required.
    B. Two colons (::) are used to represent successive hexadecimal fields of zeros.
    C. Two colons (::) are used to separate fields.
    D. A single interface will have multiple IPv6 addresses of different types.
15. What two statements about IPv4 and IPv6 addresses are true? (Choose two.)
    A. An IPv6 address is 32 bits long, represented in hexidecimal.
    B. An IPv6 address is 128 bits long, represented in decimal.
    C. An IPv4 address is 32 bits long, represented in decimal.
    D. An IPv6 address is 128 bits long, represented in hexidecimal.
16. Which of the following descriptions about IPv6 is correct?
    A. Addresses are not hierarchical and are assigned at random.
    B. Broadcasts have been eliminated and replaced with multicasts.
    C. There are 2.7 billion addresses.
    D. An interface can only be configured with one IPv6 address.

17. How many bits are in an IPv6 address field?
    A. 24
    B. 4
    C. 3
    D. 16
    E. 32
    F. 128
18. Which of the following correctly describe characteristics of IPv6 unicast addressing? (Choose two.)
    A. Global addresses start with 2000::/3.
    B. Link-local addresses start with FF00::/10.
    C. Link-local addresses start with FE00:/12.
    D. There is only one loopback address and it is ::1.
19. Which of the following statements are true of IPv6 address representation? (Choose two.)
    A. The first 64 bits represent the dynamically created interface ID.
    B. A single interface may be assigned multiple IPv6 addresses of any type.
    C. Every IPv6 interface contains at least one loopback address.
    D. Leading zeroes in an IPv6 16-bit hexadecimal field are mandatory.
20. Which of the following are IPv6 translation mechanisms? (Choose three.)
    A. 6to4 tunneling
    B. GRE tunneling
    C. ISATAP tunneling
    D. Teredo tunneling

Answers to Review Questions

1. B. Unlike unicast addresses, global unicast addresses are meant to be routed.

2. A. Packets addressed to a unicast address are delivered to a single interface. For load balancing, multiple interfaces can use the same address.

3. C. Link-local addresses are meant for throwing together a temporary LAN for meetings or a small LAN that is not going to be routed but needs to share and access files and services locally.

4. D. These addresses are meant for nonrouting purposes like link-local, but they are almost globally unique, so it is unlikely they will have an address overlap. Unique local addresses were designed as a replacement for site-local addresses.

5. B. Packets addressed to a multicast address are delivered to all interfaces identified with the multicast address, the same as in IPv4. It is also called a one-to-many address. You can always tell a multicast address in IPv6 because multicast addresses always start with *FF*.

6. C. Anycast addresses identify multiple interfaces, which is somewhat similar to multicast addresses; however, the big difference is that the anycast packet is only delivered to one address, the first one it finds defined in the terms of routing distance. This address can also be called one-to-one-of-many.

7. C. The loopback address with IPv4 is 127.0.0.1. With IPv6, that address is ::1.

8. C, D. Adjacencies and next-hop attributes now use link-local addresses, and OSPFv3 still uses multicast traffic to send its updates and acknowledgments with the addresses FF02::5 for OSPF routers and FF02::6 for OSPF designated routers. These are the replacements for 224.0.0.5 and 224.0.0.6, respectively.

9. B. RIPng uses the multicast IPv6 address of FF02::9. If you remember the multicast addresses for IPv4, the numbers at the end of each IPv6 address are the same.

10. A. EIGRPv6's multicast address stayed very near the same. In IPv4 it was 224.0.0.10; now it is FF02::A (A=10 in decimal notation).

11. B. It's pretty simple to enable RIPng for IPv6. You configure it right on the interface where you want RIP to run with the `ipv6 router rip` *`number`* command.

12. C, D, E. Unlike RIPng and OSPFv3, you need to configure EIGRP both from global configuration mode, router config mode, and interface mode, and you have to enable the protocol in router configuration with the `no shutdown` command.

13. A. To enable OSPFv3, you enable the protocol at the interface level as with RIPng. The command string is `ipv6 ospf` *`process-id`* `area` *`area-id`*.

14. B, D. To shorten the written length of an IPv6 address, successive fields of zeros may be replaced by double colons. In trying to shorten the address further, leading zeros may also be removed. Just as with IPv4, a single device's interface can have more than one address; with IPv6 there are more types of addresses and the same rule applies. There can be link-local, global unicast, multicast, and anycast addresses all assigned to the same interface.

15. C, D. IPv4 addresses are 32 bits long and are represented in decimal format. IPv6 addresses are 128 bits long and represented in hexadecimal format.

16. B. There are no broadcasts with IPv6. Unicast, multicast, anycast, global, and link-local unicast are used.

17. D. There are 16 bits (four hex characters) in an IPv6 field.

18. A, D. Global addresses start with 2000::/3, link-locals start with FE80::/10, loopback is ::1, and unspecified is just two colons (::). Each interface will have a loopback address automatically configured.

19. B, C. If you verify your IP configuration on your host, you'll see that you have multiple IPv6 addresses, including a loopback address. The last 64-bits represent the dynamically created interface ID, and leading zeros are not mandatory in a 16-bit IPv6 field.

20. A, C, D. 6to4, ISATAP (dual stack), and Teredo are translation tunnel mechanisms.

Answers to Written Lab 15

1. Unicast
2. Global unicast
3. Link-local
4. Unique local (used to be called site-local)
5. Multicast
6. Anycast
7. OSPFv3
8. ::1
9. FE80::/10
10. FC00:: /7

Wide Area Networks

THE CCNA EXAM TOPICS COVERED IN THIS CHAPTER INCLUDE THE FOLLOWING:

✓ **Implement and verify WAN links**

- Describe different methods for connecting to a WAN
- Configure and verify a basic WAN serial connection
- Configure and verify Frame Relay on Cisco routers
- Troubleshoot WAN implementation issues
- Describe VPN technology (including: importance, benefits, role, impact, components)
- Configure and verify a PPP connection between Cisco routers

✓ **Describe how a network works**

- Differentiate between LAN/WAN operation and features

The Cisco IOS supports a ton of different wide area network (WAN) protocols that help you extend your local LANs to other LANs at remote sites. And I don't think I have to tell you how positively essential information exchange between disparate sites is these days—it's vital! But even so, it wouldn't exactly be cost effective or efficient to install your own cable and connect all of your company's remote locations yourself, now would it? A much better way to go about doing this is to simply lease the existing installations that service providers already have in place and save big time.

So it follows that I'm going to discuss the various types of connections, technologies, and devices used in accordance with WANs in this chapter. We'll also get into how to implement and configure High-Level Data-Link Control (HDLC), Point-to-Point Protocol (PPP), and Frame Relay. I'll cover Point-to-Point Protocol over Ethernet (PPPoE), cable, DSL, MultiProtocol Label Switching (MPLS), MetroEthernet, and last mile and long range WAN technologies. I'll also introduce you to WAN security concepts, tunneling, and virtual private network basics.

Just so you know, I'm not going to cover every type of Cisco WAN support here—again, the focus of this book is to equip you with everything you need to successfully meet the CCNA objectives. Because of that, I'm going to focus on cable, DSL, HDLC, PPP, PPPoE, MetroEthernet, MPLS, and Frame Relay. Then I'm going to wrap the chapter up with a solid introduction to VPNs.

But first things first—let's begin with an exploration into WAN basics.

For up-to-the-minute updates for this chapter, check out `www.lammle.com` and/or `www.sybex.com/go/ccna7e`.

Introduction to Wide Area Networks

So what, exactly, is it that makes something a *wide area network (WAN)* instead of a local area network (LAN)? Well, there's obviously the distance thing, but these days, wireless LANs can cover some serious turf. What about bandwidth? Well, here again, some really big pipes can be had for a price in many places, so that's not it either. So what the heck is it then?

One of the main ways a WAN differs from a LAN is that while you generally own a LAN infrastructure, you usually lease a WAN infrastructure from a service provider. To be honest, modern technologies even blur this definition, but it still fits neatly into the context of Cisco's exam objectives.

Anyway, I've already talked about the data link that you usually own (Ethernet), but now we're going to find out about the kind you usually don't own—the type most often leased from a service provider.

The key to understanding WAN technologies is to be familiar with the different WAN terms and connection types commonly used by service providers to join your LAN networks together.

Defining WAN Terms

Before you run out and order a WAN service type from a provider, it would be a really good idea to understand the following terms that service providers typically use, as shown in Figure 16.1:

Customer premises equipment (CPE) *Customer premises equipment (CPE)* is equipment that's typically (but not always) owned by the subscriber and located on the subscriber's premises.

Demarcation point The *demarcation point* is the precise spot where the service provider's responsibility ends and the CPE begins. It's generally a device in a telecommunications closet owned and installed by the telecommunications company (telco). It's your responsibility to cable (extended demarc) from this box to the CPE, which is usually a connection to a CSU/DSU or ISDN interface.

Local loop The *local loop* connects the demarc to the closest switching office, which is called a central office.

Central office (CO) This point connects the customer's network to the provider's switching network. Good to know is that a *central office (CO)* is sometimes referred to as a *point of presence (POP)*.

Toll network The *toll network* is a trunk line inside a WAN provider's network. This network is a collection of switches and facilities owned by the ISP.

Definitely familiarize yourself with these terms, what they represent, and where they are found in Figure 16.1, because they're crucial to understanding WAN technologies.

FIGURE 16.1 WAN terms

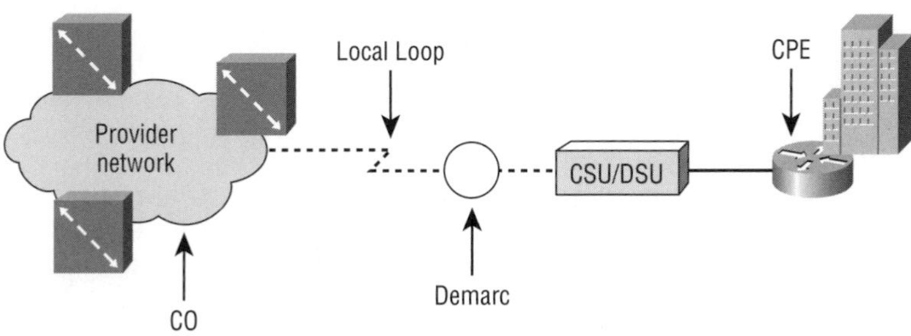

WAN Connection Bandwidth

There are some basic bandwidth terms that we use for our WAN connections:

Digital Signal 0 (DS0) This is the basic digital signaling rate of 64Kbps, equivalent to one channel. Europe uses the E0 and Japan uses the J0 to reference the same channel speed. Typically used in a T-carrier transmission, this is the generic term used by several multiplexed digital carrier systems. This is the smallest capacity digital circuit. 1 DS0 = 1 voice/data line.

T1 Also referred to as a DS1, this contains 24 DS0 circuits bundled together with a total bandwidth of 1.544Mbps.

E1 European equivalent of the T1. Contains 30 DS0 circuits bundled together with a bandwidth of 2.048Mbps.

T3 Referred to as a DS3, this has 28 DS1s bundled together, or 672 DS0s, with a bandwidth of 44.736Mbps.

OC-3 Optical Carrier (OC) 3, uses fiber, is made up of three DS3s bundled together, and contains 2,016 DS0s with a total bandwidth of 155.52Mbps.

OC-12 Optical Carrier 12 is make up of four OC-3s bundled together and contains 8,064 DS0s with a total bandwidth of 622.08Mbps.

OC-48 Optical Carrier 48 is made up of four OC12s bundled together and contains 32,256 DS0s with a total bandwidth of 2488.32Mbps.

WAN Connection Types

As you're probably aware, a WAN can use a number of different connection types, and I'm going to introduce you to each of the various types of WAN connections you'll find on the market today. Figure 16.2 shows the different WAN connection types that can be used to connect your LANs (DTE) together over a DCE network.

Here's a list explaining the different WAN connection types:

Leased lines (dedicated) These are usually referred to as a *point-to-point* or dedicated connection. A *leased line* is a preestablished WAN communications path that goes from the CPE through the DCE switch, then over to the CPE of the remote site. The CPE enables DTE networks to communicate at any time with no cumbersome setup procedures to muddle through before transmitting data. When you've got plenty of cash, this is really the way to go because it uses synchronous serial lines up to 45Mbps. HDLC and PPP encapsulations are frequently used on leased lines; I'll go over them with you in detail in a bit.

Circuit switching When you hear the term *circuit switching*, think phone call. The big advantage is cost— most POTS and ISDN dial-up connections are flat rate. No data can transfer before an end-to-end connection is established. Circuit switching uses dial-up modems or ISDN and is used for low-bandwidth data transfers. Okay—I know what you're thinking: "Modems? Did he say modems? Aren't those only in museums by now?" After all, with all the wireless technologies available, who would use a modem these days? Well, some people do have ISDN and it is still viable (and I do suppose someone does use a modem now and then), but circuit switching can be used in some of the newer WAN technologies as well.

Packet switching This is a WAN switching method that allows you to share bandwidth with other companies to save money. *Packet switching* can be thought of as a network that's designed to look like a leased line yet charges you more like circuit switching. But less cost isn't always better—there's definitely a downside: If you need to transfer data constantly, just forget about this option. Instead, get yourself a leased line. Packet switching will only really work for you if your data transfers are the bursty type—not continuous. Frame Relay and X.25 are packet-switching technologies with speeds that can range from 56Kbps up to T3 (45Mbps).

FIGURE 16.2 WAN connection types

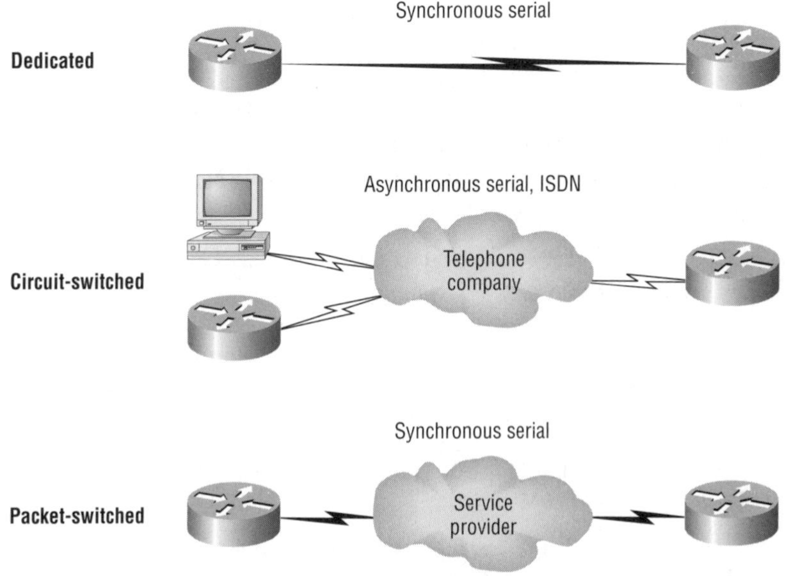

MultiProtocol Label Switching (MPLS) uses a combination of both circuit switching and packet switching, but it's not within the scope of this book's topics. Even so, after you pass your CCNA exam, it would be well worth your time to look into MPLS, so I'll talk about MPLS briefly in a minute.

WAN Support

Basically, Cisco just supports HDLC, PPP, and Frame Relay on its serial interfaces, and you can see this with the `encapsulation ?` command from any serial interface (your output may vary depending on the IOS version you are running):

```
Corp#config t
Corp(config)#int s0/0/0
```

```
Corp(config-if)#encapsulation ?
  atm-dxi       ATM-DXI encapsulation
  frame-relay   Frame Relay networks
  hdlc          Serial HDLC synchronous
  lapb          LAPB (X.25 Level 2)
  ppp           Point-to-Point protocol
  smds          Switched Megabit Data Service (SMDS)
  x25           X.25
```

Understand that if I had other types of interfaces on my router, I would have other encapsulation options, and remember you can't configure an Ethernet encapsulation on a serial interface.

Next, I'm going to define the most prominently known WAN protocols used today: Frame Relay, ISDN, LAPB, LAPD, HDLC, PPP, PPPoE, Cable, DSL, MPLS, and ATM. Just so you know, the only WAN protocols you'll usually find configured on a serial interface are HDLC, PPP, and Frame Relay, but who said we're stuck with using only serial interfaces for wide area connections? We're starting to see a lot less of serial connections today since they are not as scalable or cost effective as a FastEthernet connection to your ISP, for example.

The rest of the chapter is going to be dedicated to explaining, in depth, how cable, DSL, and basic WAN protocols work plus how to configure them with Cisco routers. But since they're important in the world beyond the latest CCNA exam objectives, I'm still going to briefly talk about ISDN, LAPB, LAPD, MPLS, ATM, and DWDM. If any of them happen to pop up in the exam objectives, no worries, I promise you'll immediately find an update regarding the information at `www.lammle.com`.

Frame Relay A packet-switched technology that made its debut in the early 1990s, *Frame Relay* is a high-performance Data Link and Physical layer specification. It's pretty much a successor to X.25, except that much of the technology in X.25 used to compensate for physical errors (noisy lines) has been eliminated. An upside to Frame Relay is that it can be more cost effective than point-to-point links, plus it typically runs at speeds of 64Kbps up to 45Mbps (T3). Another Frame Relay benefit is that it provides features for dynamic bandwidth allocation and congestion control.

ISDN *Integrated Services Digital Network (ISDN)* is a set of digital services that transmit voice and data over existing phone lines. ISDN offers a cost-effective solution for remote users who need a higher-speed connection than analog POTS dial-up links can give them, and it's also a good choice to use as a backup link for other types of links, such as Frame Relay or T1 connections.

LAPB *Link Access Procedure, Balanced (LAPB)* was created to be a connection-oriented protocol at the Data Link layer for use with X.25, but it can also be used as a simple data link transport. A not-so-good characteristic of LAPB is that it tends to create a tremendous amount of overhead due to its strict time-out and windowing techniques.

LAPD *Link Access Procedure, D-Channel (LAPD)* is used with ISDN at the Data Link layer (layer 2) as a protocol for the D (signaling) channel. LAPD was derived from the Link Access Procedure, Balanced (LAPB) protocol and is designed primarily to satisfy the signaling requirements of ISDN basic access.

HDLC *High-Level Data-Link Control (HDLC)* was derived from Synchronous Data Link Control (SDLC), which was created by IBM as a Data Link connection protocol. HDLC works at the Data Link layer and creates very little overhead compared to LAPB.

Generic HDLC wasn't intended to encapsulate multiple Network layer protocols across the same link—the HDLC header doesn't contain any identification about the type of protocol being carried inside the HDLC encapsulation. Because of this, each vendor that uses HDLC has its own way of identifying the Network layer protocol, meaning each vendor's HDLC is proprietary with regard to its specific equipment.

PPP *Point-to-Point Protocol (PPP)* is a pretty famous, industry-standard protocol. Because all multiprotocol versions of HDLC are proprietary, PPP can be used to create point-to-point links between different vendors' equipment. It uses a Network Control Protocol field in the Data Link header to identify the Network layer protocol being carried and allows authentication and multilink connections to be run over asynchronous and synchronous links.

PPPoE *Point-to-Point Protocol over Ethernet* encapsulates PPP frames in Ethernet frames and is usually used in conjunction with xDSL services. It gives you a lot of the familiar PPP features like authentication, encryption, and compression, but there's a downside—it has a lower maximum transmission unit (MTU) than standard Ethernet does, and if your firewall isn't solidly configured, this little attribute can really give you some grief!

Still somewhat popular in the United States, PPPoE's main feature is that it adds a direct connection to Ethernet interfaces while providing DSL support as well. It's often used by many hosts on a shared Ethernet interface for opening PPP sessions to various destinations via at least one bridging modem.

Cable In a modern hybrid fiber-coaxial HFC network, typically 500 to 2,000 active data subscribers are connected to a certain cable network segment, all sharing the upstream and downstream bandwidth. *HFC* is a telecommunications industry term for a network that incorporates both optical fiber and coaxial cable to create a broadband network. The actual bandwidth for Internet service over a cable TV (CATV) line can be up to about 27Mbps on the download path to the subscriber, with about 2.5Mbps of bandwidth on the upload path. Typically users get an access speed from 256Kbps to 6Mbps. This data rate varies greatly throughout the U.S.

DSL Digital subscriber line is a technology used by traditional telephone companies to deliver advanced services (high-speed data and sometimes video) over twisted-pair copper telephone wires. It typically has lower data-carrying capacity than HFC networks, and data speeds can be limited in range by line lengths and quality. Digital subscriber line is not a complete end-to-end solution but rather a Physical layer transmission technology like dial-up, cable, or wireless. DSL connections are deployed in the last mile of a local telephone network—the local loop. The connection is set up between a pair of DSL modems on either end of a copper wire that is between the customer premises equipment (CPE) and the Digital Subscriber Line Access Multiplexer (DSLAM). A DSLAM is the device located at the provider's central office (CO) and concentrates connections from multiple DSL subscribers.

MPLS *MultiProtocol Label Switching (MPLS)* is a data-carrying mechanism that emulates some properties of a circuit-switched network over a packet-switched network. MPLS is a switching mechanism that imposes labels (numbers) to packets and then uses those labels to forward packets. The labels are assigned on the edge of the MPLS network, and forwarding inside the MPLS network is done solely based on labels. Labels usually correspond to a path to layer 3 destination addresses (equal to IP destination-based routing). MPLS was designed to support forwarding of protocols other than TCP/IP. Because of this, label switching within the network is performed the same regardless of the layer 3 protocol. In larger networks, the result of MPLS labeling is that only the edge routers perform a routing lookup. All the core routers forward packets based on the labels, which makes forwarding the packets through the service provider network faster. (Most companies are replacing their Frame Relay networks with MPLS service today.)

ATM Asynchronous Transfer Mode (ATM) was created for time-sensitive traffic, providing simultaneous transmission of voice, video, and data. ATM uses cells that are a fixed 53 bytes long instead of packets. It also can use isochronous clocking (external clocking) to help the data move faster. Typically, if you are running Frame Relay today, you will be running Frame Relay over ATM.

DWDM Dense Wavelength Division Multiplexing is optical technology used to increase bandwidth using fiber backbones. DWDM works by combining and transmitting multiple signals simultaneously at different wavelengths on the same fiber link, creating a type of multilink with the signals running down the fiber. In theory, a 1.5Gbs link could have the capacity of 10Mbps. An advantage of DWDM is that it is both protocol and bit-rate independent and can run with IP over ATM, SONET, and even Ethernet.

Cable and DSL

Okay, before I talk about the principal serial encapsulation connections used on Cisco routers (HDLC, PPP, and Frame Relay), I'm going to discuss cable modems and DSL (including ADSL and PPPoE) as solutions for connections to wide area networks because I think it will really help you understand the practical differences between DSL and cable modem networking.

DSL and cable Internet services truly do have a lot in common, but they still have some basic, essential differences that are important for you to understand:

Speed Most would say that cable is faster than DSL Internet, but cable doesn't always win the race in real-world use.

Security DSL and cable are based on different network security models, and until recently, cable has been the reputed loser in this contest. But now, it's pretty much a toss-up, and both offer adequate security that meets the needs of most users. And when I say adequate, I mean that there are still some very real security issues relating to both alternatives, no matter what your ISP says!

Popularity Cable Internet is definitely "best in show" in the U.S., but DSL is beginning to catch up.

Customer satisfaction Here, the reverse is true—in the U.S., DSL is top dog. But still, do you know anyone that's really totally satisfied with their ISP?

Figure 16.3 shows how a connection can terminate from modems to either a PC directly or a router. Typically, your router would run DHCP on that interface as well as PPPoE. Both DSL and cable high-speed Internet services are available to millions of residential and business consumers worldwide, but in some areas, only one (sometimes neither) service is available.

FIGURE 16.3 Broadband access using cable or DSL

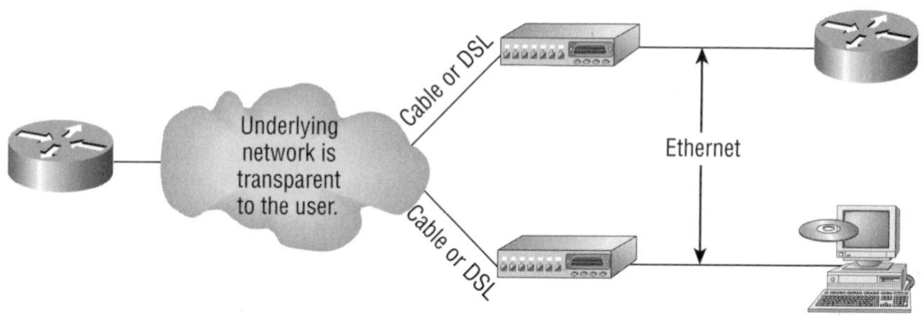

Surprisingly, some of the differences between DSL and cable modem have nothing to do with the actual technologies—it comes down to the individual ISP. All other things being equal, issues like cost, reliability, and quality of customer support for both installation and maintenance issues vary significantly from one provider to the next.

Cable

Cable is a great cost-effective connection for a small office or home office, or SOHO—yes, there is an acronym for everything! And even in larger organizations, cable (or DSL for that matter) can be great to have as a backup link.

Here are a few cable network terms:

Headend This is where all cable signals are received, processed, and formatted. The signals are then transmitted over the distribution network from the headend.

Distribution network These are relatively small service areas that usually range in size from 100 to 2,000 customers. They're typically composed of a mixed, fiber-coaxial, or

HFC architecture, with optical fiber substituting for the distribution network's trunk portion. The fiber forms both the connection from the headend and an optical node that changes light to radio frequency (RF) signals that are then distributed through a coaxial cable throughout the specific area being serviced.

DOCSIS (Data Over Cable Service Interface Specification) All cable modems and like devices have to measure up to this standard.

Figure 16.4 shows where you would find the various types of networks and how most of the terms I just listed would be used in a network diagram.

FIGURE 16.4 Cable network and terms

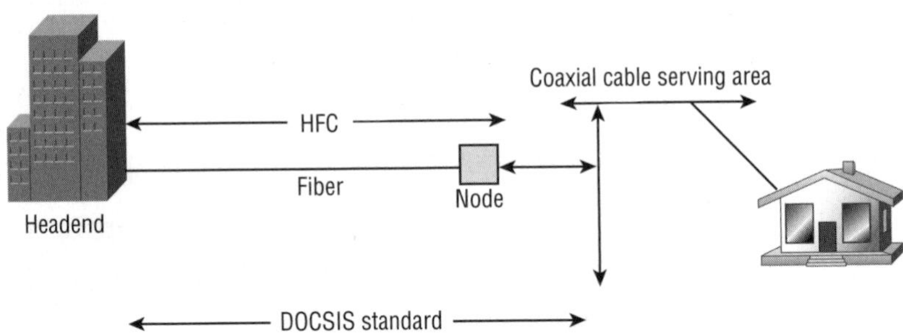

The problem is that ISPs often use a fiber-optic network that extends from the cable operator's master headend, sometimes even to regional headends, out to a neighborhood's hubsite and then arrives at a fiber-optic node, which serves anywhere from 25 to 2,000 or more homes. (Don't get me wrong, all links have problems—I'm not picking on cable—really!)

And here's another issue: If you have cable, open your PC's command prompt and type **`ipconfig`** and check out your subnet mask. It's probably a /20 or /21 class B address. Oh my. You already know that's either 4,094 or 2,046 hosts per cable network connection. Not good!

When we say "cable," we really mean using coax (coaxial) cable for transmission. And CATV, or community antenna television, is now used as a means to offer cost-effective broadcasting to subscribers. Cable is able to provide voice and data, plus analog and digital video, without requiring you to pony up your whole paycheck.

Your average cable connection gives you a maximum download speed of 20Mbps or more. And remember—you have to share that bandwidth with all the other subscribers. As if that weren't enough, there are other things like overloaded web servers and plain old Net congestion that factor in as well. But your email-checking neighbors really aren't making that much of a difference. So who or what is? Well, if you're an online gamer, you would likely notice a bit more lag during peak periods (which could be a matter of virtual life and death!). And if somebody in your neighborhood is uploading a large amount of data—like, well, an entire collection of pirated *Star Wars* movies—that could definitely max out the entire connection and bring everyone's browser to a crawl.

Cable modem access may or may not be faster or easier to install than DSL, and your mileage will vary, depending on where you live plus a variety of other factors. But it's usually more available and a tad less pricey, making it a winner by a nose. But no worries; if cable access isn't available in your neighborhood, DSL is okay—anything is better than dial-up!

Digital Subscriber Line (DSL)

Coming in second in our subscriber-based popularity contest is DSL (digital subscriber line), a technology that uses your garden-variety copper phone wires to give you high-speed data transmission. DSL requires a phone line, a DSL modem (often included with the service), either an Ethernet card or a router that has an Ethernet connection, and someone that can provide service wherever you happen to be located.

The acronym *DSL* originally meant digital subscriber loop, but now its meaning has morphed to digital subscriber line. DSL group types fall into two categories based upon upstream or downstream speed connections:

Symmetrical DSL The speed for both downstream and upstream connections are equal, or symmetrical.

Asymmetrical DSL Different transmission speeds occur between two ends of a network—downstream speed is always faster.

Figure 16.5 shows an average home user with xDSL, which is a transmission technology that moves data over copper pairs.

FIGURE 16.5 xDSL connection from home user to central office

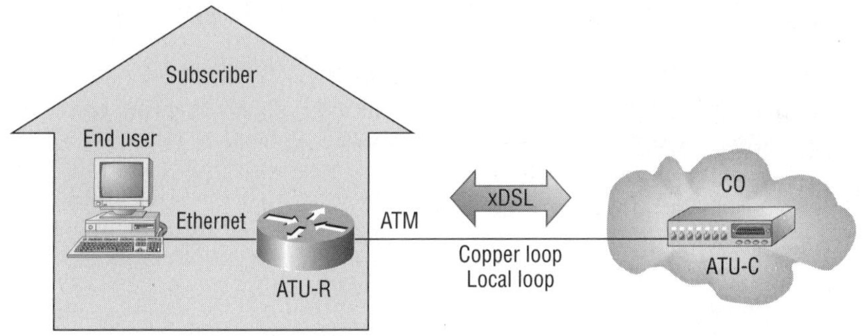

All types of DSL are layer 1 technologies.
ATU-R = ADSL Transmission Unit - Remote
ATU-C = ADSL Transmission Unit - Central

The term *xDSL* covers a number of DSL variations, such as Asymmetrical DSL (ADSL), high-bit-rate DSL (HDSL), Rate Adaptive DSL (RADSL), Synchronous DSL (SDSL), ISDN DSL (IDSL), and very-high-data-rate DSL (VDSL).

DSL flavors that don't use the voice frequencies band, like ADSL and VDSL, allow DSL lines to carry both data and voice signals simultaneously. Others, like SDSL and IDSL, that occupy the complete frequency range, can carry only data. And by the way, the data service that the DSL connection gives you is always on.

The speed that DSL service can offer depends on how far you are from the central office (CO)—the closer the better. In fact, you can blaze at rates up to around 6.1Mbps if you're physically close enough!

ADSL

ADSL supports both voice and data at the same time, but it was created to allot more bandwidth downstream than upstream because it's best for residential subscribers that usually need more downstream bandwidth for doing things like downloading video, movies, and music; online gaming; surfing; and getting emails—some that include sizeable attachments. ADSL will give you a downstream rate from 256Kbps to 8Mbps, but anything going upstream is only going to reach around 1.5Mbps max.

Plain old telephone service (POTS) provides a channel for analog voice transmission and can transmit without a problem with ADSL over the same twisted-pair telephone line. Actually, depending on the type of ADSL, not just two, but three information channels commonly utilize the same wiring at the same time. This is why people can use a phone line and an ADSL connection at the same time and not affect either service.

ATM is the Data Link layer protocol typically used over the DSL layer 1 connection from the CPE and is terminated at what's known as the DSLAM—an ATM switch that contains DSL interface cards, or ATU-Cs. After ADSL connections meet their end at the DSLAM, it switches the data over an ATM network to something called an aggregation router—a layer 3 device where the subscriber's IP connection then expires.

You know by now how important encapsulation is, so as you've probably guessed, any IP packets over an ATM and DSL connection must have this done. This happens in one of three ways, depending on your interface type and the service provider's switch:

PPPoE This will be discussed in more detail in the next section.

RFC1483 Routing RFC1483 describes two different methods for carrying connectionless network traffic over an ATM network: routed protocols and bridged protocols.

PPPoA Point-to-Point Protocol (PPP) over ATM is used to encapsulate PPP frames in ATM AAL5 (ATM Adaptation Layer 5). It is typically used with cable modems, DSL, and ADSL services and offers the usual PPP features of authentication, encryption, and compression, and it actually has less overhead in comparison to PPPoE.

PPPoE

Used with ADSL services, PPPoE (Point-to-Point Protocol over Ethernet) encapsulates PPP frames in Ethernet frames and uses common PPP features like authentication, encryption, and compression. But as I said earlier, it's trouble if you've got a badly configured firewall. This is a tunneling protocol that layers IP and other protocols that run over PPP with the attributes of a PPP link so they can then be used to contact other Ethernet devices and initiate a point-to-point connection to transport IP packets.

Figure 16.6 displays typical usage of PPPoE over ADSL. As you can see, a PPP session is connected from the PC of the end user to the router and the subscriber PC IP address is assigned by the router via IPCP.

PPPoE is used to equip custom PPP-based software with the ability to deal with a connection that's not using a serial line and to be at home in a packet-oriented network environment like Ethernet. It also allows for a custom connection with login and password for Internet connection accounting. Another factor is that the opposite side of the link's IP address is only given to it and is available only for the specific period that the PPPoE connection is open, so reusing IP addresses dynamically is permitted.

PPPoE has a discovery stage and a PPP session stage (see RFC 2516) that works like this: First, a host begins a PPPoE session, during which it has to execute a discovery process so it can determine the best server to meet the needs of the client machine's request. After that, it has to discover the Ethernet MAC address of the peer device and create a PPPoE session ID. So even though PPP delimits a peer-to-peer relationship, the discovery part is innately a client-server relationship.

Okay, before getting into serial connections, there's one last thing I want to cover—Cisco LRE.

FIGURE 16.6 PPPoE with ADSL

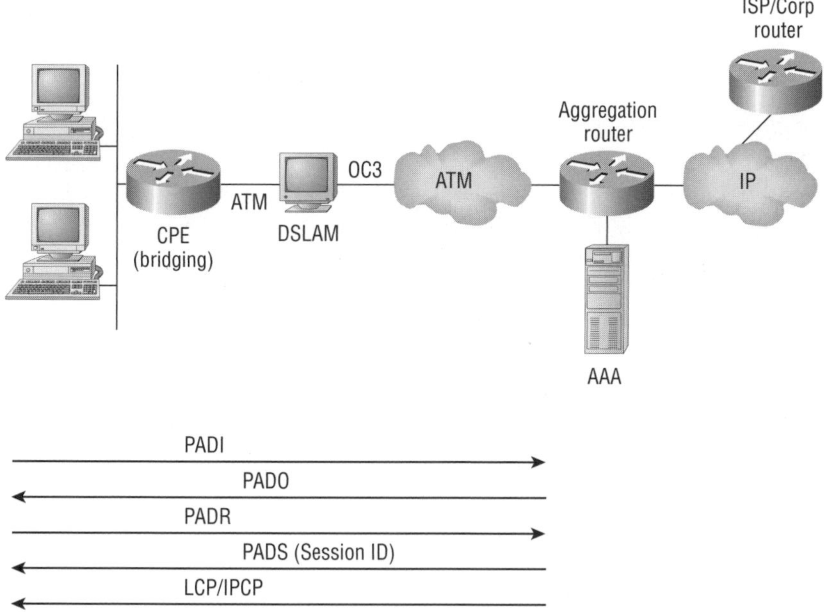

Cisco Long Range Ethernet (LRE)

The Cisco Long Range Ethernet solution employs something called VDSL (very-high-data-rate digital subscriber line) technology to significantly expand Ethernet service capacity. And LRE can achieve these impressive results: speeds from 5 to 15Mbps (full duplex) at distances up to 5,000 feet traveling over existing twisted-pair wiring!

So basically, Cisco LRE technology can give us broadband service on POTS, digital telephone, and ISDN traffic lines, and it also can operate in modes that are compatible with ADSL technologies. This flexibility is important because it makes it possible for service providers to make LRE available in structures and/or buildings that have broadband services already in place but need it enhanced—very cool indeed.

Cabling the Serial Wide Area Network

As you can imagine, there are a few things that you need to know before connecting your WAN in order to make sure everything goes well. For starters, you have to understand the kind of WAN Physical layer implementation that Cisco provides as well as ensure that you're familiar with the various types of WAN serial connectors involved.

The good news is that Cisco serial connections support almost any type of WAN service. Your typical WAN connection is a dedicated leased line using HDLC, PPP, and Frame Relay with speeds that can kick it up to 45Mbps (T3).

HDLC, PPP, and Frame Relay can use the same Physical layer specifications, and I'll go over the various types of connections and then move on to telling you all about the WAN protocols specified in the CCNA objectives.

Serial Transmission

WAN serial connectors use *serial transmission*, something that takes place 1 bit at a time over a single channel.

Older Cisco routers have used a proprietary 60-pin serial connector that you have to get from Cisco or a provider of Cisco equipment. Cisco also has a new, smaller proprietary serial connection that's about one-tenth the size of the 60-pin basic serial cable called the *smart-serial*. You have to make sure you have the right type of interface in your router before using this cable connector.

The type of connector you have on the other end of the cable depends on your service provider and their particular end-device requirements. There are several different types of ends you'll run into:

- EIA/TIA-232
- EIA/TIA-449
- V.35 (used to connect to a CSU/DSU)
- EIA-530

Make sure you're clear on these things: Serial links are described in frequency or cycles per second (hertz). The amount of data that can be carried within these frequencies is called *bandwidth*. Bandwidth is the amount of data in bits per second that the serial channel can carry.

Data Terminal Equipment and Data Communication Equipment

By default, router interfaces are typically *data terminal equipment (DTE)*, and they connect into *data communication equipment (DCE)* like a *channel service unit/data service unit (CSU/DSU)*. The CSU/DSU then plugs into a demarcation location (demarc) and is the service provider's last responsibility. Most of the time, the demarc is a jack that has an RJ-45 (8-pin modular) female connector located in a telecommunications closet.

Actually, you may already have heard of demarcs. If you've ever had the glorious experience of reporting a problem to your service provider, they'll usually tell you everything tests out fine up to the demarc, so the problem must be the CPE, or customer premises equipment. In other words, it's your problem, not theirs.

Figure 16.7 shows a typical DTE-DCE-DTE connection and the devices used in the network.

FIGURE 16.7 DTE-DCE-DTE WAN connection

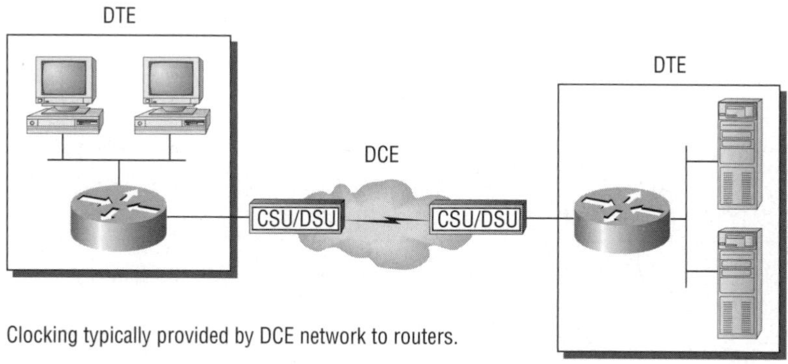
DTE
DTE
DCE
CSU/DSU
CSU/DSU
Clocking typically provided by DCE network to routers.
In non-production environments, a DCE network is not always present.

The idea behind a WAN is to be able to connect two DTE networks through a DCE network. The DCE network includes the CSU/DSU, through the provider's wiring and switches, all the way to the CSU/DSU at the other end. The network's DCE device (CSU/DSU) provides clocking to the DTE-connected interface (the router's serial interface).

As mentioned, the DCE network provides clocking to the router; this is the CSU/DSU. If you have a nonproduction network and you're using a WAN crossover type of cable and do not have a CSU/DSU, then you need to provide clocking on the DCE end of the cable by using the `clock rate` command that I showed you in Chapter 6.

Terms such as *EIA/TIA-232, V.35, X.21,* and *HSSI (High-Speed Serial Interface)* describe the Physical layer between the DTE (router) and DCE device (CSU/DSU).

High-Level Data-Link Control (HDLC) Protocol

The High-Level Data-Link Control (HDLC) protocol is a popular ISO-standard, bit-oriented, Data Link layer protocol. It specifies an encapsulation method for data on synchronous serial data links using frame characters and checksums. HDLC is a point-to-point protocol used on leased lines and ISDN dial-up connections. No authentication is provided by HDLC.

In byte-oriented protocols, control information is encoded using entire bytes. On the other hand, bit-oriented protocols use single bits to represent the control information. Some common bit-oriented protocols are SDLC and HDLC, and TCP and IP are byte-oriented protocols.

HDLC is the default encapsulation used by Cisco routers over synchronous serial links. And Cisco's HDLC is proprietary—it won't communicate with any other vendor's HDLC implementation. But don't give Cisco grief for it—*everyone's* HDLC implementation is proprietary. Figure 16.8 shows the Cisco HDLC format.

FIGURE 16.8 Cisco's HDLC frame format

Cisco HDLC

Flag	Address	Control	Proprietary	Data	FCS	Flag

• Each vendor's HDLC has a proprietary data field to support multiprotocol environments.

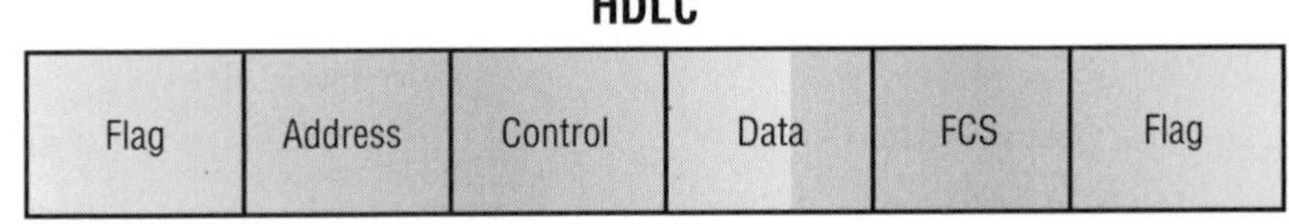

As shown in the figure, the reason every vendor has a proprietary HDLC encapsulation method is that each vendor has a different way for the HDLC protocol to encapsulate multiple Network layer protocols. If the vendors didn't have a way for HDLC to communicate the different layer 3 protocols, then HDLC would be able to operate in only a single layer 3 protocol environment. This proprietary header is placed in the data field of the HDLC encapsulation.

So let's say you have only one Cisco router and you need to connect to a non-Cisco router because your other Cisco router is on order. What would you do? You couldn't use the default HDLC serial encapsulation because it wouldn't work. Instead, you would use something like PPP, an ISO-standard way of identifying the upper-layer protocols. You can check out RFC 1661 for more information on the origins and standards of PPP. Let's discuss PPP in more detail and how to connect to routers using the PPP encapsulation.

Point-to-Point Protocol (PPP)

Let's spend a little time on Point-to-Point Protocol (PPP). Remember that it's a Data Link layer protocol that can be used over either asynchronous serial (dial-up) or synchronous serial (ISDN) media. It uses Link Control Protocol (LCP) to build and maintain data-link connections. Network Control Protocol (NCP) is used to allow multiple Network layer protocols (routed protocols) to be used on a point-to-point connection.

Since HDLC is the default serial encapsulation on Cisco serial links and it works great, why and when would you choose to use PPP? Well, the basic purpose of PPP is to transport layer 3 packets across a Data Link layer point-to-point link, and it's nonproprietary. So unless you have all Cisco routers, you need PPP on your serial interfaces—the HDLC encapsulation is Cisco proprietary, remember? Plus, since PPP can encapsulate several layer 3 routed protocols and provide authentication, dynamic addressing, and callback, PPP could be the best encapsulation solution for you instead of HDLC.

Figure 16.9 shows the PPP protocol stack compared to the OSI reference model.

FIGURE 16.9 Point-to-Point Protocol stack

OSI layer	
3	Upper-layer Protocols (such as IP, IPX, AppleTalk)
2	Network Control Protocol (NCP) (specific to each Network-layer protocol)
	Link Control Protocol (LCP)
	High-Level Data Link Control Protocol (HDLC)
1	Physical layer (such as EIA/TIA-232, V.24, V.35, ISDN)

PPP contains four main components:

EIA/TIA-232-C, V.24, V.35, and ISDN A Physical layer international standard for serial communication.

HDLC A method for encapsulating datagrams over serial links.

LCP A method of establishing, configuring, maintaining, and terminating the point-to-point connection.

NCP A method of establishing and configuring different Network layer protocols for transport across the PPP link. NCP is designed to allow the simultaneous use of multiple Network layer protocols. Some examples of protocols here are IPCP (Internet Protocol Control Protocol) and IPXCP (Internetwork Packet Exchange Control Protocol).

Burn it into your mind that the PPP protocol stack is specified at the Physical and Data Link layers only. NCP is used to allow communication of multiple Network layer protocols by identifying and encapsulating the protocols across a PPP data link.

Remember that if you have a Cisco router and a non-Cisco router connected with a serial connection, you must configure PPP or another encapsulation method, such as Frame Relay, because the HDLC default just won't work!

Next, I'll cover the options for LCP and PPP session establishment.

Link Control Protocol (LCP) Configuration Options

Link Control Protocol (LCP) offers different PPP encapsulation options, including the following:

Authentication This option tells the calling side of the link to send information that can identify the user. The two methods are PAP and CHAP.

Compression This is used to increase the throughput of PPP connections by compressing the data or payload prior to transmission. PPP decompresses the data frame on the receiving end.

Error detection PPP uses Quality and Magic Number options to ensure a reliable, loop-free data link.

Multilink Starting with IOS version 11.1, multilink is supported on PPP links with Cisco routers. This option makes several separate physical paths appear to be one logical path at layer 3. For example, two T1s running multilink PPP would show up as a single 3Mbps path to a layer 3 routing protocol.

PPP callback PPP can be configured to call back after successful authentication. *PPP callback* can be a good thing for you because you can keep track of usage based upon access charges for accounting records and a bunch of other reasons. With callback enabled, a calling router (client) will contact a remote router (server) and authenticate as I described earlier. (Know that both routers have to be configured for the callback feature for this to work.) Once authentication is completed, the remote router will terminate the connection and then re-initiate a connection to the calling router from the remote router.

If you have Microsoft devices in your PPP callback, be aware that Microsoft uses a proprietary callback known as Microsoft Callback Control Protocol (CBCP), which is supported in IOS release 11.3(2)T and later.

PPP Session Establishment

When PPP connections are started, the links go through three phases of session establishment, as shown in Figure 16.10:

Link-establishment phase LCP packets are sent by each PPP device to configure and test the link. These packets contain a field called Configuration Option that allows each device to see the size of the data, the compression, and authentication. If no Configuration Option field is present, then the default configurations will be used.

Authentication phase If required, either CHAP or PAP can be used to authenticate a link. Authentication takes place before Network layer protocol information is read. And it's possible that link-quality determination will occur simultaneously.

Network layer protocol phase PPP uses the *Network Control Protocol (NCP)* to allow multiple Network layer protocols to be encapsulated and sent over a PPP data link. Each Network layer protocol (e.g., IP, IPX, AppleTalk, which are routed protocols) establishes a service with NCP.

FIGURE 16.10 PPP session establishment

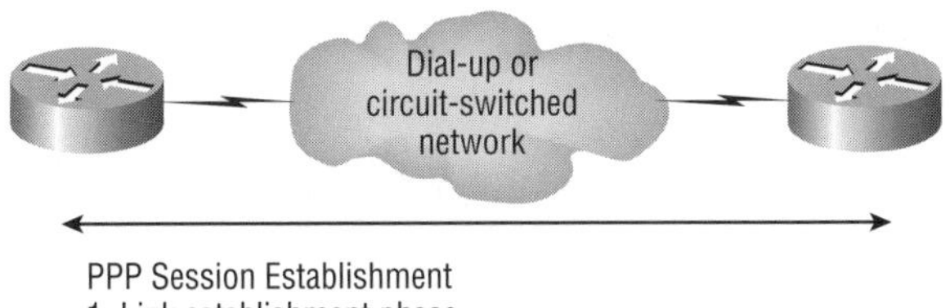

PPP Authentication Methods

There are two methods of authentication that can be used with PPP links:

Password Authentication Protocol (PAP) The *Password Authentication Protocol (PAP)* is the less secure of the two methods. Passwords are sent in cleartext, and PAP is performed only upon the initial link establishment. When the PPP link is first established, the remote node sends the username and password back to the originating target router until authentication is acknowledged. Not exactly Fort Knox!

Challenge Handshake Authentication Protocol (CHAP) The *Challenge Handshake Authentication Protocol (CHAP)* is used at the initial startup of a link and at periodic checkups on the link to make sure the router is still communicating with the same host.

After PPP finishes its initial link-establishment phase, the local router sends a challenge request to the remote device. The remote device sends a value calculated using a one-way hash function called MD5. The local router checks this hash value to make sure it matches. If the values don't match, the link is immediately terminated.

Configuring PPP on Cisco Routers

Configuring PPP encapsulation on an interface is really pretty straightforward. To configure it from the CLI, follow these simple router commands:

```
Router#config t
Enter configuration commands, one per line. End with CNTL/Z.
Router(config)#int s0
Router(config-if)#encapsulation ppp
```

```
Router(config-if)#^Z
Router#
```

Of course, PPP encapsulation has to be enabled on both interfaces connected to a serial line in order to work, and there are several additional configuration options available to you via the `ppp ?` command.

Configuring PPP Authentication

After you configure your serial interface to support PPP encapsulation, you can configure authentication using PPP between routers. First, you need to set the hostname of the router, if it's not set already. Then you set the username and password for the remote router that will be connecting to your router:

Here's an example:

```
Router#config t
Enter configuration commands, one per line. End with CNTL/Z.
Router(config)#hostname RouterA
RouterA(config)#username RouterB password cisco
```

When using the `username` command, remember that the username is the hostname of the remote router that's connecting to your router. And it's case sensitive too. Also, the password on both routers must be the same. It's a plain-text password that you can see with a `show run` command; you can encrypt the password by using the command `service password-encryption`. You must have a username and password configured for each remote system you plan to connect to. The remote routers must also be similarly configured with usernames and passwords.

Now, after you've set the hostname, usernames, and passwords, choose the authentication type, either CHAP or PAP:

```
RouterA#config t
Enter configuration commands, one per line. End with CNTL/Z.
RouterA(config)#int s0
RouterA(config-if)#ppp authentication chap pap
RouterA(config-if)#^Z
RouterA#
```

If both methods are configured on the same line, as shown here, then only the first method will be used during link negotiation—the second acts as a backup just in case the first method fails.

Verifying PPP Encapsulation

Okay—now that PPP encapsulation is enabled, let me show you how to verify that it's up and running. First, let's take a look at a figure of a sample network. Figure 16.11 shows two routers connected with a point-to-point serial connection.

FIGURE 16.11 PPP authentication example

```
hostname Pod1R1
username Pod1R2 password cisco
 interface serial 0
  ip address 10.0.1.1 255.255.255.0
 encapsulation ppp
ppp authentication chap
```

```
hostname Pod1R2
username Pod1R1 password cisco
 interface serial 0
  ip address 10.0.1.2 255.255.255.0
 encapsulation ppp
ppp authentication chap
```

You can start verifying the configuration with the `show interface` command:

```
Pod1R1#sh int s0/0
Serial0/0 is up, line protocol is up
  Hardware is PowerQUICC Serial
  Internet address is 10.0.1.1/24
  MTU 1500 bytes, BW 1544 Kbit, DLY 20000 usec,
     reliability 239/255, txload 1/255, rxload 1/255
  Encapsulation PPP
  loopback not set
  Keepalive set (10 sec)
  LCP Open
  Open: IPCP, CDPCP
[output cut]
```

The first line of output is important because we can see that serial 0/0 is up/up. But notice that the sixth line lists encapsulation as PPP and the eighth line shows that the LCP is open. This means that it has negotiated the session establishment and all is good! The ninth line tells us that NCP is listening for the protocols IP and CDP.

But what will you see if everything isn't perfect? I'm going to type in the configuration shown in Figure 16.12 and find out.

FIGURE 16.12 Failed PPP authentication

```
hostname Pod1R1
username Pod1R2 password Cisco
 interface serial 0
  ip address 10.0.1.1 255.255.255.0
 encapsulation ppp
ppp authentication chap
```

```
hostname Pod1R2
username Pod1R1 password cisco
 interface serial 0
  ip address 10.0.1.2 255.255.255.0
 encapsulation ppp
ppp authentication chap
```

Okay—what's wrong here? Take a look at the usernames and passwords. Do you see the problem now? That's right, the *C* is capitalized on the Pod1R2 username command found in the configuration of router Pod1R1. This is wrong because the usernames and passwords are case sensitive, remember? Let's take a look at the `show interface` command and see what happens:

```
Pod1R1#sh int s0/0
Serial0/0 is up, line protocol is down
  Hardware is PowerQUICC Serial
  Internet address is 10.0.1.1/24
  MTU 1500 bytes, BW 1544 Kbit, DLY 20000 usec,
     reliability 243/255, txload 1/255, rxload 1/255
  Encapsulation PPP, loopback not set
  Keepalive set (10 sec)
  LCP Closed
  Closed: IPCP, CDPCP
```

First, notice in the first line of output that `Serial0/0 is up, line protocol is down.` This is because there are no keepalives coming from the remote router. Next, notice that the LCP is closed because the authentication failed.

Debugging PPP Authentication

To display the CHAP authentication process as it occurs between two routers in the network, just use the command `debug ppp authentication`.

If your PPP encapsulation and authentication are set up correctly on both routers, and your usernames and passwords are all good, then the `debug ppp authentication` command will display an output that looks like this, called the three-way handshake:

```
d16h: Se0/0 PPP: Using default call direction
1d16h: Se0/0 PPP: Treating connection as a dedicated line
1d16h: Se0/0 CHAP: O CHALLENGE id 219 len 27 from "Pod1R1"
1d16h: Se0/0 CHAP: I CHALLENGE id 208 len 27 from "Pod1R2"
1d16h: Se0/0 CHAP: O RESPONSE id 208 len 27 from "Pod1R1"
1d16h: Se0/0 CHAP: I RESPONSE id 219 len 27 from "Pod1R2"
1d16h: Se0/0 CHAP: O SUCCESS id 219 len 4
1d16h: Se0/0 CHAP: I SUCCESS id 208 len 4
```

But if you have the password wrong, as we did previously in the PPP authentication failure example back in Figure 16.12, the output would look something like this:

```
1d16h: Se0/0 PPP: Using default call direction
1d16h: Se0/0 PPP: Treating connection as a dedicated line
1d16h: %SYS-5-CONFIG_I: Configured from console by console
```

```
1d16h: Se0/0 CHAP: O CHALLENGE id 220 len 27 from "Pod1R1"
1d16h: Se0/0 CHAP: I CHALLENGE id 209 len 27 from "Pod1R2"
1d16h: Se0/0 CHAP: O RESPONSE id 209 len 27 from "Pod1R1"
1d16h: Se0/0 CHAP: I RESPONSE id 220 len 27 from "Pod1R2"
1d16h: Se0/0 CHAP: O FAILURE id 220 len 25 msg is "MD/DES compare failed"
```

PPP with CHAP authentication is a three-way authentication, and if the username and passwords are not configured exactly the way they should be, then the authentication will fail and the link will be down.

Mismatched WAN Encapsulations

If you have a point-to-point link but the encapsulations aren't the same, the link will never come up. Figure 16.13 shows one link with PPP and one with HDLC.

FIGURE 16.13 Mismatched WAN encapsulations

hostname Pod1R1
username Pod1R2 password Cisco
 interface serial 0
  ip address 10.0.1.1 255.255.255.0
  encapsulation ppp

hostname Pod1R2
username Pod1R1 password cisco
 interface serial 0
  ip address 10.0.1.2 255.255.255.0
  encapsulation HDLC

Look at router Pod1R1 in this output:

```
Pod1R1#sh int s0/0
Serial0/0 is up, line protocol is down
  Hardware is PowerQUICC Serial
  Internet address is 10.0.1.1/24
  MTU 1500 bytes, BW 1544 Kbit, DLY 20000 usec,
     reliability 254/255, txload 1/255, rxload 1/255
  Encapsulation PPP, loopback not set
  Keepalive set (10 sec)
  LCP REQsent
Closed: IPCP, CDPCP
```

The serial interface is up/down and LCP is sending requests but will never receive any responses because router Pod1R2 is using the HDLC encapsulation. To fix this problem, you would have to go to router Pod1R2 and configure the PPP encapsulation on the serial interface. One more thing—even though the usernames are configured and they're wrong, it doesn't matter because the command `ppp authentication chap` isn't used under the serial interface configuration and the username command isn't relevant in this example.

Always remember that you just can't have PPP on one side and HDLC on the other—they don't get along!

Mismatched IP Addresses

A tricky problem to spot is if you have HDLC or PPP configured on your serial interface but your IP addresses are wrong. Things seem to be just fine because the interfaces will show that they are up. Take a look at Figure 16.14 and see if you can see what I mean—the two routers are connected with different subnets—router Pod1R1 with 10.0.1.1/24 and router Pod1R2 with 10.2.1.2/24.

FIGURE 16.14 Mismatched IP addresses

```
hostname Pod1R1
username Pod1R2 password cisco
 interface serial 0
  ip address 10.0.1.1 255.255.255.0
  encapsulation ppp
  ppp authentication chap
```

```
hostname Pod1R2
username Pod1R1 password cisco
 interface serial 0
  ip address 10.2.1.2 255.255.255.0
  encapsulation ppp
  ppp authentication chap
```

This will never work. But as I said, take a look at the output:

```
Pod1R1#sh int s0/0
Serial0/0 is up, line protocol is up
  Hardware is PowerQUICC Serial
  Internet address is 10.0.1.1/24
  MTU 1500 bytes, BW 1544 Kbit, DLY 20000 usec,
     reliability 255/255, txload 1/255, rxload 1/255
  Encapsulation PPP, loopback not set
  Keepalive set (10 sec)
  LCP Open
  Open: IPCP, CDPCP
```

See that? The IP addresses between the routers are wrong but the link looks like it's working fine. This is because PPP, like HDLC and Frame Relay, is a layer 2 WAN encapsulation and doesn't care about IP addresses at all. So yes, the link is up, but you can't use IP across this link since it's misconfigured.

To find and fix this problem, you can use the `show running-config` or the `show interfaces` command on each router, or you can use what you learned in Chapter 7—the `show cdp neighbors detail` command:

```
Pod1R1#sh cdp neighbors detail
-------------------------
Device ID: Pod1R2
Entry address(es):
  IP address: 10.2.1.2
```

Since the layer 1 Physical and layer 2 Data Link is up/up, you can view and verify the directly connected neighbor's IP address and then solve your problem.

Frame Relay

Frame Relay is still one of the most popular WAN services deployed over the past decade, and there's a good reason for this—cost. And it's a rare network design or designer that has the privilege to ignore that all-important cost factor!

By default, Frame Relay is classified as a non-broadcast multi-access (NBMA) network, meaning it doesn't send any broadcasts such as RIP updates across the network. No worries—I'm not going leave you hanging. We'll get into this more soon.

Frame Relay has at its roots a technology called X.25, and it essentially incorporates the components of X.25 that are still relevant to today's reliable and relatively "clean" telecommunications networks while leaving out the no-longer-needed error-correction components. It's substantially more complex than the simple leased-line networks you learned about when I discussed the HDLC and PPP protocols. The leased-line networks are easy to conceptualize—but not so much when it comes to Frame Relay. It can be significantly more complex and versatile, which is why it's often represented as a "cloud" in networking graphics. I'll get to that in a minute—for right now, I'm going to introduce Frame Relay in concept and show you how it differs from simpler leased-line technologies.

Along with your introduction to this technology, you'll get a virtual dictionary of all the new terminology you'll need to solidly grasp the basics of Frame Relay. After that, I'll guide you through some simple Frame Relay implementations.

Introduction to Frame Relay Technology

As a CCNA, you'll need to understand the basics of the Frame Relay technology and be able to configure it in simple scenarios. First, understand that Frame Relay is a packet-switched technology. From everything you've learned so far, just telling you this should make you immediately realize several things about it:

- You won't be using the `encapsulation hdlc` or `encapsulation ppp` command to configure it.

- Frame Relay doesn't work like a point-to-point leased line (although it can be made to look and act like one).
- Frame Relay is usually less expensive than leased lines are, but there are some sacrifices to make to get that savings.

So, why would you even consider using Frame Relay? Take a look at Figure 16.15 to get an idea of what a network looked like before Frame Relay.

Now check out Figure 16.16. You can see that there's now only one connection between the Corporate router and the Frame Relay switch. That saves some major cash!

FIGURE 16.15 Before Frame Relay

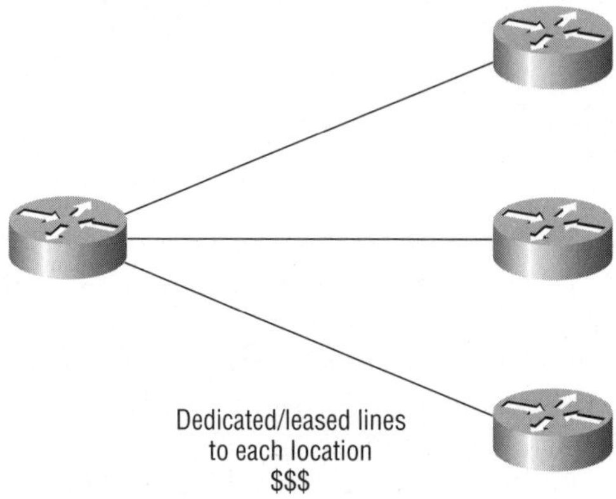
Dedicated/leased lines
to each location
$$$

FIGURE 16.16 After Frame Relay

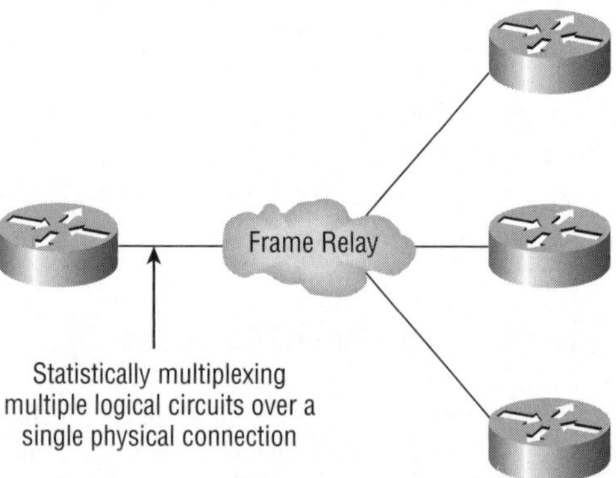
Frame Relay creates a cost-effective mesh network.
Frame Relay
Statistically multiplexing
multiple logical circuits over a
single physical connection

If, for example, you had to add seven remote sites accessed from the corporate office and had only one free serial port on your router—it's Frame Relay to the rescue! Of course, I should probably mention that you now also have a single point of failure, which is not so good. But Frame Relay is used to save money, not to make a network more resilient.

Coming up, I'm going to cover the Frame Relay technology information you need to know about when studying the CCNA objectives.

Committed Information Rate (CIR)

Frame Relay provides a packet-switched network to many different customers at the same time. This is a really good thing because it spreads the cost of the switches among many customers. But remember, Frame Relay is based on the assumption that all customers won't ever need to transmit data constantly, or all at the same time.

Frame Relay works by providing a portion of dedicated bandwidth to each user, and it also allows the user to exceed their guaranteed bandwidth if resources on the telco network happen to be available. So basically, Frame Relay providers allow customers to buy a lower amount of bandwidth than what they really use. There are two separate bandwidth specifications with Frame Relay:

Access rate The maximum speed at which the Frame Relay interface can transmit.

CIR The maximum bandwidth of data guaranteed to be delivered. In reality, it's the average amount that the service provider will allow you to transmit.

If these two values are the same, the Frame Relay connection is pretty much just like a leased line. But they can also be set to different values. Here's an example: Let's say that you buy an access rate of T1 (1.544Mbps) and a CIR of 256Kbps. By doing this, the first 256Kbps of traffic you send is guaranteed to be delivered. Anything beyond that is called a "burst"—a transmission that exceeds your guaranteed 256Kbps rate and can be any amount up to the T1 access rate (if that amount is in your contract). If your combined committed burst (the basis for your CIR) and excess burst sizes, known as the MBR or maximum burst rate when combined, exceed the access rate, you can pretty much say goodbye to your additional traffic. It will most likely be dropped, although this really depends on the subscription level of a particular service provider.

In a perfect world, this always works beautifully—but remember that little word *guarantee*—As in guaranteed rate of 256Kbps, to be exact? This means that any burst of data you send that exceeds your guaranteed 256Kbps rate will be delivered on something called a "best effort" basis of delivery. Or maybe not—if your telco's equipment doesn't have the capacity to deliver it at the time you transmitted, then your frames will be discarded and the DTE will be notified. Timing is everything—you can scream data out at six times your guaranteed rate of 256Kbps (T1) *only if* your telco has the capacity available on its equipment at that moment. Remember that "oversubscription" we talked about? Well, here it is in action!

The CIR is the rate, in bits per second, at which the Frame Relay switch agrees to transfer data.

Frame Relay Encapsulation Types

When configuring Frame Relay on Cisco routers, you need to specify it as an encapsulation on serial interfaces. As I said earlier, you can't use HDLC or PPP with Frame Relay. When you configure Frame Relay, you specify an encapsulation of Frame Relay (as shown in the following output). But unlike with HDLC or PPP, with Frame Relay, there are two encapsulation types: Cisco and IETF (Internet Engineering Task Force). The following router output shows these two different encapsulation methods when Frame Relay is chosen on your Cisco router:

```
RouterA(config)#int s0
RouterA(config-if)#encapsulation frame-relay ?
  ietf  Use RFC1490 encapsulation
  <cr>
```

The default encapsulation is Cisco unless you manually type in **ietf**, and Cisco is the type to use when connecting two Cisco devices. You'd opt for the IETF-type encapsulation if you needed to connect a Cisco device to a non-Cisco device with Frame Relay. Whichever you choose, make sure the Frame Relay encapsulation is the same on both ends.

Virtual Circuits

Frame Relay operates using *virtual circuits* as opposed to the actual circuits that leased lines use. These virtual circuits are what link together the thousands of devices connected to the provider's "cloud." Frame Relay provides a virtual circuit between your two DTE devices, making them appear to be connected via a circuit when in reality, they're dumping their frames into a large, shared infrastructure. You never see the complexity of what's actually happening inside the cloud because you only have a virtual circuit.

And on top of all that, there are two types of virtual circuits—permanent and switched. Permanent virtual circuits (PVCs) are by far the most common type in use today. What "permanent" means here is that the telco creates the mappings inside its gear, and as long as you pay the bill, they'll remain in place.

Switched virtual circuits (SVCs) are more like a phone call. The virtual circuit is established when data needs to be transmitted, then it's taken down when the data transfer is complete.

Data Link Connection Identifiers (DLCIs)

Frame Relay PVCs are identified to DTE end devices by *Data Link Connection Identifiers (DLCIs)*. A Frame Relay service provider typically assigns DLCI values, which are used on Frame Relay interfaces to distinguish between different virtual circuits. Because many virtual circuits can be terminated on one multipoint Frame Relay interface, many DLCIs are often affiliated with it.

Let me explain—suppose you have a central HQ with three branch offices. If you were to connect each branch office to HQ using a T1, you would need three serial interfaces on your router at HQ, one for each T1. Simple, right? Well, suppose you use Frame Relay PVCs instead. You could have a T1 at each branch connected to a service provider and only a *single* T1 at HQ. There would be three PVCs on the single T1 at HQ, one going to each branch. And even though there's only a single interface and a single CSU/DSU, the three PVCs function as three separate circuits. Remember what I said about saving money? How much for two additional T1 interfaces and a pair of CSU/DSUs? Answer: A lot! So, why not just go ahead and ask for a percentage of the savings in your bonus?

Okay, before we go on, I want to define Inverse ARP (IARP) and discuss how it's used with DLCIs in a Frame Relay network. Yes, it is somewhat similar to ARP in the fact that it maps a DLCI to an IP address—kind of like ARP does with MAC addresses to IP addresses. And even though you can't configure IARP, you can disable it. It runs on a Frame Relay router and maps the DLCI to an IP address for Frame Relay so it knows how to get to the IP address at the other end of the PVC. You can see IP-to-DLCI mappings with the `show frame-relay map` command.

But if you have a non-Cisco router living in your network and it doesn't support IARP, then you're stuck with having to statically provide IP-to-DLCI mappings with the `frame-relay map` command—something I'll demonstrate in a bit.

Inverse ARP (IARP) is used to map a known DLCI to an IP address.

Let's talk about DLCIs a bit more. They're locally significant—global significance requires the entire network to use the Local Management Interface (LMI) extensions that offer global significance. This is why you'll mostly find global DLCIs only in private networks.

But the DLCI doesn't have to be globally significant for it to be functional in getting a frame across the network. Let me explain: When RouterA wants to send a frame to RouterB, it looks up the IARP or manual mapping of the DLCI to the IP address it's trying to get to. Equipped with the DLCI, it then sends the frame out with the DLCI value it found in the DLCI field of the FR header. The provider's ingress switch gets this frame and does a lookup on the DLCI/physical-port combination it observes. Associated with that combination, it finds a new "locally significant" (meaning, between itself and the next-hop switch) DLCI to use in the header, and in the same entry in its table, it finds an outgoing physical port. This happens repeatedly all the way to RouterB. So basically, you actually could say that the DLCI for RouterA uses the entire virtual circuit to RouterB, even though each DLCI between every pair of devices could be completely different. The big point here is that RouterA is unaware of these differences. That's what makes the DLCI locally significant. So make a mental note that DLCIs really are used by the telco to "find" the other end of your PVC.

To discover why DLCIs are considered locally significant, take a look at Figure 16.17. In the figure, DLCI 100 is considered locally significant to RouterA and identifies the circuit to RouterB between RouterA and its ingress Frame Relay switch. DLCI 200 would identify this same circuit to RouterA between RouterB and its ingress Frame Relay switch.

FIGURE 16.17 DLCIs are local to your router.

DLCI numbers that are used to identify a PVC are typically assigned by the provider and start at 16.

You configure a DLCI number to be applied to an interface like this:

```
RouterA(config-if)#frame-relay interface-dlci ?
  <16-1007> Define a DLCI as part of the current
            subinterface
RouterA(config-if)#frame-relay interface-dlci 16
```

DLCIs identify the logical circuit between the local router and a Frame Relay switch.

Local Management Interface (LMI)

Local Management Interface (LMI) is a signaling standard used between your router and the first Frame Relay switch it's connected to. It allows for passing information about the operation and status of the virtual circuit between the provider's network and the DTE (your router). It communicates information about the following:

Keepalives These verify that data is flowing.

Multicasting This is an optional extension of the LMI specification that allows, for example, the efficient distribution of routing information and ARP requests over a Frame Relay network. Multicasting uses the reserved DLCIs from 1019 through 1022.

Global addressing This provides global significance to DLCIs, allowing the Frame Relay cloud to work exactly like a LAN. This has never been run in a production network to this day.

Status of virtual circuits This provides DLCI status. The status inquiries and messages are used as keepalives when there is no regular LMI traffic to send.

But remember, LMI is not communication between your routers; it's communication between your router and the nearest Frame Relay switch. So it's entirely possible that the router on one end of a PVC is actively receiving LMI while the router on the other end of the PVC is not. And of course, PVCs won't work with one end down. (I say this to clarify the local nature of LMI communications.)

There are three different types of LMI message formats: Cisco, ANSI, and Q.933A. The different kinds in use depend on both the type and configuration of the telco's switching gear, so it's imperative that you configure your router for the correct format, which should be provided by the telco.

Beginning with IOS version 11.2, the LMI type is autosensed. This enables the interface to determine the LMI type supported by the switch. If you're not going to use the autosense feature, you'll need to check with your Frame Relay provider to find out which type to use instead.

On Cisco equipment, the default type is, surprise, Cisco, but you still might have to change to ANSI or Q.933A, depending on what your service provider tells you. The three different LMI types are shown in the following router output:

```
RouterA(config-if)#frame-relay lmi-type ?
  cisco
  ansi
  q933a
```

As seen in the output, all three standard LMI signaling formats are supported. Here's a description of each:

Cisco LMI defined by the Gang of Four (default). The Local Management Interface (LMI) was developed in 1990 by Cisco Systems, StrataCom, Northern Telecom, and Digital Equipment Corporation and became known as the Gang-of-Four LMI, or Cisco LMI.

ANSI Annex D included with ANSI standard T1.617.

ITU-T (Q.933A) Annex A included in the ITU-T standard and defined by using the q933a command keyword.

Routers receive LMI information from the service provider's Frame Relay switch on a frame-relay encapsulated interface and update the virtual circuit status to one of three different states:

Active state Everything is up, and routers can exchange information.

Inactive state The router's interface is up and working with a connection to the switching office, but the remote router isn't up.

Deleted state No LMI information is being received on the interface from the switch, which could be due to a mapping problem or a line failure.

Frame Relay Congestion Control

Remember back to our talk about CIR? From that, it should be obvious that the lower your CIR is set, the greater the risk is that your data will become toast. This can be easily avoided if you have just one key piece of information—when and when not to transmit that huge burst! This begs the question, Is there any way for us to find out when our telco's shared infrastructure is free and clear and when it's crammed and jammed? Also, if there is a way to spy this out, how do you do it? Well, that's exactly what I'm going to talk about next—how the Frame Relay switch notifies the DTE of congestion problems—and address those very important questions.

Here are the three congestion bits and their meanings:

Discard Eligibility (DE) As you know, when you burst (transmit packets beyond the CIR of a PVC), any packets exceeding the CIR are eligible to be discarded if the provider's network is congested at the time. Because of this, the excessive bits are marked with a *Discard Eligibility (DE)* bit in the Frame Relay header. And if the provider's network happens to be congested, the Frame Relay switch will discard the packets with the first DE bit set. So if your bandwidth is configured with a CIR of zero, the DE will always be on.

Forward Explicit Congestion Notification (FECN) When the Frame Relay network recognizes congestion in the cloud, the switch will set the *Forward Explicit Congestion Notification (FECN)* bit to 1 in a Frame Relay packet header. This will indicate to the destination DTE that the path the frame just traversed is congested.

Backward Explicit Congestion Notification (BECN) When the switch detects congestion in the Frame Relay network, it'll set the *Backward Explicit Congestion Notification (BECN)* bit in a Frame Relay frame that's destined for the source router. This notifies the router that congestion is ahead. But Cisco routers won't take action on this congestion information unless you tell them to.

To check into this further, search using "Frame Relay Traffic Shaping" on Cisco's website.

Troubleshooting Using Frame Relay Congestion Control

Now let's say all your users are whining about the fact that their Frame Relay connection to the corporate site is super slow. Because you strongly suspect that the link is overloaded, you verify the Frame Relay congestion control information with the `show frame-relay pvc` command and get this:

```
RouterA#sh frame-relay pvc

PVC Statistics for interface Serial0/0 (Frame Relay DTE)

              Active     Inactive      Deleted       Static
  Local          1           0            0             0
  Switched       0           0            0             0
  Unused         0           0            0             0

DLCI = 100, DLCI USAGE = LOCAL, PVC STATUS = ACTIVE, INTERFACE = Serial0/0
  input pkts 1300          output pkts 1270        in bytes 21212000
  out bytes 21802000       dropped pkts 4          in pkts dropped 147
  out pkts dropped 0       out bytes dropped 0       in FECN pkts 147
   in BECN pkts 192        out FECN pkts 147
  out BECN pkts 259        in DE pkts 0              out DE pkts 214
  out bcast pkts 0         out bcast bytes 0
  pvc create time 00:00:06, last time pvc status changed 00:00:06
Pod1R1#
```

What you want to look for in this output is the `in BECN pkts 192` output because this is what's telling the local router that traffic sent to the corporate site is experiencing congestion. BECN means that the path that a frame took to "return" to you is congested.

Frame Relay Implementation and Monitoring

As I've said, there are a ton of Frame Relay commands and configuration options, but I'm going to zero in on the ones you really need to know when studying for the CCNA exam objectives. I'm going to start with one of the simplest configuration options—two routers with a single PVC between them. Next, I'll show you a more complex configuration using subinterfaces and demonstrate some of the monitoring commands available to verify the configuration.

Single Interface

Let's get started by looking at a simple example. Say that we just want to connect two routers with a single PVC. Here's how that configuration would look:

```
RouterA#config t
Enter configuration commands, one per line.  End with CNTL/Z.
RouterA(config)#int s0/0
RouterA(config-if)#encapsulation frame-relay
RouterA(config-if)#ip address 172.16.20.1 255.255.255.0
RouterA(config-if)#frame-relay lmi-type ansi
RouterA(config-if)#frame-relay interface-dlci 101
RouterA(config-if)#^Z
RouterA#
```

The first step is to specify the encapsulation as Frame Relay. Notice that since I didn't specify a particular encapsulation type—either Cisco or IETF—the Cisco default type was used. If the other router were non-Cisco, I would've specified IETF. Next, I assigned an IP address to the interface, then specified the LMI type of ANSI (the default being Cisco) based on information provided by the telecommunications provider. Finally, I added the DLCI of 101, which indicates the PVC we want to use (again, given to me by my ISP) and assumes there's only one PVC on this physical interface.

That's all there is to it—if both sides are configured correctly, the circuit will come up.

Check out Hands-on Lab 16.3 for a complete example of this type of configuration, including instructions on creating your own Frame Relay switch from a router.

Subinterfaces

You probably know by now that we can have multiple virtual circuits on a single serial interface and yet treat each as a separate interface—I did mention this earlier. We can make this happen by creating *subinterfaces*. Think of a subinterface as a logical interface defined by the IOS software. Several subinterfaces will share a single hardware interface, yet for configuration purposes they operate as if they were separate physical interfaces, something known as multiplexing.

To configure a router in a Frame Relay network so it will avoid split horizon issues that will not permit certain routing updates, just configure a separate subinterface for each PVC, with a unique DLCI and subnet assigned to the subinterface.

You define subinterfaces using a command like `int s0.subinterface number`. First, you have to set the encapsulation on the physical serial interface, and then you can define the subinterfaces—generally one subinterface per PVC. Here's an example:

```
RouterA(config)#int s0
RouterA(config-if)#encapsulation frame-relay
RouterA(config-if)#int s0.?
  <0-4294967295>  Serial interface number
RouterA(config-if)#int s0.16 ?
  multipoint      Treat as a multipoint link
  point-to-point  Treat as a point-to-point link
RouterA(config-if)#int s0.16 point-to-point
RouterA(config-subif)#
```

Make sure you don't have an IP address under the physical interface if you have configured subinterfaces!

You can define a serious amount of subinterfaces on any given physical interface, but keep in mind that there are only about a thousand available DLCIs. In the preceding example, I chose to use subinterface 16 because that represents the DLCI number assigned to that PVC by the carrier. There are two types of subinterfaces:

Point-to-point Used when a single virtual circuit connects one router to another. Each point-to-point subinterface requires its own subnet.

A point-to-point subinterface maps a single IP subnet per DLCI and addresses and resolves NBMA split horizon issues.

Multipoint This is when the router is the center of a star of virtual circuits that are using a single subnet for all routers' serial interfaces connected to the frame-relay cloud. You'll usually find this implemented with the hub router in this mode and the spoke routers in physical interface (always point-to-point) or point-to-point subinterface mode.

Next, I'll show you an example of a production router running multiple subinterfaces. In the following output, notice that the subinterface number matches the DLCI number—not a requirement, but it majorly helps you administer the interfaces:

```
interface Serial0
 no ip address (notice there is no IP address on the physical interface!)
```

```
 no ip directed-broadcast
 encapsulation frame-relay
!
interface Serial0.102 point-to-point
 ip address 10.1.12.1 255.255.255.0
 no ip directed-broadcast
frame-relay interface-dlci 102
!
interface Serial0.103 point-to-point
 ip address 10.1.13.1 255.255.255.0
 no ip directed-broadcast
frame-relay interface-dlci 103
!
interface Serial0.104 point-to-point
 ip address 10.1.14.1 255.255.255.0
 no ip directed-broadcast
frame-relay interface-dlci 104
!
interface Serial0.105 point-to-point
 ip address 10.1.15.1 255.255.255.0
 no ip directed-broadcast
frame-relay interface-dlci 105
!
```

Notice that there's no LMI type defined. This means that the routers are either running the Cisco default or using autodetect (if running Cisco IOS version 11.2 or newer). I also want to point out that each interface maps to a single DLCI and is defined as a separate subnet. Remember—point-to-point subinterfaces solve split horizon issues as well.

Monitoring Frame Relay

Several commands are used frequently to check the status of your interfaces and PVCs once you have Frame Relay encapsulation set up and running. To list them, use the `show frame ?` command, as seen here:

```
RouterA>sho frame ?
end-to-end      Frame-relay end-to-end VC information
fragment        show frame relay fragmentation information
ip              show frame relay IP statistics
lapf            show frame relay lapf status/statistics
lmi             show frame relay lmi statistics
map             Frame-Relay map table
pvc             show frame relay pvc statistics
```

```
qos-autosense  show frame relay qos-autosense information
route          show frame relay route
svc            show frame relay SVC stuff
traffic        Frame-Relay protocol statistics
vofr           Show frame-relay VoFR statistics
```

The most common parameters that you view with the `show frame-relay` command are `lmi`, `pvc`, and `map`.

Now, let's take a look at the most frequently used commands and the information they provide.

The *show frame-relay lmi* Command

The `show frame-relay lmi` command will give you the LMI traffic statistics exchanged between the local router and the Frame Relay switch. Here's an example:

```
Router#sh frame lmi

LMI Statistics for interface Serial0 (Frame Relay DTE)
LMI TYPE = CISCO
  Invalid Unnumbered info 0        Invalid Prot Disc 0
  Invalid dummy Call Ref 0         Invalid Msg Type 0
  Invalid Status Message 0         Invalid Lock Shift 0
  Invalid Information ID 0         Invalid Report IE Len 0
  Invalid Report Request 0         Invalid Keep IE Len 0
  Num Status Enq. Sent 61           Num Status msgs Rcvd 60
  Num Update Status Rcvd 0         Num Status Timeouts 0
Router#
```

The router output from the `show frame-relay lmi` command shows you any LMI errors, plus the LMI type. So, I have a question based on the output of the command. Is this frame-relay network working? The answer is no because the router has sent 60 inquiries and has not received even one reply from the frame-relay switch. If you see this, you need to call the provider because this is a frame-relay switch configuration issue.

The *show frame pvc* Command

The `show frame pvc` command will present you with a list of all configured PVCs and DLCI numbers. It provides the status of each PVC connection and traffic statistics too. It will also give you the number of BECN, FECN, and DE packets sent and received on the router per PVC.

Here is an example:

```
RouterA#sho frame pvc
```

```
PVC Statistics for interface Serial0 (Frame Relay DTE)

DLCI = 16,DLCI USAGE = LOCAL,PVC STATUS =ACTIVE,
INTERFACE = Serial0.1
 input pkts 50977876    output pkts 41822892
  in bytes 3137403144
 out bytes 3408047602   dropped pkts 5
  in FECN pkts 0
 in BECN pkts 0      out FECN pkts 0     out BECN pkts 0
 in DE pkts 9393     out DE pkts 0
 pvc create time 7w3d, last time pvc status changed 7w3d

DLCI = 18,DLCI USAGE =LOCAL,PVC STATUS =ACTIVE,
INTERFACE = Serial0.3
 input pkts 30572401   output pkts 31139837
  in bytes 1797291100
 out bytes 3227181474   dropped pkts 5
  in FECN pkts 0
 in BECN pkts 0      out FECN pkts 0     out BECN pkts 0
 in DE pkts 28      out DE pkts 0
 pvc create time 7w3d, last time pvc status changed 7w3d
```

If you only want to see information about PVC 16, you can type the command **show frame-relay pvc 16**. Let's take a closer look at the output of this one line:

```
DLCI = 16,DLCI USAGE = LOCAL,PVC STATUS =ACTIVE,
INTERFACE = Serial0.1
```

The PVC status field in the output of the `show frame-relay pvc` command reports the status of the PVC between the router and the frame-relay switch. The switch (DCE) reports the status to the router (DTE) using the LMI protocol. There are three types of reported statuses:

- ACTIVE: The switch is correctly programmed with the DLCI and there is a successful DTE-to-DTE circuit (router to router).
- INACTIVE: The router is connected to the switch (DTE to DCE), but there's not a connection to the far end router (DTE). This can be a router or switch configuration issue.
- DELETED: The router (DTE) is configured for a DLCI that the switch (DCE) does not recognize or is not configured correctly.

The three LMI reported statuses are CCNA objectives! Understand why you'd see each status.

The *show interface* Command

You can use the `show interface` command to check for LMI traffic. The `show interface` command displays information about the encapsulation as well as layer 2 and layer 3 information. It also displays line, protocol, DLCI, and LMI information. Check it out:

```
RouterA#sho int s0
Serial0 is up, line protocol is up
 Hardware is HD64570
 MTU 1500 bytes, BW 1544 Kbit, DLY 20000 usec, rely
  255/255, load 2/255
 Encapsulation FRAME-RELAY, loopback not set, keepalive
  set (10 sec)
 LMI enq sent 451751,LMI stat recvd 451750,LMI upd recvd
  164,DTE LMI up
 LMI enq recvd 0, LMI stat sent 0, LMI upd sent 0
 LMI DLCI 1023 LMI type is CISCO frame relay DTE
 Broadcast queue 0/64, broadcasts sent/dropped 0/0,
  interface broadcasts 839294
```

The `LMI DLCI` is used to define the type of LMI being used. If it happens to be 1023, it's the default LMI type for Cisco routers. If `LMI DLCI` is zero, then it's the ANSI LMI type (Q.933A uses 0 as well). If `LMI DLCI` is anything other than 0 or 1023, it's a 911—call your provider; they've got major issues!

The *show frame map* Command

The `show frame map` command displays the Network layer–to–DLCI mappings. Here's how that looks:

```
RouterB#show frame map
Serial0 (up): ip 172.16.20.1 dlci 16(0x10,0x400),
              dynamic, broadcast,, status defined, active
Serial1 (up): ip 172.16.40.2 dlci 17(0x11,0x410),
              dynamic, broadcast,, status defined, active
```

Notice that the Network layer addresses were resolved with the dynamic protocol Inverse ARP (IARP). After the DLCI number is listed, you can see some numbers in parentheses. The first one is 0x10, which is the hex equivalent for the DLCI number 16, used on serial 0. And the 0x11 is the hex for DLCI 17 used on serial 1. The second numbers, 0x400 and 0x410, are the DLCI numbers configured in the Frame Relay frame. They're different because of the way the bits are spread out in the frame.

You must be able to find the DLCI number used to get to a remote site by using the `show frame-relay map` command.

The *debug frame lmi* Command

The debug frame lmi command will show realtime output on the router consoles by default (as with any debug command). The information this command gives you will enable you to verify and troubleshoot the Frame Relay connection by helping you determine whether the router and switch are exchanging the correct LMI information. Here's an example:

```
Router#debug frame-relay lmi
Serial3/1(in): Status, myseq 214
RT IE 1, length 1, type 0
KA IE 3, length 2, yourseq 214, myseq 214
PVC IE 0x7 , length 0x6 , dlci 130, status 0x2 , bw 0
Serial3/1(out): StEnq, myseq 215, yourseen 214, DTE up
datagramstart = 0x1959DF4, datagramsize = 13
FR encap = 0xFCF10309
00 75 01 01 01 03 02 D7 D6

Serial3/1(in): Status, myseq 215
RT IE 1, length 1, type 1
KA IE 3, length 2, yourseq 215, myseq 215
Serial3/1(out): StEnq, myseq 216, yourseen 215, DTE up
datagramstart = 0x1959DF4, datagramsize = 13
FR encap = 0xFCF10309
00 75 01 01 01 03 02 D8 D7
```

Troubleshooting Frame Relay Networks

Troubleshooting Frame Relay networks isn't any harder than troubleshooting any other type of network as long as you know what to look for, which is what I'm going to cover now. We'll go over some basic problems that commonly occur in Frame Relay configuration and how to solve them.

First on the list are serial encapsulation problems. As you learned recently, there are two Frame Relay encapsulations: Cisco and IETF. Cisco is the default, and it means that you have a Cisco router on each end of the Frame Relay network. If you don't have a Cisco router on the remote end of your Frame Relay network, then you need to run the IETF encapsulation as shown here:

```
RouterA(config)#int s0
RouterA(config-if)#encapsulation frame-relay ?
  ietf  Use RFC1490 encapsulation
  <cr>
RouterA(config-if)#encapsulation frame-relay ietf
```

Once you verify that you're using the correct encapsulation, you then need to check out your Frame Relay mappings. For example, take a look at Figure 16.18.

FIGURE 16.18 Frame Relay mappings

```
RouterA#show running-config
interface s0/0
ip address 172.16.100.2 255.255.0.0
encapsulation frame-relay
frame-relay map ip 172.16.100.1 200 broadcast
```

So why can't RouterA talk to RouterB across the Frame Relay network? To find that out, take a close look at the `frame-relay map` statement. See the problem now? You cannot use a remote DLCI to communicate to the Frame Relay switch; you must use *your* DLCI number! The mapping should have included DLCI 100 instead of DLCI 200.

Now that you know how to ensure that you have the correct Frame Relay encapsulation, and that DLCIs are only locally significant, let's look into some routing protocol problems typically associated with Frame Relay. See if you can find a problem with the two configurations in Figure 16.19.

FIGURE 16.19 Frame Relay routing problems

```
RouterA#show running-config
interface s0/0
ip address 172.16.100.2 255.255.0.0
encapsulation frame-relay
frame-relay map ip 172.16.100.1 100
router rip
        network 172.16.0.0
```

```
RouterB#show running-config
interface s0/0
ip address 172.16.100.1 255.255.0.0
encapsulation frame-relay
frame-relay map ip 172.16.100.2 200
router rip
        network 172.16.0.0
```

Hmmmm, the configs look pretty good. Actually, they look great, so what's the problem? Well, remember that Frame Relay is a non-broadcast multi-access (NBMA) network by default, meaning that it doesn't send any broadcasts across the PVC. So, because the mapping statements do not have the `broadcast` argument at the end of the line, broadcasts, such as RIP updates, won't be sent across the PVC.

Virtual Private Networks

I'd be pretty willing to bet you've heard the term *VPN* more than once before. Maybe you even know what one is, but just in case, a *virtual private network (VPN)* allows the creation of private networks across the Internet, enabling privacy and tunneling of non-TCP/IP protocols.

VPNs are used daily to give remote users and disjointed networks connectivity over a public medium like the Internet instead of using more expensive permanent means.

Types of VPNs are named based upon the role they play in a business. There are three different categories of VPNs:

Remote access VPNs *Remote access VPNs* allow remote users such as telecommuters to securely access the corporate network wherever and whenever they need to.

Site-to-site VPNs *Site-to-site VPNs*, or intranet VPNs, allow a company to connect its remote sites to the corporate backbone securely over a public medium like the Internet instead of requiring more expensive WAN connections like Frame Relay.

Extranet VPNs *Extranet VPNs* allow an organization's suppliers, partners, and customers to be connected to the corporate network in a limited way for business-to-business (B2B) communications.

Now you're interested, huh? And since VPNs are inexpensive and secure, I'm guessing you're really jonesing to find out how VPNs are created right? Well, there's more than one way to bring a VPN into being. The first approach uses IPSec to create authentication and encryption services between endpoints on an IP network. The second way is via tunneling protocols, allowing you to establish a tunnel between endpoints on a network. And understand that the tunnel itself is a means for data or protocols to be encapsulated inside another protocol—pretty clean!

I'm going to go over the first, IPSec way in a minute, but first I really want to describe four of the most common tunneling protocols in use:

Layer 2 Forwarding (L2F) *Layer 2 Forwarding (L2F)* is a Cisco-proprietary tunneling protocol, and it was Cisco's first tunneling protocol created for virtual private dial-up networks (VPDNs). A VPDN allows a device to use a dial-up connection to create a secure connection to a corporate network. L2F was later replaced by L2TP, which is backward compatible with L2F.

Point-to-Point Tunneling Protocol (PPTP) *Point-to-Point Tunneling Protocol (PPTP)* was created by Microsoft to allow the secure transfer of data from remote networks to the corporate network.

Layer 2 Tunneling Protocol (L2TP) *Layer 2 Tunneling Protocol (L2TP)* was created by Cisco and Microsoft to replace L2F and PPTP. L2TP merged the capabilities of both L2F and PPTP into one tunneling protocol.

Generic Routing Encapsulation (GRE) *Generic Routing Encapsulation (GRE)* is another Cisco-proprietary tunneling protocol. It forms virtual point-to-point links, allowing for a variety of protocols to be encapsulated in IP tunnels.

Okay—now that you're clear on both exactly what a VPN is and the various types of VPNs available, it's time to dive into IPSec.

Introduction to Cisco IOS IPSec

Simply put, IPSec is an industry-wide standard framework of protocols and algorithms that allows for secure data transmission over an IP-based network that functions at the layer 3 network layer of the OSI model.

Did you notice I said, "IP-based network"? That's really important because by itself, IPSec can't be used to encrypt non-IP traffic. This means that if you run into a situation where you have to encrypt non-IP traffic, you'll need to create a GRE tunnel for it and then use IPSec to encrypt that tunnel!

IPSec Transforms

An *IPSec transform* specifies a single security protocol with its corresponding security algorithm; without these transforms, IPSec wouldn't be able to give us its glory. It's important to be familiar with these technologies, so let me take a second to define the security protocols and briefly introduce the supporting encryption and hashing algorithms that IPSec relies upon.

Security Protocols

The two primary security protocols used by IPSec are *Authentication Header (AH)* and *Encapsulating Security Payload (ESP).*

Authentication Header (AH)

The AH protocol provides authentication for the data and the IP header of a packet using a one-way hash for packet authentication. It works like this: The sender generates a one-way hash; then the receiver generates the same one-way hash. If the packet has changed in any way, it won't be authenticated and will be dropped. So basically, IPSec relies upon AH to guarantee authenticity. AH checks the entire packet, but it doesn't offer any encryption services.

This is unlike ESP, which only provides an integrity check on the data of a packet.

Encapsulating Security Payload (ESP)

It won't tell you when or how the NASDAQ's gonna bounce up and down like a superball, but ESP will provide confidentiality, data origin authentication, connectionless integrity, anti-replay service, and limited traffic-flow confidentiality by defeating traffic flow analysis—which is almost as good! Anyway, there are four components of ESP:

Confidentiality Confidentiality is provided through the use of symmetric encryption algorithms like DES or 3DES. Confidentiality can be selected separately from all other services, but the confidentiality selected must be the same on both endpoints of your VPN.

Data origin authentication and connectionless integrity Data origin authentication and connectionless integrity are joint services offered as an option in conjunction with the likewise optional confidentiality.

Anti-replay service You can only use the anti-replay service if data origin authentication is selected. Anti-replay election is based upon the receiver, meaning the service is effective only if the receiver checks the sequence number. In case you were wondering, a replay attack is when a hacker nicks a copy of an authenticated packet and later transmits it to the intended destination. When the duplicate, authenticated IP packet gets to the destination, it can disrupt services and other ugly stuff. The *Sequence Number* field is designed to foil this type of attack.

Traffic flow For traffic flow confidentiality to work, you have to have at least tunnel mode selected. And it's most effective if it's implemented at a security gateway where tons of traffic amasses—a situation that can mask the true source-destination patterns to bad guys trying to breach your network's security.

Encryption

VPNs create a private network over a public network infrastructure. However, to maintain confidentiality and security, we need to use IPSec with our VPNs. IPSec uses various types of protocols to perform encryption. The types of encryption algorithms used today are as follows:

Symmetric encryption This encryption requires a shared secret to encrypt and decrypt. Each computer encrypts the data before sending info across the network, and this same key is used to both encrypt and decrypt the data. Examples of symmetric key encryption are Data Encryption Standard (DES), triple DES (3DES), and Advanced Encryption Standard (AES).

Asymmetric Encryption Devices that use asymmetric encryption use different keys for encryption than they do for decryption. These keys are called private and public keys.

Private keys encrypt a hash from the message to create a digital signature that is then verified (via decryption) using the public key; Public keys encrypt a symmetric key for secure distribution to the receiving host, who then decrypts that symmetric key using their exclusively held private key. It is not possible to encrypt and decrypt using the same key. This is a variant of public key encryption that uses a combination of both a public and private key. An example of an asymmetric encryption is Rivest, Shamir, and Adleman (RSA).

As you can see from the amount of information (and I am just scratching the surface here), establishing a VPN connection between two sites takes some study time, can be difficult at times, and takes lots of practice and sometimes a large amount of patience. Cisco does have some GUI interfaces to help with this process, and they can be very helpful for configuring VPNs with IPSec—they are just beyond the scope of this book.

Cisco's Easy VPN makes it easier to configure for a company that has little admin support. There are three components to help you administrate and deploy VPNs, using Cisco products of course:

- Cisco Easy VPN Server: Cisco router with Firewall IOS or PIX/ASA Firewall acting as the VPN concentrator in site-to-site or remote-access VPNs
- Cisco Easy VPN Remote: Cisco router with Firewall IOS or PIX/ASA Firewall acting as the VPN client for the hosts on the remote network
- Cisco Easy VPN Client: Supplicant used on a PC to access a Cisco VPN Server

All of these components are there for the sole purpose of simplifying deployment.

For more detailed VPN and IPSec information above and beyond the scope of the CCNA objectives, please see `www.lammle.com`.

Summary

In this chapter, you learned the difference between the following WAN services: cable, DSL, HDLC, PPP, PPPoE, and Frame Relay. You also learned that you can use a VPN once any of those services are up and running.

I have to tell you—you must understand High-Level Data-Link Control (HDLC) and how to verify with the `show interface` command that HDLC is enabled! You've been provided with some really important HDLC information as well as information on how the Point-to-Point Protocol (PPP) is used if you need more features than HDLC offers or if you're using two different brands of routers. You now know that this is because various versions of HDLC are proprietary and won't work between two different vendors' routers.

When we went through the section on PPP, I discussed the various LCP options as well as the two types of authentication that can be used: PAP and CHAP.

And we talked about Frame Relay and the two different encapsulation methods used with it in detail. We also discussed LMI options, Frame Relay maps, and subinterface configurations. In addition to the Frame Relay terms and features we covered, I demonstrated Frame Relay configuration and verification in depth.

We finished up the chapter with a discussion on Virtual Private Networks, IPSec, and encryption and even a small discussion on Cisco's Easy VPN.

Exam Essentials

Remember the default serial encapsulation on Cisco routers. Cisco routers use a proprietary High-Level Data-Link Control (HDLC) encapsulation on all their serial links by default.

Understand the different Frame Relay encapsulations. Cisco uses two different Frame Relay encapsulation methods on its routers: Cisco and IETF. If you are using the Cisco encapsulation method, you are telling your router that a Cisco router is installed on the other side of the PVC. If you are using the IETF encapsulation, you are telling your router that a non-Cisco router is installed on the other side of the PVC.

Remember what the CIR is in Frame Relay. The CIR is the average rate, in bits per second, at which the Frame Relay switch agrees to transfer data.

Remember the commands for verifying Frame Relay. The `show frame-relay lmi` command will give you the LMI traffic statistics regarding LMI traffic exchanged between the local router and the Frame Relay switch. The `show frame pvc` command will list all configured PVCs and DLCI numbers.

Remember the PPP Data Link layer protocols. The three Data Link layer protocols are Network Control Protocol (NCP), which defines the Network layer protocols; Link Control Protocol (LCP), a method of establishing, configuring, maintaining, and terminating the point-to-point connection; and High-Level Data-Link Control (HDLC), the MAC layer protocol that encapsulates the packets.

Remember the various types of serial WAN connections. The serial WAN connections that are most widely used are HDLC, PPP, and Frame Relay.

Understand the term *virtual private network*. You need to understand why and how to use a VPN between two sites and the purpose that IPSec serves with VPNs.

Written Lab 16

Write the answers to the following WAN questions:

1. Write the command to see the encapsulation method on serial 0 of a Cisco router.
2. Write the commands to configure s0 to PPP encapsulation.
3. Write the commands to configure a username of *todd* and password of *cisco* that is used on a Cisco router for PPP authentication.
4. Write the commands to enable CHAP authentication on a Cisco serial interface. (Assume PPP is the encapsulation type.)
5. Write the commands to configure the DLCI numbers for two serial interfaces, 0 and 1. Use 16 for s0 and 17 for s1.
6. Write the commands to configure a remote office using a point-to-point subinterface. Use DLCI 16 and IP address 172.16.60.1/24.
7. What protocol would you use if you were running xDSL and needed authentication?
8. What are the three protocols specified in PPP?
9. To provide security in your VPN tunnel, what protocol suite would you use?
10. What are the typical three different categories of VPNs?

(The answers to Written Lab 16 can be found following the answers to the review questions for this chapter.)

Hands-on Labs

In this section, you will configure Cisco routers in three different WAN labs using the figure supplied in each lab. (These labs are included for use with real Cisco routers but worked perfectly with Cisco's Packet Tracer program.)

Lab 16.1: Configuring PPP Encapsulation and Authentication

Lab 16.2: Configuring and Monitoring HDLC

Lab 16.3: Configuring Frame Relay and Subinterfaces

Hands-on Lab 16.1: Configuring PPP Encapsulation and Authentication

By default, Cisco routers use High-Level Data-Link Control (HDLC) as a point-to-point encapsulation method on serial links. If you are connecting to non-Cisco equipment, then you can use the PPP encapsulation method to communicate.

The lab you will configure is shown in the following diagram.

1. Type **sh int s0** on RouterA and RouterB to see the encapsulation method.
2. Make sure each router has the hostname assigned:

```
RouterA#config t
RouterA(config)#hostname RouterA

RouterB#config t
RouterB(config)#hostname RouterB
```

3. To change the default HDLC encapsulation method to PPP on both routers, use the `encapsulation` command at interface configuration. Both ends of the link must run the same encapsulation method.

```
RouterA#Config t
RouterA(config)#int s0
RouterA(config-if)#encap ppp
```

4. Now go to RouterB and set serial 0 to PPP encapsulation.

```
RouterB#config t
RouterB(config)#int s0
RouterB(config-if)#encap ppp
```

5. Verify the configuration by typing **sh int s0** on both routers.
6. Notice the IPCP, IPXCP, and CDPCP (assuming the interface is up). This is the information used to transmit the upper-layer (Network layer) information across the HDLC at the MAC sublayer.
7. Define a username and password on each router. Notice that the username is the name of the remote router. Also, the password must be the same.

```
RouterA#config t
RouterA(config)#username RouterB password todd
```

```
RouterB#config t
RouterB(config)#username RouterA password todd
```

8. Enable CHAP or PAP authentication on each interface.

```
RouterA(config)#int s0
RouterA(config-if)#ppp authentication chap

RouterB(config)#int s0
RouterB(config-if)#ppp authentication chap
```

9. Verify the PPP configuration on each router by using these commands.

```
RouterB(config-if)#shut
RouterB(config-if)#debug ppp authentication
RouterB(config-if)#no shut
```

Hands-on Lab 16.2: Configuring and Monitoring HDLC

There really is no configuration required for HDLC (as it is the default configuration on Cisco serial interfaces), but if you completed Lab 16.1, then the PPP encapsulation would be set on both routers. This is why I put the PPP lab first. This lab allows you to actually configure HDLC encapsulation on a router.

This second lab will use the same configuration as Lab 16.1 used.

1. Set the encapsulation for each serial interface by using the `encapsulation hdlc` command.

```
RouterA#config t
RouterA(config)#int s0
RouterA(config-if)#encapsulation hdlc

RouterB#config t
RouterB(config)#int s0
RouterB(config-if)#encapsulation hdlc
```

2. Verify the HDLC encapsulation by using the `show interface s0` command on each router.

Hands-on Lab 16.3: Configuring Frame Relay and Subinterfaces

In this lab, you will use the following diagram to configure Frame Relay.

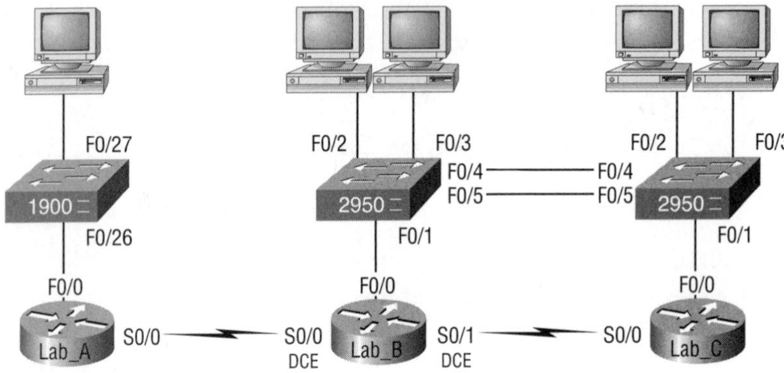

You will configure the Lab_B router to be a Frame Relay switch. You will then configure the Lab_A and Lab_C routers to use the switch to bring up the PVC.

1. Set the hostname, `frame-relay switching` command, and the encapsulation of each serial interface on the Frame Relay switch.

```
Router#config t
Router(config)#hostname Lab_B
Lab_B(config)#frame-relay switching [makes the router an
FR switch]
Lab_B(config)#int s0
Lab_B(config-if)#encapsulation frame-relay
Lab_B(config-if)#int s1
Lab_B(config-if)#encapsulation frame-relay
```

2. Configure the Frame Relay mappings on each interface. You do not have to have IP addresses on these interfaces because they are only switching one interface to another with Frame Relay frames.

```
Lab_B(config-if)#int s0
Lab_B(config-if)#frame intf-type dce
[The above command makes this an FR DCE interface, which
is different than a router's interface being DCE]
Lab_B(config-if)#frame-relay route 102 interface
  Serial0/1 201
Lab_B(config-if)#clock rate 64000
[The above command is used if you have this as DCE, which
```

```
is different than an FR DCE]
Lab_B(config-if)#int s1
Lab_B(config-if)#frame intf-type dce
Lab_B(config-if)#frame-relay route 201 interface
  Serial0/0 102
Lab_B(config-if)#clock rate 64000 [if you have this as DCE]
```

This is not as hard as it looks. The `route` command just says that if you receive frames from PVC 102, send them out `int s0/1` using PVC 201. The second mapping on serial 0/1 is just the opposite. Anything that comes in `int s0/1` is routed out serial0/0 using PVC 102.

3. Configure Lab_A with a point-to-point subinterface.

```
Router#config t
Router(config)#hostname Lab_A
Lab_A(config)#int s0
Lab_A(config-if)#encapsulation frame-relay
Lab_A(config-if)#int s0.102 point-to-point
Lab_A(config-if)#ip address 172.16.10.1
  255.255.255.0
Lab_A(config-if)#frame-relay interface-dlci 102
```

4. Configure Lab_C with a point-to-point subinterface.

```
Router#config t
Router(config)#hostname Lab_C
Lab_C(config)#int s0
Lab_C(config-if)#encapsulation frame-relay
Lab_C(config-if)#int s0.201 point-to-point
Lab_C(config-if)#ip address 172.16.10.2
  255.255.255.0
Lab_C(config-if)#frame-relay interface-dlci 201
```

5. Verify your configurations with the following commands.

```
Lab_A>sho frame ?
 ip       show frame relay IP statistics
 lmi      show frame relay lmi statistics
 map      Frame-Relay map table
 pvc      show frame relay pvc statistics
 route    show frame relay route
 traffic  Frame-Relay protocol statistics
```

6. Also, use Ping and Telnet to verify connectivity.

Review Questions

The following questions are designed to test your understanding of this chapter's material. For more information on how to get additional questions, please see this book's Introduction.

1. Which command will display the CHAP authentication process as it occurs between two routers in the network?
   - A. `show chap authentication`
   - B. `show interface serial 0`
   - C. `debug ppp authentication`
   - D. `debug chap authentication`
2. Which command is required for connectivity in a Frame Relay network if Inverse ARP is not operational?
   - A. `frame-relay arp`
   - B. `frame-relay map`
   - C. `frame-relay interface-dci`
   - D. `frame-relay lmi-type`
3. Suppose you have a customer who has a central HQ and six branch offices. The customer anticipates adding six more branches in the near future. It wishes to implement a WAN technology that will allow the branches to economically connect to HQ and you have no free ports on the HQ router. Which of the following would you recommend?
   - A. PPP
   - B. HDLC
   - C. Frame Relay
   - D. ISDN
4. Which of the following command options are displayed when you use the **`Router#show frame-relay ?`** command? (Choose three.)
   - A. `dlci`
   - B. `neighbors`
   - C. `lmi`
   - D. `pvc`
   - E. `map`

5. How should a router that is being used in a Frame Relay network be configured to keep split horizon issues from preventing routing updates?
   A. Configure a separate subinterface for each PVC with a unique DLCI and subnet assigned to the subinterface.
   B. Combine multiple Frame Relay circuits as a point-to-point line to support multicast and broadcast traffic.
   C. Configure many subinterfaces in the same subnet.
   D. Configure a single subinterface to establish multiple PVC connections to multiple remote router interfaces.
6. Which encapsulations can be configured on a serial interface? (Choose three.)
   A. Ethernet
   B. Token Ring
   C. HDLC
   D. Frame Relay
   E. PPP
7. When setting up Frame Relay for point-to-point subinterfaces, which of the following must not be configured?
   A. The Frame Relay encapsulation on the physical interface
   B. The local DLCI on each subinterface
   C. An IP address on the physical interface
   D. The subinterface type as point-to-point
8. When a router is connected to a Frame Relay WAN link using a serial DTE interface, how is the clock rate determined?
   A. Supplied by the CSU/DSU
   B. By the far end router
   C. By the `clock rate` command
   D. By the Physical layer bit stream timing
9. A default Frame Relay WAN is classified as what type of physical network?
   A. Point-to-point
   B. Broadcast multi-access
   C. Non-broadcast multi-access
   D. Non-broadcast multipoint
10. Which of the following encapsulates PPP frames in Ethernet frames and uses common PPP features like authentication, encryption, and compression?
   A. PPP
   B. PPPoA
   C. PPPoE
   D. Token Ring

11. You need to configure a router for a Frame Relay connection to a non-Cisco router. Which of the following commands will prepare the WAN interface of the router for this connection?
    A. `Router(config-if)#`**`encapsulation frame-relay q933a`**
    B. `Router(config-if)#`**`encapsulation frame-relay ansi`**
    C. `Router(config-if)#`**`encapsulation frame-relay ietf`**
    D. `Router(config-if)#`**`encapsulation frame-relay cisco`**

12. The Acme Corporation is implementing dial-up services to enable remote-office employees to connect to the local network. The company uses multiple routed protocols, needs authentication of users connecting to the network, and since some calls will be long distance, needs callback support. Which of the following protocols is the best choice for these remote services?
    A. 802.1
    B. Frame Relay
    C. HDLC
    D. PPP
    E. PAP

13. Which WAN encapsulations can be configured on an asynchronous serial connection? (Choose two.)
    A. PPP
    B. ATM
    C. HDLC
    D. SDLC
    E. Frame Relay

14. Which of the following uses ATM as the Data Link layer protocol that's terminated at what's known as the DSLAM?
    A. DSL
    B. PPPoE
    C. Frame Relay
    D. Dedicated T1
    E. Wireless
    F. POTS

15. Why won't the serial link between the Corp router and the Remote router come up?

```
Corp#sh int s0/0
Serial0/0 is up, line protocol is down
  Hardware is PowerQUICC Serial
  Internet address is 10.0.1.1/24
  MTU 1500 bytes, BW 1544 Kbit, DLY 20000 usec,
     reliability 254/255, txload 1/255, rxload 1/255
  Encapsulation PPP, loopback not set

Remote#sh int s0/0
Serial0/0 is up, line protocol is down
  Hardware is PowerQUICC Serial
  Internet address is 10.0.1.2/24
  MTU 1500 bytes, BW 1544 Kbit, DLY 20000 usec,
     reliability 254/255, txload 1/255, rxload 1/255
  Encapsulation HDLC, loopback not set
```

A. The serial cable is faulty.

B. The IP addresses are not in the same subnet.

C. The subnet masks are not correct.

D. The keepalive settings are not correct.

E. The layer 2 frame types are not compatible.

16. In which of the following technologies is the term *HFC* used?

A. DSL

B. PPPoE

C. Frame Relay

D. Cable

E. Wireless

F. POTS

17. A remote site has just been connected to the central office. However, remote users cannot access applications at the central office. The remote router can be pinged from the central office router. After reviewing the following command output, which do you think is the most likely reason for the problem?

```
Central#show running-config
!
interface Serial0
 ip address 10.0.8.1 255.255.248.0
 encapsulation frame-relay
 frame-relay map ip 10.0.15.2 200
!
Router rip
Network 10.0.0.0

Remote#show running-config
!
interface Serial0
 ip address 10.0.15.2 255.255.248.0
 encapsulation frame-relay
 frame-relay map ip 10.0.8.1 100
!
Router rip
Network 10.0.0.0
```

A. The Frame Relay PVC is down.

B. The IP addressing on the Central/Remote router link is incorrect.

C. RIP routing information is not being forwarded.

D. Frame Relay Inverse ARP is not properly configured.

18. Which of the following is an industry-wide standard suite of protocols and algorithms that allows for secure data transmission over an IP-based network that functions at the layer 3 Network layer of the OSI model?

A. HDLC

B. Cable

C. VPN

D. IPSec

E. xDSL

19. Which of the following describes the creation of private networks across the Internet, enabling privacy and tunneling of non-TCP/IP protocols?
    A. HDLC
    B. Cable
    C. VPN
    D. IPSec
    E. xDSL

20. Referring to the following diagram, what functions does the Frame Relay DLCI provide with respect to RouterA?

    A. Identifies the signaling standard between RouterA and the frame switch
    B. Identifies a portion of the virtual circuit between RouterA and the frame switch
    C. Identifies the encapsulation used between RouterA and RouterB
    D. Defines the signaling standard between RouterB and the frame switch.

Answers to Review Questions

1. C. The command `debug ppp authentication` will show you the authentication process that PPP uses across point-to-point connections.

2. B. If you have a router in your Frame Relay network that does not support IARP, you must create Frame Relay maps on your router, which provide known DLCI-to-IP address mappings.

3. C. The key is "there are no free ports" on your router. Only Frame Relay can provide a connection to multiple locations with one interface, and in an economical manner no less.

4. C, D, E. The `show frame-relay ?` command provides many options, but the options available in this question are `lmi`, `pvc`, and `map`.

5. A. If you have a serial port configured with multiple DLCIs connected to multiple remote sites, split horizon rules (discussed in Chapter 8) stop route updates received on an interface from being sent out the same interface. By creating subinterfaces for each PVC, you can avoid the split horizon issues when using Frame Relay.

6. C, D, E. Ethernet and Token Ring are LAN technologies and cannot be configured on a serial interface. PPP, HDLC, and Frame Relay are layer 2 WAN technologies that are typically configured on a serial interface.

7. C. It is very important to remember when studying the CCNA exam objectives, and when configuring Frame Relay with point-to-point subinterfaces, that you do not put an IP address on the physical interface.

8. A. Clocking on a serial interface is always provided by the CSU/DSU (DCE device). However, if you do not have a CSU/DSU in your nonproduction test environment, then you need to supply clocking with the `clock rate` command on the serial interface of the router with the DCE cable attached.

9. C. Frame Relay, by default, is a non-broadcast multi-access (NBMA) network, which means that broadcasts, such as RIP updates, will not be forwarded across the link by default.

10. C. PPPoE encapsulates PPP frames in Ethernet frames and uses common PPP features like authentication, encryption, and compression. PPPoA is used for ATM.

11. C. If you have a Cisco router on one side of a Frame Relay network and a non-Cisco router on the other side, you would need to use the Frame Relay encapsulation type of IETF. The default is Cisco encapsulation, which means that a Cisco router must be on both sides of the Frame Relay PVC.

12. D. PPP is your only option because HDLC and Frame Relay do not support these types of business requirements. PPP provides dynamic addressing, authentication using PAP or CHAP, and callback services.

13. A, B. Please do not freak out because ATM is an answer to this question. ATM is not covered in depth on the CCNA exam. PPP is mostly used for dial-up (async) services, but ATM could be used as well, though it typically is not used anymore since PPP is so efficient.

14. A. ATM is the Data-Link layer protocol that's typically used over the DSL layer 1 connection from the CPE and terminated at what's known as the DSLAM—an ATM switch that contains DSL interface cards, or ATU-Cs.

15. E. This is an easy question because the Remote router is using the default HDLC serial encapsulation and the Corp router is using the PPP serial encapsulation. You should go to the Remote router and set that encapsulation to PPP or change the Corp router back to the default of HDLC.

16. D. In a modern network, hybrid fibre-coaxial (HFC) is a telecommunications industry term for a network that incorporates both optical fiber and coaxial cable to create a broadband network.

17. C. Even though the IP addresses don't look correct, they are in the same subnet, so option B is not correct. The question states that you can ping the other side, so the PVC must be up—option A can't be correct. You cannot configure IARP, so only option C can be correct. Since a Frame Relay network is a non-broadcast multi-access network by default, broadcasts such as RIP updates cannot be sent across the PVC unless you use the broadcast statement at the end of the `frame-relay map` command.

18. D. IPSec is an industry-wide standard suite of protocols and algorithms that allows for secure data transmission over an IP-based network that functions at the layer 3 Network layer of the OSI model.

19. C. A VPN allows or describes the creation of private networks across the Internet, enabling privacy and tunneling of non-TCP/IP protocols. A VPN can be set up across any type of link.

20. B. As I mentioned many times in this chapter, and you need to remember this: DLCIs are locally significant only and define the circuit from the router to the switch only. They do not reference a remote router or DLCI. RouterA would use DLCI 100 to get to the RouterB networks. RouterB would use DLCI 200 to get to the RouterA networks.

Answers to Written Lab 16

1. `sh int s0`
2. ```
   config t
   int s0
   encap ppp
   ```
3. ```
   config t
   username todd password cisco
   ```
4. ```
   config t
   int serial0
   ppp authentication chap
   ```
5. ```
   config t
   int s0
   frame interface-dlci 16
   int s1
   frame interface-dlci 17
   ```
6. ```
   config t
   int s0
   no ip address
   encap frame
   int s0.16 point-to-point
   ip address 172.16.60.1 255.255.255.0
   frame interface-dlci 16
   ```
7. PPPoE or PPPoA
8. HDLC, LCP, and NCP
9. IPSec
10. Remote access VPNs, site-to-site VPNs, and extranet VPNs
   ```

About the Companion CD

IN THIS APPENDIX:

- ✓ What you'll find on the CD
- ✓ System requirements
- ✓ Using the CD
- ✓ Troubleshooting

What You'll Find on the CD

The following sections are arranged by category and summarize the software and other goodies you'll find on the CD. If you need help with installing the items provided on the CD, refer to the installation instructions in the section "Using the CD" later in this appendix.

Sybex Test Engine

The CD contains the Sybex test engine, which includes the two bonus exams.

Electronic Flashcards

These handy electronic flashcards are just what they sound like. One side contains a question, and the other side shows the answer.

PDF of the Glossary

We have included a glossary of terms in PDF format. You can view the electronic version of the glossary with Adobe Reader.

Adobe Reader

We've also included a copy of Adobe Reader so you can view PDF files that accompany the book's content. For more information on Adobe Reader or to check for a newer version, visit Adobe's website at `www.adobe.com/products/reader/`.

System Requirements

Make sure your computer meets the minimum system requirements shown in the following list. If your computer doesn't match up to most of these requirements, you may have problems using the software and files on the companion CD. For the latest and greatest information, please refer to the ReadMe file located at the root of the CD-ROM.

- A PC running Microsoft Windows 98, Windows 2000, Windows NT4 (with SP4 or later), Windows Me, Windows XP, Windows Vista, or Windows 7
- An Internet connection
- A CD-ROM drive

Using the CD

To install the items from the CD to your hard drive, follow these steps:

1. Insert the CD into your computer's CD-ROM drive. The license agreement appears.

Windows users: The interface won't launch if you have autorun disabled. In that case, click Start ➢ Run (for Windows Vista or Windows 7, Start ➢ All Programs ➢ Accessories ➢ Run). In the dialog box that appears, type `D:\Start.exe`. (Replace *D* with the proper letter if a different letter is used for your CD drive. If you don't know the letter, see how your CD drive is listed under My Computer.) Click OK.

2. Read the license agreement, and then click the Accept button if you want to use the CD.

The CD interface appears. The interface allows you to access the content with just one or two clicks.

Troubleshooting

Wiley has attempted to provide programs that work on most computers with the minimum system requirements. Alas, your computer may differ, and some programs may not work properly for some reason.

The two likeliest problems are that you don't have enough memory (RAM) for the programs you want to use or you have other programs running that are affecting installation or running of a program. If you get an error message such as "Not enough memory" or "Setup cannot continue," try one or more of the following suggestions and then try using the software again:

Turn off any antivirus software running on your computer. Installation programs sometimes mimic virus activity and may make your computer incorrectly believe that it's being infected by a virus.

Close all running programs. The more programs you have running, the less memory there is available to other programs. Installation programs typically update files and programs, so if you keep other programs running, installation may not work properly.

Have your local computer store add more RAM to your computer. This is, admittedly, a drastic and somewhat expensive step. However, adding more memory can really help the speed of your computer and allow more programs to run at the same time.

Customer Care

If you have trouble with the book's companion CD-ROM, please call the Wiley Product Technical Support phone number at (800) 762-2974.

Index

Note to the reader: Throughout this index boldfaced page numbers indicate primary discussions of a topic. Italicized page numbers indicate illustrations.

A

B

C

D

E

F

L

M

N

O

P

R

S

T

U

V

W

Wiley Publishing, Inc.
End-User License Agreement

The Absolutely Best CCNA Book/CD Package on the Market!

Get ready for your Cisco Certified Network Associate exam with the most comprehensive and challenging sample tests anywhere!

The Sybex Test Engine features:

- All the review questions, as covered in each chapter of the book
- Challenging questions representative of those you'll find on the real exam
- Two practice exams available only on the CD
- Use Glossary for instant reference

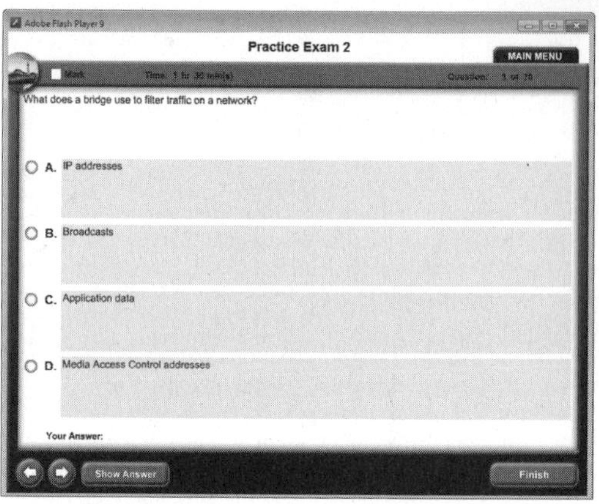

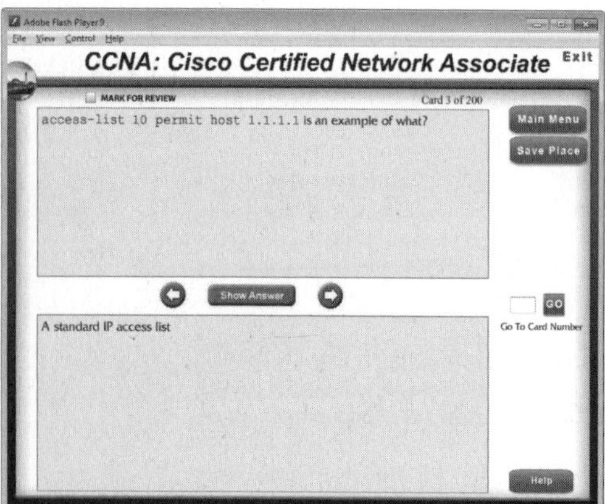

Preview copy of Todd Lammle's CCNA Audio and Video series.

- Over 30 minutes of instructional video from networking guru Todd Lammle
- Over a half hour of CCNA audio review in MP3 format

Use the Electronic Flashcards to jog your memory and prep last-minute for the exam!

- Reinforce your understanding of key concepts with these hardcore flash-card-style questions.
- Now you can study for the CCNA exam any time, anywhere.

2 Glossary

10BaseT Part of the original IEEE 802.3 standard, 10BaseT is the Ethernet specification of 10Mbps baseband that uses two pairs of twisted-pair, category 3, 4, or 5 cabling—using one pair to send data and the other to receive. 10BaseT has a distance limit of about 100 meters per segment. See also: *Ethernet* and *IEEE 802.3*.

100BaseT Based on the IEEE 802.3u standard, 100BaseT is the Fast Ethernet specification of 100Mbps baseband that uses UTP wiring. 100BaseT sends link pulses (containing more information than those used in 10BaseT) over the network when no traffic is present. See also: *10BaseT*, *Fast Ethernet*, and *IEEE 802.3*.

100BaseTX Based on the IEEE 802.3u standard, 100BaseTX is the 100Mbps baseband Fast Ethernet specification that uses two pairs of UTP or STP wiring. The first pair of wires receives data; the second pair sends data. To ensure correct signal timing, a 100BaseTX segment cannot be longer than 100 meters.

A

A&B bit signaling Used in T1 transmission facilities and sometimes called "24th channel signaling." Each of the 24 T1 subchannels in this procedure uses one bit of every sixth frame to send supervisory signaling information.

AAA Authentication, Authorization, and Accounting: A system developed by Cisco to provide network security. See also: *authentication*, *authorization*, and *accounting*.